T0189329

Lecture Notes in Computer Science 602

Edited by G. Goos and J. Hartmanis

Advisory Board: W. Brauer   D. Gries   J. Stoer

I. Tomek (Ed.)

Computer Assisted Learning

4th International Conference, ICCAL '92
Wolfville, Nova Scotia, Canada, June 17-20, 1992
Proceedings

Springer-Verlag

Berlin Heidelberg New York
London Paris Tokyo
Hong Kong Barcelona
Budapest

Series Editors

Gerhard Goos
Universität Karlsruhe
Postfach 69 80
Vincenz-Priessnitz-Straße 1
W-7500 Karlsruhe, FRG

Juris Hartmanis
Department of Computer Science
Cornell University
5149 Upson Hall
Ithaca, NY 14853, USA

Volume Editor

Ivan Tomek
Jodrey School of Computer Science, Acada University
Wolfville, Nova Scotia BOP 1X0, Canada

CR Subject Classification (1991): K.3, I.2, D.2

ISBN 3-540-55578-1 Springer-Verlag Berlin Heidelberg New York
ISBN 0-387-55578-1 Springer-Verlag New York Berlin Heidelberg

© Springer-Verlag Berlin Heidelberg 1992
Printed in Germany

Typesetting: Camera ready by author/editor
Printing and binding: Druckhaus Beltz, Hemsbach/Bergstr.
45/3140-543210 - Printed on acid-free paper

Preface

ICCAL, the International Conference on Computers and Learning, is a forum for the exchange of ideas and presentation of developments in the theory and practice of computer uses in education; its focus is post-secondary education. ICCAL '92 is being held at Acadia University in Wolfville, Nova Scotia, Canada, June 17-20, 1992.

ICCAL '92 is the fourth in a series of International Conferences on Computers and Learning. The previous ones were held in Hagen (Germany 1990), Dallas (USA 1989), and Calgary (Canada 1987). Due to ICCAL's success, future meetings will be held annually and enlarged in scope. The next one will be in Orlando, Florida, in June 1993 under the name ED-MEDIA-World Conference on Educational Multimedia and Hypermedia; it will be sponsored by the Association for Advancement of Computers in Education. Further information about ED-Media is available from Dr. Hermann Maurer, IIG, Schießstadtgasse 4a, A-8010 Graz, Austria, fax number: (0043 316) 82 5394, or e-mail address: hmaurer@iicm.tu-graz.ac.at

ICCAL '92 whose proceedings are presented in this volume, features forty-five submitted and six invited papers. Another twenty-nine short papers are included in the supplementary proceedings (not included in this volume). We thank the authors of all submissions for their contributions.

Papers were selected from one hundred submissions by the following program committee: I. Benest (UK), M. Brown (USA), P. Carlson (USA), S. Cerri (Italy), B. Clark (Canada), N. Coulter (USA), G. Davies (UK), M. DeBlasi (Italy), N. Gardner (UK), A. Derycke (France), J. Hammond (Australia), F. Hill (USA), D. Jonassen (USA), E. Luque (Spain), G. Kovacs (Hungary), R. Hartog (Netherlands), H. Hamburger (USA), F. Makedon (USA), H. Maurer (Austria), G. McCalla (Canada), R. Mizguchi (Japan), A. Montgomery (Australia), D. Norrie (Canada), M. Mulhauser (Germany), G. Oberem (South Africa), Th. Ottmann (Germany), D. Paramskas (Canada), M. Petruk (Canada), C. Prescott (Thailand), B. Shneiderman (USA), I. Tomek (Canada), S. Wills (Australia), C. Unger (Germany), B. Woolf (USA), M. Yazdani (UK). We thank them all for the careful reading of their share of the numerous submissions and for adherence to the short deadlines.

Much appreciated are also the contributions of the steering committee consisting of H. Maurer (Austria), D. Norrie (Canada), F. Makedon (USA), and Th. Ottmann (Germany), and the advisory board whose members are D. Bitzer (USA), A. Bork (USA), W. Clark (Canada), G. Davies (UK), K. Friend (USA), H. Six (Germany), G. Kovacs (Hungary), W. Srisa-an (Thailand). Special thanks go to Dr. Hermann Maurer, the indefatigable spirit of the conference.

The conference would not be possible without a lot of invisible help behind the scenes. I wish to thank in particular A. Germani, M. Elammari, T. Morse, S. Nassar, P. Proszynski, and my wife Jana.

Finally, thanks to A. Hofmann from Springer-Verlag for cooperation in the preparation of this volume.

Wolfville, April 1992   Ivan Tomek

Contents

Why Hypermedia Systems are Important*

H. Maurer

IIG (Institutes for Information Processing),
Graz University of Technology, Austrian Computer Society and
Joanneum Research, Schieszstattg. 4a, A-8010 Graz, Austria
email: hmaurer@iicm.tu-graz.ac.at

Abstract

In this paper we argue that the original vision of hypertext-pioneers in North America and Europe (yes, Europe also has had its hypertext visionaires!) that a non-linear widely distributed corpus of information accessible "everywhere by everyone" is still very much alive and becoming more and more a reality, even if some of the glamour has been stolen by stand-alone developments as started by Hypercard. We further contend that the advent of computer supported multi-media systems does provide not just acute alternative to present information but an enrichment of our sensory and communicative possibilities that will impact society in a major way. We finally conclude that the merging of large wide-spread hypertext systems with computer supported multimedia technology into powerful hypermedia systems will indeed provide a new kind of infrastructure for working, communicating, and thinking whose influence on how mankind will live, work, teach, and learn could be quite dazzling.

---

*The support of my hypermedia work by the Austrian Federal Ministry for Science and Research is gratefully acknowledged.

1   Introduction

In this section we briefly review how hypertext systems developed historically; and how they are more and more merging with multimedia technology into potentially large-scale hypermedia systems with a rich spectrum of applications.

This is by no means intended to be a history of hypermedia, or a general survey. For such purposes we refer to [Conklin88], [Maurer91],[Maurer91c], [Nielsen90], or [Tomek91]. We do feel, however, that this is a good opportunity to address a few issues that are rarely mentioned. In particular that (i) the idea of networked and linked non-linear collections of informations was conceived on both sides of the Atlantic independently; it has not been entirely successful on either side, yet has resulted in viable but completely different spin-offs in North America and Europe; and that (ii) the use of digital multimedia technology and advances in networks and data-compression are finally opening the possibility to realize some of the dreams of early visionaries.

Bush [Bush45] is usually credited as the first to write in concrete terms about a technological system (not yet computerised) allowing to store and access large amounts of cross-linked information to augment the human intellect. And Engelbart's NLS system [Engelbart68] was probably the first version of what one might call a simple hypertext system: it did allow to store chunks of information and navigate through them using "links" and other techniques.

During the late 60's and early 70's a number of researchers realized the tremendous additional possibilities becoming available through progressive networking. It is this idea of having a sophisticated network-component in addition to the paradigm of connecting chunks of information by means of "links" that resulted in concepts for the first genuine hypertext systems: systems allowing distributed storage and access to a rich variety of (initially textual) information, with chunks of informations connected by a variety of mechanisms usually refered to as "links".

It is curious to note how different this idea developed in North America and in Europe. Let us first look at North America. In the USA, Ted Nelson was certainly one of the early hypertext visionaries [Nelson65], [Nelson72], seeing hypertext as a new universal medium for general publication; his efforts to implement and make available a suitable hypertext system Xanadu on a large scale [Nelson87] have not been entirely successful, yet his ideas have inspired many researchers. His flamboyant personality and rhethoric [Nelson87] have done much to spread the gospel of hypertext (and a bit of concern that maybe hypertext is pushed with "too much hype"). His water analogy (that water is needed everywhere and hence has been made available everywhere at the turn of a watertap; that the same is true of information and that "hypertext systems are the waterworks for the mind; the computer screen the spigot or showernozzle") has become as much a classic as his hope that working with hypertext systems may eventually bring "noids" and "fluffies" together. ("Noids" are "technoids with an exaggerated notion of what is clear-minded thinking ...with a negligible concern for history, art and human freedom"; "fluffies" are people whose "cognitive style leans towards ...idealistic terms. And they do not like computers or screens"; according to Nelson, noids and fluffies have only one thing in common: "Each sees the other group as 'those people in their little corner, unaware of the big wide world"'.)

In the seventies and eighties large networked hypertext efforts including also other "media", like pictures (i.e. hypermedia undertakings) started at a number of prestigious institutions in the USA. (See [Conklin88], [Nielsen90], or [Tomek91] for surveys; some of the major efforts are described in [Champine90], [Haan92], [Shneidermann89], and [Ziegler90]; see also the special issues on hypermedia systems [CACM88], [CACM90], [CACM91], [CGR91b], [IEEE91], and [JMCA91].)

Although quite successful for some purposes in their mainly educational settings, none of them managed a break-through on a grand scale, none created an avalanche of hypertext usage as envisaged by some of the hypertext pioneers. Such wide-spread use is still to come – and will come, as we point out in section 4.

In the meantime, another event changed the world of hypertext, maybe even the meaning of the words hypertext and hypermedia: Apple introduced Hypercard. Hypercard and its many followers on both Apple and other platforms provide most of the functionality expected from a full-fledged hypermedia systems except for the fact that they are designed as stand-alone (one-user) systems. Thus, the important network/information-sharing/communicational and cooperational features are, by necessity, missing. Nevertheless Hypercard and its followers – due to its easy use and its distribution policy (Hypercard came bundled with every Mac) – have become widespread to an extent that Hypercard has become almost synonymous to hypermedia systems, at least for some people. Let us emphasize that we do not subscribe to this point of view: a genuine hypermedia system must support a large number of users on a networked basis.

Let us now turn to Europe in the early seventies. The notion of easy-to-use networked systems providing informational, communicational and transactional aspects was first conceived, as a bold vision, by Sam Fedida of British Telecom. In contrast to the USA, where such ideas were pursued by prestigious research institutes at the very top of the state-of-the-art level (hence by definition with no immediate mass-audience), Sam Fedida was instrumental in pushing through a much more down-to-earth approach [Fedida75]: his idea was to provide a nation-wide, eventually world-wide, network of computers, accessible to the general public via ordinary phone lines and using somewhat modified TV-sets or such as terminals. Thus, videotex was born. Although by no means a real success story (growth has been much more sluggish than predicted) some 6 million Europeans are using videotex now. And videotex offers, albeit on a very modest technical platform most of the features usually stipulated for a hypermedia system, including delivery of non-textual data, and the integration of communicational and cooperational features. Taking into account that videotex provides access to terrabytes of information (e.g. complete phone books of a number of countries, complete property-registers for some countries, dozens of encyclopedias, etc., etc.) it comes close to Ted Nelson's dreams of Xanadu ... but the technology used is too simple, the system not user-friendly enough to satisfy more sophisticated needs.

In a nut-shell the situation concerning hypermedia systems is this: both in North America and Europe a number of "genuine" networked state-of-the-art hypermedia systems are in prototype-usage. We mention Hyper-G [Maurer90b], [Kappe91], and Nestor/Hector [Mühlhäuser90] as European examples, and particularly World Wide Web ("W3") [WWW] operated by CERN. W3 is tying together hypermedia systems in the whole world (including the Minnesota-originated Gopher system with by now over 20 sites). It is maybe the first attempt at creating a world-wide hypermedia system, yet has a number of serious limitations. Thus, the truly high-power, wide-spread hypermedia system still remains a vision: rather, all hypermedia-efforts, sofar, have produced a variety of commercial spin-offs, at most: in addition to opening ways for electronic publishing and exhibition support [Maurer91b] the most significant results originating in North America are stand-alone systems such as Hypercard, and the most significant result originating in Europe is Videotex.

Thus, the high hopes of hypermedia-pioneers have been perverted into hypermedia systems without net (Hypercard-like systems), or into hypermedia systems with archaic user-interfaces and functionality (Videotex-like systems).

Why should we, then, still believe in grand visions? We should and we can, since our now available software, hardware and know-how will allow us to develop successfully what failed with videotex because of still inadequate technology. Putting it differently: widely networked systems with the user-friendliness of modern stand-alone or local-area hypermedia systems will become increasingly available.

2 Why hypertext systems are important

By hypertext system we mean in this section a system as proposed by Ted Nelson: a distributed data-base of chunks of information (if more than textual information is supported we speak of hypermedia systems), cross-referenced by various types of links, accessible by a large number of persons (as passive users or as authors) and supporting a variety of navigational, manipulational, communicational and cooperational activities. We can follow links, thus browsing "associatively" through some information space (much like maybe thinking processes work in our brains), we can rearrange and anotate information for later use, or we can just query the data-base, thus overall extending our intellect much in the sense of [Bush45]; and we can communicate and cooperate with others over arbitrary distances: everyone of us now using high-speed computer-nets for email or cooperation via e.g. remote logins does appreciate some of those facilities already; and that a hypermedia approach to such features would enhance their usability should be clear [Maurer90]. (For a survey of the state-of-the-art in computer supported cooperative work see [CSCW91]).

If hypertext systems become as widespread and ubiquitous as proposed by some researchers, Nelson's vision of hypertext as the ultimate medium for eletronic publishing does not seem that far-fetched anymore, hypertext as "Gutenberg 2" might indeed become reality: not just bringing some but "all" books onto everyone's desk! "All published information just a mouse-click away" [Nelson87].

Universal availability of large hypermedia data-bases may be less science-fiction than it sounds: with lap-top computers soon integrated via cellular telephones into a global communication network this would be quite feasable. Observe that the possibility to "instantaneously" check on information could change our whole communicative patterns. When receiving information we may be able to verify its correctness, when transmitting information it will be easier to be specific and accurate. How much will we learn to rely on this "extension to our brain?"

Hypermedia systems offer a number of other potentially significant "philosophical" advantages: the fact that readers may leave notes for others may well be helpful in judging the value of a controversial report in a hypermedia newscast; many complex issues of modern society are not linear in nature, but consist of many mutually interwoven aspects: clearly such situations (a law-case, the working of a piece of machinery, ...) can be described much better using a multi-dimensional web of chunks of information than using linear text; Marshall McLuhan has pointed out that linear text has narrowed our view of the world: hypertext is the first chance to "de-linearize" the way we communicate ideas.

How much of above is wishful speculation or will at least partially come true only future developments will show!

In the meantime, hypertext systems are already successfully used for electronic publishing on a smaller scale: electronic encyclopedia systems – the most famous one maybe Hyperties [Shneiderman89] - or collections of maps are ideal applications. One of them is a highly flexible modulare scheme for using individualized encyclopedias as described in [Mülner89].

3 Why computer-supported multimedia systems are important

Everyone realizes that diagrams or pictures, let alone animated diagrams or movieclips, are powerful tools for conveying information in many situations. Thus it is clear that the integration of such materials, and others (e.g. sound and speech) into information systems has been a dream for decades. This dream is now rapidly coming true: large capacity storage media (like Giga-byte sized harddisks or CD ROMs), high quality compression techniques, particularly for still pictures [Wallace91] and movieclips [LeGall91], special purpose chips allowing decompression fast enough for showing television quality movies by displaying some twenty medium-resolution colour raster images per second [LeGall91], [Green92], [Poole91], and the rapid market-penetration of inexpensive high-quality graphic cards and monitors are allowing an increasing media mix on wide-spread hardware platforms.

Thus, the days when the incorporation of high-quality picture material or movies into hypertext systems was only possible by using analog sources (particularly videodiscs) and required much special hardware are nearing an end. Fully digital multimedia systems and tools are emerging [Poole91], [Green92].

Although everyone agrees that the wide-spread use of pictures, diagrams, animation and movies will increase the value and applicability of hypermedia systems we think that the real impact of such a media-mix is still underestimated by most people. We believe that the easy retrieval and manipulation of pictoral material in all its forms will deeply influence mankind in how knowledge is archived and communicated. The reason for this credo is based on a simple physiological observation whose significance is often overlooked: mankind is lacking one very important organ! [Maurer91d], [Maurer92].

To be more specific: our second most important sensory organ, the ear, has an active counterpart: the mouth, which is capable of generating utterances understood by the ear. Our most important sensory organ, the eye, has no analogous counterpart: humans have no physiological construct to display any kind of picture!

Is it not disturbing that we can produce "concrete" sounds (speech) and "abstract" sounds (music) using the vocal chords but that we are not equipped to display – in real time – high quality pictures, either "concrete" or "abstract", let alone being able to project animated pictures? Some may be tempted to answer that we can indeed produce visual information by using gestures, facial expressions, bodystance or such. Note, however, that those are what we would call "secondary" visual signals: much like the sound of hitting the table with a fist or clapping hands are crude "secondary" acoustic signals.

Let us face the fact that we can store images based on reality in our head, that we can "conjure" up images of things we have never seen; that we can "imagine"(!) things that no one has ever experienced. Yet, when it comes to externalizing these images we are markedly deficient and must resort to gestures and antics.

The only way we have had in the past to communicate mental imagery in a lasting fashion was to code it into words, and words into writing, or to draw a picture, to use sculpting techniques, or to record something as photos or movies (making it difficult to leave room for abstraction and creativity), or more recently, to use computer graphics and visualization – and animation tools.

This is the main point to understand: humans are heavily visually based beings: about half of the human neocortex is devoted to visual information processing. We have an unconscious desire to "feed" our eyes with visual information, and this is one of the reasons for the appeal of movies and television. Yet despite all of this desire to accept visual stimuli and our excellent equipment for receiving them, we are sadly lacking a "picture generating organ".

However, this is no reason for despair. Humans are lacking many facilities of potential great value: we have no wings to fly and no gills to swim underwater; yet we have developed airplanes, submarines and SCUBA equipment as "surrogates" or "crutches" to overcome the mentioned deficiencies.

It is our contention that computer-supported multimedia systems are going to become better and better substitutes for our missing picture generating organ. As software tools and interface-mechanisms continuously improve the externalization of mental imagery will become progressively easier. Initially, and right now, this means that the effort required to express our ideas using pictures, diagrams, animation sequences, movies, etc. is going to reduce more and more; eventually (maybe) the tools will become sophisticated enough to be used in real-time: in the same way as we are more or less capable of externalizing our thoughts in realtime by speaking (note that for a good presentation we do need some preparation!) we might someday be able to externalize our thoughts by producing, in real time, a presentation consisting of acoustic and visual elements using a suitable technological surrogate for our missing picture generating organ.

Real-time multimedia "production" may or may not prove to be elusive. The main point remains the same: multimedia tools are going to allow the presentation and communication of information (i.e. knowledge) in a much more efficient way; and thus are bound to play a major role in the life-long information acquisition processes (i.e. learning) we are all involved in.

It has to be understood that the visual component of a computer supported multi-media system is not limited to ordinary digitized photos and movies: such photos and movies of real-life situations are valuable in some cases but lack the necessary level of abstraction in others. At least as important are other techniques for visualization, among them:

  (i) diagrams, maps, and abstract pictures;

 (ii) process visualization tools;

(iii) data visualization tools;

 (iv) 3D modelling, animation, and abstract movies.

It is curious to note that the area of computer visualization which encompasses all of the above is often not sufficiently integrated into hypermedia efforts. Still more surprising, specialists in computer visualization are rarely aware of the full range of aspects covered by points (i) – (iv).

It seems appropriate to at least superficially deal with a few of the issues involved:

Diagrams, maps, and abstract pictures
This is probably the best understood aspect. A variety of tools for "drawing", up to and including CAD techniques (supporting everything from city-planning to VLSI chip design) are available, and so are various "paint" programs: the former packages tend to use an object oriented approach (not necessarily in the sense of software-engineering but in the sense of geometric objets), the latter packages usually work on a pixel level. To our knowledge no system has succeeded in "seamlessly" combining the two approaches, sofar.

Process – visualization tools
Showing animated diagrams is one of the most effective ways of explaining processes, whether it is a production process in a plant, a phenonmenon in the natural sciences or in medicine, the working of a computer algorithm, etc.

The development of CAI packages has been a major driving force in this area [Huber87], [Huber89], [Kappe90], [Makedon87]. Reasonable "animation tools" do now exist on various levels (as on-screen editors, as special-purpose "programming" languages or as combination of both). Typical such tools are e.g. the "Animator" by Autodesk (PC based), the "Macro Mind Director" (Mac based), or workstation based 3D animation packages for professional applications such as the "Advanced Visualizer" (Wavefront Technologies Inc.), "Explore" (Thomson Digital Image), or "Studio" (Alias). However, no widely accessible package for e.g. efficient "$2\frac{1}{2}$–D" animation-editing as typically required for diagram animation is yet available: much research and development is still required in this area.

An important subarea of process-animation is the visualization of computer algorithms. Best results – from a pedagogical point of view – are obtained by using some of the general tools just mentioned. However, displaying any process nicely and in detail involves much manual work. An alternative approach, first taken in Balsa [Brown88] and later refined in systems such as Tango [Stasko90] is to try to automatically generate visualizations of programs by adding a kind-of "interpreter" to the programs akin to debuggers, but using graphical facilities to show the working of the program.

Although it is fair to say that the visualizations produced are usually inferior to ones produced specifically for a certain algorithm, the production effort is minimal. Hence the techniques now available in algorithm animation will ordinarily not be used so much to explain algorithms to the novice but rather to gain a deeper understanding of the process involved. Indeed, one of the main resulting applications is algorithm debugging and optimization. Visualization techniques are also used more and more for explaining the parallel execution of programs, see e.g. [Szelenyi91].

Data visualization tools

Bar-chars, pie-charts, graphs of all kind, etc. have been used for a long time to visualize simple numeric data.

In many areas of science, however, huge amounts of high-dimensional data, i.e. data representing a large number of parameters, are produced. To interpret the important features of the data obtained, new visualization techniques are of paramount importance. An excellent annotated bibliography which may serve as introduction to this field is [Nielson90]. Good surveys are [Frenkel88] and [Crawford90]. Special journal issues on scientific visualization are [CGR91], [CGR92], [Computer89]. A classic paper is [Chernoff73] in which it is suggested to use cartoon faces with variable attributes (shape of face, length of nose, shape of eyes, shape of mouth, etc.) to represent data of up to 12 dimensions. The papers [Cunningham91], [Haber90] and [DeFanti89] are other nice papers describing special aspects of visualization problems. In [Domik92] practical problems of visualization are described using a concrete project in Astrophysics.

It is worth noting and has been an intriguing experience for us that the time-element can be used effectively for certain visualization problems. One such problem we have encountered was to try to visualize and "understand" a 4-dimensional (4D) polytope. We developed a program which permits us to move a 3D hyperplane through the 4D object from any direction at any speed, and displaying the 3D "cut" determined by the hyperplane in perspective drawing. Thus, the 4D polytope can be inspected by moving the hyperplane, the screen showing how the object which is cut out changes. After exploring the polytope long enough an interesting phenomenon happens: we begin to understand the polytope in the sense that we can predict what we will see, even if we sweep the hyperplane through the polytope in entirely new directions. Thus, our brain has digested, in a way, the necessary information of the polytope: humans can see 4 dimensions, after all!

3D modelling, animation and abstract movies

Much of 3D modelling and animation belongs to core areas of CAD and computer graphics. We thus just refer to two major books [Hill90] and [Foley90] in this area. Observe that sophisticated systems for creating animated scenes with real-life quality are being used for areas as diverse as military training applications, the production of pictures and movie clips for purposes of art, entertainment, education and advertisement. Again we refer to professional animation packages such as "Advanced Visualizer", "Explore", or "Studio" mentioned earlier. For details on realistic human computer animation see e.g. [Thalmann91], for a glimpse into the world of Art [Linehan90].

There is one issue which we want to mention a bit more detailed since it has been largely ignored, sofar: it is the concept of abstract movie.

We can look at this notion from a number of points of view. Observe first that there is general agreement that after reading a book, viewing a movie produced on the basis of that book is usually disappointing. We believe that one reason for this phenomenon is that in going from the book to the movie, the level of abstraction changes, hence limiting the viewers' imagination. "A tall person" turns into a concrete actor or actress, "a gentle flowing river" into a concrete version thereof, etc. If we are to succeed to convey ideas at the desired level of abstraction we have to learn to introduce and work with appropriate abstract moving images.

Observe next that we have concrete pictures (photos, or realistic paintings) and abstract pictures (e.g some cubistic painting as a sample of a totally abstract picture, or some expressionistic or impressionistic painting, inbetween "real life" and "totally abstract"). We do not have any substantial experience beyond cartoons with the equivalent semi- or totally abstract movies yet! What would a cubistic, expressionistic or impressionistic film be like? We can imagine that such films may be quite beautiful, may be able to convey information in a very deep and abstract (i.e. individualizable) fashion; yet such films are likely to require a learning process before they can be understood.

Still looking at it differently, static symbols such as letters or abstract icons convey a lot of information; how much more will micons (moving icons) be able to convey, once we have learnt to use and understand ("read") them!

Much research and experimentation will be necessary before we are fully able to exploit the potential of abstract movies beyond the trivial level of diagrams and slightly stylized (cartoon-like) movies.

However, there is also much promise. Let us for a moment consider a micon-paradigm for "loving", symbolized by "reaching out and embracing": speed, strength and other parameters (is the reaching out "one-way" or "mutual"?) all give much information on what this "loving" is like.

A scene of two persons (themselves maybe stylized) embracing each other will show the degree of emotions towards each other more clearly than words could express; a scene of a flower gingerly embracing the sun, but cordially embracing shadow and water may be a much better way of showing the prefered habitat of that flower than a verbal description, etc.

We are just starting to learn how to use pictures for expressing various notions; and we have a still longer but interesting route to go to learn how to use abstract and animated versions of pictures for expressing ideas, i.e. for human to human communication. However, the very fact that suitable use of multimedia technology will improve our ability to communicate ideas is the real reason why multimedia research is such an exciting and potentially revolutionary area.

4 Hypermedia - combining hypertext and multimedia

Emerging technologies are starting to permit to use large-scale networks supporting distributed data-bases with hypertext-kind of links between chunks of information; they also permit to store and transmit (in compressed form) visual and audio data in digitized form in large quantities, and are enabling a playback of pictures, audio- and movieclips in real time. Hypertext and fully digitized multimedia systems are slowly merging into hypermedia systems providing easy access to all kinds of information, communicational and cooperational infrastructure, and a mix of media suitable for expressing ideas and information much better than by written or spoken word alone.

The original dream of hypertext pioneers was that hypertext may help to delinearize our thinking that has been deformed by the linearity of text, that we may see complex issues as what they are: a web of supporting, conflicting and interwoven arguments and of pieces of information, that large quantities of easily accessible information will become a huge extension of our personal memory. Thus, hypertext was seen as extending our brain. Looking at it from today's point of view this vision can be modified: hypermedia has the potential to not only extend our brain but, maybe much more important and more realistic, to extend our communicational facilities by providing a surrogate for the missing picture generating organ and by allowing to link not just pieces of information, but through networks, to also link people in joint cooperative endeavours, synchronously or asynchronously.

Experiences with huge data-bases have been, overall, disappointing: completeness, consistency, obsolescence and clumsiness of use have plagued most really big attempts at creating "universal data-bases". For that reason we believe more in those aspects of hypermedia systems that do not require "complete" data-bases, i.e. applications for the purpose of information and teaching on selected topics, and of communication and cooperation, with a heavy dose of multi-media thrown into all of them. We strongly believe that hypermedia will be successful and stay with us in these areas, not just as a system, but as general paradigm [Maurer90].

References

[Brown88]   Brown, M.H.: Algorithm Animation, MIT Press, Cambridge, Mass. (1988).

[Bush45]   Bush, V.: As we May Think; Atlantic Monthly 176, 1 (July 1945), 101-108.

[CACM88]   Special Issue on Hypertext, C.ACM 31, 7 (1988).

[CACM90]   Special Issue on Hypertext, C.ACM 33, 3 (1990).

[CACM91]   Special Issue on Digital Multimedia Systems, C.ACM 34, 4 (1991).

[CGR91]   Special Issue on Scientific Visualization, IEEE Computer Graphics
                and Applications 11,3 (1991).

[CGR91b]   Special Issue on Multimedia, IEEE Computer Graphics and Appli-
                cations 11, 4 (1991).

[CGR91c]   Special Issue on Visualizing Complexity, IEEE Computer Graphics
                and Applications 11, 5 (1991).

[Champine90]   Champine, G.A., Geer, D.E., Ruh, W.N.: Project Athena as a
                Distributed Computer System; IEEE Computer 23, 9 (1990), 40-
                51.

[Chernoff73]   Chernoff, H.: The Use of Faces to Represent Points in a K-
                Dimensional Space Graphically; J. American Statistical Association
                68, 342 (19973), 361-368.

[Computer89]   Special Issue on Scientific Visualization, IEEE Computer 22, 8
                (1989).

[Conklin88]   Conklin, E.J., Begemann, M.L.: gIBIS: A Hypertext Tool for Team
                Design Deliberation; Proc. of Hypertext'87, TR88-013, University
                of North Carolina, Dept. of Computer Science (March 1988), 247-
                252.

[Crawford90]   Crawford, S.L., Fall, T.C.: Projection Pursuit Techniques for the
                Visualization of High Dimensional Datasets; in: [Nielson90].

[CSCW]   Special Issue on Collaborative Computing; C.ACM 34, 12 (1991).

[Cunningham90] Cunningham, S., Brown, J.R., McGRath, M.: Visualization in
                Science and Engineering Education; in [Nielson90].

[DeFanti89]   De Fanti, T.A. Brown, M.D. McCormick, B.H.: Visualization – ex-
                panding Scientific and Engineering Research Opportunities; IEEE
                Computer 22, 8 (1989), 12-25.

[Domik92]   Domik, G.O., Mickus-Miceli, K.D.: Design and Development of
                Data Visualization Systems in a Workstation Environment; J.MCA
                (1992) (to appear).

[Engelbart68]   Engelbart, D.C., English, W.K.: A Research Center for Augmenting
                Human Intellect; AFIPS Proceedings, Fall Joint Computer Confe-
                rence (1968), 395-410.

[Fedida75]   Fedida, S.: An Interactive Information Service for the General Pu-
                  blic; Proc. European Conf. on Communication Networks (1975),
                  261-282.

[Foley90]   Foley, J.D., Van Dam, A.: Computer Graphics; Addision Wesley,
                  Reading, Mass. (1990).

[Frenckel88]   Frenckel, K.A.: The Art and Science of Visualizing Data; C.ACM
                  31, 2 (1988), 110-121.

[Green92]   Green, J.L.: The Evolution of DVI System Software; C.ACM 35
                  (1992), 53-67.

[Haan92]   Haan, B.J., Kahn, P., Rilly, V.A., Coombs, J.H., Meyrowitz, N.K.:
                  IRIS - Hypermedia Services; C.ACM 35, 1 (1992), 36-51.

[Haber90]   Haber, R.B., McNabb, D.A.: Visualization Idioms: A Conceptual
                  Model for Scientific Visualization Systems; in [Nielson90]

[Hill90]   Hill, F.S.: Computer Graphics; Macmillan, New York (1990).

[Huber87]   Huber, F., Maurer, H. : On Editors for Presentation Type CAI;
                  Angewandte Informatik 11 (1987), 449-457.

[Huber89]   Huber, F., Makedon, F., Maurer, H.: Hyper-COSTOC: A Com-
                  prehensive Computer-based Teaching Support System; J.MCA 12
                  (1989), 293-317.

[IEEE91]   Special Issue on Multimedia Information Systems, IEEE - Compu-
                  ter 24, 10 (1991).

[JMCA91]   Special Issue on Hypermedia Systems, J.MCA 14, 2 (1991).

[LeGall91]   Le Gall, D.: MPEG: A Video Compression Standard for Multimedia
                  Applications; C.ACM 34, 4 (1991), 47-58.

[Kappe90]   Kappe, F., Maurer, H.: Animation in Hyper-G – An Outline; Proc.
                  Future Trends in Information Technology, Oldenburg Pub.Co.,
                  Vienna-Munich (1990), 235-248.

[Kappe91]   Kappe, F., Maurer, H., Tomek, I.: Hyper-G: Specification of Re-
                  quirements, Proc. Conference on Intelligent Systems, CIS'91, Vesz-
                  prem, Hungary (1991), 257-272.

[Linehan90]   Linehan, T.E.: Digital Image – Digital Cinema; C.ACM 33, 7
                  (1990), 30-37.

[Makedon87]   Makedon, F., Maurer, H., Ottmann, T.: Presentation Type CAI in
                  Computer Science Education at University Level; J.MCA 10 (1987),
                  283-295.

[Maurer90]   Maurer, H., Tomek, I.: Broadening the Scope of Hypermedia Principles; Hypermedia 2,3 (1990), 201-221.

[Maurer90b]   Maurer, H., Tomek, I.: Some Aspects of Hypermedia Systems and Their Treatment in Hyper-G; Wirtschaftinformatik 32 (April 1990), 187-196.

[Maurer91]   Maurer, H., Tomek, I.: Hypermedia Bibliography; [JMCA91], 161-216.

[Maurer91b]   Maurer, H., Williams, M.R.: Hypermedia Systems and Other Computer Support as Infrastructure for Museums; [JMCA91], 117-137.

[Maurer91c]   Maurer, H., Tomek, I.: Hypermedia – from the Past to the Future; Proc. New Results and New Trends in Computer Science, Graz, Austria, LNCS 555, Springer Pub.Co. (1991), 320-336.

[Maurer91d]   Maurer, H., Carlson, P.: Computer Visualization, a Missing Organ, and Cyber-Equivalency; IIG Report 295, Graz (1991).

[Maurer92]   Maurer, H., Carlson, P.: Computervisualisierung: die Krücke für ein fehlendes Organ?; technologie & management (1992), to appear.

[Mühlhäuser90] Mühlhäuser, M.: Hyperinformation in Instructional Tools Environments; Proc. ICCAL'90, Hagen, Germany, LNCS 348, Springer Pub.Co (1990), 245-264.

[Mülner89]   Mülner, H.: A System of Interactive Encyclopedias; Austrian-Hungarian Computer Conference, Budapest (1989), 181-190.

[Nelson65a]   Nelson, T.H.: A File Structure for the Complex, the Changing and the Indeterminate; Proc. 20th ACM Natl. Conference (1965), 84-100.

[Nelson72]   Nelson, T.H.: As We Will Think; Online 72, Proc. Intl. Conf. on Online Interactive Computing, Brunel University, Uxbridge, England (September 1972).

[Nelson87]   Nelson, T.H.: Literary Machines; Edition 87.1, 702 South Michigan, South Bend, IN 46618 (1987).

[Newcomb91]   Newcomb, S.R., Kipp, N.A., Newcomb, V.T.: The 'HyTime' Hypermedia/Time-based Document Sturctured Language; C.ACM 34, 11 (1991), 67-83.

[Nielsen90]   Nielsen, J.: Hypertext and Hypermedia; Academic Press (1990).

[Nielson90]   Nielson, G.M., Shriver, B. (eds.): Visualization in Scientific Computing; IEEE Computer Society Press, Los Alamitos, California (1990), 5-30.

[Poole91]   Poole, L.: Quicktime in Motion; Mac World (Sept. 1991), 154-159.

[Shneiderman89]   Shneiderman, B., Brethauer, D.; Plaisant, C., Potter, R.: The HyperTIES Electronic Encyclopedia: An Evaluation Based on Three Museum Installations; J. of the American Society for Information Science 40 (1989), 3.

[Stasko90]   Stasko, J.T.: Tango – A Framework and System for Algorithm Animation; IEEE Computer 23, 9 (1990), 27-39.

[Szelenyi91]   Szelenyi, F., Zecca, V.: Visualizing Parallel Execution of Fortran Programs; IBM J. Res. Develop. 35, 1/2 (1991), 270-282.

[Thalmann91]   Magnenat-Thalmann, N., Thalmann, D. (Eds.): Computer Animation'91, Springer Pub.Co. (1990).

[Tomek91]   Tomek, I., Khan, S., Müldner, T., Nassar, M., Novak, G., Proszynski, P.: Hypermedia – Introduction and Survey; [JMCA91], 63-100.

[Wallace91]   Wallace, G.K.: The JPEG Still Picture Compression Standard; C.ACM 34, 4 (1991), 30-44.

[WWW]   World Wide Web – W3; Login via telnet under info.cern.ch

[Ziegler90]   Ziegler, L., Weiss, G.: Multimedia Conferencing on Local Area Networks; IEEE Computer 23, 9 (1990),52-61.

Project CALC: Calculus as a Laboratory Course

Lawrence Moore and David Smith
Department of Mathematics
Duke University
Durham, NC 27706

Abstract

Calculus is the study of change. The concepts of calculus enable us to model processes that change and to describe properties of these processes that remain constant in the midst of change. Now change has come to the **learning** of calculus -- change driven by the need to respond to the revolution in technology and fueled by funds from the United States National Science Foundation. What should be changed? How and how fast? What should remain constant? In this paper we describe one answer to these questions: Project CALC, a new calculus course developed at Duke University. The key features of our approach are real-world problems, hands-on activities, discovery learning, writing and revision of writing, teamwork, and intelligent use of available tools.

Goals

As we discussed the nature of the new course and worked on materials, we gradually formulated a number of goals.

1. **We wanted the students to be able to use mathematics to structure their understanding of and investigate questions in the world around them.** This meant that the students should work on real-world problems with real data.

2. **We wanted the students to use calculus to formulate problems, to solve problems, and to communicate the solution of problems to others.** This meant that we needed to spend some time developing the physics setting, the economics background, or the biological models necessary to understanding the problem. It also meant that the students needed to write up their investigations in coherent readable English.

3. **We wanted the students to use technology as an integral part of this process of formulation, solution, and communication.** Computers and sophisticated calculators have changed they way we relate to the world. The students need to

concentrate on what they need to know to use these tools intelligently and with confidence; they should not engage in John Henry-like competition of pencil and paper versus technology.

4. We wanted the students to work and learn cooperatively. Talking to each other about mathematics is a strange new idea for most students. Once they get started and develop a learning community, they learn as much or more from their peers as they do from their instructors.

With these goals in mind, we developed a three-semester calculus program based on a laboratory science model. In our case, the laboratory is a computer laboratory. Here the students, working in pairs, explore real-world problems with real data, conjecture and test their conjectures, discuss their work with each other, and write up their results and conclusions on a technical word processor. This laboratory experience drives the rest of the course. It shapes the contents and the approach of the text and the format of the classroom activities.

In the classroom, we were struck by the difference between teaching and learning. For years we and our colleagues had concentrated on what the teacher was doing. What makes a good lecture? How can we cover all the topics packed into the syllabus in a logical manner? Now we began to concentrate on the student. What activities should students be doing to help them construct the mathematical knowledge needed? As we thought about this and experimented, we lectured less and less. More time was given to student activities in groups -- gathering data on the period of pendulums in terms of the length (for use later in the lab), balancing plywood cutouts to locate the experimental center of mass (to compare later with the theoretical center), calculating the rate of decrease of the distance between two planes approaching an air traffic control tower and deciding whether they will collide. We were more likely to be out among the class talking to the students than to be in front lecturing.

Details of the course at Duke

At Duke the course meets for three 50-minute periods in a classroom equipped with one computer for instructor demonstrations. Each section (maximum of 32 students) splits into two lab groups; each group has a scheduled two-hour lab each week. Each lab team (two students) submits a written report almost every week; three or four of these a semester are formal reports that involve submission, review by the instructor, and resubmission for a grade. The remaining reports are "fill in the paragraph", often finished during the lab period itself.

In the classroom, we try to limit lecturing to brief introductions of new topics and responses to demands for more information. Teams of four work on activities that lead to a variety of reports. In weeks that do not include a test, each student has a week-long assignment of routine computations and exercises embedded in the reading. One class period each week is "group office hours"; the instructor responds to student problems, but does not initiate new material.

During the first semester, the students use *Mathcad* for the mathematical portion of the labs and write up their reports on EXP. During the second semester we add *Derive*, right after the students have begun to wrestle with the problem of finding antiderivatives. In the third semester we add still more software, *MPP* for parametric curves and numerical evaluation of double and triple integrals, and *Surface Plotter* for the investigation of surfaces. The labs are currently equipped with PS2 Model 30's, each with a coprocessor, connected to a 386 file server.

In the first year of the project (1989-90), we taught two sections of the new course at Duke. The next year (1990-91) we increased this to seven sections of Calculus I and one of Calculus III. During the past academic year (1991-92), we taught five sections of Calculus I, one section of Calculus II (for entering students with advanced placement), and two sections of Calculus III. The department has voted to extend the new course in 1992-93 to all entering students beginning with Calculus I (about half of entering Duke students taking calculus -- seventeen sections) with a further extension to all first-year calculus sections in 1993-94.

Test sites and dissemination

We began our development in cooperation with the North Carolina School of Science and Mathematics, a state supported school for high school students with ability and interest in science and mathematics. They have now gone on to develop their own version of the course materials, similar in spirit to our development, but targeted at the high school student.

During the academic year 1991-92, ten different colleges and universities used our materials. In particular, Bill Barker at Bowdoin College in Maine has adapted our laboratory materials to a *Mathematica* environment. Next year, we expect to see the development of lab materials for the HP48S calculator; other software platforms under consideration are *Mathcad 3.0 for Windows* and *Maple 5.0*.

We expect to see the number of test sites significantly increased next year. During the week of June 8 – 12, 1992 we will conduct a workshop at Duke for 32 faculty interested in using our materials. We have held similar workshops for the past two years for our own faculty and graduate students working with the project classes.

Project materials

At the present time our materials include

1. *The Calculus Reader.* This reader supports the three semester course with material the students actually have to read. Reading is an important part of the course, not something that can be ignored if you concentrate on the prototype examples.

2. *Instructor's Manual.* This is a general introduction to the course and a week-by-week description of how the lab and classroom activities relate. We have included class-by-class suggestions for student activities.

3. Lab materials for the *Mathcad/Derive* version of the course. This includes instructions for the student and disk copies of the computer files.

4. Lab materials for the *Mathematica* version of the course are available from Bill Barker at Bowdoin College.

5. Instructions for a variety of classroom projects and activities.

D. C. Heath will handle the distribution of the preliminary version of the *Reader* in 1992-93 and will publish the entire set of materials in Fall 93.

Project CALC publishes a newsletter twice a year with a mailing list of over 700 names. If you would like to be included on the list, contact us at

      Project CALC
      Department of Mathematics
      Duke University
      Durham, NC 27706
      919-660-2825
      lang@math.duke.edu

The Structures of Advanced Multimedia Learning Environments: Reconfiguring Space, Time, Story, and Text

Janet H. Murray
Senior Research Scientist
Department of Humanities
Director, Athena Language Learning Project

Stuart A. Malone
Head Programmer, Athena Language Learning Project

Athena Language Learning Project
Massachusetts Institute of Technology
18 Vassar Street, Room 20B-231
Cambridge, MA 02139

As humanities education reflects increasing concern with cultural diversity and with fostering an understanding of multiple perspectives on the world, educators are increasingly drawn to multimedia environments. This is true across the disciplines. In *language learning* the new communicative methodologies strive to prepare students not only to study the literature of a foreign culture, but also to interact with contemporary speakers of the language in a culturally appropriate manner. Such an approach necessitates the use of film and video materials as well as print examples of "realia" (real objects from everyday life, such as train tickets and newspaper ads) as a source of the language as it is actually used by native speakers in their natural environment. It fosters a sense that the French spoken by a priest and a plumber, by friends and strangers, in public and in private, differ from one another in ways that reveal much that is important to know about the culture. *Literature* has long incorporated the study of narrative art in film, and along with *history* is moving toward cultural studies in which visual material and examples of popular culture, as well as art produced in film and video, are as important as print sources as objects of analysis.

As the objects of study have become more various the technology for accessing them has become more capable. In particular, interactive video, delivered for now on videodisc but eventually available in mammoth digital archives, offer an accessibility to visual material undreamed of only a decade ago. By combining the computer with the videodisc player (and eventually with digital sources of moving video) we have created a new medium in which text, still, and moving video can be synchronized, displayed, annotated, and recombined in ways that we are only beginning to discover.

The emergence of this new medium carries with it a need for the invention of new structures to exploit both the greater quantity of materials and the multiplicity of access that computers can offer. This chapter explores the structures we have invented at MIT for advanced multimedia learning projects in the humanities. These structures were developed for particular applications but also can be seen as multi-purpose building blocks of the new medium.[1]

Spacial Structures

The language learning videodiscs produced at MIT explore two genres, *interactive fiction* and *interactive documentary*. [Fur88, Mur90] In both of these forms we have found it useful to give students mobility in a simulated world, to locate them psychologically by giving them a strong sense of place and an ability to move through specific spaces. Both our documentary and our fictional discs, therefore, exploit spacial metaphors as important organizing devices. The two most important metaphors are the **map** and the **footpath**. The footpath is used in a technique known as **surrogate travel**, which can be used for exterior public spaces or for interior private (and even fictional) spaces.

In the disc *Dans le quartier St. Gervais*, the student is allowed to explore a neighborhood of Paris. Access is in several modalities. One key modality is the **map.**

[1] All of the structures described in this paper are the result of collaborative work. Gilberte Furstenberg and Douglas Morgenstern are the language teachers who have been the primary shapers of the French and Spanish videodiscs, respectively. Ayshe Farman-Farmaian was the producer and co-designer of *A la rencontre de Philippe*; Michael Roper was the co-producer and director of *Dans le quartier St. Gervais;* Rus Gant was the producer of *No recuerdo.* Benjamin Davis of the MUSE Consortium at MIT also played a role in shaping these projects, particularly in their workstation versions. Charles Kerns, formerly of Stanford, currently with Apple Computer played a key role in developing the first Macintosh version of Philippe. Our collaborators on the Shakespeare Interactive Archive Project are Renaissance scholars Peter Donaldson and Larry Friedlander, designer of the groundbreaking Stanford Shakespeare Project. The Athena Language Learning Project has for its principle sponsor the Annenberg/CPB Project. It is also received significant support from Apple Computer, Digital Equipment Corporation, International Business Machines Corporation, the Consortium for Language Teaching and Learning, the Florence Gould Foundation, and the National Endowment for the Humanities.

In this mode the student can select a video clip from a menu that represents the actual geographic location of the store or church or streetcorner where the video was shot. Maps are embedded in one another, starting with an overview and moving to increasingly fine levels of detail.

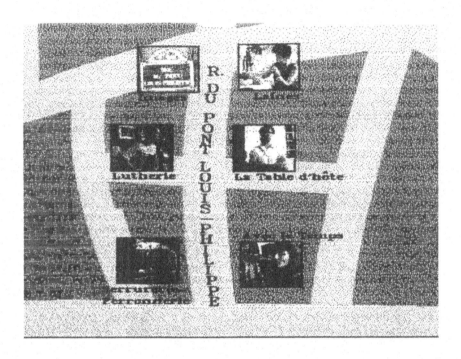

This allows the student to get a notion of the general geography of the area before choosing specific segments. The advantage of the map as an organizing principle is that it is immediately grasped and provides the student with a navigational system familiar from everyday life. It is therefore useful in minimizing the disorientation problems that plague hypermedia design, while still preserving freedom of exploration. A map allows the designer to suggest pre-determined paths (such as progress down a particular street) without prescribing them. As a result the student is free to progress in a straight line, systematically exploring one small area and then another, or to jump around from place to place. In either case, the student is provided with a picture of the whole and can place their individual explorations in the larger context. [App87, Land90]

The same St. Gervais neighborhood can be explored "on foot" rather than by map, using a **surrogate travel** method (also referred to as a "movie map") based on the pioneering work of MIT's Aspen Disc, made by the Architecture Machine Group, a forerunner of the Media Lab.[Lip80] In this modality, the user is placed in the position of a pedestrian, and moves step by step down a footpath by clicking on arrows on the computer screen. The arrows are displayed as part of a street map, thereby allowing the user to form a concept of their geographic position. The video screen shows what would appear to a person standing in that location. The student is given the illusion of moving through a space by the successive display of a sequence of still images that mimic a walk through the area. (Figure 1). The user can always move backwards as well as forwards and at some places has the choice of moving left or right.

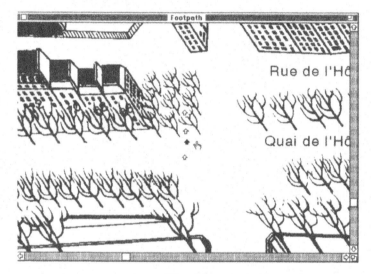

Figure 1

The advantage of surrogate travel is the feeling of psychological immersion in a simulated reality, in this case, the helpful illusion of actually visiting the country where the studied language is spoken. The detail of the movie map is also an advantage in teaching culture. Its disadvantage is its "pedestrian" point of view, in the metaphoric as well as the literal sense of the term. It is too constricting and uninvolving to move step by step through a place that has been recorded in such a rote, uninterpreted fashion. Therefore we have supplemented the footpath with *short video essays* in which the camera moves freely, focusing in on such details as a gargoyle on a cathedral or a tea-pot shaped shop sign that convey the subjective feel of a place as interpreted by the video filmmaker. Video essays can also provide ambient sound which is difficult to link up to the still images of the movie map. These essays are available from the map menus and are described as "Son et Images" (sound and images of the place).

Since the interviews, footpath images, and video essays are all anchored in map-based representations of the neighborhood, the user may not distinguish among these modes of exploring the space. Ideally all of them would blend into one integrated sense of the neighborhood which would include its geography, subjective feel, and its inhabitants.

The sense of psychological immersion created by giving the student control over a physical space is especially valuable in the context of fiction. In the interactive fiction *A la rencontre de Philippe*, a **map** is also used at certain times in the story in which the student is expected to visit different places in Paris in an attempt to help the protagonist find a new apartment. The map we are using is similar to one that Parisians use except that it has been made interactive and expanded for pedagogical purposes. As in Paris, the students are asked to first to determine the arrondissement of the street they wish to visit. They then choose the arrondissement by clicking on its number on an interactive map, and receive a description of the character of the chosen neighborhood with an interactive list of those streets that play a part in our story.

One of the most important story locales is the apartment Philippe has been sharing with his girlfriend Elizabeth. This apartment is presented in a manner similar to the **surrogate travel** of *St. Gervais*. The rooms of the apartment have been photographed so that the students can step through them and experience the illusion of walking around an authentic Parisian apartment. We have also made it possible to jump from room to room in order to move more purposefully. Again the method is to represent the space schematically on the computer with interactive arrows that indicate your position and allow you to move, and to provide on the video screen the view that you would see if you were standing in the position indicated by the currently blackened arrow. (Figure 2)

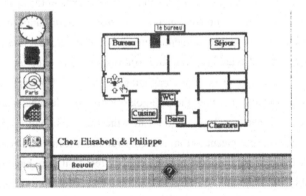

Figure 2

Another way in which we have sought to enhance the students' sense of immersion in a concrete world is by creating **simulated, interactive objects**. These objects can be seen on the video as photographed real objects (which are sometimes used by the protagonist, increasing the viewer's sense of their reality). They also exist in scanned-in reproduction on the computer screen where the can be used interactively by the student. In the study on the desktop are several such objects: a copy of the Figaro newspaper that can be opened to examine simulated apartment ads, a message machine that can be operated by clicking on its familiar buttons, and a telephone on which one can dial numbers within the story (which will lead to simulated answering machine messages and a text box of the computer screen in which one can type in a message) and numbers outside the story (in which case one will hear the "not in service" message used in Paris) (Figure 3). In *No recuerdo* a fax machine serves a similar purpose. These simulated objects add to the verisimilitude of the story and provide an element of surprise, while facilitating tasks that require language comprehension.

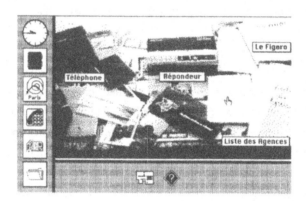

Figure 3

Of course there are clear learning tasks involved in moving through the space provided in the documentary and fictional environments, including accessing information in answer to teacher's assigned tasks, listening to authentic speech in a clear context and coming to an understanding of the gist of what has been said. But the student's experience is not of using a reference tool or taking a quiz or even of completing an exercise. The experience is framed as a **visit** because the spacial rather than the pedagogical structure dominates the presentation. Although more research needs to be done to identify the student's relationship to the materials, anecdotal evidence gleaned from student evaluation forms and comments to instructors and developers supports the notion that they feel as if they have been somewhere, that they have taken an imaginary journey. This assumption increases our responsibility to make the simulated environments as diverse, authentic, and non-stereotypical as possible.

Temporal Structures

Along with space the other great organizer of human consciousness is of course time, and so it not surprising that in establishing landmarks in a confusingly unstructured new medium we have relied on time as one of our principal coordinates.

In *St. Gervais* we make wide use of historical time. In addition to interviews and video and still renderings of the life of the contemporary neighborhood, we have over 600 still images of historical significance, recording the life of the neighborhood from the seventeenth century to the present. These historical slides have text files associated with them that are written in intermediate level French describing everything from life in the literary salons to the daily life of artisans. The student accesses this information by a kind of time travel that parallels the spacial travel.

Because this is a hypermedia system, there are several ways to discover and explore the historical material. First of all, a student using the foot path would be alerted to historical material by a special sign that appears on the map. The student could click on this historical sign and move back and forth between annotated contemporary and historical views of the same location. Either through the map or through a lattice of cultural topics the students are given access to a navigational window that lets them change either time or place as they move around in the collection of historical slides. This allows access that bypasses the map and footpath, subordinating the schematization of space to questions of temporal change in a variety of locations.

In the fictional world of *Philippe* and *No recuerdo* time is at least equally important, but it is *storytime* rather than historical time that the student is aware of. In both simulations a clock is provided (seen on the upper lefthand of the *Philippe* screens reproduced here) and certain activities — appointments, interviews, visits to particular locations — can only take place during certain hours. The story clock controls the plot and keeps the story progressing in a predictable way toward a conclusion which in *No recuerdo* is set for a particular hour. The clock provides a structure within which the various permutations of the story can be contained.

But time in a fictional world is not governed by the sun. In the case of *Philippe*, in which all the action takes place within a single day, time is measured in two ways, corresponding to the two modes in which the story is presented. For the parts of the story presented as video segments (interrupted by questions posed to the student) the time is predetermined. A particular scene always takes place at the same time of day and runs for the same amount of fictional time. But Philippe also includes two periods of time in which the student is left "alone" to explore Philippe's apartment and to move around Paris. These time periods are bounded by appointments, and the student is given a fixed amount of time in which to explore. How is this time counted? Each possible action — making phone call, looking around Philippe's apartment, visiting a realtor or another apartment, etc. — is given a certain number of minutes, and the displayed clock advances accordingly until the student is reminded that it is time for their next appointment. In this way the fictional world is made more concrete, and the teacher can ensure that the student performs a certain number of desirable activities, while leaving open the choice of activities performed by any individual student.

In addition to the clock in the corner of the screen, the student has available an "agenda" or diary which records everything that happens during the day. This tool allows the student to review video segments from previous scenes, while still remaining within the sequence of events that marks his or her individual experience of the story. Any event listed in the sequence can be clicked on for reviewing. Afterwards the student is returned to the "current" story time — the time from which he or she began the review.

Taken together the spacial and temporal structures, both taken from familiar objects, provide powerful organizers of the students' experiences. Although it will require more intensive study to fully understand how simulated space and time are understood by individual students and how they affect the learning process,.
it seems likely that the psychological experience of immersion which these structures create also contributes significantly to students' motivation.

Story Structure

Narrative form is in itself an important organizing structure. Interactive fiction combines the expectations of conventional narratives (e.g. character, conflict, resolution) with innovative structures that allow viewers to affect the progress and outcome of the story.

Philippe and *No recuerdo* are both interactive stories (although *No recuerdo* also has some documentary elements based upon brief explorations of Bogota). *Philippe* is designed in an exploratory style. Although the student is asked to help the protagonist solve his problems there is no single right solution. Choices that the student makes all have consequences but there are many satisfying ways to end the story. In *No recuerdo* the student is under more pressure to find out a particular piece of information, but lack of success provides as much narrative interest as success. In either case it is involvement with the story that is rewarded, and the rewards are intrinsic. The more you understand and respond, the rich the fictional world revealed to you.

In any interactive fiction, the big question for the designer is how to build in the student's interventions. One method is to give the student a role in the story, preferably one that includes problem-solving of some kind. The camera then represents the student and the actors address the student by looking into the camera. Both Philippe and Gonzalo (the protagonist of *No recuerdo*) look in the camera at times and directly address the student, who has a definite role to play in the drama. In *Philippe,* the student represents a visiting friend, in *No recuerdo* an investigative reporter.

First person video (as this approach is called) can be limited as a language learning technique becausewe want to show interactions between two or more authentic speakers, including speakers in intimate situations, which would be awkward to portray if the camera is meant to be a person rather than an observer. For this reason we have filmed some scenes in third-person point of view, with the student a proverbial fly on the wall, observing the scene but not really in it.

In cases where characters address the viewer directly the interaction begins to take on the form of a conversation. *Conversational form* is one of the emerging subgenres of interactive fiction, and it offers great promise to language teachers because the discourse features of conversation are often the focus of language instruction.[Mur91] In *Philippe* we limit conversations to one or two interchanges, all of them answers to questions that Philippe directly poses such as "Where is the check for the plumber?"

But in *No recuerdo* we are attempting to structure the story around several conversational interviews between the reporter and Gonzalo in which the student will be given the task of actively eliciting information. Although *No recuerdo* was originally designed for use with a natural language processing system that could parse and to some degree "understand" students' questions, both interactive stories are currently being implemented on the Macintosh with interfaces in which the student's part of the conversation will be chosen from a menu of possible remarks.

Another way of having the student affect the story is by creating an exploratory environment, a *microworld* to use Papert's term [Pap80], in which the student is free to try out a number of things, all of which have interesting effects. In *Philippe* the period in which the student can explore the desktop and can visit realtors and rental apartments provides such a microworld. If the student call a particular realtor, opportunities will arise later in the story. If the student listens to the answering machine, then he or she will gain information that will affect later developments. If the student calls a mutual friend of Philippe and Elizabeth after learning some key information, then the friend will help them make up. None of these are moments of obvious branching, yet all are changes in the configuration of the story resulting from the student's choices and actions.

Of course our effort is to combine the pedagogical task with narrative function, making the student's interactive participation in the story overlap with the learning task. In *No recuerdo* the student is a newspaper reporter and has to communicate with a demanding editor who exchanges faxes with the student-reporter. The student must compose faxes that are acceptable paraphrases of interviews with important characters, and must direct interviews so that informants answer the questions that the editor has posed. These tasks require the use of basic language skills, but they also make sense in terms of the story. When the student has trouble with one of these tasks the story is held up and the student is given pedagogical help in the form of fictionally appropriate communications from the editor. It is hoped that the overlap between the pedagogical and the fictional will aid in motivation and in focusing the student on the communicative nature of the task.

When dealing with fiction with a pedagogical purpose it is important to ally the pedagogical tasks with the imaginative realm of the story. What the student does to demonstrate or practice comprehension should be an intrinsic part of the fictional world and have a clear effect on the story. It should also be borne in mind that users like to play through the fiction several times, exploring different branches, and to compare their experiences of the story with other users (which can be useful for establishing communicative tasks across an intriguing knowledge gap in language classes). Student participation should therefore be designed so that successive plays provide additional information.[2]

Textual Structure: Interactive Indexing and Topical Navigation

A documentary videodisc like *St. Gervais* can be thought of as a databank. Students are sent to such a disc with particular exercises, adapted to their level and learning task. The databank itself need contain no exercises, only supple means of access that will facilitate the learning tasks various teachers assign.

In thinking about ways to make the material of *St. Gervais* available to students we can look to analogies in structures designed for books The most obvious kind of information we would want to retrieve are topics and themes discussed in the interviews. Here it is useful to think about textbook readers for use in composition or introductory literature courses which are printed with more than one table of contents, such as one by author or chronology and one by topic or genre. A hypermedia data base also needs multiple contents and also multiple indices, and these structures must be available to the user from many points of access.

St. Gervais has an *index by topics* that is available at the top level, but also from any interview. One can review all the topics and who speaks to each one, or one can see just the topics list that deals with what the current interviewee is discussing, presumably in order to choose another interviewee who speaks to the same theme. For the historical information the topics are arranged like a *lattice* (Figure 5) since subtopics like " the Family in the 17th century" belong under two general topics, "The Family," and "Daily Life in the 17th Century." Both of these arrangements would be difficult to duplicate in a linear form like the book. They are meant to take advantage of the webbing of information that hypermedia systems allow.

---

[2]A good example of this kind of educational application is the early history application *The Wouldbe Gentleman*, designed by Caroline Lougee and Michael Carter at Stanford University, which allows a student to try to succeed economically and socially in ancien régime France. good example, no interactive video but true microworld

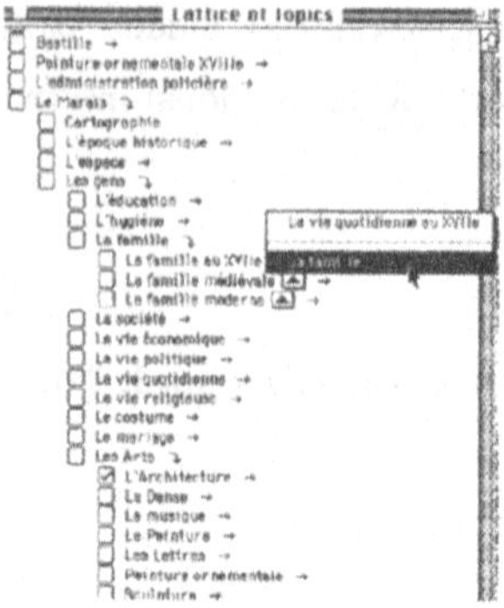

Figure 5

In fact from a language learning point of view even a fictional videodisc like *Philippe* (or *No recuerdo*) is to some extent a data base. It is a repository of authentic language use that can be indexed and cross-indexed according to a multitude of language teaching categories: grammatically, functionally, communicatively. The *Multiple Functions Index* of *Philippe*, for instance, includes grouped examples of greetings, leave-takings, requests for help, hesitations, and use of tricky idioms or colloquial expressions. In this way the disc has a usefulness beyond its structure as a story, and in an environment with easier access to multiple videos than we currently can sustain, could be part of an extensive reference library of the spoken language. More ambitiously, as these discs increase one could create cross-cultural indices that would show the same functional situation (e.g. greeting a friend) in several cultures and subcultures.

Textual Structure: Moving in Both Directions between Words and Images

One of the key capabilities of an advanced educational hypermedia system is that you must be able to go from text to video and from video to text. This is so little the norm that some hardware and software systems do not even allow for the possibility of the video to text move. Yet there are several situations in which this is utterly essential and which point to the centrality of this functionality for humanities applications in the future, including language learning and literary applications.

Conclusion

The emerging structures of advanced multimedia teaching environments in the humanities are following key trends in the profession: the move to communicative language teaching using authentic language spoken by native speakers; the interest in culture as a totality incorporating visual as well as textual material; the emphasis on interdisciplinary collaboration; the need to think in global terms and to reinforce awareness of multiple perspectives. One challenge posed by these new modes of inquiry is how to maintain such broad perspectives without becoming disoriented. Part of the solution to that problem will be the definition of structures of hypermedia that will facilitate a rich engagement with varied and dense materials without overwhelming ourselves. We must establish conventions by which we can feel in possession of clear landmarks without being forced through the same pre-marked paths. Only further use and sophisticated testing of hypermedia materials will reveal to us the best way to facilitate this exploratory yet oriented approach to learning. The joy of working with hypermedia can make us feel as if we are at liberty in an enchanted forest. The success of the medium as a long-lasting learning environment will depend upon to invent the right sort of roadsigns and compasses.

Works Cited

[App90] Apple Computer, *Human Interface Guidelines: the Apple Desktop Interface* (Addison-Wesley, 1987) recommends using visual metaphors drawns from everyday objects and actions.

[Fur88] Gilberte Furstenberg, Douglas Morgenstern, Janet H. Murray, "The Athena Language Learning Project: Design Issues for the Next Generation of Computer-Based Language Learning Tools," Chapter in *Modern Technology in Foreign Language Education* ACTFL/NTC, 1988

[Lan90] George P. Landow, "The Rhetoric of Hypermedia: Some Rules for Authors," in Paul Delany and George P. Landow, *Hypermedia and Literary Studies,* MIT Press, 1990.

[Lip80] Andrew Lippman, "Movie-Maps: An Application of the Optical Videodisc to Computer Graphics," ACM, April, 1980.

[Mur90] Janet H. Murray, "Emerging Genres of Interactive Videodiscs for Language Instruction, *Multimedia and Language Learning,* published by the Institute for Academic Technology, University of North Carolina at Chapel Hill, 1990.

[Mur91] Janet H. Murray, "Anatomy of a New Medium: Literary and Pedagogic Uses of Advanced Linguistic Computer Structures" *Computers and the Humanities,* XXV, 1, 1991

[Pap80] Seymour Papert, *Mindstorms: Children, Computers, and Powerful Ideas,* N. York: Basic Bks,1980

Adjusting to the Paradim Shift in Teaching and Learning
or
What do I do Now???

Presented by
Dr Milton W. Petruk
Professor, Faculty of Education
University of Alberta
Edmonton, Alberta, Canada T6G 2G5

The primary theme of my presentation is change. Specifically, I want to focus on technological change and the way that it is affecting us as educators today, and more important, the way it will affect us throughout the remainder of this decade.

It is often useful, particularly from the standpoint of gaining perspective, to look back at our past, and while I am not a historian, I would like to draw your attention to some features of the education system as it has evolved over the past several decades. Perhaps the one of the most significant characteristics of it was that it existed in an environment where direct access to information, primarily books, was relatively scarce. To make this point, I often refer to the high school which I attended just over 3 decades ago. The entire school library in this high school contained less books than I currently have in my own personal library! And I might add that while a public library did exist, its collection was not much better. The only other learning resources that were readily available to students in that high school were teachers. In that time frame, most teachers had studied either at a Normal School or a University, where they had access to comparitively extensive libraries. Teachers knew everything! This was a time when if one wanted to know something about anything, one asked the teacher.

The way in which educational institutions, at all levels, were organized reflected this reality. Schools and univerisities alike consisted of classrooms which could accomodate groups of students and learning consisted of listening to the teacher tell the students what they needed to know. Learning was demonstrated by being able to recall what one had been told by the teacher and neither the available resources nor the climate were conducive to encouraging students to become independent learners.

To fully appreciate the significance of the pedagogical model which I have described one must recognize that the context within which these schools existed was one which is often referred to today as the Industrial Age. World War II had just ended and domestic production and manufacturing were growing at an incredible rate in an attempt to satisfy the demands of post-war society for consumer goods. But industry needed workers and their primary source of workers were schools. Ideally, the school would produce students who could read and write well enough to meet the demands on the job and who would conform to the discipline of a production plant. Industry did not need, nor was it prepared to pay for more than the basic minimum education.

The First Change - The Information Explosion

Today, it is common to hear at we are living in the midst of an unprecedented information explosion. Frequent colorful quotes dramatize the exponential growth of new information that our society is generating each year. The impact on educational institutions has been dramatic. The publishing industry was quick to catch the wave of this information explosion, publishing just about everything that anybody wanted to write. One of the rapid growth areas of today's educational institutions have been libraries, although, often they all feel that they are not able to grow as quickly as they should. Another rapid growth are is the pulp and paper industry as it attempts to meet the demand for more paper. This, of course, raises many other concerns such as the concern about the effect of the pulp and paper industry on the ecology. It is ironical that we continue to cut down forests in order to manufacture paper so that we could publish more articles about the negative effects of the pulp and paper industy on our ecology!

Unlike the situation that existed 3 or 4 decades ago, educational institutions now no longer face a shortage of books. Instead, they are concerned with the cost of housing all the books they have, the cost of keeping the collection current, and the time it takes to extract specific information which they need. It is unlikely that many of us read more than one book a day. Assuming a career of 35 years, the most that we can possibly read in an entire lifetime is 13,000 books. The Library of Congress catalog lists more than 200 times this number of books and it is expected to double over the next 5 years. Clearly, we will never catch up.

The Second Change - Digital Electronics - Microcomputers

It is only since the end of World War II that digital electronics, specifically in the form of digital computers first came into existence. While the first digital computers had little practical value, advances in digital electronics have produced a variety of small, low cost digital electronic devices which add another dimension to the information explosion described earlier. Information can and is increasingly being stored digitally and I have often told my friends in the book publishing industry that if they don't change the business that they are in, before the end of this decade, and this century, they will be out of business. Today, the key concept that is emerging in relation to microcomputers is multimedia. A digital microcomputer today can not only store textual or pictorial information electronically, it can also store digitized audio, animation, and full-motion video complete with sound track.

I want to explore the notion that the information explosion I referred to earlier is often viewed as being one-dimensional but in reality is two-dimensional. When we think about the information explosion, we normally think of the dimension that describes the amount of new information which is being produced. The second dimension that I am referring to involves digital electronic technology which makes it possible to transform old information and represent new information in ways which are easier to understand. For example, instead of relying on words and static pictures to describe electron flow in an electrical circuit, as one would do in a book, one can construct an animated graphic image on the screen, annotated with voice that allows the student to watch and hear the effect. One can then make the presentation interactive allowing the student to verify his or her own understanding of the concept by directly controlling the activity on the screen. It is this second dimension of the information explosion brought about as a result of interactive multimedia and digital microcomputers that promises to have the greatest impact on the way we think about teaching and learning. What's more, it is environmentally clean.

The Third Change - A Post Industrial, Global Economy

The industrial economy, depended for its survival, on the availability of raw material, cheap labour and availability of markets. Today, North America is quickly realizing that this is not enough. Ten years ago, the North Americal auto industry produced approximately 70% of the cars sold in North America. Today that figure is approximately 30%. Survival in today's global market, where raw materials can be transported easily from North America to Japan and finished product can equally easily be transported from Japan to North America, depends on our ability to be competitive and the key to being more competitive lies in more effective teaching and learning.

If our economy is to survive during the next decade, it will not do so because of our access to raw material alone. It will not do so because of access to large markets alone. It will survive because of our ability to maintain a workforce that is extremely well-trained and is capable of inventing a better way. The alternative, one which none of us is anxious to accept, is to resign ourselves to a lower standard of living.

So What Do I Do Now

At the beginning of this paper, I described the kind of education paradigm that most of us grew up with and many of us are living with today. The paradigm places the teacher at the centre of the teaching-learning process. In this paradigm, the teacher is the primary source of information and learning that takes place outside the direction of a teacher is not generally acknowledged as having occurred. The paradigm is designed to establish a learner-dependency on the teacher and while learners today have far better access to learning resources than I did 3 decades ago, they still think of "taking a course", a teacher-centered activity as the principal means of upgrading.

What is quickly evolving is a learner-centered paradigm of the teaching-learning process. In such a paradigm, the primary purpose of formal schooling is to teach the learner how to be an independent learner, one who knows how to teach him or herself whatever is necessary by interacting directly with the two-dimensional information resource I described earlier. Such a paradigm shift in education will not be greeted with enthusiasm since doing so means that the role of the teacher will change, the role of the learner will change, the nature of curriculum will change and the administrative structure of educational institutions will change. But change we must, for both our economic and our intellectual survival depends on it.

This is perhaps best described by paraphrasing a saying from the World Health Organization "Teach a person something, and you have satisfied their intellectual need for now but teach a person how to teach themselves and you have satisfied their intellectual needs for a lifetime".

Engagement and Construction:
Educational strategies for the post-TV era

Ben Shneiderman[1]
Department of Computer Science
University of Maryland
College Park, MD 20742

Introduction

We all remember the empty faces of students seated in rows, intermittently taking notes, and trying to retain disjointed facts. This old lecture style seems as antiquated as a 19th century clockwork mechanism; familiar and charming, but erratic and no longer adequate. The orderly structure of industrial age mechanisms and the repetitiveness of the assembly line are giving way to the all-at-once immediacy of McLuhan's non-linear electrified global village [McL64]. The early electronic media such as radio, stereos, and television have created a snap-crackle-and-popular culture that is enjoyable, but passive. The post-TV era will be different. Computing and communication technologies offer opportunities for engagement with other people and the power tools to construct remarkable artifacts and experiences.

Educators can now create engaging processes for their students that will motivate them to work together and explore the frontiers of knowledge. Students from elementary schools through college can apply computing technology (word processors, spreadsheets, databases, drawing programs, design tools, music composition software, etc.) to construct high quality products that they can proudly share with others. Advanced communications tools (electronic mail, network access, bulletin board systems, videotape recorders, TV broadcasts) support engagement among students, connection to the external world, information gathering, and dissemination of results.

Defining Engagement

My definition of engagement focuses on *interaction with people*; students working together, as they must in the workplace, community, and family. Paired collaborations, team projects, and class presentations can teach valuable skills that are now left to sports teams and after

[1] Also Head of the Human-Computer Interaction Laboratory and a Member of the Systems Research Center. Parts of this paper were derived from [Shn92a].

school clubs. Secondly, students can interact with people outside the classroom; by visiting adults in the workplace, interviewing community leaders, and communicating with students in other schools, cities, states, and countries. Instead of requiring conjugation of French verbs, teachers might set the goal for students to make a videotape about their community in French to send to students in Canada or Togo. The students would have to learn conjugation, but they would work as a team to create a product of which they could all be proud. Instead of memorizing the sequence of British monarchs, students might create a hypermedia document with a timeline, photos, music, and biographies that could be stored in the library for future students to access or expand. Instead of merely reading about the disease patterns in urban areas, students might collect data from local hospitals on patterns of flu outbreaks and build a simulation model of disease epidemics in communities as a function of age, gender, and sociological factors, with the goal of reporting results at community meetings, to medical groups, in local newspapers, or in electronic bulletin boards.

In support of these projects students would have to work together and also reach out to others to collect information from librarians, city officials, physicians, scientists, bankers, business leaders, etc. Imagine how a report on World War II would be enriched by an interview with a D-Day participant in a retirement home. Imagine how an ecology report would be enlivened after a discussion with a local park naturalist, a political science project would become livelier after an interview with a local or state politician, and biology would become more meaningful after a visit with a hospital lab technician. The experience of speaking to adults at work would be educational, the process could improve social and communication skills, and the discussions are potentially illuminating for everyone involved.

The second aspect of engagement is the cooperation among students needed to complete projects. When working in teams students can take on more ambitious projects, can learn from each other, and must make their plans explicit to coordinate. Engagement with fellow students can help make learning more lively and effective as a model for the future world of work, family, and community.

The rich environment of computers and networks is already being used to support engagement across cities and countries. For example, approximately 10,000 elementary school children at 150 sites collected and exchanged acid rain data. In another project, high school students in the U.S. were paired with Russian students for email exchanges. A science project involved hundreds of sixth graders simultaneously measuring the length of a shadow and exchanging data to measure the earth's diameter.

Electronic mail opens up new possibilities for cooperation among students, guidance from teachers, and communication with national or international leaders. For example, students in my graduate seminar on user interface design undertook the common task of reading research journal papers and critiquing them, but interest in the task increased when they were required to send their critiques to the authors by email. The discussions were deeper, the usual off-hand attacks were softer in tone, but sharper in insight. The replies and contact with leading professionals gave my students a sense of importance and maturity.

Defining Construction

The second part of my theme is construction, by which I mean that <u>students create a product from their collaboration</u>. This may not seem so different from current expectations of writing a computer program or a term paper. But when coupled with the engagement theme, I mean <u>constructing something of importance to someone else</u>. Instead of having database management students write the same safe class project, my students have implemented database management programs for the University's bus service, generated a scheduling program for a local TV station, prepared an online information retrieval program for a suicide prevention clinic, and developed record keeping software for a student scuba club.

Instead of writing a term paper on computer applications for the elderly, two of my students in a Computers and Society course offered computing lessons for elderly residents of a local apartment complex. Then the students prepared a report for the director of the complex, with a copy for me to grade. Several teams of students worked with their former high schools or elementary schools to suggest ways to improve the use of computers. One student wrote computer programs to manage lists of volunteers and contributors for a local soup kitchen. One student challenged the University's legal policy about student access and privacy rights with respect to their accounts. Another student wrote a handbook about educational software for parents of deaf children, while another pair of students prepared a hypertext guide to coping with computer software viruses. Computer tools enable construction of ambitious projects; there is a special sense of pride when students produce an animated hypertext, laser-printed report, or collect/disseminate data through networks.

In addition to these semester-long projects, there are many opportunities for short-term construction projects ranging from the traditional programming exercise done as a team project to class presentations by students on normal lecture material. Requiring a team of two students to present a topic to the entire class can make the topic appealing for the whole class, and the designated students will be likely to take their responsibility seriously. Turning work into a communal experience is made practical by the presence of word processors/text editors because making suggested revisions has become easy.

Cooperative groups in general studies

College level computer science has been my academic domain, so it might seem that these notions are only suitable for that age group and subject. However, I feel that engagement and construction are appropriate at most ages and in most fields. In fact, related ideas have been proposed by many reports on education during the past decade. The Final Report of the Study Group on the Conditions of Excellence in American Higher Education, National Institute of Education wrote that "Active modes of teaching require that students be inquirers - creators, as well as receivers of knowledge." That report also stressed projects, internships, discussion groups, collaborations, simulations, and presentations (Figure 1). Similarly, the Principles for Good Practice in Undergraduate Education presented by the American Association for Higher Education (Figure 2) pushed for cooperation among students and active learning projects.

1) Student Involvement
- involving students in faculty research projects
- encouraging internships
- organizing small discussion groups
- requiring in-class presentations and debates
- developing simulations
- creating opportunities for individual learning projects

2) High Expectations
3) Assessment and Feedback

Figure 1: Conditions for Excellence in Undergraduate Education, *Involvement in Learning: Realizing the Potential of American Higher Education*, Final Report of the Study Group on the Conditions of Excellence in American Higher Education [NIE84].

Encourage Student-Faculty Contact
Encourage Cooperation Among Students
Encourage Active Learning
Give Prompt Feedback
Emphasize Time on Task
Communicate High Expectations
Respect Diverse Talents and Ways of Learning

Figure 2: Principles for Good Practice in Undergraduate Education [AAH87].

Exploration and Creation

The spirit of engagement is to enable students to experience the challenge of exploratory research and the satisfaction of creative accomplishment. I believe that imaginative teachers can find ways in every discipline and at every grade to create an atmosphere of exploration, novelty, and challenge. Whether collecting scientific data or studying Greek theater, there are provocative open questions that students can attempt to answer. My undergraduate students regularly conduct empirical studies related to my research in user interface design [Shn92b] and their work is published in scientific journals. Only one in ten projects leads to a publishable result, but the atmosphere of exploration at the frontier of research produces a high level of engagement even for introverted and blase computer science students at my state university. Similarly, my 12-year old daughter did her 7th-grade science project on spaced vs. massed practice with 3rd-graders in her school learning to type.

The concepts of exploration and creation are well-established in the education literature from John Dewey to Seymour Papert. Piaget wrote that "Knowledge is not a copy of reality. To know an object, to know an event is not simply to look at it and make a mental copy, or image, of it. To know an object is to act on it. To know is to modify, to transform the object, and to understand the process of transformation, and as a consequence to understand the way the object is constructed [Pia64]." The phrase "discovery learning" conveys the key notion that "whatever knowledge children gain they create themselves; whatever character they develop they create themselves" as Wees wrote in his aptly titled book *Nobody Can Teach Anybody Anything* [Wee71].

Summary

The post-TV media of computers and communications enables teachers, students, and parents to creatively develop education by engagement and construction (Figure 3). Students should be given the chance to engage with each other in team projects, possibly situated in the world outside the classroom, with the goal of constructing a product that is useful or interesting to someone other than the teacher. Challenges remain such as scaling up from small class projects to lecture sections with hundreds of students, covering the curriculum that is currently required by many school districts, evaluating peformance, and assigning grades. However, there seems to be no turning back and, anyway, the children of the Nintendo and Video Age are eager to press fast forward.

Students want to engage with people to:

| Create | Communicate | Plan | Help | Initiate |
| Explore | Build | Discover | Participate | Collaborate |

Students will be engaged by constructing products:

Writing   (poems, plays, essays, novels, newspapers, diaries)
Drawing   (pictures, logos, portraits, maps, birthday cards)
Composing   (music, songs, operas, hypermedias, videos)
Designing   (buildings, furniture, games, animations, family trees)
Planning   (class trips, charity events, vacations, parties, elections)

Teachers should promote:

Engaging in the world   (lobby a Senator, raise environmental awareness,
                             call City Hall to report a problem)
Helping where needed   (teach computing to the elderly, improve recycling,
                             increase awareness of drug abuse or AIDS)
Caring for others   (raise funds for the homeless, improve medical care)
Communicating ideas   (write to a newspaper editor, make a class speech,
                             produce a cable TV show)
Organizing events   (prepare a bake sale or lecture series)

Multimedia technologies can empower students:

Enable students to create multimedia reports
Encourage media-supported class presentations
Develop communication through electronic mail
Provide experience in searching databases
Explore information networks and bulletin board systems
Promote use of word processing, drawing, spreadsheets, ...

Project orientation enhances engagement:

Help an elementary school to improve computer use
Teach elderly users word processing
Find or develop aids for a handicapped person
Revise university policy on information protection and privacy
Improve university administration, registration, ...
Evaluate and suggest improvement to bank machines,
     library systems, public access terminals, voicemail, ...
Write guide for parents about kids' software
Review workplace practices for computer users

Figure 3: Strategies for increasing Engagement and Construction

45

References

[AAH87] American Association for Higher Education. Principles for Good Practice in Undergraduate Education, 1987.

[McL64] Marshall McLuhan. *Understanding Media: The Extensions of Man*, McGraw-Hill Book Company, New York, NY, 1964.

[NIE84] National Institute of Education. *Involvement in Learning: Realizing the Potential of American Higher Education*, Final Report of the Study Group on the Conditions of Excellence in American Higher Education, 1984.

[Pia64] Jean Piaget. Cognitive development in children: the Piaget papers, In R. E. Ripple and V. N. Rockcastle (Editors), *Piaget rediscovered: a report of the conference on cognitive studies and curriculum development*, Ithaca School of Education, Cornell University, pp. 6-48, 1964.

[Shn92a] Ben Shneiderman. Education by Engagement and Construction: A Strategic Education Initiative for a Multimedia Renewal of American Education, In, Barrett, Ed (Editor), *The Social Creation of Knowledge: Multimedia and Information Technologies in the University*, MIT Press, Cambridge, MA, 1992.

[Shn92b] Ben Shneiderman. *Designing the User Interface: Strategies for Effective Human-Computer Interaction, Second Edition*, Addison-Wesley Publ. Co., Reading, MA, 1992.

[Wee71] W. R. Wees. *Nobody Can Teach Anybody Anything*, Doubleday Canada, Toronto, Ontario, 1971.

BUILDING KNOWLEDGE BASED TUTORS[1]

Beverly Park Woolf
Department of Computer Science
University of Massachusetts
Amherst, Massachusetts 01003, USA

Building a Tutoring System

We have evolved a generic and consistent foundation for representing, acquiring, and reasoning about tutoring knowledge. The big payoff has been that we can now apply the framework and evolving theory to several domains. We are not invested in promoting a particular tutoring strategy, nor do we advocate a specific intelligent tutoring system design. Rather, we build tools that allow for a variety of system components, teaching styles, and intervention strategies to be combined into a single framework. For example, Socratic tutoring, incremental generalizations, and case-based reasoning are just a few of the teaching strategies we have experimented with using this framework. Ultimately, we expect the machine to reason about its own choice of intervention method, to switch teaching strategies, and to use a variety of tactics and teaching approaches, while making decisions about the most efficacious method for managing one-on-one tutoring.

We are aided in our work by colleagues in three states who apply the tools we develop to new domains and new user groups. For example, colleagues at San Francisco State University have sent us several carefully-built physics simulations on top of which we placed the tutoring formalism described here. These colleagues help us evaluate the tutors. Using an iterative methodology in which formative evaluation augments tutor development, we have designed systems that tutor about statics, thermodynamics, time management, statistics, genetics, algebra word problems, and explanations. In

---

[1]This work was supported in part by a grant from the National Science Foundation, Materials Development Research, No. 8751362. It was also supported in part by the Air Force Systems Command, Rome Air Development Center, Griffiss AFB, New York, 13441 and the Air Force Office of Scientific Research, Bolling AFB, DC 20332 under contract No. F30602-85-0008 which supported the Northeast Artificial Intelligence Consortium (NAIC). Partial support was also received from University Research Initiative Contract No. N00014-86-K-0764.

A longer version of this paper appeared in *Intelligent Tutoring Systems: Evolutions in Design*, H. Burns, J. Parlett and C. Redfield (Eds.), Lawrence Erlbaum: NJ., 1991.

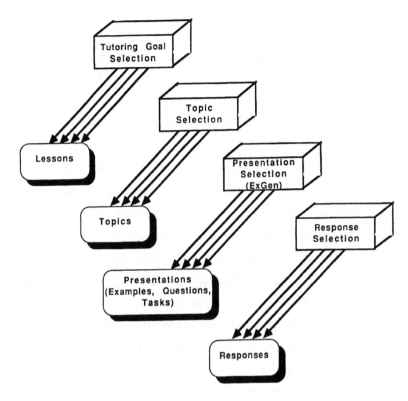

Figure 1: Representation and control in a tutoring system.

this paper we describe that methodology along with the generic tutoring foundation.

Development Cycle for Artificial Intelligence Systems

Development of an intelligent tutor, like development of any Artificial Intelligence system, requires several iterative cycles: computer scientists and instructional designers first collaborate on the design and development of the system, additional collaboration is required to test the system with students, and then the original implementation is modified and refined based on information gained through testing. This cycle is repeated as time permits.

For example, a professor at City College of San Francisco used the statics tutor (discussed below) in a classroom and noticed weaknesses in the simulation's ability to inform the student. She augmented the system with verbal discourse, adding examples or explanations, making diagnoses, and clarifying system response. She gave us a list of her additional discourse moves to be incorporated into the next version of the tutor.

Representation and Control

Artificial Intelligence programs require that a teaching expert define the knowledge to be used along with the control structures which define the way an interpreter will traverse that knowledge. Knowledge representation refers to how such knowledge is stored by a system to allow it to model the domain, human thinking, learning processes, and tutoring strategies. Knowledge bases might store concepts, activities, relations between topics, and other quantities needed to make expert decisions. In tutoring, they might store a variety of lessons, topics, presentations, and response selections available to the tutor (see Figure 1). Control refers to passage of an interpreter through those knowledge bases and its selection of appropriate pieces of knowledge for making a diagnosis, a prediction, or an evaluation. For tutoring, control structures might be specified at the four levels indicated in Figure 1, separately defining control for selection of lesson, topic, presentation, and response selection.

Currently, our control structures are motivated by specific instructional and diagnostic goals; thus, for example, one control structure produces a predominantly Socratic interaction and another produces interactions based on presenting incrementally generalized versions of new concepts or examples. Control structures are specific to a particular level of control and are used separately to define the reasoning to be used for selecting a lesson, topic, presentation, or response.

Acquiring and encoding this large amount of knowledge, or the knowledge acquisition process, is difficult and time consuming. We have built a number of tools that facilitate representing, acquiring, and reasoning about tutoring knowledge (see Figure 2). For each knowledge base (lessons, topics, presentation, or response) we consider the nature of the knowledge that must be accessed, such as the examples or questions (from the presentation knowledge base) or the activity the tutor must engage in, such as to motivate or teach a topic, or to provide follow-up. We have built tools, shown at the bottom of Figure 2, to support most activities listed in the figure. Only a few such tools will be described in this paper, namely TUPITS, Response Matrix, and DACTN.

We divide the discussion into two parts, separately describing tools for representing

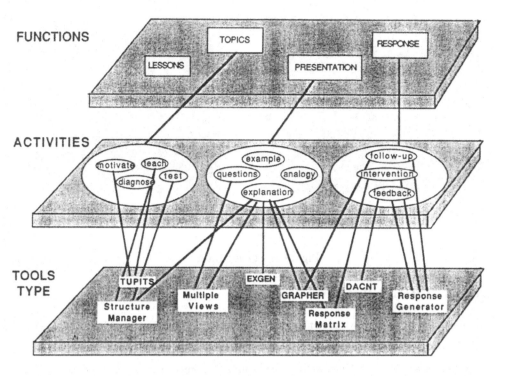

Figure 2: Tools for the representation and control of tutoring knowledge.

tutoring primitives (lessons, topics, and presentations) and then tools for representing discourse knowledge.

Tools for Representing Tutoring Primitives

We define **tutoring primitives** as basic elements needed for communicating knowledge, such as topics to be taught, specific tutoring responses, and possible student errors. Our knowledge bases hold a variety of examples, knowledge types, tasks to be given to the student, and discourse states describing various human-machine interactions.

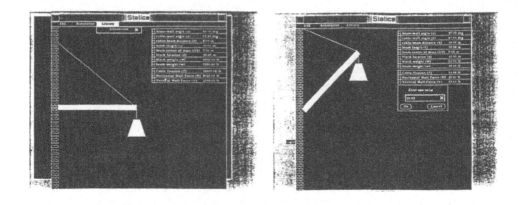

Figure 3: Statics tutor.

Example Tutoring Primitives

As an example of how tutoring primitives are used, we describe two tutors we have built in conjunction with the Exploring Systems Earth (ESE) Consortium[2] [Duc87]. These tutors are based on interactive simulations that encourage students to work with 'elements' of physics, such as mass, acceleration, and force. The goal is to help students generate hypotheses as necessary precursors to expanding their own intuitions. We want the simulations to encourage students to 'listen to' their own scientific intuition and to make their own model of the physical world before an encoded tutor advises them about the accuracy of their choices. These tutors have been described elsewhere [WCu87; WMu87] and will only be summarized here.

Figure 3 shows a simulation for teaching concepts in introductory statics. In this example, students are asked to identify forces and torques on the crane boom, or horizontal bar, and to use rubber banding to draw appropriate force vectors directly on the screen. When the beam is in static equilibrium there will be no net force or torque on any part of it. Students are asked to solve both qualitative and quantitative word problems.

---

[2]San Francisco State University, the University of Massachusetts, and the University of Hawaii were members of the Exploring System Earth Consortium, a group of universities and industries working together to build intelligent science tutors. The consortium is supported by the Hewlett-Packard Corporation.

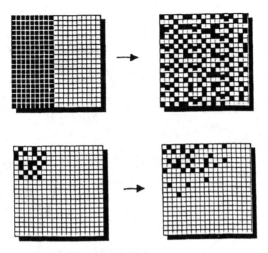

Figure 4: Thermodynamics tutor.

If a student were to specify incorrect forces, either by omitting force lines or by including the wrong ones, the tutor makes a decision about how to respond. There are many possible responses depending on the tutorial strategy in effect. The tutor might present an explanation or hint, provide another problem, or demonstrate that the student's analysis leads to a logical contradiction. Still another response would be to withhold explicit feedback concerning the quality of the student's answer, and to instead demonstrate the consequence of omitting the 'missing' force; i.e., the end of the beam next to the wall would crash down. Such a response would show the student how her conceptions might be in conflict with the observable world and to help her visualize both an internal conceptualization and the science theory.

A second tutor is designed to improve a student's intuition about concepts such as energy, energy density, entropy, and equilibrium in thermodynamics. It makes use of a very simplified but instructive simulated world (Figure 4) consisting of a two-dimensional array of identical atoms similar to that of Atkins [Atk82]. Like the statics tutor, the thermodynamics tutor monitors and advises students about their activities and provides examples, analogies, or explanations. In this simplified world the atoms have only one excited state; the excitation energy is transferred to neighboring atoms through random 'collisions.' Students can specify initial conditions, such as which atoms will be excited and which will remain in the ground state. They can observe the

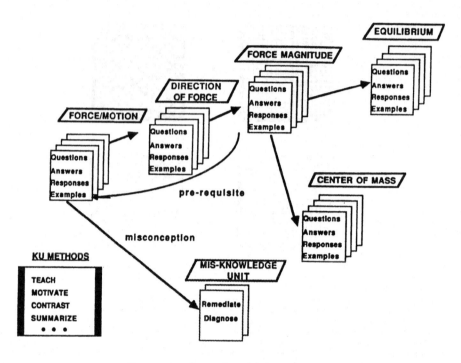

Figure 5: Hierarchy of frames.

exchange of excitation energy between atoms, and can monitor, via graphs and meters, the flow of energy from one part of the system to another as the system moves toward equilibrium. In this way, several systems can be constructed, each with specific areas of excitation. For each system, regions can be defined and physical qualities, such as energy density or entropy, plotted as functions of time.

Representing and Reasoning about Tutoring Primitives

For each domain, we represent topics, examples, explanations, and possible misconceptions in the four knowledge bases shown in Figure 1. We use a network of Knowledge Units frames to express relationships between topics such as prerequisites, corequisites, and related misconceptions (Figure 5). An important notion about the network is that it is declarative—it contains a structured space of concepts, but does not mandate any particular order for traversal of this space.

The network describes tutorial strategies in terms of a vocabulary of primitive discourse moves such as Teach, Motivate, Contrast, and Summarize. It is implemented in a language called TUPITS[3] which was built as a framework to facilitate development of numerous tutors. It is an object-oriented representation language that provides a framework for defining primitive components of a tutorial discourse interaction. These components are then used by the tutor to reason about its next action.

As shown in Figure 5, each object in TUPITS is represented as a frame and each frame is linked with other frames representing prerequisites, co-requisites, or triggered misconceptions. The primary objects in TUPITS are:

- Lessons which define high-level goals and constraints for each tutoring session;

- Knowledge Units (KUs);

- MIS-KUs, which represent common misconceptions, wrong facts or procedures, and other types of 'buggy' knowledge;

- Examples, which specify parameters that configure an example, diagram, or simulation to be presented to the student;

- Questions, which define tasks for the student and how the student's behavior during the task might be evaluated; and

- Presentations, which bind an example together with associated questions.

MIS-KUs, or "Mis-Knowledge Units," represent common misconceptions or knowledge 'bugs' and ways to remediate them. Remediation is inserted opportunistically into the discourse. The tutoring strategy sets parameters for this aspect of Knowledge Unit selection by indicating whether such remediation should occur as soon as the misconception is suspected, or wait until the current Knowledge Unit has been completed.

Control is achieved through information associated with each object which allows the system to respond dynamically to new tutoring situations. For instance, Knowledge Units, or topics represented as objects, have procedural 'methods' associated with them that:

- teach their own topic interactively;

- teach their own prerequisites;

- explain knowledge didactically;

---

[3] TUPITS (Tutorial discourse Primitives for Intelligent Tutoring Systems) was developed by Tom Murray to run on both Hewlett-Packard Bobcats and Apple Macintosh IIs.

- test students for knowledge of that topic;

- summarize themselves;

- provide examples of their knowledge (an instantiation of a procedure or concept);

- provide motivation for a student learning the topic; and

- compare this knowledge with that of other Knowledge Units.

A specific tutoring strategy manifests itself by parameterizing the algorithm used to traverse the knowledge primitives network based on classifications of and relations between knowledge units. Several major strategies have thus far been implemented. For example, the tutor might always teach prerequisites before teaching the goal topic. Alternatively, it might provide a diagnostic probe to see if the student knows a topic. Prerequisites might be presented if the student doesn't exhibit enough knowledge on the probe. These prerequisites may be reached in various ways, such as depth-first and breadth-first traversal. An intermediate strategy is to specialize the prerequisite relation into 'hard' prerequisites, which are always covered before the goal topic, and 'soft' prerequisites, taught only when the student displays a deficiency.

Acquiring Tutoring Primitives Knowledge. Knowledge acquisition of tutoring primitives knowledge or acquiring and encoding the questions, examples, analogies, and explanations used in a particular domain is still a difficult problem. We need to know not only the primitives used by the expert, but also the reasoning used to decide how and when to present each primitive. We achieve knowledge acquisition for tutoring primitives through a graphical editor built into TUPITS which is used by the instructional designer to encode and modify both primitives and the reasons why one primitive might be used over another. The graphical editor allows a teacher to generate and modify primitives without working in a programming language. The system currently presents a user with a sheaf of "cards" listing a series of primitives. The user chooses a card and brings the primitive into an edit window, from which he/she builds new primitives.

Tools for Representing Discourse Knowledge

Our tutors are beginning to represent and reason about alternative responses to the student. Choices are concerned with how much information to give and what motivational comments to make. For instance, the machine must decide whether or not to:

- talk *about* the student's response;

- provide *motivational* feedback about the student's learning process;

- say *whether* an approach is appropriate, *what* a correct response would be, and *why* the student's response is correct or incorrect;

- provide hints, leading questions, or counter-suggestions.

Motivational feedback may include asking questions about the student's interest in continuing or providing encouragement, congratulations, challenges, and other statements with affective or prelocutionary content. Control is modulated by the active tutoring strategy, which in turn places constraints on what feedback or follow-up response to generate. The strategy may also specify that system action be predicated on whether the student's response was correct, or whether any response was given.

Reasoning about Discourse Level. As a start to this process we have defined several high-level response strategies and tactics as shown in the Response Matrix (Figure 6). For example, we have designated an informative response tactic as one in which the machine will elaborate, give reasons, and congratulate the student. For each concept represented in the machine, some of these primitive responses are available and the machine will generate the requested tactic. However, we also advise the system about strategies such as Socratic tutoring, being brief, and being verbose. Here we indicate a priority ordering; thus to be Socratic, the machine must place highest priority on the tactic called coy and secondary rating on the tactic to be informative. If there is a conflict between the checks and the crosses in the matrix shown in Figure 6, that notation with the highest priority will win.

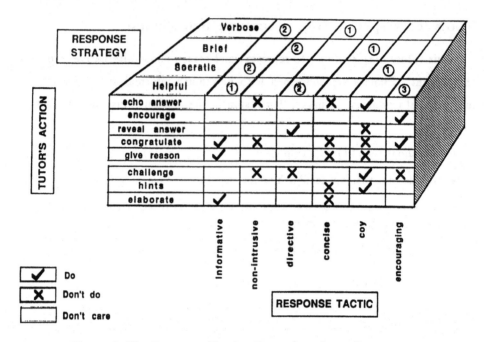

Figure 6: The Response Matrix: Reasoning about discourse.

Managing Discourse

We realize that a more flexible and responsive discourse management technique is critical to a tutoring or consultant system. By discourse management, we mean the system's ability to maintain interactive discourse with the user and to custom-tailor its responses beyond the generalized discourse levels suggested above. Ideally, the system should tailor its response to the idiosyncracies of a particular user. Machine discourse and response need not be in natural language to be effective [Ser83].

For example, the system should ensure that an intervention relates directly to an individual's personal history, learning style, and on-line experience with the system. It should dynamically reason about a user's actions, the curriculum, and the discourse history. In doing this the tutor should make each user feel that her unique situation has been responded to appropriately and sensitively. In this way the system simulates one-on-one human tutoring behavior. The mechanism we use to do this is called a DACTN, *Discourse ACtion Transition Network*, which represents and controls human-machine dialog. Figure 7 shows a DACTN for responding to a user about an inventory test of

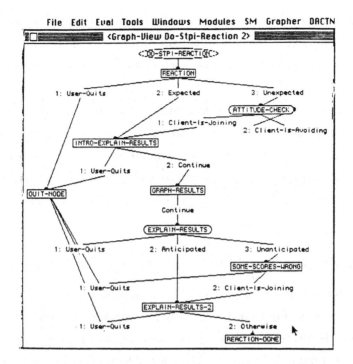

Figure 7: <u>D</u>iscourse <u>AC</u>tion <u>T</u>ransition <u>N</u>etwork: DACTN.

questions that she took in the TEV (Time, Energy, and Vision) system implemented by our group. This graphic is taken directly off the screen of that system.

Sometimes the intervention steps designated by a DACTN are based on a taxonomy of frequently-observed discourse sequences which provide default responses for the tutor [WMu87]. The discourse manager reasons about local context when making discourse decisions. Here local context is an aggregate of the client profile and response history.

The DACTN represents the space of possible discourse situations: Arcs track the state of the conversation and are defined as predicate sets while nodes provide actions for the tutor. The discourse manager first accesses the situation indicated by the arcs, resolving any conflicts between multiply-satisfied predicate sets, and then initiates the action indicated by the node at the termination of the satisfied arc.

Arcs represent discourse situations defined by sets of predicates over the client profile and the state of the system. For instance, the value of the arc "CLIENT-IS-AVOIDING" (top half of Figure 7) is determined by inferring over the current state of the profile and recent user responses. Placing actions at the nodes rather than on the arcs, as was done in the ATN [Wds70], allows nodes to represent abstract actions which can be expanded into concrete substeps when and if the node is reached during execution of the DACTN. For example, the node "EXPLAIN RESULTS" (middle of Figure 7) expands into yet another complete DACTN to be executed if this node is evaluated in the course of the intervention.

Each user response causes the user model to be updated, which in turn affects the interpretation and resolutions of subsequent interactions. DACTNs allow discourse control decisions to be based on a dynamic interpretation of the situation. In this way the mechanism remains domain-independent and flexible enough to allow dynamic rebuilding — decision points and machine actions can be modified through a graphics editor, as explained in the next section.

Acquiring Discourse Knowledge

Knowledge acquisition for discourse knowledge involves first identifying and then encoding the reasons why an instructor makes decisions about responding to the student and how the teacher decides when such interventions will take place. We facilitate the knowledge acquisition process by use of a graphical editor in which the instructor selects interventions and modifies the dialogue "on-line." This editor facilitates piecewise development and evaluation of the system, thus providing an opportunity for a wide circle of people, including psychologists, teachers, curriculum developers, and instructional scientists, to participate in the process of developing the system. The DACTN in Figure 7 shows a specific instance of this graphics editor.

The teacher adds a new question or statement directly on the screen. Arcs and nodes are added by simply buttoning the mouse on the graphical element to be changed. Graphical inputs are directly translated into LISP code by the system. The instructor is led through a series of prompts designed to elicit possible interventions and client responses. Each response has associated with it two pieces of information: a classification of the response, which is based on the current user profile, and the profile updates related to the choice of this response. Using a small set of classifications, i.e., EXPECTED, INDICATES-CONFUSION, AVOIDANCE, etc., the expert indicates his understanding of the meaning of each user response. These classifications may depend on the current user profile or other indications of context. The profile modifications may include updates based both on the classification of the response and those specific to this question and response.

Because DACTNs provide a structured framework for representing dialogues, the visual dialogue editor allows an expert to work on knowledge acquisition without having to work with knowledge engineers. In this way, we continue to elicit new interventions from our experts even as development and evaluation of the system proceeds.

The dialogue editor enables the domain expert to directly manipulate a graph of the dialogue where each question, statement, or action is represented in an editable node, and each arc (also editable) represents a discourse situation that could result from the client's response. As each question is added, the graph is updated so the expert always has a view of the current state of the intervention. The underlying DACTN is created dynamically so that at any point in the editing it can be executed against default profiles, allowing the expert to check the appropriateness of the machine's responses.

Summary

We have described existing tools for representing, acquiring, and reasoning about tutoring knowledge. Tutoring knowledge has been described both in terms of content (i.e., topics, questions, and examples) and in terms of context (i.e., tutoring strategies and discourse interventions). Current tools provide a generic framework which allows development of multiple tutors. Several application systems have been described, namely those in statics and thermodynamics, along with a few tools, namely TUPITS, DACTNs, and the Response Matrix. The tools and applications provide a test-bed for exploring new issues and testing new tutoring functionality. Ultimately, we expect to build systems which can reason about the choice of tutoring strategy based on a clear representation of a student's cognitive knowledge. No extant system yet has this capability.

References

[Atk82] Atkins, T. (1982). *The second law*. San Francisco: Freedman.

[Duc87] Duckworth, E., Kelley, J., & Wilson, S. (1987). AI goes to school. *Academic Computing*, pp. 6-10, 38-43, 62-63.

[Ser83] Servan-Schreiber, D. (1983). Artificial intelligence in psychiatry. *Journal of Nervous and Mental Disease*, 174: 191-202.

[Wds70] Woods, W. (1970). Transition network grammars for natural language analysis. *Communications of the ACM*, 13(10): 591-606.

[WCu87] Woolf, B., & Cunningham, P. (1987). Multiple knowledge sources in intelligent tutoring systems. *IEEE Expert*, 2, Summer: 41-54.

[WMu87] Woolf, B., & Murray, T. (1987). A framework for representing tutorial discourse. *International joint conference in artificial intelligence (IJCAI-87)*. Los Altos, CA: Morgan Kaufmann, pp. 189-192.

Learning Styles and Computer-Based Learning Environments

Lesley Allinson

Department of Psychology

University of York

York, YO1 5DD, England

tel. 44-904-433161

email: lja1@uk.ac.york.vax

Abstract

Learning Support Environments need to support the learner not only for a variety of tasks (both learning and information retrieval), but also by providing flexibility so they can determine their own navigational or learning strategy with which to accomplish these tasks. Following a review of the background to our understanding of individual learner differences and individual learning strategies and styles, an investigation of user behaviour and its relationship to individual learning style is reported. Entwistle's Approaches to Study Inventory was employed to select test subjects as this questionnaire attempts to incorporate various dimensions of a student's approach to study, deep/surface processing, the serial/holist dimension (as proposed by Pask), and various strategic and motivation elements. Those subjects selected for their *high reproducing* approach to study, showed a preference for a more linear and structured presentation of the information and navigated the screens at a slower rate. The *high meaning* group demonstrated more active use, especially for their initial period of system use, showed greater use of the *self-determined* hypertext linkages as a navigational strategy, and appeared to be more actively searching the material.

Introduction

We demonstrate in this paper through the application of the Approaches to Studying Inventory, that students' styles of learning, using CAL systems, do differ and that they manipulate the material to be learnt in different ways. In a conventional learning situation (e.g., learning from reading text) we can have little idea of the detailed processes utilised by the learner. Do they skim the article first or slowly work from start to finish? Do they exhibit common strategies for gaining an overview? With computer-based material, the activities and techniques involved can be recorded in fine detail. The flexibility of a hypertext system together with opportunities for multiple navigational strategies provided by a range of 'navigational tools' may well permit and encourage the user to adopt a 'best method' to suit their individual approach.

What we cannot claim is that the provision of these tools will necessarily lead to the development of good strategies in the learners (it would be perverse for us to suggest that this would be possible), but that the interface and its available navigational tools can play a part in affecting appropriate use. Our definition of appropriate will, however, vary as a function of both task and user characteristics. Different students or even the same student with increasing familiarity with a particular problem or knowledge domain, or students with differing needs, will adopt different learning strategies. Indeed, a single student may exhibit a flexible approach. Our aim here is a restricted one, namely, to demonstrate that the variability of system usage is to some extent dependent on user characteristics as well as task requirements. A hypertext-based CAL system needs both to support the user in a variety of user activities such as exam revision or essay preparation, and be flexible enough to allow the user to pursue their individual approaches to these activities. Designers of CAL systems need to be alert to the users' varying requirements and approaches. Practising educators will not want any such reminder.

1 Previous Studies

In previous work we have discussed the design and development of our own hypertext-based learning support environment [Ham-All88a]. System design was grounded in our cognitive principles generated from our understanding of human cognition and our educational goals [All-Ham89] and realised in an examplar system - the **Hitch-hiker's Guide**. This system is referred to as a learning support environment as it is intended to supplement conventional teaching methods rather than to replace them, and to be a flexible system where the locus of control can be shifted effortlessly between the user and the computer. Considerable emphasis has been placed on making the interface as transparent as possible and on the provision of a range of navigational tools embedded within the metaphor of a *travel holiday,* where the information frames represent places to visit and the various facilities - indexes (selectable entries), maps (graphical representations of the local information network providing 'footprinting' information), tours (author-defined sequences) and hypertext links (selectable words/pictures embedded within the text) represent the ways and means of travelling around. (See [Ham-All87] for an elaboration of the role of metaphor in interface design and [Ham-All88b] for the specific use of metaphor within the Hitch-hiker's Guide itself.)

Extensive evaluation of the system has demonstrated that users do use all of the system facilities and in a manner appropriate to their current task [Ham-All89, All90]. Hence, the increased use of tours for exploration and learning and the increased use of the index facility for direct information seeking. These effects were obtained when subjects were provided the full set of navigations facilities hence establishing that novice subjects could utilise the full system in an appropriate way, and with no apparent detriment to their subjective ratings of ease and success. Although we were able to show effects due to task, it was also clear from the individual data collected that differences between the users could not solely be accounted for by the task in hand.

2   Learning Styles and Strategies

A cognitive style is a general habitual mode of processing information. Learning strategies are simply cognitive styles applied when individuals go about learning. In a sense, styles are latent and strategies are manifest. A variety of cognitive styles has been suggested; for instance, Messick et al. [Mes76] define 19 different dimensions. Though the independent nature of such a variety of cognitive styles has been criticised in that they may simply be differing aspects of a general cognitive ability, they remain useful in exposing the different learning styles which can be adopted. Witkin's work [Wit76] on *field-dependent* and *field-independent* cognitive styles concentrates on the differences in the way an individual structures and analyses information. Pask and Scott [Pas-Sco72] identified *holist* and *serialist* strategies in problem solving. Pask argues that the holist and serialist strategies are the manifestations of underlying differences in the ways people approach learning and problem solving. Though there is evidence that some people consistently demonstrate one form of thinking as opposed to the other, many individuals will change their cognitive style to suit the current task [Web-Wal81]. What is important in the context of CAL is not whether these distinctions represent true differences in cognitive style but that they are observable.

Certainly, different types of *learning strategies* do exist. Säljö [Säl79] found that whereas adults with an extended education realised that different types of learning were important for different tasks, unsophisticated learners viewed learning to involve only rote memorization.

The awareness that students show about the selection of appropriate strategies is similar to the *cue-consciousness* described by Miller and Parlett [Mil-Par74] in relation to students' preparation for examinations. They identify two distinct groups of students. The first group is receptive to, and actively seeks out, cues and hints from their tutors regarding forthcoming examinations, these they term as *cue-seeking*; whereas the second, who are less sophisticated strategists and do not pick up on available hints, are termed *cue-deaf*. Based on interview techniques Marton and Säljö [Mar-Säl76], focusing on the referential aspect of outcome, were able to discriminate students on the basis of their approach to, and process of, reading articles. This distinction was that students adopted either a *deep level of processing* which started with the intention of understanding the meaning of the article and reformulating the arguments with respect to previous knowledge and experience, or a *surface level of processing*, in that it was their intent to memorise the parts of the information that they considered salient guided by the types of questions they had anticipated. The distinction between *deep* and *surface levels of processing* was replaced in a later paper by *deep* and *surface approaches* [Mar-Säl84].

The work of Entwistle and his colleagues [Ent-Ram83] is an attempt to obtain evidence for the existence of differing learning styles by studying a wider range of disciplines and to explore the issue of robustness and stability of these characteristics. In particular, the work led to the development of an inventory, based on student interviews, which explored the relationships between the various dimensions of approaches to studying including the inter-relationships between the concepts identified by Marton (*deep* and *surface* processing) and Pask (*holists* and *serialists*). It also included items based on a modified version of the *cue consciousness* ideas of Miller and Parlett, developed into a more general dimension of a *strategic approach to assessment* [Ram79]. Further items based on motivational factors (*intrinsic/extrinsic*) and *internality* and *openness* were included, influenced by the work of Biggs [Big76]. This Approaches to Studying Inventory attempts to draw together the two main components consistently found as predictive of academic success, namely organised study methods and active learning processes [Wei-Und85], as well as a set of motivational aspects. A detailed history of the development of this inventory is provided in [Ent88].

The four factors that emerged are termed *orientations* to indicate a consistency of approach and also to acknowledge the existence of both approach and motivation as components in three of the factors. The first factor, *Meaning Orientation*, had high loadings on Marton's concept of a Deep Approach to learning and its two associated processes (namely, Relating Ideas and Use of Evidence). Also associated with this factor were Comprehension Learning and Intrinsic Motivation. For the second factor, *Reproducing Orientation*, the highest loadings bought together Surface Approach, Operational Learning and Improvidence – all indicating an atomistic way of tackling academic work. The associated motivational subscales were Fear of Failure and Extrinsic Motivation. Entwistle argues that although in theory operational learning is necessary for a versatile deep learning approach, this relationship with surface learning would indicate that students who prefer a serialist strategy may, perhaps through lack of time, adopt a reproducing mode of operation. The remaining two factors are less distinct.

This Inventory has been used by other research workers [Mor80, Wat82, Wat83, Dia84]. Their results generally confirm the importance of *Meaning* and *Reproducing Orientations* with less general agreement on the remaining two factors. More support for the validity of an inventory type of approach comes from the work of Biggs [Big78, Big87] who, using an independently developed inventory, reported three main factors – *Deep*, *Surface* and *Achieving* (which combines Organisation and Competition). What is important for our current purposes is that these differences appear to be robust – despite their differing theoretical background, individual emphasis and variations in experimental design and analysis. The use of the Approaches to Study Inventory will furnish us with a legitimate means of classifying users into categories that represent clearly differing learning strategies and approaches.

3 Present Study

3.1 Selection of subjects

Completed questionnaires were obtained from 310 first year students at York. The analysis by Entwistle (and also the case in most other studies using this inventory) combined the raw question responses into their respective totals for each subscale. This distorts the factor analysis in two ways. Firstly, it assumes that all questions in each subscale relate equally to one factor; and secondly, it makes it impossible to remove questions that are biased. For this study, factor analysis was performed on the uncollapsed questionnaire responses, after the removal of eight biased questions (the full inventory contains 64 questions). Principal axis factoring, with oblique rotation, was employed using SPSS^X. The analysis produces four well-formed factors, though Factor 3 is composed of only three question responses. Factors 1 and 2 are referred to as meaning and reproducing orientation factors respectively. They are comparable with the similarly named factors obtained in other studies.

Two distinct groups with the largest differences in these two orientations were selected. This was based on responses to the two sets of questions which contributed to the two principal factors. The two groups are characterised as:–

Group 1   High reproducing orientation – Low meaningful orientation
Group 2   High meaningful orientation – Low reproducing orientation

Care was taken to ensure that the two groups were well balanced in terms of male-female and science-arts splits. The disproportionate number of female arts undergraduates reflects the distribution in the original subject pool. Also, as the main learning material was concerned with physiological subject matter, undergraduates taking a biology or psychology degree, or possessing A-level biology, were omitted. The profiles of the two groups employed in the subsequent experiments are given in Table 1.

Table 1   Scores for the two selected subject groups

	Group Score				Meaning Orientation Score				Reproducing Orientation Score				Male/ Female		Science/ Arts	
	Min.	Max.	Mean	σ	Min.	Max.	Mean	σ	Min.	Max.	Mean	σ	M	F	S	A
Group One	-3.81	-2.04	-2.60	0.61	0	6	3.78	1.83	7	11	9.28	1.18	6	12	7	11
Group Two	1.82	3.29	2.58	0.55	9	13	11.0	1.41	1	4	2.00	0.97	8	10	7	11

3.2   Experimental materials

The Hitch-hiker's Guide was transferred to HyperCard (the original Hitch-hiker's was written in Pascal for non-IBM compatible machines), and two stacks produced. The first was designed to be practice material. The intention in this investigation was to study established navigation strategies, hence the second stack was the main experimental vehicle. This second set of materials covered information on the **Physiological Feedback Mechanisms in Humans** and represented a demanding and realistic learning task. The material was designed to present both factual content and also elements that required a deeper understanding of the concepts involved. Following the thirty minute learning phase, subjects were given a short questionnaire to complete. The first five questions were as follows:–

- How easy was the computer system to use?
- How successful do you think the computer was in presenting the material?
- How does learning material in this way compare with learning the same material from a book?

- Did you enjoy using the system?
- How difficult was the material you were asked to learn?

Subjects were finally given a five-page question sheet consisting of 25 questions. Answers to all the questions could have been found within the information presented. Questions varied in their presentation so that either they required the subject to phrase a specific answer to a question or they required the recall of specific facts. An attempt was made to provide a balance between those questions where the answer required only a simple recall of presented facts to those where a correct response might indicate a deeper understanding of the material.

The experiment hence consisted of four main sections – a practice computer session, a learning session on the computer, a short break during which time they completed the subjective questionnaire and the final question paper. The total time of the experiment was about one and half hours, and the subjects worked individually.

3.3   Subjective questionnaire and examination findings

The only significant difference between the groups, for the subjective questionnaire, was for the question "How difficult was the material you were asked to learn?" The Group 1 (High Reproducing) subjects rated the material more difficult. This result was significant at the 5% level (Independent samples t-test, $p = 0.022$). As there was no difference in learning outcome as measured by the subsequent examination results, this could imply that Group 1 subjects expended more effort in attempting to learn the material. Scores on the question paper indicated a wide range of correct answers, from an overall score of 18% – 92%, with an average of 57%. No significant differences were found between the scores obtained for the different groups. This finding was as expected; indicating that the differences in Attitudes to Study, as isolated by the Entwistle questionnaire, were not simply reflecting general ability level. The main purpose of this testing session was to produce a realistic learning phase. The scores obtained in this test would indicate that the learning phase had indeed been taken seriously by the vast majority of subjects tested.

3.4   Navigation strategies

The system automatically generated a log-file of each subject's navigation throughout the thirty minute interaction with the learning material. From these log-files, a significant difference was found in the total number of screens viewed by the two groups, subjects in Group 1 (high reproducing) seeing significantly fewer screens ($F(1,34) = 5.144$, MSE = 2095.9, $p < 0.05$). Despite there being a significant difference between groups with regard to the total screens viewed, there is no significant difference between the two groups with regard to the percentage coverage of the available information. This seems to imply that Group 2 (high meaning) traversed the screens more in an attempt to elicit the information.

Using a minimum keystroke model of efficiency, efficiency in a hypertext system is increased by the provision of guidance and access tools. Pure hypertext systems necessitate the repetition of screens by promoting a predominantly trial and error approach to navigation combined with simple navigational strategies such as back-tracking (i.e., the only approach available to elaborate structure from the materials). If we measure efficiency as available information screens as a percentage of total information screen seen, a significant difference between the groups exists $(F(1,34) = 8.681, MSE = 119.44, p < 0.01)$. Group 1 (high reproducing) subjects showing greater efficiency. However, it is not at all clear what the efficiency indices of learning should be. Interface designers have long based their design on information processing theory and not on the individual differences of approach or indeed learning theory [Cov90]. The repeated presentation of the information may help the student structure and assimilate the information. We have no evidence to support such a claim except rather tenuously as there is no evidence to suggest that this *inefficiency* effects the learning outcome as there are no significant differences between the groups on measures of learning outcome.

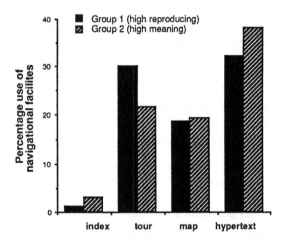

Figure 1   *Percentage usage of facilities shown by the two subject groups*

3.5 Navigation methods

From an analysis of the percentage of interactions using specific navigational facilities, a graph of facility usage was generated (see Figure 1). Significant differences were found for the extent of usage of both tours and indexes between the two groups. Group 1 (high reproducing) showed significantly greater use of the tour ($F(1,34) = 4.526$, MSE $= 123.7$, p < 0.05); whilst Group 2 (high meaning) showed significantly greater index usage ($F(1,34) = 4.275$, MSE $= 5.1$, p < 0.05). It appears that subjects in Group 1 do conform to the expected pattern, that is showing a preference for a linear and structured presentation of the materials. Subjects in Group 2 indicated a tendency to utilise the less well structured hypertext navigation though the differences between the groups was not significant.

3.6 Longitudinal analysis of log-files

Table 2 shows the total interactions occurring within the four 7.5 minute slots of user activity. The initial number of interactions (i.e., the first 7.5 minutes) are the same for both groups. However, Group 2 (high meaning) subjects show a consistently increased rate of activity over Group 1 (high reproducing) subjects for each of the subsequent time slots.

Table 2   *Total interactions for each of four successive time intervals*

	slot 1	slot 2	slot 3	slot 4
Group 1 (reproducing)	18.2	18.6	21.1	21.0
Group 2 (meaning)	20.0	32.0	33.5	32.5

Figure 2 shows the use of the individual navigational facilities for the two groups. For all facilities Group 2 (high meaning) students demonstrate a faster uptake of usage. This is shown by the steeper curve for each of these facilities between slots 1 and 2. After 15 minutes, the graphs show a parallel relationship for map usage and back-one usage; reflecting the different overall interactions of each group. The graphs show that the expected parallel pattern of usage for tours and index does not occur; usage by the two groups is equivalent at 22.5 minutes and, in fact, a cross-over occurs at 30 minutes. This reflects the significant difference that was found for tour usage between the two groups. Note that following an initial inspection at the start of the session, no student in Group 1 (high reproducing) used the index facility during the remaining 75% of the session.

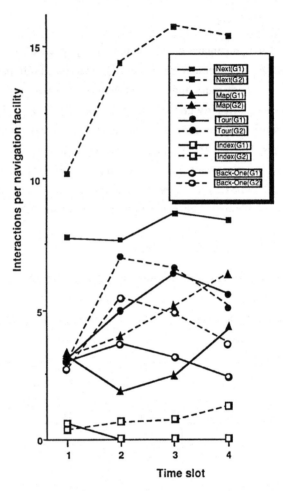

Figure 2   *Use of navigational facilities over the four successive time slots*

Finally, one other property of this longitudinal analysis of log-files is the ability to observe trends. Usage of some facilities appears to be tailing off. The reduction in the use of tours (for both groups) in the final time slot might indicate that the tours had all been completed by this stage (i.e. reflecting facility usages dependence on the actual size and content of the hypertext). The most interesting feature is the increasing uptake of the map facility with time. Here, we have evidence that the map is being increasingly used as an aid not only to navigation but as a learning tool.

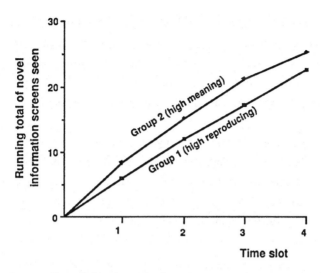

Figure 3   *Consolidated novel information screens as function of time*

A further trend is illustrated in Figure 3. Here, the consolidated novel information screens per time slot is plotted for both groups. Group 2 (high meaning) saw 40% more screens than Group 1 (high reproducing) during the first time slot, but thereafter the rate of seeing new information screens was essentially constant over the remaining time for both groups (Group 1: 5.48 new screens/slot, $r = 0.999$; Group 2: 5.62 new screens/slot, $r = 0.987$).

4   Conclusions

The two groups were well-balanced in terms of their arts/science and male/female distributions so it can be confidently predicted that differences between the groups are due to their differing attitudes to study as identified by Entwistle's Approaches to Study Inventory. There were no differences in the learning outcome between the two groups, as measured by their performance in the examination paper. This seems to support the view that differences in the responses to the Inventory are not concerned with simply a general level of ability. The subjects' perceptions of the system, as judged by their responses to the subjective questionnaire, revealed that there was little difference between the groups. Analysis of the log-files, however, showed some of the effects which had been predicted. Group 1 (high reproducing) demonstrated a preference for a more linear and structured presentation of the learning material and made greater use of the tour facility. Group 1 saw fewer screens than Group 2 (high meaning), though there was no difference in the actual information coverage. Hence, Group 1 could be said to be the more efficient of the two groups. Alternatively, Group 2 could be said to be more active in that their *start-up* was quicker (i.e., activity in the first 7.5 minutes) and made greater use of hypertext links and the index facility. However, after this initial burst of activity by Group 1, both groups saw very similar numbers of novel information screens per unit time. Group 2 appear to be actively searching the material in order to form their own internal structure of the material, while Group 1 seem to be more content to follow prescribed paths and study each screen in more detail.

Experimental psychology progresses through a process of the gradual accumulation of evidence. In isolation, the findings presented here may be heavily bound to the specific experimental conditions. Much work remains to be done, but we must be vigilant in not falling into the trap (as previously happened with programmed learning systems) that students are a homogeneous group with uniform strategies and needs.

References

[All-Ham89] L. J Allinson, N. V. Hammond. *A learning support environment: the Hitch-Hiker's Guide*. In (R. McAleese, ed.) *Hypertext: theory into practice*. Intellect Books, 1989, pp. 62-74.

[All90] L. J. Allinson. *Designing and evaluating the navigational toolkit*. In Proceedings of the NATO Advanced Educational Workshop "Cognitive Modelling and Interactive Environments", Mierlo. 1990.

[Big76] J. B. Biggs. *Dimensions of study behaviour: another look at A.T.I*. British Journal of Educational Psychology. 1976, Vol. 48, pp. 68-80.

[Big78] J. B. Biggs. *Individual and group differences in study process*. British Journal of Educational Psychology. 1978, Vol. 48, pp. 266-279.

[Big87] J. B. Biggs. *Student Approaches to Learning*. Australian Council for Educational Research, 1987.

[Cov89] L. Coventry. *Some effects of cognitive style on learning UNIX*. International Journal of Man-Machine Studies. 1989, Vol. 31, pp. 349-365.

[Dia84] D. Diaz. *The identification of approaches to learning adopted by Venezuelan university students*. University of Wales Institute of Science and Technology, 1984.

[Ent88] N. Entwistle. *Motivational factors in students' approaches to learning*. In (R. R. Schmeck, ed.) *Learning Strategies and Learning Styles*. Plenum, 1988, pp. 21-51.

[Ent-Ram83] N. J. Entwistle and P. Ramsden. *Understanding Student Learning*. Croom Helm, 1983.

[Ham-All87] N. V. Hammond and L. J. Allinson. *The travel metaphor as design principle and training aid for navigating around complex sytems*. In (D Diaper and R Winder, eds.)

People and Computers III. Cambridge University Press, 1987, pp. 75-90.

[Ham-All88a] N. V. Hammond and L. J. Allinson. *Development and evaluation of a CAL system for non-formal domains: the Hitch-hiker's Guide to cognition*. Computers and Education, 1988, Vol. 12, pp. 215-220.

[Ham-All88b] N. V. Hammond and L. J. Allinson. *Travelling around a learning support environment: rambling, orienteering or touring*. CHI'88: Human Factors in Computing Systems. ACM Press, 1988, pp. 269-273.

[Ham-All89] N. V. Hammond and L. J. Allinson. *Extending hypertext for learning: an investigation of access and guidance tools*. In (A. Sutcliffe and L. Macaulay, eds) *People and Computers V*. Cambridge University Press, 1989, pp. 293-304.

[Mar-Säl76] F. Marton and R. Säljö. *On qualitative differences in learning: 1. Outcome and process*. British Journal of Educational Psychology. 1976, Vol. 46, pp. 4-11.

[Mar-Säl84] F. Marton and R. Säljö. *Approaches to learning*. In (F Marton, D Hounsell and N Entwistle, eds.) *The Experience of Learning*. Scottish Academic Press, 1984, pp. 36-55.

[Mes76] S. Messick et al. *Individuality in Learning*. Jossey Bass, 1976.

[Mil-Par74] C. M. Miller and M. R. Parlett. *Up to the mark: a study of the examination game*. SRHE, 1974.

[Mor-Gib80] A. Morgan, G. Gibbs and E. Taylor. *Students' approaches to studying the social sciences and technology foundation courses: preliminary studies*. Institute of Technology, The Open University, 1980.

[Pas-Sco72] G. Pask and B. C. E. Scott. *Learning strategies and individual competence*. International Journal of Man-Machine Studies. 1972, Vol. 4, pp. 217-253.

[Ram79] P. Ramsden. *Student learning and perceptions of the academic environment*. Higher Education. 1979, Vol. 8, pp. 411-428.

[Säl79] R. Säljö. *Learning about learning*. Higher Education. 1979, Vol. 8, pp. 443-451.

[Wat82] D. Watkins. *Identifying the study process dimensions of Australian university students*. Australian Journal of Education. 1982, Vol. 26, pp. 76-85.

[Wat83] D. Watkins. *Assessing tertiary study processes*. Human Learning. 1983, Vol. 2, pp. 29-37.

[Web-Wal81] W. G. Webiter and A. D. Walker. *Problem solving strategies and manifest brain assymetry*. Cortex. 1981, Vol. 14, pp. 474-479.

[Wei-Und85] C. E. Weinstein and V. L. Underwood. *Learning strategies: the 'how' of learning*. In (J. W. Segal, S. F. Chipman and R. Glaser, eds.) *Thinking and Learning Skills*. Lawrence Erlbaum, 1985.

[Wit76] H. A. Witkin. *Cognitive style in academic performance and in teacher-student relations*. In (S Messick et al., eds) *Individuality in Learning*. Jossey-Bass, 1976

Text and Graphics In Instructional Design

Alana M. Anoskey and Richard Catrambone
School of Psychology
Georgia Institute of Technology
Atlanta, GA   30332 USA
tel. (404) 894-2680
email: gt3762c@prism.gatech.edu

Abstract

This paper addresses textual and graphical representation formats in instructional design. First, it describes background research in information display and instructional design. Second, it integrates guidelines suggested from past research and proposes a methodology for designing instructional material with regard to textual and graphical content. The paper then describes a pilot experiment conducted to examine the validity of the methodology in optimizing instructional design.

Introduction

Technological progress has increased consumer exposure to electronic equipment both at home and in the workplace. Efficiently operating electronic devices is often neither easy nor intuitive, however. Although user's manuals provide "how-to-use" information, it is unlikely that users read this information in its entirety [Wri81]. In addition, instructions do not necessarily provide effective guidance, even when users read them in full [Kam75].

Previous research shows that instructional material may be ineffective because it is either ignored or misunderstood. This leads to the question: If instructional information is available, why are people unable to put that information to use? Rouse [Rou86] states that the critical issue is the form in which instructional information is presented. Instructional form must be appropriate to the user because it ultimately affects the comprehensibility and usefulness of the information. Thus, consideration of the content of the instructional material as well as the possible representational (textual or graphical) forms it can take may enable designers to optimize readability and comprehensibility, and produce instructions that effectively communicate usage information.

Instructional Design

While developing help screens for a software application, Keister [Kei89] found that technical writers often overloaded instructional material with technical detail. Users might cast aside complex, detailed instruction written by technical writers because it includes information that seems irrelevant to the immediate use of the system. This suggests that instructional writers should match the representation and content of the instructions to the goals and technical abilities of the audience. It is proposed here that instructional designers can produce effective instructional material if they consider how to represent, integrate, and display instructional information.

The work of Wickens, Sandry and Vidulich [Wic83] was conducted to develop display design guidelines that would facilitate information perception and processing, and optimize task completion. Wickens et al. conducted an experiment to observe competition between encoding and response modalities. Subjects performed a simulated flight task in which they were presented information either aurally or visually and had to make either verbal or manual (spatial) responses. Best performance occurred when subjects verbally responded to aural information and manually responded to visual information, that is, when the perception and response modalities were compatible.

These results suggest that an important design guideline is high compatibility between the form of the displayed stimulus and the human processing modality. Wickens et al. named this the principle of stimulus-central processing (S-C) compatibility. This principle might assist instructional design because it addresses the way the displayed form of information relates to perception and processing modalities. For the visual presentation of procedural instructions, the S-C compatibility principle suggests that verbal information is best presented textually and spatial information is best presented graphically.

It is hypothesized that instructions designed with regard to stimulus-central processing compatibility are processed directly, avoiding translation to the proper S-C compatible modality. Such direct processing suggests that processing time and frequency of processing errors will be reduced as compared to non-direct, translational processing. The present experiment was conducted to test these predictions and to determine whether Wickens et al.'s S-C compatibility principle is useful in instructional design.

Representing Instructional Information

Instructional material may convey introductory, operation, maintenance and perhaps troubleshooting information. Some of this information is verbal, such as the name of a system component. Other information is spatial, such as the location of a power switch. There has been some effort to construct information taxonomies and to observe the effects on task performance of varying the representational form of instructions. Three of these efforts are discussed below.

Booher [Boo75] compared the relative effectiveness of printed words and pictures in conveying procedural information. In an experiment, subjects who received highly graphical instructions performed a flight simulation control-display task significantly faster than subjects who received highly textual instructions. However, the fastest subjects also made the most errors. The most accurate subjects were those who received highly graphical instructions with related (non-redundant) textual information. This is in accord with Larkin and Simon's [Lar87] hypothesis that highly graphical instructions minimize task completion speed because diagrammatic representations enable short search and recognition times. Related textual statements maximize accuracy because they limit the number of ways graphical instructions may be interpreted.

Bieger and Glock [Bie85] have developed a taxonomy for classifying the types of information present in instructional elements. This taxonomy is summarized below.

Inventory information:	depicts objects or concepts
Descriptive information:	depicts object or concept detail
Operational information:	directs an agent to act
Spatial information:	specifies location, orientation or composition
Contextual information:	provides organization in time
Covariant information:	relationships between objects
Temporal information:	specifies time course of states or events
Qualifying information:	modifications due to attribute specification
Emphatic information:	directs attention to specific attributes

Bieger and Glock applied this taxonomy to the design of procedural instructions, and found that only four of these informational categories were essential to building complete instructional statements. These were the inventory, operational, spatial, and contextual categories. These categories basically represent "what," "how," "where," and "when" information, respectively. (Bieger and Glock did not include the temporal category because time can be represented in the contextual information category.)

In addition, Feiner and McKeown [Fei90] have developed an artificial intelligence application that coordinates textual and graphical forms of explanation. COMET (COordinated Multimedia Explanation Testbed) was designed to generate equipment maintenance and repair instructions by combining textual and graphical information components in accord with user preference ratings. Feiner and McKeown's users identified six categories of information and preferred representational forms:

location information	graphics only
physical attributes	graphics only
simple actions	text and graphics
compound actions	text and graphics
abstract information	text only

conditional   text for connectives,
                               text and graphics for actions.

The preference ratings show that subjects preferred the display of certain information in only one mode, and not both text and graphics modes concurrently. Further, Feiner and McKeown found that subjects preferred spatial information to be represented by graphics and explanatory or verbal information represented by text. This agrees with Wickens, et al.'s [Wic83] S-C compatibility principle. Feiner and McKeown's categories of information can be mapped to Bieger and Glock's [Bie85] categories as shown below:

location information   ≈   spatial category information,
physical attributes   ≈   descriptive information,
actions   ≈   operational and temporal information,
conditionals   ≈   contextual and covariant information, and
abstract actions   ≈   qualifying information.

This mapping does not include Bieger and Glock's inventory and emphatic categories because these categories are inherent to representations. The correspondence between the Bieger and Glock and Feiner and McKeown taxonomies supports their use as a classification scheme in developing effective procedural instructions.

Objective

The purpose of this study was to investigate some aspects of how the representational form of instructions may affect task performance. Specifically, this research examined how variations in the use of text and graphics (pictures) in procedural instructions affect the speed and accuracy of subjects' performance of a computer task. Procedural instructions were presented to subjects as text, graphics, or as a combination of the two, and the speed and accuracy of subjects' performance was assessed. Instructional information was classified and represented according to Table 1.

Table 1. Summary of Information Presentation Guidelines

Source	Guideline
Wickens, Sandry, and Vidulich (1983)	Represent verbal information with text. Represent spatial information with pictures.
Bieger and Glock (1985)	Include the essential categories of inventory, operational, spatial, and contextual information.
Booher (1975), Feiner and McKeown (1990)	Represent location, physical attributes, action, and relationship information with pictures. Represent rationale for action, conditional explanation, and abstract information with text.

Manipulation of the representational form of instructions is the between-groups independent variable including four format conditions: purely textual, purely graphical, combined textual and graphical, and the reverse of the textual and graphical condition. In the reverse condition, information that was represented by text in the combined textual and graphical condition was represented by graphics, and vice versa. The completeness of the instructions, whether or not a given set of instructions supplied all information that was critical to task completion, was also manipulated. The completeness manipulation was included to examine the ability of subjects to infer information within a particular representation format, given incomplete instructional phrases.

Method: Subjects

Forty volunteer subjects without knowledge of Guide hypermedia construction software (Owl International, Inc.) were given experimental credit for participation and were randomly assigned to eight experimental conditions.

Subjects' computer experience, experience with hypertext software environments, and handedness were recorded.

Design

A 4-by-2 cross of instructional material format (text only, graphics only, text and graphics combined, and the reverse of the text and graphics combination), and relative instructional completeness (complete vs. incomplete) produced eight experimental conditions. Subjects were divided among these conditions, each subject receiving instructions in only one format: text-only-complete (TOC), graphics-only-complete (GOC), text & graphics-complete (TGC), text & graphics reverse-complete (TGRC), text-only-incomplete (TOI), graphics-only-incomplete (GOI), text & graphics-incomplete (TGI), and text & graphics reverse-incomplete (TGRI). The dependent variables in this experiment were time-on-task and task accuracy.

Materials

The experimental task was performed with Guide hypermedia construction software, operating on an IBM PS/2 80 computer, equipped with a keyboard and a mouse. Task completion speed, number of errors, and time spent reading instructions were recorded by the computer. The Guide task was chosen because it was procedural and easily explained, and the software had the facilities for flexible presentation of instructions and recording subject behavior.

The experimental task required each subject to make mouse-activated buttons in a hypertext document. This document consisted of 15 "pages" superimposed in a virtual stack, with the name and a brief description of a type of fruit on each page. If made correctly, the buttons would place another page at the top of the stack when clicked with the mouse. At the top of the computer screen were a "Previous" button and a "Next" button to allow subjects to navigate through the hypertext fruit document. When subjects clicked the mouse on either of these buttons, the pages of the hypertext document turned accordingly (see Figure 1).

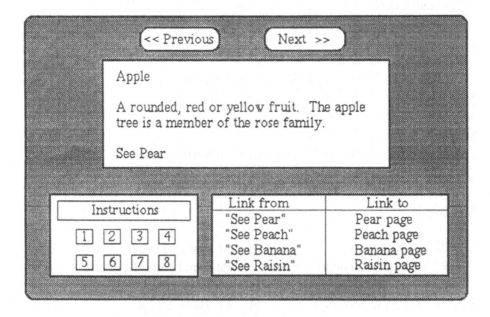

Figure 1. Diagram of Experimental Computer Screen.

Subjects received instructions from a control panel located in the lower section of the screen. The control panel consisted of 8 buttons corresponding to the 8 instructional steps required to complete the experimental task. Subjects were required to click on these buttons sequentially to view the steps involved in the task. One instructional step was visible at a time.

Bovair and Kieras [Bov81] detail the procedure for propositional analysis of textual information. Propositional analyses are performed to identify the basic textual elements contained within a body of text. Such an analysis of the experimental task instructions was necessary to insure the creation of graphical instructions that were analogous to textual instructions with regard to propositional content. The eight steps of text required for performing the button-making task were propositionally analyzed (these eight steps were derived from the reference manual for the Guide software). The analysis produced a total of 21 basic propositional elements as shown in Table 2.

Table 2. Propositional analysis of instructional text.

<u>Instructional Text</u>

S1. Go to Source page
S2. Highlight "Link from" words
S3. Pull down "Make" menu and Select "Reference Button"
S4. Pull down "Make" menu and Select "Start a Link"
S5. Go to "Link to" page
S6. Click "Link to" page top
S7. Pull down "Make" menu and Select "Reference Point"
S8. Pull down "Make" menu and Select "Link From Reference Button"

<u>Analysis</u>

S1: P1 (go-to $ page)   S5: P1 (go-to $ page)
     P2 (mod page Source)   P2 (mod page "Link to")

S2: P1 (highlight $ words)   S6: P1 (click $ page)
     P2 (mod words "Link from")   P2 (mod page "Link to")
                                          P3 (mod P1 top)

S3: P1 (pull-down $ menu)   S7: P1 (pull-down $ menu)
     P2 (mod menu make)   P2 (mod menu make)
     P3 (select $ reference-button)   P3 (select $ reference-point)

S4: P1 (pull-down $ menu)   S8: P1 (pull-down $ menu)
     P2 (mod menu make)   P2 (mod menu make)
     P3 (select $ start-a-link)   P3 (select $ link-from-reference-button)

The 21 basic propositional elements were classified by information type, and were assigned an optimal representational form according to the guidelines in Table 1. Simple pictures were created for each propositional element and were used where required to accommodate the eight instructional conditions. Textual elements were used together with the graphics in the instructional phrases in the combined conditions, but none of the phrases contained redundant information (the information in the text was not identical to the information in the graphics). Text was used within a graphic instructional element wherever the software dictated. For example, the word "make" was used in a graphic depiction of the menu because that word itself is used in the software interface. Complete instructions contained all of the propositional elements enumerated in the propositional analysis. Incomplete instructions were created by omitting the abstract action terms "go to" and "pull down," and the object term "page" for each of the conditions.

It is hypothesized that steps missing the abstract action text or graphic ("go to," "pull down," and "page") would be more difficult to follow than their corresponding complete steps. For example, the term "go to" was omitted from step 1 of the TGI instruction, whereas it was included in the TGC instruction (see Figure 2). In addition, the the turned-up corner in the TGC instruction was omitted in the TGI instruction, requiring subjects to reason that the TGI instruction was referring to the Source page. Requiring subjects to infer information should make the incomplete steps more difficult to follow.

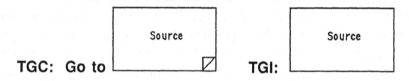

Figure 2. Step 1 Presentation Examples

Procedure

Subjects were briefed by the experimenter of the nature of the experimental task and the Guide software. They were then seated at the computer. The experimenter verbally instructed the subjects on how to use a mouse to move the pointer on the screen, select (highlight) text, and use pull-down menus. Subjects were instructed to view the steps involved in the experimental task by clicking on the numbered boxes on the control panel.

The experimental task required subjects to create functional "reference" buttons in the hypertext fruit document described in the Materials section. Reference buttons allow users to jump from one location in a document to another when they are activated with the mouse. As shown in Figure 1, the two lists of words that subjects needed to complete the experimental task were located to the right of the control panel. Unlike the instructional steps, these two lists were always visible. Subjects had to make the words in the "Link from" list into reference buttons, and the corresponding words in the "Link to" list into the end locations for those reference buttons. Subjects were required to navigate through the fruit document using the "Previous" and "Next" buttons to complete the experimental task. A correctly made reference button would jump to its corresponding destination when clicked with the mouse. For example, if the subject correctly made "See Peach" into a reference button, the peach page would be brought to the top of the page stack when the subject clicked on "See Peach." Subjects were required to create four reference buttons.

The task was self-paced, but the subjects were asked to complete each button as efficiently as possible. Time and accuracy data for each trial were recorded by the computer. A training trial was not included because part of the intent of this experiment was to observe how quickly subjects could learn a task given a particular instructional format. All four button-making trials were included in the analysis. After subjects completed the experimental task they were debriefed by the experimenter.

Predictions and Analyses

Work by Booher [Boo75], Wickens et al. [Wic83], Bieger and Glock [Bie85] and Feiner and McKeown [Fei90] suggests that subjects who received textual and graphical instructions in the hypothesized optimal representation would perform the task in a shorter amount of time and with fewer errors than subjects who receive solely textual, solely graphical, or reverse-combination instructions. In accord with Booher, it was expected that the graphics only group would complete the task faster than the text only group, but that the latter would make fewer errors than the former. Furthermore, subjects who received complete instructions were expected to perform the experimental task faster and more accurately than their counterparts. Thus, significant effects of both instructional format and completeness were expected. Finally, a format-by-complexity interaction was not expected because completeness was altered similarly for each format.

Analysis of the pilot data failed to show significant differences in task performance between groups. Analysis of variance revealed that neither format ($F(3,32)=0.67$, $p<0.58$) nor completeness of instructions ($F(1,32)=0.23$, $p<0.64$) affected the time required by subjects to complete each task step. A practice effect was observed, however, $F(3,96)=36.21$ ($p<0.001$), with subjects performing the button-making task faster throughout the experiment. Additionally, the number of reference buttons successfully completed did not differ between groups overall, $F(7,32)=1.48$ ($p<0.19$).

Discussion

Given the small number of subjects included in the pilot study, it is wrong to conclude that designing instructional material with regard to textual and graphical content is frivolous. The lack of other expected effects of instructional format suggests including a larger number of subjects in future experimentation. Such experimentation will be conducted, and interested parties are encouraged to contact the first author for the analysis of additional results.

The experimental task was designed to be engaging to the subjects. However, ensuring this quality may have made a molecular analysis of task performance difficult to achieve. A more simple procedural task may lend itself to more direct analysis of subject action, may produce significant effects of instructional format and completeness, and may indeed show that the proposed methodology is beneficial to instructional design.

Significant group effects would support using the Wickens et al. [Wic83] Stimulus-Central Processing Compatibility Principle to design instructional material for computer applications. The methodology for design of instructional material proposed here, however, is not limited to computer applications. Significant experimental results would also suggest using the S-C principle for the successful design of instructional material outside of the computer domain. Results could apply to the design of computer hardware and software usage manuals, as well as electronics user manuals, and equipment maintenance and repair manuals. There may even be implications for icon, symbol, and sign design in the computer, education, and engineering domains.

References

[Bie85] G. R. Bieger and M. D. Glock. *The Information Content of Picture-Text Instructions.* Journal of Experimental Education. 1985, Vol. 53, No. 2, pp. 68-76.

[Boo75] H. R. Booher. *Relative Comprehensibility of Pictorial Information and Printed Words in Proceduralized Instructions.* Human Factors. 1975, Vol. 17, pp. 266-277.

[Bov81] S. Bovair and D. E. Kieras. *A Guide to Propositional Analysis for Research on Technical Prose.* University of Arizona, Technical Report No. 8, 1981.

[Fei90] S. K. Feiner and K. R. McKeown. *Generating Coordinated Multimedia Explanations.* Proceedings of the 6th IEEE Conference on Artificial Intelligence Applications. 1990. pp. 290-303.

[Kam75] R. Kammann. *The Comprehensibility of Printed Instructions and the Flowchart Alternative.* Human Factors. 1975, Vol. 17, No. 2, pp. 183-191.

[Kei89] R. S. Keister. *The Content of Help Screens: Users Versus Developers.* Proceedings of the Human Factors Society, 33rd Annual Meeting, Denver, Colorado. October 1975. pp. 390-393.

[Rou86] W. B. Rouse. *On the Value of Information in System Design: A Framework for Understanding and Aiding Designers.* Information Processing & Management. 1986, Vol. 22, No. 2, pp. 217-228.

[Wic83] C. D. Wickens, D. Sandry, and M. Vidulich. *Compatibility and Resource Competition Between Modalities of Input, Central Processing and Output: Testing a Model of Complex Task Performance.* Human Factors. 1983, Vol. 25, pp. 227-248.

[Wri81] P. Wright. *"The Instructions Clearly State..." Can't People Read?.* Applied Ergonomics. 1981, Vol. 12, No. 3, pp. 131-141.

This research was aided by a Grant-in-Aid of Research from Sigma Xi, The Scientific Research Society.

Assessing Program Visualization Systems as Instructional Aids

Albert Badre[1], Margaret Beranek[2], J. Morgan Morris[3], John Stasko[1]

[1]Graphics, Visualization, and Usability Center
College of Computing
Georgia Institute of Technology
Atlanta, GA 30332-0280

[2]Computer Information Systems Department
Georgia State University
Atlanta, GA 30303

[3]Department of Mathematics and Computer Science
Georgia State University
Atlanta, GA 30303-3086

Abstract

Recently, program visualization systems have received much attention as learning tools and as software understanding aids. How to evaluate these systems, however, is an open and unexplored area. In order to determine what factors may be important, we conducted an exploratory study using XTango, an algorithm animation system. First, we asked professors to complete surveys intended to solicit information regarding current practices in the teaching of algorithms. Next, we observed two groups of students: one group received a handout and viewed an animation of the Shellsort algorithm, the other received the same handout and listened to a lecture featuring drawings on the blackboard. The students were queried on their understanding of the sort and their impressions of the animation system. Comments indicated a high perceived value for the system, with most students favoring its use as a teaching tool. It was clear from students' responses that an algorithm animation system can be used more effectively as a supplement in the classroom environment than as a substitute for the teacher. The results of this study identified changes to the animation system that will help integrate it into the classroom environment, and provided several important factors to consider in future empirical studies.

Introduction

Recently, *program visualization* systems[Mye90] have garnered increasing attention as aids for software understanding and for teaching computer science. Program visualization systems provide graphical views of the constituents, methods, and techniques of computer programs. They enable end-viewers to "look inside" the mysterious black-box of a program and visualize its inner workings in a convenient, (hopefully) understandable visual format or metaphor.

Program visualization systems range from showing programs at a low level of detail, such as showing data structure manipulations, to showing programs at a more global level, such as showing the program's purpose and methodologies[SP91]. Systems presenting a more global, high-level abstract view are called *algorithm visualization* systems. Often, these systems present a continuous, smooth view of a program during its execution, thus earning the name *algorithm animation*.

Over the past ten years, a number of algorithm visualization systems have been created[LD85, Dui86, Bro88, HHR89, Sta90]. Each concentrates on a slightly different aspect of the problem of viewing program execution, and all have their individual merits. The clear focus to this work, however, has been on improving the systems technology and visual techniques involved. Somewhat lost has been the original motivation for the systems—how to improve software understanding through pictures. Although many systems have been designed, no systematic evaluation of the systems' utility has been conducted. No formal end-user testing has been performed. Essentially no followup to the claim that these systems improve software understanding has been checked. The small amount of system evaluation done to date is largely anecdotal.

Perhaps the most extensive application of algorithm visualization technology was the use of the Balsa system[BS85, Bro88] as an aid for teaching algorithms at Brown University in the mid-1980s. Classes were taught in a large auditorium with Apollo, and subsequently Sun, workstations. Each lecture was accompanied by visualizations of the algorithm(s) being taught that day. Informal, anecdotal results of this application were good; students frequently mentioned how the visualizations helped them understand how the algorithms worked. No formal study or attempt to quantify how much the visualizations helped was conducted, however.

Instructors in a class on analysis of algorithms at San Diego State University utilized the MacBalsa[Bro88] system (a descendant of Balsa) and a local system called Algorithms Lab to help teach algorithms[WU90]. The instructors noted that the better students seemed to derive more and learn more from the addition of the computer visualizations. The authors believed that the minimal computer science background of the weaker students somewhat lessened the cognitive gains made by these students. The students' impressions of the visualizations were difficult to quantify precisely. The instructors noted, "Motivation and enthusiasm defy simple measurement." The visualization systems, however, did receive favorable feedback from the students; most felt the visualizations added to the course.

One reason for the lack of user testing in algorithm visualization is the sheer difficulty involved. What are the appropriate visualizations to utilize? How do we measure program understanding? What criteria are used for evaluation? How is the evaluation properly and fairly conducted? We believe that these difficulties are the reasons for the lack of significant system testing, and this has motivated the exploratory study we report in this paper. Rather than performing an evaluation of an animation system immediately, our goal was to learn how to evaluate an algorithm animation system.

We wanted to learn how experienced teachers might utilize this technology as an aid in the classroom. We wanted to learn how to evaluate a student's understanding of a program, and we wanted to learn what problems might arise in performing such testing.

We also wanted to learn what constitutes a good algorithm animation. How should a student be able to interact with the system? What further capabilities would be beneficial? For example, adding sound and help facilities would make a system more of a multimedia tool, and might significantly improve usefulness.

Existing work in algorithm visualization has given us intuition about the answers to these questions. But as has frequently been shown, intuition is not always correct. Consequently, we set out on this study to gather important evidence for confirming or disputing our beliefs. We focused on identifying the factors that would be important in conducting a more formal, empirical study. In a subsequent project, we will use the information we gathered to perform an exhaustive testing of the impact of an algorithm animation system on instruction.

1 Exploratory Study

The exploratory study consisted of two parts: a survey of faculty for current teaching practices, and an observational study of students interacting with an algorithm animation system. The faculty survey on teaching practices strived to identify current teaching methods for algorithms, specifically, uses of drawings, pictures and conceptualizations of algorithms. The observational study investigated the effectiveness of computer animation to enhance algorithm comprehension in a classroom environment. The computer animation was implemented on top of the algorithm animation system, XTango[SH90] that helps to design graphical representations of data structures and algorithms. The animations were presented to students as a supplemental learning tool, and the students were tested to determine their knowledge and ability to conceptualize the algorithm presented to them. The algorithm was also presented to a second group in a regular classroom environment using blackboard lecture style.

1.1 Faculty Survey

An important part of this study was to identify current methods of teaching algorithms and to identify appropriate conceptualizations of the algorithms to be used in the computer animation. These conceptualizations, or mental models, indicate how the professor visualizes the algorithms and how they transfer their vision of the algorithms to their students. To acquire this information we surveyed professors who have taught algorithms courses at two different universities. The survey consisted of two parts. Part one asked for information about the professors' background in teaching algorithms, the teaching methods used, their use of teaching aids such as textbooks, drawings and diagrams, overhead transparencies, and the use of supplemental notes.

Part two consisted of a list of four algorithms. The professors were requested to draw a diagram to emulate their conceptualization of the algorithms. The drawing could be accompanied by verbal explanations and/or color. The drawing could be static, or it could be a dynamic conceptualization, with motion indicated by the use of multiple drawings, arrows, etc. This helped us identify appropriate conceptualizations of algorithms and data structures to be used in computer animations.

Results and Discussion

Eleven professors responded to the questionnaire. In terms of current practices, the most common teaching method (36%) was a combination of lectures, textbook and use of drawings and diagrams. 82% of the professors used a textbook to supplement lectures, 81% also used drawings and diagrams as a supplement, while only 26% used overheads and only 27% used other supplementary materials. From this, along with the results from part two of the survey, we can conclude that most of the professors attempt to show the dynamic nature of the algorithms through the use of a series of drawings. Only one professor indicated that he had used any form of computer animation or graphics package in the classroom or laboratory to supplement his lectures. This would indicate that in the teaching of algorithms it is necessary to somehow show the dynamic nature of the operations of these algorithms, but very few, if any, professors are currently using any form of computer graphics package as an aid.

With regard to general conceptualizations, all of the respondents used separate phases or steps in their drawings to indicate dynamic representations for at least one algorithm. 86% of the total conceptualizations described did contain dynamic components. Four professors responded with conceptualizations of the Shellsort, which we chose as the algorithm to represent in our study. Other sorting methods, including bubble sort, selection sort, and insertion sort, are frequently taught in introductory programming courses. Since the Shellsort is usually taught at the data structures level, it was less likely that the Shellsort would be familiar to the students. The concepts involved in the Shellsort may be learned quickly, requiring knowledge of either a bubble sort or an insertion sort. In the Shellsort, subarrays are sorted in each pass, until the entire array is sorted in the final pass. The subarrays are formed using elements a specified distance apart. A sequence of distances are chosen, with the last distance having a value of 1 so that the entire array is sorted. For example, the sequence of distance values could be 40, 13, 4, 1. Each subarray is sorted using either bubble sort or insertion sort.

Of the four Shellsort conceptualizations that the professors described, two used bars of various sizes lined up on a horizontal axis. The height of the bars represented the values to be sorted. Exchange of the bars, or data values, during the sort was indicated by a change in color or circling the bars to be exchanged. A third representation lined up the numbers of the data values on a vertical axis and indicated an exchange using arrows. The fourth representation was from Knuth[Knu73]. We chose the first representation as the one used in our animation.

1.2 Observational Study

The case study group consisted of students from three separate undergraduate data structures classes. They are an appropriate audience for this study, since students usually get their initial exposure to many algorithms in a data structures course. Eleven students volunteered to participate. Approximately 64% of the students were in a Computer Science degree program and 36% were in a Computer Information Systems degree program.

The algorithm animation system we used in our study is the XTango system[SH90]. XTango supports color, two-dimensional views of programs in a workstation-based windowing environment. In our experiments, end-users were viewing animation previously created and designed to help explain different algorithms. XTango is a descendant of the original Tango system[Sta90], and it is a simpler and more portable system. XTango functions directly on top of the X11 Window System, and it generates color or black-and-white animations without any intermediate software. XTango is available via anonymous ftp, and over 200 installations worldwide have acquired the system. It has been used for teaching computer science courses, illustrating the workings of an operating system, illustrating robot planning, doing VLSI chip drawings, etc. As more institutions acquire it, we anticipate further new and interesting usages.

Figure 1 shows a frame from the XTango animation of the Shellsort. In it, the array of values to be sorted is illustrated by a row of rectangles in the top half of the window. Each rectangle's height has been scaled to correspond to the value it represents. The animation illustrates the Shellsort by lowering all the elements in an equidistant subarray, keeping their horizontal orientation constant, and then exchanging and sorting those elements below. When the subarray has been sorted, it is raised back into the main array, and the next set of elements descends. This continues, using subarrays of decreasing spacing size, until the entire array is sorted. The frame we show has caught a lowered subarray of elements being sorted.

In our study, five of the students received a handout describing the Shellsort plus a blackboard lecture depicting the effects of the sort for a specific data set. The other six students received the same handout, but instead viewed an animation of the Shellsort using XTango. Following the presentations, all of the students were asked to answer three questions. The first question asked that the students perform a Shellsort with a different data set and a particular subarray distance sequence by rearranging the numerical values, and showing the results of each step on a sheet of paper. In the second question, the students were presented with a set of rectangular bars representing data values, and asked to show the results of the sort for those values pictorially. The third question asked for the students to describe why the distances chosen for the Shellsort should not be relatively prime. After answering these questions, the students were given a questionnaire to gather subjective information about animations. They were also asked for their comments regarding the use of animations in a classroom setting.

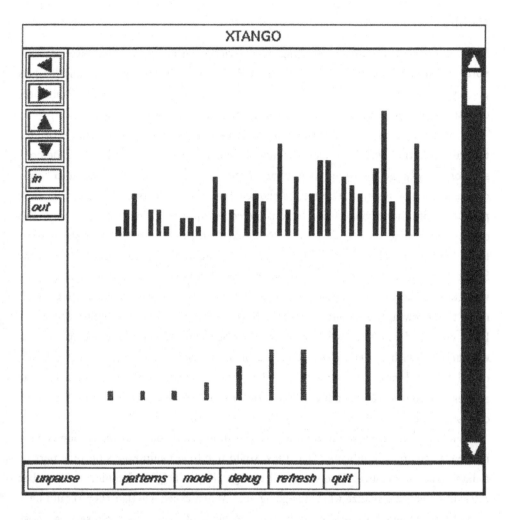

Figure 1: Sample animation frame from the XTango Shellsort animation. A subarray of elements being sorted has been lowered. When this set is in order, it will rise back in place.

Results

Performance results varied depending on individual background. Most students reported their expected grade to be at least a B. These good students were observed to perform well regardless of whether they used the animation. Further, the technically-oriented students also performed well irrespective of their use of animation.

A primary focus of this observational study was to determine typical attitudes toward animation systems. The blackboard students were presented with a demonstration of XTango following completion of the experiment, so that they also could comment on the system. The results showed that the students enthusiastically support the animations when asked to rank perceived quality. When asked to rank the quality of XTango on a scale from poor to excellent, no student ranked the system toward the poor end of the scale, with most assigning a rank of very good or excellent. Similarly, most ranked the system as being understandable and efficient. One student who ranked the quality of the system as fair and who found the system confusing made the following statement: "From the beginning of the graphic program execution I was unsure of what was what; more labeling of visual elements would help. If text was included with the animation, it would be appropriate for the classroom. I didn't completely understand the animation – I had more questions about it than it could answer." Other students indicated that the use of color was confusing at first, and others indicated problems with the system response time.

Students were also asked to comment on the appropriate role of an animation system in the classroom. All indicated that they would like to see animations become part of a data structures course. One stated, "I thought it was helpful. I couldn't remember rules, but I could visualize what was going on." When asked whether they should be a part of a separate laboratory or integrated into the traditional classroom setting, most were in favor of integrating them into the classroom. One student differed, stating, "I think they would be helpful in the classroom. Personally, I could use a separate animation system with textual explanations added, but I would like to have someone around to ask a question." Most students preferred the typical group interaction that takes place in the classroom, with one student saying, "We still need a teacher and group to benefit from discussion from others."

2 Conclusion

2.1 Lessons Learned

Discussion

The faculty survey results suggest that the current practice for teaching algorithms is a combination of lectures, textbooks, and drawings. This information, although anticipated, helps define the instructional environment expected by a student learning computer algorithms. Any instructional strategies incorporating animations should follow this model in order to match students' expectations.

The use of drawings in the classroom seems necessary to impart the dynamic qualities of an algorithm in execution. These dynamics are the basis for the existence and use of algorithm animation systems such as XTango. For any given algorithm there may be multiple representations of the objects and actions during execution. The survey results indicated no definitive representation of any of the algorithms. Most of the replies were influenced by depictions provided in textbooks or through prior experience with animation systems. Although none of the responses contradicted the views frequently used in XTango, more research is needed to explore the qualities that comprise an effective view for an algorithm.

The results of the observational study identify a high perceived value for XTango, with many students stating that they would like to see similar animations integrated into data structures courses. Such reports are crucial to the use of animation systems, and enthusiasm could translate into long-term performance gains during a data structures or algorithms course.

Little effort has been directed toward evolving animation systems into effective teaching tools. The responses from students using such systems are the ultimate test of their value. Although the responses about XTango were highly favorable, many suggestions were made that could enhance the effectiveness of XTango as an educational tool. Some suggestions for improvement include better response time, consistent use of labels to accompany states and actions during an animation, and textual explanations of the algorithms. Such reports are consistent with usability principles and with current classroom practices. Adding value labels to the Shellsort animation would be beneficial, according to student comments. Value labels are appropriate for small data sets intended to demonstrate the mechanics of an algorithm. Value labels are impractical, however, with large data sets, particularly when the animation compares several algorithms presented simultaneously on the screen.

The observational study provided valuable insights into formal studies intended to gauge the effects of animation on performance. Important variables to control include academic and technical background, since they will obscure any other variables which may affect performance. Data about spatial abilities should be collected and analyzed. It is possible that poor visualizers would benefit most from the explicit visual representations made possible by animation systems. Data regarding prior experiences with visual technologies, including game-playing and educational systems, should be collected from the participants.

Many algorithms may have inherent visual qualities for which animations can enhance learning and performance. For example, a common view of the heap sort uses a visual representation of the heap, with elements gradually migrating to the sorted array. One student who took part in the observational study who was only moderately enthusiastic about the Shellsort animation was highly impressed with the heap sort animation used in XTango. It is difficult to determine whether this difference may be attributed to the relative quality of the views for Shellsort and heap sort, or if the heap sort algorithm is more suited to a visual representation. A formal study should examine several algorithms in order to gain more insight into this issue. Additionally, the experimental task must be constructed carefully in order to identify any performance benefits of animations.

Summary

The following is a summary of what we have learned in this initial attempt to evaluate animation systems.

- Many instructors report the use of lectures, textbooks, and drawings to aid the teaching of algorithmic concepts.

- The views reported by instructors report no definitive views and do not contradict those currently used in XTango.

- Students were receptive and enthusiastic towards animations, and would like to see them included in the classroom.

- Performance results are difficult to relate to the effects of an animation, since many factors may influence learning. The factors that must be considered in an empirical study include include:

  1. Academic and technical background.

  2. Spatial abilities.

3. Prior experience with visual technologies.

- Some algorithms may have more of an inherent visual quality than others. This implies differences in performance benefits by students for animations of different algorithms.

- Generating an experimental task that evokes differences in visual representations may prove difficult or artificial.

- Several features of XTango animations may be improved or manipulated to determine their effects.

  1. The addition of labels to images.

  2. The addition of textual explanations of the algorithms.

  3. Improvements in system response time.

  4. The adjustment of execution time for the algorithm.

  5. The relationship between large and small data sets and the implications for labeling.

- Students prefer that animation tools such as XTango augment the current instructional environment and do not want them to replace the classroom setting. Students seem to prefer the benefits of group interaction for answering questions.

2.2 Future Work

The observational study cited here is the initial step in our project to examine the use of animation to promote the comprehension of algorithms and, more encompassing, the use of computer animation to enhance learning in a classroom environment. The major objectives of the study are to determine if learning is increased, if learning is increased over time, if there is a difference in learning between different algorithms, what types of views better promote comprehension, and ultimately, whether animation should occupy an important place in a computer science classroom environment.

The next step in this line of research is developing a longitudinal study in a classroom environment, similar to the study of animations and physics in [RBA90]. We will make appropriate changes to the animations as suggested by this study, to make the graphical images easier to interpret and provide for a more responsive system. These changes include the addition of more text and legends to the animations. An implementation in a classroom environment will provide us with a sizable user community and the ability to conduct a longitudinal study.

We will increase the generalizability of the software as a learning tool for algorithms and, to control for learning differences between different algorithms, use it to teach several different algorithms. A second change we may explore is the use of a videotape of the animations for use in a classroom environment. The videotape will become part of the instruction received in classes, and it would allow us to reach a larger audience. We still plan to have students view animations on-line as well, because of the interactive nature of some of the animations. In addition to being tested on comprehension of the algorithms, the students will also be tested at a later dates to determine whether animations lead to changes in retention over time.

This observational study has also suggested future improvements to the animation system itself. We plan to explore the inclusion of sound, voice, textual information, and on-line help to make the system more of a multimedia tool. Such improvements could make the animation system a valuable instructional unit, which a student could independently progress through at an appropriate pace.

Acknowledgements

Reid Turner implemented the XTango Shellsort animation. We thank him for his contribution.

References

[Bro88] Marc H. Brown. *Exploring algorithms using Balsa-II.* Computer. May 1988, Vol. 21, No. 5, pp. 14-36.

[BS85] Marc H. Brown and Robert Sedgewick. *Techniques for algorithm animation.* IEEE Software, January 1985, Vol. 2, No. 1, pp. 28-39.

[Dui86] Robert A. Duisberg. *Animated graphical interfaces using temporal constraints.* In *Proceedings of the ACM SIGCHI '86 Conference on Human Factors in Computing Systems*, April 1986, Boston, MA, pp. 131-136.

[HHR89] Esa Helttula, Aulikki Hyrskykari, and Kari-Jouko Raiha. *Graphical specification of algorithm animations with Aladdin.* In *Proceedings of the 22nd Hawaii*

International Conference on System Sciences, January 1989, Kailua-Kona, HI, pp. 892-901.

[Knu73] Donald E. Knuth. *Sorting and Searching*. Addison-Wesley, Reading, MA, 1973.

[LD85] Ralph L. London and Robert A. Duisberg. *Animating programs using Smalltalk*. Computer, August 1985,Vol. 18, No. 8, pp. 61-71.

[Mye90] Brad A. Myers. *Taxonomies of visual programming and program visualization*. Journal of Visual Languages and Computing, March 1990, Vol. 1, No. 1, pp. 97-123.

[RBA90] Lloyd P. Rieber, Mary J. Boyce, and Chahriar Assad. *The effects of computer animation on adult learning and retrieval tasks*. Journal of Computer-Based Instruction, Spring 1990, Vol. 17, No. 2,pp. 46-52.

[SH90] John Stasko and J. Douglas Hayes. *The XTANGO Algorithm Animation System, User Documentation*. GVU Center, College of Computing, Georgia Tech, Atlanta, GA, December 1990.

[SP91] John T. Stasko and Charles Patterson. *Understanding and characterizing program visualization systems*. Graphics, Visualization, and Usability Center, Georgia Institute of Technology, Atlanta, GA, Technical Report GIT-GVU-91/17, September 1991.

[Sta90] John T. Stasko. *TANGO: A framework and system for algorithm animation*. Computer, September 1990, Vol. 23, No. 9, pp. 27-39.

[WU90] Roger E. Whitney and N. Scott Urquhart. *Microcomputers in the mathematical sciences: Effects of courses, students, and instructors*. Academic Computing, March 1990, Vol. 4, No. 6, pp. 14-18,49-53.

AT LAST! A COMPUTER AID FOR THE TEACHING OF ELECTRONICS WHICH ANSWERS ALL THE NAGGING QUESTIONS ABOUT CAPACITORS.

Catherine BALLE, Françoise DUBREUIL, Bruno BOURET
Université de Paris 7
U.F. de Didactique des Disciplines
DRUID Tour 45-46 1er étage porte 116
2, place Jussieu - 75251 PARIS CEDEX 05 France
Phone:33 1 44 27 61 32
Fax:33 1 44 27 57 40
Telex:Pariset 270075F Paris
E.mail:DUMONT a FRCICRP81

Abstract

"PENELOPS 2" - Produit d'ENseignement de l'ELectronique Opérant Par Simulation - is a new aid for the teaching of Electronics by computer simulation. It is in the process of being developed by the DRUID laboratory - Développements et Recherche sur les Utilisations de l'Informatique en Didactique - of the University Paris 7 and the Electronics Department of the University Paris 6.

It is intended for students up to and including the M.A. level.

It deals in an original way with the functioning of electrical capacitors which have either a vacuum or an isothermal isotropic homogeneous dielectric insulator.

It explains clearly:

- the phenomena that produce the charges on the plates

- how the capacitor "cuts" the direct current component of the signals and allows the alternative current component "to pass".

It analyses the principal uses of the capacitor:

- uncoupling of the circuits

- insulation between amplification stages

- integration and average value of the signals
- derivation of the signals
- filtering of the signals
- various other applications

It is innovative: it helps the student to understand the subject by the realistic visualization of undetectable microscopic phenomena which control the functioning of the capacitor, such as the variations of the electric field and the resulting displacement of the charges.

The educational impact of these visualizations is reinforced by the dynamic simulations of the interactive Practical Exercises and Seminars.

The displayed phenomena are explained by on-screen reminders corresponding to the"Mathematics", "Electrostatics" and "Electronics of electrical circuits and components" courses.

All the simulations guarantee a complete scientific explanation.

It is developed using the "DRUID" authoring system and it runs on a standard Personal Computer. The purpose of "PENELOPS 2" is to complement the existing educational methods used at University in an attempt to reinforce their pedagogical effectiveness.

Introduction

Working within the framework of Universities Paris 6 and Paris 7's policy of introducing new teaching techniques, the " DRUID" laboratory - Développements et Recherche sur les Utilisations de l'Informatique en Didactique - of Paris 7 and the Electronics Department of Paris 6 are developing and experimenting with new educational aids [1], [2].

The most recent of these aids, described in this article, is a new courseware which teaches Electronics by computer simulation.

It is called "PENELOPS 2" - Produit d'ENseignement de l'Electronique Opérant Par Simulation.

It is intended for the teaching of Electronics at University up to the M.A. level.

Its originality lies in the choice of subject and in the way in which it deals with it: it answers all the student's questions regarding the functioning of capacitors which have either a vacuum or an isothermal isotropic homogeneous dielectric insulator.

By means of dynamic simulations it visualizes the fundamental microscopic phenomena which are usually undetectable.

It backs-up the student's knowledge of these visualizations by interactive exercises in the form of Practical Exercises and Seminars.

This software is developed using the "DRUID" authoring system.

This authoring system is particularly intended for teachers who are not computer specialists and who wish to create their own educational software.

1 Educational Objectives

Electronics teachers know all too well that students find a number of subjects baffling. The subject of the capacitor is the best example of this.

This software is the answer to all the following problems, typical of those encountered by students:

- what are the phenomena that produce the charges on the plates
- how does the capacitor "cut" the direct current component of the signals and allow the alternative current component "to pass".

It studies thoroughly the principal uses of the capacitor:

- uncoupling of the circuits
- insulation between amplification stages
- integration and average value of the signals
- derivation of the signals
- filtering of the signals
- various other applications.

2 Whom Is This Software Intended For ?

All levels up to and including masters.

It can be usefull for:

- independent self- study
- all university students who wish to illustrate by computer simulated experiments their lectures or prepare sessions for Practical Exercises, in order to better understand the content.

3 How Does It Work ?

This software gives a complete demonstration of the functioning of the capacitor and of its principal application circuits. It offers the student four learning levels, depending on his familiarity with the subject:

3.1 Visualization of Microscopic Phenomena

This computer simulation is the backbone of the educational usefulness of the software: it helps the student to understand the subject by the realistic visualization of undetectable microscopic phenomena which control the functioning of the capacitor, such as the variations of the electric field and the resulting displacement of the charges.

The computer screen displays in interactive windows the logistical support necessary for the experiment, and a "Help" function for the student (see figure 1).

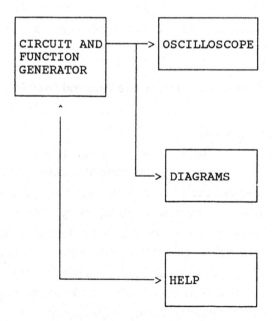

Figure 1: the interacting windows

The logistical support comprises of the following windows:

- a circuit where the mobile charges are "materialized" in a concrete way and move exactly as they do in reality when under the influence of an electric field.

- a multifunction generator which supplies the circuit

- a double trace oscilloscope which allows the user to observe the voltage at any point in the circuit.

- a graphing area which is dedicated to specific diagrams (see paragraph 5)

The apparatus are displayed as they appear in reality. Their characteristics are real (input and output impedance, bandwidth...)

The computer simulation works in real time: every modification of the experimental parameters, using the mouse, has an immediate effect on the phenomena and on the variables.

Each window can be accessed, enlarged or set aside temporarly by selecting an icon.

The student performs all these operations. He has to adjust the experimental parameters. The "Help" function provides him with information on adjusting the experimental parameters and with aid for calculations.

A series of tests ensures microscopic phenomena are well understood.

3.2 Computer Simulation of Interactive Practical Exercises

It allows the student:

- to observe "in slow motion" all the macroscopic effects which are characteristic of the functioning of the circuit (transient or periodic response).

- to acquire the know-how of electronics specialists: choosing the best experimental parameters, adaptating impedances, measuring, determining characteristics, studying how the circuit functions, defining limits.

The student is able to carry out a genuine Practical Exercise which mimics a laboratory. The student can call up on screen displays of all the laboratory equipment which is usually used during the Practical Exercises,as well as a "Help" function (see figure 1). He has at his disposal:

- a realistic circuit with components that have ajustable values

- a multifunction generator which supplies the circuit

- a double trace oscilloscope

- a graphing area which is for Bode's diagrams (module and argument)

In this computer simulation:

- the apparatus are displayed as they appear in reality and their characteristics are real (input and output impedance, bandwidth)

- the student can work alone or with the "Help" function.

The "Help" function shows:

- the successive manipulations necessary for carrying out properly an experiment which is the equivalent of a complete lesson.

- the principal formulae of the experiment (transfer function, attenuation, phase displacement, bandwidth, cut-off frequency, input and output impedance...).

- each display can be opened or closed by an icon.

- the computer simulation works in real time: every modification of the experimental parameters has an immediate effect on the transfer function of the circuit, the signals displayed on the oscilloscope, and on the Bode's diagrams.

3.3 Computer Simulation of Interactive Seminars

The student is offered a series of interactive exercises adapted to the subject, and may, when necessary, request to see the solution.

An optional function "evaluation" allows the computer to assess the work done. This gives the student a better idea of how well he is progressing.

3.4 On-Screen Keys Refering to the Corresponding "Mathematics", "Electrostatics" and "Electronics of Electrical Circuits and Components" Courses

After calling up the key, the student is asked to choose from two possibilities:

- the lessons which correspond exactly to the simulation on screen
- any other lecture from a collection which supports the software.

4 The Menu

This software simulates the functioning of the capacitor and its principal uses. Its menu gives the choice of the subject and the type of training.

4.1 The Main Menu

In the main menu (see figure 2) the student is asked to choose the subject:
- the study of the functioning of the capacitor
    . charging processes
    . direct current insulation and signals transmission
- the study of the applications
    . uncoupling of the circuits
    . link between amplification stages
    . derivation of the signals
    . integration and average value of the signals
    . filtering of the signals
    . various other circuits.
and the learning level:
    - visualization of microscopic phenomena
    - simulated Practical Exercises
    - simulated Seminars
    - course Keys

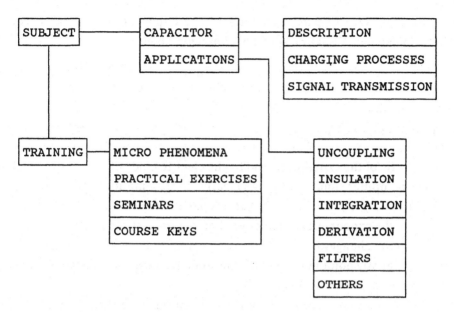

Figure 2: the main menu

4.2 The Secondary Menus

For the themes "Charging Processes", "Seminars" or "Course Keys" there is a secondary menu which offers a more precise choice (see figure 3).

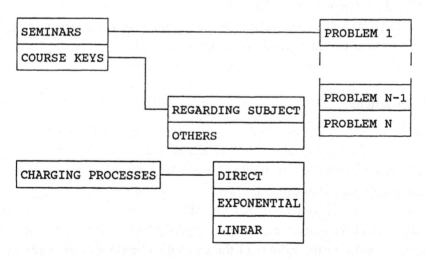

Figure 3: the secondary menus

5 An Example Of Computer Simulation: "The Exponential Charging Process Of The Capacitor - Visualization Of Microscopic Phenomena"

This process can be observed in a circuit consisting of a resistor in series with a capacitor.

The mobile charges are "materialized" on screen for every part of the circuit: as in reality, their movements are governed by the equations characteristic of the experiment and by the electric field.

The computer simulation shows clearly "in slow motion" the migration of the mobile charges to and from the various parts of the circuit, as well as:

- the exponential progressive charging process of the plates

- the changes in voltage across the circuit at any given moment

- at any point in the circuit, the student can see the real time changes in the voltage and electric field

This computer simulation gives a thorough demonstration of the exponential charging process of the capacitor plates.

6 The "DRUID" Authoring System

This educational product has been developed using the "DRUID" authoring system, available on IBM-PC compatibles equipped with 640 kb RAM and EGA graphics monitor.

"DRUID" provides a highly stimulating learning environment [3], [4]. It offers resources that facilitated the design of our project.

6.1 Simulations

The visualization part of PENELOPS 2 is chiefly composed of simulations produced with the help of a user friendly graphics editor, offering colour graphics and animated displays.

The authoring system is capable of communicating with an external program which calculates and displays simulations based on the student's choices. Checks on the validity of the student's choices can be made by the system, and exploratory comments can be delivered before or after simulations take place.

6.2 Answer Analysis And Individualized Comments

The system allows the analysis of open-ended messages and of numerical values along with the possibility of displaying sophisticated remedial comments taking into account information regarding the student's previous work using the courseware. A sort of student model (profile) can be elaborated to help the system to individualize pathways and comments.

6.3 The Supervisor

The authoring system has a built-in mechanism for detecting whether the student is making a request or a natural language entry, and allows the courseware to be flexible and adapted to different learning contents.

6.4 Formative Evaluation Tools

The inherent logic underlying permits the automatic recording of the paths followed by the student through the software with reference to the data prepared by the author. A relatively sophisticated record keeping system, together with sorting and statistical procedures, are incorporated in the authoring system. Using this information, the author can evaluate the effectiveness of his teaching approach, and the teacher can evaluate the student's progress.

Conclusion

This original software for the teaching of Electronics by computer simulation was conceived by a lecturer in Electronics at the University Paris 6, to satisfy the real needs of students.

Its educational objectives are perfectly targeted so as to be a teaching aid for students up to the M.A. level.

This software is especially exciting because it takes full advantage of the computer's graphics capability and will be the ideal complement to current university teaching methods

References

[1] C. Balle, *Conception of an original Electronics teaching tool through computer simulation dealing with operational amplifier and its fundamental applications*, Proceedings of the IFIP 5th WCCE - Sydney - Australia - July 1990, volume 2, p 42-43.

[2] C. Balle, R. Bonnaire, H. Perrin, *Development of a new Electronics teaching tool: educational simulation of operational amplifier and of its fundamental applications circuits*, Proceedings of the 7th ICTE, Brussels, Belgium, March 1990,volume 2, p 140-142.

[3] G. Musso, R. Luft, J-P Rabine, D. Cabrol et F. Dubreuil, *La Technique des objectifs pédagogiques - Didacticiel d'autoformation* - publié en 1989 par le C.D.I.G.C. ISBN n° 2-908156-00-8.

[4] J-P Rabine, M. Rouillard, D. Cabrol, F. Dubreuil, *a N.M.R. spectrum analysis: A problem solving partner based on the student's approach*. Computer in Education, F. Lovis and G.D. Tagg (eds), IFIP 1988,61-66.

An Object Oriented Approach To Produce Educational Hypermedia Software

Beltran Thierry, Péninou André

Laboratoire A.P.I., Université Paul Sabatier / IUT A

50 chemin des Maraîchers, 31 062 Toulouse, France

Phone : 62 - 25 - 88 - 85 (or 86) / Fax : 62 - 25 - 88 - 01

Abstract

First, we present the architecture developed for the 'COMPTA' and 'SYSTEMDENT' systems. These ITSs (Intelligent Tutoring Systems), named 'Hybrids', have been implemented using an authoring system connected to an expert system generator. They have allowed us to improve the production of ITSs from the **author's point of view** (prototyping and realization stages) thanks to the possibility of reusing both structures and knowledge from a hybrid system to another one.

This paper describes principally our works in improving the interaction and the management of the dialogue in the Hybrid ITSs. We discuss a hypertext-like interaction in order to build ITSs less directive and therefore improve the communication from the **learner's point of view**. So, we propose an architecture for a hybrid system, in which Hypermedia information can be combined with some directive forms aimed at direct instruction and control in given fields. This architecture enables a hypermedia-based educational software to act sometimes as a learning system, sometimes as a teaching one.

Introduction

Intelligent Tutoring Systems (ITSs), because they are very complex and designed to perform only specific tasks, are not often developed beyond laboratory prototypes. An *ad hoc* approach has been the rule, and no well-ordered plan existed for developing them. As they were made for specific purpose, it is difficult or impossible to reuse the elaborated architectures and techniques. Thus, the main problem is to elaborate models, knowledge bases and system architectures for ITSs which could be reused. Our approach is experimental and led us toward an ICAL system model named **Hybrid** (see § 1). It offers a framework for the knowledge representation which can be reused in other systems. However, we found deficiencies in Hybrid systems concerning the management of interactive dialogues.

We think the integration of Hypertext in Hybrid ITSs would be interesting for knowledge presentation and information seeking, and then allowing the learner more initiative. What then should be the architecture supporting an educational hypermedia software ?

1 The Notion Of Hybrid ITSs

ITSs can be described (at least theoretically) by four models or expertises [Wen87], [Nic88] :

- the domain model which contains knowledge about the word (interconnected concepts) and information about reasoning processes. This model allows the system to generate and solve exercises related to the domain concerned,
- the student model, in which information about the learner is used in order to adapt the system. Several dimensions in the variability in knowledge states can be studied : scope, incorrect knowledge and the notion of viewpoints,
- the communication model which can be viewed as a student-specific database maintained by communication processes to support further decisions. The user interface is the module designed to support the dialogue between the system and the learner.
- the didactic model referring to teaching strategies intended to have a direct effect on the student. From this model and according to the context, the system can decide a didactic operation, for example, fixing a new target for the learner.

Several solutions may be chosen for developing these models, but the evolution of an ITS is always a long and complex process. Our approach (an experimental one), based on the connexion between an authoring system and an expert system generator has led us to the definition of the **concept of Hybrid ITSs**. We distinguish [Can90a] *local knowledge,* describing the behaviour of the learner during a transaction (answers, timing, learner's choices, ...) and *global knowledge* defining the transmission of information, that is to say the author's model. Global knowledge contains :

- *Predefined learning paths* which define both synchronized stages in the presentation of knowledge and control of these stages which adapts the system according to the learner's behavior,

- *Dynamic modules* which take into account instructional methods, that provide a remedy for learning problems which cannot be resolved by predefined learning paths.

In the field of Hybrid systems, studies of [Can90a] have led to a formal representation of both local and global knowledge (using frames and rules), and a specific methodology for the design and development of such systems. Furthermore, this concept of Hybrid representation allows us to produce several types of ICAL systems. Several Hybrid ITSs have been successfully developed, we can notice :

- COMPTA, an ITS designed to teach how to perform accountancy transactions [Lav90],
- SYSTEMDENT, a distance learning and help resource (in the French public network Télétel) concerning dental anaesthetic risks regarding the several drugs taken by a patient [Pul89], [Can90b].

In these Hybrid systems, the predefined learning paths are represented by frames built by the authoring system and the dynamic part is a set of rules in the expert system.

2 Improving User Interaction In The Hybrid ITSs

Although the architecture developed for the Hybrid ITSs improves the representation of knowledge and also allows the reuse of their components, it does not lead to the realization of highly interactive systems : Hybrid ITSs are in a general way much too directive. This problem is due essentially to the need of controlling at the same time both user interaction (local knowledge) and predefined learning paths (global knowledge). The systems produced are not able to handle a dialogue which can be initiated either by the learner (learning system) or by didactic modules (teaching system).

So, the architecture developed for the knowledge representation in a Hybrid ITS makes the author's work easier but *does not improve the efficiency of the system from the learner's point of view.* It is therefore questionable that the work needed to build a Hybrid ITS is worth the effort... These remarks have led us to consider the *interaction with the learner* as the main problem to be studied. We present our solutions concerning the definition of an architecture which allows the separation of the management of the interaction with the learner from the regulation of the transmission of knowledge, while keeping the advantages of the structure of the Hybrid ITSs. We think that a Hypertext-oriented interaction can be an answer to the needs of the Hybrid ITSs previously presented. For this purpose, we have introduced in [Bel91a&b] the notion of **Hypermedia-based educational software**. In order to let either the learner or the system take the initiative in the exploration or the presentation of the course, we have built new types of links, which we term *pedagogical links* (see below).

3 An Architecture For Hypermedia-based Educational Software

The teaching/learning environment being studied is made up of three systems : a *Hypermedia system* dedicated to presentation of knowledge and information retrieval, a *CAI/ICAI system* which ensures pedagogical control, and a *supervision system* which monitors the interaction between the learner and the educational software (this system acts as an interface between the two others) (see figure 1).

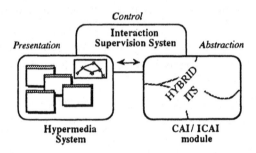

Fig.1 : The general architecture for Educational Hypermedia software.

This architecture is not concerned with the structure of the CAI/ICAI components (answer analysis, student model, ...) so the *functions of the resulting system are not fixed in advance* and can easily be adapted to the authors' needs or to the learning situations required: the CAI module can be simple (classical courseware) or complex (Hybrid ITS). This division between mediatic part and didactic part is of great interest for the production of advanced educational software. From the author's point of view, the architecture we propose makes the designing and the prototyping stages easier to formulate. The author can *study separately the mediatic aspects of the course and the didactic behavior of the system.*

Educational Hypermedia software is unique in its use of new link types which allow sharing control between the learner and the Hypermedia software. While classical links are used by the learner without any control in the system, all the links introduced here are managed by the supervision system.

New link types for a control shared between the user and the system:

In our architecture shown in figure one, a *Learning Unit* is a Hyper-database focused on a precise point of the course and can either force the student to look into specific items or leave him free to browse through any of them. Sometimes, some paths or nodes have to be presented to the student (for example : guided tours, exercises, advice, ...), others can only be proposed to him (help, documentation, dictionaries, table of contents, ...). For this purpose, we have introduced new types of links : some of them are used only by the learner without any control of the system (*classical links*), others are activated by the system (**pedagogical links**). In this way, freedom of the learner in manipulating courseware depends on the type of links chosen by the author.

A link is a connection between two nodes (reference link) or two sets of nodes (hierarchical link). In 'classical' Hypermedia systems, links are activated only by the user. In the Educational Hypermedia system, all pedagogical links are controlled by the supervision system in order to direct the learner in the course. Each of these links is represented by rules in the supervision system and is activated by the events received from the presentation level.

The **Pedagogical reference links** are activated by the learner (the user interface objects send events of the type 'Next'). The node to be presented is fixed by the author for a given path in the Learning Unit. According to the rule base currently in use (by the supervision system), different effects can be achieved by the same interaction (each learning path has a set of rules attached to it in the supervision system). The **Conditional reference links** are activated according to a condition. A link of this type is used for linking two pedagogical nodes in a particular context ; they characterize 'context sensitive' links. When an event of type 'Next' is received, the choice of the node to be displayed is made by the system according to the context (conditions imposed by the author). An **Answer link** is a connection between two nodes. The first node contains one or several interface objects (or **dialogue entities**) with which the learner has to interact (see § 3.2). The dialogue entities can be questions, sensitive areas, interactive elements, ... The interaction with each of these elements results in the sending of a particular event (of type 'Answer'), reflecting the learner behavior. When all the expected events have been received by the supervision system, the answer link is activated (the system can wait for several questions distributed into several nodes before activating the interaction analysis, by means of CAI components). The **Rerouting links** are only used by the system. A rerouting link is automatically activated by the system as soon as one or several conditions are verified.

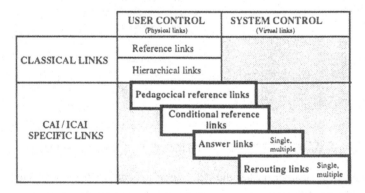

	USER CONTROL (Physical links)	SYSTEM CONTROL (Virtual links)
CLASSICAL LINKS	Reference links	
	Hierarchical links	
CAI / ICAI SPECIFIC LINKS	Pedagocical reference links	
	Conditional reference links	
	Answer links Single, multiple	
		Rerouting links Single, multiple

Fig.2 : The links used by an Educational Hypermedia software.

Concerning the new types of link, more details can be found in [Bel91a&b].

Answers links and dialogue entities:

Answer links are represented, at the interface level by **dialogue entities** developed for this purpose (see fig.3). We have defines several types of dialogue entity (Multiple Choice Questions, Interactive Areas, ...) composed of several user interface objects (buttons, fields, check boxes, pictures, sounds, ...). Each entity controls the interaction with the learner by itself (help, syntactic control, scrolling, modification of appearance, ...) and sends 'answer' events independently of the user components of the interface. The dialogue entities send events to the control system and then are connected to the educational module. Such entities are represented in the PAC model developed by J. COUTAZ [Cou88], (see fig.3).

In this model an interactive system is composed of a hierarchy of PAC objects. Each PAC object is composed of an *Abstraction* representing internal data, a *Presentation* defining the data presentation at the user interface level, and a *Control* which is an interface between the system and the presentation. When a user interacts graphically with a PAC object (fig.3), the control returns the changes to the associated Abstraction and transmits them to the hierarchy. Reciprocally, when the system modifies a value, each Control returns the modifications to the associated Presentations. The advantages of this model are :

- a modular design and realization of interactive systems, as well as
- a separation between the control of the user interface and the functions of the system.

Therefore, we used this model in order to adapt hypermedia functionalities to the needs of Hybrid ITSs, that is to allow the control of the learner and at the same time to have CAI functionalities, while keeping a hypertext-like interaction. Figure 3 shows a dialogue entity (structured PAC object) of type MQC-SA-CB (a Multiple Choice Question with a Single Answer and Check Boxes presentation : only one answer is accepted).

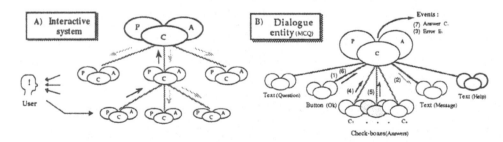

Fig.3 : The 'PAC' model and the representation of a dialogue entity (type MQC-SA-CB).

For example : if the learner pushes the 'Ok button' (1) without having selected any answer, the entity activates the error message (2) and sends an event of type error (3). Each time a check box is selected, the corresponding PAC object controls its own appearance and alerts the entity in which the answer is stored (4), (5) ; when another check box has already been selected, the entity sends an event in order to unselect it (only one answer can be chosen by the learner). Finally, when the learner validates his choice (6) the entity alerts the environment by means of an event of type answer (7). In the case of a MCQ-MA-CB dialogue entity (Multiple Answers) several choices are accepted and then several answer events can be sent by the entity. The dialogue entities are customized by the author of the course and integrated into the nodes of the Educational Hyperdocument. When the learner interacts with those elements, the events generated are processed by the supervision system.

The supervision mechanism:
We have chosen an event-based mechanism for the implementation of the Educational Hypermedia architecture. The pedagogical links are not physical because they are not encoded in the Hypermedia system. Each pedagogical link does not directly activate a predefined node. While low level interactions (mouse, keyboard input, ...) and classical links are managed by the Hypermedia system, events concerning higher level interaction (answers, errors, topic choices, ...) are sent to the supervision system which contains a knowledge base associated with the Learning Unit currently in use (see fig.4). This knowledge base contains predefined learning paths (*Continuation Rules*) and *Breakpoint Rules* which activate the CAI components that interpret the interaction and then make a decision concerning which Learning Unit is to be presented or the strategy to be adopted. Moreover, several knowledge bases can be associated with a Learning Unit, each of them can define a new behaviour for the system.

Here we present an object oriented approach for the realization of such an architecture an discuss its advantages from both the learner's and author's point of view.

4 An Implementation

In order to test the different sides of the proposed architecture, a prototype of the educational hypermedia architecture is being developed on a Unix workstation HP9000. We are using an object oriented environment : Spoke[1] [Spo90]. This environment is composed of a programming language (Spoke-Kernel), a library (SpokeWindows) based on MOTIF for management of graphic objects, and a library (SpokeEngine) implementing an expert system generator.

The development of the Educational Hypermedia software architecture in the Spoke environment:
The CAI/ICAI modules ([A] on fig.4) are supported by rule bases developed using the SpokeEngine library ; nevertheless, some particular aspects can be directly encoded with objects (Spoke language). The supervision system [B] is also supported by a set of rule bases

---

Spoke is a registred trade mark of Alcatel ISR and laboratories of Marcoussis.

(each one controlling a Learning Unit). The transmission of information concerning user interaction to the dynamic modules (for interpretation) is supported by the propagation mechanism available in SpokeEngine.

The dialogue entities [C] and the new types of links [D] are developed using SpokeWindows and Spoke-Kernel (see next paragraph). A hypermedia-like system could be developed easily thanks to SpokeWindows [E] (each node is a window). Finally, the communication between [C]-[D]-[E] is based on the message sending mechanism. The event communication between [C-D-E] and the supervision system [B] is based on the event management mechanism [F] and makes use of the Spoke exception handling mechanism.

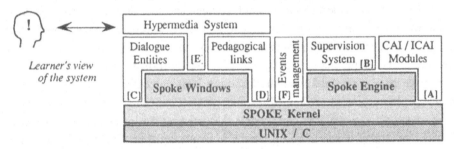

Fig.4 : The physical support of Educational Hypermedia software using Spoke modules.

Design and realization of the classes of dialogue entities:

Each type of PAC object which can be used for defining a dialogue entity is attached to a specific class hierarchy. For example, all displayed buttons (answers, validation, ...) are defined in a separate hierarchy describing their interactive capabilities (the multiple inheritance of graphic objects is available in SpokeWindows). From a general class called 'entity' (which defines communication with the supervision system), we describe the behaviors of the dialogue entities to be used, for example Multiple Choice Questions and Interactive Areas (see fig.5) with single or multiple answers.

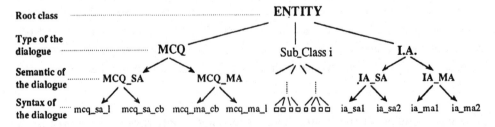

Fig.5 : An Object Oriented representation of dialogue entities.

The characteristics of structure and behavior are grouped in a general class when they are shared by several classes. The leaves of this tree are instanciable classes from which an author can create a dialogue entity. This entity inherits from the several levels of the hierarchy defining the 'type' of the dialogue (general form of the envisaged dialogue), the 'semantics' of the dialogue (general behaviors of the control of interaction), and the 'syntax' of the dialogue (external aspect and associated behaviors of the dialogue entities satisfying the 'semantic' requirements). When designing an answer link, an author has to choose the type of dialogue, that is to say, the class of the entity and then, make use of an editor to customize the components. For this purpose, we have developed an editor which can be used by an author : he has only to modify the appearance of the dialogue entity (colours, position, ...) or parameters such as the number of graphical elements ; all the behaviors are inherited from the hierarchy. (We can find in the annex the MQC-SA-CB dialogue entity editor, and a sample of generated dialogue entity).

5 Analysis Of The Hypermedia Educational Architecture

The architecture described, based on the PAC model, separates the learner interaction (surface level) from the teaching/learning control (deep level). Predefined learning paths are supported by the supervision system and are separated from the control of the user interaction (both logically and physically). The supervision system observes the learner's behaviors by means of the events received, which represent local knowledge independent of details of the interface.

The CAI components communicate only with the supervision system and receive high level information (answers, behavior, errors in manipulation, ...), they are not concerned with the low level interaction (text scrolling, button or menu selection, ...) or the user interface components. Events received when a dialogue with the learner are independent from the class of the entity being used ; they depend only on the content of the components. Thus, it is possible to modify the user interface by replacing a dialogue entity with another, in that way changing the style of the interaction. On the other hand, it is possible to change the behavior of the system, by modifying the rule set in the supervision system, with no change at the user interface level.

An important aspect of our architecture is the correspondence between the theoretical (modelization of the knowledge), the logical (system architecture) and the physical levels (see figure 6).

From our experiences in the field of hybrid systems and the developments in progress concerning the described architecture, we can notice some of the advantages due to the adaptation of the Hypermedia system :

- learner responsibility is noticeably enhanced by the use of a hypermedia system ; the use of predefined classes of dialogue entities permit a uniform interaction,
- low level interaction being taken into account by the hypermedia (by means of

dialogue entities), allows the didactic model to be studied separately from the interface and thus can be reused,

- the dialogue entities provide standard frames for communication with the user, allowing the use of a large number of varied contents and displays.

	Represented by		Supported by

THEORETICAL MODEL	LOGICAL ARCHITECTURE		PHYSICAL SUPPORT
Presentation level *(communication with the learner)*	*Presentation System*	Hypertext-like interaction *(classical links, dialogue entities associated with supervision rules)*	Hypermedia System *(taking into account the control of the dialogue entities)*
Learner's behavior *(local knowledge)*		Events sent by the dialogue entities *(independent of the user interface)*	Event based communication *(between the Hypermedia and the supervision systems)*
Predefined Learning Path	*Supervision System*	Pedagogical reference links, conditional links *(and answer links)*	Set of rules activated by the events received
Dynamic interpretation of user interaction		Calling on the CAI / ICAI modules for information interpretation	'Breakpoint rule' activation and transmission of events to the CAI / ICAI modules

Fig.6 : From the model to the realization of the Educational Hypermedia software architecture.

During the production stage, this architecture provides the following improvements :

- standardization of events simplifies the implementation of the predefined learning paths (a dialogue entity belongs to a predefined class and therefore is able to return only a predefined set of events),
- the separation of the several components of the theoretical model of a Hybrid ITS enables an author to engage in a continuous and logical production process,
- the use of dialogue entities simplifies the user interface production according to the predefined learning paths requirements,
- reuse of the different parts of an educational hyperdocument is made easier (reuse of user interface realizations such as dialogue entities, reuse of didactic strategies, for example a set of supervision rules).

6 Conclusion

The system presented here is only a prototype which demonstrates a first proof of the validity of the proposed architecture. The complete formalization of the three-system architecture will require time and efforts to unify current research in this field. Nevertheless,

two aspects of our contribution are worth being emphasized :
- the architecture proposed provides both an effective teaching tool (use of CAI components) and an attractive learning tool (Hypermedia-based interaction),
- a unified architecture allows the reuse of several parts of the realizations.

Although a complete system has not as yet been developed, we think our efforts to integrate Hypermedia into educational software, constitutes an important step towards new integrated authoring/learning environments. An important goal of our works now is to complete a formal representation of the Educational Hypermedia system. The final aim is to make an operational model which would allow an exchange of Educational hyperdocuments between different systems, or to make two different Educational Hypermedia systems directly communicate. Our purpose is not to propose a new model for the hypertext representation but extend an existing one [Hal90], [Lan90] taking into account interaction control as we have defined it.

In conclusion, we have presented an architecture designed to improve :
- interaction with the learner (defining an adaptation of Hypertext to ICAL),
- the modelization of knowledge in order to help the authors during the production stage ('Hybrid' model),
- communication between the systems of user presentation and those controlling the educational process, through the standardization of the means of the exchanged events.

References

[Bel91a] Beltran T. *Hypermedia and Learning : an architecture for hybrid systems*, Proceedings of the CALISCE'91 conference, 9-11 sept. 1991, Lausane.

[Bel91b] Beltran T. *Une architecture pour le guidage de l'apprenant dans un système Hypermédia éducatif*, journées scientifiques "Hypermédias et apprentissages", 24-25 sept. 1991, Chatenay-Malabry.

[Can90a] Canut M.F. *Spécification formelle de systèmes d'EIAO pour l'Atelier de Génie Didacticiel Intégré*, Thèse de doctorat de l'Université Paul Sabatier, Toulouse III.

[Can90b] Canut M.F., Péninou A. *Systemdent : an intelligent tutoring system for diagnosis learning, at a distance, of risks in the use of dental anesthetics*, Expersys90, IITT International, Grenoble.

[Cou88] Coutaz J. *Interface Homme-Ordinateur : Conception et Réalisation*, thèse de l'université J.Fourier, Grenoble.

[Hal90] Halasz, Swartz *The Dexter hypertext reference model*, NIST'90, Hypertext Standardization Workshop, 16-18 Juill. 1990.

[Lan90] Lange D. *A formal model for hypertext*, NIST'90, Hypertext Standardization Workshop, 16-18 Juill. 1990.

[Lav90] Lavielle A. *Spécification de l'expertise pour un tuteur intelligent en passation d'une écriture comptable*, DEA informatique, UPS Toulouse III.

[Nic88] Nicaud J.F., Vivet M. *Les tuteurs intelligents : réalisations et tendances*, Numéro spécial TSI : Applications de l'informatique à la formation, Vol 7/1, Dunod-Afcet, pp.21-45.

[Pul89] Pulicani F. *Conception d'un système d'EIAO en anesthésiologie dentaire à l'usage du praticien*, DEA informatique, UPS Toulouse III.

[Spo90] Documentation of Spoke, Spoke Engine, SpokeWindows, Spoke Environment, Release 3.1.0, Alcatel -ISR, 34 cours B. Pascal, 91025 Evry, France.

[Wen87] Wenger E. *Artificial Intelligence & Tutoring Systems*, Morgan Kaufmann Publishers, INC.

ANNEX : Dialogue entity editor and MCQ-SA-CB dialogue entity sample

(MCQ editor for entities with single or multiple answers with a presentation based on check boxes or scrollin text. Four classes of dialogue entities can be created)

A Cognitive Model of Programming Knowledge for Procedural Languages

Koen Bertels, Philip Vanneste*& Carlos De Backer
University of Antwerp
Prinsstraat 13
2000 Antwerp, Belgium
e-mail: Bertels at BANUFS11.bitnet

Abstract

Recently many studies focusing on diverse aspects of programming knowledge were published. However, none of them proposes a complete model in which the contents and overall structure are defined. One of the first (and only) attempts to define such a model was made by Shneiderman, where he defines Programming Knowledge to contain two distinct knowledge bodies. We complement this model by defining the link between the syntactic and semantic knowledge. This link is constituted by the Semantically Augmented Programming Primitives (SAPP's). The paper is concerned in the definition of this 'missing link' in programming knowledge.

Keywords : programming knowledge, cognitive model, human problem solving, knowledge based CAI-systems.

1 Cognitive Research and Intelligent Tutoring Systems

In this paper we present a cognitive model of programming knowledge for procedural languages (PK).[1] Programming knowledge is the knowledge an expert programmer uses when writing, interpreting or debugging programs. A cognitive model of such knowledge is a (static) description of the concepts and strategies the programmer uses while programming.

One may wonder why one would like to construct a cognitive model of programming knowledge. The construction of such a model may be relevant for the development of Intelligent Tutoring Systems (ITS) for Programming which can, among other things, present a programming problem to a student who then tries to solve it. One of the tasks of the ITS is to analyse the proposed solution, which requires the use of domain

---

*K.U. Leuven Campus Kortrijk, Universitaire Campus, 8500 Kortrijk, Belgium

[1] We only look at the programming kowledge as used with procedural languages. Though it is likely that there will be similar concepts and structures when using declarative languages, further research in this area is needed. Therefore, when we use the concept 'programming knowledge', we always mean programming knowledge for procedural languages.

structure	multi leveled [Shneiderman 1977]
	semantic-syntactic [Shneiderman 1977]
	generalisation hierarchy [Jonckers 1986]
contents	programming plans -cliches [Soloway 1983]
	rules of programming discourse [Soloway 1983]
	units [Jonckers 1987]
	problem solving strategies [Soloway 1983]
	programming primitives [Knuth 1968]

Table 1: Previous Studies on Cognitive Aspects of Programming

knowledge, in casu PK. Part of the cognitive model as described in this paper was implemented in a program analyser, called **Camus** [Bertels 1991a] [Bertels 1991b].

Not only for program analysis can such a model be used, but also for the actual tutoring itself because it may provide the novice-programmer with more adequate concepts to build programs with.

Introductory programming courses normally start with explaining the syntax of a particular programming language and then proceed with the discussion of a number of standard routines, such as sorting an array, searching in a file and so on. Little or no emphasis is given to the problem solving activities which constitute an important part of writing computer programs. Providing the student with more operational concepts and appropriate problem solving strategies may thus be considered a vital part of the currciculum taught in programming courses.

2 Previous Research

For our purposes, we use the Newell and Simon model of problem solving, [Newell 1972], and focus on the contents of Long Term Memory, which contains the knowledge that is used when solving problems. This knowledge can be described in terms of *symbol structures, elementary information processes* and *primitive symbols*. At the most elementary level we find primitive symbols which have a fixed meaning and designate information at a microscopic level. These symbols are static in nature and can be used to construct more dynamic concepts, namely the elementary information processes (EIP's). The EIP's can generate the macroscopic performance of the Information Processing System. The EIP's can be combined to form symbol structures, which is higher level and more complex knowledge and can be accessed by mere reference.

In the past, a number of studies focused on certain aspects of PK. Table 1 summarizes the most important results.

- **Semantic-Syntactic Model** : The model of programming knowledge as presented by Shneiderman claims that there are two distinct parts in programming knowledge [Shneiderman 1977](See Figure 1).

  One part contains the semantic aspects of that knowledge and the other part only contains syntactic information about the different programming languages. Shneiderman describes the overall structure of semantic programming knowledge as multi-layered where the highest level contains information about the goals to

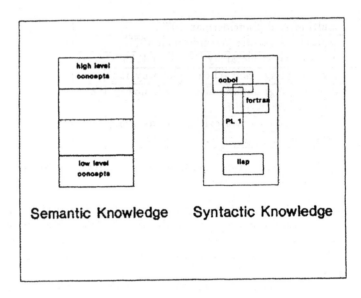

Figure 1: The Syntactic-Semantic Model of Programming Knowledge

be achieved, and the lowest level contains information about the meaning of, for example, an individual assignment.

- **Programming Plans** : There seems to exist knowledge at the level of an individual statement, but also at the level of a number of instructions. This chunking of information in programming was also shown by Shneiderman. The idea of chunking was further formalised by Soloway and called programming plans which are stereotypic ways to solve particular programming problems [Soloway 1983].

- **Units** : Programming plans can be combined in a number of ways in order to achieve certain programming goals. Relating a number of programming plans to a particular data structure results in units [Jonckers 1987]. This systematic collection of programming plans can be more efficiently organized using a generalisation hierarchy which groups structurally related programming plans [Jonckers 1986]. Finding a maximum or minimum value in an array or count the number of elements of that array are all specialisations of the more abstract programming concept 'enumeration of an array'.

- **Rules of Programming Discourse** : Rules of programming discourse specify in an informal way a number of programming conventions, such as the use of variable names, the use of documentation, and so on [Soloway 1983].

- **Problem Solving Strategies** : Problem solving strategies allow the programmer to formulate solutions in terms of previous solutions [Soloway 1983]. The amount of new code to be written can thus be restricted dramatically.

However, in the previously discussed studies two elements are not specified or at least not taken into account. First, nowhere is specified what the constituent parts of the

Newell and Simon Model	Cognitive Model of Programming Knowledge
primitive symbols	programming primitives
elementary information processes	?
symbol structures	programming plans, units

Table 2: Analogy between Newell and Simon Model and our Proposed Model of PK

programming plans are. Second, it is implicitly assumed that there is no link between the syntactic and semantic knowledge bodies.

When applying the Newell and Simon model to programming knowledge, only two elements can be identified so far and are shown in Table 2. First, programming plans and units can be seen as the symbol structures. Secondly, at this stage we can only propose a hypothetical analogy between primitive symbols and the programming primitives. Each of these syntactical primitives have a fixed meaning and are used in some way in the symbol structures. However, the way they are used is not very clear yet. Therefore, what remains to be specified are the elementary information processes that operate on these primitive symbols and which constitute the symbol structures. We then automatically define the missing link between semantic and syntactic PK.

This paper is dedicated to the presentation of such a complete cognitive model. To this purpose, an experiment was conducted using verbal protocol analysis to describe the thought processes and the concepts used by the expert programmer when interpreting and debugging programs. For a detailed discussion of the experimental settings we refer to [Bertels 1991a].

3 A Session with an Expert Programmer

In this section, we discuss a session which is exemplary for the way the subjects interpreted (and debugged) computer programs. The expert programmer was asked to think aloud when analysing a small program that computes the average. This program is depicted in Figure 2.

Starting point of this analysis is the first instruction and when interpreting the loop, the programmer immediately checks on the two looprules[2] : " a loop... do while new...what is strange at first sight is that there is no new read-statement inside the loop... The loopcontrolvariable gets a new value through an increment... "
The computation of sum and count leads the programmer to think that an average is being calculated. " sum and count... I think an average is calculated... " Then he starts looking for evidence for this hypothesized goal :"...and it is confirmed by this "if" where the average is actually computed in the then branch... "
Having established the goal of the program, he now goes back to the beginning of the loop and starts the interpretation process again. "do while new... different from 999...this is a stop condition... we increment count by 1 and...I compute the sum...

---

[2]When using a while-loop, one normally checks whether the variable that controls the loop has a value upon entry, and secondly, whether that variable is given a new value inside the loop.

```
1. count:=0
2. sum:=0
3. read new
4. do while new ≠ 9999
5.        count:=count+1
6.        sum:=sum+new
7.        new:=new+1
8. enddo
9. if count > 0
10. then
11.          avg:=sum/count
12. endif
```

Figure 2: Erroneous Average Computation

Ah,...I increment new by one. So, I am summing all numbers between 5 (his test example) and 9999, and count them too... " Now he has completed his interpretation of the program and he can compare it with his own programming plan to compute averages :*" it seems odd to compute this kind of sum to get an average. Normally, you compute an average of a set of unspecified data".*

4 Descriptive Analysis of the Programmer's Vocabulary

One of our hypotheses that needed verification was to establish the nature of the elementary information processes that are used as building blocks in higher knowledge structures, namely the programming plans.

The experiment suggests that expert programmers, while interpreting a computer program, use a particular vocabulary that cannot be fully defined in terms of the traditional programming primitives, such as an assignment, a read/write-instruction. They rather use programming primitives which have been semantically augmented. Programming plans can then be described in terms of these concepts which we name **semantically augmented programming primitives (SAPP's)**. In other words, we can deduce the semantics of an instruction out of its syntactical occurence.

The anecdotal description as presented in the previous section can be complemented with information about the frequency of use of these SAPP's by each subject.

In what follows, we provide a more detailed analysis of the vocabulary used by our subjects which by no means can be considered to be exhaustive.

4.1 Division of Assignments

When confronted with an assignment in a program, we found that the subjects hardly ever used the concept "assignment" as such. They divided it into a number of different occurences, each bearing a different semantic value, of which we will discuss a limited number.

- **initialization**: assignments in which a variable is given a constant value, like 0 or 1, are called initializations.

- **count-instruction** : a count-instruction is a special case of an assignment because the variable on the left hand side also appears on the right hand side where it is being summed with the constant 1. When reading instructions like this, the subjects uttered phrases like *"we count the number of valid inputs"* or *"it seems to be counting something"*.

- **sum-instruction** : this is the next occurence of an assignment. Again the syntactical structure is quite similar to the increment but with a difference, namely that the constant is replaced by a multi-valued variable.

4.2   Read-instruction

When the variable of the read-instruction is also the loopcontrolvariable then this read is considered to be either a pre-read or a post-read.[3] The pre-read refers to the read-instruction which is placed before the while-condition and the post-read refers to the read-instruction of that same variable inside the loop. In any other case, no specific concept was used for this particular instruction.

4.3   Role Definitions

It was also established that when using these concepts, the subjects attached a specific role to variables as well. These roles summarize the way the variables are used and what their purpose might be in the program. Following from the above descriptions, typical roles are *countvariable* and *sumvariable*. When linked with an array, this role may be extended to the *index of an array*. In defining a role for a variable, the mnemonic value of the variable name is also taken into account though this is not really necessary. Evidently, one variable can have multiple roles. An example of multiple roles is where a variable is used at the same time as a countvariable and as an index of an array.

4.4   Iteration : Unification instead of Division

Contrary to what one might have expected, programmers tend to treat the different loopstructures in a uniform way.[4] Whereas one can distinguish between three syntactically different loops, the subjects were actually reasoning in other terms, thus abstracting away from any functionally irrelevant difference. Most of the concepts programmers use when discussing loops have to do with the way one can enter and exit the loop. This is best illustrated by the fact that every programmer explicitly checked when the loop could be entered and when it could be exited.

In deciding upon entry, the subjects checked how the loopcontrolvariable was given its initial value. When entry was shown to be possible, they then checked to see whether it was possible to exit the loop. To this purpose they checked on how the variable got a new value inside the loop. They also took into account whether this instruction was

---

[3] This semantic augmentation is only found when while-loops are used.

[4] A lot of recursive calls can be converted in loop-based control structures. Therefore, we did not explicitly take recursivity into account in our analysis.

conditional or not. A typical utterance is : " *Read rainfall....a sentinel in the while (he thinks of the entry condition)... we should then find another "read rainfall" (inside the loop), yes..., but it is made conditionally."* Whenever it is relevant, like in the case of an average calculation, the minimum and maximum number of loop passes are specified. *"...if you immediately input the sentinel, we divide by zero... "*

4.5 Selections : Individual Constraints

Though the results with respect to selections are incomplete and further experiments are needed to validate certain conjectures, we suggest the following interpretation of selections.

Selections are often transformed into constraints which are then connected with individual instructions or a block of instructions. The following excerpt illustrates this. The subject is interpreting an erronuous part of the program in which the programming plan to compute a maximum is supposed to be found. The error is that in the then-part of the selection a sum-instruction is also included. *" if rainfall is greater than highest then highest gets the value of rainfall. That seems normal. But then total is total plus rainfall. So if it's lower than highest, it is not being included in the total computation."* The programmer obviously knows how a maximum is to be computed. So he links the if-condition to the *maximum assignment instruction.* He then proceeds to the next line and tries to find a sensible interpretation. We can thus hypothesize that individual instructions are linked to a constraint which is a translation of the if-condition. This also determines the quality of the variables used in these instructions : *"..if r is greater than 0 then d is d plus 1...d is the number of positive inputs... "*

5 Elementary Information Processes in Programming

In the previous section, we have defined the nature of the elementary information processes which are used as basic vocabulary and, consequently, as building blocks of the symbol structures, in casu the programming plans. To incorporate these concepts in a cognitive model, we introduced the SAPP's. A SAPP in the program interpretation process comprises traditional programming primitives whose meaning have been augmented and which are used as basic building blocks in the program interpretation process. A more formal definition of the different SAPP's is as follows.

SAPP's : In general, SAPP's are semantic augmentations of programming primitives, embodying a higher meaning. We distinguish between *single SAPP's* and *compound SAPP's*.

1. **Single SAPP's :** are the traditional, one-line programming primitives that have a higher semantic value. This includes the semantic augmentations of assignments, read-instructions and the role definitions of variables.

2. **Compound SAPP's :** are the traditional control structures. For every compound SAPP a standardized description can be generated, thus transcending the

programming concept	augmented programming concept
assignment	initialization
	count-instruction
	sum-instruction
	increment
read	pre-read
	post-read
variable	sum-variable
	count-variable
	minimum-maximum variable
	index of array
loop	stopvalue-sentinel
	exit condition
	entry condition
	loopcontrolvariable(s)
	number of passes through loop
selection	guard
	quality of variable

Table 3: An Overview of some Semantically Augmented Programming Primitives

specific syntactic occurence. For the loop structures, the following attributes are used.

- entry condition
- exit condition
- sentinel(s)
- loopcontrolvariable(s)
- number of passes through loop

As explained above, every selection is translated into a constraint under which instructions are executed.

Examples of some of the SAPP's can be found in Table 3.

6 Programming Knowledge : a Multi-leveled, Inverted Pyramid

Out of empirical studies reported on in the introduction of this paper and out of the empirical evidence of our experiment, multiple characteristics of programming knowledge emerge.

6.1 Pyramidal Structure of the Cognitive Model

The establishment of a relationship between the different constituent parts of a cognitive model of programming knowledge is a fundamental question. Before we propose

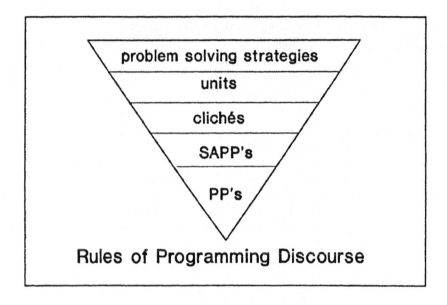

Figure 3: Pyramidal Structure of Programming Knowledge

our cognitive model, consider again Shneiderman's syntactic-semantic model as shown in Figure 1. The overall organization of programming knowledge, as suggested by Shneiderman [Shneiderman 1977], is clearly multileveled. However, the following considerations based on the model of Shneiderman may not hold true :

1. this model indicates that the amount of knowledge at each level remains constant,

2. there are no links between the syntactic and semantic knowledge,

3. Shneiderman does not explicitly incorporate his concept of program chunks into this model and the contents of the different levels are not described.

To incorporate the previous considerations, consider a **multi-leveled, inverted pyramid** as basic overall structure of a cognitive model for programming knowledge. This structure is shown in Figure 3.

- **Multi-leveled :** We distinguish between different levels of programming knowledge. The lowest level in our model contains the programming primitives or the syntactic programming knowledge. The second level in our structure contains the SAPP's. They are closely related to the programming primitives because, considered at the syntactic level, they are identical and they are defined on a single instruction basis.
  However, the SAPP's embody more information than the programming primitives. They condense information about their function and summarize both data and control flow. Consider the following example of a SAPP. A count-instruction

requires the presence of an initialization for the count-variable, which must precede the execution of the count-instruction. These two instructions represent the data flow. Furthermore, it is trivial to use a count-instruction without any kind of loop control structure. The count-instruction as such requires the presence of at least one loop structure. Consequently, control flow information is embedded in the concept of a SAPP.

A single SAPP or a combination of SAPP's may serve as beacon in the program understanding process and, even more important, SAPP's are the basic building blocks out of which programming plans are made. They form the prime constituents of the cliché based reasoning process and may be considered to be the missing link between the syntactic and semantic programming knowledge.

- **Inverted Pyramidal :** The inverted pyramidal structure represents the fact that at each higher level, the amount of incorporated information expands. Let's consider and slightly modify Shneiderman's example that illustrated the three layers in semantic knowledge, and show that the amount of information indeed expands at each level : at the lowest level the programmer understands the meaning of an assignment; at the intermediate level he knows how to use this assignment to create an array, and at the highest level the programmer is capable of extending the notion of arrays to matrices and to matrix-operations like inverting. Understanding an assignment implies that a programmer knows basic programming concepts like a variable and how to store a value in it by using the assignment statement. Understanding an array means understanding that it consists of many, single memory addresses that can be accessed by using indices. The programmer must understand the concept of an assignment quite well in order to be able to apply it to the creation of an array. The matrix concept again incorporates more knowledge than the mere 'array' concept. It is an abstraction of the concrete occurence of an array.

7 Existing Intelligent Tutoring Systems

Though this is not the place to provide a detailed discussion of existing intelligent tutoring systems (ITS) for programming, we will discuss a number of them and explain to what extend they use concepts as explained above.

Well known examples of ITS in programming are Proust [Johnson 1986], Laura [Laurent 1980], Lisptutor [Reiser et. al 1985] and Talus [Murray 1988]. We will only discuss the first two because they analyse programs written in a procedural language. The concept of plans (and sub-plans) is explicitly used Proust but not in Laura. The latter transforms every program in a graph and then tries to transform that graph into some kind of standardized form which can then be compared to the graph representation of a correct program. Any difference in the student program graph with the correct program graph is considered to be an error. Because Laura only uses a graph representation for computer programs, it implies that Laura does not reason in terms of the basic instructions nor explicitly uses the semantics of programming plans.

As far as Proust is concerned, plans and subplans are the basic concepts used in program analysis. As we have explained above, programming plans are constructed using

SAPP's. Therefore, any approach using programming plans must in some way use SAPP's as basic building blocs, which is also the case with Proust. However, note the following differences :

- The typology of instructions and control structures is not based on psychological evidence and is often determined ad hoc leading to inaccurate classifications[5].

- Proust's reasoning still takes place at the code-level. In no way can Proust make abstraction of a particular occurence of an instruction which results in a lot of incorrect analyses[6], whereas abstraction constitutes the major advantage of the use of SAPP's in program analysis.

8 Conclusion

In this paper, we have presented a cognitive model of programming knowledge that contains the relevant knowledge structures and concepts that human expert programmers use when programming. Using verbal protocol analysis, we made the very simple and straightforward observation that these expert programmers reason in terms of SAPP's out of which higher knowledge structures are formed. These SAPP's may be considered to be the missing link between the semantic and syntactic programming knowledge as originally described by Shneiderman [Shneiderman 1977].

We conclude by formulating a hypothesis which may be topic for further research and which was formulated at the beginning of this paper. We hypothesize that in giving the novice programmer the appropriate cognitive concepts and strategies, this will most likely result in a better understanding of programming.

References

[Bertels 1991a]   Bertels K.; *Qualitative Reasoning in Novice Program Analysis*; Ph.D.-thesis, University of Antwerp, june 1991.

[Bertels 1991b]   Bertels K., Vanneste Ph.& De Backer C.; *The Development of a Program Analyzer*; Proceedings of the PEG-91 Conference, Rapallo, Italy, june 1991.

[Bouwman 1985]   Bouwman; *The use of Protocol Analysis in Accounting*; Accounting and Finance, May 1985, pp.61-84.

[Jonckers 1986]   Jonckers Viviane; *Generalisations Hierarchies in Knowledge Based Programming*; AI-memo no. 86-4, 1986, 14 p.

[Jonckers 1987]   Jonckers Viviane; *A Framework for Modeling Programming Knowledge*; V.U.B. A.I.-Lab, Technical Report 87-1, 1987.

[Johnson 1986]   Johnson W. L.; *Intention-Based Diagnosis of Novice Programming Errors*; Morgan Kaufmann Publishers, 1986.

---

[5] We refer, for example, to the loop classification.
[6] Again we refer to [Bertels 1991a] for more information.

[Knuth 1968]   Knuth ; *Fundamental Algorithms*; Reading, Massachusetts, 1968, 2nd. ed., 634 p.

[Laurent 1980]   Laurent, Adam; *Laura : a system to debug programs*; Artificial Intelligence, no. 15, 1980, pp.75-122.

[Murray 1988]   Murray; *Automatic Program Debugging for Intelligent Tutoring Systems*; Morgan Kaufmann Publishers, San Mateo, 1988, 344 p.

[Newell 1972]   Newell & Simon; *Human Problem Solving*; Englewood Cliffs NJ, Prentice Hall, 1972.

[Reiser et. al 1985]   Reiser, Anderson & Farrell; Dynamic student modelling in an intelligent tutor for LISP programming, *Proceedings of the International Joint conference on Artificial Intelligence-85*, Los Altos, Morgan Kaufmann, vol. 1, pp. 8-14.

[Shneiderman 1977]   Shneiderman; *Teaching Programming : a spiral approach to syntax and semantics*; Computers and Education, vol.1, 1977, p.193-197.

[Soloway 1983]   Soloway E., Bonar J. & Ehrlich K.; *Cognitive Strategies and Looping Constructs : An Empirical Study*; C.A.C.M., Vol. 26, Nr. 11, 1983, pp. 853-860.

[Wills 1987]   Wills, Linda; *Automated Program Recognition*; MIT-AI laboratory, Massachusetts, Technical Report 904, 1987, 199 p.

Programming by Experimentation and Example

Cynthia Brown, Harriet Fell, Viera K. Proulx, Richard Rasala
College of Computer Science, Northeastern University
Boston MA, 02115 USA
tel. (617) 437-2462
Internet: brown@corwin.ccs.northeastern.edu, fell@corwin.ccs.northeastern.edu
vkp@corwin.ccs.northeastern.edu, rasala@corwin.ccs.northeastern.edu

Abstract

In this paper we describe our long term project aimed at improving the teaching of the first year computer science courses. The project is based on extensive individually designed animation and visualization programs. All programs are written in THINK Pascal for the Macintosh, using QuickDraw toolbox. There are written in a good modular style with documentation that enables students to use the source code in their own programs. A separate collection of tools enables students to easily create graphical user interfaces. The programs can be used during lectures, in closed labs, as examples of programming style, and as tools to be used by students.

We describe three examples of the use of our modules. The first is a MiniPaint programming project students program after only six weeks of instruction. It gives them great freedom to design their own graphic user interface, teaches them about software engineering and provides a challenge for all levels of learners. The second example presents several different visualizations used in presenting recursion. The programming assignment, drawing of recursive trees, reinforces student's understanding of the difference between passing parameters to recursive procedure by value vs. by reference. The third example is a program that demonstrates all sorting algorithms typically introduced in the first year course, and a number of ways it can be used in teaching.

Introduction

Over the past several years our group has been experimenting with new methodology for teaching introductory computer science courses. To this end we developed a large collection of interactive visualization software modules that have a multitude of uses. Our aim is to bring the best methods for teaching science and engineering into the computer science classroom. In science courses, students not only listen to lectures, but also spend a substantial amount of time in lab, conducting experiments that provide motivation or verification for theories presented in the lectures. In engineering courses, students learn to build more complex objects from simpler ones - they do not have to build everything from the bottom level up. And in both cases, students are exposed to examples and exercises that are relevant and realistic.

The new ACM curriculum recommendations [TUCK91] promotes this type of teaching methodology - especially the closed laboratory component. Sheila Tobias [TOB90] shows how a more experiential learning style can improve the student success rate, especially among 'nontraditional' students.

Three Problems in Teaching Introductory Computer Science

The first problem is that the dynamical behavior of computer algorithms and the temporal changes in the associated data structures is usually presented in a static lecture format with drawings and diagrams on a chalkboard. In some universities, general purpose algorithm animation systems are also used to illustrate algorithms. Many of these systems specialize in illustrating either the algorithm behavior, or the data structure [e.g. AUG-YED88, BAE-SHER81, BEN-KER87, BRO88, BRO-SEG85, NAP90, NAP89, REI86, STA90]. They may allow the user to view the dynamical changes in the values of selected variables, or display them graphically, or trace the order of execution of the program statements and the contents of the procedure call stack or other relevant variables. The display is usually tied to the dynamic changes in the current values of a particular data structure or it is tied to a particular steps in the implementation of the algorithm in a specific programming language.

In contrast, our visualizations represent the problem domain of a particular algorithm, and illustrate the key steps in the algorithm as reflected in this representation. Each one of our modules is designed <u>individually</u> to model a particular concept. Each visualization program is designed for interactive experimentation by students either in a closed laboratory session or on their own time. The programs can also be used for dynamic illustration of a concept presented in a lecture. The speed of the visualization in most cases is controlled by the user. The size of the animation step is determined by the concept that is being illustrated not by the internal structure of the program. This gives the student an opportunity to deduce an algorithm from the observed dynamic illustration and to verify their understanding by experimenting with different variations of the inputs to the visualization program. Students may also validate theoretical results by running a series of experiments and plotting the results.

The second problem that we feel needs to be addressed is the nature of typical programming assignments in introductory computer science courses. The programming projects in first year textbooks typically are not very exciting. Most of the input and output is in the text format and the resulting programs are essentially identical. Many students get frustrated, bored, and disillusioned. The first year computer science course seldom conveys the excitement most active computer scientists encounter in their daily work. Computer professionals in the workplace build on the work done by others - they modify existing code, add new procedures to existing programs and design new user interfaces. Our modules are designed to give this rich experience to first year computer science students.

All of our software is written in THINK Pascal for the Macintosh. We make extensive use of the simple QuickDraw procedures to generate visualizations. There are three different components in our modules. The interactive visualizations are written in such a way that the students can not only run them as is, but can also read the programs, modify them, or use some of the procedures to build their own programs. When appropriate, tools are provided for performance evaluation so that students can collect realistic experimental data for verifying mathematical analysis of particular algorithms. A separate collection of tools contains procedures that simplify building the user interface: windows, input-output, mouse usage, and timing controls. These tools are available to students, but they are not expected to understand their internals.

This rich collection of software gives the students an opportunity to work on the most interesting parts of a particular problem, while using the existing tools and programs to perform the more mundane tasks. In other instances the software serves as a model and motivation for their projects. In any case, they start learning about stubs and drivers, about reusable software, and about abstract data structures from the very beginning. They are also constantly exposed to examples of good programming style, and to examples of partitioning of a program into procedures, modules, and tools.

This framework also allows us to address the third problem typically encountered in the first year computer science classroom, namely a lack of realistic examples of the uses of computer science in the different areas of human endeavor. Biological modeling is illustrated by Conway's Game of Life. The MiniPaint programming assignment exposes students to the problems one encounters when designing graphical user interfaces. A maze search problem illustrates the various methods employed in finding a route between two cities. A traffic intersection simulation illustrates uses of queues in programming.

In addition, our approach supports individualized instruction. Our modules give a lot of support, and opportunities for reinforcement of the basic concepts to those that are novices. On the other hand, the software framework gives a number of challenging opportunities to the brightest students. Besides writing more challenging programs, they can study the software and learn about many complex issues, they would not have the opportunity to explore in ordinary courses.

Three Examples of Use of Our Methodology and Our Visualizations in Teaching

We now present three examples of our methodology and of the use of our software. When a new topic is presented, the visualization software is used to illustrate the concepts. The software may be used in a lecture or in a closed laboratory. In either case, the software that performs the visualization is made available to students from a network server. Students always have access to software tools and the source code. When appropriate, executable applications are also provided to eliminate the need for compilation. The only time students are not allowed to see the source code is when they are asked to program their own version of a particular set of procedures. In that case a compiled applications serves as a guide for what is to be accomplished.

In the first example, the visual display is a vehicle for giving students an early opportunity to work on an interesting piece of software, doing their own design, and integrating their own work with existing software. In the second example, several dynamic visualizations are used to explain different aspects of recursion. The programming assignment, especially its visual component, reinforces the new concepts.

In the third example an animation is used to introduce and study different sorting algorithms in a dynamic experimental manner. A separate 'Time Trials' version of the software is used for timing experiments.

Example 1: MiniPaint Project

The objective of this programming project is to give students an opportunity to integrate all the basic Pascal concepts they have learned during the first six weeks of the course. At this point they have covered the assignment statement, the control structures (loops, decision statements), the use of procedures, and passing parameters to procedures (at least by value). They have also written several programs that used QuickDraw procedures to draw pictures. Over the first six weeks they have had numerous opportunities to read programs given to them by the instructor, to modify such programs, or to incorporate given procedures into their own projects.

The assignment is to write a very simple mouse controlled paint program. The user can paint circles, rectangles, and ovals, clear the screen, and quit. At the beginning the left end of the drawing window shows the five corresponding icons. Creative students may add additional features and icons. The icons are represented as simple rectangles with a drawing or text inside. The user selects the type of figure using mouse click, then selects the position and size of the figure with two more mouse clicks. Students have previously studied a Pascal program that paints circles, ovals and rectangles in locations identified by mouse clicks. They have access to this program in both printed and electronic version and are encouraged to use any parts they find suitable.

With this background, what are the main problems students have to address in order to solve the problem? They have to decide what kind and how many icons they will use, and what action each icon will represent. They have to write the procedure that reads the mouse location, highlights the selected icon, and calls the procedure that performs the selected action. Only simple arithmetic is needed to identify the correct icon. Each action procedure can be written and debugged independently - indeed a lot of code here can be copied from the model program. Designing a control program that orchestrates all these actions poses the greatest challenge.

Students greatly enjoy working on this program. They concentrate on design issues, on the structure of the whole program, and on adapting existing procedures to fit their needs. By the time they are done they have created a nice piece of software - most of it of their own design. And it is fun to run it (see Figure 1).

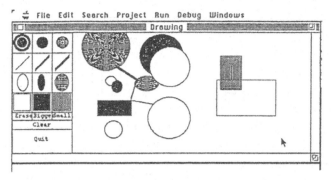

Figure 1. MiniPaint Project (Tom Farrell, November 1990).

When all of the projects are turned in, we spend one lab class looking at the different solutions. We ask each group of students to run several projects written by others and write down their comments. This usually turns into a hands-on lab on user interface design. Students may complain that some programs draw over the icons, or they wonder what the other student did to avoid it. Some interfaces require too many mouse clicks and are confusing to the user. Others may not clear the screen correctly. Students learn from both the successes and the mistakes of their peers. Students that are new to programming learn a lot from observing the additional features built by their more experienced classmates.

Overall, the students could see in practice a number of software engineering principles: reuse of software, testing procedures using stubs and drivers, examples of good documentation in the code supplied to them, proper modularization, use of tools, design of user interface.

Example 2: Recursion

There are a number of different concepts students have to learn to truly understand recursion. These include partitioning of a problem into subtasks at the next lower recursion level, backtracking, the nature of the procedure call stack during recursion, and scoping of variables between different recursive calls. We have several programs that let the students experiment with these concepts in different settings.

The visualization of the Towers of Hanoi illustrates dynamically the movement of the disks. The mouse button controls stepping through the algorithm, unless the user decides to 'zoom through' by pressing the *caps lock* key. The text under the picture

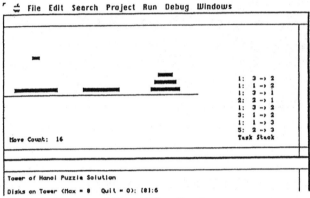

Figure 2. Towers of Hanoi Visualization.

explains the current task, while the stack of currently active procedure calls is displayed on the right. A count of the number of moves completes the picture (Figure 2). Students first try to discover the algorithm by manipulating five or six disks of different sizes. The visualization confirms their solution and allows them to study the underlying implementation.

Another program illustrates backtracking by performing an exhaustive search for all solutions to the Eight Queens problem (Figure 3). The user can actually vary the size of the chess board up from size 2 to size 10. The user can follow the backtracking in single step mode, in slow motion, or as fast as possible. As queens are added or removed from the board, all squares attacked by the currently positioned queens are shaded gray. When a solution is found, it is compared to all previous ones for possible symmetries. If the solution is symmetric to an earlier one then that solution is also displayed. When the

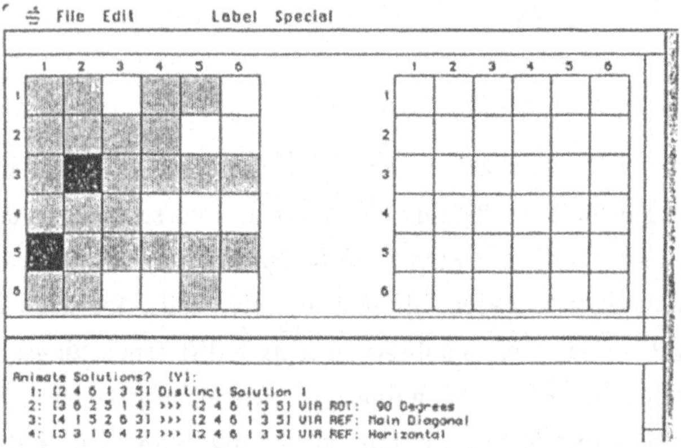

Figure 3. The Eight Queens Problem Visualization.

exhaustive search is complete, the user can see a recapitulation of all solutions that are genuinely distinct.

Once the students begin to understand recursion they are given a program that recursively draws the snowflake curve using an implementation of the Logo Turtle abstract data structure (Figure 4). Students are next asked to write a program that draws a recursive tree. A tree consists of a trunk and a fixed number of smaller subtrees growing from it. There is a subtle difference between the snowflake and the tree. In the snowflake curve, the turtle continues on its trek using only recursive procedure calls. In contrast, when drawing a tree, the Logo Turtle must return back to the top of the trunk before it can draw the second (or third) subtree. The difference between passing the parameters by value rather than by reference is startling. We have used this assignment for a couple of years now. Typically, some of the students walk out of the class and complete the assignment within an hour. Others - often equally capable students - live in frustration for a couple of days, drawing wilted trees leaning to the left, until the right idea clicks ("Aha!" time). Once this happens, these students can also complete the project in an hour.

Figure 4. Recursive Snowflake Curve (Levels 1, 2, 3).

Students are encouraged to experiment with different trees by varying the number of branches, the angle between them, the reduction scale for the next level, the initial angle of the first branch (Figure 5). and by introducing randomness into any of these choices. Some of the resulting trees look very natural. This serves as a first introduction to the study of fractals and scientific visualization (Figure 6).

Example 3: Sorting Algorithms

There are three different components we use to study and investigate sorting algorithms. There are two programs - an interactive animation program and a Time Trialsprogram to permit performance comparisons. In addition, manipulative materials are used to introduce sorting concepts.

The interactive demonstration programs displays all sorting algorithms typically

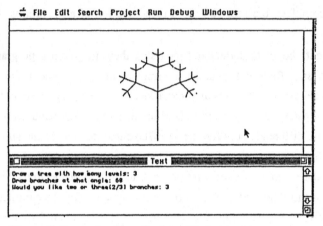

Figure 5. Recursive Tree Project (Chris Hopkins, March 1990).

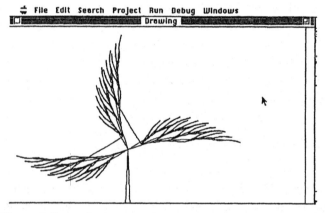

Figure 6. Recursively Drawn Palm Tree (Bob Pitas, March 1989).

covered in the first year curriculum. The array to be sorted is represented as a bar chart. As the algorithm progresses a number of visual clues help the user understand what is happening. These include highlighted bars representing numbers that are being compared, pivot elements displayed on the side, and in some cases a solid horizontal bar over the numbers yet to be sorted. Text explaining what is happening appears below the chart. For small arrays the numerical values are displayed below each bar (Figure 7). The maximum size of the array to be sorted is 450 - the limitation imposed by the number of pixels on the small Macintosh screen (Figure 8). User can run the same algorithm several times on different sets of data, or run several different algorithms on the same set of data.

The Time Trials version of this program contains the same sorting code and

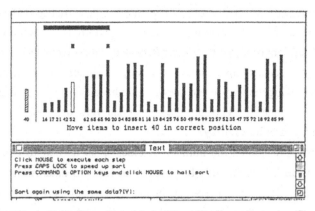

Figure 7. Sorting Algorithms Visualization - Insertion Sort on 35 Items.

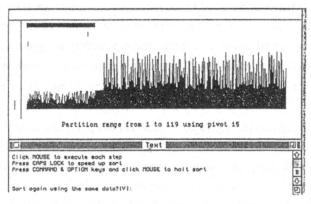

Figure 8. Sorting Algorithms Visualization - Quicksort on 450 Items.

allows the user the same choices as the demonstration program. However, all calls to the graphic display have been replaced with data collection and timing code. This program can be used to do accurate performance comparisons of a number of different algorithms for a number of different input sets. A special feature of the Time Trials program is that various enhancements to the quicksort algorithm can easily be contrasted.

We first introduce sorting to our students through manipulative materials. Students are given a strip of sixteen numbered slots and about fifty squares with numbers on them. We ask them to sort fifteen numbers placed on the strip by moving a number only into an empty place. They count their moves and try to minimize them. To be more realistic, they may be required to keep the numbers face down. Once the students understand the limitations of a computer solution, they observe the animation program.

After running an algorithm for a couple of times, the students can usually deduce the method and mimic it on their strip. The students can then see the implementation of the algorithm in a programming language, or try to implement it themselves. This method works for all of the simple sorting algorithms. The strip becomes useful again for introducing heapsort. By drawing the strip as a binary tree students have a great visual aid which helps them make the connection between the conceptual view of a heap as a tree and its explicit representation as a linear array.

The animation program records the number of clock ticks needed to complete each algorithm. The array to be sorted may be filled with random data, sorted data, inverted data, or user input. Students can see easily the differences between average cases, best cases, and worst cases. One interesting phenomenon surfaces when students compare the timing of the animation program versus that of the Time Trials program. Selection sort does much better than expected in the animation. Investigation shows that this is because selection sort does very few data swaps. In an animation, swaps are very expensive since bits must be moved around the screen. hence, selection sort gets an unfair advantage over the other sorts in the animation. This anomaly emphasizes to students that performance testing must be done in configurations that match the characteristics of the actual applications.

The programming assignments we give our students at this point aim at increasing their awareness of the need for analysis and testing of algorithms before they are used in applications. The assignments also guide students into writing reusable code. We start by asking them to write a program in which the input, output, and sorting phases are clearly separated into different procedures. The sorting program used in this assignment is one of the simple sorting algorithms.

Next they replace the simple sort with quicksort. We ask them to implement the quicksort both recursively and nonrecursively, and to record the maximum size of the stack. We ask them to write the program in two ways - saving the subtask on the left, and saving the larger subtask for later processing. They are asked to run the different version for a number of different inputs and to plot the stack size results. Students learn that implementation details can sometimes be important in determining whether an algorithm will be robust in practical applications.

In the next assignment, quicksort is replaced by a heapsort. Students display the heap once it is built, and compare runs on different inputs - including presorted array or inverted array.

Finally, the students are asked to run a number of different algorithms with different sets of data using the Time Trials program and plot the results, possibly using a spreadsheet. Using Time Trials is similar to a physics lab that verifies the laws of motion deduced theoretically in lecture.

Conclusion

We have presented several examples of our methodology for teaching introductory computer science and of the software module we are developing to use in these courses. A number of other modules are being built - some are in use now, some are under development, some are planned. We have seen a great difference in our students over the past few years. They are much more enthusiastic about their programming projects and display great satisfaction with the work they complete. In many cases, the amount of time needed to introduce a topic has been drastically reduced. The student's ability to build useful software soars. Last year two of our best student combined code from a number of different modules with their own procedures to create a very nice animation of graph algorithms.

We are hoping to find a good way to conduct objective evaluation of our approach to teaching computer science. We plan to make our software and the accompanying materials available to all instructors interested in using our modules in their classroom and will ask them to document their experiences and write to us their observations and comments.

References

[AUG-YED88]   Moshe Augenstein and Langsam Yedidyah, *Automatic Generation of Graphic Displays of Data Structures Through a Preprocessor*, SIGCSE Bulletin, February 1988, Vol. 20, No. 1, p. 148.

[BAE86]   Ronald M. Baecker, *An Application Overview of Program Visualization*, Computer Graphics, July 1986, Vol. 20, No. 4, p 325.

[BAE-SHER81]   Ronald M. Baecker and David Sherman, *Sorting Out Sorting*, 16mm color sound film, 30 minutes, 1981. (Shown at ACM SIGGRAPH '81 in Dallas, TX and excerpted in ACM SIGGRAPH Video Review No.7, 1983.)

[BEN-KER87]   Jon L. Bentley and Brian W. Kernighan, *A System for Algorithm Animation: Tutorial and User Manual*, Computer Science Technical Report No. 132,

AN EXPERIMENT OF COOPERATIVE LEARNING WITH HYPERCARD

D. Clément, C. Viéville, P. Vilers
Trigone Laboratory - University of Lille I
59655 Villeneuve d'Ascq - France
Phone : +33.20.43.49.21
Fax : +33.20.43.48.66
E-mail : vieville@frcitl81.bitnet

Abstract

In Distant Open Learning system, the lack of socialization between learners appears to be one of the major faults. If the socialization is very important to construct knowledge, it is also essential from other points of view such as political, economical or ethical.

So, the learning resource center could be used by the pedagogical teams as the best place to promote collective work. This kind of work provides means which allow learners to locate their level with regard to the group.

In order to progress in this direction, we have adapted existing tools mainly designed for the office automation domain to our educational needs. These software tools which allow cooperative work are also named "groupware".

After a review of the "groupware" concept, we will describe a system we have set up to facilitate cooperation between learners involved in the same task.

This system has been experimented with using Hypercard in a learning resource center where learners have tools to cooperate in a real time mode, and we have focused our attention particularly on the coordination of the learners' points of view.

The first results of that study are related as well as the perspectives of development of such systems.

INTRODUCTION

For three years, the research-team of the Trigone laboratory of the Lille I University has been working on the setting up of communication systems and tools for distance and Open Learning.

Our aim is a large program of pluridisciplinary research named the "CoCoNut Project" in which numerous specialists (Computer experts, psychologists, pedagogues) work in order to promote socialization in the distance learning process [Derycke 90].

The key-concept of our approach is the concept of cooperative autonomy :

- We have chosen to design and experiment with systems that allow each learner to manage and conduct personally his learning, to work alone at any time, to elaborate solutions, or work only on one aspect of a task.

- But, at the same time, we wish to offer to each learner either the opportunity to compare the solutions he has elaborated with those of other learners working on the same task or articulate the results of a sub-problem he has dealt with the results of other sub-problems treated by other learners.

Thus, in our distance learning system, every learner can work either in a private mode or in a collaborative / cooperative mode.

As seen before, our principal aim is to be able to put together individuals geographically distant but engaged in the same learning.

Thus, the concept of virtual classroom is emerging as a social electronic space in which there are discussions and groupwork on a defined topic (concept discussions, case-studies...).

I - COOPERATIVE WORK VERSUS COOPERATIVE LEARNING

This concept of electronic and cooperative workplace comes from the domain of the office automation with the emergence of the notion of "groupware".

This rise of groupware is due to the reflexions and work of a multidisciplinary domain : the CSCW (Computer-Supported Cooperative Work) whose aim is to use the computer not only in order to automate tasks but also to support cooperation between people doing the same task [Ellis 91].

I.1 - CSCW : the concept of groupware

Used first in the field of office automation, the "groupware" can be conceived as the specialization of a computer-mediated system of communication which supports a specific cooperative activity (for example : group decision support system, collaborative writing of a paper).

The CSCW systems are human-to-human communication systems working either in real-time (example : the audio or video conference) or in deferred-time (electronic mail).

They put in interaction a group of people, sharing the same goal. These people can be in the same room : they need tools dedicated to support meetings. They can be either in the same building (the group-network) or in very different locations (for a taxonomy of the different domains of the CSCW, see [Kraemer 88]).

In the educational domain, we can notice that pioneers have proposed for a long time to use electronic mail, or better, CMCS (Computer-mediated conference system), for education.

R. Hiltz has already shown the potential and deficiencies of [Hiltz 86] and popularized the concept of "virtual classroom".

Regarding the more recent research projects in the CSCW domain, it appears that some new cooperative tools specialized in some professional activities are being developed. For example, it is the case of brainstorming with Colab [Stefik 87], argumentation support with G. Ibis [Yakemovic 90]. It seems that the majority of these activities can be transposed in the educational field.

The evolution of the two domains, office automation and educational technologies, shows some convergence due to the adoption of very close paradigms. For example, starting from our concept of "cooperative autonomy" we have designed the Nanoreseau which constituted a group network devoted to facilitate a group pedagogy [Derycke 88]. Soon, in the CoCoNut project [Derycke 90, Derycke 92] we will set up a distant learning system supported by the technologies of information and communication. This project borrows computer tools from the CSCW domain and adapts them to Cooperative distant learning.

I.2 - Cooperative learning : the challenge

We know that different modes of cooperative learning have always existed : group dynamics, case-studies, collaborative problem-solving, and sometimes the pedagogy of the project. We argue that the trade-guild and the on-site learning are also forms of learning where all the actors can be in turn teacher or learner.

Nevertheless, for economical reasons (problem of classroom size), the learning process is often seen as a process of knowledge transfer between a transmitter (teacher) and a receiver (learner). The relations between learners are often seen as trouble, disturbance or, as Van Eckevoort [Delta 87] said, as "noise in the system".

So, it appears that cooperative learning has to take place in the educational process, for several reasons : political, ethical and economical :

- In initial education, the cooperation between children makes them citizens able to live in a democracy. The modern world requires some important relational capabilities. The relations between races, genders, nations are becoming central. As Dewey wrote "living in the classroom is the democratic process in microcosm, and the heart of democratic life is in group cooperation" ;

- At the economic level, in order to assume the competitiveness of firms, it is necessary for workers to acquire not only technical or procedural skills but also skills in team-working [Galegher 90]. Here also, Cooperation and Learning are interdependent. Indeed, in the economic domains where information is the raw material and the source of added value, the worker has to acquire new capacities related to data-processing (transversal skills). So, these new capacities are learned by adults in interaction with the other potential actors of the educational process (teachers, tutors, professional experts, peers...).

So Cooperative learning is becoming a necessary challenge.

II - SOME THEORETICAL FOUNDATIONS OF COOPERATIVE LEARNING

Ours is a constructivist and interactionist point of view :

- Constructivist because, like J. Piaget, we argue that it is when he works directly on the reality, by trying to solve some difficulties that a learner can progress in accessing to the knowledge and in acquiring intellectual skills. Thus, he constructs the schemes which will help him to be efficient in some classes of situation.

- Interactionist because, like G. Mugny et W. Doise [Mugny 85], we admit an important role for the interindividual relations and for the interpersonal conflicts in the building of knowledge. Several partners doing the same task can progress only if they formulate different points of view on the perception they have of the task and its solution.

These different points of view bring them to co-ordinate their primarily divergent perspectives in order to have access progressively to a mental representation, as objective and integrated as possible, of the objects they work on.

However, for this "socio-cognitive conflict" to occur and lead to progress for the learners, everyone of them has to be in a state of mind making him able to formulate his own position and to pay attention to the others' point of view. Finally, it is necessary to create a pedagogical environment where the learners have all the facilities to leave a side their own approach (necessary partial of the problem) in order to explore and have access to the others' perspectives.

What is important according to Doise and Mugny is to build together an integrated vision of the analyzed situation i.e. the need to offer to the learners a work space where they will share their representations and/or solutions of the problem and then decide in favour of the optimal solution, selected as a correct one by everybody.

These theoretical foundations justify the technological choices we have made, i.e. the setting of a shared space with the opportunity, thanks to the hypertext/hypermedia, to have, at any moment, the possibility of associating to an individual work, on each workstation, a representation of the collective work being elaborated [Derycke 90].

But speaking about cooperative learning does not mean leaving the learners alone in front of the task/problem. We also have to set up a guidance as a mediation between the learner and the object of learning.

The work of Vygotsky [Vygotsky 85] and Bruner [Bruner 87] insists on the need for such an external guidance and on the social dimension of the learning process. So the cognitive changes depend on the nature of the relations with others. This function of mediation, scaffolding (Bruner), permits us to connect the environment with our own cognitive states.

By his role as expert, the mediator (human or computer in our study) guides and structures the learner's activities.

This guidance brings the learner from an actual cognitive level to what Vygotsky calls "the Zone of Proximal Development" that is :

"The distance between the actual development level as determined by independent problem-solving and the level of potential development as determined through problem-solving under adult guidance or in collaboration with more capable peers" [Vygotsky 81].

The art of scaffolding is in managing subgoals and facilitating interaction between peers engaged in the same problem solving.

III - PRESENTATION OF A "POOR-MAN" PLATFORM FOR "HYPERMEDIA AND COOPERATIVE LEARNING"

We have designed a collective system for learning, connected in network, in order to facilitate interaction between peers, running with Hypercard and to which we have added a software allowing coordination between learners.

III.1 - The collectivisation apparatus of Hypercard

Jointly with the CoCoNut Project, whose goal is to create a specialized platform for cooperative learning, we have also wished to experiment with another system working with standard material.

So, we have set up a Cooperative learning apparatus that uses only existing software tools.

III.1.1 - The necessary functionalities

To design a program collectively in a group with Hypercard, i.e. build together a structure stack, we have set up a relatively simple hardware and software platform. In the classroom, we have placed five Macintoshes ; we would like every user to have access to a shared work place where he will be able to cooperate with others for programming.

So everyone has a private space but can also work in the public space by activating a window that represents the screen of the Macintosh dedicated to cooperation. In this space, the cards can be handled by all the members of the group as if they were working on the host computer.

Likewise, each user can copy parts of the program in his private space.

III.1.2 - The implementation

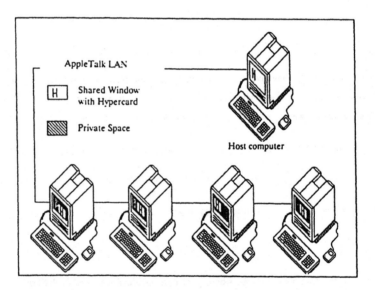

AppleTalk LAN

H   Shared Window
     with Hypercard

     Private Space

Host computer

System allowing multi-user access to Hypercard

The five computers are linked by the local appletalk network that offers the means of exchanging data between them and sharing some peripheral equipment such as a printer. We have used the software named "Timbuktu" [Farallon 89] that allows remote access to a station and remote control from a keyboard or mouse.

The connection provided by this software is dissymmetrical. One of the stations has to be the host of a second one. And the latter can control the host from its keyboard or its mouse.

On the host computer, it is as if there were two keyboards and two mice. So, in our classroom, we have a host station that supports the public space. This computer runs with Hypercard and all the others activate Timbuktu and control the host station.

During this session, a window is opened on each screen and everyone can see on his own screen the copy of the host window.

All the keyboards and mice can control the host station. So, the collective work has to be organized by one of the members of the group. This protocol is heavily backed up by the voice conversation.

The learners have to respect some discipline while working. When a user does not pilot the host, he takes his mouse out of the window in order not to disturb the others' work.

On the screen, a user can see two mouse-pointers : that of his own mouse in his private space and that of the telepointer of the host-machine. So, telepointing is possible and allows a user to point an object by circling it, for example.

IV - EVALUATION

Our purpose is, first, to evaluate the capabilities of the Timbuktu software in facilitating the cooperative learning and possibly to point out the deficiencies it can have ; and secondly to determine the possibility of using this apparatus for the prototyping (mock-up) of specialized tools for Collaborative Learning before their integration into the CoCoNut Platform.

IV.1 - Method

IV.1.1 - Subjects

A group of five students, at the graduate level in Instructional Technology of the University of Lille I who have little previous experience of Hypercard.

IV.1.2 - Protocol

During a course session on the collective design of a technical handbook of a video-recorder using Hypercard, each student has previously had a reflexion and has elaborated a handbook. Then, all the students are dispatched on the five workstations. Meanwhile, a big video screen permanently displays the operations and data running in the public space (i.e. the screen of the host computer) in order to recenter, at certain time, the students on the different stages of the task [Stefik 87].

A tutor is present in the room in order to answer to the questions of the students and manage the communications.

IV.1.3 - Data collecting

We collect two types of data :

- Video-record of the session at two levels :
    . the group interaction
    . each workstation.

- Recording of the operations run in the shared space (data displayed on the big video screen).

IV.1.4 - Data analysis

We analyse two principal aspects of the collectivisation apparatus :

- Firstly, the mode of cooperation that the system induces, the help and hindrances it introduces into the communication between learners.

- Secondly, the cognitive aspects induced by this type of task, namely the simultaneous management of the private and public spaces and the representation of the role that everyone has developed.

IV.2 - Results

IV.2.1 - The deficiencies of the actual system

We can point out some important deficiencies of Timbuktu : in fact, this software only redirects the input/output flow. It really does not allow us to share the objects of the public space. It is not possible to recover, by the classic operations of cut/past operations, the elements in the album of the host machine. The communication between the two spaces (private and public) is only possible through a data transfer that is merely a functionality offered by Timbuktu.

There is no tool for managing the collective work. All that organization is to be assumed by the users who have to adopt a discipline of their choice.

The window of the private space can be dimensioned but then we cannot be certain than all the users see the same things. On the other hand, Timbuktu always displays the zone where the pointer is and the screen zone where the learner is working.

We have also noticed that, when a Hypercard script loops, it becomes impossible to change the screens of the connected users. Moreover, the "play" operation of hypertalk is not transmitted to the connected stations.

IV.2.2 - Temporal data

We have calculated the ratio between the time the learners spend acting on the apparatus versus the time of verbal interactions (not using the system) :

. using the collective apparatus :	60 %
. verbal interactions :	40 %
. total time :	100 %

So, the time really spent using the system is relatively short.

IV.2.3 - Mode of cooperation

Finally, the learners use the system in order to see, in part the actions of everyone designing the technical handbook, but especially for visualizing the results of the actions.

Only one of the collaborators acts on the system, in the public space, and the other collaborators are only seeing what he is doing, giving sometimes criticisms.

The private space is never used.

IV.2.4 - Cognitive aspects

Social cognition is very difficult with such a system. Planning and negociation are always realized through the verbal channel or the blackboard. The system serve in consulting information stored in the data base, elaborating the successive specifications and detecting problems related to the specifications.

But the learners were not able to act simultaneously on the shared objects of the tasks, or to present really their own solutions of the problem.

In fact, the privatisation of the public space (the use of the public space by only one participant) do not permit everyone to have a good understanding of the successive states and transformations of the objects of the tasks.

V - CONCLUSION

The deficiencies of that software, if they don't hinder a collective use of hypercard, nevertheless denote certain weakness. As in the development systems and in the implementation, nothing has been done for the cooperative work. The level of access of the Timbuktu type softwares is too low to permit one to share the objects of the application. We think that the development system of the computers will have to offer some cooperative functionalities in order to facilitate the group work.

However, our purpose is to experiment with other traditional types of software (ideas organizer such as THINK-THANK, MORE, SPREAD SHEETS) in order to determine :

- the constraints in the writing of multi-user applications,
- the balance between verbal protocols and those supported by computers (conference manager - "Floor" algorithms...).

The key principle is to offer to the user a real guidance.

So, around a shared space achieved by some groupware, we have to re-introduce the role of the human mediator - such as a teacher or the peers - and a suitable environment that leads to human interaction and the construction of shared knowledge and social cognition according to our theoretical choices.

References :

[Bruner 87] Bruner J., Le développement de l'enfant : savoir faire, savoir dire, PUF, 1987.

[Derycke 88] Derycke A., Viéville C., Poisson D., Stach C., N'Guyen M., Le Nanoréseau : utilisations pédagogiques d'un réseau local. Technique et science informatique, Vol. 7, n° 1, Dunod, 1988, pp. 7-20.

[Derycke 90] Derycke A., Viéville C., Vilers P., Cooperation and communication in open learning : the CoCoNut project. Proceeding of the WCCE 90 - IFIP - Sidney - July 1990 - edited by North-Holland - pp. 957-962.

[Derycke 92] Derycke A., Viéville C., Vilers P. : Coopération et communication dans l'enseignement à distance : le projet CoCoNut. Génie Educatif N° 3, à paraître 1992, Editeur EC2.

[Ellis 91] Ellis C.A., Gibbs S.J., Rein G.L., Groupware some issues and experiences. Communication of the ACM, January 91, Vol. 34, n° 1.

[Farallon 89] Farallon : Notice of the software Timbuktu - 1989.

[Galegher 90] Galegher J., Kraut R., Egiolo C. : Intellectual team-work : social and technological foundations of cooperative work, Lawrence Erlbaum Associate, Hillsdale NJ, 1990.

[Hiltz 86] Hiltz S.R. : The virtual classroom : using computer mediated communication for University. Journal of Communication, 36(2), 1986, pp. 95-104.

[Kraemer 88] Kraemer K.L., King J.L. : Computer based systems for cooperative work and group decision making. ACM Computing surveys, Vol. 20, N° 2, June 1988, pp. 115-146.

[Mugny 85] Mugny G., Psychologie sociale du développement cognitif - Peter Lang, 1985.

[Stefik 87] Stefik M. & al. : Beyond the chelkboard : computer support collaboration and problem solving in meetings. Communication of the ACM, Vol. 30, N° 1, January 1987.

[Vygotsky 81] Vygotsky L.S., The Genesis of higher Mental Functions, In J. Wertsch (Ed) The Concept of Activity in Soviet Psychology, New York, Sinclaire Inc.

[Vygotsky 85] Vygotsky L., Pensée et Langage. Editions sociales, 1985.

[Yakemovic 90] Yakemovic B.K., Conklin E.J. : Report on a development project use of an issue-based information system. Proceeding of the CSCW'90 ACM Conférence, Los Angeles, October 7-10, 1990, pp. 105-118.

An ITS for Engineering Domains
Concept, Design and Application

Thomas Diessel, Axel Lehmann

Federal Armed Forces University, Munich

Computer Science Department

Germany

E-mail: diessel@informatik.unibw-muenchen.de

Abstract

This paper describes the concept of an intelligent tutoring system (ITS) for application in highly innovative technical domains, e.g. for training operators of public communication systems. The basic approach taken for student and tutor modelling is discussed, as well as the knowledge acquisition process for elicitation and representation of domain and tutor knowledge regarding domain specific restrictions. Finally, results of a test and a prototype implementation are presented.

1 Introduction

Most intelligent tutoring system (ITS) implementations are developed for application in 'classical' knowledge domains (e.g. geometry, LISP programming) characterized by the availability of time-independant, basic knowledge. Other implementations prevent new knowledge from falling into oblivion. In contrast, when using an ITS for teaching highly innovative disciplines (e.g. computer and communications systems) several specific restrictions have to be considered:

○ **Instability and Time Dependancy of Product Knowledge**

Most implemented 'classical' ITS deal with stable knowledge, mostly with facts (e.g. in teaching domains as LISP, algebra, geometry). For most technical application domains, completeness and time dependency of product knowledge depend on the products life cycles.

○ **Distribution and Inconsistency of Product Knowledge**

Especially for complex systems, product knowledge is distributed among various knowledge sources. As a result, consistency and completeness are not guaranteed.

○ **Multiple Usability of Product Knowledge**

Knowledge elicitation for structuring the basic domain knowledge should be processed only once taking into account different expert or knowledge based system applications applying this product knowledge (e.g. as diagnostic expert systems, intelligent tutoring systems or intelligent operation systems).

○ **Knowledge Categories and Knowledge Sources**

Engineering and product knowledge of innovative domains is composed of factual, temporary, fragmentary, unstable and heuristic knowledge resulting from extremly short product life cycles. Consequently, knowledge is distributed among various knowledge sources, especially among specialists mostly in a non-documented form.

○ **Concurrent Knowledge Acquisition**

An effective ITS application requires permanent updates. This demands permanent knowledge acquisition processed concurrently to product development and application.

As part of a joint research project with Siemens AG, Munich, different ITS approaches for the training of operators in the operation and maintenance of public telecommunication systems had to be evaluated taking into account these restrictions. For demonstration purposes, a test environment (*NTU*, see Sec. 2.2) and a prototype version (*USCHI*, see Sec. 3.4) of the suggested ITS approach were developed. Both systems benefit from the experiences obtained by the development of expert systems ([BFKL89], [BDFK91a]) and conventional computer aided instruction (CAI) systems (*KEE-Tutorial*, [MaWe90]).

2 Basic ITS Approach and Test

With respect to the specific restrictions resulting from the characteristics of innovative engineering domains (as discussed in Sec. 1), a conceptual ITS model was developed. For testing the conceptual model, the shell *NTU* (Neubiberg Test Unit) was implemented. *NTU* was applied for testing teaching-strategies assuming a fictitious domain structure.

2.1 Conceptual ITS Model for Engineering Domains

The proposed conceptual model is based on a hierarchical subdivision of the domain structure or the teaching subject respectively, into chapters C_i each covering a specific and strongly limited topic. This results in a hypertext similar structure of a course as shown in Fig. 1.

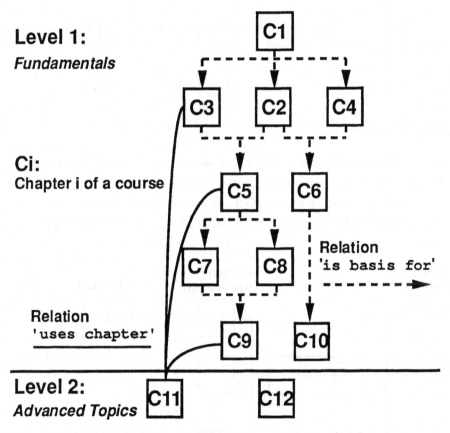

Figure 1: Hierarchical Structure of a fictitious Knowledge Domain / Course

Two categories of chapters are distinguished:

- O Fundamentals (all chapters are structured according the relation 'is basis for')
- O Advanced topics (related to the fundamental chapters by the relation 'uses chapter')

Each chapter in both levels is represented by different elements (T, L, R, A) (see Fig. 2 and 3). In level 1, a fundamental chapter consists of several lessons L_j each of them having different styles of information representation R_r. At the end of each chapter, tasks or examinations T_d with different degrees of difficulty have to be performed by the student.

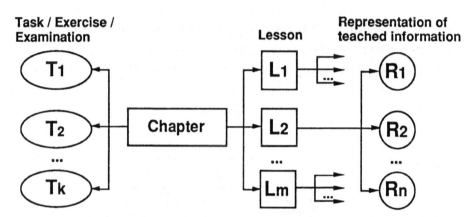

Figure 2: Level 1-chapters

The advanced topic chapters of level 2 have a slightly different structure. These include special lessons representing special approaches or examples of a special application A_s. These applications explain advanced topics to the student using convenient representations schemes R_r of chapters in level 1 (see Fig. 3). The lessons A_s can be regarded as 'pointers' to lessons L_i.

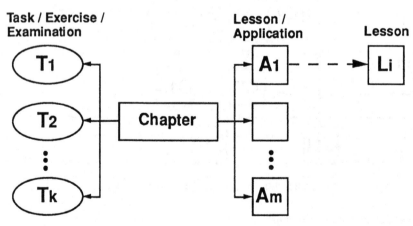

Figure 3: Level 2-chapters

In our approach, the dynamics of a teaching process result from choosing one of the following teaching strategies of a human tutor:

- ○ Application top-down: An application using knowledge of fundamental chapters is described. The required fundamentals are only explained if required.
- ○ Application bottom-up: First, the required fundamentals are explained followed by their application.
- ○ Introduction bottom-up: A complete introduction into the domain is given starting with basic chapters from the fundamentals.

2.2 Test Environment (NTU)

NTU was especially developed as a test shell of the conceptual ITS model summarized in Sec. 2.1. Functionality and system control of *NTU* is shown in Fig. 4.

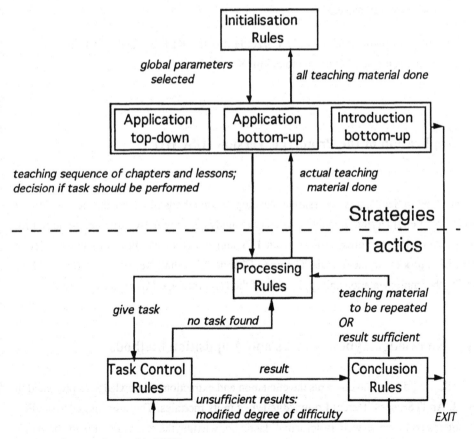

Figure 4: System Control in NTU

NTU uses several rule sets divided into two classes: the rules of the strategic layer determine the sequence of the instructed chapters; the rules of the tactic layer reason on the student's performance and control the local actions within a lesson.

Strategic teaching rule sets

○ Initilization (initialization of the student model setting values for the aim, application, teaching strategy, teaching style, degree of difficulty and other parameters.)

○ Strategy (application top-down, application bottom-up, introduction bottom-up)

Tactic teaching rule sets

○ Processing (present the teaching material in a representation form R_r to the student)

○ Task Control (manage the task provision using a task T_d)

○ Conclusion (evaluate the task results; reasons on the appropriate form of representation, teaching style, degree of difficulty and the lessons to be repeated for the individual student.)

NTU has been implemented on a SUN 3/260HM using KEE 3.1 and Sun CommonLISP 2.1.3. Further details of *NTU* can be found in [Könn90].

3 Application of the Prototype Version (USCHI)

As discussed in Sec. 1, it is necessary to develop new methods of knowledge acquisition for an ITS in an engineering domain. This chapter analyses knowledge structures required for domain knowledge representation in an ITS and gives an example of the knowledge acquisition process in the domain 'Common Channel Signaling Network Control (CCNC)'. Finally, the implementation and application of the ITS prototype *USCHI* are described.

3.1 Knowledge Types, Sources and Acquisition Methods

The following discussion concerns the elicitation and extraction of knowledge as presented in Sec. 2. An ITS uses different **knowledge types** in its modules. The tutor module (see Fig. 7) contains common as well as domain didactic knowledge, the expert module the domain's technical knowledge. The tutor module uses knowledge about common didactic for the control of the teaching process. This knowledge is supposed to be common for different knowledge domains. In general, there is also available didactic knowledge specific for a knowledge domain. It has to be acquired for each application domain seperately and has to be represented in either the tutor or in the expert module.

There are different **knowledge sources** which can be distinguished as primary and secondary sources. Primary knowledge sources create or collect original knowledge. Secondary knowledge sources present knowledge that has been retrieved from a primary knowledge source and converted in a form useful for specific applications.

Primary knowledge sources are:

○ Human Experts - The experts can be engineers or teachers. They usually offer their knowledge in an unstructured form. This knowledge (including didactic and domain knowledge) has to be elicited and converted. Different methods for knowledge elicitation are discussed below.

○ Data Bases - A data base contains knowledge in a structured form. This knowledge is mostly factual knowledge about a specific domain. It can be compiled by humans or automatically by machines, e.g. it can be retrieved by an expert system or an ITS.

○ Documentation - There a different types of documentation (e.g. specifications, manuals) that contain different knowledge types written for different groups of readers: developers, engineers, users, customers, etc. There are also different abstraction levels for product documentation (e.g. for novice or experienced users). Documentations are mostly written in prose. These presentations can be used within an ITS [LeGB90].

Secondary knowledge sources can be:

○ Knowledge Based Systems or Expert Systems - The knowledge base of an expert system (XPS) contains domain knowledge. If appropriately (e.g. application independent) represented this can be used or transformed for a specific ITS application.

○ CAI Systems - Presentations of domain knowledge applied in CAI systems can be mostly re-used in an ITS.

Knowledge acquisition is performed by a knowledge engineer as the ITS developer. Experts are engineers and teachers. The following knowledge acquisiton methods can be applied for the elicitation of domain expert knowledge; but not all methods are applicable to elicit the tutors strategies and tactics:

O Observation and Tracing: The knowledge engineer observes experts or teachers performing their tasks.

O Explanation and Justification of Actions: The knowledge engineer observes the working expert who has to explain and to justify each action taken for problem solving. This very time-consuming but efficient procedure [BDFK91b] is not really applicable in the classroom.

O Interviews

O Questionnaire

3.2 Prototype Domain

The knowledge and application domain of the ITS prototype *USCHI* is the operation of the common channel signaling system #7 in a digital switching system (e.g. EWSD from Siemens) [Dies91]. Opposite to previous signaling systems the signaling information is transmitted separately from voice or data on a special channel (see Fig. 5). One part of an operator course named 'CCNC' is concerned with training technicians how to operate the Common Channel Signaling Network Control (CCNC).

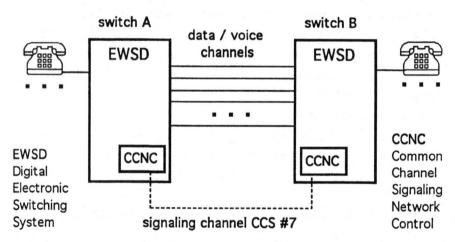

Figure 5: Common Channel Signaling System #7 (CCS #7)

The structure of the course, selected as application domain for the prototype implementation of the suggested conceptual ITS model, was structured according our approach in Fig. 1. In Fig. 6, the course structure is shown. It contains only chapters from the fundamental level 1 of the structure model given in Sec. 2.

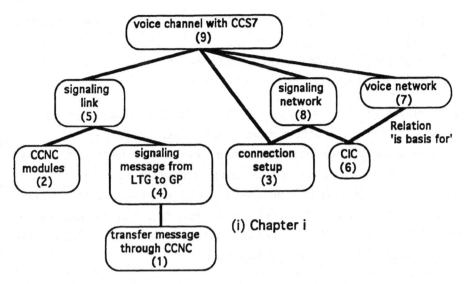

Figure 6: Chapture structure of the Prototype Domain 'CCNC'

3.3 Knowledge Acquisition Process

Knowledge elicitation for *USCHI* was stepwise performed by the knowledge engineers:

1. Study of introductory readings and manuals (for understanding the domain)
2. Participation in classroom lessons of the 'CCNC' course (for structuring the domain knowledge into chapters)
3. Unstructured interviews with the teacher of 'CCNC' (to determine common didactic rules)
4. Questionnaire including structured interviews for the teacher (for elicitation of domain specific didactic knowledge).

The questionnaire was not given to the teacher before starting the interview, avoiding misunderstandings and having chances for further inquiries. It was developed after the first unstructured interview with the teacher when the teacher's basic didactic principles in the classroom were discussed. The questionnaire covers the following topics:

O Number of the chapter
O Expected task solution time (After that time the teacher will discuss the task with the student.)
O Chapter's relative importance the teacher gives to chapter (Relatively unimportant chapters can be skipped depending on the time limits available.)

○ Type of the chapter (E.g. detailled chapters for advanced students and repetitative chapters.)

○ Categories of the student answers and results for given tasks (The results are classified into five categories. The teacher was asked for the definition of these.)

Typical errors made by students were discribed by the teacher and classified using this scheme of the questionnaire. In addition, resulting reactions were described.

The evaluation of the questionnaire confirmed the proposed structure for the domain shown in Fig. 6. This approach should prevent from getting inconsistence in the domain structure. The result of the interviews and the questionnaire evaluation was expressed by 18 rules (LISP). The knowledge elicited by following this acquisition procedure included common didactic and domain didactic. The written class room course for the domain 'CCNC' was used as basis material for the domain knowledge acquisition.

3.4 Architecture of *USCHI*

USCHI ('Unterricht durch SCHülergerechte Instruktion', instruction by student adapted teaching) was the first ITS prototype for applying our conceptual model according Sec. 2.

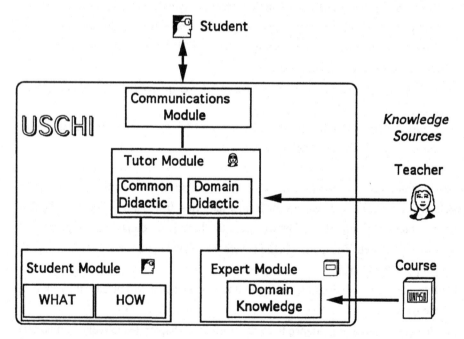

Figure 7: Architecture of USCHI

The goals for the *USCHI* implementation are:

- ○ Demonstration of our conceptual approach
- ○ Getting experiences using an ITS in an engineering domain
- ○ Comparing efficicency and acceptance of an ITS in contrast to a conventional CAI system.

The architecture of *USCHI* and its knowledge sources are shown in Fig. 7. *USCHI*'s student model is divided in two parts: The WHAT part is summarizing what chapters a student has worked on and what he already should know. The other part states HOW the student learns, e.g. the preferred style of chapter presentation. This module separation is according to the suggestion of [Vass90]. Each chapter got three forms of information representations: theoretical, figurative and practical. The chapter structure based on that of *NTU*'s fundamental level is shown in Fig. 8.

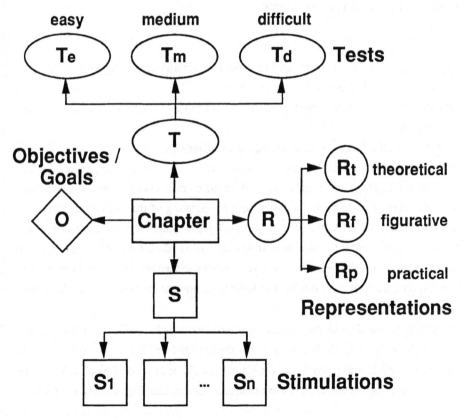

Figure 8: Structure of USCHI's Chapters

The selected presentation or teaching style can be influenced by the student using teaching buttons [ScJo90], e.g. 'to easy', 'to difficult', 'uninteresting'. There are three implemented test levels offering tasks and examinations with different degrees of difficulty. Some tasks have additional questions. This structure includes the chapters objectives O. The different forms of representations R and tests T are limited to three different types. Furthermore, there are information representations S offering additional stimulating tasks and comments to the student.

USCHI runs on a SUN 3/260 with Sun CommonLISP 2.1.3 and KEE 3.1 or a SUN SPARCstation 1 with LISP 4.0 and KEE 4.0. It can be demonstrated in our institute. A detailed description of USCHI is given in [West91].

4   Conclusions and Future Work

This paper proposes a new conceptual ITS modell especially regarding requirements of teaching and training students in innovative engineering domains. It describes the general approach, its test and prototype implementation for the application domain 'Common Channel Signaling Network Control (CCNC)'.

Our current research efforts are concentrated on the adaption and transformation of already existing knowledge bases for inclusion in an ITS's expert model. A prototype named CLIO ('ConfiguratiOn LearnIng') is currently designed for the domain 'configuration of a switching system's coordination processor'. To ensure proper operating of the switching system, its units have to be in defined states. When configuring the system e.g. for operation or for diagnostic purposes not all state transitions are allowed. CLIO will use rules for representation of domain knowledge. These rules will be extracted from an already existing diagnosis expert system of this domain. The basic structure and the didactic knowledge will be applied from USCHI.

The teacher's understanding of the student's misconceptions is based on experiences. After being a teacher for a while she/he knows what the required lessons are to correct typical student's errors. This learning process of the teacher should be processed by an ITS too. For that reason, we will implement and test a dynamic and adaptive teaching strategy in CLIO.

References

[BDFK91a] M. Berberich, Th. Diessel, A. Lehmann et. al. *Expertensystem-Prototyp zur Fehlerdiagnose und Wartungsunterstützung in rechnergesteuerten Vermittlungssystemen.* KI. Vol. 3/91, pp. 34-40. ISSN 0933-1875.

[BDFK91b] M. Berberich, Th. Diessel, A. Lehmann et. al. *Erfahrungen bei Planung, Entwicklung und Test eines Expertensystems zur Fehlerdiagnose und Wartungsunterstützung in rechnergesteuerten Vermittlungssystemen.* KI. Vol. 4/91, pp. 32-40. ISSN 0933-1875.

[BFKL89] M. Berberich, A. Lehmann et. al. *An Expert System Approach for Maintenance Support of EWSD Switches.* IEEE - International Conference on Communications (ICC '89), Boston (USA), June 1989.

[Dies91] Th. Diessel. *Intelligente Lehrsysteme - Entwicklung, Aufbau und Anwendung.* Federal Armed Forces University, Munich, UniBwM Internal report no. 9111, December 1991.

[Könn90] T. Könneke. *Grundkonzepte für intelligente Lehrsysteme.* Federal Armed Forces University, Munich, Diploma-thesis UniBwM ID-30/90, 1990.

[LeGB90] K.A.M. Lemmen, W.J. Gillisen and K.L. Boon. *The Direct Use of Already Existing User Manuals for Computer Aided Instruction and Information Retrieval with the Aid of Hypermedia.* Proceedings ICCAL '90, Hagen (Germany), pp. 277-287.

[MaWe90] A. Mayer and M. Westermann. *Erweiterung des KEE-Tutorials zur Einarbeitung in wissensbasierte Systeme.* Federal Armed Forces University, Munich, thesis UniBwM IT-17/90, 1990.

[ScJo90] R.C. Schank, R.C. and M.Y. Jona. *Empowering the Student: New Perspectives on the Design of Teaching Systems.* The Institute for the Learning Sciences, Northwestern University, Evanston, IL (USA), August 1990.

[Vass90] J. Vassileva. *A Classification and Synthesis of Student Modelling Techniques in Intelligent Computer-Assisted Instruction.* Proceedings ICCAL '90, Hagen (Germany), pp. 202-213.

[West91] M. Westermann. *USCHI: Ein wissensbasiertes Lehrsystem für die Domäne "Steuerung der zentralen Zeichengabekanäle in Vermittlungssystemen".* Federal Armed Forces University, Munich, 1990, Diploma-thesis UniBwM ID-25/91.

Acknowledgements

We would like to thank our students Michael Westermann and Thorsten Könneke for their fruitful and engaged cooperation and prototype implementations.

Structuring the Subject Matter

U. Dumslaff, J. Ebert

Computer Science Department

University of Koblenz

D-W5400 Koblenz, Rheinau 3–4, Germany

Tel.: +49 261 9119–436

Email: uro@infko.uni-koblenz.de

Abstract

The three main paradigms of computer based tutoring systems are computer assisted instruction, hypertext, and intelligent tutoring. Each of these uses a characteristic combination of models and representations for the four instructional architecture components, namely the subject matter, the learner model, the didactic expertise, and the communication interface. A brief survey on these main paradigms emphasizes their subject matter components. These considerations are used to develop a graph based subject matter structuring approach for conceptual as well as for procedural knowledge as the core of a computer based tutoring system architecture.

1 Introduction

Every kind of instructional system allows the identification of four different necessary components, namely the subject matter, the knowledge about the learner, the didactic expertise, and the communication interface (see [Wenger87]). The *subject matter knowledge* offers the topics and themes to communicate about, directed by the instructional objectives. The *knowledge about the learner* is essential for understanding the learner's comprehension of the subject matter and for reasoning about her/his learning capabilities. The *didactic expertise* is responsible for topic selection and presentation, taking the subject matter knowledge and the learner's knowledge into consideration. The *communication interface* arranges an adequate and efficient dialogue between the learner and the tutoring system regarding the objectives and the learner's capabilities.

These components form also the basis for most computer based tutoring system and may be realized in different ways, following various theories and models and using different representation techniques. There are *three main paradigms* of computer based tutoring systems:

- the conventional *computer assisted instruction* (CAI) systems,
- the *hypertext based instruction* (HBI) systems, and
- the *intelligent tutoring* systems (ITS).

Each of these approaches has its own history driven by the research and development activities in the respective fields.

In this paper we motivate and describe a graph based subject matter structuring approach, using results from these main paradigms. For that purpose, the next section gives a brief survey on these, focussing on the subject matter knowledge component. A graph based subject matter structure model is introduced in section three. Section four describes an overall computer based tutoring system architecture around the subject matter graph as an instance of the instructional architecture. The ideas are summarized in the conclusion.

2 Forms of computer based tutoring systems

The characteristic shapes of the instructional components as realized by the three main paradigms of computer based tutoring systems are outlined in the following. Starting with the particular goals of each approach, we skeletonize the respective realization of the necessary instructional components. This requires the characterization of subject matter representation, the description of didactic knowledge representation (or application), the explanation of the information used about the learner, and the communication efforts.

CAI systems — The origins of CAI systems can be found in behaviorism research and its linear programmed instruction [Skin58]. Linear programmed instruction was transferred on computers and extended by branching structures, allowing anticipated reactions on the learner's behavior. Today, CAI systems still follow the same principles though they now use sophisticated media support and modern computer technology [Bier91].

Subject matter in CAI-systems is encoded in a collection of so-called frames consisting of text fragments, graphics, and perhaps video sequences. These frames contain e.g. definitions, explanations, examples, problem solving demonstrations, and questions related to the subject matter. They form a pool of independent and unordered items of the knowledge to be learned. The (human) subject matter expert, who maps her/his knowledge into the system via computer presentable frames, is responsible for the frame contents (see [AlTr85]). An explicit representation of this knowledge is not available. Hence, poor support for reasoning about the encoded knowledge is available.

Instructional objectives and the learner profile are the basis for frame pool structuring using branching structures and applying didactic expertise. The learner model is reduced to a statistical model of the frames displayed and the answers given on questions. These data drive the path selection strategy through the branching structure of frames. Communication between the CAI system and the learner is realized by frame presentation, controlled by the branching structure and the primitive learner model, and by question answering facilities using simple interaction techniques.

Hypertext systems — The term hypertext denotes the nonlinear representation of arbitrary documents. This involves the existence of a nonlinear document structure of nodes, which contain document fragments, and links between these nodes. Nielsen considers a hypertext as a belief network to the extent that if two nodes are linked together, then we believe that their contents are related in some way [Niel90, p.140].

As in CAI systems subject matter is not represented explicitly. The goal is to design and implement a nonlinear document containing the subject matter topics. The CAI system frames correspond to hypertext nodes as containers for text and graphic fragments (possibly extended by interaction fragments like e.g. the question answering tasks). The step beyond the CAI frame pools are the node links, which reflect an expert's view on the domain. Therefore, the knowledge is encoded in large data bases realizing the above mentioned belief networks.

Hypertext usage for computer based tutoring systems (see also [JoMa90]) means the application of two divergent didactic strategies, namely discovery learning (if this is a strategy at all) and guided tutoring, involving the pre-selection of suited paths. The most important information about the learner are the nodes visited and the paths used. Both together preserve an image about the learner's navigation strategy through a hypertext. Since hypertexts are primarily documents, the communication interface supports presentation and orientation facilities, where the latter ensure that the learner always knows her/his position in the hypertext.

Intelligent tutoring systems — Unsatisfied with the results of the activities in the domain of CAI systems, Carbonell proposed in his well known paper [Carb70] the *information structure oriented paradigm* for computer based tutoring systems using semantic networks as a model for explicit knowledge representation. He encouraged new directions in the communicational framework between human and machine in the instructional context. One consequence was the attempt to consider and implement the instructional system components as separate exchangeable software modules.

In contrast to CAI systems and hypertext systems, ITSs use an explicit knowledge representation for the subject matter. The goal is to develop cognitive models simulating human problem solving within a given domain. Typically, knowledge is distinguished into declarative knowledge, procedural knowledge and qualitative process models [Ande88]. Declarative knowledge represents concepts and facts, which are appropriately organized so that reasoning about them is enabled. Procedural knowledge is knowledge of how to perform welldefined complex tasks. Qualitative process models are responsible for the causal knowledge which allows to reason about processes, especially the comprehension of cause-effect chains.

The didactic knowledge of ITSs is either deeply encoded in that part which controls the tutorial interaction, inheriting the basic ideas from traditional CAI by refining the topic sequencing algorithms, or it is realized as an explicit didactic module by using rule-based models of didactic expertise. Learner models in ITSs have three aspects. These are the information about the learner, its representation and the diagnostic process [Wenger87]. The goal is to reconstruct the knowledge really acquired by observing and interpreting the learner's activities. Furthermore, ITSs try to enable a human-like communication based on natural language capabilities.

3 Subject matter graphs

In the following, we introduce a subject matter structuring approach. For this, we define a graph of vertices and edges representing the subject matter structure. This graph is divided into two different graph types, one denoting a *concept structure* and the other a *procedural task*. Although the two graph types can be defined separately, their integration forms the complete *subject matter graph* by using special edge types between them.

Concept graphs — Concepts are, as defined in [Brac85], formal objects used to represent objects, attributes, and relationships of the domain being modeled. A concept graph exactly reflects these demands by having object classes as nodes and relationships as edges. The *concept nodes* contain the attributes of a concept, where an *attribute* is composed of an *attribute name* and an associated *attribute domain*.

Hence, a concept graph node is described by $C(a_1:d_1,\ldots,a_n:d_n)$, where C is the concept name and a_i is an attribute name with its associated domain d_i.

The skeleton of a concept graph is based on the *subtype*, the *supertype* and the *part-of* relationships. Their definitions are based on the attributes of the particular concepts involved. The subtype relationship between two concept graph nodes represents the fact, that two objects have similar features and one of them is a specialization of the other, perhaps having some additional attributes. A formal definition of C_y *is a subtype of* C_x is:

$$
\begin{aligned}
isSubtype(C_x, C_y) \;\Rightarrow\; & C_x(a_1 : t_1, \ldots, a_n : t_n) \\
\wedge \;\; & C_y(a_1 : t_1^y, \ldots, a_n : t_n^y, b_1 : d_1^y, \ldots, b_k : d_k^y) \\
\wedge \;\; & \forall i, 1 \le i \le n : t_i^y \subseteq t_i
\end{aligned}
$$

C_y inherits the attributes of C_x, where the attribute domains are equal or subsets of those from C_x, and C_y has the additional attributes b_i. The supertype relationship between two concept graph nodes is the inverse of the subtype relationship. The part-of relation is based on the fact that every attribute denotes a part of a concept. If a concept itself is used as an attribute domain, this will be represented as a part-of edge between this attribute and the associated concept node (see [DuEb91]).

An example of a concept is the *finite automaton* FA [HoU179], which has the subtypes deterministic FA and nondeterministic FA. It has the attributes *state* (Φ), *input alphabet* (Σ), *start state* (S), *final state set* (F) and *state transition function* (δ). The state transition function δ of the *deterministic* finite automaton (DFA) always delivers exactly one succeeding state on an input, whereas a *nondeterministic* finite automaton (NFA) yields a set of succeeding states. Thus, the concept FA has the concept structure: $FA(\Phi{:}2^{\mathcal{N}}, \Sigma{:}2^{ch}, F{:}2^{\mathcal{N}}, S{:}\mathcal{N}, \delta{:} ((\mathcal{N} \times ch \to \mathcal{N}) \cup (\mathcal{N} \times \Sigma \to 2^{\mathcal{N}})))$, depicted as a concept graph in Fig. 1 (where $\mathcal{N}$ is a finite number set and ch a final character set).

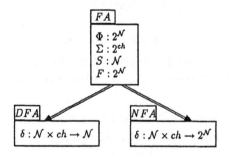

Fig. 1: A concept graph for FA with DFA and NFA as subtypes

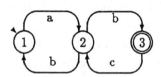

Fig. 2: An instance N_1 of the concept NFA

An *instance* of a concept is an example with an assigned value for every attribute from its associated domain. An instance N_1 of the concept NFA is depicted in Fig. 2 as a state transition diagram.

Concept hierarchies are extendable by *user defined relations* between concepts as proposed by (extended) Entity Relationship Models or by semantic data models as described in [ElNa89]. For example, a finite automaton specifies exactly one *regular language*, consisting of sequences, alternatives and iterations of symbols [HoUl79]. Fig. 3 indicates this *many to one relation* between FA and regular languages (RL). Such relations beyond the hierarchy relations are sometimes inherited by all subtype concepts. Here, $DFAs$ as well as $NFAs$ describe regular languages.

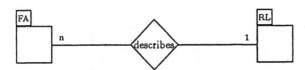

Fig. 3: A concept graph for the *describes* relation between the concepts FA and RL

Procedure graphs — Procedures are goal driven and well defined methods or algorithms which modify or construct concept instances in a well describable manner. Thus, procedures model the knowledge about how to perform a given task. The procedure graph represents this kind of knowledge.

A complex procedure is decomposable into its particular *actions*. Before an action can be performed, some *preconditions* have to been met. The result of an action is its *effect*. A procedure works on concept instances and an action works on the attributes of these concept instances by changing or initializing their values. Preconditions and effects can be specified by predicate logic calculus expressions, where the preconditions express the demands on the *input data* and the effects describe features of the *output data* with respect to the input data of an action.

The nodes of a procedure graph are the particular actions which consist of the action name, its preconditions and its effects. The action name is extended by a *signature* which declares the mapping between the input attribute domains and the output attribute domains the action works upon. An action node template is depicted in Fig. 4.

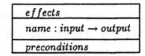

Fig. 4: A template for action nodes

Essential for performing successfully a procedural task is the application of the actions in a correct order where usually more then one action ordering is possible [Spen88]. An action can be performed only if its preconditions are satisfied. An action's effects may be be part of the preconditions of other actions. So, there exists a relationship between the actions of a procedure in that way, that the effects of one action or the conjunction of the effects of more than one action form the preconditions of other actions. Furthermore, there exists an information flow between the actions. The output of one action could be part of the input of one or more other actions. The effects of an action are formulated on the output data (with respect to the corresponding input data) and the preconditions are formulated on the input data. Altogether, a procedure graph can be regarded as a nonlinear plan structure.

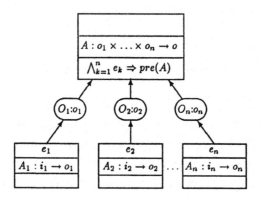

Fig. 5: The effect–precondition relationship between actions ($e_1 \wedge \ldots \wedge e_n \Rightarrow pre(A)$)

These relationships between actions and input/output data are represented as directed edges between action nodes and data nodes in a data flow procedure graph as sketched in Fig. 5. A procedure graph is well defined if all elements of the action set of the corresponding procedure are interconnected by such edges and at least one action node has as its effect the goal of the complete procedure. If necessary, an action can again be treated as a procedure specifiable and refinable with the same means (e.g. if an attribute domain is a concept and an action has to modify this complex concept).

Since a procedure graph gives a declarative description of particular procedure actions and their relationships, the action nodes can be attached with operational descriptions. This can be done by applying conventional software engineering methods like control flow charts, Nassi-Shneiderman diagrams or any programming language.

Subject matter graphs — Either single concept graphs or procedure graphs together with concept graphs form the subject matter graphs. For the second case some relations between concept nodes and data nodes have to be introduced and realized as edges. Since at least one concept node denotes the input type of a procedure, a concept node can be linked by an input edge with the associated input data node. Similary, the output data node of the procedure graph is connected with that concept node which represents the output of the procedure (these edges are bold face in Fig. 6).

An example of a procedure employes the introduced concepts DFA and NFA. This procedure *NfaToDfa* (with its procedure graph in Fig. 6) transforms one NFA instance N into an *equivalent* $(\equiv)$ DFA instance D [HoUl79].

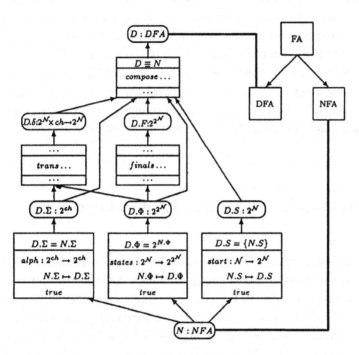

Fig. 6: A subject matter graph for *NfaToDfa* using the concept FA from Fig. 1.

The essence of this procedure *NfaToDfa* is that every set of NFA-states which is reachable from one state $(N.\Phi)$ by an input symbol $(\in N.\Sigma)$ in N is treated as a unique state $(\in D.\Phi)$ in D. For this, the action *states* computes the new states, *start* builds the new start state, the alphabet is taken over by *alph*, the final states of D are computed by *finals*, and *trans* determines the changed state transition function for D with respect to the new states. Finally, *compose* builds the equivalent DFA D by arranging the previously computed parts.

A procedure can also be depicted as an action node. To differentiate a procedure node from an action node, the first is double framed. Therefore, Fig. 7 is a delineation of the procedure node for *NfaToDfa* where Fig. 6 presents the corresponding refinement.

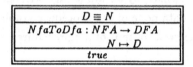

Fig. 7: A procedure node for *NfaToDfa*

Summary — Subject matter graphs as introduced above offer a basis for subject matter structuring. They support concept structuring by dividing concepts into their attribute components and using their domains to describe relations between different concepts. On the other hand, they support the structuring of methods or algorithms by dividing them into their particular actions and describing the data flow between these actions including the relationships between the respective preconditions and effects. A person who has the task to build a computer based tutoring system can use these means for organizing the subject matter knowledge component.

4 Implications for the instructional architecture

The implications and effects of subject matter graphs on the remaining instructional components are outlined in the following. Although the focal point of this paper is on the support of knowledge structuring and organization, the described approach has interesting implications for the remaining instructional components which can be arranged around this knowledge structuring approach to achieve a sound instructional architecture.

Learner model — The concept graph delivers a solid basis for representing the learner's knowledge with respect to a concept structure. It is clearly identifiable which concepts are mastered on which level, which attributes are known and which relationships between concepts are understood. Similary, a procedure graph can be used to represent the learner's comprehension of a procedure regarding the particular actions, their underlying plan structure (e.g. partial order) and the concepts involved. Hence, diagnosis is supported for determining the learner's *preknowledge*, for declaring the *learning objectives* and for processing *learner's progress* (see [DuEbMe91]).

This dynamic information about an individual learner and the associated modifying operations can be represented as an overlay on a subject matter graph. Furthermore, a set of rules allows reasoning on the learner model e.g. if the learner knows a procedure she/he knows the input/output concepts. If the learner does not know the input/output concepts, one can infer directly that she/he does not know the associated procedure(s).

Didactic expertise — While the learner's preknowledge and the objectives are a kind of static information about the learner which is anticipated or defined by the designer, the learning process is highly dynamic. The main objectives of concept learning are the mastering of discrimination and generalization tasks [MeTe77]. Starting with the learner's preknowledge, this requires to find an efficient arrangement of explanations, definitions, examples, counter examples and practices to introduce the new information about concept attributes and their dependencies on the one hand and about concepts with their relationships on the other hand.

Essential is the support of embedding this new information into the learner's (pre)knowledge about the domain. Responsible for this is the didactic expertise which directs the interaction between the learner and the tutoring system and reacts adequately on the learner's progress with respect to the objectives. The didactic knowledge is representable as a set of rules which can be applied on a learner model and a subject matter graph. The result of this application is a plan [PeMc86], consisting of teaching and learning operations [DuEbMe91]. Such a set of rules reflects a didactic strategy (e.g. a bottom-up strategy from the attributes to a concept or a top-down strategy from a concept to its subtype concepts). Usually, more than one didactic strategy should be available and the designer has to select one or has to develop her/his own didactic strategy as a set of rules. The strategy application results in a plan proposal which is modifiable by the designer.

The same interpretation is obviously possible with the procedure graphs including the connected input and output concepts. The main objectives of procedure learning are transferrable procedure learning skills within a domain [VaBr80]. This can be reached by using similar ideas as in concept learning and teaching. If the objective is the mastering of a whole procedure it is easily inferrable that all actions, the possible ordering, including the semantics of the corresponding relationships, and the concepts it is applied on have to be treated during the learning process. In this case also plans are computable which reflect different didactic strategies. As an example, a procedure can be introduced in a bottom-up data driven style starting with the input concepts or it can be learned and teached by a method driven strategy in a kind of backward chaining by concentrating on the construction of the output concept instances. Here also the proposed plans are modifiable by the designer.

Nevertheless, the most powerful facility comes from a learner progress diagnosis which allows the definition of criteria for didactic strategy changes. This results in on-line replanning by using another set of rules representing didactic expertise.

Such criteria are e.g. the stagnancy of the learning process, the reaching of learning impasses or the learner herself/himself requests a method change.

Communication interface — Didactic expertise has the to decide in every instructional situation which topic to communicate about and how to interact with the learner. The first task is covered by the didactic planner which follows a strategy to traverse a subject matter graph and to select the topics. The second task lies in the responsibility of the tutoring system designer. For this, tiny dialogue fragments, containing text and graphics for definitions, examples, practices, or tests, can be attached to every part of a subject matter graph. Anchor points for attaching dialogues in a subject matter graph are the concept nodes, their attributes including the domains, action nodes as well as their parts, data nodes, and all types of edges.

These dialogue fragments can be composed of presentation and interaction items. The learning and teaching operators, mentioned in the context of didactic strategies, employ these dialogue fragments for the communication about subject matter between the learner and the tutoring system. It is finally the didactic strategy which decides the balance of interaction between the learner and the tutoring system. The interaction diagrams of [Jacob86] are employed as an adequate model for the overall dialogue structure of a tutoring system, coordinating the particular fragments.

Overall architecture — Subject matter graphs together with the above outlined aspects of tutoring systems form a complete instance of the basic instructional architecture. Each component is clearly isolatable with respect to its tasks and features and can be defined separately. The subject matter graph is the core of the architecture. The designer's tasks are sketched as well as their support, which is deliverable by using this architecture (see [DuMe91]). Another valuable aspect is the maintainability and reusability of developed parts. A didactic strategy can be applied on different subject matter graphs, the dialogue fragments can be modified locally since the relevant information is always nearby in the subject matter graph and additionally, information about the learner or the intended objectives can be modified directly.

5 Conclusion

It is quite natural, that each computer based tutoring system structures its subject matter. In CAI systems this is realized by the designer's frame ordering, applying some didactic strategies. HBI systems usually are only restricted to labeled links, where the wide range of information may have very little semantic structure [CaRa90].

ITS development is usually a labor-intensive, hand-crafted task with little reusability and maintainability features. The effects of this specific properties are well known.

The subject matter structuring approach with subject matter graphs proposed here intends to merge these ideas by taking the best of all, resulting in an architecture for a limited form of ITS. The subject matter graph is built on a proper, formally defined syntax and an associated semantics (as in ITS). The graph based nature of subject matter structuring including the attaching of dialogue fragments allows a restricted form of idea structuring (as in HBI systems). The status of natural language processing today is not so far developed, that one is able to order and install a corresponding tool. This is the reason why we prefer to use tiny dialogue fragments (as in CAI systems) which are directly related to the underlying subject matter structure. The realization of explicit learner models and explicit didactic knowledge is reached only by ITS. Our approach follows these ideas with the available means.

Domains which are representable by subject matter graphs can be found in engineering sciences, computer sciences or technical domains. It seems, that they have to be well structured and defined axiomatically (as in existing ITS). Future work tries to find ways to open the spectrum without loss of clarity.

Acknowledgment — The authors want to thank Dirk Meyerhoff for many discussions and valuable comments

References

[AlTr85] S.M. Alessi and S.R. Trollip. *Computer-based Instruction: Methods and Development*. Prentice Hall, Englewood Cliffs, NJ, 1985.

[Ande88] J.R. Anderson. The expert module. In C.M. Polson and J.J. Richardson, editors, *Foundations of Intelligent Tutoring Systems*, chapter 2, pages 21–53. Lawrence Erlbaum, Hillsdale, New Jersey, 1988.

[Bier91] D.J. Bierman. To be intelligent or not to be intelligent: Is that the question? In Forte [Forte91], page 25.

[Brac85] R.J. Brachman. On the epistemological status of semantic networks. In *Readings in Knowledge Represantation*, chapter 10, pages 191–215. Morgan Kaufmann, Los Altos, CL, 1985.

[CaRa90] D.A. Carlson and Sudha Ram. Hyperintelligence: The next frontier. *Communications of the ACM*, 33(3):311–321, 1990.

[Carb70] J. Carbonell. AI in CAI: Artificial intelligence approach to computer-assisted instruction. *IEEE Trans. on Man-Machine Systems*, 11(4):190–202, 1970.

[DuEb91] U. Dumslaff and J. Ebert. Courseware development by concept structuring. In Forte [Forte91], page 115.

[DuEbMe91] U. Dumslaff, J. Ebert, and D. Meyerhoff. Nonlinear plan generation for concept teaching (in german). In R. Gunzenhäuser and H. Mandl, editors, *Vierter Workshop der Fachgruppe "Intelligente Lernsysteme" der Gesellschaft für Informatik*, Rauischholzhausen, 1991.

[DuMe91] U. Dumslaff and D. Meyerhoff. A tutoring system architecture to support the design process. In H.-J. Bullinger, editor, *Proceedings of the 4th International Conference on Human-Computer Interaction, Stuttgart, September 1991*. North Holland, Elsevier Science Publishers, Amsterdam, 1991.

[ElNa89] R. Elmasri and S.B. Navathe. *Fundamentals of Database Systems*. Benjamin/Cummings, Redwood City, CL, 1989.

[Forte91] E.N. Forte, editor. *CALISCE '91 – Proceedings of the International Conference on Computer Aided Learning and Instruction in Science and Engineering*. Presses Polytechnique et Universitaires Romandes, Lausanne, 1991.

[HoUl79] J.E. Hopcroft and J.D. Ullmann. *Introduction to Automata Theory, Languages and Computation*. Addison-Wesley, Reading, MA, 1979.

[Jacob86] R.J.K. Jacob. A specification language for direct manipulation interfaces. *ACM Transactions on Graphics*, 5(4):283–317, October 1986.

[JoMa90] D.H. Jonassen and H. Mandl, editors. *Designing Hypermedia for Learning*, volume 67 of *F NATO ASI*. Springer, Berlin, 1990.

[MeTe77] M.D. Merrill and R.D. Tennyson. *Teaching Concepts: An Instructional Design Guide*. Educational Technology, Englewood Cliffs, NJ, 1977.

[Niel90] J. Nielsen. *Hypertext and Hypermedia*. Academic Press, San Diego, CA, 1990.

[PeMc86] D.R. Peachey and G.I. McCalla. Using planning techniques in intelligent tutoring systems. *International Journal of Man-Machine Studies*, 24:77–98, 1986.

[Skin58] B.F. Skinner. Teaching machines. *Science*, 128:269–277, 1958.

[Spen88] F. Spensley. Dominie: Trainer interface. CITE Report 44, Institute of Educational Technology, The Open University, Milton Keynes, July 1988.

[VaBr80] K. VanLehn and J.S. Brown. Planning nets: A representation for formalizing analogies and semantic models of procedural skills. In R. Snow, P.A. Federico, and W. Montague, editors, *Aptitude, Learning, and Instruction: Vol.2. Cognitive Process Analysis of Learning and Problem Solving*, volume 2, chapter 18, pages 95–137. Lawrence Erlbaum, Hillsdale, NJ, 1980.

[Wenger87] E. Wenger. *Artificial Intelligence and Tutoring Systems*. Morgan Kaufmann, Los Altos, California, 1987.

MIDI Draw: Designing an Impressionistic Medium for Young Musicians, Artists, and Writers

William J. Egnatoff

Faculty of Education, Queen's University

Kingston, K7L 3N6 Ontario, Canada

tel: (613) 545-6722

FAX: (613) 545-6584

email: William.Egnatoff@QueensU.Ca

Abstract

MIDI Draw is an impressionistic medium in the making—a computer program for color drawing and writing linked to a MIDI-based electronic synthesizer. A series of robust prototypes of modestly varying functionality is being developed based on use in various contexts: music composition, art, and creative writing at home and in the classroom; integrated arts-based teacher education; and research on child development. Children, artists, musicians, and teachers are influencing the design.

A well-designed medium in an engaging, supportive context enables creative expression by constraining it to a comfortable and manageable space. The creative spaces bounded by an electronic keyboard synthesizer, a computer-based color drawing program, and a word-processor change when the three media are integrated. But what is created within this hybrid space is governed mainly by the social context and individual imagination, capabilities, and experience. What insight might be gained into collaborative learning and into the interacting development of children's musical, artistic, and literary expression by examining the use of MIDI Draw for impressionistic play with sound and color, for illustrating or scoring musical compositions, for creating orchestrated paintings or illustrated stories or cartoon strips, and for whatever means children might invent?

Introduction

Daddy, I call it "play-all-day school".
> Daughter, age 7, characterizing a one-week summer school

I believe children are happiest and learn most when they direct their own activity. I would even say that creative, imaginative play is the essence of childhood and is at the heart of learning. Some creative expression is plastic—musical improvisation and composition, invention of musical notation, writing poetry and stories, drawing, and painting—and some, dramatic—dancing, acting, mime, puppetry. In integrated arts-based education, one form of play often flows into another and school subject boundaries dissolve in the activity space constructed by children and teachers together.

Play often leads to the collaborative gathering and construction of tools and artifacts that further shape the play. When children play with tools that adults use, they are making their own sense of adult activity and making personal connection with the adult world. MIDI Draw, an evolving tool for plastic expression, is being designed in collaboration with children and teachers to encourage children to see themselves equally as artists, writers, and musicians. Research accompanying the software development is designed to explore the social and cognitive mechanisms that influence what children do with the software and to search for evidence of parallels and interaction among musical, artistic, and literary development in particular contexts.

The paper is in four sections. The first provides the context of the work: making tools for creative expression; children's play with synthesizers, computer drawing programs, and word processors; and integrated arts-based education. The second section describes the development of the program: the emerging conception of MIDI Draw, the design criteria, the series of prototypes, the programming environment, and the appropriateness of such a project for secondary school computer science. The third section lists actual and imagined uses of the program related to diverse subjects and accommodating various ways of learning. The fourth section delineates research questions on the development of creative expression.

Electronic Tools for Creative Expression

If the computer has a role to play in the crafts of children, it is to make the creation and sharing of their works more accessible.

Upitis

New expressive tools come from adult play-all-day schools. Nuclear physicist Hugh Le Caine (1914-1977) was eventually given a free hand by the National Research Council of Canada to dedicate himself to inventing electronic musical instruments begun on his own. His instruments, meeting exacting technical requirements of composers and performing artists, are ancestors of current electronic instruments, recorders, and editors. Similarly, the vision of Douglas Engelbart and the self-directed work of Alan Kay and colleagues at the Xerox Palo Alto Research Centre have given us object-oriented programming and the now familiar way of seeing into and interacting with a computer through overlapping windows and the mouse. Using such well-crafted, professional tools one can move quickly from design to realization of new tools for creative expression.

MIDI Draw links three electronic media—the electronic synthesizer keyboard, the computer drawing program, and the word processor—for which the main ergonomic problems have been solved. Children take well to each of these media and what they do is rooted in extensive experience with sound, image, and text. An electronic synthesizer has a keyboard of comfortable size with many keys and buttons with which children can generate interesting and reproducible results without special instruction. A synthesizer accommodates individual or collaborative improvisation, composition, and performance of music and exploration of sound and rhythm. A computer drawing program extends drawing on paper. Children learn quickly to control a mouse to generate lines by gesture and to choose color, pattern, thickness, shade and specialized shapes by pointing and clicking. A word processor permits revision, writing in any order, and production of perfect copy, although its usefulness depends very much on the task, typing skills, and approach to writing (Chandler, [Cha90]).

The tools comprising MIDI Draw are of educational value to children for several reasons (Upitis, [Upi89]): (1) they are used by professionals and so children can identify their activity with creation of the music, art, and writing that surrounds them; (2) they permit ideas to be expressed in many forms and worked out in any order; (3) they are enjoyable to use; and (4) skill can be acquired quickly enough that attention soon shifts from tool to task.

MIDI Draw is intended for creative play at home and at school. In both settings, "it is important to create an atmosphere where children can feel free to choose tools appropriate to their purposes" (Upitis, [Upi89], p. 154). Parents and teachers should endeavor to create a supportive community of children who are given time, materials, and opportunity to pursue their creative urges and to build connections between various sorts of experience (Upitis, [Upi90]). Children are free to learn because their activity is constrained physically and socially to a space that has a comfortable size and feeling. The media should not be so flexible nor the play so unbounded that children resort to what Alan Kay [Kay91] calls "clay pushing". Such integrated arts-based teaching does not require exceptional artistic talent but it does demand a vision of how diverse bits of activity spread over days or months connect to one another. Lawler's intimate study of the learning of his own children [Law85] has demonstrated convincingly that learning results from the gradual linking and reorganization of bits and pieces of knowledge operating in a wide range of contexts.

Designing MIDI Draw

My current notion of MIDI Draw as a hybrid of music, drawing, and writing tools evolved from narrower interests. I first wanted a tool to create musical notation without using an established symbol system as found in much music software. I began to think about a "gestural composer" program, but could not conceive of a sensible mechanism by which the composer could determine what gestures would create what music. I then decided to use a MIDI keyboard as the music source and to link notation with music more weakly simply by choosing a location on the screen for each recorded music block (my term for a bit of music). The appropriate notation could then be drawn at that location and the music could be played back by clicking on the assigned spot. I saw that my program would allow musical and visual creativity to inspire each other. Finally, wanting to accommodate song writing and influenced by children's picture books and the variety of ways in which text and image come together in children's creative work, I felt that the program should also support writing.

I questioned further elaboration of the program.. Would it be useful to be able to group music blocks to enable composing by creating larger and larger units? Should bits of drawing be recorded as objects that could subsequently be copied, cut, moved, or resized? Should bits of music be associated with these objects rather than with particular screen locations? Such questions will be explored through testing a series of prototypes in various contexts.

MIDI Draw has obvious limitations. What one creates with it cannot be taken out of the computer; it can only be moved to another system with the same synthesizer. (Each model of synthesizer has its own set of voices!) The weak coupling of music and drawing eliminates what most music programs provide, a "dynamic interaction between the notation on the screen and the sounds [one] hears" (Upitis, [Upi89], p. 156). In drawing mode, it offers no control of brush pressure and angle. Screens cannot be printed out in full color without expensive printers or plotters. Therefore, what is done should be seen more in terms of process than product, although children will be able to demonstrate their work.

The main design criteria are personal interest, simplicity, balance of the three media, robustness, and adaptiveness. The program must be enjoyable for me to use for drawing, writing songs, learning other languages, and playing with my own children. The program is to be simple enough that anyone using it can soon handle all the technical possibilities it offers. The program provides for comparable flexibility and subtlety and expression in each of the three media. For example, it records inflection (key velocity) and changes in voice just as it permits choice of brush width and color. The program must be sufficiently robust to work well for possibilities not envisaged by the designer. Most important, the path of development must reflect what is learned from people using the program for various purposes in various contexts. Early suggestions included saving, allowing multiple pages, having a "palette" of music blocks, and allowing the length of a line to determine the length of repetition of an ostinato figure.

Early in the design, I decided to create a series of version, beginning with Version -7, each having features distinct form its predecessor. Each version except the first is produced in stand-alone form so that it can be tested at various sites. Version 0 will include those features that teachers and children have found most interesting. Specifications will be written for a commercial product based on the final prototype. The main features and refinements included in each new version are revised as development proceeds. The following table was created while Version -6 was being developed.

Version	Additional Features	Refinements
-7	select mode from menu: record from MIDI synthesizer and place on screen, draw with wide pen and random pattern, playback by clicking; location of recording indicated by change in cursor shape	
-6	full color drawing with variable pensize and texture; saving; cutting, copying, and pasting music blocks and selected regions of the drawing; all options selected from icons on the screen	longer music blocks, music blocks visible in play mode, sensible cursor shapes to indicate mode
-5	text on drawing (not editable) or in moveable resizeable text windows (fully editable)	choice of font, font size, and font style; print screen
-4	sequencing and grouping of music blocks, repetition of a music block governed by length of a line	revoicing of music block; linking to another MIDI music program (exporting and importing of music blocks)
-3	object-oriented drawing	couple/uncouple music blocks and drawing blocks
-2	multiple windows with links	
-1	Logo animation	
0	(selection of most useful features)	

Practical and educational considerations influenced the choice of Object Logo (Paradigm Software, [Par90]) as the programming environment. It is an object-oriented extension of Logo that includes procedures for MIDI communication, 24-bit color, Macintosh QuickDraw graphics, windows, menus, and the mouse. Stand-alone applications may be developed and freely distributed. Though not trouble-free, Object Logo is inexpensive and continues to evolve with the Macintosh operating system which may extend its market niche to include that of IBM products. Finally, others who have access to Object Logo can extend the program, for example, by including animation created using turtle geometry.

As a teacher of secondary school computer science education, I like to undertake projects similar in scope to what advanced high school students and their teachers might tackle. In this way, I can teach about project work from my own experience. The development of MIDI Draw illustrates prototyping in a modern, object-oriented programming environment through a series of functionally adequate stages shaped by an emerging context of use. As a major project by a team whose members have diverse expertise, it could fit well, for example, within the framework of the senior course of study, *Computers and problem solving: A case-study approach* [Ont87]. It is an interdisciplinary project, related to art, music, and language arts, and indirectly to physics (acoustics) and mathematics (symbol systems) leading to a tool peers may use to awaken hidden artistic talent. Finally, it could lead entrepreneurial students to a commercial venture.

Growing a Niche: Envisioned Uses

Then Miss Chirp gave everyone a sheet of paper and coloured chalk and asked them to draw the magic sounds they had heard.

The drawings were the strangest you could ever imagine. I have seen some of them and although none are exactly the same, I know that when you look at them and put your fingers in your ears, count to ten and hold your breath, they suddenly start to make sounds for you., And even if you haven't heard the sound of the stars washing in the water, you can hear the sound in the pictures. It is the strangest music you could ever want to hear. Much stranger than flutes or clarinets or violins.

R. Murray Schafer

Thus ends "Edward's Magic Orchestra" [Sch86, pp. 325-331], written for an 8-year-old who wrote Schafer to say simply that his teacher had played Schafer's music and he liked it. That impressions and thoughts in one mode may invoke impressions and thoughts in another underlie the following activities that could be supported by MIDI Draw. The examples vary in form (recording, playback, drawing, writing), purpose (creative expression, learning a skill, making a report or collection, exploring), and social context (individual, group demonstration or performance, collaborative creation, design for group activity).

- Record a melody and draw a picture of it or invite someone else to do so.

- Create a sound-scape of a park, a busy intersection, a forest, a farmyard, or sounds and sights following a first snowfall.
- Make a musical picture-dictionary of synthesizer voices, cartoon characters, musical phrases, sound-colors, rhythm-shapes, letters of the alphabet, or dance rhythms.
- Make a collection of folk songs from various countries with characteristic illustrations and text in the original language.
- Make a cartoon in which some characters speak in English, some in French, some in pictures, and some in music
- Draw a picture and ask someone else to compose music or a poem to go with it.
- Invent musical notation for one of your compositions and teach someone else how to read it.
- Write, illustrate, and orchestrate a story. Read it to your friends or a younger child.
- Use MIDI Draw as a scratchpad for improvising and composing.
- Write a poem and ask others to illustrate it and set it to music.
- Make a storyboard for a puppet theatre or musical production.

Testing the Vision: Research on Children's Creative Expression

Two sorts of questions underlie the development of MIDI Draw. The first concerns finding a niche for computer-based muti-media tools. In what settings and for what tasks can MIDI Draw be adapted to work well? The second concerns how one form of specialized intelligence (Gardner, [Gar83]) interacts with another. How can MIDI Draw activities illumine the development of musical, verbal, and spatial intelligence?

Both sorts of questions are variations on those set out by diSessa [DiS90, p. 301-2]:

What exactly is it that children will be doing with this software? What will they think they are doing with it? Why should they do what you think they should do? How is it exactly that they should learn from what they do? What happens if they have different purposes and if they should see the program in a different light than you intend?

Underlying the work is the notion that "creative thinking is made possible by constraints" (Boden, [Bod91], p. 217) given by task, tool, social context, and individual experience and capacity. The network of constraints, though too complex to specify fully, determines what is possible and what is likely. The art of good teaching is to know what constraints are critical: the art of good research is to uncover important constraints that the teacher or software designer may have overlooked. The researcher must therefore work moment-by-moment with teachers and children.

Classroom studies and writing on music in education point to the existence of a niche for MIDI Draw. In a detailed two-year study in elementary school classrooms, Carmichael, Burnett, Higginson, Moore, & Pollard, [Car85] demonstrated that talented teachers could acquire the technical knowledge and adapt their methods to support the use of computers for creative expression linked to mathematics, art, creative writing, and music. Logo was the main tool but word processors, drawing programs, and, to a limited extent, a music system with electronic keyboard were also used. Schafer [Sch86] and Upitis [Upi90] have demonstrated in classrooms and other settings that the sorts of creative expression described by Carmichael *et al* are more coherent and meaningful when teachers and children want to do the same things together and when children are encouraged to direct their own learning, to create their own tools, and to design and direct their own productions.

How does bringing several arts together enrich children's learning? First, each art has a clear developmental path of increasing specificity and structural differentiation. Gardner [Gar80] has traced the progression in children's art and Upitis [Upi91] has drawn parallels between the development of musical notation and spelling (Gentry, [Gen82]). Second, Weir [Wei87] has shown how simple animation sequences can enable story writing. She explains that story scripts are stored in memory with emotional attachments and when those emotions are evoked by a suggestive animation sequence, the script comes alive. Such mobilization of knowledge should also be visible in some of the suggested MIDI Draw activities. For example, stereotypical musical fragments are used as emotional signatures of dramatic moments and so should be just as evocative as is animation. Does increasing structural differentiation in one art support the same in another when they are deliberately linked? As least, if one art mobilizes production in another, then that can only lead eventually to development.

When my son (then aged 5:8) sat with me and drew three figures on the MIDI Draw screen and after drawing each began to improvise at the synthesizer keyboard, he was more focussed and reflective than on other occasions when he was playing the synthesizer alone. What he had drawn seemed to shape his playing. By collecting many examples of this sort, it should be possible to sort out some of the mechanisms by which the arts interact in the growing minds of children.

The work described here reflects a broad concern: How can we maintain "a social space for childhood...in our modern technological era—a space where the child can become *at home* in the world, where she can also be the subject, not only the object, of history" (Suransky, [Sur82], p. 171)? How can we cultivate children's aesthetic sensibilities in our noisy world? I believe we should begin by recognizing the centrality of creative expression in child development, by joining work and play, by crossing subject boundaries, and by linking the arts with mathematics, science, and social studies. Artistically sensitive children and teachers are the best guides.

References

[Bod91] Boden, M. A. *The creative mind. Myths and mechanisms.* New York: Basic Books, 1991.

[Car85] Carmichael, H., Burnett, J.,Higginson, W., Moore, B., & Pollard, P. Computers, children , and classrooms: A multisite evaluation of the creative use of microcomputers by elementary school children. Toronto: Queen's Printer for Ontario, 1985.

[Cha90] Chandler, D. Student writers and the word processor. A review of research for the classroom teacher. [Unpublished manuscript. Faculty of Education, University College of Wales, Aberystwyth.] 1990.

[DiS90] diSessa, A. Social niches for future software, in Gardner, M., Greeno, J., Reif, F., Schoenfeld, S., DiSessa, A., & Stage, E. (eds.). *Toward a scientific practice of science education.* Hillsdale, NJ: Lawrence Erlbaum Associates. 1990. pp. 301-322.

[Gar80] Gardner, H. *Artful scribbles, The significance of children's drawings.* New York: Basic Books. 1980.

[Gar83] Gardner, H. *Frames of mind—The theory of multiple intelligences.* New York: Basic Books. 1983.

[Gen82] Gentry, J. R. An analysis of developmental spelling in GNYS AT WRK. *The reading teacher,* 1982, Vol. 36, No. 2, pp. 192-200.

[Kay91] Kay, A. Computers, networks and education. *Scientific American* , 1991, Vol. 265, No. 3, pp. 138-143, 146, 148.

[Law85] Lawler, R. W. *Computer Experience and Cognitive Development: A Child's Learning in a Computer Culture.* 1985. Chichester, England: Ellis Horwood.

Standardized Architecture for Integrated Open Courseware

Omar ElHani (*,**), Guy Gouardères (**)

* : BULL SA, 7 rue Ampère, courrier: K2/136, 91343 MASSY (FRANCE)

** : Laboratoire A.P.I., IUT "A", Université Toulouse III, 50 chemin des Maraîchers

31062 TOULOUSE (FRANCE)

Tel : (33)-1-69-93-82-25

Fax : (33)-1-69-93-84-47

Abstract

In recent years, hypermedia has been grown in interest in Advanced Research on learning. Furthermore the extension of hypermedia toward intelligent hypermedia becomes more than obvious, to meet perfectly specific requirements of learning, such as the learner modelling, diagnosing and guiding the learner in his investigation.

Independently of any existing systems, this paper specifies a layered conceptual architecture, based on integrating Hypermedia Systems and Intelligent Knowledge Based Systems skills, for courseware purpose. This architecture may apply for a wide range of Computer Assisted Learning courseware (CAL) as well as for Intelligent Tutoring System (ITS).

As far as the knowledge representation is crucial for this architecture, two formalisms are chosen because of their complementarity. The object formalism is chosen to represent static and predefinned knowledge, whereas the rule formalism applied for modelling dynamic knowledge and reasonning processes either in the framework of the domain knowledge, the learner modelling or teaching stratégies expertises.

To foster interoperability in an open and distant learning, an interchange format fitting to this architecture, making use of existing and forthcoming standards in the area of multimedia, is manipulated for exchange between different production or learning platforms.

[Ont87] Ontario Ministry of Education. *Computer studies Ontario academic course 1987. Computers and problem solving: A case-study approach.* Toronto, Ont.: Ontario Ministry of Education. 1987.

[Par90] Paradigm Software. Object Logo, Version 2.5 [computer software]. Cambridge, MA: Paradigm Software. 1990.

[Sch86] Schafer, R. M. *The thinking ear.* Toronto, Ont: Arcana Editions. 1986.

[Sur82] Suransky, V. P. (1982). *The erosion of childhood.* Chicago: University of Chicago Press. 1982.

[Upi89] Upitis, R. The craft of composition: Helping children create music with computer tools. *Psychomusicology. Microcomputers in psychomusicology research* , 1989, Vol. 8, No. 2, pp. 151-161.

[Upi90] Upitis, R. *This too is music.* Portsmouth, NH: Heinemann. 1990.

[Upi91] Upitis, R. The development of invented music notations: A cousin to invented spellings. [Paper presented at the Annual Meeting of the American Educational Research Association, April 3-7, Chicago, IL; submitted to *Arts & Learning*] 1991.

[Wei87] Weir, S. *Cultivating minds: A Logo casebook.* New York: Harper & Row. 1987.

Introduction

European Community's Research and Development have been focussing, these last years, on the area of advanced learning technology based on the information technology, telecommunication and broadcasting. The DELTA (Development of European Learning through Technological Advance) project has been interested in the trans-European *flexible open and distance learning*, to achieve a high level of appropriate capabilities among the workforce. Research is therefore needed to reduce the production cost of the learning materials, to make them more efficient and to foster *interoperability* enabling their distribution through the appropriate networks and to make easy their execution on different platforms. The courseware representation presented hereafter is resulting from the Exploratory Action phase of the DELTA LEAST project.

1.   Courseware Representation

The purpose of the courseware representation is to provide a *common conceptual architecture* that can meet the requirement of a wide range of courseware whether it is conventional generally called as CAL or intelligent generally called as ITS. Furthermore, the representation should   propose an interchange format to facilitate the courseware interchange between heterogeneous systems.

The architecture presented below takes advantages of integrating *Multimedia/Hypermedia* and *Intelligent Knowledge Based Systems* (IKBS) technologies to achieve this purpose. In fact researchers and developers have expressed, these last years, that hypermedia represents good prospects for education [Beltrand, 91], [Reaume, 91], [Kibby, Mayes, 90]. Due to its advanced multimedia interface, knowledge organization and access in an associative way, and its script language which is procedural, hypermedia may fulfil the CAL requirements. However it suffers from limitations that make it insufficient for ITS. That is why hypermedia should be extended toward IKBS. Several researchers have felt and recommended this requirement [Boyle, Snell, 89], [Barden, 89], [Nicolson, 89].

1.1.   Guidelines for Courseware Representation

To overcome the problem of none compatible workstations and execution environments, standards are needed to guarantee interoperability and interworking between heterogeneous systems either at the learning or at the authoring level. For interchange purposes, courseware is transformed into standard data types, independent of any system, called here *interchange format*. This latter should make use of the existing standards in the field of multimedia information and a standard of representing complex data structures such as ASN.1 (Abstract Syntax Number 1, ISO 8824). For multimedia components of courseware, several standards exist right now such as ODA (Office Document Architecture, ISO 8613), SGML (Standard Generalized Markup Language, ISO 8879), and especially MHEG (Multimedia Hypermedia information coding Expert Group) which is perfectly fitted to multimedia and hypermedia objects of the courseware architecture we will present later.

However, standards which are missing in the framework of IKBS, should be subject of further research. So far, some efforts have been exerted for this purpose [Knaus, Jay, 90].

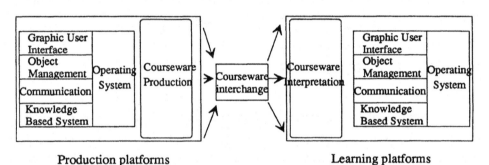

Production platforms   Learning platforms

Figure 1 - Interoperability and courseware interchange

2.   Kind of Knowledge of CAL and ITS

We often distinguish between two main categories of courseware: CAL and ITS [Wenger, 87]. CAL may be characterized as containing static knowledge and a pre-defined interaction pattern. All the knowledge about the domain and the pedagogical strategies is implemented in its final form. The ways in which the learner may react are determined beforehand as well as the reactions of the system. However, in ITS (part of) the knowledge is dynamic and requires AI (Artificial Intelligence) representations. Generally in ITS a distinction is made between four kinds of expertise: domain knowledge, learner modelling, teaching strategies, communication knowledge. These expertises do not necessarily have to correspond with the architecture of a particular ITS, nor do all ITS's possess all kinds of knowledge in an intelligent way.

CAL and ITS are overlapping, and the distinction between them is not always clear cut. Often, in terms of knowledge representation, a "hybrid" formalism, which established the integration and cooperation between two complementary languages, one is procedural, and the other is declarative, is chosen [Canut, 90]. That is why the Object formalism (i.e., procedural) and the rule formalism (i.e., declarative) are chosen in the layered courseware architecture below. The first is mainly used to represent static knowledge, and the second mainly for modelling dynamic reasoning process.

3.   Layered Courseware Architecture

As a first level of decomposition, this architecture may be split into three logical levels: Presentation, Hypermedia and Knowledge Base.

Knowledge Base
Hypermedia
Presentation

Figure 2 - Levels of the courseware architecture

The presentation level is devoted to describe the content of multimedia interactive objects as they will be shown to the learner on his workstation, and how each object will interact with the learner.

The Hypermedia level permits sequencing and navigation through these interactions taking into account the learner's inputs.

The Knowledge Base level uses Artificial Intelligence skills to meet the requirements of intelligent tutoring systems.

As refined decomposition, the presentation level is divided into two layers that distinguish between basic and composite learner-computer interactions.

Thus, as shown in figure 6 (see below), it is a hierarchical architecture built around four layers: Basic Presentation objects (i.e., layer 1), Composite Presentation objects (i.e., layer 2), Hyper objects (i.e., layer 3), Knowledge Base (i.e., layer 4).

3.1.   Layer Components

In respect with the Object Oriented Language skills with classes and inheritance, layers 1, 2 and 3 are described as a collection of autonomous and active objects with related services. Each object is an instance of a related class. All classes and meta-classes are predefined and independent from a specific learning application .

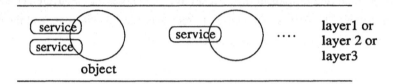

Figure 3- Objects in the layered architecture

For layer 4, three main knowledge-based and interdependent components are highlighted: domain knowledge, teaching strategies, learner modelling. The separation between them remains conceptual. Each component, as a collection of rules and facts conforming to the declarative approach, can do specific services without any ad hoc functions.

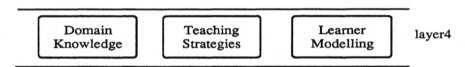

Figure 4 - Knowledge Base's general structure

3.2. Communication between Layers

During the courseware execution, layer components interact between them by means of message sending, for services invocation. A layer component (i.e., object of the three bottom layers or a rule of layer 4) has to send a specific message, to an object for a service activation. Then the receiver replies with a report which carries the relevant results of the service activated. Messages are generally propagated from higher layers to lower layers and reports in the reverse way.

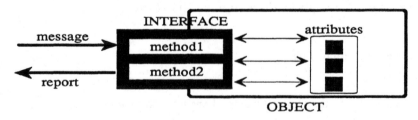

Figure 5 - Communication between the components of layers

3.3.   Specific Services of each Layer

3.3.1.   Layer 1: Basic Presentation Objects

A basic presentation object is an elementary information to be used through the learner-computer interface. It is necessarily atomic, monomedia, either of an output or an input kind:
- **basic output object** such as a text, graphic, still picture, audio sequence or an audiovisual sequence.
- **basic input object** such as a button, input character string, menu selection, multiple selection, form filling, location or a numerical value.

services:
- In reply to an invocation from higher layers, it restitutes the content of the basic output object on the relevant output device (e.g., screen, loudspeaker) or
- ensures the acquisition of input data from a learner using the relevant input device (e.g., keyboard, mouse) and returns them as a report to the upper layers for analysis.

3.3.2.   Layer 2: Composite Presentation Objects

For purpose of building composite multimedia learner-computer interaction, a composite object has a tree structure. Intermediate components are also composite, and terminal components are basic (see figure 6). A composite object can be monomedia or multimedia. By means of multimedia synchronization, a composite object may gather not only output information from different media, but also input information. Multimedia synchronization describes the time at which some outputs, or more generally some outputs and inputs are to be activated in the progression of a presentation. A composite object is handled as a whole by a learning application and may be of three types:
- **Composite Output object**: Gathering basic or composite presentation objects of only output kind (e.g., two or more blocks of text; a still picture + audio sequence).
- **Composite Input object**: Combining basic or composite presentation objects of only input kind (e.g., two chained menu selections).
- **Composite Interactive object**: Combining basic or composite presentation components from output and input kind (e.g., graphic + subsequent menu selection).

services:

In reply to an invocation from an hyper object, a composite object invokes its direct sons for the presentation of their contents in an order respecting the multimedia synchronization. Then the resulting input data are returned back to the Hyper object for further analysis.

3.3.3. Layer 3 : Hyper Objects

The purpose of an Hyper object is mainly deciding what will be the next learner-computer interaction taking into account the current results of interaction and the pedagogical goal. Like in hypermedia systems, hyper objects are structured as nodes of a *network* (see figure 6). Links, with related activation conditions acting upon results of interactions, are objects and allow to navigate through several dependent learner-computer interactions. Three kinds of Hyper objects can be distinguished:

- **Learning-page:** Object of an output kind, giving information about what is to be taught. It may be *an example or an explanation about a domain concept.* It refers either to a basic output, composite output or even interactive presentation object from lower layers.

- **Solicitation :** Object of an input kind, devoted to assess the learner's comprehension about what is already taught. It may be a *simple question, an exercise,* or *a problem to solve.* Author's expected responses, which are objects too in our architecture, are attached to a solicitation object. A solicitation object refers either to a basic input, composite input or interactive presentation object from lower layers. However a solicitation may be made up by the learner himself, in such a case, the hyperobject is an instance of a class of frame that the learner will fill in to express his solicitation, and related expected responses are calculated dynamically.

- **Module:** As a collection of relevant and organized Learning-pages and/or Solicitations, in layer3, a module is an object specialized in *teaching a specific domain concept.*

services :

Hyper objects are entities which are involved when results of input data come back from the presentation objects. Two main services Hyper objects support:

- Analysis of input data, made by the current solicitation object, in comparison with expected response objects. These latter may be either stored beforehand by the author or calculated dynamically by layer 4 .

- Decision making respecting the analysis. Two levels of decision should be highlighted:

. Local decision : What will be the next Learning Page or Solicitation following the current one in the current module. This kind of decision is made by the current solicitation object as looking for the link object which activation conditions are true.

. Global decision : When a module is finished a next module is chosen. Which one is chosen depends upon the learner's behavior to all previous solicitations in the current module. This decision is made by the current module object as looking for the link object which activation conditions are verified.

3.3.4. Layer 4 : Knowledge Base

Intelligent Knowledge Base are substantial to an ITS. It has the ability to supervise the functioning of the three bottom layers of the courseware architecture, to make more dynamic the learner-computer interactions, and to adapt them to the individual learner. An example is given in §3.7. to illustrate the layer 4's control of the courseware execution.

Layer 3 and Layer 4 have some common services such as the analysis of input data and making local or global decision, but implemented in different ways. An hyper object provides these services only if the learner's response is expected and the static link is foreseen by the author. In such a case, the current Hyper object has the ability to make decision without involving the Knowledge base which is only informed of the learner's response to update the learner model, and of such local decision.

Otherwise layer 4 is the only means to deal with dynamic and unexpected responses (i.e., dynamic link). Thus, when the Hyper object discovers, after analysis, that the response is unexpected, it will not make decision itself, but it will forward the learner response to the Knowledge base for diagnosis and decision making.

services :

As well known in the education literature, briefly services are:

- domain knowledge : to present domain knowledge to the learner such as examples or problems, to solve problems and explain solutions, and to evaluate dynamically the responses and paths the learner gives for the problems he has to solve.

- teaching strategies : sequencing concepts of the domain to be taught, making dynamic decisions when layer 3 is unable to do it.

- learner modelling : modelling knowledge of the learner (i.e., what is known, not known or badly known) to adapt the learning application to the individual learner, diagnosing the learner's problem solving process especially when his response is unexpected.

3.4.   Module Notion

As it is shown in figure 6, a learning application may be devoted to teach one or several domain concepts. A domain concept is either factual (i.e., factual knowledge) or procedural (e.g., exercise, problem to solve). The section of courseware which is centered around a domain concept is called *module*. A module is represented by an object in layer 3 entailing both statistics about the learner's behavior toward the module and a method to make global decision. A module is also represented by some knowledge in layer 4.

3.5.   Pedagogical Unit Notion

From the learner's point of view, a courseware may be seen as a sequence of dependent or independent modules. *A module is seen as a sequence of Pedagogical Units (PU). A Pedagogical-Unit is a learner-computer interaction,* which may be either an example shown to a learner, an explanation (i.e., Learning-Page), a question to answer , an exercise or a problem to solve (i.e., Solicitation) about the related concept.
From the system's point of view, a PU is seen as a vertical section of the architecture.

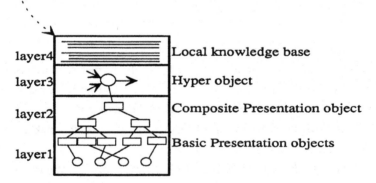

(a) The learner view : pedagogical units, modules and concepts

(b) The system view :pedagogical unit structure

Figure 6 - The learner and the system views of courseware

3.6. Local and Global Knowledge Bases

In terms of what is specific and what is generic to a Pedagogical Unit, layer 4 may be divided into two parts:

* **LKB**: It should include knowledge which are specific to a Pedagogical Unit such as domain facts: pre-stored by the author or set dynamically by the domain expertise when the exercise is made up, they are used to select rules from the Global domain Knowledge Base and to activate them in order to solve the specific exercise or problem tackled in this Pedagogical Unit. LKB may include results of interactions such as the learner's response, delay of time of response, type of response. These latter facts are instantiated when the response comes back from the Hyper object. LKB may include rules too. It may be represented as a temporary memory. When the Pedagogical Unit is desactivated some of its knowledge (e.g., learner's response) are included in the GKB, in the sense to be exploited by the following Pedagogical Units for diagnosing and making decision.

* **GKB** : Rules and facts, about the domain knowledge, the learner modelling and the teaching strategies, which are shared by all Pedagogical Units.

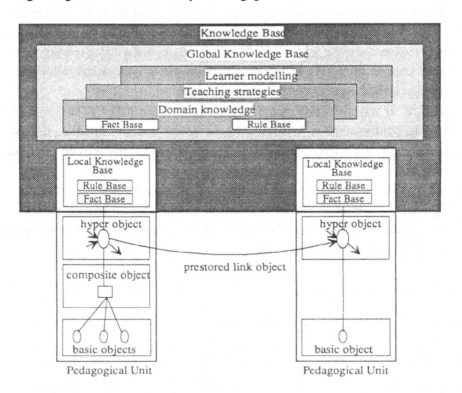

Figure 7 - Local and global knowledge bases

3.7.   Courseware Execution Example

To illustrate sequencing between components of layers and interactions between them through message sending, we apply the architecture to a simple intelligent courseware example teaching the concepts of quadratic equation (i.e., $ax^2 + bx + c = 0$) as shown in the figure below.

Layer 4: First, the teaching strategies component decides to present a certain kind of problem (i.e., with 1, 2 or no solutions). After this, the domain knowledge generates the problem by instantiating the problem-frame with random generated numbers (i.e., a, b, c) which allow to instantiate the local knowledge base. Then the domain knowledge solves the problem which solutions are x1, x2, and a rule generates a structured message entailing a, b, c, x1, x2 values, sent to the correspondent hyper object.

Layer 3: The hyper object gets expected correct responses (i.e., x1, x2 values) from the message, instantiates the expected response objects, and forwards the message to the presentation object.

Layer 2 and layer 1: Then, the composite object propagates the message with a, b, c values until reaching the concerned basic objects. These latter fill in blanks of the presentation-exercise-frame with a, b, c values as it is shown to the learner on the workstation, and present the exercise to the learner with the text of the exercise, a dialog box and validation buttons. Once the learner fills in the answer1 and answer2, the composite object puts them in a structured report and sent them to the hyper object.

layer 3: If the response is expected (i.e., correct), the hyper object will let layer4 know about this positive result to update the learner model, and will make the decision by activating an existing link object, if any. Otherwise, it will only forward the report to layer4.

layer 4: If the learner has given an incorrect answer, layer 4 has to determine the cause (i.e., lack of knowledge, misconception, forgetting), to update the learner's model, and to make a tutorial decision to decide which kind of feedback and what kind of new problem (i.e., what is the next Pedagogical Unit ?).

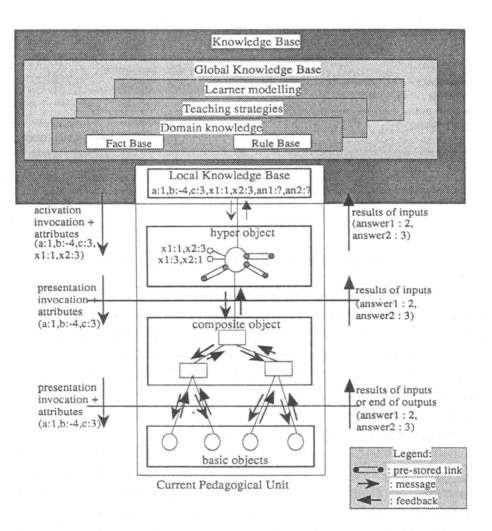

Figure 8 - Interactions between components of a Pedagogical Unit

4. Courseware Interpretation

To exchange a courseware between different platforms, an interchange format is used. This latter is then interpreted, during execution, by a specialized program called an *interpreter*. This latter is a portable program running on different platforms and transforms the interchange format into a format conforming to the available tools of the execution environment.

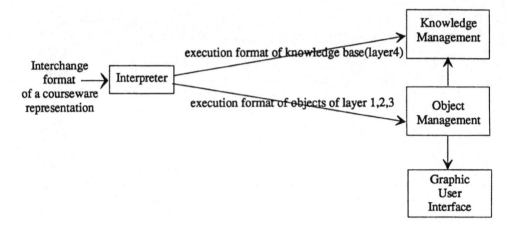

Figure 9 - Courseware interpretation and execution

As resources, three major components should be enhanced:

Object Management: it executes services and manages data of each object of layer 1 , 2 or 3. Since presentation objects (i.e., layer 1 or 2) must be handled through the Graphic User Interface, the Object Management calls the appropriate functions of the GUI to display presentation objects and gets then the results of inputs. Moreover the Object management should communicate with the Knowledge Management because there is a necessity of interaction between Hyper objects and the Knowledge Base in case of an intelligent courseware.

Graphical User Interface: for example Microsoft Windows, Unix Motif or X-window, OS/2 Presentation Manager. In accordance with the Object Management invocations, it permits the presenting of real presentation information on the learner's workstation and the transfer of input data as feedback to the Object Management for further processing.

Knowledge Management: for example an Expert System Generator such as Guru, Nexpert object, or Kool. Entailing mainly an inference process it allows dynamic reasoning acting upon the factual knowledge and the reasoning knowledge coming from the layer 4 of the courseware architecture.

Conclusion

The courseware architecture described above relies upon a layered architecture and an interchange format. The architecture aims that a kind of cooperation takes place between two separated environments which are hypermédia and intelligent knowledge based system. It may be validated by integrating a hypermedia system like ToolBook

(Asymetrix) and an Expert System Generator like Nexpert Object (Neuron Data). However, the architecture is rather independent of any existing market systems. An interchange format is recommended to develop courseware in an open environment. MHEG standard seems to be perfectly fitted to the specification of multimedia/hypermédia objects. However no standardization effort has been made about Knowledge Based Systems, that will slow down the development of intelligent courseware in an open environment.

References

[Barden, 89] R. Barden. *Using Hypertext in building Intelligent Training Systems.* Interactive Learning International, Vol. 5, pp. 109-115. 1989.

[Boyle, Snell, 89] C. Boyle and J. Snell. *Knowledge Based Navigation under hypertext.* Hypertext II, York, West Yorkshire, UK. June 89.

[Canut, 90]. M.F. Canut. *Spécification formelle de systèmes d'enseignement intelligemment assisté par ordinateur pour l'Atelier de Génie Didacticiel Intégré.* Doctorat de l'Université Paul Sabatier, laboratoire A.P.I, Toulouse III, Juin 1990.

[Kibby, Mayes, 90]. M.R. Kibby, J.T. Mayes. *The learner's view of hypermedia.* Learning Technology in the European communities. DELTA Conference, pp.53-63 October 1990. Kluwer Academic publishers.

[Knaus, Jay, 90]. R. Knaus, C. Jay. *Transporting Knowledge Bases: a Standard.* AI Expert, pp. 34-39, November 1990.

[LEAST 3.1] DELTA LEAST, deliverable no. 11. *Representation of basic information.* 1990

[LEAST 3.2] DELTA LEAST, deliverable no. 12. *User interfaces.* 1990

[LEAST 4.4] DELTA LEAST, deliverables n° 22 and 23. *Courseware representation.* 1991

[MHEG] Multimedia and Hypermedia information coding Expert Group. ISO/IEC JTC1/SC2/WG12. *Information processing - coded representation of multimedia and hypermedia information objects.* Working document <S.4> draft version, September 1991.

[Nicolson, 89]. R. I Nicolson. *Toward the third generation: the case for Intelligent Knowledge Based Hypermedia.* Hypertext II, York, West Yorkshire, UK. June 1989.

[Rhéaume, 91] J. Rhéaume. *Hypermédia et stratégies pédagogiques.* Premières journées Hypermédia et Apprentissages. Paris 1991.

[Wenger, 87] E. Wenger. *Artificial Intelligence and Tutoring Systems: Computational and Cognitive Approaches to the Communication of Knowledge.* Morgan Kaufmann Publishers, Inc. Los Altos, California.

Formal Techniques In Higher Education: A Proposal (*)

Paola Forcheri and Maria Teresa Molfino

Istituto per la Matematica Applicata del Consiglio Nazionale delle Ricerche

Via L.B. Alberti, 4 - 16132 Genova (Italy)

tel. +39-10-515510/517639

email:FORCHERI@IMAGE.GE.CNR.IT

email:MOLFINO@IMAGE.GE.CNR.IT

Abstract

An educational environment, called THEOPRO, able to perform formal proof processes in algebraic domains described by a finite set of equations, has been designed and implemented. The system is intended to be used in mathematics courses at University level. Unlike most automatic deduction tools, THEOPRO is easy to operate, it produces solutions by using techniques similar to those employed by human experts, and it explains the reasoning and the knowledge behind the solution of a problem. The discussion of the system is aimed at analysing those features which are required in automatic theorem provers, so that they may improve the learning of algebraic concepts and formal proof techniques.

Introduction

Automatic deduction tools are conceived as professional aids for doing mathematics: the computer is used to verify conjectures, and to carry out the most tedious and mechanical parts of the work. This hind of tool is usually quite difficult to be handled; it produces efficient solutions by employing methods different from those of human experts and do not show the reasoning employed in solving a given task. The student who approaches an automatic proof system has somewhat different needs than those of the professional mathematician.

(*) This work has been partially supported by "Progetto Finalizzato Sistemi Informatici e Calcolo Parallelo of C.N.R., under grant n.90.00750.69

Students are not familiar with sophisticated tools and are, or should be, interested in the methods employed to obtain a result rather than in the result itself. Students should be induced to experiment different techniques to reach the same conclusion and should be allowed to modify problem solving techniques in order to compare the differences. Finally, students' attitude in problem solving should move from a perceptive view to a deductive analysis.

With this in mind we designed THEOPRO, an automatic theorem prover capable of performing formal proof processes applied to algebraic problems.

THEOPRO can be used to make students work on the following problems:

- To find examples of numerical domains which satisfy the defining axioms for a specified class of algebraic structures. For example, to find out a numerical domain and a composition law in it such that the numerical domain has a ring structure.

- Given a domain, to verify properties. For example, to prove that the sum of two natural numbers is even if, and only if, either both the addenda are odd or both even or to verify the De Morgan laws in the boolean domain or to prove the distributivity of the sum with respect to the product in rings.

- Given a domain, to find out properties. For example, to complete the defining equations of the group structure or to make integers with the sum inherit the group properties.

- To classify all structures which satisfy a particular set of defining axioms. For example, to define a domain as union or enrichment of already known domains.

- Given a domain, to identify it in terms of known classifications. For example to identify a structure for which the boolean domain is a model or to identify a structure for which the integers modulo two are a model.

- Given a numerical domain and an abstract structure, to analyse their relationship. For example, to prove that naturals are a monoid with respect to the sum or to prove that the set of even integers is a subgroup of the integer additive group.

- To compare the proofs of the same properties depending on the knowledge used. For example, to prove that by adding to the opposite of the sum of two numbers the first one I obtain the opposite of the second one in two ways: at first, by using only the defining equations of the integer domain; then, by using the fact that integers are a group with respect to sum.

The system was developed on SUN 3/60 under operating system UNIX.

THEOPRO is described herebelow. Specifically, we will analyse the pedagogical problems taken into account and the corresponding technical solutions adopted. Finally, the potential of the system will be illustrated through practical examples of application. The analysis of THEOPRO provides an operative contribution to the discussion on the educational role of automatic provers, their features, and the techniques employed to render these systems valuable tools to improve the learning of algebraic concepts and formal proof techniques at University level.

1 Overview of the system

A formal proof is a sequence of proof statements which uses the premisses and intermediate results. The goal of a proof is to show the validity of the assertion in question. In our context, assertions (properties) to be proved are equations, and the premisses of the proof are equational axioms. Assertions are proved by using equational deduction and induction. Under suitable hypotheses, we can impose directionality to the premisses, and replace equational deduction with computations, through the use of rewriting [Ehr-Mah85]. This presents two main advantages: first of all, we can carry out automatic proof processes in a way which is quite similar to that adopted by the human mind; secondly, it must be noted that computing by equations is one of the abilities that students acquire in the early school years. As a consequence, it seems worthwhile to follow this approach in building an automatic proof system apt to be used in the introduction of formal systems.

In accordance with these ideas, the THEOPRO system proves properties of algebraic domains described by a finite set of equations. Properties are proved by using rewriting and induction.

1.1 The proof environment

To prove properties of an algebraic domain, different premisses are used by students, depending on their expertise and knowledge. Some of them use only the equations which define the domain, thus carrying out long and inefficient proofs which are difficult to check. Some others use the knowledge they previously acquired on the domain, that is the properties already proved, to speed up the proof process. Finally, some students try to use general knowledge about algebra, and obtain efficient proofs by relying on the features common to the domain at hand and other domains.

To simulate these models of reasoning, the environment of any property we want to prove is a description of an algebraic domain and this description comprises the equational definition of the domain and its already known properties. Algebraic domains are numerical, such as natural numbers, integer numbers and so on, or abstract structures, such as semigroup, monoid, group and so on. For each domain, the equational definition is given by the user; the system automatically enriches the description of the domain, by adding to it the properties already proved.

The equational definition is constituted by the signature and by a set of equational axioms which give meaning to the operation symbols. The signature comprises a name referring to the generic element of the domain and the names and the arities of the operations. If the domain is numerical, we distinguish between constructors, that is operations which allow us to constructively obtain the set of elements, and defined operations [Hue-Hul82]. Both structures and numerical domains may be hierarchically defined, as extensions of structures or predetermined numerical domains, respectively. Figure 1 shows the equational definition of the numerical domain *intsum*.

```
OBJECT integer IS
SORT int
CONSTRUCTOR
0: --> int;
succ: int --> int;
pred: int --> int.
QUOTIENT
succ(pred(X))=X;
pred(succ(X))=X.

OBJECT intsum IS
ENRICHMENT OF integer
OPERATION add:int x int --> int IS AXIOM
add(0,X)=X;
add(succ(X),Y)=succ(add(X,Y));
add(pred(X),Y)=pred(add(X,Y)).
OPERATION opp:int-->int IS AXIOM
opp(0)=0;
opp(succ(X))=pred(opp(X));
opp(pred(X))=succ(opp(X)).
OPERATION double:int-->int IS AXIOM
double(0)=0;
double(succ(X))=succ(succ(double(X)));
double(pred(X))=pred(pred(double(X))).
```

Figure 1. Equational definition of the numerical domain *intsum*. It is incrementally defined, starting from the definition of the numerical domain *integer*. The numerical domain *intsum=(int, 0, pred, succ, opp, add, double)* we define consists of a base set *int*, an operation with arity zero *0:-->int*, four unary operations *succ: int-->int; pred: int-->int; opp: int-->int; double: int-->int;* and one binary operation *add: int x int-->int*.

Furthermore, the structures can be seen as the union of other previously defined structures. Figure 2 shows the equational definition of the abstract structure *group*.

```
CLASS semigroup IS
SORT gr
OPERATION comp: gr x gr --> gr IS AXIOM
comp(comp(X,Y),Z)=comp(X,comp(Y,Z)).

CLASS group IS
USES CLASS semigroup
OPERATION e: --> gr IS AXIOM
comp(e,X)=X.
OPERATION i: gr --> gr IS AXIOM
comp(i(X),X)=e.
```

Figure 2. Equational definition of the abstract domain *group*. In this example, the phrase *USES CLASS semigroup* enables the *group* definition to inherit the sort name, operation symbol and axiom of the *semigroup* definition. The *group* definition consists of a base set *gr*, a binary operation *comp:gr x gr-->gr* which is associative, a neuter element *e* and an inverse operation *i*.

The description of a domain is automatically enriched when a new property is proved. This property can be either a property which has been proved from the defining axioms of the domain or a property which has been inherited through the links, should they have been already proved, with another domain. The process which permits to enrich the description of a domain is illustrated in the following paragraph 1.2.

1.2 The proof process

Solving complex problems requires the capability of organizing, generating, verifying and using knowledge. In mathematics, knowledge is generated by building formal models and conjecturing theorems; the knowledge is used to verify and formulate definitions and to construct proofs. As a consequence, mathematics teaching/learning must focus on these conceptual processes.

To help students to understand the different processes which contribute to the formation of mathematical knowledge, the proof process aims at solving problems of two different classes: to verify properties of a domain, starting from its description, and to generate properties of a numerical domain, by proving that the numerical domain is a model for an abstract structure.

In the first case, the student states the environment of the proof and formulates the property. The verification process is carried out by the system. If positive, the description of the domain is enriched with the newly proved property.

In the second case, the student indicates a numerical and an abstract domain, and a functional association between them. The system verifies whether the numerical domain is a model for the abstract one in this way: the correctness of the functional association is checked; the axioms of the abstract structure are particularized according to the association; an attempt is made to verify if this particularization holds in the numerical system. If so, we are guarantee that all properties of the abstract structure hold in the numerical domain. An example of the effect of the process is shown in Figure 3: the inherited properties of the *intsum* domain have been automatically generated by THEOPRO as it has been proved that *intsum* is a model for the *group* domain, when the *group* domain is described as shown in Figure 4.

A DESCRIPTION OF THE NUMERICAL DOMAIN INTSUM			
Signature	**Defining equations**	**Properties**	
		Proved	**Inherited**
base set:	succ(pred(X))=X		add(opp(X),add(X,Y))=Y
int.	pred(succ(X))=X	add(opp(X),X)=0	add(X,0)=X
constructor:	add(0,X)=X	add(add(X,Y),Z)=add(X,add(Y,Z))	opp(opp(X))=X
0:int;	add(succ(X),Y)=succ(add(X,Y))		add(X,opp(X))=0
succ:int->int;	add(pred(X),Y)=pred(add(X,Y))		add(X,add(opp(X),Y))=Y
pred:int->int.	opp(0)=0		opp(add(X,Y))=add(opp(Y),opp(X))
defined operations:	opp(succ(X))=pred(opp(X))		
opp:int->int;	opp(pred(X))=succ(opp(X))		
add:intxint->int.	double(0)=0		
double:int->int.	double(succ(X))=succ(succ(double(X)))		
	double(pred(X))=pred(pred(double(X)))		

Figure 3. Description of the *intsum* domain seen as a group with respect to the sum. Proved properties are the properties which have been proved to verify that the *intsum* domain is a group. Inherited properties are automatically obtained from the group structure by particularising the properties which correspond to the rewriting rules associated of the group structure.

In both cases, proofs are carried out by using a many-sorted version of the Boyer and Moore theorem prover, which performs a proof by using induction and rewriting. [Ant87; Boy-Moo75].

The main idea underlying the proof process is that of orienting the equations which constitute the premisses of a proof (defining equations and properties already proved for a given domain) and interpreting them as a rewriting system. This interpretation can be given only if the rewriting system satisfies suitable conditions [Ave-Mad90], that is if every term can be reduced to a unreducible term and equal terms are reduced in a unique way. Unfortunately, this last property is not always verified by the rewriting system obtained by orienting the equations. Due to this problem, a control mechanism has been implemented; the mechanism is based on an incremental version of the Knuth-Bendix completion algorithm [Knu-Ben70], that, in case of success, builds a set of rewriting rules satisfying the properties, by adding new equations and orienting them.

Figure 4 shows the description of the *group* domain obtained as the result of the validation of the equational definition of Figure 2.

DESCRIPTION OF THE ABSTRACT STRUCTURE GROUP		
Signature	Defining equations	Lemmas
base set:	comp(comp(X,Y),Z)=comp(X,comp(Y,Z))	comp(i(X),comp(X,Y))=Y
gr.	comp(e,X)=X	comp(X,e)=X
operations:	comp(i(X),X)=e	i(i(X))=X
comp: grxgr --> gr;		i(e)=e
e: --> gr.		comp(X,i(X))=e
i: gr --> gr.		comp(X,comp(i(X),Y))=Y
		i(comp(X,Y))=comp(i(X),i(Y))

Figure 4. A description of the abstract structure *group*. The lemmas are properties obtained by deriving the computational model of the *group* structure from the set of defining equations.

1.3 Building a proof

To make students acquire the capability of formally handling mathematical problems, mathematics teacher should guide them to autonomously choose the knowledge which is to be used to carry out a proof, to analyse the common features of different domains, and to employ knowledge about these features in order to formulate definitions and to construct proofs.

To this end, THEOPRO places a series of commands at user disposal, to allow him to establish the environment of a proof, to explore relationships between domains, to verify conjectures, and so on. Given a problem to be solved by using THEOPRO, the solution process adopted by a user is represented by the sequence of commands given to the system.

As it is shown in Figure 5, commands pertain to three different classes: commands for defining domains (EDIT, SHOW); commands for verifying the computational properties of a domain (COMPLETE, VERIFY); commands for analysing mathematical properties of a domain (BINDING, PROVE).

Input	Aim	Output
EDIT intsum	To access the editor for giving the equational definition of the *intsum* domain shown in Figure 1.	*Object INTSUM created*
SHOW intsum	To see the description of the *intsum* domain.	print_out of the description of the *intsum* domain.
COMPLETE group	To complete the equational description of the algebraic structure *group* specified in Figure 2.	*OK completion*
VERIFY intsum	To verify the validity of the definition of the *intsum* domain w.r.t. the computational model.	*OK no errors on spec*
PROVE intsum add(double(X),double(Y))= double(add(Y,X))	To verify if the *double* operation is closed w.r.t. the *add* operation defined on *intsum*.	print_out of the proof (see Figure 6)
BINDING intsum TO group [int] TO [gr] [add,0,opp] TO [comp,e,i]	To verify if *intsum* domain is a model of *group* according to the given association.	print_out of the proofs of the "proved properties" shown in Figure 3

Figure 5. The commands and their effects: some examples.

1.4 Analysing a proof

A formal proof is a long and tedious process of the mechanical application of a scheme and its iteration. As a consequence, students are not usually required to perform these kinds of processes, and they are made to learn the concept of proof by analysing examples carried out by the teacher. Due to the nature of the process, the examples shown by the teacher are too simple and too few to enable students to handle complex problems, which require the iterative application of a proof scheme: this fact is one of the main causes of the inability to apply correctly induction when more than one iteration is required.

To make students analyse complex examples of proofs, THEOPRO has been endowed with the capability of producing the print-out of a proof, as a side-effect of the computation. The print-out of the proof shows the individual steps of the solution with their justifications: at first the environment of the proof is visualized (the arrows are employed to clarify that equational deduction is replaced by computation); then, the property to be proved is displayed; finally, the complete proof process is shown.

When the system decides to use induction as proof method, it informs the user by giving a message, by indicating the variable on which induction will be applied and the induction cases. The rewriting rules applied in an inductive proof are explicitly indicated. Figure 6 shows an example of print_out of a proof.

```
The axioms are:
 ax_1 succ(pred(A0)) -> A0
 ax_2 pred(succ(A1)) -> A1
 ax_3 add(0,A2) -> A2
 ax_4 add(succ(A3),A4) -> succ(add(A3,A4))
 ax_5 add(pred(A5),A6) -> pred(add(A5,A6))
 ax_6 opp(0) -> 0
 ax_7 opp(succ(A7)) -> pred(opp(A7))
 ax_8 opp(pred(A8)) -> succ(opp(A8))
 ax_9 double(0) -> 0
 ax_10 double(succ(A9)) -> succ(succ(double(A9)))
 ax_11 double(pred(B0)) -> pred(pred(double(B0)))

The theorem is:
 add(double(B1),double(B2)) = double(add(B1,B2))
Begin induction on B1
Induction on B1 case 0
 (L) add(double(0),double(B2))      << subst B1 with 0 <<
 (R) double(add(0,B2))      << subst B1 with 0 <<
 (L) add(0,double(B2))       << reduct by ax_9 <<
 (R) double(B2)      << reduct by ax_3 <<
 (L) double(B2)      << reduct by ax_3 <<
 *** equality obtained ***
Induction on B1 case succ(B3)
 (L) add(double(succ(B3)),double(B2))      << subst B1 with succ(B3) <<
 (R) double(add(succ(B3),B2))      << subst B1 with succ(B3) <<
 (L) add(succ(succ(double(B3))),double(B2))      << reduct by ax_10 <<
 (R) double(succ(add(B3,B2)))      << reduct by ax_4 <<
 (L) succ(add(succ(double(B3)),double(B2)))      << reduct by ax_4 <<
 (L) succ(succ(add(double(B3),double(B2))))      << reduct by ax_4 <<
 (R) succ(succ(double(add(B3,B2))))      << reduct by ax_10 <<
 (L) succ(succ(double(add(B3,B2))))      << ind. hyp. on  B1 for B3 <<
 *** equality obtained ***
Induction on B1 case pred(B3)
 (L) add(double(pred(B3)),double(B2))      << subst B1 with pred(B3) <<
 (R) double(add(pred(B3),B2))      << subst B1 with pred(B3) <<
 (L) add(pred(pred(double(B3))),double(B2))      << reduct by ax_11 <<
 (R) double(pred(add(B3,B2)))      << reduct by ax_5 <<
 (L) pred(add(pred(double(B3)),double(B2)))      << reduct by ax_5 <<
 (L) pred(pred(add(double(B3),double(B2))))      << reduct by ax_5 <<
 (R) pred(pred(double(add(B3,B2))))      << reduct by ax_11 <<
 (L) pred(pred(double(add(B3,B2))))      << ind. hyp. on  B1 for B3 <<
 *** equality obtained ***
End induction on B1
QED
```

Figure 6. Print_out obtained by giving the command:
PROVE intsum add(double(B1),double(B2)) = double(add(B1,B2)).
The environment of the proof and the assertion to be proved are displayed. At every proof step, the user is shown: the label of the side (L for left and R for right) of the equation under examination; the expression obtained in one deductive step; a comment indicating the deduction.

2 Examples of application

THEOPRO aims at helping students to improve the learning of the following abilities.

- To formalize a problem, as the system requires the user to model a domain by using a formal language which allows to: clearly state the objects of the domain and the operations on them; distinguish among syntactic and semantic interpretation; use inductive definitions; model properties as equations; rely on relationships among domains.

- To choose a solution process, as the user is asked to identify a sequence of commands which allows stating the environment in which to prove an assertion.

- To understand that not every equational description of a domain has a corresponding computational model, as the environment of a proof must be validated.

- To read and interpret a proof process based on induction and rewriting rules, as the system explains the knowledge and the deductions performed to carry out these kinds of proofs.

- To use knowledge about algebra, as students are given the possibility of referring to abstract structures in order to build proof environments.

2.1 Examples of use

We shall illustrate the possibilities offered by THEOPRO by discussing three examples. The first example shows how THEOPRO makes possible the analysis of the relationship between numerical domains and abstract structures; the second illustrates the possibility of using different environments to carry out the same property. Both examples refer to the domains already discussed. Finally, the third example provides hints on different formalizations of the same problem, both as regards proof environment and model of the property.

Example 1

Show that the set of even integers is a subgroup of the integer group.

The problem can be solved by showing the following: a) integers are a group w.r.t. the sum; b) even integers are a group w.r.t. the sum.

a) To this aim students can rely on knowledge about both the integer domain and the group structure, in order to establish a relationship, between operations on integers and operations on groups, which makes it possible to conclude that integers are a group. Consequently, students build an equational model of integers, with the sum and the opposite (see Figure 1); then, they have to find out an equational description of the group structure (see Figure 2). Both descriptions must be validated w.r.t. the computational model (Figure 4 shows the effect of the validation process applied to the *group* domain). Finally, students must state the relationship between operations on the group structure and operations on integers which allows to prove that the sum induces a group structure on integers. (Figure 3 shows the description of the *intsum* domain obtained as side-effect of this proof).

b) To handle this task students are required to give a constructive definition of the even numbers (see, for example, the *double* operation shown in Figure 1) and to formalize, by means of equations, the properties which allow to prove the closure of the even numbers w.r.t. the sum (see Figure 6) and the closure of the opposite operations.

Example 2

Verify that by adding to the sum of two integer numbers the opposite of the second one you obtain the first.

We propose two different ways of handling the problem.

For example, some students use a formalization for integers similar to that shown in Figure 1, and try to prove the property in this environment. (by referring to the formalization in Figure 1, the property is modelled by the equation: add(add(X,Y),opp(Y))=X).

Otherwise, students can use general knowledge about algebra: in this case, they have to find out an equational description of the group structure (see Figure 2) and to state the relationship between operations on the group structure and operations on integers which enables us to prove that integers are a group (see Example 1, part a). Knowledge on groups is then used to speed up the required proof.

Example 3

Prove that the sum of two natural numbers is even if and only if either both are even or odd.

To solve this problem, some students express the idea of even and odd numbers by means of two predicates and formulate the above statement as a relationship between the true value of the even predicate applied to the sum of two addenda and the true values of the even and odd predicates applied to the addenda. In this case, the environment of the proof is a domain built from the equational definitions of both the natural and boolean domains.

Another modelling of the same problem is obtained by giving a constructive definition of even and odd numbers as multiples of 2 and successor of multiples of 2 respectively, and by expressing the above statement as a set of properties of the addition.

3 Concluding remarks

Artificial intelligence based tools are used in mathematical higher education following mainly two different approaches: on the one hand, automatic theorem provers, which assist students who carry out proofs in the field of geometry, are proposed and experimented; on the other hand, attention is focused on the analysis of the educational possibilities of symbolic manipulation systems, which guide students to solve problems involving symbolic computations [Wen87]. Geometry oriented automatic provers are experimented mainly with secondary school students (aged from 17 to 19) [And-Boy85, Py91], while symbolic systems seem particularly suitable for use with University students of mathematics courses [Kim82, Sup90].

Until now, only scant attention has been paid to the possibility of using automatic proof systems to assist University students in the learning of formal systems. THEOPRO constitutes an operative contribution to research in this field.

The system is conceived as a lab to make experiments on proofs in formal domains, as students can freely choose the knowledge to be used in a proof and to modify it, thus understanding its role in mathematical activity. A limitation of the present prototype is due to the fact that students cannot intervene during the proof process. To overcome this problem, THEOPRO will be endowed with the capability of allowing users to interactively carry out a proof by choosing both the knowledge to be used and the proof steps to be performed.

An interesting development of the work is that of integrating the reasoning capability of THEOPRO with that of performing numerical computations. As it is known, if different computing facilities are available from different software tools, a considerable amount of time and efforts is required to learn how to deal with such tools and students are led to focus attention on technical problems rather than on the topics of interest. The possibility of using integrated environment should partly eliminate these obstacles, thus facilitating the use of computing environments in math courses.

References

[And-Boy85] John R. Anderson, C.Franklin Boyle, Gregg Yost. *The Geometry Tutor.* Proceedings of International Joint Conference on Artificial Intelligence. 1985, Vol.1, pp.1-7.

[Ant87] Sergio Antoy. *Automatically Provable Specifications.* Ph.D. Thesis Department of Computer Science, University of Maryland, 1987.

[Ave-Mad90] J. Avenhaus, K. Madlener. *Term Rewriting and Equational Reasoning.* Formal Techniques in Artificial Intelligence. Banerji R.B. (Ed.), North Holland, 1991, pp.1-43.

[Boy-Moo75] Robert S. Boyer, J.Strother Moore *Proving Theorems about LISP Functions.* JACM 22-1, 1985, pp.129-144.

[Ehr-Mah85] Hartmut Ehrig, Barnd Mahr. *Fundamentals of Algebraic Specifications 1.* Springer-Verlag, 1985.

[Hue-Huo82] Gerard Huet, Jean-Marie Hullot. *Proofs by Induction in Equational Theories with Construstors.* Journal of Computer and System Science. 1982, Vol. 25, pp.239-266

[Kim82] Ralph Kimball. *A Self-improving Tutor for Symbolic Integration.* Intelligent Tutoring Systems, D. Sleeman and J.S. Brown (Eds.), Academic Press, 1982, pp.283-307.

[Knu-Ben70] Donald E. Knuth, Peter B. Bendix. *Simple Word Problems in Universal Algebras.* Computational Problems in Abstract Algebras, Leech J. (Ed.), Pergamon Press, 1970, pp.263-297.

[Py91] Dominique Py. *Adaptative Training for Geometry Problem-solving in MENTONIEZH.* Proceedings of PEG91, Rosa Maria Bottino, Paola Forcheri, Maria Teresa Molfino (Eds.), 1991, pp.295-403.

[Sup90] Patrick Suppes. *Uses of Artificial Intelligence in Computer-Based Instruction.* Artificial Intelligence in Higher Education, V. Marik, O. Stepankova and Z. Zdrahal (Eds.), Springer-Verlag, 1990, pp.206-225.

[Wen87] Etienne Wenger. *Artificial Intelligence and Tutoring Systems.* Morgan Kaufmann Publishers, 1987.

QUIZ, a Distributed Intelligent Tutoring System

Michel Futtersack (*), Jean-Marc Labat (**)

(*) LIUM	(**) LAFORIA
Université du Maine	Université Pierre et Marie Curie
Route de Laval BP 535	4, place Jussieu
72017 Le Mans Cedex, France	75252 Paris Cedex, France
tel. (33) 16 43 83 32 21	tel. (33) 1 44 27 70 02
email: futtersack@laforia.ibp.fr	email: labat@laforia.ibp.fr

Abstract

QUIZ is a Distributed Intelligent Tutoring System for learning bridge bidding. A set of generic tasks is distributed among four specialists (a tutor, a problem solver, an explainer and a problem generator), who perform their tasks in parallel. These agents are heterogeneous. They own a private working memory and communicate by asynchronous messages passing. Increasing flexibility is a key point in improving the pedagogical capacities of ITS. The strategic level of flexibility results from the determination of the curriculum, the choice of the pedagogical strategy and the degree of expertise used in the problem solver. The choices made at this level must be based mainly upon the student model. The tactical level of flexibility results from the choice of exercise, the advising, the corrections and the explanations. In QUIZ, the pedagogical actions are gathered and sequenced by means of plans, which are chosen by metarules and dynamically assembled from pieces that are memorized in libraries.

Introduction

QUIZ is an Intelligent Tutoring System for learning bridge bidding. Its aim is to help all players, whether they be absolute beginners or experienced players, to improve their bidding capacities in the "fifth major" convention. The main factor, which influenced the choice of our domain is the very diversity of teaching knowledge involved. The learners too, differ according to their degree of experience and motivation: bridge can be a source of distraction, a way of meeting other people or a competitive activity.

We began by developing an actual expert system to solve bridge bidding problems, enabling the learner to submit his own exercises. This is the first source of flexibility in the teaching process. Another source of flexibility with QUIZ is its ability to adapt itself to a particular student. We defined several tutorial strategies which are represented explicitly in pedagogical plans and materialize. Finally, we designed a very open and modular architecture to define bases for a general shell of Intelligent Tutoring Systems.

1 Distributed Intelligent Tutoring Systems: A new paradigm

The problem that faces an Intelligent Tutor is that of directing a human student towards a given state of knowledge in a given domain. This problem can be divided into various sub-problems calling upon skills varied in nature: the elaboration of an instructional plan, the generation of a "made-to-measure" exercise, the "pedagogical" solving of an exercise (solve at the level of the student), the providing of varied and targeted explanations.

In traditional learning, the teacher is alone in front of his/her class and the difficulty lies in creating personalized teaching activities. With QUIZ, we imagined a quite different teaching/learning situation, as an interaction between a learner and a team of teachers, each specializing in pedagogical skills, and cooperating towards a common goal. Distributed learning aims to allocate functions (expose knowledge, devise exercises and problems, solve these problems, provide explanations) to different agents. Those functions generally are present in the same human teacher. The standard architecture for an ITS -expert module, pedagogical module, student model and interface- simulate a sole but multi-function intelligent entity; these different functions are insured in a sequential fashion.

The new paradigm of **Distributed Intelligent Tutoring System** (DITS) is drawn from Distributed Artificial Intelligence [Agha 86] [Ferber 89], which sees the solution of problems as the result of cooperation between autonomous agents. This approach would appear of great interest in the conception of artificial teaching systems, which propose highly reactive training environments, thank to the parallelizing of numerous tasks : for example, while the explanatory agent presents the solution to an exercise, the pedagogical agent can perform a pedagogical evaluation to bring the student model up to date with his/her progress, then ask the agent responsible for generating exercises to provide a problem adapted to the present situation. Finally, the pedagogical agent can ask the solver agent to begin solving a new problem (while the explainer is still presenting the student with comments on the previous exercise).

2   Structure and Functions of a QUIZ's Agent

The communication model between QUIZ's agents differs from the blackboard approach used in ITS as in SCENT-3 [McCalla and Greer 1988]. It is drawn from Semiotics [Buyssens 70]. There is a two-phase mechanism. The first phase is the setting up of a communication network. It is based on the mutual recognition of all agents wishing to communicate. The establishment of this connection can be made by the exchange of conventional signs that we call "signals" in the QUIZ system. The second phase is an exchange of information (facts and knowledge) between agents in a communication situation.

The structure of a QUIZ agent enables this communication to take place at two levels. As shown in Figure 1, each QUIZ's agent is comprised of a signal-box, a set of mail-boxes, a set of programs that represent the different behaviors of the agent, and a program called "controller". The controller defines the general internal functioning of the agent, i.e. how it consults its signal-box and what behavior it adapts when it becomes aware that signals are arriving from other agents.

3   Heterogeneous Knowledge-Based Systems

The production of an ITS requires the help of a team of experts [Woolf & Cunningham 1987]: this means the cooperation of at least one specialist in the domain and a pedagogue. Each expertise can be decomposed into several sub-expertises. Therefore a good teacher should know how to plan a lesson, be capable of monitoring and scrutinizing specific indicators (signs of lassitude, mental blockage). He also should know how to evaluate the student's performance and make deductions concerning the learner's cognitive and affective state. The specialist on the other hand, should be capable of solving a problem in a pedagogical fashion [Labat & Futtersack 1990], i.e. by using only the concepts and know-how attained by the learner. The same problem can thus be solved from different viewpoints and at different levels of abstraction.

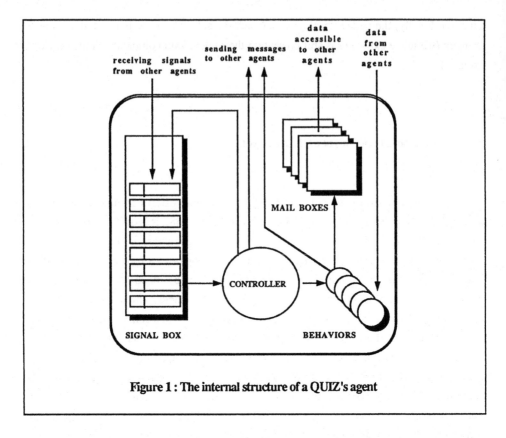

Figure 1 : The internal structure of a QUIZ's agent

All these diverse expertises can be expressed using different formalisms of knowledge representation in A.I. We are convinced that a good methodology for the elicitation and the coding of an expertise begins with the natural expression used by the expert and then a formal language that most closely resembles that of the original can be chosen.

We claim that each DITS specialist should have its own language for knowledge representation and its own inference mechanisms. For example, to describe their teaching activity, human pedagogues use plans and objectives to express themselves. However, for reasoning about the student, the teacher bases his/her deductions on information received through student's behavior. A language based on production rules is perfectly adapted to this step of the teaching process. To represent pedagogical knowledge, we used the dynamic pedagogical planner KEPLER-ELFE, which we describe later. To solve bidding problems in bridge, the experts perform a data driven reasoning. They have no particular objective, apart from attaining the best contract, but this cannot be easily decomposed into sub-goals. As bridge is a game of incomplete information, the experts could be inclined to make hypotheses and backtrack when they possess more information. Then to represent knowledge in the domain (resolution expert system and explanation expert system) we chose the SNARK forward-chaining inference engine [Laurière & Vialatte 1986], which allows hypotheses management.

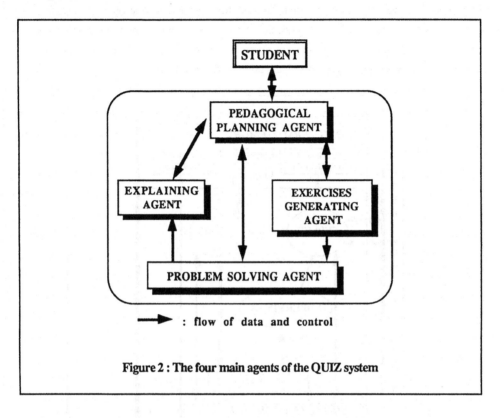

Figure 2 : The four main agents of the QUIZ system

QUIZ comprises four main agents such as is shown in Figure 2.: a tutor, a problem solver and an explainer, which are expert systems, and a problem generator. Thus QUIZ agents are by nature very heterogeneous as they use radically different languages and reasoning paradigms.

4 KEPLER-ELFE: A Dynamic and Interactive Pedagogical Planner

The pedagogical planner KEPLER-ELFE comprises three knowledge interpreters such as is shown in Figure 3.: a task interpreter (SUPERVISOR), a plan interpreter (KEPLER [Vivet 1988]) and a rule interpreter (ELFE). The SUPERVISOR manages an agenda that represents the strategic level of the pedagogical planner (teach what?). SUPERVISOR selects the tasks which it submits to KEPLER, which in turn solves the problem with dynamic planning: it elaborates a plan by retrieving and assembling sub-plans from a library (see Figure 4.). If several pedagogical plans are candidates for the same objective, KEPLER chooses the best one by using pedagogical metarules taking into account the student model and the learning context. To monitor the planning activity, KEPLER calls upon ELFE, which reasons about the world: student model and context of the session.

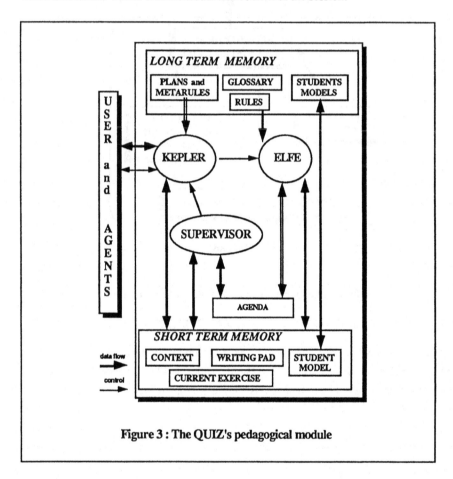

Figure 3 : The QUIZ's pedagogical module

The learner can interrupt the planner after each pedagogical action. KEPLER-ELFE then indicates the current pedagogical strategy (a list of objectives to be reached), the current objective and the tactic (a pedagogical plan) chosen to attain this objective. The learner can contest this plan by forcing the system to abandon the current objective. The learner does this by inserting a new objective or deleting the current one. Thus the learner participates fully in the pedagogical planning process, which is indispensable when taking into account the inadequacy of pedagogical knowledge available in the system. KEPLER-ELFE is then an interactive pedagogical planner.

```
(Topen%1 (meta_descriptors    (nb_exercises high) (level beginner))
    (to (teach_openings) try on
        (introduce openings)
        (present openings_level_1)
        (propose_exercices openings 3)
        (present openings_level_2)
        (propose_exercises openings 3)
        (student_evaluation)))
```

Figure 4 : An example of pedagogical plan

5   The Pedagogical orientation of the Problem Solving Agent

Initially, the solver was devised to be integrated in a tutor. We adopted a pragmatic approach, by remaining as close as possible to the expert's approach in spite of the limitations of knowledge based systems [Cerri 1988]. In particular, we avoided transforming qualitative on quantitative information. We above all excluded any "invention" in variables, which failed to interpret the expertise of a bridge player (no quantitative aggregation for multicriteria analysis). This aspect is of fundamental importance in providing pertinent explanations. Before selecting a bid, the solver should locate all possible bidding contracts, thus allowing a defined analysis of the learner's answer, by comparing his bid with those introduced by the solver. Finally, in the context of a pedagogical system, several levels of solution should be available for the same problem. Consequently, a novice bridge student should not directly aim for the same degree of knowledge as a top level player. The acquisition of this knowledge should proceed in an incremental manner, each stage being in itself coherent yet incomplete. Moreover, in the case of a novice, a commonsense bid should not be rejected, even if it does not satisfy certain technical criteria. We thus envisage at least two levels of solution. The first level contains the complete expertise for a tournament player of competition. The second level represents the knowledge of a rubber bridge player. It is obtained by constraint relaxation.

6   The pedagogical knowledge in QUIZ

In this paragraph, we first set forth the pedagogical principles on which our model is based. Secondly we introduce the two levels of pedagogical knowledge (strategic, tactic) and finally we present our student modelling.

6.1   The bases of our pedagogical choices

The basic idea in this study is:

"There is no one single good method in pedagogy"

Departing from this statement, our elements of reflection were based on the following factors:

* Teaching and learning are complementary and not contradictory.

* Whatever the kind of pedagogy involved, the learner must necessarily build his/her own know-how himself. Therefore, he/she should be left with as much initiative as possible within the context of interactions, because, in the last analysis, we can never say definitely what entirely suits him/her.

* Education implies defining objectives. These objectives, defined preferably in terms of targeted competence, assume the division of the subject being taught into independent units, called modules, regrouped into planned series of apprenticeship activities.

* Offering the learner a diversified choice of apprenticeship itineraries should be the constant preoccupation of the teacher. To do so, modules defined in terms of competence should possess several equivalent versions.

6.2   The strategic level

A choice is qualified as strategic if it involves the whole situation and if it is little subject to modification. In this category, we find the favorite pedagogical mode which determines and controls each session, the decomposition of the domain which depends on the didactic, the determination of the curriculum and certain aspects relating to the affective part in the student model (see § 7).

Four major strategies are present in QUIZ.

The "**study**" mode is the most directive. It is founded on expository logic: each notion is the subject of a lesson with definitions, examples, exercises and tests. The tutor maintains control of the situation, even if he decides to use other modes or to hand over to the learner.

The "**guided apprenticeship**" mode is based on the notion-core concept. The tutor or the learner chooses a theme at the beginning of the session. From there, the tutor organizes the session, by proposing exercises which enable the tackling of majors aspects.

The "**free apprenticeship**" mode is the third one. Unlike the preceding mode, there is no unifying theme. An agenda is unnecessary. The learner proposes his own hands (thirteen cards) or asks the generator for random supplementary data.

In the "**consultation**" mode, QUIZ is used only to play with. The student model is not used nor modified. The player can propose hands or constraints (in this case, the data generator creates hands which respect specifications). He can make the machine bids alone (with two hands) or take the place of one player.

As in the modular teaching theory, we considered it necessary to operate decomposition at two levels. At the first one, we decomposed the domain into themes. Each theme is a coherent group of knowledge, relatively independent from that contained in the others, and requiring several learning sessions. At the second level, each theme is decomposed into a group of teaching units, called "modules". These are homogeneous units, sufficiently small in size to be assimilated in a single pedagogical episode.

The notion of curriculum can only make sense for the "study" and "guided apprenticeship" modes. The agenda is the structure which enables curriculum management. QUIZ, therefore, is, according to the typology suggested by Murray [Murray 1989], "agenda based" and not "plan based" although the main formalism of the pedagogical model is the plan. The curriculum is determined by an expertise given in production rules which use the decomposition of the domain in themes and the student model. It is composed of an ordered list of themes.

6.3 The tactic level

Unlike the strategic level, the tactic level involves short term decision-making, which can be often contested, without long-term effects. This level is comprised of the task selector once the curriculum has been fixed, and the choice of plans to accomplish the task in question. The principle tasks are aids, explanations and exercise correcting.

Aid is sometimes accessible to the learner but it is the student who should formulate the demand in an explicit manner. Aid is provided in the form of texts, either information on concepts (recall of definitions at different degrees of details) or information on the use of strategies in these concepts. Finally, the learner can consult a glossary.

In QUIZ, the explanation expertise did not immediately use the trace of the expert system but rather insists on the final achievement of the solver. An object containing pertinent information for explanations is created during the resolution and attached to each topic used by the expert system of explanation. If the learner asks "why?", the first reply is a general commentary of the situation. If the learner wants more details, he can ask for information concerning strategy, prior knowledge (which match this strategy) or the consequences of the bid. These three categories of reasons - strategy, prior knowledge, expected consequences of the action made - constitute a good approach to the "why?" problem.

Numerous tactics enable correction: the answer is given with no commentary; the answer is given with a recall of previous lessons; the same question is reiterate without information; tests concerning the necessary prerequisites for the solution are posed; another exercise is given as an example or a counter-example. In QUIZ, all these tactics exist except the last one, which is the most difficult to put into operation due to the precise typology of the required exercises. Three or four of these tactics are implemented according to the exercise.

7   Student modelling

The location of an exact modelling of the student's cognitive structure in research on ITS does not, to our mind, appear of primary importance. Even the human teacher has an approximate knowledge of the student's cognitive states. Therefore, after the development of a pedagogical module, we approach the problem of student modelling in a pragmatic manner. At the cognitive level, we chose an "overlay model", which gave us a simple but robust image of the learner.

According to Meirieu's propositions [Meirieu 1989], we built a student model with around twenty attributes regrouped semantically in four sections :

* General situation: this section includes identification of the learner and the conditions in which he/she will play.

* Cognitive domain: although the game of bridge necessitates competence in different modes of reasoning, the only competence represented is the ability to learn. This is

expressed in number of times the learner has rapidly or more slowly mastered the particular know-how directly related to bridge. The system deals with a summary of the performances on each theme. The overlay model refers to the concepts of bridge and respects the pedagogical decomposition of the domain. Finally, the system provides a global estimation of the learner's level (absolute beginner, beginner, average player or experienced player).

* Affective domain: the objectives the student wishes to attain, the chosen pedagogical mode, the degree of motivation, the use of help and explanations, are all necessary aspects of information the pedagogical module requires to adapt to the learner.

* Historic: this section contains data for initializing the context at the beginning of each session and should be conserved from one session to the next.

The most relevant events, which occur during a pedagogical episode are registered in an intermediate memory called "block-notes". During the evaluation phase the student model is up-dated by means of production rules.

Example :

IF   the learner makes numerous mistakes
            and (s)he asks for neither help or explanations
            and the current pedagogical mode is free apprenticeship
THEN   pedagogical mode <-- guided apprenticeship

8   Implementation

QUIZ is implemented on an IBM 4381 machine under the system VM/CMS. Each agent is installed in an independent virtual machine. Thus, QUIZ can be considered as an actual distributed multi-machines system.

Our implementation used several programming langages: VM/LISP for KEPLER-ELFE and the pedagogical routines, REXX for the communication primitives among virtual machines, VM/C for several procedures (translation from KEPLER-ELFE's knowledge representation to SNARK's one).

The knowledge bases for bridge bidding and explanations comprise more than five hundred rules of first order. We wrote about two hundred plans and rules for representing pedagogical knowledge.

9   Conclusions

We were able to reach the following conclusions from the development of our QUIZ system. First and foremost, the Distributed Intelligent Tutoring System is an operational paradigm to represent and integrate different expertises in an Intelligent Tutoring System. Secondly, the two-level communication by asynchronous message passing allows parallel functioning of agents, essential for obtaining acceptable response time by the system. Thirdly, the dynamic and interactive pedagogical planner is a good conceptual framework for representing the curriculum in an Intelligent Tutoring System. Finally, the KEPLER-ELFE's language is rich enough to express a large range of pedagogical knowledge in a declarative manner: plans, rules and metarules.

References

[Agha 86] Gul Agha. *Actors: a Model of Concurrent Computation in Distributed Systems*, MIT Press, Cambridge, Massachusetts, 1986.

[Buyssens 70] Eric Buyssens. *La communication et l'articulation linguistique*, Presses Universitaires de Bruxelles, 1970.

[Cerri 88] Stefano A. Cerri. *The Requirements of Conceptual Modelling Systems.in Artificial Intelligence and Human Learning*, J. Self editor, 1988.

[Ferber 89] Jacques Ferber. *Objets et agents: une étude des structures de représentation et de communications en IA*, Thèse d'état, Paris, 1989.

[Futtersack & Labat 1989] Michel R. Futtersack, Jean-Marc Labat. *QUIZ : Une architecture multi-experts pour un tuteur intelligent enseignant les enchères au bridge*, AFCET RF-IA Congress, Paris, 1989.

[Labat & Futtersack 1990] Jean-Marc Labat, Michel R.Futtersack.*Résolution pédagogique*.APPLICA Congress, Lille,1990.

[Laurière & Vialatte 1986] Jean-Louis Laurière, Michèle Vialatte. *SNARK, a language to represent declarative knowledge*. IFIP, North Holland, 1986, pp 811-816.

[McCalla 1988] Gordon I. McCalla, Jim E. Greer. *Intelligent Advising in Problem Solving Domains : the SCENT-3 Architecture"*.ITS 88, Montreal, 1988.

[Meirieu 1989] Philippe Meirieu. *Apprendre...oui, mais comment ?* E.S.F. Editions, Paris, 1989.

[Murray 1989] William R. Murray. *Control for Intelligent Tutoring Systems : a Blackboard-based Dynamic Instructionnal Planner*", 4th International Conference on AI and Education, Amsterdam, 1989.

[Vivet 1988] Martial Vivet. *Knowledge-based tutors. Towards the design of a shell.* International Journal of Educational Research, 1988, Vol 12, n°8, pp. 839-850.

[Woolf & Cunningham 1987] Beverley Woolf, Patricia A. Cunningham. *Multiple Knowledge Sources in Intelligent Teaching Systems.* Conference of the American Association of Artificial Intelligence, Seattle, 1987.

INTELLIGENT TUTORIAL SYSTEM IN MEDICINE THROUGH AN INTERACTIVE TESTING PROGRAM: HyperMIR

Joan C González, Joan J Sancho, Joan M Carbó, Alex Patak and Ferran Sanz.
Departament d'Informàtica Biomèdica. Institut Municipal d'Investigació Mèdica.
Universitat Autònoma de Barcelona. P. Marítim 25. 08003. Barcelona. Spain.

Abstract

In Spain, as in many countries, the only pathway to reach postgraduate specialization in medicine is through a National MIR Exam (a multiple choice test). This exam exerts a great impact both in the teachers and students attitudes during the undergraduate period, promoting a test-oriented rather than a patient-oriented learning.

We developed an interactive auto-test system, HyperMIR, that acts as a tutor devising a personalized and permanently updated study plan. Our program includes a database of 11500 questions, previously validated and classified by their importance and difficulty by 20 sixth year medical students and 6 physicians.

The singularity of HyperMIR versus other "auto-test programs" is its ability for assessing the knowledge of the student in each curricula subject, comparing it to the needed knowledge to pass the MIR, and building a study plan and schedule based on the potential gain attainable by devoting time and effort in the study of particular subjects.

HyperMIR has been tested by 30 sixth year medical students using the program 10h./week/student. They answered a questionnaire about the usefulness of HyperMIR. All students considered the program helpful to prepare the MIR exam and all found HyperMIR easy to use. The program was qualified with an average of 4.5 over 5.

Introduction

Computer-Assisted-Instruction (CAI) is a teaching method used since the 1960s. A number of papers reported that this form of instruction has been greeted with high enthusiasm by students and that they have viewed it as an useful extension of traditional teaching methods [Xak90] [Pie88] [Gar87]. This kind of education allows students to save time by individualizing instruction, which has long been established as the optimum method of learning [Wau82].

In medicine, CAI is being developed under two main strategies: Knowledge Transfer (clinical patient simulations, physiological simulations, electronic textbooks, interactive tutorials and medical knowledge bases), and Knowledge Assessment (Multiple Choice Questions (MCQ) programs or other assessment programs).

CAI helps the acquisition of basic concepts in medical education. Using CAI is an active, self-directed and motivated learning experience, that provides immediate feedback in a non competitive environment, allowing students to evaluate their own progress during the learning process [Wal90] [Lir90] [Mar82].

Many kinds of test have been designed to evaluate the knowledge acquisition during the learning process. MCQ Tests are widely used as a form of exam in Medical Sciences, both at undergraduate and graduate levels.

In Spain, as in many countries, the only pathway to reach postgraduate specialization in medicine is through the Residency Training Program (RTP). Graduate medical students must pass a National Exam (called MIR: Medical Internship and Residency Exam) which is composed by 250 MCQ with 5 possible answers with wrong answer penalty. The test accounts for 75% of the final score and academic scores from the undergraduate curriculum account for the remaining 25%. RTP vacancies in each hospital are strictly allocated by final score. About twenty thousand graduates take the exam yearly and only about three thousand pass it. Therefore, the MIR exam has a great impact both in the teachers and students attitudes during the undergraduate period. The reputation of Medical Schools is strongly dependent from the number of its graduates able to embark the RTP. Professors are faced with the dilemma of focusing the instruction of medical students for the MIR Exam or prepare them as general practitioners instead. Even, there are some medical schools that have decided to prepare their students more for passing the MIR exam rather than for having the necessary practical medical knowledge, hoping that they will take this knowledge during the specialization period.

Many computer programs have been designed to help pass MCQ Tests. These programs have not enjoyed wide acceptance because in general they were too simple and they did not constitute a great help for the students, representing a potential loss of time to prepare this kind of exams seeing and answering questions in front of the computer's screen without getting any guidance other than the final score.

It is obvious that the best solution for this problem would be to arrange a tireless and personal tutor for each student who could guide and direct the preparation's process of these exams in an explanatory way following objective and reasoned criteria. This tutor would be ideally giving advice about the correct answer, identifying subjects where the student should concentrate his/her effort, designing a specific study plan to optimize the study time. We can not provide such a personal tutor for all students and classical MCQ programs will never guide a student during all the learning process.

Those considerations lead us to develop an interactive system, HyperMIR, to help medical students to prepare the MIR Exam, with a personalized learning schedule. The program acts as a constant and tireless tutor and it devises a study plan to follow-up for passing the exam. This system will allow the faculty to prepare physicians according with the WHO guidelines without wasting efforts in exam-oriented teaching.

The objectives were to offer a program able to: 1) Assess the student's initial knowledge to adapt the difficulty level of future questions 2) Determine in which areas of the curriculum the student needs to concentrate the effort in order to pass the exam and suggest a personalized study plan 3) Follow-up the progress in the study plan 4) Continuously reassess the progress in those weak areas and update accordingly the study plan 5) Offer the opportunity of eventually taking a MIR-like exam as a global evaluation and 6) Provide the right answer together with an appropriate explanation with bibliographic support.

Material and Methods

The choosed graphical user interface was HyperCard$^{(TM)}$ in Apple$^{(TM)}$ Macintosh (Apple Computer, Cupertino, CA) to implement HyperMIR.

We used for the development of HyperMIR: a Macintosh IISi computer with 5 MB RAM and 80 MB hard disk. The minimum hardware requirements to run HyperMIR are: a Macintosh Plus computer with 1 MB of RAM and a hard disk with 10 MB free.

The Multiple Choice Questions database includes a public domain pool of 9000 MCQ and an historical MIR database of 2500 MCQ. These questions were stored in ASCII Text format and they have been converted to be used in HyperMIR. For that purpose several utilities were used:

DOS Mounter® (Dayna Communications, Inc), which allowed reading MS-DOS diskettes on Macintosh computers, MacLink Plus/PC EU 4.50© (Data Viz, Inc, Trumbull, CT), to transform MS-DOS ASCII Text format to Macintosh Text format and Word Perfect 1.03® (Word Perfect Corporation, Orem, Utah), to insert codes into the text, so it could be easily managed by our program.

Versions of HyperMIR for IBM/PC compatibles (MS-DOS, MS-WINDOWS), UNIX machines (X Windows) and DEC VAX (VMS) are currently being developed.

Design Problems and Solutions

In order to generate accurate MIR exam simulations it was necessary to know two parameters of the MIR exam: the percentage of questions dealing with each subject and the degree of difficulty of each question within each subject.

The process of entering, validating and performing a subject classification of the questions from 10 MIR exams (1980-1989) were carried out by a selected group of 20 sixth year medical students and 6 physicians, using a simple program we called MIR Validation and was supervised by the authors. After validation, 127 questions (1.1%) were rejected, mainly because obsolescence, inconsistency or duplication. Furthermore, they validated the remaining questions from the data bank. In the validation of the data bank, each member of the group spent a mean of 38h/volunteer. At the same time, each question was assigned an "initial difficulty score". From this starting point, the difficulty score of each question is permanently updated by the percentage of wrong answers it received.

From this validation, it was observed that some questions were classified in different subjects depending on the student. It was intended to limit subjectivity bracketing together those subjects with major overlapping, coming out with a new classification of the medical curricula, reflecting the perception of it from the students point of view. This way, there were established four new "MIR subjects": Microbiology and Infectious Diseases, Gynecology and Obstetrics, Epidemiology and Statistics and finally Pathology and Histology.

In order to make sound recommendations, it was necessary to identify the subjects in which the study effort will be more productive, taking into account its importance, difficulty and the initial knowledge of each subject by the student. The result can be expressed numerically as the "potential gain" for each subject for each student .

After analyzing the performance of students with a prototype of HyperMIR, it was proposed that the potential gain of studying a particular subject is inversely proportional to the logarithm of the initial knowledge about that subject (in percentage of right answers) and directly proportional to the importance of the subject (in percentage of questions of that subject over the total questions in the MIR exam), to model this relationship the following formula was devised:

$$PG = (SI * \log (MK)) - (SI * \log (IK))$$

Being, SI = Subject Importance, percentage of questions by subject over the total questions of the exam, MK = Maximum Knowledge = 100%, IK = Initial Knowledge, percentage of right answers over the total questions by subject.

Table 1 shows examples of potential gain in extreme situations and a three dimensional plot representation of the gain is shown in Figure 1.

SUBJECT IMPORTANCE	INITIAL KNOWLEDGE	POTENTIAL GAIN
90%	10%	90
90%	90%	4,12
10%	10%	10
10%	90%	0,46

Table 1: Examples of potential gain in extremes situations. Subject Importance: percentage of questions by subject over the total questions of the exam. Initial Knowledge: percentage of right answers by subject over the total questions of the exam.

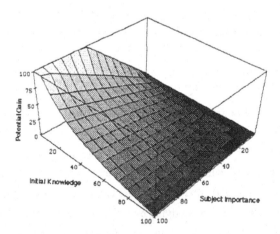

Fig. 1: Three dimensional plot of the potential gain values obtained for each combination of initial knowledge and subject importance.

Program Description

Program modules are implemented in two different types of stacks: "Welcome" stores all information generated by and offers results and recommendations to students; "MIR-Exam and MIR-Subject" import the text-based database and presents the questions to the student.

The program creates a card for each student, placing his/her personal details, and registering a log of the activity, reflecting the date of each session and the time spent, the study plan, the test taken and the scores achieved in each area.

In the first interaction with HyperMIR, the student must take an examination of 300 random questions covering all subjects (12 questions for each one of the 25 subjects included in the MIR exam) to assess his/her initial knowledge. Once completed, HyperMIR establishes a pattern of the students performance and so, HyperMIR will be able to generate tests adapted to learner's initial knowledge.

In the next interaction, the student must take a MIR exam simulation with 250 random questions with identical number of questions by subject of a real MIR. Once finished, HyperMIR compares the scores in each subject with the specific requirements for the MIR Exam, identifying the areas with insufficient achievement. From this comparison, HyperMIR builds a study plan of suggested areas of study, which is based on the potential gain for each subject. (Fig. 2).

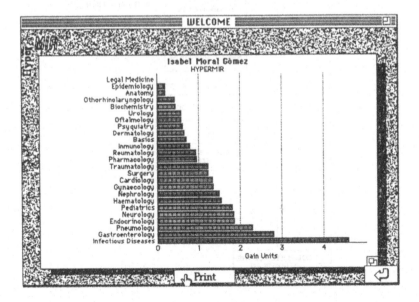

Figure 2: Graphical representation of the gain of one student by subjects.

In successive sessions the student follows the study plan suggested by HyperMIR to obtain maximum effectiveness. Then, the student takes short sets of 40 questions covering specifically each area suggested, to improve his/her knowledge. Those short tests are built according to the score of the initial assessment, and increase in complexity until the score achieved is considered good enough by HyperMIR to pass that particular area of the MIR exam.

The list of suggested areas to study is updated after passing each set. If a student does not agree with the difficulty level of his/her questions, he/she can take again an initial evaluation to reassess their knowledge.

At any time the user is allowed to take a real MIR exam from the historical database among 1980-1991 years, with time limitation and penalty for wrong answers, to get a personal feeling of progress.

At the end of each test, the user can review the answers accompanied by help screens with explanations related to each question. The teaching strategy is represented in figure 3.

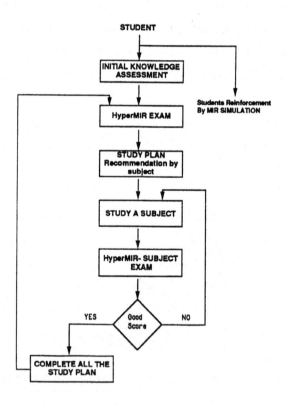

Figure 3: Overall teaching strategy.

Practical Results

We are very encouraged by the results obtained so far. HyperMIR has quickly caught the interest of students. The learning curve proved to be smooth and the average time for mastering the interface was well under one hour.

The program was developed in about six months. The process of testing the program is being carried out by a group of volunteers of 30 sixth year medical students, which are using the program about 10h./week/student.

A questionnaire about the usefulness of HyperMIR was designed for these students to answer. Results of the questionnaire indicate that students found the computer-assisted instructions easy to use. This fact, allows students to concentrate on the content rather that struggle with the mechanics of using the computer. All the students considered that the program could be helpful to prepare the MIR exam. The program received a distinctly favorable response from the students, with the average overall rating being 4.5 on a five-point scale. They qualified the quality of the questions database with 4 points and they thought they could be using the program during 3 or 4 hours continuously.

Discussion

Some papers covering CAI evaluation in medical sciences suggested that this instructional method may be more efficient and effective than more traditional forms of instruction, since less teaching time was required to attain the same results [Mar82]. However, CAI requires well-trained personnel, good programs for development, a good computer system, and adequate funding to provide complete evidence of its effectiveness with a convincing demonstration [Pie88].

Our purpose with the creation of HyperMIR is offering it as a supplement to traditional teaching, traineeship or preparation for MCQ exams in general and for the MIR Exam in particular. HyperMIR should be considered as a support tool that guides students towards a better planning of their study time, following objective parameters. In the process, HyperMIR will let students cultivate attitudes and skills that will sustain a lifetime of learning in medicine.

We choosed HyperCard$^{(TM)}$ and Apple$^{(TM)}$ Macintosh because it has the advantage to be freely distributed with the purchase of each Macintosh microcomputer, and its becoming almost a standard in multimedia systems for medical teaching. This tool will allows us to easily supplement HyperMIR with sounds and images .

Our conclusion is that with HyperCard$^{(TM)}$ is feasible and easy to develop a CAI program, which works as an assistant tutor and corrector of all kind of exam with MCQ.

In the future, is our intention to: 1) Translate our program to other languages (German, French) to be used in similar critical MCQ tests; 2) Expand HyperMIR scope, allowing professors to enter their own questions and explanations into the database permitting the use for the examination of students and converting it to HyperEXAM; and 3) Do a periodical validation of the program.

References

[Xak90] Xakellis GC and Gjerde C. Evaluation by Second-Year Medical students of their Computer-Aided Instruction. Academic Medicine. 1990, Vol 65, pp 23-6.

[Pie88] Piemme TE. Computer-Assisted learning and Evaluation in Medicine. JAMA 1988, Vol 260, pp 367-72.

[Gar87] Garret TJ, Asjford AR and Savage DGA. Comparison of CAI and tutorial in Haematology and Oncology. Journal of Medical Education. 1987, Vol 62, pp 918-22.

[Wau82] Waugh D. Pedagogy, self-education and the information explosion. Pharos. 1982, Vol 45, pp 20-1.

[Wal90] Walsh RJ and Bohn RC. CAI: a role in teaching human gross anatomy. Medical Education. 1990, Vol 24, pp 499-506.

[Lir90] Liras A. CAI and Scientific Method in Medical School. Academic Medicine. 1990, Vol. 65, pp 687.

[Mar82] Marion R, Niebuhr BR, Petrusa ER and Weinholtz D. Computer-based instruction in basic medical science education. Journal of Medical Education. 1982, Vol. 57, pp.521-6.

DCE: A Knowledge-Based Tutoring and Advisory System
- Tutoring Strategies and Architecture -

Rul Gunzenhäuser and Alfred Zimmermann
Department of Computer Science (Informatik)
University of Stuttgart
Breitwiesenstrasse 20-22
D-7000 Stuttgart 80
Germany
Telephone: +49 (0711) 7816-331
Telefax: +49 (0711) 7801045
email: rul@ifi.informatik.uni-stuttgart.dbp.de

Abstract

DCE (Dynamic Critic Expert) is an intelligent tutoring and advisory system based on a special designed dialog model. It supports explorative learning and problem solving within a flexible simulation environment. DCE offers different tutoring strategies and therefore provides a better transparency than traditional help and explanation systems do.

Based on this model, the control of the learner's activities is taken over by our Dynamic Critic Expert Model (DCEM). The explorative learning environment acts like a coach and provides critique based explanations about correct and false parts of the solution. Errors are corrected by the expert component. In addition, we have extended some traditional navigation facilities to focus the learning information and to integrate different types of learning information in a consistent way.

We have mapped the functionality of DCEM to a prototype architecture based on the conceptual model of a blackboard. The knowledge based learning system is applied in the context of risk adapted therapy planning and control in pediatric oncology. The paper describes the tutoring strategies, the DCEM constraint, and the architecure of the DCE system. This report is rounded off by some remarks about other applications.

Introduction

The design of DCE - a knowledge-based tutoring and advisory system for risk adapted therapy planning and control in pediatric oncology - integrates computer aided problem solving, different types of tutoring information, and a consistent user interface.

DCE forms an intelligent explorative learning environment for students, nurses, and doctors. These people have to master complex details and rules about pharmacological combinations, surgery operations, radiation therapies, and supportive therapies. [Treuner, 86]. All these details - including time dependencies - are described in protocols for oncologic therapies. The applied therapy has to be individually adapted to each case to minimize the risks.

The explorative environment DCE offers a variety of learning and tutoring strategies [Michalski 87] like learning from examples, learning by observation and discovery, and learning by experimentation within a flexible simulation environment. It is based on a special designed dialog model, the Dynamic Critic Expert Model (DCEM), which contains expert knowledge (e.g. about therapy plans), knowledge about individual users (e.g. students as novice users), and knowledge about tutoring strategies (e.g. for critiquing).

In order to consider the various dependencies between these heterogeneous knowledge types, a special blackboard architecture was designed and implemented. This architecture enables a close integration of of guided discovery, didactic deep tutor information, focusable hyper-tutoring information, dynamic critique based explanations, and inconsistency resolution.

1 Tutoring strategies for explorative learning

The tutoring strategies of DCE are based on guided exploration. As understood by [Cronbach 77], problem solving is a process of:

- analyzing (i.e. recalling similar situations and structuring the problem),
- synthesizing (i.e. generating alternative solutions),
- classifying, and fixing the solution.

In explorative learning [Neber 81] people develop initiatives and thinking activities. These processes are inductive and hypothetical: The exploring learner usually adopts and applies some basic problem solving knowledge, and induces new hypotheses. These assumptions are confirmed or corrected during the simulation process, e.g. in the oncologic therapy planning. During the explorative learning process, the user's competence advances and flows into the real case application of the acquired knowledge. This process is rather cyclic and influenced by the acquired knowledge and additional tutoring information.

At the beginning of the learning process, within DCE the exploration goal is formed by determining instances of system variables. The intended exploring process then starts from this initial goal. In the next steps, the user specifies basic (i.e. mandatory) inputs from which the expert component is able to derive automatically the solution of the studied case.

The user then tries to find out and to specify fragments of the solution, e.g. the supposed dose of a chemotherapy. Depending on the completeness of this specification the explorative environment reacts and supports different problem solving methods. The tutoring strategies are adapted to two different types of user activities:

- The novice user solely enters mandatory inputs. The system presents all the inferred problem solving actions. Guided by didactical instructions, the novice user analyzes as many system variables as needed. He can use helps and explanations related to the selected context.

- The more experienced user obtains the opportunity to check his acquired knowledge specifying result elements (optional inputs), gained by hypothetical processes. The explorative environment offers a critique based explanation dialog including praise and corrections.

The complete control of the learner's activities is taken over by the Dynamic Critic-Expert-Model (DCEM). The learning environment acts like a coach and provides feedback about correct and false parts of the solution. False elements are corrected by the expert component.

The tutor conceptually contains abstract and deep information. Abstract tutor information like instructions, helps, explanations, and critiques are refined by deep information e.g. introductions, motivations, lessons, and repetitions. The presentation sequence and the content of deep tutorial information depends on the tutoring history and a user model.

The user can easily influence the sequence of the tutor's presentations. He is also able to navigate using a focus-based multiple hypertutoring facility. Different exploration paths can be followed in parallel to keep the initial learning goal. Additionally, the user is supported by traditional services like tutoring notes, text markers, and an index. The explorative user may reduce the simulation-time-factor to accelerate the exploration.

2 The Dynamic Critic-Expert-Model (DCEM)

2.1 The DCEM constraint

DCEM is built upon two well known classes of knowledge based systems: planning expert systems and critiquing systems.

Planning expert systems [Hertzberg 89] derive planned actions from problem descriptions. They are related to a given case and use explicitly represented domain knowledge (Fig. 1). Critiquing systems [Miller 84] conclude consistency specifications (critiques) from problem descriptions and the user's opinion (supposed actions) about the given descriptions. The critique presents explanations about significant differences between the user's judgement and the system's derivations. As users have to specify the complete solution about a given case, critiquing systems are very useful for specialists.

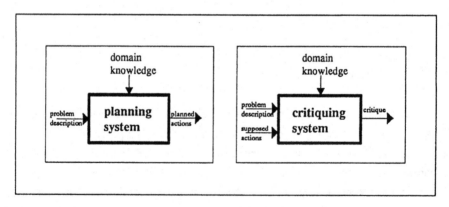

Fig. 1: Planning and Critiquing Expert Systems

DCEM includes an expert planning mode and a critiquing mode. It extends the functionality of both enabling to optionally specify result elements. DCEM is conceptionally based on the idea of constraint networks [Güsgen 88]. In order to get a flexible system design, we have mapped the DCEM's global functionality to a blackboard architecture.

Actions a(t) either derive automatically from the mandatory inputs im(t) or can be specified according to the actual user's knowledge and behaviour as optional inputs io(t) (Fig. 2). The consistency analysis of the explored case is embedded in the tutoring dialog. The tutor information T(t) includes: critiques, instructions, explanations, helps, introductions, motivations, lessons, and repetitions as we have seen. All constraint variables depend on time.

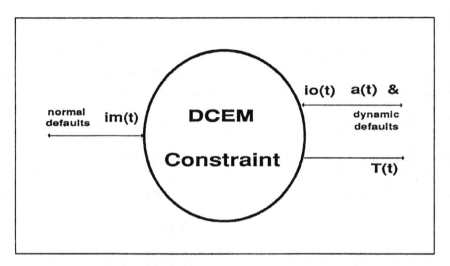

Fig. 2: The DCEM Constraint

2.2 Model description of DCEM

All variables of the DCEM constraint can be represented as input/output sets. They are specified with relation to a definite user who is exploring a specific case (e.g. a patient) in an explicitly represented expert domain (e.g. a specific oncologic therapy protocol).

We note the basic sets of DCEM as following:

(1) $Im(t) = \{ im_1(t), im_2(t), ... , im_{i(t)}(t) \}$: the mandatory inputs at time t,

(2) $Io(t) = \{ io_1(t), io_2(t), ... , io_{j(t)}(t) \}$: the optional inputs, and

(3) $A(t) = \{ a_1(t), a_2(t), ... , a_{k(t)}(t) \}$: the derived user's actions.

The number of elements (cardinality) and the contents of elements (instancies) of the above sets are time-dependent.

The tutor information subsets are:

(4) $T(t) = \{ C, Ins, E, H, Int, M, L, R \}$.

These subsets are primarily induced from the elements of the critic-expert model, the user's inputs, and the dynamical maintained user model. The infered tutor information obviously depends indirectly on time. The elements of the tutor can also be noted as sets:

(5) $C = \{ c_1, c_2, ... , c_l \}$: the set of all critiques,

(6) $Ins = \{ ins_1, ins_2, ... , ins_m \}$: the instructions,

(7) $E = \{ e_1, e_2, ... , e_n \}$: the explanations,

(8) $H = \{ h_1, h_2, ... , h_o \}$: the helps,

(9) $Int = \{ int_1, int_2, ... , int_p \}$: the introductions,

(10) $M = \{ m_1, m_2, ... , m_q \}$: the motivations,

(11) $L = \{ l_1, l_2, ... , l_r \}$: the lessons, and

(12) $R = \{ r_1, r_2, ... , r_s \}$: the repetitions.

In DCEM we define the optional inputs as powerset (i.e. the family of all subsets) of the user's executable actions:

(13) $Io(t) = \mathcal{P}(A(t))$

From card $A(t) = k(t)$ and card $Io(t) = j(t)$ results card $Io(t) = 2^{k(t)}$. We extend (13) to:

(14) $Io(t) = \mathcal{P}(A(t)) = \{ S_1, S_2, ... , S_{2^{k(t)}} \}$ where S_i are subsets of $A(t)$,

$S_1 = \{\}$ (empty set),

$S_2 = \{ a_1(t) \}$,

. . .

$S_{2k(t)} = \{ a_1(t), a_2(t), \dots, a_{k(t)}(t) \}$.

Based on the previously defined sets, we delimit the exploration range of DCEM. It is based on the already mentioned existing expert system modes.

Case 1: The planning expert system approach. The user enters the mandatory inputs Im(t); the system concludes the actions A(t), and the user executes these actions. We have:

(15) $Io(t) = \{\}$ i.e. $P(A(t)) = \{\} = \{ S1 \}$.

Case 2: The exploring system approach. The user specifies a more or less complete solution. The system acts like a coach providing necessary critiquing and correcting information:

(16) $Io(t) = \{ S_2, \dots, S_{k(t)}, \dots, S_{2k(t)-1} \}$

Case 3: The pure critiquing mode. The environment examines a complete user's solution and derives consistency check explanations:

(17) $Io(t) = \{ S_{2k(t)} \}$ i.e. $Io(t) = A(t)$.

DCEM substantially expands the cases 1 and 3 and provides the user with the ability to explore up to $2^{k(t)}$ simulated situations in relation to his dynamical learning activity.

The functionality of DCEM is based on the following functions:

(18) Planning and controlling (PC)   : $Im(t) \to A(t)$, and

(19) Exploring (EXP)   : $Io(t) \times A(t) \to C$.

Exploring (EXP) is based on the (PC) planning and controlling. The domain of function exploring is the subset of the cartesian product of optional inputs Io(t) and the system derivated actions A(t). The range of function exploring consists of useradapted critic information, the elements of set C.

3 Blackboard architecture

The problem domain and the DCEM tutoring aspects recommend to separate the required knowledge in different types. In order to consider the dependencies between heterogeneous types, a special architecture of a blackboard system [Engelmoore, Morgan 88] was developed.

The scheduler contains a knowledge base of activation rules which are used to activate different knowledge sources. This activation is determined by the focus, a kind of actual abstract update information of the blackboard.

Different knowledge sources KS contain specialized knowledge bases and related inference engines: KS TimeManager orders all possible actions of a day, considering some special designed time intervalls and pseudo-time points [Allen 85], [Treuner 86]. KS PlanControler filters the causal constraint actions [Hertzberg 89] from the time related actions. Here, the most parts of the problem solving domain knowledge are represented . KS DoseManager computes the quantitative constraint actions, e.g. individual case dependent doses of chemotherapy or radio-therapy.

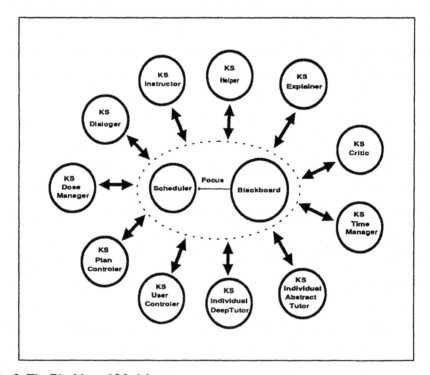

Fig. 3: The Blackboard Model

A dialog module - KS Dialoger - [Gunzenhäuser, Böcker 88] transforms the abstract information from the blackboard into an individual dynamic and episodic graphic user interface based on direct manipulation. (Fig. 4). KS Instructor derives instructions in neutral form. Then the system translates the neutral information into an useradapted instruction. KS Helper delivers neutral help information. Context dependent information related to selectable attributes or tutor information are based on a help model [Bauer 88] which manages user adapted and focused hyper-help information. KS Explainer enables an exploring investigation of inputs, actions, and tutor information. User demanded explanations are completed by automatic critiquing explanations from KS Critic which delivers a neutral critique and a critique context. Inconsistencies from the critique context can be solved later.

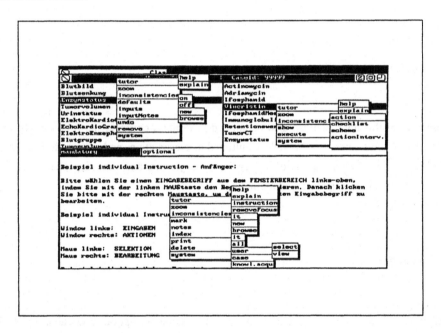

Fig. 4: The Explorer Window

KS IndividualAbstractTutor adapts the neutral tutor information to the individual user's attributes. During the presentation of the abstract tutor information, the user is able to demand deeper tutor information. These information types are managed by KS IndividualDeepTutor.

The user is able to navigate between dynamically related concept nodes in two complementary domains - in the problem solving space within a flexible simulation environment, and in the learning space of the tutor subsystem. The active user who explores alternative situations navigates in the problem solving space. The exploring user may additionally navigate in the learning space where the relevant information is represented by a medium like hypertext.

The user model [Schwab 89] consists of data stored on blackboard areas like GeneralUserModel and DomainExperience. KS UserControler watches the user's behaviour, his learning activities and his interaction preferences. Attributes of a typical user - stereotyp [Rich 89] - are initial values of the user model. Its maintenance leads to a nonmonotonic behaviour of the user model and is based on an overlay model.

The interactive components and the blackboard repository were prototypically implemented using the Smalltalk-V environment. The system is applied in the field of pediatric oncology therapy planning and controlling.

4 Conclusions

Results from this approach can also be applied in projects covering the following topics: Extended dialog and user models, multimedia presentation and interaction models, synthetic tutor information based on learning subsystems, and time dependent learning processes including forgetting and reminding.

References

[Allen 85] J. F. Allen: Maintaining Knowledge about Temporal Intervalls. In R. J. Brachman, H. J. Levesque (Eds.), Readings in Knowledge Representation pp 509-521. Morgan Kaufmann Los Altos, 1985.

[Bauer 88] J. Bauer: Konzepte und Prototypen interaktiver Hilfesysteme. Dissertation. Fakultät für Mathematik und Informatik der Universität Stuttgart, 1988.

[Cronbach 77] L.J. Cronbach: Educational Psychology. Harcourt Brave Jovanovich. New York, 1977.

[Engelmoore, Morgan 88] R. Engelmoore, T. Morgan (Eds.): Blackboard Systems. Addison Wesley Publishing Company, 1988.

[Güsgen 88] H.W. Güsgen: CONSAT - A System for Constraint Satisfaction. Dissertation, Fachbereich Informatik, Universität Kaiserslautern, 1988.

[Gunzenhäuser, Böcker 88] R. Gunzenhäuser, H.-D. Böcker (Eds.): Prototypen benutzergerechter Computersysteme. Walter de Gruyter Berlin-New York, 1988.

[Hertzberg 89] J. Hertzberg: Planen: Einführung in die Planerstellungsmethoden der künstlichen Intelligenz. B.I. Wiss. Verlag, Mannheim Wien Zürich, 1989.

[Michalski 87] R. Michalski: Learning strategies and automated knowledge acquisition. In G.L. Bradshaw, P. Langley, R.S. Michalski, S. Ohlsson, L.A. Rendell, H.A. Simon, J.G. Wolff (Eds.), Computational models of learning, pp. 1-19. Springer Verlag Bern, 1987.

[Miller 84] P.L. Miller: A Critiquing Approach to Expert Computer Advice: ATTENDING. Pitman Advanced Publishing Program, Boston London Melbourne, 1984.

[Neber 81] H. Neber (Eds.): Entdeckendes Lernen. Beltz Verlag, Weinheim und Basel, 1981.

[Rich 89] E. Rich: Stereotypes and User Modeling. In A. Kobsa, W. Wahlster (Eds.), User Models in Dialog Systems, pp. 35-51, Springer Verlag Berlin Heidelberg New York, 1989.

[Schwab 89] Th. Schwab: Methoden zur Dialog- und Benutzermodellierung in adaptiven Computersystemen. Dissertation. Fakultät Informatik der Universität Stuttgart, 1989.

[Treuner 86] J. Treuner: Cooperative Weichteilsarkomstudie CWS-86 -Studienprotokoll. Studienkommision der Gesellschaft für Pädiatrische Onkologie, Tübingen, 1986.

[Zimmermann 89] A. Zimmermann: Exploratives Lernen aufgrund eines dynamischen Kritiker-Expertenmodells. In R. Gunzenhäuser, H. Mandl (Eds.), Dritter Workshop der Fachgruppe Intelligente Lernsysteme der Gesellschaft für Informatik e.V. vom 8.-9.6.1989 Tübingen, S. 133 - 143.

Discourse Style and Situation Viewpoint for a Conversational Language Tutor

Raza Hashim and Henry Hamburger
Department of Computer Science
George Mason University
Fairfax, Va 22030
email:rhashim@gmuvax2.gmu.edu
henryh@aic.gmu.edu

1 Perspective, Rationale and Organization

What should a conversational foreign language tutoring system say next? The choice is constrained by two sets of considerations: the demands of conversational continuity and the language progress of the student. An introduction to these potentially conflicting requirements is the topic of an earlier paper [1]. The present study provides a more technical analysis of the conversational side of the problem by developing a framework with two key conversational structures: interaction mode and conversational viewpoint. In the course of the investigation, it also becomes necessary to examine issues of knowledge representation and implementation for a two-way, two-medium communication system, one that lets tutor and student converse spatially and linguistically.

At the outset, the reader may well wonder just what a conversational language tutoring system might look like and why one should expect it to be useful. One may also seek some clue to how it is organized, to gain perspective on the role played by discourse and viewpoint, the main subject matter of this paper. We take up these preliminary questions briefly, in turn.

The purpose of a conversational - or immersive - language learning environment is to help the student to understand and use a new foreign language directly and automatically, as opposed to carrying out conscious mental translation or computation of grammatical formulas. To this end, we get the computer to provide some of the immersion activities that successful language tutors often use, involving familiar physical objects used to act out familiar scenarios. Following these methods, we make use of the student's own (first) language only to set the stage, and leave the explicit teaching of grammar to others. Immersion must be gradual, with exposure and comprehension of language preceding its production. Gradualness also means introducing new words and patterns one at a time, in situations where they can be figured out from the rest of the sentence in the context of the visual activity and the continuity of the subject matter in the conversation. It is this need for conversational continuity that motivates the work below.

To fix ideas, it may help to have a concrete example of the kind of objects and scenarios that are involved here. In one microworld that we call Washroom World, there is a figure whose movable hand enables him to turn on the water and to pick up, use and put down various objects like the soap, towel or toothbrush as needed. Such actions can combine to form composite actions that result in getting his face or teeth clean, and so on. The hand can be controlled by either student or system, and the sequence of events is quite flexible. Foreign language descriptions, comments, commands and questions are tightly interwoven with the screen events.

Space does not permit proper treatment of the second and third preliminary questions, those of motivation and organization. On motivation, see our earlier work [2] and the broader discussion by [3]. The approach is best suited for the early stages and can be used with other systems - as well as teachers and books - that complement it.

As for organization, viewing matters very coarsely, one may say that the system has three broad functions: to handle input, make internal updates and decisions, and generate output. Breaking these down in turn, input involves handling what the student says and does. This means robust natural language understanding with error analysis as well as interpretation of graphics (mouse) actions, each interpreted in their mutual context. As for output, it too is bimodal and involves corresponding challenges. Internally, the system is responsible for maintaining models of the situation, the discourse, and the student, and for making tutorial decisions about what to say and do. The preceding few sentences suggest ten modules, five each for the internal duties and for input/output. Each of the ten offers ample opportunity for complex reasoning. To make such an ambitious undertaking manageable we are making some judicious compromises and proceeding in stages. A pilot system has been built that provides some useful immersion experiences. A more modular, flexible and elaborate system is under construction.

2. The Structure of What to Say

The system and the student need to maintain a coherent dialog so that both parties have a physical and linguistic context in which to interpret and formulate new sentences. A concrete physical situation is important, since the dialog is in the new language, which the student doesn't understand completely. The partially animated graphical interaction on the computer screen indicates the physical context in which both the system and the student formulate and interpret utterances. The linguistic context, on the other hand, gradually develops as both parties succeed in communicating their intent to each other. This requirement of maintaining a shared context is present for conversation in general [4] but is more important for language tutors since they need a language-independent source of information about what is being said, to support the learning of new language aspects without translation.

Section 2.1 introduces our approach to the problem of conversational continuity and states some principles for achieving clarity in the conversation. The next section deals with microworlds, discussing what aspects need to be represented, including goals and actions. In section 2.3, we present dialog schemas and interaction types that have been developed to maintain conversational continuity. The final subsection indicates how language diversity can be achieved by alternative views of an event and its results.

2.1 Approach and Principles

To achieve conversational continuity the FLUENT system needs to (1) structure the student-tutor discourse, and (2) decide which aspect of the current situation to talk about. We structure the student-tutor discourse by maintaining a three-level discourse representation. At the top level is the dialog schema, a skeletal plan of the student-tutor interaction. A dialog schema is composed a flexible sequence of interchanges between the student and the tutor. Each interchange, in turn, comprises of a small number of turns, possibly as few as one, by each party. Each turn is a linguistic and/or spatial output by either the student or the tutor. The second issue, what particular aspect or view of the situation to talk about, is the responsibility of the view selector, which must be sensitive both to student needs and to the discourse structure just sketched. In the process of constructing the student-tutor dialog we adhere to the following principles that help maintain clarity.

For educational continuity:

1. Present input to the student in order of increasing linguistic complexity.
2. Present only one new linguistic aspect in a sentence and only a few in a lesson.
3. Assume comprehension of an aspect before demanding its production.

For conversational continuity:

4. Keep students aware of the discourse structure.
5. Make comments that are relevant to the current situation.
6. In a new situation, make view selection relatively repetitive.

To control the ambiguity of the visual channel:

7. Keep the number of objects low.
8. Talk about physical objects and their visible properties before talking about abstract or invisible properties.
9. Also defer talk of abstract actions and goals.

2.2 Representing the Domain: Goals and Actions

In this section we describe how to represent goals and actions in the microworld. Examples described in this section will be used in sections 2.3 and 2.4 to show how to talk about these goals and actions. The state information of the objects in the microworld has been represented as a simple object system with inheritance. Since our use of this approach to states is familiar and straightforward, we focus on goals and actions.

In a microworld, like the Washroom World mentioned above, we can talk about the goal that is being currently pursued, such as washing the face, the action that is being carried out, such as picking up an object from the cabinet, or the state of a particular object, such as the face being dirty. In order to communicate effectively at these three levels, we maintain three levels of domain representation. At the top level is a model of the goals that can be pursued in the microworld. In the Washroom World example mentioned earlier, these goals include washing one's face, combing hair, brushing teeth, etc. With each goal there is a goal structure that tells the system how to achieve that goal, using primitive actions and/or other (sub)goals.

The action rules form the second level of representation in the system. There are rules for actions such as picking up and putting down objects, as well as manipulating the states of switches such as the faucets and the light switch. At the third level is a frame-based representation of the underlying microworld, which keeps track of the visible properties of the objects in the microworld, like the cup being on the shelf, as well as invisible properties, like the surface state of the hand being wet.

A specific example of a goal structure is in Figure 1, which consists entirely of executable Prolog code. The goal in this example is to get a movable object - say a cup or a plate - soapy, using a sponge. The object to be soaped must meet the conditions in the "pre" list, which indicates the the object is to be held in the stationary hand and should be dirty. The "sub" indicates how soaping is actually carried out, as a sequence of familiar actions. The microworld has a cabinet, a sink, a sponge, and a bucket of soapy water. The character has a stationary hand, which can hold one item at a time, and a mobile hand, which can pick up one item at a time.

Two points are worth mentioning about this goal structure. First, it does not recognize an arbitrary sequence of actions as achieving a goal. A system constructed in this way will only recognize its predefined goal structures. In order to recognize arbitrary sequences as goals we would need a deeper model of the domain. Second, it is possible to define the goal, say soap(X), as that of getting the surface-condition slot of the object X as soapy using the predefined action rules of the system. We have chosen not to do this since planning a sequence of actions in the microworld to achieve a particular goal can be a nontrivial task. For details on microworld planning see [5].

The second level of representation correspond to actions that can be observed graphically. These actions include things such as pick-up, put-down, brush-teeth, soap-by-sponge, etc. Figure 2, which also is executable Prolog code, shows a typical action in the system. Since the character in the microworld has only one mobile hand, we have chosen to represent it by the constant, "m_hand". The rule transfers an object to the mobile hand from the thing that previously contained it.

The preconditions show that for this rule to be used, the mobile hand must be empty, the object to be transferred must be movable, and it must be located at the "From" object. In case the preconditions are met, the system can execute the rule. To do so, it issues the corresponding "act" and "mouse" commands to the graphics component to carry out the action graphically, and updates the knowledge base by carrying out all the items in the "post" or postconditions section of the rule.

The system can also use this rule in reverse to detect a pick-up action that is carried out by the student graphically. In order to do this it makes sure that the student's graphics actions matched the "mouse" and "act" component of this rule, and that all the preconditions are met. If this is the case, the system can update the knowledge base accordingly by asserting the postconditions.

```
goal_is        soap_by_sponge(Object)

pre            is_movable(Object) and
               is_dirty(Object) and
               in(s_hand,Object)

sub            action:pick_up(sponge,cabinet) and
               action:soap_sponge(sponge,soap_water_bucket) and
               action:soap_by_sponge(Object) and
               action:put_down(sponge,cabinet) and
               action:put_down(Object,sink)

post           Query =.. [Object, surface, =, [soapy]] and
               call(Query).
```

Figure 1: Goal Structure for Soaping a Movable Object.

1. The code given in this figure is executable Prolog code. Variable names begin with upper case letters while constants are lower case.

2. "goal_is", "pre", "sub" and "post" are user defined operators.

Choosing the level of detail is an important issue in the design of a microworld. The primitive graphic actions in our microworld are visit and mouse actions. It is possible to describe all actions in the system as a combination of these primitives. This, however, would mean reasoning from first principles about the state of the world, complicating the tasks of both microworld reasoning and language processing. We therefore model all actions with rules like the one in figure 2, expressing a higher level action in terms of graphic primitives and microworld states. Such rules represent complex actions that are applicable in rather special circumstances. Beside the one shown, other complex, specific rules deal with actions like wetting movable objects, soaping objects by hand when the surface of the hand is soapy, and so on. For interpreting student actions, these rules are preferred over the broadly applicable primitives. Modeling actions at this level simplifies language processing as well as reasoning, since languages typically have verbs at this level of abstraction.

```
rule          pick_object

do            goal(pick_up(Object,From))

mouse         mouse(mouseDown)

act           visit(m_hand,Object)

pre           value(m_hand, contains, =, empty) and
              value(Object,is_prop, =,Props) and
              member(is_movable,Props) and
              value(From,contains, =, Object)

post          Fact =.. [From,contains, =,Object] and
              retract(Fact) and
              assert(hand(contains, =,Object)).
```

Figure 2: Rule to Pick-up an Object.

1. The code given in this figure is executable Prolog code. Variable names begin with upper case letters while constants are lower case.

2. "rule", "do", "mouse", "act", "pre" and "post" are user defined operators with appropriate precedence levels.

2.3 Dialog Schemas and Interaction Modes

In the previous section we looked at the knowledge representation needed to carry out various goals and actions in an immersion style microworld. This section covers the dialog schemas, interaction types, and views which are discourse tools needed to talk about goals, actions and states. We begin with dialog schemas, which guide communication with the student, and more specifically with the example in figure 3.

At the heart of the dialog schema in figure 3 are two types of interactions. In the presentation mode, the system simply describes a particular view of the current activity and the student simply acknowledges this presentation, while in the commander mode the tutor issues a command and the student carries it out graphically. In order to simplify the presentation of this example, it is assumed that the student will perform each graphic action successfully without errors in the commander mode. In the actual situation this might not be the case. We can use discourse management strategies to make local plan repairs in case of incorrect student responses and ensure that the student remains on track, for details see [6].

1.presentation(goal:Goal, agent:Agent,
                    view:[describe_goal_to_do])

2. presentation(object:Object,slot:Slot, value:Value,
                    view:[describe_state_value])

3. commander(goal:Goal,
                    view:[describe_action]).

4. presentation(object:Object,slot:Slot, value:Value,
                    view:[describe_state_value_now]).

5. presentation(object:Object,slot:Slot,value:OldValue,
                    view:[describe_state_value_before]).

6. presentation(goal:Goal,
                    view:[describe_goal_action]).

Figure 3: A dialog schema that uses Presentation and Commander mode

Suppose we instantiate this schema with the goal soap-by-sponge, with the object "glass" and slot "surface", and agent as the student. This can result in the bimodal dialog of figure 4. The sentences in the figure are to be produced by a natural language generation generator operating on the output representation produced by our system. We are collaborating with the Athena Language Learning Project [7] whose generator is capable of this kind of output.

A few specific comments may help with understanding figure 4. Items (3-7) correspond to the commander mode interaction while the other utterances correspond to the presentation mode. We will look at the commander mode interactions (3-7) first. In these pairs the tutorial command is followed by the student performing the appropriate graphic actions in response. The expression "visit(X,Y)" is generated when a rectangular frame for object X overlaps one for object Y. In item (7) student actions must trigger both pick-up and put-down to take the glass from the stationary hand and put it in the sink. As a result of each tutorial command and student response, several updates occur in the microworld, and several tutorial comments become possible, by using different views, as explained in section 2.4.

Tutor	Student
1. You will soap the glass.	\<acknowledge\>
2. It is dirty now.	\<acknowledge\>
3. Pick up the sponge.	visit(m_hand,sponge), mouse(mouseDown)
4. Soap it in water.	visit(sponge,soap_water)
5. Take the sponge to the glass.	visit(sponge,glass)
6. Put it back in the cabinet.	visit(sponge,cabinet), mouse(mouseDown)
7. Put the glass down in the sink.	visit(m_hand,glass),mouse(mouseDown) visit(glass,sink), mouse(mouseDown)
8. Now the glass is soapy.	\<acknowledge\>
9. It was dirty, before.	\<acknowledge\>
10. You soaped it with a sponge.	\<acknowledge\>

Figure 4: A sample dialog based on the schema

If we add more interaction types more interesting discourse schemas can be created. Some of these occur in the current pilot system but are not implemented with the kind of flexibility and generality we ultimately seek. Quizmaster is defined as a type of interaction that allows the tutor to ask students questions which they can respond to graphically or linguistically. The Oracle interaction would let the student ask questions, either picking from a menu of options, or by typing in questions, and the system responds. In the Movecaster mode, which is currently implemented with some generality, the system comments on the graphic actions done by the student. Celebrity would be the reverse of Movecaster, allowing the student to talk about system moves; the system would check for appropriateness. In the Servant mode the student issues the commands and the tutor carries them out, again with the possibility of commenting on the goal, action and states that are relevant. Some of these interaction types and some views are less demanding of student progress than others, and the system designers can choose to hand-craft dialog schemas of increasing difficulty using these ideas.

2.4 Views

There is a great diversity in what the tutor can say at various times. For one thing, the dialog schema given in Figure 3 can be used with other goal structures, for example, structures for washing or drying objects. In this section we will see that even at one particular time there are many conversationally relevant utterances that can be produced by the language tutor. For example, after the interaction in line (3) of Figure 4, any of the following sentences is reasonable:

1. The sponge is in the hand.
2. You picked up the sponge from the cabinet.
3. The sponge is no longer in the cabinet.
4. You are holding the sponge.

Each of these utterances corresponds to a different view of the resulting situation. Such utterances can be generated by the tutor with more advanced students. With beginning students, a good tutorial strategy would be to stick to the basic command and very little follow up. In case the student doesn't carry out the anticipated action, it would seem useful for the system to generate an utterance describing what the student actually did. Figure 5 gives a selection from among dozens of possible views involving goals, actions, time and the state of objects. Commenting on less obvious aspects of the situation can provide important language exposure to the student. However, some of these views might be difficult to understand for the beginner since they correspond to the physical situation only in an indirect way.

A view structure is essentially a frame, implemented in the same Prolog style as the action rules and goals. One slot contains the interaction type and view information. Another slot specifies what information about the current situation will need to be consulted, typically the kind of action and its current (actual) arguments. A third slot specifies how to put the information from the first two together to construct a semantic structure to send to the natural language generator. It should be noted that the dialog schema given in Figure 3 can be used with other goal structures, for example, structures for washing or drying objects. Moreover, looking at the list of views in Figure 5 one can see that if they are incorporated into the dialog schema given in Figure 3 many more conversationally relevant utterances can be produced by the language tutor.

Goal-Oriented Views:
- starting subgoal
- subgoal transition within the same goal
- goal completion
- violation of goal-based expectations

Action-Oriented Views:
- action that was carried out
- non-occurrence of anticipated action
- same operator with another argument, negated

Temporal View:
- this action follows its predecessor

State-Oriented Views:
- new state of the object that has been acted upon
- previous state of the object acted upon
- composite observation ("Now, there are two ...")
- preceding state no longer holds

Figure 5: Views possible in a goal-oriented microworld

3 Summary

Discourse style and situational viewpoint are key elements of an immersion-style language tutor. In order to achieve conversational continuity, such a system needs to maintain a model of goals, actions and states in the microworld along with tools to manage discourse. The discourse management tools include various dialog schemas composed of interaction types. These schemas guide the communication protocol between the student and the tutor. Another tool is the type of view that one takes of what occurs in the microworld. The various view types in our taxonomy provide a mechanism for generating comments on those aspects of the microworld that are relevant while using a particular interaction type. In sum, we have devised a variety of interaction types and views and shown how to use them in the construction of a bimodal, bidirectional communication system for immersive foreign language learning.

References

1.   Hamburger, H. and Maney, T. (1991) Twofold Continuity in Immersive Language Learning. J. Computer-Assisted Language Learning 4,2: 81-92.

2.   Hamburger, H. and Hashim, R. (1992) Foreign langauge tutoring and learning system. In M. Swartz and M. Yazdani (Eds.), Intelligent Tutoring Systems for Foreign Language Learning. New York: Springer-Verlag.

3.   Richards, J.C. and Rodgers, T.S.(1986) Approaches and Methods in Language Teaching: A Description and Analysis. Cambridge: Cambridge Language Teaching Library.

4.   Grosz, B. and Sidner, C. (1987) Attention, intentions, and structure of discourse. Computational Linguistics 12,3: 175-204.

5.   Wilensky, R. (1983) Planning and Understanding: A Computational Approach to Human Reasoning. Reading, MA: Addison Wesley.

6.   Novick, D. (1988) Doctoral Dissertation, University of Oregon, Eugene, Oregon.

7.   Felshin, S. (1991) The Lingo Manual. The Athena Language Learning Project, MIT.

Open Structured CAI System for Kanji Learning

Toshihiro Hayashi, Yoneo Yano
Tokushima University
2-1, Minamijosanjima, Tokushima 770 Japan
tel. [+81]886-23-2311 ext. 4712
e-mail: kanji@n65.is.tokushima-u.ac.jp

Abstract

Kanji learning is the most difficult part of learning Japanese for foreigners and the method of learning kanji in Japan isn't suitable for foreigners. We are developing a new environment for foreigners to learn kanji using a computer. When we Japanese see an unknown kanji, we can infer the meaning and pronunciation of the kanji from its parts. learning the parts of kanji is important and it is better to learn kanji systematically using a knowledge of their parts. We are developing two systems for kanji learning, one is a kanji dictionary system including the knowledge if kanji parts, the other is a kanji learning CAI system 'Kanji Laboratory' with a new environment wherein students can construct kanji by putting parts together. With regard to the kanji dictionary system, we focus on two points as follows: (1) A kanji has three levels of hierarchical structure. (2) The meaning and pronunciation of kanji parts are related to those of kanji. With regard to the Kanji Laboratory, we are developing an environment in which kanji can be learned freely. The Kanji Laboratory is oriented to an open structured CAI which gives students an environment wherein students can learn positively.

Introduction

Recently, the number of foreigners who are learning Japanese has increased. In our research, the targets are foreigners who don't use kanji in their mother tongue. Japanese is often considered a difficult because of some of its characteristics, namely:

1. Japanese grammar is radically different from that of a European language.

2. Japanese has complicated levels of formality.

3. Japanese has a complicated character system.

Especially, with regard to 3, Japanese consists of hiragana, katakana and kanji. There are about fifty characters in the Japanese hiragana and another fifty in katakana, and there are thousands of kanji. Of these kanji, there are two thousand kanji used in daily life. The number of kanji is very great as compared with the number of English alphabet. Therefore, kanji learning is one of the most difficult aspects of learning Japanese for foreigners.

In Japan, Japanese students are subjected to an intense cycle of memorization, drilling, and testing of kanji required for daily life in nine years at school. Although this learning method has some problems, such as the useless memorization of small and trivial parts of kanji, Japanese students can learn many kanji. But this method isn't suitable for foreigners. Because, foreigners must learn kanji is too short a period.

Most foreigners here are not children but adults. They have common sense and a lot of knowledge about social life. Therefore, they can learn many objects systematically to complete learning in a short period. Kanji consist of some parts such as strokes and radicals. There are not many kanji parts compared with the number of kanji. We think that understanding the part structure of kanji is important to the learning of kanji systematically. Foreigners can learn kanji easily and effectively in a short period if they understand the kanji parts. It is difficult to realize this learning environment using traditional education materials and dictionaries, but we can use a computer for developing this environment.

We are developing a kanji dictionary system [Hayashi-Yano91a] and a kanji learning CAI system for foreigners [Hayashi-Yano91b]. Generally, kanji learning has three types of learning targets, namely, the writing of kanji, the meaning and pronunciation of kanji, and the usage of kanji. There are some CAI systems teaching the writing of kanji[Zeng-et al90, Yamasaki-et al90]. In our CAI system, students can learn kanji, their pronunciation and meaning through understanding the part structure of kanji.

1   Kanji

We are developing a kanji dictionary system as a knowledge base of our kanji learning CAI system. This kanji dictionary system contains knowledge about kanji parts. Kanji are constructed from kanji parts according to a kanji construction method except for basic kanji. Therefore we have considered kanji construction methods in order to develop a knowledge base module for a kanji dictionary system.

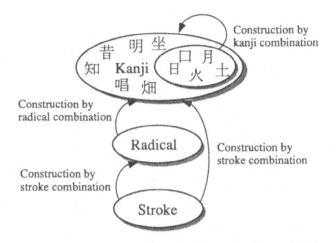

Figure 1: Hierarchical Structure of Kanji

1.1 Kanji construction method

Kanji are formed according to four construction methods: *Syokei*, *Shiji*, *Kaii*, and *Keisei*. *Syokei* is to construct a kanji by formalizing the shape of an object. *Syokei* is a foundation of kanji construction. *Shiji* is to construct a kanji by converting the property of an object to a shape. *Shiji* represents an abstract concept by a concrete symbol. *Kaii* is to construct a kanji by combining more than two kanji. *Kaii* is used to construct kanji with a new meaning derived from the meaning of the combined kanji. *Keisei* is to construct a kanji by combining one part that represents the meaning and another part that represents the pronunciation.

1.2 Structure of kanji

Kanji consist of strokes, radicals and kanji. A radical is called 'bushu' in Japanese. Fig.1 shows three levels of hierarchical structure of kanji.

Strokes are the most primitive structure. A stroke can be written by one touch of the pen. Strokes have no meaning and no pronunciation. We have defined twenty strokes in Table 1. Kanji and radicals are represented as combinations of these strokes.

A radical is the upper level structure of strokes and radical are parts of kanji. If a kanji is constructed by *Keisei* or *Kaii*, its radical carries information about meaning and pronunciation to the kanji. Some radicals have names such as '*ninben*' and '*sanzui*'. Radicals are classified by their location in kanji. Table 2 shows the classification of radicals. For example, the radicals located on the left side of a kanji are called '*hen*' and the radicals located on the right side of a kanji are called '*tsukuri*', in Japanese.

Table 1: Strokes

Stroke	Name	Example	
―	Yoko	二 (ni)	三 (san)
│	Tate	木 (ki)	川 (kawa)
亅	Tatehane	小 (syo)	利 (ri)
＼	Migiharai	入 (nyu)	全 (zen)
ノ	Hidariharai	人 (hito)	久 (kyu)
⼅	Migihane	冷 (rei)	場 (jyo)
＼	Ten	点 (ten)	凡 (bon)
⼛	Kagi	国 (kuni)	凸 (totsu)
⼚	Kagihane	同 (do)	永 (ei)
⌞	Shitakagi	医 (i)	凶 (kyo)
∟	Marukagi	亡 (bo)	七 (nana)
⌐	Makagi	甬 (yo)	字 (u)
⻌	Mukagi	仏 (hotoke)	育 (iku)
⌇	Tekagi	犯 (han)	手 (te)
∟	Rekagi	氏 (shi)	表 (hyo)
⌞	Tsuribari	礼 (rei)	心 (kokoro)
⼁	Kagibari	与 (yo)	考 (ko)
⼂	San	及 (kyu)	道 (michi)
⼃	Kunoji	女 (onna)	巡 (jun)
乙	Ahiru	風 (kaze)	九 (kyu)

Kanji are the top level of the structure. Many kanji are constructed by a combination of radicals. Some kanji have no radical. These kanji are constructed by a combination of strokes. In some cases, a kanji is part of another kanji.

1.3 Attribute of kanji

Attribute of kanji indicates the meaning and the pronunciation of kanji. We Japanese can in many cases infer the meaning and the pronunciation of unknown kanji from kanji parts. This fact depends on the kanji construction method *Keisei*. The meaning and the pronunciation of kanji are inherited from radical to kanji in many cases.

2 Knowledge representation of kanji

In our kanji dictionary system, kanji knowledges are represented as triplets and these triplets are managed using TRIAS [Yamamoto-et al89].

Table 2: Radical

Radical	Shape	Example	Kanji
Hen	◧	丿 亻	冷 凝 行 征
Tsukuri	◨	卩 殳	印 即 段 殺
Kanmuri	⬓	冖 宀	冠 冥 安 定
Ashi	⬒	日 皿	昔 普 盛 監
Kamae	◰	匸 囗	医 巨 園 国
Tare	◳	厂 广	雁 原 広 屋
Nyo	◲	廴 辶	延 廻 道 近

2.1 Triplets and TRIAS

A triplet consists of entity, attribute and value, formalized as

$$(e, a, v) = (entity, attribute, value)$$

Attributes refer entities to values. For two triplets $(1)(e_1, a_1, v_1)$ and $(2)(e_1, a_2, v_2)$ whose entities(e_1) are the same, if the value of $(1)(v_1)$ equals the attribute of $(2)(a_2)$, it is said that "The two triplets are linked from (1) to (2)". The searching function of the linked triplet is called 'association'.

TRIAS handles all data in triplet format and manages a database. TRIAS is a tool for developing a database system [Yamamoto-Kashihara89a]. TRIAS can execute fast data access, because its database module has an ML-tree (Multi Linked-tree) [Yamamoto-Kashihara89b] structure.

Any triplet may be used as a search condition in TRIAS. The elements e, a, v of a triplet can have '*' as a meta-character. '*' matches with all strings. For example, $(E, A, *)$ matches with all triplets of which entity is E and attribute is A, and $(*, *, *)$ matches with all triplets. We call these searches 'asterisk searches'.

2.2 Triplet representation of kanji

We represent the structure of kanji in terms of stroke and radical. We represent a kanji using radical. Sometimes, a radical itself is a kanji. Some kanji cannot be separated into radicals. They are represented using only strokes. We represent a radical by the

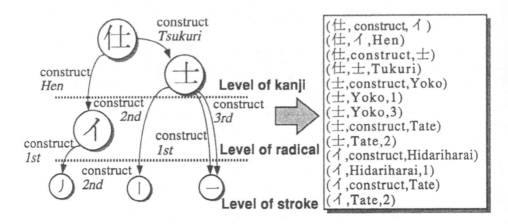

Figure 2: Triplet Representation of Kanji Structure

stroke which constructs the radical. Fig.2 shows an example of triplet representation of the structure of a kanji.

2.3　Triplet representation of kanji attributes

A Kanji has a meaning and a pronunciation. These attributes must be represented in relation to the structure of the kanji. We select the attributes from each structure and represent them as triplets.

Kanji have these attributes: pronunciation(Chinese reading and Japanese reading), meaning and number of strokes. We call these attributes 'basic attributes' and call other attributes 'extension attributes'. Extension attributes are such things as usage, the method of kanji construction. Radicals have basic attributes: name, meaning and pronunciation. Kanji which are radicals also have these attributes. Triplet representation of kanji attributes is shown in Fig.3.

3　Kanji dictionary system

Fig.4 shows our kanji dictionary system. The kanji search consists of two processes which are called 'condition search' and 'data search'. A condition search finds a target kanji using some conditions. A data search gets the data of the target kanji.

Some condition searches are as same as general dictionary references. We call these searches 'basic searches' such as search by pronunciation, strokes and radical. Other searches are called 'extension searches' such as search by meaning.

In Fig.4, a student is going to input a search condition by meaning after searching for a kanji which is constructed by 4 strokes. In our kanji dictionary system, a

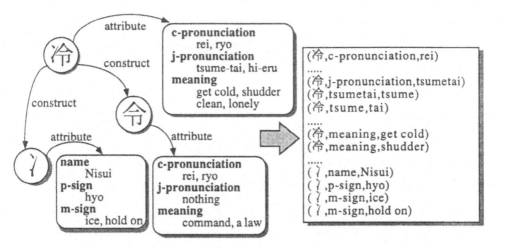

Figure 3: Triplet Representation of Kanji Attributes

student can select a condition button by mouse click. In partcular, if a student clicks on a kanji then the mouse cursor changes from normal cursor type to the kanji cursor type. A student can search the kanji data by clicking a search button using the kanji cursor. When a student selects the radical condition, the student can also use a kanji cursor.

4 Kanji Laboratory

Kanji Laboratory is a CAI system for kanji learning. Its main targets are foreigners who don't use kanji characters in their mother tongue. We are developing a micro world as an environment for kanji learning. Students can construct kanji by combining kanji parts in this environment. We think that foreigners can learn kanji through reiteration of this type of action.

But our system doesn't consider that a student will acquire kill in the writing of kanji. Because acquisition of skill in writing kanji is too hard to learn when compared with that of writing other characters. Instead of this skill acquisition, we focus on the student's understanding of the part structure. Therefore, inputting kanji or kanji parts isn't done by handwriting but by direct manipulation using a GUI in the Kanji Laboratory. Kanji part learning is useful for learnig kanji systematically, because by means of knowledge of kanji parts a student can avoid useless learning. Kanji Laboratory is not an all-round kanji CAI system but one of the tools for learning knowledge of kanji such as that of kanji parts. We think that student can learn kanji effectively using our system.

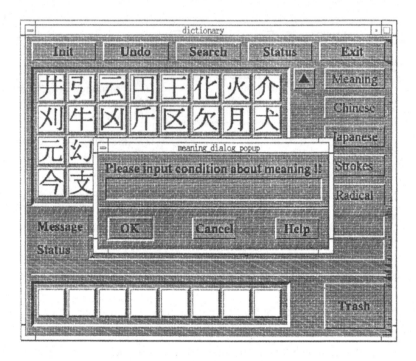

Figure 4: Kanji Dictionary System

Kanji Laboratory is oriented to environmental CAI, micro world type CAI, open structured CAI[Yamamoto-Kashihara89c]. Fig.5 shows the system configuration of Kanji Laboratory. Kanji Laboratory consists of a free learning environment, a learning monitor module, a student model, a learning management module and knowledge of teaching strategy.

4.1 Free learning environment

A student can learn kanji and their parts through a free learning environment, the interface module of Kanji Laboratory. This environment consists of a notebook field, a kanji making field, a dictionary field, a question field and a dialogue field. The configuration of this environment is shown in Fig.5.

4.1.1 Note book field

This field stores kanji and radical which are constructed by students. In the initial state, the notebook field stores only strokes. Students can start to construct kanji and radicals using these strokes. When students construct kanji, the saved kanji and radicals are used again. We think that students can learn about kanji parts and their

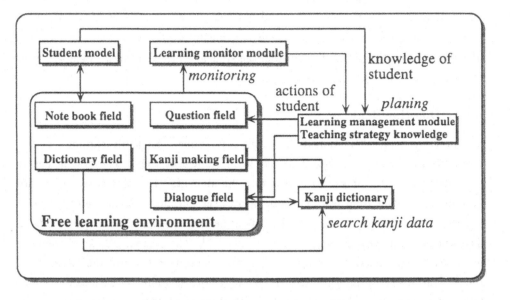

Figure 5: Configuration of Kanji Laboratory

hierarchical structure through these actions. A notebook field has the same search functions as a kanji dictionary system for searching for kanji and radicals which are used again. Students can get the target kanji and radical by using a condition search.

4.1.2 Kanji making field

Students can construct kanji and radical by inputting some parts in this field. Students take some parts for kanji construction from the notebook field. This field can't produce kanji when there are errors derived from incorrect input of kanji parts in the following two cases:

- There is not such a kanji in the knowledge base.

- There is a kanji which has the inputted kanji parts but the sequence of the inputting is not the same as in the correct writing sequence.

In these cases, the system has a dialogue with the student in the dialogue field. The constructed kanji and radical are automatically stored in the notebook field.

4.1.3 Dictionary field

The student can directly use the kanji dictionary system in this field. When students are working in another field, students can move to the dictionary field and can search for kanji without restriction. The students can get by themselves hints informing them of kanji construction. Our system is going to acquire some data to infer the understanding status of the student from the student's behavior, such as knowledge of the search condition which is used.

4.1.4 Question field

The previous fields offer students a positive environment for kanji learning. In this environment, the student cannot always learn kanji effectively. The system has to give effective advice for kanji learning to some students. But this advice must not prevent the student from learning kanji freely. The question field is one of the fields for the guidance of kanji learning. There are some kanji questions in the question field. The student freely chooses questions from this field. The student gets kanji from the notebook field or constructs kanji in the kanji-making field to solve the question. If the student answer a question with the wrong kanji, then our system has a dialogue with the student about this wrong kanji. Our system guides the student towrads the production of correct kanji and acquires some data to infer the understanding status of the student, just as in the dictionary field.

4.1.5 Dialogue field

This, along with the question field, is one of the fields devotes to guidance in kanji learning. This field has the following functions in relation to the dialogue with students. The first function is to have a dialogue with students when they have constructed some kanji which the knowledge base doesn't have. Our system asks why the student has constructed the kanji or focuses on the question which the student wanted to solve. The second function is to evaluate the learning status of the student. Thus, this field mainly executes an operation which performs a dialogue with students.

4.2 Learning monitor module

This module monitors the behavior of a student in the free learning environment and records the history of the student's actions. Generally, in a free environment, the student can perform various actions, such as noises, which then interfere with the inference of the understanding status of the student. In our system, the student's actions are simplified by using a GUI which is based on mouse operations.

4.3 Student model

The status of this model is that of understanding kanji. Our system mainly leads to the acquisition of understanding status of kanji attributes such as meaning and pronunciation, and also leads to the acquisition of an understanding status of radicals by inference from the history of student actions with the learning monitor module and by dialogue with student in the dialogue field. The student model is generated by these understanding statuses.

4.4 Learning management module

This module sets up a learning plan using the action history and the student model. And the learning management module always generates a learning plan in accordance with the teaching strategy knowledge. Our system is based on a student's positive learning. Our system doesn't have any teaching strategy for direct instruction but, mainly, for indirect instruction. In this way, Kanji Laboratory monitors the student's actions and plans guidance in kanji learning for the student.

5 Conclusion

In this paper, we described the development of two systems for foreigners to learn kanji.

With regard to a kanji dictionary system, we focused on kanji parts. In our kanji dictionary system, kanji are systematically represented as combinations of parts. Kanji parts carry information about meaning and pronunciation. In our kanji dictionary system, a student can search using various types of key. Our kanji dictionary system has new types of key, such as that for meaning, which can't be used in a traditional kanji dictionary. Therefore foreigners can flexibly search for kanji.

With regard to Kanji Laboratory, we offer a new environment for kanji learning. Students can learn kanji positively. In this environment, students can take various actions to learn kanji. Through the kanji learning, the system can assess the kanji knowledge of the student and can plan effective guidance for kanji learning.

We think that these systems are good tools to guide kanji learning and that a new kanji learning method is realized by using them.

References

[Hayashi-Yano91a] Hayashi T, Yano Y. *Development of a Kanji DictionaryFocusing on the Method of Constructing Japanese Kanji*, ICOMMET'91 Proc. International Conference on Multimedia in Education and Training, pp.121-126, 1991.

[Hayashi-Yano91b] Hayashi T, Yano Y. *A Micro world for Kanji Learning*, 22th Annual International Conf. International Simulation & Gaming Association (ISAGA'91), 1991.

[Yamamoto-Kashihara89a] Yamamoto Y, Kashihara A. *Development of KACE : Knowledge Acquision type CAI System*, Journal of JSCAI Japan, No.6, pp.12-20, 1989(in Japanese).

[Yamamoto-Kashihara89b] Yamamoto Y, Kashihara A. *Batch Deletion for ML-tree*, Trans. IEICE Japan, J72-D-1, pp.140-143, 1989(in Japanese).

[Yamamoto-Kashihara89c] Yamamoto Y, Kashihara A. *A Modeling of Knowledge Stability in Open Structured CAI*, Trans. IEICE Japan, J-72-D-II, No.9, pp.1459-1471, 1989(in Japanese).

[Yamamoto-et al89] Yamamoto Y, Kashihara A, Kawagishi K, Tsukamoto N. *A Tool of Personal Database:TRIAS*, Trans. IPSJ Japan, No. 30, pp.734-742,1989(in Japanese).

[Yamasaki-et al90] Yamasaki T, Yamamoto M, Inokuchi S. *Computer Coaching for Beautiful Handwriting of Japanese Characters in Elementary School*, Proc. of 5th World Conf. on Computers in Education(WCCE90), pp.725-728, 1990.

[Zeng-et al90] Zeng J, Zang X, Inoue T, Sanada H, Tezuka Y. *A Computer Generation model of Brush used Handwritten Chinese Characters and Its Application in Education*, computer processing of handwriting(Proc. 4th IGS Conf.), World Scientific Publishing Co., pp.363-400, 1990.

THE SUM OF THE PARTS IS GREATER THAN THE WHOLE IN ONLINE GRADUATE EDUCATION

Lois Ann Hesser, Robert P. Hogan, Al P. Mizell
Abraham S. Fischler Center for the Advancement of Education
Nova University
Fort Lauderdale, Florida
tel: (800) 541-6682

Abstract

Distance education programs have been available to the adult learner in various subject areas and delivery formats for nearly 300 years. The advent of the computer and recent advances in technology and telecommunications provides new avenues for pursuing this form of education.

Since its inception, Nova University has been particularly involved in developing better strategies to meet the needs of distance learners in its master's and doctoral programs. The development of the Electronic Classroom has provided a vehicle that is an important enhancement of the normal telecommunications interaction, providing an online environment closely patterned after the actual environment of the traditional classroom.

The Programs in Child and Youth Studies began to offer a technologically delivered alternative to its usual site-based cluster delivery system in February 1991. An intensive 3-year longitudinal study has been developed to track the effectiveness of this new delivery model. Preliminary returns indicate positive attitudes among students who have been involved in the pilot cluster, and more frequent communication between students, faculty, and staff members. The research design provides a comparison of attitudes and academic accomplishment between two site-based and two technologically delivered models, in a one-way analysis of covariance. The design is quasi-experimental, as groups are intact allowing no random assignment.

Introduction

> The next generation of education programs -- called *online education* or
> *computer-based distance learning* -- is anything but dull and hackneyed.
> This is education on the brink -- technology tapped and harnessed to
> bring learning to people who are too busy to attend traditional school or
> who don't have access to conventional campus environments. (Roberts,
> 1991, p. 19)

While the term *distance education* still seems to carry the connotation of an
avant garde form of educational delivery, the concept has been used and applied for
nearly 300 years. Accounts of correspondence courses, the earliest form of education
at a distance from the teacher, can be found in the March 20, 1728, *Boston Gazette*
(Battenberg, 1971) and in the delivery of Isaac Pitman's shorthand courses in 1840
England (Dinsdale, 1953). With organizations such as Chautauqua, the International
Correspondence Schools, and later offerings by traditional schools such as Illinois
Wesleyan and the University of Wisconsin (Rumble, 1986), distance education to meet
the needs of the adult learner and the working professional became a significant factor
in the educational scene in the United States.

Computer-assisted distance education graduate programs are offered today by a
growing number of universities throughout the United States and Canada. It is seen by
the National University Continuing Education Association (NUCEA) as a clearly
identifiable area within the field of education, and not just a supplement to conventional
learning (Markowitz, Almeda, Logan, Loewenthal, & Young, 1990). Early definitions
(Feasley, 1982; Evans, 1986) emphasize the fact that student and instructor are
physically separated, and instructional content is coordinated and managed at another
location. More recent definitions (Keegan, 1990; Markowitz, 1990; Rumble, 1989)
stress the interaction of technical media to provide communication between teacher and
learner.

The addition of technological media in recent years has fired the debate
concerning the appropriateness of distance education. Can the student receive
maximum benefit and adequate learning from instruction in which interaction with the

instructor is partially or wholly mediated by a technological device? The query, while appearing to address the problem, is a poor hypothesis, ignoring the growing problems and dissatisfaction with the conditions of instruction in the traditional setting, assuming their greater effectiveness rather than comparing the two instructional modes.

Moore (1968), in support of his discourse on tutoring, noted that Rousseau's *Emile*, a classic in education, provides as its major insight the discovery that traditional school methods are unavoidably inadequate because they are applied to many people at once. Each person, he concluded, really learns by his or her self, encouraged by others, stimulated, perhaps, by competition or fear, but never in quite the same as any other individual. Indeed, Carroll (1963) contended that homogeneous grouping was actually an impossibility due to individual learning rates and capacities.

Like it or not, the computer has precipitated the entrance of an age of learning that is fundamentally independent of time and space, an age described by Kearsey (1985) as one of "distributed learning" (p.1). The value of individualization is realized when a student can engage in learning at any time or in any place that may fit his/her own unique needs whether at home, at work, or in a center for learning.

While there are clear advantages to the implementation of distance learning, there are critical questions which must also be addressed - questions concerning pedagogical soundness, quality, and cost effectiveness (Dirr, 1987; Ely, Leblanc, & Yancey, 1989; Levin, 1986; Piele, 1989). This paper will describe the distance education programs initiated by Nova University, and the blending of a number of technological components presently used to provide doctoral level study for students in the Child and Youth Studies program. The response to the program, although still in its infancy, has been consistently positive, leading us to feel that the delivery process is resulting in an educational program that is "greater than the sum of its parts" (Mizell, Marcus, Hesser, and Hogan, p. 2).

Nova University and Distance Education

Nova University was founded in 1964 in Fort Lauderdale, Florida. Its basic *raison d'etre* was to offer educational programs to those for whom traditional educational formats were unavailable or unfeasible. The university has grown from its early offering of one Ph.D. program to the status of a major university serving over 10,000 students annually.

Nova's first distance education program was initiated in February 1972. Its *cluster format* model provided direct instruction at a geographically central location for a group of students one Saturday a month. By June of that year, a higher education doctoral program was begun using this model and, by 1974, 14 distant sites were opened to accommodate a field-based master's program. Today, approximately one-half of the student body receives a major portion of instruction through this distance education format.

In 1983, Nova expanded its offerings to incorporate high technology. The first doctoral degrees in the country to be offered primarily through the use of telecommunications were the Doctor of Arts in Information Science and the Doctor of Education in Computer Education. This was expanded shortly to include a master's of science degree and four additional doctoral degrees.

While not all of Nova's programs use telecommunications as a mode for instructional delivery, many do require their students to become computer literate in their professional area. The teacher education master's program (Graduate Education Modules or GEM) require six credit hours in administrative and classroom uses of technology. The School of Business and Entrepreneurship requires all doctoral students to complete a four-hour research course via telecommunications. Based upon the success of these efforts, the Higher Education doctoral programs are preparing to offer one of their three-credit seminars through telecommunications, as a first step toward an online delivery model.

The National Cluster in Child and Youth Studies

In 1986, the Early and Middle Childhood doctoral program was renamed and revised to include specialization components to better meet the needs of a student population growing in its diversity of services to children and youth. A technology component was also added, consisting of two, 2-credit courses to be completed during the first two years of study. Plans were begun to offer this new program in Child and Youth Studies (CYS) with a telecommu-nications option for geographically disadvantaged students for whom monthly travel to an established regional center was economically or physically unfeasible. These plans came to fruition in February 1991 when the first cluster in this program to use electronic delivery for instruction met on campus in Fort Lauderdale, Florida. The 18 students, who reside in 11 different states and two Canadian provinces, became known as the *National Cluster*.

Students receive instruction in two formats. Twice a year, during the fall and spring terms, the group participates in 3 to 4 days of intensive instruction at the Fort Lauderdale campus. During the summer, students follow the same schedule as all other clusters, consisting of a 5-day instructional program concentrated on their selected specialization, followed by a 5-day institute in which seminars alternate between an emphasis on advocacy for children and youth, and trends and issues in leadership. The remainder of the instruction and communication is through telecommunications.

It is important that National Cluster students become familiar with the UNIX operating system. This system provides access to various applications such as electronic
mail, bulletin boards, online conferencing, and specific programs available on UNIX such as Electronic Library, Electronic Question, Electronic Student, and Writer's Workbench.

These applications and programs are augmented for the National Cluster by access to a unique form of communication, developed by Nova, called the Electronic Classroom*, commonly referred to as ECR. It is this component that provides the synergy and cohesiveness of a traditional classroom experience to the distance instruction format of the National Cluster.

The Electronic Classroom

When computer-based instruction was first used for distance education, the primary communication forms were electronic mail and computer conferencing. It was quickly found that for many students, the absence of real-time interaction was a real disadvantage. While telephone conferencing allowed interaction between teacher and student in a one-on-one situation, the lack of class interaction and the benefit of discussion and debate within the group was perceived as a definite drawback.

To address this situation, Nova embarked upon research to modify the UNIX environment so that it could provide a traditional classroom experience without the physical presence of the student, accommodating the real-time interaction between a teacher and a class of 20 or more students. The result of this was the Electronic Classroom. The hypothesis underlying the development of the ECR was:

> Good things that happen in a classroom cannot be replaced by electronic
> mail and computer conferencing or even one-on-one communication --
> things like the student's seeing opposing views on issues or listening in
> on challenging statements that are made by classmates (or by the
> teacher), and that general feeling of belonging to a community.
> (Scigliano, Joslyn, & Levin, 1989, p.65)

The ECR system was expected to emulate as closely as possible a traditional classroom setting. Two options, however, make it possible to improve the educational process in ways that cannot be duplicated conveniently in that traditional classroom.

Capitalizing upon the power inherent in the UNIX system, each ECR session can be recorded and made available to all Novavax users. This allows the student to re-run a session for review, or "sit in" on a class that was missed. New faculty members can observe how a session was developed and handled, giving them valuable background for their own input. A second option is for the instructor to demonstrate to students various program and software operations while remaining in the ECR. For example, an instructor of statistics might demonstrate data manipulation through the use of the SPSS-X package that is available for the VAX/UNIX system.

Another option available to the instructor is the provision for small group discussions within the scheduled online session. The ECR system allows for up to 27 "classrooms" to be in operation at one time. By reserving three or four classrooms for the time period, students can exit to an assigned room, carry on their discussion, and then re-enter the main classroom to present their findings. Faculty can also relinquish "teacher" status to a student in the main classroom for student presentations, with the provision of resuming their control at any time.

Effectiveness of Electronic Delivery for the CYS Program

While the use of electronic media has received acceptance from much of the educational community, there is to date insufficient data to prove or disprove the educational value of these media. In the study reported by MacFarland (1990) concerning the efficacy of ECR, subjects viewed the medium as being "superior to traditional instruction in view of access and equivalent to traditional instruction in view of learning behaviors and outcomes" (p. 13).

The Programs for Child and Youth Studies are embarked on a much broader study, encompassing not only the effectiveness of electronic media (particularly electronic mail and the Electronic Classroom) in the delivery of instruction, but also a comparison of the National Cluster delivery method as a whole with the traditional cluster in which instruction is totally classroom presented.

The research design will seek to answer the following questions:

1. Is the National Cluster delivery model as effective as the normal site-based delivery system?

2. Is the turn-around time for submission of materials by the student and response by faculty or advisor significantly reduced from the traditional use of the postal system?

3. Does the use of electronic media increase student/faculty student/advisor interaction to a greater degree that student/faculty student/advisor interaction in a site-based cluster?

Four clusters of students will be considered in the study over the 3-year life of their program. Clusters A and B are both based in Fort Lauderdale, and began within 2 weeks of each other in February 1992. Cluster A is a site-based model; Cluster B is a technology-based model. The instructors who teach Research and Evaluation, Human Development, Technology, and Political Processes and Social Issues will be the same for both groups. The only exception will be in the Leadership study area, where the same duplication was not possible. A site-based Cluster (C) from another location will be considered as a control for Cluster A, and a technology-based Cluster (D), that will begin in October 1992, will act as a control group for Cluster B. No effort will be made to match the faculty assigned to Clusters C and D with either Cluster A or B. It is anticipated that the first data for clusters A and B will be collected and analyzed by July 1992. You may contact the authors for a copy of the results.

Several instruments are in place at the present. All groups will take the *Myers-Briggs Type Indicator*, the *Kolb Learning Styles Inventory* and the *Torrance Hemisphericity: Your Style of Learning and Thinking* instruments at the beginning and the end of their 3 years of study. Study area and study guide evaluation forms will be used, as well as pre and posttests assessing entrance/exit knowledge of study area material. The research design is quasi-experimental as the groups are intact, thereby allowing no random assignment. The design of this study can be depicted as follows:

$$
\begin{array}{ccc}
O_1 & X_1 & O_2 \\
O_1 & X_2 & O_2 \\
O_1 & X_3 & O_2 \\
O_1 & X_4 & O_2 \\
\end{array}
$$

$^{*}O_1$ and O_2 = pretest and posttest.
$^{*}X_1$, X_2, X_3, and X_4 = treatment groups.

Figure 1. Research Design

A self-assessment instrument of technology knowledge will be administered to the technology-based Cluster (B) at the beginning and at the one-year mark of instruction. This will be compared with the results of the data for the same time period collected from the first, or pilot, National Cluster. The same instrument will be administered to Cluster A.

A log is kept by the practicum department that records dates for all interactions between students and their advisors, whether by regular mail, electronic mail, or telephone. The data will be used to assess any differences in both frequency and time interval experienced in student/advisor interaction.

Future Directions

The computer-based, distance education component of the Child and Youth Studies programs is still in its infancy. Only small numbers of students and faculty have participated in the program to date. Bugs still need to be worked out of the delivery and training system. The research upon which we have embarked should begin to provide important answers for us in the near future.

Certain advantages have already been noted. In one instance, a student on the west coast sent work to his advisor on the east coast by email and received the advisor's review within 24 hours. The student then made the necessary corrections and two days later sent the revised work to the advisor. The advisor was now attending a conference, but had brought along a laptop with a modem — the student received approval the following day. Normal time for this process using regular mail would have been increased by at least an additional 10 to 12 days.

National Cluster members appear to communicate with faculty and each other more frequently that students in the traditional site-based clusters. Certainly, ease of communica-tion is one factor. We must also consider that, because the program is new, we may be experiencing a Hawthorne effect that will disappear with time.

Nova University recognizes the urgent need to provide better access to education for adult learners, especially as the gap between the necessary job skills and the education of the adult population increases. The increased mobility of our society adds another dimension to that problem.

It is vital that we keep abreast of delivery modes that can provide quality education that will also be cost-effective for student and university alike. It is also important to recognize that there is no *super medium*. Best strategies recommend that a wide range of media incorporated in a planned and integrated manner will provide the optimum variety of educational approaches (Moore, 1987). Spikes (1990) is convinced that the "training organization of the future, the classroom of the future, the education of our citizens of the future will be technologically driven" (p. 14). Distance learning through the use of appropriate technology is a growing field. The future is wide open, and Nova plans to be one of the forerunners.

References

[Bat71] R. W. Battenberg. *The Boston Gazette*, March 20, 1728. Epistolodidaktika, 1971, *1*, 44-45.

[Car63] J. B. Carroll. *A model of school learning*. Teachers College Record, *64*, 1963.

[Ded89] C. Dede. *The evolution of distance learning: Technology-mediated interactive learning*. A report for the study: Technologies for Learning at a Distance. Science, Education and Transportation Program for the Office of Technology Assessment, Congress of the United States. (ERIC Document Reproduction Service No. ED 325 099), July 1989.

[Din53] W. A. Dinsdale. *Inception and development of postal tuition*. The Statist, 1953 pp. 572-575.

[Dir87] P. J. Dirr. *Critical questions in the evaluation of distance education*. In T. Gibson (Ed.), Third Annual Conference on Teaching at a Distance: Evaluation of Teaching/Learning at a Distance. Madison, WI: University of Wisconsin, School of Education, August 1987, pp. 29-46.

[Ely89] D. P. Ely, G. Leblanc, & C. Yancey. *Trends and issues in educational technology*. (Report No. ISBN 0-937597-26-0). Washington, DC: Office of Educational Research and Improvement. (ERIC Document Reproduction Service No. ED 326 212)

[Eva86] Evans, A. *Media managers and distance education*. Media Management Journal, 1986, *5*, pp. 22-23.

[Fea83] C. Feasley. *Serving learners at a distance*. (Report, No. 5). Washington, DC: ASHE-ERIC Higher Education Research, 1983

[Kea85] G. Kearsey. *Training for tomorrow: Distributed learning through computer communications technology*. Reading, MA: Addison-Wesley, 1985

[Kee90] D. Keegan. *A theory of distance education: From Peters to Peters*. In M.G. Moore (Ed.), Contemporary issues in distance education in North America. Pergamon Press, 1990.

[Lev86] H. Levin. *Is CAI cost effective?* Phi Delta Kappan, 1986, *6*, pp. 26-30.

[Mac90] T. W. MacFarland. *Computer-based distance education in real-time: The electronic classroom*. Fort Lauderdale, FL: Nova University, 1990.

[Mac88] W. Mackay. *Diversity in the use of electronic mail: A preliminary inquiry*. ACM Transaction Office Information System, 1988, *6* (4), pp. 780-797.

[Mar90] H. Markowitz. *Distance education staff handbook*. University of Illinois, 1990.

[Mar90] H. Markowitz, M. B. Almeda, S. Logan, N. Loewenthal, & R. Young. *The status of independent study: 1990 and beyond*. Final report of the Task Force on the Status of the Division of Independent Study. Washington, DC: National University Continuing Education Association, Independent Study Division. (ERIC Document Reproduction Service No. ED 316 658), 1990.

[Miz92] A. P. Mizell, D. Marcus, L. A. Hesser, & R. P. Hogan. *Distance teacher education: Σ > the WhOle*. Unpublished manuscript, Nova University, Abraham S. Fischler Center for the Advancement of Education, Fort Lauderdale, FL, 1992.

[Mor87] M. G. Moore. *New technology: Lessons from the Open University*. Paper presented at the annual conference on New Technology in Higher Education: Acquisition, Integration, and Utilization, Orlando, FL, February 16-17 1987.

[Mor68] W. G. Moore. *The tutorial system and its future*. Oxford Pergamon Press Ltd., 1968.

[Pie89] P. K. Piele. *The politics of technology utilization: From microcomputers to distance learning. Trends and issues series, No. 3* (Report No. ISBN 0-86552-100-x). Washington, DC: Office of Educational Research and Improvement. (ERIC Document Reproduction Service No. ED 318 132), 1989.

[Rob91] S. Roberts. *Brain waves*. Compute, April 1991, *4*, pp. 19-24.

[Rum89] G. Rumble. *On defining distance education*. American Journal of Distance Education, 1989, *3*, 2, pp. 8-21.

[Rum86] G. Rumble. *The Planning and management of distance education*. London: Croom Helm, 1986.

[Sci89] J. A. Scigliano, D. L. Joslyn, & J. Levin. *The non-school learning environment: ECR*. Technological Horizons in Education, 1989, *2*, pp. 63-67.

[Spi90] W.F. Spikes. *Training in the twenty-first century: Where do we go from here?* Paper presented at the annual meeting of the American Association for Adult and Continuing Education, Salt Lake City, UT. (ERIC No. ED 328 673) October 31 1990.

Development of GeoBlock:
a Micro-World
for Learning and Teaching Geometry

Kazuyoshi Hidaka
Tokyo Research Laboratory
IBM Japan
5-11, Sanban-cho, Chiyoda-ku
Tokyo 102, Japan

Abstract

GeoBlock is a micro-world software tool for learning and teaching geometry, and has
been prototyped on personal computers. It was designed according to the concept of
direct manipulation of geometric figures under geometric constraints. A block is constructed to correspond to each complicated figure that is under geometric constraints,
and it can be changed, re-used, and observed interactively on the computer's display.
From practical use in classrooms, we are convinced that GeoBlock is effective in two
phases of geometry lessons. One is the phase of discovering rules among geometric
webs that the students have not yet studied. The other is the phase of assimilating
geometrical facts that they have already studied. GeoBlock shows one way in which a
computer can help students to learn geometry, and can help teachers to give persuasive
geometry lessons.

1 Introduction

Computers are coming to be used widely in various educational fields. Teachers like to
use them because they make classes more interesting and effective, and students are also
fond of them because of their beautiful and exciting graphics capabilities and because

they are fun to use. We think that practical activities are very important in helping students to become familiar with geometric concepts, to assimilate theorems, and to acquire the ability to reason geometrically. Here, we include the direct and interactive manipulation and observation of geometric figures under the term "practical activities." Computers and their interactive graphics capabilities can be a foundation for developing tools that enable teachers and students to manipulate and observe geometric figures directly and interactively. We developed one such "micro-world" tool specifically for two-dimensional geometry, and named it "GeoBlock" [Hid90].

A wide variety of programs are available for drawing figures on personal computers. However, they are not suitable for use in the study of geometry, because they do not allow the user to manipulate geometric structures directly. For example, it is difficult for a user to make a segment P3-P4 that is a perpendicular bisector of segment P1-P2 and whose length is half that of segment P1-P2 (Figure 1(a)). Moreover, P3-P4 cannot be changed automatically when segment P1-P2 is changed (Figure 1(b)). In GeoBlock, P3-P4 can be defined as the perpendicular bisector of segment P1-P2, and the length of P3-P4 can be set in relation to P1-P2; for example, it is possible to specify that P3-P4 has half the length of P1-P2. Furthermore, segment P3-P4 can be changed as shown in Figure 1(c). A capability for constructing and automatically redrawing figures under a constrained geometric structure is needed in a system that manipulates geometric figures. A capability for linking figures is also needed, so that a figure can be used as a part of another figure and the number of complicated drawing steps thus reduced.

"Geometric Supposer" [Sch89] is a typical application of a computer as a tool for learning geometry. It is easy to use, because all figures are drawn by the system, but users cannot manipulate the geometric objects (figures) directly as they wish. Moreover, the number of types of figures is limited by the system. (The effects of this geometry tool software are reported by L. P. McCoy [McC91].)

Cabri-Geometry [Cabri] is another software tool that aims to provide a geometric micro-world. It allows a user to construct all the figures that can be made with a ruler and a compass. However, constructing a figure requires a lot of work, because all figures must be constructed without the useful and sophisticated support of a computer.

Since the work of I. E. Sutherland [Sut63], much research has been done on constraint-based graphics; examples include ThingLab [Bor86] and Juno [Nel85]. Systems based on variational geometry [Lig80,Lin-Gos81] and rule-based systems [Arb-Win87,Inu-Kim88] have been developed for the design and modification of mechanical parts. However, there is still no general consensus on what constitutes a good interface for direct manipulation of geometric figures under geometric constraints, and research in this area is continuing. GeoBlock facilitates man-machine communication by allowing direct manipulation of a geometric structure.

Viewed as a constraint management system, GeoBlock provides "one-way constraints" and uses "eager evaluation" [Zan-Mye90]. Therefore, the x-y coordinates values of each control point are re-evaluated immediately when the status of one control point is changed.

In this paper, we describe the implementation of GeoBlock and its practical use in classrooms.

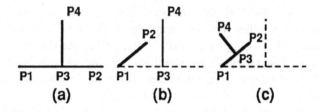

Figure 1.   Drawing a Perpendicular Bisector

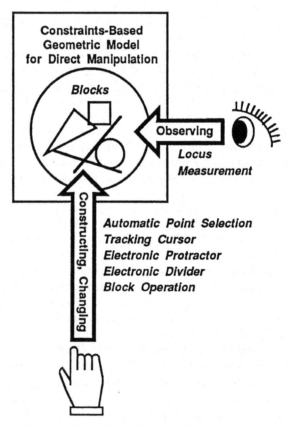

Figure 2.   GeoBlock Functions

2 Implementations

2.1 Overview of GeoBlock

Figures that are manipulated in the study of geometry are bounded by geometric constraints, such as "a line that crosses another existing line at an angle of 30 degrees," "a point that bisects the segment AB," and "an intersection of two segments or a segment and circle." In GeoBlock, such complicated figures are defined as "blocks," and can include or be included in other figures. A block is divisible into primitive blocks, such as points, segments, and circles. Each primitive block is defined by control points. A control point can maintain the above geometric constraints.

In Figure 1(a), the figure consisting of segments P1-P2 and P3-P4 is a block. Segments P1-P2 and P3-P4 are primitive blocks (segments), and P1, P2, P3, and P4 are control points. P3 is defined as the midpoint of segment P1-P2. P4 is defined as a point located on a line through P3 perpendicular to P1-P2 and at a certain distance from P3. These points are determined in the order P1, P2, P3, and P4. That is, geometry in GeoBlock is defined by control points and the order in which they are drawn.

In order to implement a geometric micro-world that can be used naturally and easily by students and teachers, we analyzed the construction process on paper, established a geometric model, and developed construction tools, functions for animation, and functions for evaluating values (such as length, angle, and ratio).

All of GeoBlock's user-level functions are shown in Figure 2. Figure 3 shows the GeoBlock screen.

2.2 Principles

The basic principle of GeoBlock is "learning by constructing, changing, and observing geometric figures under geometric constraints." We arrived at this principle, by pursuing the idea that students become familiar with geometric concepts, assimilate theorems, and acquire the ability to reason geometrically only through practical activities under specific conditions–geometric constraints. In accordance with the above basic principle, we established three design principles in order to implement a good user interface for manipulating geometric figures under geometric constraints. These design principles are "direct object access," "a position-sensing protocol and object-action sequence," and "constrained cursor control." The following geometric model and advanced functions for drawing and observing geometric figures are founded on these principles.

2.3 Geometric Model

By analyzing the operations for drawing geometric figures that appear in geometry textbooks, primitive drawing operations can be defined and listed as in Table 1. To implement each drawing operation on the computer, we classified control points into ten types according to their geometric constraints (Table 2). GeoBlock uses a geometric model that is defined by control points which hold information on the relations among graphics objects, namely, constraints.

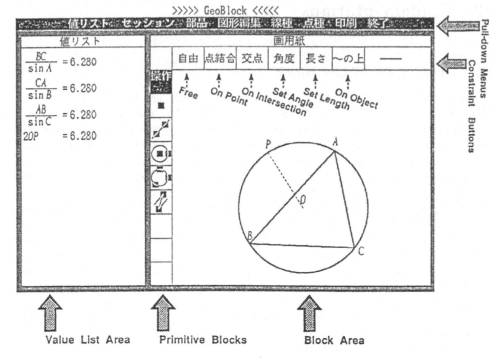

Figure 3.   GeoBlock Screen

Table 1: Primitive Drawing Operations

Number	Operation
1	Select a point defined by coordinates on a plane
2	Select a vertex
3	Select an intersection point (of two lines, a line and a circle, or two circles)
4	Select a point on a segment that divides the segment in some ratio
5	Select a point on a circle that divides the circle in some ratio
6	Set the angle between an existing line and a new line
7	Set the length of a segment
8	Select a point that is located on a line and is used as the starting point of another line perpendicular to the first
9	Select a point that is located on a circle and is used as the point of contact with a tangent to the circle
10	Draw a line (segment, straight line, or half line) by using two points defined on a plane
11	Draw a circle with the center and one point on the circumference given, or a circle with three points on the circumference given, by using defined points on a plane

Table 2: Control Points

TYPE	DEFINITION
1	A point defined by the absolute values of coordinates
2	A point located exactly on an existing point (such as a vertex)
3	An intersection of two lines
4	An intersection of a line and a circle
5	An intersection of two circles
6	A point that is located on a segment and divides it in a certain ratio
7	A point that is located on a circle and divides this circle in a certain ratio
8	A point that is located on a line crossing another line at point P with some specific crossing angle, and is at a certain distance from P
9	A point that is located on a line and is used as the starting point of another line perpendicular to the first
10	A point that is located on a circle and is used as the point of contact with a line

2.4   Drawing Figures under Geometric Constraints

All operations for drawing and setting constraints are performed with a mouse. A primitive block can be drawn by pushing the primitive block button and clicking the mouse at the positions of the control points that define the primitive block. Primitive blocks are a point, a segment (including a straight line or a half line), a circle with the center and one point on the circumference given, a circle with three points on the circumference given, and polygons.

While the control points are being defined, geometric constraints can be set interactively by pushing the constraint buttons and using GeoBlock's construction tools. These tools are (1) a TRACKING CURSOR to select points on a segment or circle that divide it in some particular ratio, (2) an ELECTRONIC PROTRACTOR to define the angle at which a segment crosses an existing segment, (3) an ELECTRONIC DIVIDER to define a segment length by relating it to an existing segment, and (4) an AUTO-MATIC POINT-SELECTION MECHANISM to use existing vertices and intersections in new figures. A characteristic of these tools is that they automatically operate on the display whenever they are needed. Here, we take an example of constructing a block by using construction tools (Figure 4(a)-(j)).

Tracking Cursor

In Figure 4(a), an arbitrary triangle has been drawn. A user is defining the point D. If he places D exactly on the segment AB and pushes the "On Object" button, he can display a tracking cursor and a track along the segment (Figure 4(b)). The length of the track is same as that of the segment AB. The user can move the cursor discretely along the track to the position of a graduation by dragging a mouse. He can then select the exact position of the graduation (that is, the midpoint of the segment AB). Finally, he can make a segment DE that crosses the segment AB at its midpoint (Figure 4(c)). In the same way, the midpoint of the segment AC is defined and named as E. Another segment is drawn by connecting the points D and E (Figure 4(d)).

Electronic Protractor

When an end point (F) of a segment is being defined (Figure 4(d)), if the "Set Angle" button is pushed and the reference line is selected, an electronic protractor is shown on the display (Figure 4(e)). In this figure, the electronic protractor is shown with its base line parallel to the segment DE, because this segment is selected as the reference line of the electronic protractor, and its center is located on E (the starting point of the segment to be drawn). The user can set the angle between segment EF and segment DE to an exact value (such as 30, 60, or 90 degrees), by dragging the tracking cursor of the electronic protractor. Figure 4(f) shows that the segment EF is constructed as a parallel line to the segment DE.

Electronic Divider

When the user is drawing a segment, he can get an electronic divider on the display, as shown in Figure 4(g), by pushing the "Set Length" button and selecting a reference segment from the existing segments. The electronic divider is parallel to the segment being drawn at the time (EF) and its starting-point is located at the starting-point of

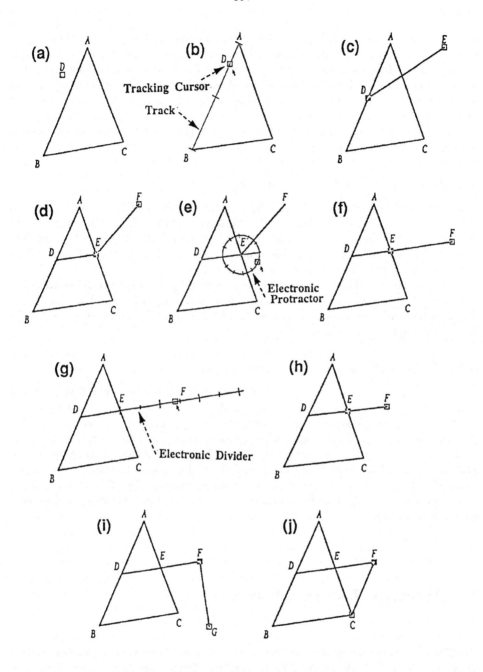

Figure 4. Construction Process

this segment (E). There are large graduations and small graduations on the electronic divider. The distance between adjacent large graduations is the same as the length of the segment DE, because the user has selected DE as the reference segment. The distance between a small graduation and an adjacent large graduation is half the length of the segment DE. The user can select any position for a large or small graduation by dragging the tracking cursor of the electronic divider. A user can set the length of segment EF to be the same as that of segment DE (Figure 4(h)). He can change the graduations of the tracking cursor, electronic protractor, or electronic divider.

Automatic Point Selection Mechanism

This tool operates when a user is defining a point. In Figure 4(i), the user is defining a point G. If he pushes the "On Point" button after placing G on the vertex C, the new point (G) is set to the existing point (C) (Figure 4(j)). If he pushes the "On Intersection" button after placing a new point on a point of intersection of lines and/or circles, he can set the new point at the intersection.

A figure named "Block" that has been constructed by following the above steps can be changed while preserving the geometric constraints. By using the block in Figure 4(j), students can experimentally confirm that BCFD forms a parallelogram even if the shape of triangle ABC is changed.

2.5 Observation of Geometric Figures

There are two kinds of observation: qualitative and quantitative. The first approach is realized by using "animation and locus," and the second by using a "value list."

A user can plot the loci of some moving graphics objects and observe the transformation process qualitatively. Figure 6(b) shows an example of "animation and locus."

In the value list area, the numerical values of blocks are shown by using the Mathematical Formula Editor (MFE [Nak89]) and the mathematical formula evaluator (see Figure 3). The numerical values are updated automatically when figures are changed on the display. By using these functions, students can examine their ideas on geometric figures numerically.

3　Practical Use in Classrooms

GeoBlock has been practically used in junior high school classrooms. One example is shown in Figure 5(a), (b) (from a lesson taught at Shimonaga Junior High School by Mr. H. Sawamori). First, students drew a star. Then, they conjectured the sum of the five interior angles and discussed their ideas each other. Next, they examined the value in the value list. Then, they changed the shape of the star, and saw that the value was always the same. They were able to assimilate geometrical facts by repeating the observation. In this example, GeoBlock was used as a tool for introducing a theme, and for convincing students of geometrical facts.

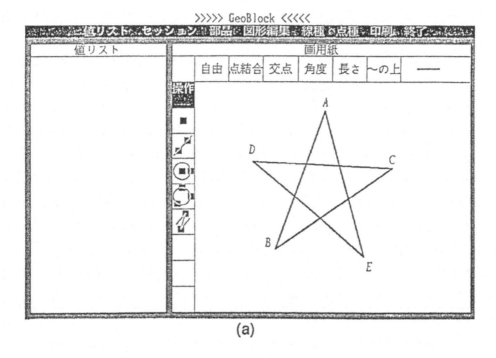

(a)

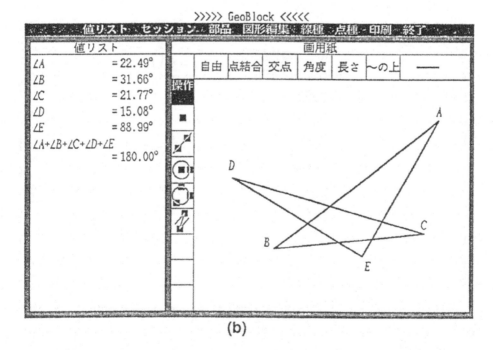

(b)

Figure 5. Practical Use in a Classroom (Example 1)

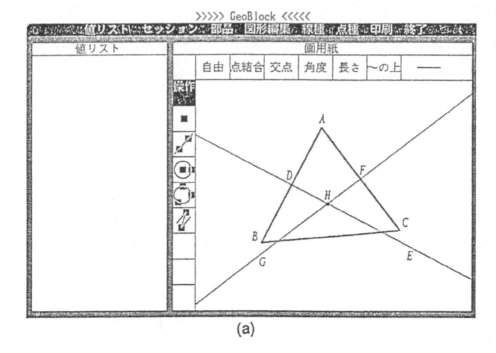

(a)

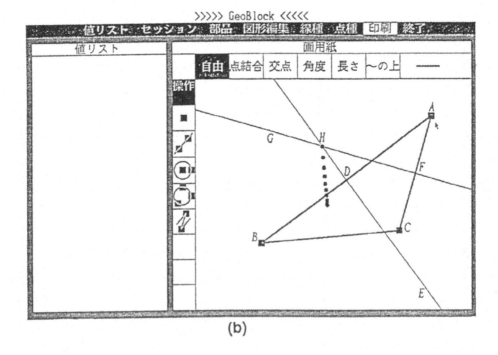

(b)

Figure 6. Practical Use in a Classroom (Example 2)

Another lesson was given by Mr. M. Sasaki at Takehaya Junior High School (Figure 6). First, students draw an arbitrary triangle (ABC) and two perpendicular bisectors: DE and FG. H is defined as the intersection point of DE and FG (Figure 6(a)). Then, they considered what could be said about the positions of H while they were changing the shape of the triangle ABC. Some of them were able to discover that H was always located on the perpendicular bisector of the segment BC (Figure 6(b)). Others were able to assimilate the fact by repeating the manipulation and observation. The details of this lesson were reported by M. Sasaki [Sas91]. He says that GeoBlock provides functions for cognitive technologies for mathematics education and motivates students to learn geometry.

The above two examples show that GeoBlock can be a micro-world for learning geometry, in which students can discover and assimilate geometrical facts through manipulating geometric figures directly by themselves.

4 Conclusion

GeoBlock provides teachers and students with a geometric micro-world in which they can construct, change, and observe complicated geometric figures bound to each other by geometric constraints. The key feature of GeoBlock is direct manipulation of figures under geometric constraints.

From practical use, as illustrated in the above examples, we are convinced that GeoBlock is effective in two phases of geometry lessons. One is the phase of discovering rules among geometric webs that the students have not yet studied. The other is the phase of assimilating the geometrical facts that they have already studied.

We intend to make the maximum use of the computer's abilities to store information (in this case, geometric constraints), to reproduce geometric figures based on this information, and to present elaborate geometric figures very quickly. These abilities are never available in the process of drawing geometric figures on a piece of paper with only a straightedge and a compass.

Acknowledgements

I would like to thank Muneaki Sasaki (Takehaya Junior High School), Takeshi Ise, Katsuki Suzuki (Hakodate-Kita Junior High School), Hideo Sawamori, Toshiyuki Inoue (Shimonaga Junior High School), and Masahiro Udo, Toshiyuki Sanuki, Yasutomo Nakayama, and Masanori Akaishi (IBM Japan), for useful discussions.

References

[Hid90] K. Hidaka. *A Tool for Learning Geometry, The Journal of Science Education in Japan, Vol. 14, No. 2, Japan Society for Science Education, 1990.*

[Sch89] J. L. Schwartz. *Intellectual Mirrors: A Step in the Direction of Making Schools Knowledge-Making Places, Harvard Educational Review, Vol. 59, No. 1, pp. 51-61, Harvard College, 1989.*

[McC91] L. P. McCoy. *The Effect of Geometry Tool Software on High School Geometry Achievement, Journal of Computers in Mathematics and Science Teaching, Vol. 10(3), Spring 1991.*

[Cabri] *Cabri-Geometre: An Interactive Notebook for Learning and Teaching Geometry, User's Manual for Version 2.0: Laboratoire de Structures Discretes et de Diactique: Institut D'Informatique et de Mathematiques Appliquees de Grenoble Universite Joseph Fourier-CNRS, 1988*

[Sut63] I. E. Sutherland. *Sketchpad: A Man-Machine Graphical Communication System, Lincoln Laboratory Technical Report, No. 296, Massachusetts Institute of Technology, 1963.*

[Bor86] A. Borning. *Graphically Defining New Building Blocks in ThingLab, Human-Computer Interaction, Vol. 2, pp. 269-295, New Jersey: Lawrence Erlbaum Associates, Inc., 1986.*

[Nel85] G. Nelson. Juno: *A Constraint-Based Graphics System, SIGGRAPH Computer Graphics, Vol. 19, No. 3, pp. 235-243, 1985.*

[Lig80] R. A. Light. *Symbolic Dimensioning in Computer-Aided Design, M.S. Thesis, Massachusetts Institute of Technology, 1980.*

[Lin-Gos81] V. C. Lin, D. C. Gossard, and R. A. Light. *Variational Geometry in Computer-Aided Design, Computer Graphics, Vol. 15, No. 3, pp. 171-177, 1981.*

[Arb-Win87] F. Arbab and J. M. Wing. *Geometric Reasoning: A New Paradigm for Processing Geometric Information, Design Theory for CAD, International Federation for Information Processing, 1987.*

[Inu-Kim88] M. Inui and F. Kimura. *Geometric Constraint Solving for Constructing Geometric Models, Proceedings of Graphics and CAD Symposium, pp. 181-190, Information Processing Society of Japan, 1988.*

[Zan-Mye90] B. V. Zanden and B. A. Myers. *A Constraints Primer, Computer, pp. 74-75, November 1990.*

[Nak89] Y. Nakayama. *Mathematical Formula Editor for CAI, Proceedings of ACM CHI'89, pp. 387-392, 1989.*

[Sas91] M. Sasaki. *A Practical Use of a Computer in Mathematics Education, Tokyo Gakugei Journal of Mathematics Education, Vol. 3, pp. 87-97, 1991.*

SODA: A Computer-Aided Design Environment for the Doing and Learning of Software Design*

Luke Hohmann, Mark Guzdial, Elliot Soloway
University of Michigan
Highly Interactive-Computing Environments
Research Group
Ann Arbor, MI 48109-2110
email: hice@csmil.umich.edu

Abstract

SODA (Software Design Laboratory) is a Design Support Environment (DSE) that supports novice programmers learning software design skills. SODA is based on a formal model of software design derived from studies of expert programmers. SODA explicitly supports students in this model of software design through a series of integrated workspaces and an explicit process model. In addition to supporting students doing software design, SODA also supports students learning software design skills through scaffolding that encourages articulation and reflection on the design process.

1   Introduction

A transition is taking place in education: classrooms are moving from didactic instruction to a more constructivist, project-oriented learning model in which students are asked to design and construct artifacts [Far90]. While providing motivating opportunities for learning, project-oriented curriculum places new demands on teachers and students: how do we support students as they design and construct such artifacts?

SODA (Software Design Laboratory) was created to support students in the process of software design. As novice software designers, students have significant difficulty with

---

*This research was supported by NSF Grant #MDR-9010362, Apple Computer Corporation, and Electronic Data Systems Corporation.

identifying appropriate modularizations to make during the design process [Per88] and putting together and coordinating the modules into a coherent solution [Spo-Sol85]. Traditional programming environments provide little more than a simple text editor, with no additional support for dealing with modularization. Such an environment is not optimized to the design process, and thus provides no real assistance to the student.

SODA is a *Design Support Environment* (DSE), a special kind of Computer-Aided Design (CAD) tool that focuses on supporting the design activities of the user. The support that is given to the user is called *scaffolding*, and is characterized by support that users need in order to be successful but cannot yet provide for themselves [Far90, Col88]. In SODA, scaffolding is focused on supporting the student so that they can successfully create programs while gaining expertise in learning our model of software design. Scaffolding helps the student understand the underlying components of a domain (e.g., the Pascal programming language) and the processes used to assemble these components into finished products (e.g., working programs).

Student outcomes from using a precursor to SODA, the GPCeditor (Goal-Plan-Code editor), have been promising. The GPCeditor was used for three years in an introductory programming class in Community High School in Ann Arbor, Michigan. While students in an average high school programming class can be expected to complete five to seven programs, students in the GPCeditor class complete about twenty working programs. Students in the GPCeditor class produced high quality programs and performed well in writing programs outside of the GPCeditor.

The organization of this paper is as follows. Our model of software design is presented in section 2. In section 3 we describe how SODA supports student doing and learning software design as they engage in the software design process. Student outcomes from the GPCeditor and expected outcomes from SODA are outlined in Section 4. The paper concludes with a discussion of future research directions.

2 The SODA model of software design

The SODA model of software design is based on studies of expert software designers working on complex design tasks [Ade-Sol85]. This model of the software design process is presented in Figure 1. The top half the figure presents major activities, with sub-activities beneath them. The bottom half the figure relates the various types of software support provided by SODA to these sub-activities. There are three types of major activities in software design: Problem Decomposition, Composition, and Debbuging. Each of these is described below.

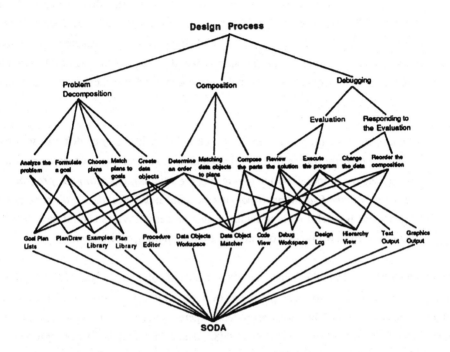

Design Process

Figure 1: Software Design Model <-> SODA Features Chart

- *Problem Decomposition:* When generating design solutions for a new problem, our model describes experts reviewing cognitive libraries of program solution techniques developed through experience. By first concentrating their search on previously solved plans experts are able to reduce complexity by using plans with known characteristics [Ade-Sol85].

If no plan is found the decomposition process continues and a new modularization is generated. [Par72, Bro75] discuss several criteria that can be used to generate good designs. Of primary importance is generating designs that decompose a problem into manageable subproblems. Because novices have little experience in generating designs, they need special tools to help them develop clear decompositions. Figure 1 indicates that problem decomposition is characterized as *Analyzing the problem,*

Formulating goals, Choosing plans, Matching plans to goals and *Creating data objects.*

- *Composition:* Once goals and plans have been identified, experts compose them into a coherent whole and then review the resultant solution to ensure that it meets established criteria. The composition process consists of *Determining an order, Matching data objects to plans* and *Composing the parts.* Experts develop strategies for ordering plans (composition) and selecting appropriate data objects to place into these plans (matching). Novices can benefit from an environment that makes the composition and matching processes *easy.*

- *Debugging:* As programs increase in complexity it becomes difficult to write a program correctly on the first try. Debugging is an iterative process, consisting of *Evaluating* the proposed design (*Reviewing the solution, Executing the program*) and *Responding to the Evaluation* (*Changing the data* and/or *Reordering the composition*). Experts use powerful tools to facilitate this process; novices should have access to these same tools within the context of their programming environment.

These three activities form the foundation of our model of software design. However, moving between these activities can cause problems, even for expert programmers. To maintain an effective understanding of the software product, experts utilize many different representations of the overall structure of the design [Swa-Bal82, Bro86]. Examples of these representations include function call graphs [Sol88] and the actual source code itself. Novices rarely use multiple representations of their problem solution. SODA presents multiple representations of the software design and links them dynamically so that changes in one representation are immediately reflected in another. Our goal is to encourage an understanding of both the decompositional and compositional structures of the overall software design.

3　How SODA supports the doing and learning of software design

SODA attempts to support the student as they engage in software design, but also support the student's learning. The former consists of supporting the student as they develop a knowledge of Pascal and the processes used to construct well-designed programs. The latter consists of an interaction between the instructor, the curriculum, and meta-learning strategies that are embedded in the SODA user interface [Sch90, Sol-Guz91].

Supporting the doing

SODA supports the doing of software design by explicitly supporting our model of software design, providing specialized tools for learning the Pascal language, presenting programming plans in a manner that encourages reuse, and providing sophisticated debugging tools for the student.

Explicit support of the design model:
SODA supports our model of software design by providing an explicit operational framework for the novice programmer. By operational framework we mean the objects the student uses or creates in the environment, the operations that can be performed on these objects, and the manner in which operations are structured to complete the task of designing a program (see *Controlling the students design process*).

The objects in the SODA framework consist of goals, plans, and the data objects used in and by the program. *Goals* define what is to be accomplished, *plans* define the specific algorithms required to properly realize a goal, and *data objects* are the constants and variables used in and by student programs. Students create goals and plans in a recursive process in which a high-level goal is implemented by a single plan; this plan, in turn, can be implemented through subgoals. The recursion results in a Goal-And-Plan (GAP) Hierarchy displayed to the student where leaf nodes represent Pascal language constructs. Data objects can be created at any time to meet the expected needs of a goal or to specify a plan.

Figure 2 presents a screen snapshot of SODA. This picture shows how SODA explicitly supports our design model through the menubar at the top of the screen: main activities become menus while subactivities become menu items under a specific menu. For example, during *Problem Decomposition* the activity *Formulate a goal* is invoked by selecting the *Decompose* menu and selecting *New Goal*. Other windows of SODA displayed in Figure 2 are:

- Goal-Plan Lists (upper left), which display the purpose of each goal and plan within a specific level of the design hierarchy. This window is used during the decomposition process and as a navigational aid.

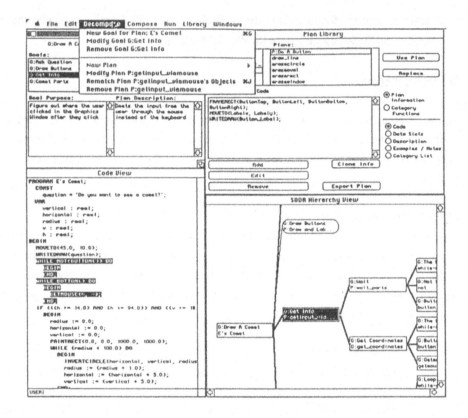

Figure 2: Screen snapshot of SODA,
featuring a student generatedprogram to draw a comet

- Code View (lower left), which presents the Pascal program and is used during the composition process to order the code and during the Debugging process to reflect on the overall solution.
- Hierarchy View (lower right), which presents the Goal-and-Plan Hierarchy and is used to facilitate reflection.

- Plan Library (upper right), which contains Pascal language plans and student generated plans.

The Goal-Plan Lists, Code View and Hierarchy View present three different representations of the program to the student. They are linked, such that a selection or modification in any one is reflected in the other two. This linking serves two purposes: it encourages reflection on the developing program and minimizes the chance that the student will generate opaque modularizations because they are able to relate each component of the design to the overall design [Bou-She89]. A list of SODA windows is presented in Appendix A.

Specialized tools for learning Pascal - PlanDraw:
A large portion of the SODA curriculum is based on Macintosh graphics. Looping constructs can be combined with graphics primitives to produce startling graphics effects, allowing exploration of programming concepts in a motivating context. Our previous experiences with the GPCeditor demonstrated that students have difficulty in three areas related to programming graphics on the Macintosh: (1) students have trouble understanding the Macintosh coordinate system, which is different from the more familiar Cartesian system, (2) it is sometimes difficult to correlate graphics shapes with the Pascal code fragment(s) that draw the shape, and (3) students are discouraged from exploring different graphics effects if the cost of explicitly programming each such effect is high.

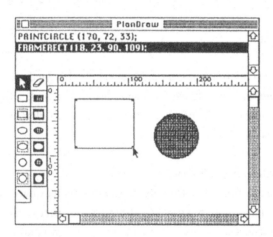

Figure 3: PlanDraw

PlanDraw (Figure 3) was designed to simultaneously address these issues. It is an object-based drawing package in which the shapes that can be drawn are equivalent to the shapes that can be generated from Pascal constructs that perform graphics functions. When a student draws a shape, the Pascal code fragment necessary to implement that shape is presented above the PlanDraw drawing area. Shapes and code fragments are dynamically linked, and shapes generated in PlanDraw can be directly incorporated into the program.

Encouraging software reuse - Plan Library:
The Plan Library stores Pascal language and student generated plans. It is organized around a set of *categories* (e.g. Input, Graphics, Output) that are designed to aid the student in locating plans. Our implementation also reinforces an important tenant of software design: because Pascal language plans must be obtained from the plan library before they can be used in the program, students are encouraged to think about reuse early in the design process.

Providing sophisticated debugging tools - Data Objects and Debug Workspaces:
SODA supports the debugging process in the Data Objects Workspace and the Debug Workspace. While debugging, students can observe the values of variables as they are changed during program execution in the Data Objects Workspace. The Debug Workspace presents two representations of the temporal execution of the program: a dynamic stack, that shows each plan as it is executed, and a trace of the program execution. This information can be printed and compared to the program to help aid the student in the debugging process.

Supporting the Learning

SODA supports the learning of design through a specially designed curriculum and a tight control over the students' processes as they engage in design activities. SODA supports meta-learning strategies such as articulation and reflection through characteristics of its user interface. [Bra-Cun87, Lan-App86].

Specially designed educational curriculum:
The SODA curriculum is organized towards developing increasingly complex programs throughout the semester while stressing the design skills necessary to cope with this complexity. It is worksheet-based and self-paced, with the instructor playing the role of a mentor, providing help for students on an individual basis. Students complete worksheets and the store the results of these worksheets (programs, program output, etc). in their project notebooks. These notebooks these are used both for grading and research. Each worksheet has a different focus, and the worksheets alternate between Pascal and software design concepts, following a natural progression. There are approximately 31 worksheets and 41 assignments during a 15 week semester.

Controlling the students design process:
SODA enforces our model of design through the enabling and disabling of menus and menu items that correspond to distinct activities in the model. For example, the menu item for

creating a *New Goal* is always available in the Decompose menu, but the menu item for creating a *New Plan* is only enabled when a goal has been created, is selected, and has no matching plan. Menu items are named to reflect their context, making explicit that the connection between a plan and the goal it realizes. SODA provides tight process control of the the design process: one cannot simply add code to the Code View, but rather one must first identify goals, then plans, and then put the pieces together. This tight ordering can benefit students who have not yet internalized the different stages of the design process [Cor-Sno86] .

Articulation and Reflection:

Articulation is a process in which students are encouraged to produce explicit descriptions (externalizations) about their design process. Reflection, which is related to articulation, involves comparing one's own activities to a model of the desired activities. Both of these work together to enhance the students' understanding of their own design process and the problem they are working on [Far-90].

Articulation is supported in SODA during the generation of the goal-plan design. Students are asked to name and describe goals, plans, and data objects. This articulation encourages reflection, since accurately describing a component requires reflection on how that component fits into the overall design. Further reflection occurs as students examine the relationship between their decompositional structure (Hierarchy View) and the compositional structure (Code View).

4 Student Outcomes

SODA was introduced at Community High School in September of 1991; we have no publishable results, but student outcomes of a precursor to SODA, the GPCeditor, have been studied. A brief review of our results is presented in this section.

The GPCeditor is based on a similar model of software design, and features similar kinds of support structures (e.g. a plan library, multiple linked representations) for the student. SODA was built to address limitations of the GPCeditor[1]. Because there is a high degree of similarity

---

[1] Specifically, common operations such as creating a new goal might take as long as 5 minutes in the GPCeditor for a large program. The GPCeditor does not contain PlanDraw, a Data Objects Workspace, a Debug Workspace, a Design Log and has a primitive Plan Library.

between the GPCeditor design model and the SODA design model, we feel confident that we can discuss expected outcomes of SODA in terms of actual outcomes from the GPCeditor.

Students in the GPCeditor class are expected to complete more than twenty working programs during the semester. At the end of the semester, students use LightSpeed Pascal in order for us to explore the question: 'Can students write programs without the support of the GPCeditor?' If we count the lines of code in the final program generated by the students, we see that approximately 1/3 wrote final programs at the 850 statement level, 1/3 wrote final programs at the 250 statement level, and 1/3 wrote programs at the 150 statement level. *Thus, 2/3 of the class were able to produce a significantly sized program without the aid of the GPCeditor!* Moreover, these programs did not exhibit "spaghetti code;" rather, these programs exhibited a highly modular structure [Sol-Guz91].

We expect that students using SODA will complete the same number of assignments as students using the GPCeditor. However, because SODA supports more of the design process and provides better debugging tools, we anticipate that students will be able to handle more complex assignments and generate larger programs using SODA as compared to the GPCeditor. We expect a similar increase in the size and quality of students programs when they make the transition to more traditional programming environments.

5   Future Research

To further support the student in developing expert-like design skills, what follows are some major themes that are being explored in the development of a successor to SODA.

In the early use of SODA, students are novice software designers - their design processes become more fluid, and they begin to transition from creating high-level goals to directly generating several lines of source code [Ade-Sol85]. As students become more expert-like in their own processes, we have found that the enforced process control of SODA can become more of a hindrance than a help. We would like this kind of scaffolding to fade, allowing the student to engage in the design process without control from the environment.

Most software is written by professional programmers working in teams, collaborating on the design of the system and sharing the programming responsibilities [Bro75, Fai85]. While students in the SODA class are encouraged to share plan libraries, there is no real support for collaborative design. We would like to support collaboration among students, allowing them to engage in even more expert-like behavior.

6 Summary

Providing support for novice designers is crucial if they are (1) to be successful in doing their projects and (2) to learn the domain expertise necessary to progress in their design abilities. SODA and its predecessor, the GPCeditor, demonstrate that we can provide sophisticated Design Support Environments for novice designers engaged in the doing and learning of software design skills. Furthermore, student outcomes from these environments demonstrate that they are effective - students can construct sophisticated, modular programs both within the DSE and in traditional programming environments.

References

[Ade-Sol85] Adelson, B. and Soloway, E. *The role of domain experience in software design.* IEEE Transactions on Software Engineering. November 1985.

[Bou-She89] Boulay, B., O'Shea, T., Monk, J. *The Black Box Inside the Glass Box: Presenting Computing Concepts to Novices,* Studying the Novice Programmer, 1989.

[Bra-Cun87] Bransford, J., Cunningham, R. *BRIDGE: A programming environment for novice programmers.* LRDC Technical Report, 1987.

[Bro75] Brooks, F. *The Mythical Man-Month,* Addison Wesley,1975.

[Bro86] Brooks, F. *No Silver Bullet: Essence and Accidents of Software Engineering,* Information Processing, 1986.

[Col88] Collins, A. *Cognitive Apprenticeship and instruction technology.* BBN Technical Report #6899, 1988.

[Cor-Sno86] Corno, L & Snow, R. Adapting teaching to individual differences among learners. In *Handbook of Research on Teaching.* Wittrock, M. (Ed). Macmillan: New York, 1986.

[Fai85] Fairley, R. *Software Engineering Concepts .* Mc-Graw Hill, 1985.

[Far90] Farnham-Diggory, S. *Schooling,* Harvard University Press, 1990.

[Lam84] Lampson. B. *Hints for Computer System Design.* IEEE Software. January, 1984.

[Lan-App86] Langer, J.A., Applebee, A.N. Reading and writing instruction: toward a theory of teaching and learning. In *Review of Research in Education*, 13:171-194. Rothkopf, E. (ed.) Washington, DC: AERA. 1986.

[Par72] Parnas, D. *On the Criteria to be Used in Decomposing Systems Into Modules*, CACM, 15(2) 1053-58, 1972.

[Per88] Perkins, D.N., Faraday, M., Hancock, C. Hobbs, R., Simmons, R., Tuck, T., Villa, E. *Nontrivial pursuit: The hidden complexity of elementary logo programming.* ETC Technical Report. August, 1988.

[Sch90] Schank, R. *Teaching Architectures.* Technical Report #3, Northwestern University Institute for the Learning Sciences. August, 1990.

[Sim69] Simon, H.A. *The Sciences of the Artificial.* The MIT Press: Cambridge, Mass. 1969.

[Spo-Sol85] Spohrer, J.C., Soloway, E. *Putting it all together is hard for novice programmers.* Invited Paper. In Proceedings on the IEEE International Conference on Systems, Man, and Cybernetics. November 12-15, 1985. Tucson, AZ

[Sol-Ehr84] Soloway, E. and Ehrlich, K. *Empirical Studies of Programming Knowledge.* IEEE Transactions on Software Engineering, September, 1984.

[Sol87] Soloway, E., Spohrer, J., Littman, D. *E Unum Pluribus: Generating Alternative Designs.* Cognitive Sciences Conference. 1987.

[Sol88] Soloway, E., Pinto, J., Letovsky, S., Littman, D. and Lampert, R. *Designing Documentation to Compensate for Delocalized Plans.* Communications of the ACM Vol 31 Number 11. November 1988

[Sol-Guz91] Soloway, E., Guzdial, M., Brade, K., Hohmann, L., Tabak, I., Weingrad, P., Blumenfeld, P. *Technological Support for the Learning and Doing of Design .*

[Sol86] Soloway, E., *Learning to program = Learning to construct mechanisms and explanations.* Communications of the ACM, 29(9):850-858. September

[Swa-Bal82] Swartout, W. and Balzer, R. *On the Inevitable Intertwining of Specification and Implementation.* Communications of the ACM, Vol 25. Number 7, 1982.

Appendix A: SODA Windows

Though SODA provides a large number of windows, the environment is not complex since each window in SODA represents a specific tool for either learning or doing software design (or both!) Furthermore, students are not overwhelmed with these windows on the first day of class: the curriculum introduces each window in the context of learning new Pascal language components or new software design skills. In this appendix the major SODA windows and the functions they provide are briefly described.

Window Title	Function
Goal-Plan List	• A navigational tool for decomposition and composition within a particular plan. • A reflection tool that presents the purpose of each goal and the description of each plan.
PlanDraw (Figure 3)	• Presents explicit representation of the Macintosh graphics coordinate system. • Associates graphic shapes and the Pascal plans that generate these shapes. • Encourages exploration in the software design process.
Examples Library	• A component of the Plan Library, the plan examples library demonstrates each of the basic plans available for use in SODA in a small, working program.
Plan Library (Figure 2)	• Contains all Pascal plans used by the student. • Provides information on how to reuse plans, the data objects a plan requires, and what the plan does. • Repository for student generated plans.
Procedure Editor	• Allows students to create procedures, specifying input and output parameters.
Data Objects Workspace	• Allows students to create data objects and helps manages their scoping.
Data Object Matcher	• Used to match data objects to plan slots when instantiating a plan for use in a program.
Code View (Figure 2)	• Represents the composition structure of the design generated by the student.
Debug Workspace	• Presents an explicit representation of the program stack and a trace of the program output to aid the student in debugging.
Design Log	• Displays student actions within the environment to facilitate reflection on their problem solving process.
Hierarchy View (Figure 2)	• Represents the overall decomposition structure of the software design. • Allows students to rearrange the decompositional structure of the design.
Text Output	• Textual Input/Output occurs in this window.
Graphics Output	• Graphical Input/Output occurs in this window.

A GRAPHICAL CAL AUTHOR LANGUAGE

David Jackson and Michael A Bell

Dept. of Computer Science
University of Liverpool
PO Box 147
Liverpool L69 3BX
ENGLAND

ABSTRACT

Many CAL packages are implemented using an author language, which allows the developer of the package easily to create and alter lessons that are to be presented to the user. Typically, such a language must provide statements to send text to the screen, get input from the user, match this input against the expected answers and take the appropriate actions, etc., but it is suggested that recent advances in the development of both hardware technology and programming languages have meant that most author languages now have a severely outdated and 'low-tech' feel to them. Attempts to address this problem — and these appear to be few and far between — suffer other failings such as lack of generality or portability.

In this paper, we describe a new CAL author language that is aimed at exploiting the powerful graphical and other facilities offered by modern microcomputers and workstations. Thus, the language enables the author to specify the size and position of multiple windows; to direct text, diagrams and program output to any of these windows; to provide interaction via menus; and so on. Simple examples of use of the language in developing courseware are given. A highly portable interpreter for the language has been implemented, details of which are described in a subsequent section.

Keywords: Computer-Assisted Learning (CAL); author languages

1. Introduction: the need for a new authoring language

Languages for writing CAL software packages — the so-called *author* languages [Bar87] — have been around for some time now. Examples of the more successful of these languages include MICROTEXT [Bev83] and PILOT [Con84]. It is unfortunate, however, that recent advances in the development of computer technology and techniques have greatly outpaced any developments in authoring languages, to the extent that most of them now have a distinctly 'low-tech' feel. In particular, the graphical facilities offered by many of today's workstations and microcomputers are generally not capable of being exploited to their full potential by most authoring systems.

The flavour of a typical author language is given by the following extract of a PILOT program (taken from [Bar87]):

```
*START
T: Hello
*STARTA T: GOODMORNING
*BEGIN TH: Type your name...
*STARTB T(#Z>0): GOODMORNING#
J: *START
J(#Y=4): *BEGIN
U: *JIM
```

The code is largely difficult to read and exhibits little of the structure that is nowadays deemed to be an essential property of a good programming language. This makes the code hard to understand, maintain and adapt. It is also very restrictive in the fact that it is usable only within a VDU-style (i.e. non-graphical) environment, although a later version of PILOT (called GPILOT) added some simple graphic commands. Other languages [Mak87] may improve on certain aspects, but they fare little better in general. In fact, the situation is such that the majority of courseware seems to be written in local dialects of BASIC. This gives the advantage of access to powerful microcomputer sound and graphics, but at the expense of extreme lack of portability in a language that is not noted for its encouragement of good programming practice.

The state of the art in courseware authoring systems is probably best represented by the Hypercard system running on the Apple Macintosh computer, which *does* make exceedingly good use of the graphics, sound, etc. of that particular machine. However, its associated scripting language — Hypertalk[App88] — still does not fulfil the specification of what we consider a truly general-purpose graphical CAL language. Hypertalk is not only machine-dependent, it is *package*-dependent; that is, it cannot be used as a stand-alone language in the same way that PILOT can, since Hypertalk scripts are written as 'handlers' of events that are generated from pre-built Hypercard front-ends. Similarly, the constructs of the language are very much oriented to objects that are provided by the Hypercard environment, so that there are references to cards, stacks, fields, and so on.

Thus, there seems to be a niche for a new CAL author language, for which the following design requirements may be specified:

- The language should be simple to use, with computational and flow-of-control statements tailored to use in a CAL context. Constructs such as while-loops, procedures and functions, that promote the development of well-structured and modular programs should be emphasised.

- An integral set of statements within the language should provide the author with comprehensive control of a workstation/microcomputer WIMP environment. For example, there should be statements to open a window with a particular size and location, to direct text and pictures to individual windows, to create menus, and to detect and respond to user interaction via the mouse or keyboard.

- As far as possible, the language should be machine and system independent, although it is desirable to have a mechanism to enable the author to invoke commands and utilities provided by the host system

With these requirements in mind, we have designed a new authoring language and implemented a prototype interpreter system for it. Portability of the interpreter was a major consideration, and it is therefore written in C to run under Unix using the X-Windows system. In the following sections of this paper, we give an overview of the language, along with some examples that demonstrate its use, and describe briefly the implementation of the interpreter.

2. Language overview

Many of the fundamental statements present in the language resemble those that are found in other more conventional imperative programming languages. To avoid confusing authors who have little prior programming experience, variables are implicitly declared as and when they appear in the script, and are automatically given a type that corresponds to the type of the expression that is assigned to the variable. The usual range of arithmetic and boolean operators is available, plus several pre-defined constants such as PI, and a large number of mathematical functions such as sin, cos, log, sqrt, etc. A typical assignment statement might be

```
result = pi * log(x)
```

In general, an end-of-line acts as a statement terminator; that is, only one statement may appear on a single line of the file. The syntax of loops and if-statements are similar to those of Pascal and Ada. Input and output statements are also analogous, except that since CAL applications may operate in a multi-window environment, output operations must specify the window to which the calculated values are being transferred. For example:

```
count = 1
while count <= 5 loop
   print(text, count)
   new_line(text, 2)
   count = count + 1
endloop
```

prints the numbers 1 to 5, separating successive numbers by two blank lines, in a window called 'text'. Similarly:

```
print(text, "Do you want to see a diagram (y/n) ?")
get_text(q)
if q == "y" then
   display(picture, "pics/diag1")
endif
```

sends the diagram contained in the file "pics/diag1" to the window called 'picture'. Note that no window is specified when getting input from the user with the *get_text* statement: it was decided that, to avoid confusion, all keyboard input by the user would be restricted to a single entry window; other forms of input (e.g. via menus) are still possible, however.

A miscellany of commands exists for creating and initializing the windows, menus, etc., that a script may subsequently manipulate. These have been designed to make the author's task of setting up the user interface as straightforward as possible. For instance, there are a number of *coordinate-independent* statements for creating windows, e.g.

```
window2r("win_a")
window4tl("win_b")
```

The first of these routine calls creates a window with the name "win a", that is half of a full screen in size (indicated by the '2' in the routine name) and which takes up the right half of the screen. The second statement sets up a quarter-screen sized window in the top left (hence the 'tl' in the routine name) corner of the screen.

For the majority of courseware applications, the author will not have to use any of the interface initialization commands just described; on start-up, the interpreter system looks for a *default* file which specifies exactly how this interface should appear. That is, it declares the windows, menus, title bars, and so on that will be used, and where they are to placed on the screen layout. This file is a purely textual one that can be altered by the author to suit the needs of the application. An example default screen layout is shown in Figure 1.

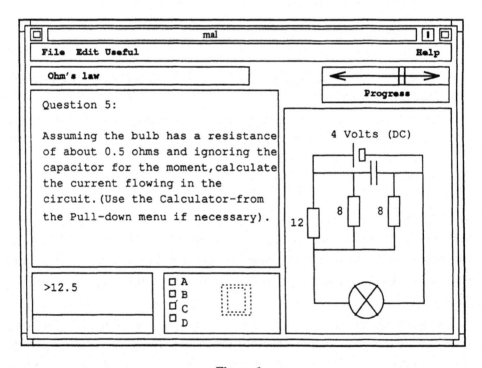

Figure 1

In this particular example, the default configuration comprises: a title bar ("Ohm's Law"); a menu bar via which the user can invoke system utilities or a built-in help menu; a text window that displays the course material; a picture window containing a circuit diagram; a progress indicator; a multiple-choice box; and a text input box. Another example making use of a similar default configuration is given in the next section.

It has been mentioned that the language design is intended to support modular development of courseware, and to this end the language incorporates procedure and function declarations with provision for recursion and parameter passing. An example of a call to a recursive function is as follows (for simplicity, parameters are referred to by position, e.g. $1 is the first parameter, etc.):

```
func factorial() begin
   if $1 == 0 then
      return (1)
   else
      return($1 * factorial($1 - 1))
   endif
endfunc

print(text, "factorial 3 = ")
print(text, factorial(3))
```

3. Example of use

A trivial example of the sort of script that one might write using our graphical CAL language is presented in Listing 1.

```
clear(all)
score = 0
print(title, "     Mathematical Tutor")
print_line(text, "        Algebraic Expressions")
print_line(text, "        --------------------")
new_line(text, 3)
print_line(text, "If a basket containing 100 apples was to distributed")
print_line(text, "among three people 'a', 'b' and 'c', how many would")
print_line(text, "'c' hold if 'a' holds 22 and 'b' holds 43")
display(picture, "pics/apples")
new_line(text)
a = 22
b = 43
result = 100 - a - b
print_line(text, "Type in the number held by 'c' and click on 'Enter'")
get_number(no_of_apples)
new_line(text)
if no_of_apples == result then
    print(text, "Correct!")
    score = score + 1
else
    print_line(text, "Wrong!")
    print_line(text, "The answer should be 35!")
    new_line(text)
    print_line(text, "If you require an explanation, type y and click
                      on 'Enter'")
    get_text(ans)
    if ans == "y" then
      print_line(text, "First you must calculate the number of
                        apples which")
      print_line(text, "'a' and 'b' have. This is 22 + 43 which
                        is 65.")
      new_line(text)
      print_line(text, "The total number of apples is 100 thus 'c'
                        would have")
      print_line(text, "100 - 65 apples, giving 35.")
      new_line(text)
    endif
endif
```

Listing 1.

The code constitutes a lesson in elementary arithmetic, and makes use of a default configuration file to set up the interface. The format of this is shown in Figure 2, and it contains a menu bar, a title bar (referred to in the script as 'title'), a user text entry window with an associated 'Enter' button, a text window (referred to as 'text'), and an illustrations window (with the label 'picture').

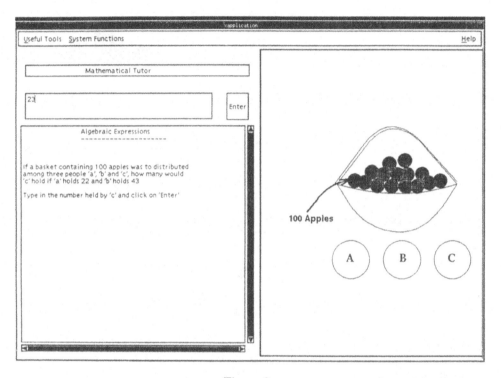

Figure 2

The program begins by clearing all windows with the statement *clear(all)*, initializing a *score* variable, and writing a title to the title bar. The arithmetic test itself is written to the text window, and an appropriate diagram is presented in the display window. The program then waits for the student to answer the question by typing in a number and clicking on the 'Enter' button. This is the point reached in Figure 2, from which it will be seen that, despite the availability of a calculator that can be invoked through the menu bar, an incorrect response has been typed. The program continues by highlighting this error and providing an explanation of the correct answer if the student so desires. Figure 3 shows the status of the screen at the completion of this activity; note that when no input is requested of the user, the 'Enter' button disappears.

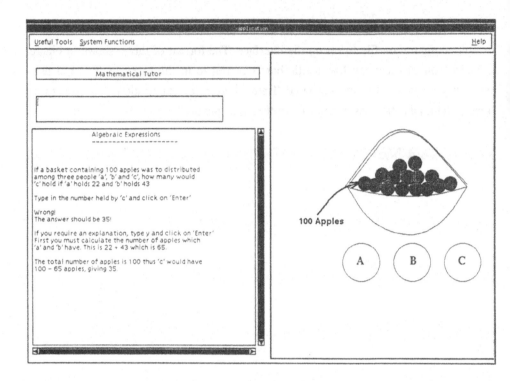

Figure 3

4. Implementation

A considerable amount of effort has been put into making the implementation of the interpreter system robust, maintainable and highly portable. The system has been developed using high level tools wherever possible, and comprises two main components:

- The language interpreter itself. This has been built using the Unix compiler-generation tools Lex[Les75] and Yacc[Joh75]. It converts the source CAL script into intermediate virtual code which is subsequently interpreted to run the program.

- The graphical front end. This takes the form of an X-Windows server process, built using the OSF Motif Widget set [You90]. It is the job of this process to update the screen display and handle user input.

The two components run in parallel and communicate via Unix *sockets*. Figure 4 gives an overview of the system, and depicts a situation in which the interpreter is sending an encoded instruction along a socket to the X process, requesting it to print a text string in a certain window.

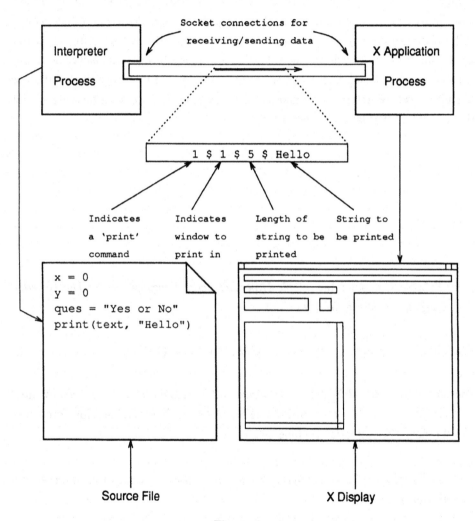

Figure 4

5. Conclusions

It seems clear that there is still much to be done in advancing the state of the art of courseware both to match the needs of its end-users and to exploit more fully the power offered by current desktop computers. As we have discussed, CAL author languages are a prime example of software technology lagging behind hardware technology, and their improvement could do much to foster the production of visually stimulating and exciting courseware. The language we have described in this paper is still undergoing development, and we hope that feedback that is gained from its use in generating courseware will provide valuable ideas for its furtherance. Nevertheless, we feel that it takes a step in the right direction, especially in its recognition of the now ubiquitous WIMP environment, and it will be interesting to see what the next generation of CAL author languages brings.

References

[App88]Apple Computer Inc., *Apple Hypercard Script Language Guide: The Hypertalk Language*, Addison-Wesley (1988)

[Bar87]P Barker, *Author Languages for CAL*, Macmillan (1987)

[Bev83]N Bevan and R Watson, *The design and evaluation of a microcomputer based authoring system for trainers*, Proc. IFAC/IFIP Conf. on 'Training for Tomorrow', Lerden, The Netherlands (June 1983)

[Con84]T Conlon, *PILOT - the language and how to use it*, Prentice-Hall International, Englewood Cliffs, NJ (1984)

[Joh75]S C Johnson, *Yacc: Yet Another Compiler-Compiler*, Comp. Sci. Tech. Rep. No. 32, Bell Laboratories, Murray Hill, New Jersey (1975)

[Les75]M E Lesk, *Lex - A Lexical Analyzer Generator*, Comp. Sci. Tech. Rep. No. 39, Bell Laboratories, Murray Hill, New Jersey (Oct. 1975)

[Mak87]G J Makinson and H L Morarji, *Experiences of a new authoring system for computer-assisted learning*, Proc. 1986 Conf. Computers in Higher Education, Lancaster University, published as *Trends in Computer-Assisted Education*, R Lewis and E D Tagg (eds.), Blackwell Scientific Publications (1987), pp. 180-188

[You90]D A Young, *The X Window System: Programming and Applications with Xt, OSF/Motif Edition*, Prentice-Hall, Englewood Cliffs, NJ (1990)

A Knowledge Base Approach to Learning to Program in Prolog

Donna M. Kaminski

Computer Science Department

Western Michigan University

Kalamazoo, Michigan   49008 U.S.A.

tel. (616) 387-5645

email: kaminski@gw.wmich.edu

Abstract

A second programming language should be considerably easier to learn because the programmer has built up a knowledge base of language-independent stereotypic structures and rules for handling commonly needed programming tasks (e.g., processing a list, branching, keeping a running total). However, transference of this underlying goal/plan knowledge is more complex for an unconventional language such as Prolog. Some traditional programming activities can be implemented quite directly by just learning the appropriate Prolog syntax - e.g., modularizing, parameter passing, using arithmetic expressions. But the mechanisms for accomplishing many other common tasks such as repetition, conditional execution, use of a counter, variable initialization, are handled quite differently in Prolog. In addition, certain of Prolog's built-in features, e.g., unification, search, backtracking, have no direct counterpart in traditional languages and vice versa, e.g., arrays, global variables.

This paper provides discussion and examples of key plans and strategies for the beginning Prolog programmer's knowledge base in each of these areas. Such a "toolbox" provides them with GOAL/PLAN and PLAN/TEMPLATE rules, guiding them as to when a particular structure is useful and how it is used for both existent traditional programming knowledge and new Prolog-specific knowledge. It is argued that an explicit presentation of such knowledge, in addition to the syntax and semantics of the language, greatly aids the programmer learning to program in Prolog.

Learning a Second Language

Learning a second programming language is categorically different from learning a first language primarily because the learner already knows how to "program", per se. Much of that knowledge is directly transferable to the new language [Sch-Wie89]. Since the second language is usually encountered after considerable programming practice, a more directed focus on the syntax of the new language and the types of problems for which it's most suited is possible. It becomes more a matter of "learning a new language" rather than "learning to program in a new language".

This programming knowledge base is a key difference between novice and experienced programmers [Ehr-Sol84, Sol-Ehr-Bon-Gre84, Sol86]. To an experienced programmer each problem's solution is not totally unique, but rather, incorporates pieces from previously solved problems used successfully in the past, including techniques for very simple concepts like handling a variable assignment, up through high level knowledge like sorting (i.e., algorithms). The concern here is with a more intermediate level of programming knowledge, e.g., using a counter, looping to read and process data, keeping a running total, searching a list. Language-independent canned solution plans for these stereotypic sub-problems are used as building blocks for planning and constructing algorithms for new problems [Sol86]. And their generic labels (rather than their implementations) are the primitives used by experienced programmers in conceptualizing the solution.

It is argued that this knowledge base approach is useful in teaching programming by explicitly providing the learner with canned solution plans for typical programming situations [Kam89, Sne80, Sol85, Sol86]. In effect, provide the learner with a set of GOAL/PLAN and PLAN/TEMPLATE rules:

    IF _ this _ is the GOAL you're trying to do
        THEN _ here _ is the PLAN for accomplishing that goal.

    IF _ this _ is the PLAN in the algorithm
        THEN _ here _ is the TEMPLATE for implementing that plan.

Such explicit instruction is typically done for higher level knowledge (i.e., data structures and algorithms), but is usually not explicitly addressed for intermediate-level concepts. This knowledge acquisition approach is also useful in learning a second language, helping in the transference of programming knowledge. Programmers already have the cognitive structures (the GOAL/PLAN rules) and know how to implement them in the first language (the PLAN/TEMPLATE rules), but need to know the syntax for implementing them in the new language. They also need to acquire rules and templates for constructs unique to the new language. Typical introductory texts do not usually use this knowledge base approach to presenting the language but rather focus on syntax and semantics, assuming that the programmer's knowledge base will develop through experience.

Learning Prolog

Because Prolog is a rather unconventional language, the programmer's existent knowledge base is not entirely directly usable for Prolog programming. In some cases, rules just need new implementation templates. These may directly parallel traditional implementation details or be quite different because of Prolog's unique capabilities and/or lack of them. Other rules need entirely new plan structures. And, in other cases, new goal/plan rules need to be introduced to take advantage of Prolog's built-in features and declarative nature.

Although Prolog is ideally a declarative language and hence considerably different in structure and approach from traditional languages, it does allow a significant procedural component. Prolog implementation details for such procedural control constructs as straight sequential processing, fixed count and conditional iteration, conditional execution, and subprogram calls are particularly important since this is primarily how traditional programmers conceptualize control flow in problem solving. But because of Prolog's built-in features, such as unification, recursion, search and backtracking, the implementations of these structures is not always obvious. (Few authors specifically address these [Cov-Nut-Vel88, Mun86]). And Prolog also allows for other types of control not found in traditional languages (in part, in order to work with Prolog's "natural", inherent way of behaving): e.g., the cut to force determinism (or correctness or efficiency), "fail" to force backtracking for looping, forced success ("true") to force continued straight-line processing. Such constructs need to be described not only in terms of the syntax and semantics of the particular predicates. More importantly, rules must be provided explaining what functions they are used for, when they should be used as well as templates for how they are used. Prolog programmers need such generic canned solution plans in their knowledge base in order to "think in Prolog".

In order to take full advantage of Prolog's unique declarative capabilities, a true understanding of its inherent unification, variable instantiation, search, backtracking and goal-seeking mechanisms is needed. Such constructs do not already exist in the learner's programming knowledge base. Problems must be conceptualized using this new paradigm; conventional programmers must unlearn some of their ways of thinking about programming and problem solving. (Several projects have successfully used Prolog as a first programming language and/or for teaching non-computer science students to program [Enn86, Pai-Bun87, Sch-Mal-Sha86]). Specific plan knowledge must be explicitly presented for commonly used operations and stereotypic code structures, guidelines for solving certain characteristic subproblems must be presented as well as strategies for avoiding common pitfalls and typical bugs [Brn-Bun-Pai-Lyn87, Sch-Gol-Fun90]. For example, guidelines and templates might be provided for such tasks as recursion for rule definitions (as well as for procedural looping), unification for comparison and assignment (rather than actively "doing" these operations procedurally), guarding rules with pre-conditions, "global variable" vs. parameter implementation of counters, cases for using facts as data storage, simulating stacks and queues with facts, using unification (as well as recursion) for list processing, the advantages and disadvantages of doing work on the way down vs. up in recursion and when each is preferable, initializing at the bottom of recursion, etc.

Whether a procedural or declarative approach is used, Prolog programming utilizes many of the same design techniques and structures as are used in conventional programming, e.g., top-down and bottom up design, incremental development using dummy stubs and drivers, a modular approach including both internal and external components, parameter passing for module independence and external libraries of commonly used routines for extending the language. Prolog implementation details must be highlighted for these.

Traditional programmers have also developed cognitive plan structures for commonly required tasks such as keeping a running total, reading and processing input data until the end of file, and using a counter. They also have specific conceptions about what variables are and how they can be used inside a program. Such constructs as data storage alternatives, variable assignment, variable comparison, re-using variables within a rule, global vs. local variables and input-output parameters are handled differently in Prolog and need to be assimilated into the programming knowledge base so that they too seem "intuitive" to the programmer.

Thus there are two types of plan knowledge relevant to the new Prolog programmer: those aspects which utilize existing cognitive structures and those aspects which are totally new and require a new way of thinking. In the former case, coverage of Prolog implementation details is needed with explicit discussion of how these fit into their existent cognitive framework for programming. In the latter case, the learner needs to add to their knowledge base a true understanding of Prolog's built-in capabilities and how these can be harnessed to accomplish the desired goals, in addition to plan knowledge for specific structures commonly used in declarative, logic programming.

Examples

Examples from each of the categories of goal/plan knowledge are presented below to demonstrate the types of knowledge which should be explicitly provided to supplement introductory Prolog text material (where absent) - i.e., familiar vs. new structures, similar vs. new implementations. Sample code has been kept simple for ease of presentation here. (A more extensive set of examples has been developed [Kam92, Mun86]).

List Processing

List processing operations can be subdivided on several dimensions based on what they are to accomplish including:

yes/no	vs.	answer(s)
single answer	vs.	multiple answers
visit some members	vs.	visit all members
may succeed	vs.	will succeed

       return answer(s)   vs.   build a new list
       etc.

These reflect WHAT the programmer wants to accomplish with the rule. Each represents a commonly needed programming goal. The programmer needs a plan for HOW to accomplish each of the goals. For example, suppose the goal is to build a new list given an input list, where each element of the new list is a function of the corresponding element in the original list. A plan/template for how this could be done might be as follows:

```
build_corr_list([], []).
build_corr_list([Head | Tail], NewList) :-
    build_corr_list(Tail, List),
    NewElement is. . . ,                % some function of Head
    NewList = [NewElement | List].
```

By using a non-tail-recursive structure, the base case can serve to both detect when the input list is empty and to then initialize the new list. New elements will then be added to the front of it on the way back up the recursive call returns. Thus the new list is in an order corresponding to the input list. (An alternative tail recursive template might also or instead be provided).

       Since list processing is a very common Prolog task, there should obviously be quite a few goal/plan rules for the programmer to assimilate into his/her programming knowledge base. Each of the list processing tasks represents a goal which a Prolog programmer might want to do. Their programming knowledge base would include a rule indicating which plan to use, e.g.,

       IF "build corresponding list" is WHAT you want to accomplish
         THEN "plan B_C_L" is HOW to do it

With experience in using the rule, the programmer begins to conceptualize the problem solution in terms of the rule labels, e.g., "build_corr_list", just as he/she did for commonly used tasks in traditional procedural programming, e.g., use a counter.

Modularity

       Because Prolog can be interpreted procedurally as well as declaratively, traditional programming knowledge regarding top-down design, the development of independent internal and external modules, parameter passing, local variables, etc. is applicable in learning to program in Prolog. A program (whether declarative or procedural aspect) might thus be viewed as corresponding to the form:

```
main_program :-
        procedure1(in_param, out_param),
        procedure2(out_param),
        ...
        procedureN.
procedure1(param_1, param_2) :-
        procedure1A(param_1),
        ...
        procedure1N(param_1, param_2).
    ...
```

where any procedure may instead be just an in-line statement rather than a call to another procedure.

Viewed declaratively, rules are defined in terms of a set of assertions (facts) and other sub-rules, which are themselves defined in terms of... The head of a rule corresponds to the name of the procedure, the body of the rule corresponds to the sequence of steps defining the procedure, and a query (or a rule named in the body of a higher level rule) corresponds to a call to a procedure. The programmer's knowledge base would thus contain a rule of the form:

IF the goal is to program using modularity
    THEN here is a plan/template/example for accomplishing the task.

Corresponding to external subroutines, Prolog programs can be subdivided into any number of physically separate files, allowing for several programmers to work independently and for exploitation of a library of commonly used rules (e.g., list processing operations, fancy I/O routines, an expert system shell). The main program can automatically load the latest versions of the sub-programs by including the following commands at the beginning of the main program:

```
:- reconsult ('listproc.library').
:- reconsult ('niceio.pro').
```

Further discussion of related concepts and their goal/plan/template rules should follow including local variables, parameter variables (naming, matching arity and order), consistent instantiation, the use of dummy stubs (rules) during development, sharable/reusable external modules, and incremental development.

Conditional Execution

Prolog's handling of modularity and related concepts is not all that different from that used in traditional languages. However, carrying out conditional execution can be implemented in Prolog in several ways: one which somewhat parallels the traditional implementation, and a more efficient technique which uses Prolog's unique built-in unification mechanism. For example, to carry out the conditional statement,

> If the input is 1,
>> then the result is 100,
> otherwise the result is 200,

the following could be embedded in-line in the code:

> ((Input = 1, Result is 100);
> (Input \= 1, Result is 200)),

This parallels the traditional implementation and is useful only for simple conditions. The following format is useful for extending to more complex conditions, nesting and/or simulating CASE statements. To express the above statement the embedded calling clause,

> if_check (Input,Result),

calls the rule defined as:

```
if_check (Input,Result) :-
    Input = 1, !,              % IF condition
    Result is 100.             % THEN statement
if_check (Input,Result) :-
    Result is 200.             % ELSE statement
```

A simulated CASE statement including compound conditions such as the following:

> If the input is 0
>> then the result is 100;
> if the input is 1 or 2,
>> then the result is 200;
> if the input is between 3 and 7,
>> then the result is 300;
> otherwise   the result is 0.

can be defined similarly. However, a simpler, more efficient version using unification for both the item comparison and the variable assignment is shown below. The above IF/THEN/ELSE statement could be defined as:

```
if_check (1,100) :- !.
if_check (_,200).
```

i.e., if the first calling parameter, Input, unifies with the 1 in the first clause, then the second calling parameter, Result, will be instantiated to 100, then stop. Otherwise the parameter Input will always unify with the anonymous variable and then bind Result to

200. The CASE statement above could be written as follows:

```
if (0,100) :-
                !.
if (Input,200) :-
                (Input = 1; Input = 2), !.
if (Input,300) :-
                Input > = 3, Input = < 7, !.
if (_,0).
```

All of the above examples provide a final ELSE clause which is important to ensure the success of the overall rule. For example, a simple IF rule

```
If the input is 'yes'
    then the result is 'ok'
```

might tempt a Prolog beginner to implement it as follows:

```
if_check(yes,ok).
```

(or similar to this if embedded), assuming that they can generalize from the above Prolog rule in conjunction with their knowledge about traditional IF procedures. However, the above rule could fail, which would cause the calling rule to fail without finishing the rest of that rule, which would cause. . . So common pitfalls should be provided to the learner to aid in their plan knowledge assimilation.

By providing examples which demonstrate a range of possibilities (e.g., simple and boolean conditions, IF/ELSE and CASE, a typical beginner's bug), a generic template can be assimilated into the programmers plan knowledge for conditional statements.

Conclusions

As with any area, the knowledge acquisition process for learning to program in Prolog can be inductive, in which the learner develops and extends his/her knowledge through experience, or more direct, through the explicit presentation of that knowledge to the learner. It is argued here that the second method is more effective for learning a second programming language, particularly for a non-traditional one like Prolog. The learner must develop a new way of thinking about problem solving, a new set of tricks, tools and building blocks for program planning and development. But they already have a considerable base on which to build, making it easier to assimilate the new knowledge.

Just as data structures and algorithms are explicitly presented to computer science students, so too should this intermediate level of semantic programming knowledge. This can effectively be done through supplemental material, building on an existing introductory Prolog text.

Several examples were shown to demonstrating the types of goal/plan "rules" along with templates/examples for implementation. A much larger set of such rules has been developed and is being extended, particularly regarding Prolog's unique aspects [Enn86]. Other important constructs in the Prolog programmer's knowledge base include such things as various approaches to looping, simulating FOR and WHILE loops, using a counter, keeping running totals, guaranteeing the success of a rule, simulating global variables, record structures, handling negative facts, self-starting programs, typical pitfalls and bugs [Brn-Bun-Pai-Lyn87, Sch-Gol-Fun90], why $I=I+1$ doesn't work, assigning values in recursive procedures, using an open world assumption, classification of list processing goals [Sol85], a simpler way to use the cut, etc. These, of course, are relatively low level concepts, but are particularly useful to explore with the beginning Prolog student. After developing the basic Prolog expertise, explicit presentation of higher level plan knowledge is of great value, e.g., traditional data structures and algorithms and, for artificial intelligence, knowledge representation and search techniques. Many texts do present such material [Bra90, Cov-Nut-Vel88]. The Prolog "toolbox" concept (or library of commonly used routines) is also very helpful in further developing Prolog programming skills [Coe-Cot88, Cov-Nut-Vel88].

References

[Bra90] I. Bratko. *Prolog Programming for Artificial Intelligence*, New York: Addison-Wesley, 1990.

[Brn-Bun-Pai-Lyn87] P. Brna, A. Bundy, H. Pain, L. Lynch. *Programming Tools for Prolog Environments*, Advances in Artificial Intelligence, J. Hallam & C. Mellish (eds.), New York: Wiley, 1987, pp. 251-264.

[Coe-Cot88] H. Coelho, J. Cotta. *Prolog by Example*. New York: Springer-Verlag, 1988.

[Cov-Nut-Vel88] M. Covington, D. Nute, A. Vellino. *Prolog Programming in Depth*, Glenview, IL: Scott, Foresman, 1988.

[Ehr-Sol84] K. Ehrlich, E. Soloway. *An Empirical Investigation of the Tacit Plan Knowledge in Programming*, Human Factors in Computer Systems, J. Thomas & M.L. Schneider (eds.), New York: Ablex, 1984, pp. 113-133.

[Enn86] R. Ennals. *Teaching Logic as a Computer Language in Schools*, Logic Programming and its Applications, M. VanCaneghem & D. Warren (eds.), Norwood, NJ: Ablex, 1986, pp. 129-144.

[Kam89] D. Kaminski. *Canned Procedural Structures as Meta-Language for Programming*, Proceedings of the Western Educational Computing Conference, 1989, pp. 9-13.

[Kam92] D. Kaminski. *Knowledge Structures for Introductory Prolog Programming*, in progress, 1992.

[Mun86] T. Munakata. *Procedurally Oriented Programming Techniques in Prolog*, IEEE Expert, Summer 1986, pp. 41-47.

[Pai-Bun87] H. Pain, A. Bundy. *What Stories Should We Tell Novice Prolog Programmers?*, Artificial Intelligence Programming Environments, R. Hawley (ed.), Chichester, England: Ellis Horwood, 1987, pp. 120-130.

[Sch-Mal-Sha86] Z. Scherz, O. Maler, E. Shapiro. *Learning with PROLOG - A New Approach*, Journal of Computers in Mathematics & Science Teaching, 6:1, 1986, pp. 31-37.

[Sch-Gol-Fun90] Z. Scherz, D. Goldberg, Z. Fund. *Cognitive Implications of Learning Prolog - Mistakes and Misconceptions*, Journal of Educational Computing Research, 6:1, 1990, pp. 89-110.

[Sch-Wie89] J. Scholtz, S. Wiedenbeck. *Learning a New Programming Language*, Designing and Using Human-Computer Interfaces and Knowledge Based Systems, G. Salvendy & M.J. Smith, Amsterdam: Elsevier, 1989, pp. 152-159.

[Sne80] B. Sneiderman. *Software Psychology: Human Factors in Computer and Information Systems*. New York: Little, Brown, 1980.

[Sol-Ehr-Bon-Gre84] E. Soloway, K. Ehrlich, J. Bonar, J. Greenspan. *What Do Novices Know About Programming?*, Directions in Human-Computer Interaction, A. Badre & B. Sneiderman (eds.), Norwood, NJ: Ablex, 1984, pp. 27-54.

[Sol85] E. Soloway. *From Problems to Programs via Plans: The Content and Structure of Knowledge for Introductory LISP Programming*, Journal of Educational Computing Research, 1:2, 1985, pp. 157-172.

[Sol86] E. Soloway. *Learning to Program = Learning to Construct Mechanisms and Explanations*, Communications of the ACM, 29:9, 1986, pp. 850-858.

Self-adjusting Curriculum Planning in Sherlock II

Sandra Katz, Alan Lesgold, Gary Eggan, Maria Gordin, Linda Greenberg

Learning Research and Development Center

University of Pittsburgh

Pittsburgh, PA 15260, USA

tel. (412) 624-7054

email: katz@unix.cis.pitt.edu

Abstract

What are the main criteria for effective automatic curriculum planning? We propose that there are two criteria—one cognitive, the other motivational: (1) selection of tasks that are at the appropriate difficulty level for the student; i.e., challenging, but not frustrating and (2) enough variety in the chosen tasks to sustain the student's interest. The first objective is the more difficult to meet, because it depends upon the system's ability to adaptively model the student's strengths and weaknesses in the domain being taught. However, student modeling is fraught with uncertainty, brought on by such factors as ambiguity in interpreting student actions, careless errors, forgetting prior knowledge, and insufficient evidence.

We suggest four design principles that can help to make curriculum planning less dependent upon accurate and complete student models: (1) holistic vs. componential instruction, (2) interpretation of student performance relative to expert performance, (3) use of local, rather than global assessment as the criteria for advancement, and (4) letting students have some say in the design of their curriculum. We illustrate these principles by describing the curriculum planner in **Sherlock II**, an intelligent coached practice environment for electronic fault diagnosis. In addition, we show how task variety can be sustained via the design of the problem set, and by filtering the set of candidate "next" problems according to their distinctive features. Finally, we conclude with some observations about how student input into curriculum planning could be used to update the student model.

Keywords: intelligent tutoring systems; student modeling and cognitive diagnosis; instructional planning; curriculum; performance monitoring

Introduction

Individualized instruction is commonly named as the main goal driving the development of a technology for intelligent tutoring systems (ITS's). A prerequisite for achieving this goal is to enable tutoring systems to construct and dynamically refine a model of students' understanding of domain concepts, and mastery of basic skills. Equipped with the ability to model the student, an "intelligent" tutor can then use this model to tailor various teaching functions to each student's needs, such as (1) selecting the appropriate level of hinting and explanation, (2) determining advancement and dynamically planning the student's curriculum, and (3) giving the student feedback on her current performance and overall progress.

However, there is a great deal of uncertainty involved in interpreting student actions and responses. Factors contributing to uncertainty include careless errors and lucky guesses, changes in student knowledge due to learning and forgetting, and patterns of student responses simply unanticipated by the designers of the student modeling knowledge base. Because student models are fraught with uncertainty, it is important that other system modules that use these models be robust. To take an extreme case, if the student is doing well and knows this, but the student modeling engine hasn't yet "caught up" with the student's ability and issues her a poor progress report, the system will lose credibility to the student.

Comparing the other two system functions that depend upon the student modeling module (listed above), instruction (hinting and explanation) and curriculum planning, the first might seem to be the more robust against errors in the student model. If the system misjudges the student's ability level, and gives the student an insufficiently detailed hint or explanation, the student can ask for help again, phrase her question differently, etc.. On the other hand, if the tutor gives the student a task which is too hard or too easy, the student will still have to do it, and successive tasks will likely remain misaligned with the student's actual ability. We suggest that this apparent lack of recoverability to modeling errors in curriculum planning at least partly explains why far less attention has been given to developing a technology for automatic curriculum planning than for other tutoring system functions.

The main objective of this paper is to show how the curriculum planning module of an ITS can be more robustly designed, so that it is less dependent upon accurate and complete student models. We propose four principles for achieving this aim:

1. **Holistic vs. componential instruction**: anchoring instruction in realistic, complete tasks, rather than in skill-isolating exercises.

2. **Comparative assessment**: interpreting student performance relative to simulated expert performance, instead of in absolute terms.

3. **Local versus global criteria for advancement**: basing decisions about advancement on the student's performance on the current task, rather than on a cumulated rating across tasks.

4. **Student input into designing the curriculum, and into student modeling**: using student self-assessments to adjust the evolving curriculum plan and, when expected performance conflicts with actual performance, to then adjust the student model.

In the remainder of this paper, we discuss these principles in more detail, and illustrate them by showing how they were incorporated within the curriculum planning module of **Sherlock II**, an intelligent coached practice environment for electronic troubleshooting [Les-EKR]. In addition, we show how we attempt to meet another criteria of effective curriculum planning: *variety*, in order to sustain student interest. Finally, we conclude with some observations about how student input into curriculum planning could be used to adjust the student model.

Toward More Robust Curriculum Planning

What are the main criteria for effective automatic curriculum planning? We suggest that there are two—one cognitive, the other motivational:

(1) Problems should be at the *appropriate difficulty level* for students—i.e., sufficiently challenging, but not so far beyond the student's ability level as to be frustrating.

(2) Problems should be *varied*, so as to maintain the student's interest and sense that she is making progress.

Achieving the first goal is the more difficult, since it depends upon the system's ability to model the student's knowledge state, and to dynamically adapt this model to changes in student competency. To recap the argument presented in the **Introduction**: since there is a great deal of uncertainty inherent in student modeling, the curriculum planner needs ways of being more robust. We proposed four principles for increasing robustness. In this section, we will discuss how each one could contribute to more robust planning.

1. *Holistic versus componential instruction.* Within the last few years, "situated learning" [Brown-CD89] has become increasingly popular as a theory for instructional design. The basic idea is that much real-world (non-classroom) learning is embedded in a context of social activity, rather than taught as abstract knowledge to be applied later. As such, situated learning, such as apprenticeships, can be viewed as an antidote to inert (unused) knowledge, a major problem with traditional classroom instruction. Several system developers, including our group at the Learning Research and Development Center, have been building ITS's upon these notions of situated learning and cognitive apprenticeship (e.g., [Laj-Les90]; [Les-EKR]).

In addition to addressing the problem of inert knowledge, and more relevant to our purposes in this paper, situated learning helps to make curriculum planning more efficient and less dependent upon detailed student models. It does this by limiting the amount of knowledge components (concepts and skills) that need to be taken into account during task selection, since many will be common across problems.

For example, in our electronic troubleshooting tutor, **Sherlock II,** students *always* have to take measurements, interpret readings, trace through schematics, etc.—no matter how hard or easy the problem. (The computor coach, Sherlock, is available to provide advice when the student asks for it.) In apprenticeship-style learning environments such as **Sherlock II,** which have students practice on realistic, complete tasks, the job of problem selection becomes more contained than in systems that sequence tasks skill by skill, according to some model of the order in which these skills are typically acquired. Instead of having to take into account how the student is doing on each knowledge component that constitutes expertise in the domain, the curriculum planner in an apprenticeship-style tutor need only focus on the student's competency in those knowledge components that determine problem difficulty. Some features that account for problem difficulty in **Sherlock II** include the location of the electronic fault, the type of test equipment that the technician has to use (e.g., the oscilloscope is more complex than the handheld meter), and what types of circuit components the technician will have to test in order to locate the fault (e.g., switches are more complex than relay cards).

The tutor can focus on the student model's assessment of the student's ability in these subskills, and two or three others related to problem difficulty, and ignore the rest of the student model when it comes time to choose the next problem.

2. *Comparative assessment.* Although holistic instruction limits the number of competency variables in the student model that need to be considered during curriculum planning, it does not address the problem that the subset of relevant modeling variables (i.e., those that determine task difficulty) are still prone to inaccuracies and uncertainty in the student model. Very often, uncertainty stems from simply not having enough evidence to go by in inferring the student's ability on some knowledge component. However, if the system is capable of simulating an expert's performance on the same problems that the student has worked on, it can then use the "expert's" competency model as a basis for interpreting the student's competency model.

For example, suppose that both student and "expert" have solved only two Sherlock problems that involve malfunctioning switches. At this point, the system "believes" that the student is slightly below average on faulty switch problems. However, it also "believes" that the simulated expert has only average ability on faulty switch problems, simply because not enough evidence has been accrued yet to raise the "expert's" score to expert level. So what should the curriculum planner infer about the student's ability on faulty switch problems? If the planner were to look at the student's score in absolute terms, it would infer that the student needs more practice on switch problems. However, if the planner were to consider the student's performance *relative to* that of the simulated expert—expressed, perhaps, as a ratio of scores—it would notice that there is not much difference between the two—at least not yet. It would therefore wait and see if, in future faulty switch problems, it gets more evidence of a bigger performance gap. Only when this gap falls below a certain threshold would switch problems be removed from the "needs more practice" list. Thus, through comparative assessment, the curriculum planner can be made more robust against the problem of uncertainty in the student model due to insufficient evidence.

3. *Local versus global criteria for advancement.* Another way to make the curriculum planner more robust against uncertainty in the student model is to restrict the model's role in the planning process. Assuming that the set of tasks is ordered by increasing difficulty, we suggest that the student model be used to filter the candidate set of next tasks according to features that the student needs to practice, as described in the example above. However, the

student model should not be used to "locate" the student within the ordered problem set. In an earlier version of **Sherlock II** that underwent preliminary field trials, we learned the hard way that direct mapping between the student's scores on particular modeling variables (knowledge components) and the ordered problem set offers the curriculum planner up as prey to errors in these scores.

How, then, should the student's "place" within a problem set ordered by increasing difficulty be determined? We suggest that this be done *locally* rather than globally—i.e., by focusing on the student's performance on the most recent (current) problem, instead of on her cumulative modeling scores across problems. The rationale for doing this is simple. If the student does very well on the current problem, she is probably ready to advance; if she does poorly, then she has probably been advanced too far already—is in "over her head," so to speak—and should be moved back. Once the student has been placed within the range of problems that she is ready for, the student model can then be used to filter the problems within this range according to features that the student needs more practice on. Interpreting the student's rating on these features relative to the "expert's" ratings should help to increase the reliability of assessment.

4. *Student input into curriculum planning and the student model.* Perhaps the simplest and most natural way to increase robustness in curriculum planning is to allow students to give input into the design of their curriculum. There are two main benefits to be gained from doing this. First, the student might know more than the system does about her ability, especially when there simply have not been enough opportunities yet for the student to show the tutor what her ability is on particular knowledge components. Second, welcoming student input is good for motivation.

The challenge presented by handling student input into curriculum planning is to determine when to allow student self-assessments to continue to bias the curriculum, and when not to. After all, the trainee will be peeved if she gets a harder problem, handles it pretty well, but still gets easier ones thereafter because the system has not yet enough confidence to "promote" her. On the other hand, if the trainee misjudged her ability, that error should not produce a long-term bias to give her harder problems than it appears she can handle.

The key to enabling the curriculum planner to accurately distinguish between the two situations described in the preceding paragraph is to make it sensitive to discrepancies between *expected performance*—i.e., the planner's assessment of where in the curriculum the student should be placed—and *actual performance*—i.e., how well the student does on easier/harder problems than the planner "thinks" she is ready for. Below, we describe our approach to doing this in **Sherlock II**, as well as some initial ideas we have for using accurate student self-assessments to update the student model.

The second criterion for effective problem selection named at the beginning of this section, *variety*, can be achieved mainly through the design of the problem set. The main design principles that contribute to variety in the problem set include:

1. **Limit the size of the problem set.** If there are too many problems, especially too many of the same type, the student will not be able to move onto new types of problems quickly enough.

2. **Order problems in a way that ensures some mixture of features.** Usually, several factors will determine problem difficulty. These factors can be weighted in such a way that running the ordering routines produces a problem set whose features are distributed, instead of clustered among adjacent problems.

3. **Keep a backup set of "ringer" problems, and randomly select from this set at regular intervals.** Ringer problems capture idiosyncratic situations that could happen in the real world, but are less common than those in the regular problem set. Choosing a problem from this surprise set every so often could awaken a dozing student.

In the next section, we will illustrate these principles for increasing variety and robustness in curriculum planning, by describing the curriculum planner in **Sherlock II**.

An Example: Curriculum Planning in Sherlock II

To set the stage for this example, we first give a brief overview of the tutor. A more detailed description can be found in [Les-EKR].

Overview of Sherlock II. **Sherlock II** is a coached practice environment developed to train avionics technicians to troubleshoot faults in a complex electronic testing system—in particular, a test station that checks out aircraft modules. The test station contains approximately 70ft^3 of circuitry. However, not all of this circuitry is needed to carry out each checkout procedure. So, the essential task confronting the trainee is to construct a mental representation of the active circuitry—what we refer to as the *active circuit path*—and to troubleshoot this path until she locates the fault. Sherlock's job is to scaffold the process of learning effective troubleshooting strategies and how to construct an abstract representation of the problem space.

Sherlock II is a realistic computer simulation of the actual job environment. (The system is written in Smalltalk/V286, an object-oriented programming language, and runs on 386 workstations equipped with Sony videodisc hardware.) Sherlock presents students with a series of exercises of increasing complexity. There are two main episodes in each **Sherlock II** exercise: *problem-solving* and *review*. During problem-solving, the student runs a series of checkout procedures on the aircraft unit suspected of malfunction. Using interactive video, the student can set switches and adjust knobs and dials on test station drawers, take measurements and view readings. These and other options, including being able to ask for advice, are available through a menu-driven interface.

During the review phase of an exercise, which we call *reflective follow-up*, a trainee can replay her problem solution step by step. At each step, Sherlock provides an evaluation of what the trainee did and explains to the student *why* an action was flagged as suboptimal or inappropriate (e.g., *This test was redundant*). A number of information sources are available to the trainee as well, so that she can figure out why a test was considered redundant, premature, inappropriately executed, etc. For example, the student can ask what an expert would have done instead. Also, she can examine simplified diagrams of the circuitry which are organized to provide good abstract representations of the active circuitry. Finally, in addition to these opportunities for reviewing one's own performance, there is also the opportunity to simply run through an expert's solution to the problem, with the same informational resources available at each step of the expert solution.

The basic scheme for curriculum planning. The best way to think about **Sherlock II**'s curriculum planner is to envision a slide scale, whose pointer at any given time is centered around the subset of problems that Sherlock "thinks" the student is ready for. (Problems are ordered by increasing difficulty.) We refer to this pointer as the *selection point*. The selection point moves up or down the "scale," in response to the student's performance on the current problem. If the student's performance is above a certain threshold, Sherlock will move her up (rightward). If below threshold, Sherlock will move her down (leftward); otherwise,

Sherlock will keep the student at about the same level.

The range of problems to the right and left of the selection point constitute what we call the *selection set*. This is the set of candidate next problems. Sherlock filters the selection set according to two factors: (1) student need (focus on features that the student needs to practice) and (2) variety (adjacent problems should not be too similar). One problem is then chosen at random from the filtered selection set.

After the student solves this problem, Sherlock shows her the slide scale, whose selection point indicates where Sherlock thinks the student should be placed next in the curriculum. The tutor then gives the student the option of moving the selection point left or right, if the student thinks she is being given problems that are too hard or too easy for her, respectively. Finally, after the student solves the selected problem, Sherlock readjusts the selection point, if the student's performance shows that her self-assessment was correct and she should indeed be getting harder/easier problems.

In the remainder of this section, we will discuss several aspects of this process in more detail; in particular:

· how to design and order the problem set so as to ensure variety and increasing difficulty

· how to initialize the placement of the selection point (i.e., determine where the student should start off from)

· how to determine where the selection point should be, after the student solves a problem

· how to choose the next problem from the selection set

· how to handle student input into the planning process, without falling prey to inaccurate self-appraisals

Design of the problem set. Sherlock automatically orders the set of problems it "knows" about by increasing difficulty, so problems can be added and deleted very easily. To enable Sherlock to automatically order the problem set, the system designers must classify each problem along a series of qualitative dimensions—i.e., features that determine how difficult a problem is to solve. Each problem can then be automatically assigned a difficulty rating by tallying the points associated with its features.

Sherlock II recognizes four categories of difficulty features: (1) the initial fault indication (e.g., a bad waveform), (2) the types of measurements involved (e.g., only resistance measurements on the multimeter required; oscilloscope must be used), (3) the type of component faulted (e.g., switch, simple relay card), (4) the location of the fault in the test station (e.g., the path between the aircraft unit and the digital multimeter). These categories are listed in order of increasing strength in determining problem difficulty. Within each category, each specific feature is also ranked, again according to its strength in determining problem difficulty. For example, in category (3), simple relay card faults are ranked second; switch faults ranked fifth—again by increasing difficulty.

The difficulty value for each feature is computed by multiplying its category's rank by its rank within the category. For example, the difficulty value for a faulted switch is 15 (category rank x rank in category; 3 x 5). Sherlock calculates the difficulty rating for each problem by tallying the difficulty value of its individual features.

In **Sherlock II**, the sorted problem set is divided evenly into four difficulty levels, for the purposes of issuing progress reports and to initialize the student's placement within the problem set. More specifically, this abstract division enables the tutor to tell the student during the review phase (reflective follow-up) that she has progressed to Level 3 problems, for example, which the student understands as "high intermediate." The use of levels for placement initialization will be described next.

Initial placement of students. We pretest students by having them run through two Sherlock problems without hinting available. One problem is at difficulty Level 1, the other at Level 3. If the student goes over threshold on one problem, Sherlock starts her at Level 2. If she goes over threshold on both problems, Sherlock also starts her at Level 2, but additionally increases the rate at which the student will advance through the problem set. Otherwise, Sherlock starts the student at Level 1.

Post-problem placement. After the student solves a problem, Sherlock will "slide" the selection point up (to the right) or down (to the left), depending upon the student's performance on the current problem. A student's performance on a problem can be represented as a ratio comparing the number of points that were "charged" for the simulated expert's (Sherlock's) solution, over the number of points charged for the student's solution. These 'points' coincide with appropriate troubleshooting actions— such as extending a card for testing, and replacing a faulty component with a shop standard—as well as with inappropriate behaviors, such as testing a component more than once, replacing a component that is working properly, setting up test equipment for the wrong type of test, etc. Sherlock's score will almost always be less than the student's, since it will not contain any charges for inappropriate actions, but it will never be zero. If the ratio of the expert's points to the student's points is .75 or greater, Sherlock slides the selection point up (right) by a certain number of problems; between .5 and .75, the selection point stays the same; otherwise, Sherlock moves the selection point down (left). Currently, we move the selection point by five problems in either direction, unless we want to advance the student more quickly (e.g., if she did well on the Level 1 pretest), in which case we set this parameter to seven. We need to fine-tune these advancement parameters by running student problem traces through the system.

Student control over curriculum planning. As stated earlier, the student can move the selection point up or down by any amount, thereby requesting harder or easier problems than Sherlock would otherwise give her. How do we handle student input so that accurate self-appraisals can be used to adjust the curriculum, and inaccurate self-appraisals not be allowed to corrupt it? The student's performance on the requested problem determines the new placement of the selection point. There are four cases to consider.

1. *The student asks for a harder problem and does better than predicted.* Sherlock adjusts the selection point closer to the student's selection, using the formula shown in (1), where $\hat{s}_{i+1}$ refers to Sherlock's initial placement of the selection point; δ refers

$$s_{i+1} = \frac{2\hat{s}_{i+1} + \delta}{2} \tag{1}$$

to the difference between Sherlock's selection point and the student's relocation of it; and s_{i+1} refers to the corrected problem placement level (selection point).

2. *The student asks for a harder problem and does poorly.* Sherlock adjusts the selection point only slightly up from its current level, using equation (2). The basic idea is not to set

$$s_{i+1} = (1-\varepsilon)s_i + \varepsilon\hat{s}_{i+1} \tag{2}$$

the student back (i.e., lower than s_i), because the problem was obviously over her head. s_{i+1} again refers to the corrected problem placement level (selection point); s_i refers to the location of the selection point during the last problem the student solved; and $\hat{s}_{i+1}$ refers to Sherlock's original choice of where to place the selection point for the next problem. The corrected selection point (s_{i+1}) will be set a bit higher than Sherlock's original estimate ($\hat{s}_{i+1}$).

c. *The student asks for an easier problem and performs well, but not so well as to suggest that the problem was too easy for her.* Sherlock adjusts the selection point closer to the student's selection, using a similar equation to (1). (The plus sign should be minus.)

d. *The student asks for easier problem and "aces" it.* Sherlock sets the selection point back to her original placement, $\hat{s}_{i+1}$, before the student asked for an easier problem.

Choosing the next problem. Sherlock chooses the next problem at random from the selection set, after this set has been filtered so that only problems that meet the following two criteria remain:

(1) *Must have at least one qualitative feature (listed above, in the section entitled, "Design of the problem set") that the student has not yet reached a threshold level of competency on.* Sherlock cumulates the student's scores on each category of problems (e.g., switch fault problems; problems that require use of the oscilloscope). Until the student's cumulated score reaches .75 on a problem category, problems within that category are legitimate selections.

(2) *Must be "psychologically different" from previous problems.* We ran into an interesting situation during our initial field trials of **Sherlock II**. It turned out that some problems seemed to be identical to students, because the same component was faulted in each case, even though the precise nature of the fault was different. For example, a circuit containing a relay card with an armature that is microwelded up will appear the same as one containing the same relay card with an armature microwelded down. This is because fault diagnosis is at the circuit card level in **Sherlock II**, not at the subcomponent (e.g., relay) level. Consequently, to sustain variety, the selection set needs to be filtered so that its problems contain a fault in a different component than in previous problems.

If the selection set is empty after filtering, Sherlock chooses a problem from the set of "ringer" problems.

Conclusions and Future Directions

We have proposed several means of increasing the curriculum planner's robustness against inaccuracies in the student model, and for ensuring that the resulting curricula are sufficiently varied to maintain student interest. At the time of this writing, **Sherlock II** is nearing completion and will be field-tested shortly thereafter. Consequently, it remains to be seen which combination of principles are actually effective in achieving these aims.

We expect that student input into curriculum design will prove to be an asset in keeping the planner on-track. If we are right, then it seems like the next reasonable step would be to enable the system to reflect the lessons that the planner learns from the student back into the student model. The basic approach to doing this would be to "back-propagate" the corrected placement (selection point) through a network of student modeling variables until the ratings on these variables are consistent with the corrected placement.

Although the notion of 'back-propagation' stems from connectionist modeling, we expect that the same effect could be achieved more efficiently using another AI technique for reasoning under uncertainty—namely, Bayesian belief networks (for a brief introduction, see [Charn91]). Although belief networks have been used in various reasoning systems, their potential usefulness for student modeling is now only beginning to be explored. We are excited by the prospect that in future tutors the student modeling module will not only serve the curriculum planner, but the latter will also be able to, in return, correct the student model when it does not match demonstrated competence.

References

[Brown-CD89]. J. S. Brown, A. Collins, P. Duguid. *Situated Cognition and the Culture of Learning*, Educational Researcher, Vol. 18, 1989, pp. 32-41.

[Charn91] E. Charniak. *Bayesian Networks without Tears*. AI Magazine. Vol. 12, No. 4, 1991, pp. 50-63.

[Laj-Les90] S. P. Lajoie, A. Lesgold. *Apprenticeship Training in the Workplace: Computer-Coached Practice Environment as a New Form of Apprenticeship*. Machine-Mediated Learning, Vol. 3, 1990, pp. 7-28.

[Les-EKR] A. M. Lesgold, A.M., G. Eggan, S. Katz, G. Rao. *Possibilities for Assessment Using Computer-Based Apprenticeship Environments*. To appear in W. Regian & V. Shute (Eds.), Cognitive Approaches to Automated Instruction. Hillsdale, NJ: Erlbaum.

Integrating an Educational Simulation into a Logic Design Course

Philip A. Lawson
Department of Computer Studies
Loughborough University of Technology
Loughborough, Leicestershire,
LE11 3TU, United Kingdom
tel: (UK) 0509 222699
fax: (UK) (G3) 0509 211586
email (Janet): P.A.Lawson@uk.ac.lut

Abstract

This paper describes the philosophies underlying the transition from a hardware laboratory to computer simulation within the Logic Design module of a Computer Systems course and the development of SimLog™, a Computer Aided Learning application, for Apple Macintoshes™. The current emphasis on software engineering means that the majority of students are not going to use this theory in any electronic engineering sense and as such have a certain reluctance to deal with hardware based laboratory classes. Good computer simulation of traditionally laboratory based subjects offer many advantages to both the student and the establishment alike. When implemented on existing teaching work-stations, multiple facilities can be created at almost zero cost. Emphasis within a simulation can placed upon maintaining realism whilst incorporating sound educational tenets. A certain element of fun can be embodied to assist with student acceptance.

The place of Logic Design in a Computing course

An aspiring software engineer requires a basic understanding of the internal architecture of modern computer systems. However, such students may not need the detailed knowledge of functional components, architectural performances and system construction that is taught in Electronic Engineering courses. Never-the-less, they should acquire a conceptual appreciation and working description of typical computer machinery.

In the Department of Computer Studies at Loughborough University of Technology, computer systems modules account for 20% of the undergraduate course. Traditionally these have started in the first year with an introduction to Logic Design and progressed to details of Computer Architectures, Memory Systems, Peripheral Systems and the interactions with Operating Systems. Further options in the subsequent years covered such subjects as Microprocessor Applications which again entails an element of circuit design.

The rôle of a hardware laboratory

The Logic Design module introduces the students to the fundamental building blocks used in computer systems. In the past this module was complemented by laboratory sessions where the students were set practical tasks in the construction of hardware circuits using logic elements. Each element carried a single integrated circuit of the low order TTL family and a set of colour coded sockets. The elements were interconnected using colour coded wires of various lengths with stackable coloured plugs on each end. The physical act of constructing a hardware circuit significantly reinforced the students' grasp of the theory taught in the Logic Design module. They learnt to appreciate the physical size of devices that are used inside computers and the true complexity of their interconnections. The students worked individually where possible but sometimes in small groups. They tackled a number of sequenced exercises ranging from initial investigation of the behaviour of simple gates up to quite complex constructions of decoder-drivers and memory based sequencers. Initially only basic logic device types were provided but as certain stages were completed more complex devices from the MSI range, such as Static RAMs and ALUs, were made available.

This 'real world' approach not only reinforced the theory but also helped to relate theory to practice. Being forced to deal with actual devices from a specific logic family, the student was made aware that there are certain traits and difficulties to be overcome. For example, having designed a circuit from first principles, mathematical manipulative techniques must be applied to ensure that the circuit can actually be constructed from the logic devices available. Once the circuit had been constructed, the student could test the signal being propagated at a particular input or output in the circuit by attaching an audible or visual mimic. This was very helpful in tracing the progress of a signal in a small simple circuit yet, in large complex circuits, the large number of such mimics required could make it difficult to associate a light with a particular point in the circuit, especially where the lights were all grouped together on another element. In some circuits, where a signal fed back into the circuit at some stage, the rapidity of the propagation made it difficult to perceive exactly what was happening. An oscilloscope trace could be used to capture and display such events but many students found it difficult to relate the screen picture to the circuit on the bench. There were also some features of this 'real world' laboratory that actively hindered the students' educational progress. Operational features of particular chips, such as active-low signals, threshold levels, propagation times and switch bounce contributed little to the fundamental understanding sought yet had to be appreciated by the student attempting to build circuits using real components. At times their discernible effects were so intrusive as to form a substantial barrier to the students' understanding of the underlying theory. The students experienced repeated frustration with the broken wires and damaged chips, which they were too inexperienced to detect. The cost of repair and replacement, on an hour by hour basis was a very real concern. From the lecturer's point of view, the students were never able to construct a sufficiently complex circuit, such as a simple central processor and memory, so as to forge that final leap in understanding towards the 'mechanics' of micro-programmed computer architecture.

Replacing a hardware laboratory with a simulation

In 1987 a programming laboratory with 35 Apple Macintosh workstations was acquired. This provided the opportunity to evaluate more critically the educational rôle, within the Logic Design module, of the then aging hardware laboratory with a view to replacing it with a highly interactive simulation which could use the facilities provided by the Mac [Bry 86, Laws-Par 90, Cas et al 86]..

It was intended that any simulation should retain and build upon the advantages of the hardware laboratory whilst eliminating its shortcomings. This meant that where educational objectives could be better met by presenting the student with a consistent set of rules, then this should be adopted in preference to strict adherence to reality. Detail, which would be vital to a skilled electronic engineer but is considered irrelevant and intrusive to an introductory level student, should be excluded from the simulated environment. All signal states would have to be visible and bear no resemblance to voltages, since it is sufficient for such a student that an LED should be turned on by the logic level output from a device. The devices can be idealised, their power supply and any other redundant connections suppressed. Indeed, the pictorial representation of the simple logic gates in the simulation could be portrayed by the well known device shapes found in text books. As an extension of this idea, the more complex devices, such as flip-flops, counters and decoders, are displayed not just as a rectangular box but as a small image of their internal functionality. This pictorial representation, together with the visible state of inputs and outputs, not only enables the simulated construction of logic circuits to be more intuitively associated with the theory taught in lectures but also eliminates the 'black box' nature of the old logic design hardware.

Integrating a simulation into a Logic Design module

SimLog [Laws-Par 91], as the simulation program came to be called, was designed as a learner-controlled Logic Design problem solving aid. It exploits the belief that "learning most frequently derives from people expressing what is important to them within the confines of a medium which both enables and constrains their expression" [Lawl 84]. SimLog allows the student total freedom in the construction of logic circuits within a complete microworld [Pap 80]. Given the microworld objects, in this case a set of logic and input/output devices, the student can experiment by connecting them together to establish their functionality both individually and in various configurations. Individual devices can be combined to create more complex objects, which the student should recognise as functionally the same as devices required in the real world, for example registers. More importantly, the simulation faithfully emulates the behaviour of the circuit (both as component parts and as a whole) and provides visual feedback of the resultant effects, as can be seen in Figure 1.

A high priority in designing the user interface was given to ensuring that the interaction techniques could be quickly acquired and, once learnt, would prove effective. That is, the interface would enable the user to carry out the logic design work with minimal conscious attention to the paraphernalia of the interactive terminal and the command language [Fol et al 84, Kan-Ode 89]. To obviate the need for the user to have previously acquired a dexterity at the keyboard, it was decided that the human-computer interaction should be predominantly mouse driven with a minimum of keyboard input.

Only the minimum of essential knowledge, required to use the simulation, is explicitly brought to the student's attention. A single introductory exercise includes how to use menus; how to select devices, singly or in groups, and drag them across the screen to the desired location; how to 'wire up' inputs to outputs, by drawing rubber band lines, and to remove unwanted connections. Certain features are left for the students to discover for themselves either by chance, as a result of their own inquisitiveness, or through reading the user manual, although the prescribed exercises do much to prompt such discoveries. This approach is effective in encouraging the students to actively explore the microworld which, being 'indestructible', they have far less hesitation in doing than was true of the hardware laboratory.

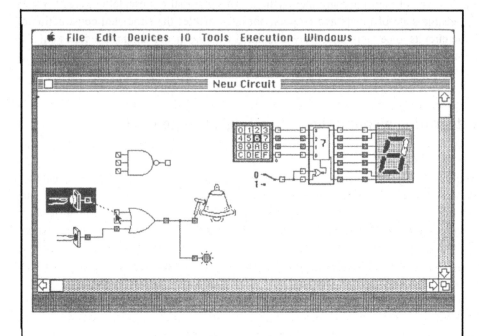

Figure 1   SimLog's User Interface

The above illustration highlights many aspects of the user interface. Clearly visible are the input and output boxes for various types of Logic and I/O devices. Logic Ones, logic Zeros and Unconnected states are portrayed in different ways in order that the state is always visible. Connections are drawn using 'rubber band lines' dragged by the mouse cursor, but these are stylized by a routing algorithm as soon as the placement is complete. Input and Output devices such as the Button, LED, Bell and 7-Segment Display change their form as their logical state changes.

However, unstructured experimentation within a simulation is not necessarily conducive to effective learning and SimLog is not a CAL system [Tai 87]. Therefore, the simulation is integrated into the lectures and tutorial sessions associated with the Computer Systems modules. Each tutorial has the same format - preparation prior to use of SimLog, its actual use, and written report afterwards. The balance of the work in each of these three stages varies with the level of the student's learning both with respect to their expertise in the theory of logic design and their facility with the features of the simulation package. In recognition of the learning curve involved in each aspect, user access to the microworld of logic circuitry provided by the simulation has been structured through a password system. Each tutorial session has its own password so that the students can be given access to a controlled range of devices. Initially the students are only allowed simple logic gates plus a few input and output devices. Their tutorial tasks at this stage allow time to learn the basic features of SimLog and the WIMP interface. The tasks are simple and closely defined as it is appreciated that the students' facility with the system will be uppermost in their minds. The teaching ethic at this stage is the rule/example/practice approach. For example, the students are required to demonstrate that the AND gate in the simulation conforms to its truth table definition. In doing this the students are not only reinforcing information that they have assimilated about such gates in lectures but also learning how the simulation represents the 'facts' that they have been taught. The preparation away from the computer is more extensive for subsequent sessions. As in any logic design course, the students are required to use traditional methods, such as truth tables, Karnaugh maps and mathematical manipulation, to design a logic circuit.

The students are encouraged to experiment with circuit designs, to discover what happens, to compare results obtained against their expectations and explain any discrepancies. On-line help is limited to reference truth tables and in general SimLog offers no guidance or criticism of their undertakings. The aim is purely to allow complete freedom of action and to then clearly amplify the effect for all to see.

The advantages of using a simulation

Experience with SimLog has now shown that the simulation helps to maintain the students' level of interest in logic design throughout the course. The range of simulated input and output devices incorporated retains the connection with reality, previously experienced in using the logic hardware that the simulation replaced. The practical problems associated with constructing and exercising a 'real' logic circuit are hidden by idealising the workings of equivalent logic devices in the simulation. This enables the student to concentrate on the requirement to understand the theory of circuit logic whilst eliminating problems such as power supplies, fan out, switch bounce and noise which are arguably not the concern of such a student at this stage.

Since all the input and output states of devices are visible in the simulation, time is no longer wasted by the students using a device without realising that it was not functioning properly. This was a frustrating problem for both students and supervisors using the hardware system. Also, students cannot unknowingly destroy an output in the simulation since it produces immediate visible and audible evidence that a particular configuration has resulted in the destruction of part of the circuit. The embarrassment suffered (eventually by all in the class) is a sufficient motive for the student to understand the problem and rarely repeat the mistake.

The simulated circuit is completely interactive in its operation. The circuit is always 'live' so that signal changes can be observed, as connections between inputs and outputs are modified, without having to go through any form of compilation or evaluation cycle. Despite the complexity of both the program and constructed circuits, SimLog responds virtually instantaneously to the user's actions, a feature that was paramount in the design.

The most important benefit derived from the integration of the simulation into the logic design course has been the assistance it has provided the students in conceptualising the dynamic workings of individual logic devices and hence fully understanding their significance and rôle in larger circuits. The students are able to watch the changes that occur in a logic circuit during a signal propagation resulting from the modified

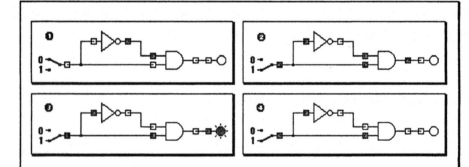

Figure 2 Race Conditions displayed in Step Mode

Race conditions normally occur so fast that they can only be observed using oscilloscopes. The simulator, working in step-mode allows the student to follow the signals as they propagate and thus observe the momentary 'glitch' that occurs in diagram 2 due to the delay added by the invertor. This signal would be so short-lived in a hardware circuit that, to the naked eye, the LED would not be perceived to have changed state. The hold state is portrayed such that the logic and I/O devices are always self consistent but new signals from changed outputs are not propagated. This results in an unreal but acceptable view of the behaviour of interconnections.

state of an input. They observe that the propagation continues until the circuit once again attains a stable state. An inherently unstable circuit, which could be difficult to conceptualise, is more easily understood with a visual demonstration that can be run in slow motion compared with an equivalent hardware circuit. This feature is particularly useful in demonstrating race conditions and circuits containing feedback loops where simulated oscilloscope probes can be attached to outputs.

The simulation also allows the student to elect to view the propagation in false time by selecting the step-mode. In this mode the propagation is displayed in stages. The student controls the execution of each stage and is therefore able to inspect in detail the changes that have occurred at each level of propagation before requesting the next stage to be displayed. This is particularly useful in observing the transient states in such circuits as NOR gate rings and short cycling counters which contain feedback loops, see Figures 2 and 3.

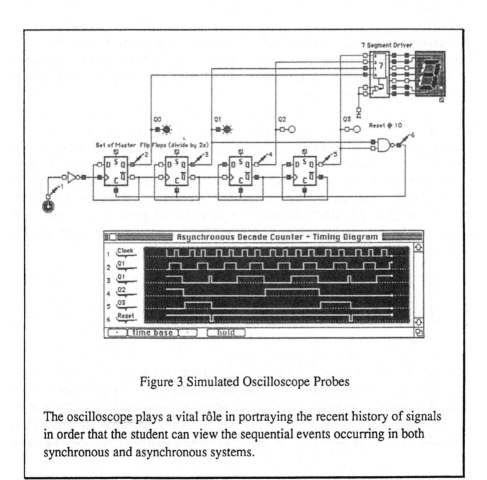

Figure 3 Simulated Oscilloscope Probes

The oscilloscope plays a vital rôle in portraying the recent history of signals in order that the student can view the sequential events occurring in both synchronous and asynchronous systems.

SimLog enables the student to save a logic circuit to disc and recall it later. This is a significant improvement on the hardware facilities where the student was not able to save the circuit constructed in a laboratory session since the individual components were frequently required for subsequent classes. It further allows the student to transport the circuit for demonstration to the tutor and, vice-versa, allows the lecturer to disseminate circuits developed in the lectures (using SimLog and video projectors) to the students via the computer network. The use of SimLog within the teaching environment provides the student with a clear view of the dynamics of circuit logic and, eventually, a much deeper insight than could ever be achived through the more traditional media of the lecture room.

From within the simulation a printed copy of a circuit diagram can be obtained. Snapshots, taken a different stages during a propagation, together with simulated oscilloscope timing diagrams are particularly useful. These can be included in subsequent reports of the laboratory sessions to demonstrate the student's command of the subject matter and also for reference at a later date.

If necessary the student can also use the simulation program outside timetabled laboratory sessions. This means that learning can be geared to the student's individual needs. Those requiring the extra reinforcement of replaying' a circuit are free to do so and can work at their own pace.

However, there is one aspect of the logic design laboratories that was noticeably missing in the SimLog sessions - group work. The time restriction imposed in the old laboratory system and the amount of equipment available, meant that for some experiments the students had to work in groups. This resulted in far more discussion and shared ideas than occurs in the present SimLog laboratory. Here each student has their own computer and effectively their own inexhaustible supply of components and as a result, for the vast majority of the time, they are engrossed in silent, solitary endeavour.

Conclusions

Whilst the adjunct of a specialized laboratory course for the teaching of basic logic design is seen as invaluable it is clear that the benefits are only truly achieved if the students' experience of this structure is favourable. Repeated failure to achieve goals either through over-complexity or malfunction seriously undermines the educational principles. Whilst computer simulations are not without their problems, the underlying reliability of both the equipment and the program's behaviour do much to enhance the students' appreciation of the taught material.

Certainly, a more thorough treatment of the behaviour of circuits would be required if the emulation was in any way to act as a testing ground for 'professional' designs. It would have to encompass a wider range of device parameters if it were to be used for electronic engineering courses. It must be said in defence of the current design philosophy that perfectly acceptable application programs exist for the design and emulation of electronic circuits. These are usually extremely thorough, complex and expensive. What was required was a package that could adequately provide sufficient scope for students to produce working designs with the minimal amount of effort and learning overheads.

In designing a highly interactive simulation the effort expended upon the ease with which the novice could operate the system, based upon intuitive or systematic responses, appears to have been worthwhile. SimLog, now available from Oxford University Press (UK) has taken over four years to complete. The main reason for this lies in the thorough developmental stages that were undertaken. Each academic year, some 60-80 students used SimLog for a period of 10 weeks at a time. Apart from debugging, the feedback obtained, on both a daily and more formal basis, has provided a significant foundation for the design decisions.

In summary, the implementation of a simulation as a total replacement for the hardware laboratory has been highly successful and has achieved many of the set targets. Importantly, the benefits of simulation, both in the form of user acceptance, educational utility and the enhanced ability to demonstrate otherwise difficult concepts have completely justified the investment in time and paved the way for further endeavour.

References

[Bry 86] R. Bryant. *Simulations in Education.* in 5th Canadian Symposium on Instructional Technology, Ottawa, Canada, 1986

[Cas et al 86] G. Castelli, G. Gazzano and C. Tibald. *Simulation in Teaching: The Idea of Laboratory and its Implementation on Low Cost Machines.* 5th Canadian Symposium on Instructional Technology, Ottawa, Canada, 1986

[Fol et al 84] D.F. Foley, V.L. Wallace and P. Chan. *The Human Factors of Computer Graphics Interaction Techniques.* IEEE Computer Graphics and applications , 1984

[Kan-Ode 89] E. Kantorowitz and S. Oded. *The Adaptable User Interface.* Communications of the ACM Vol 32 No 11, 1989

[Lawl 84] R. Lawler. *Designing computer-based microworlds*. New Horizons in Educational Computing, M Yazdani (ed), Horwood, 1984

[Laws-Par 90] P.A. Lawson and L.M. Parks. *Interactive microworlds for teaching Logic Design*. in CALEE 90 Delft University of Technology 1990

[Laws-Par 91] P.A. Lawson and L.M. Parks. *SimLog - An Educational Logic Simulator*. Oxford University Press 1991

[Pap 80] S. Papert. *Mindstorms: Children, Computers, and powerful Ideas*. New York: Basic Books, 1980

[Tai 87] K. Tait. *The study station concept in computer-based learning*. University Computing, 9, 25-28, 1987

An Algorithm Animation Programming Environment

Moon-chuen Lee

Dept. of Computer Science, The Chinese University of Hong Kong

Shatin, Hong Kong

Email: mclee@cucsd.cuhk.hk

Abstract

To understand a computer algorithm written in a static text format is often difficult as it may demand the reader much effort to trace what the algorithm is meant to do. However, through algorithm animation, a student can easily visualize what a given algorithm does and can thus learn the algorithm in a more relaxed way. This paper proposes AAPE, a versatile programming environment which comprises a suite of primitives, for the construction of programs for algorithm visualization and animation. With this environment, the program development time can be drastically reduced. Moreover, the primitives, based on an object-oriented design, are found easy to use and to maintain. Programs developed through AAPE can make use of graphics, animation, audial and algorithm text tracing techniques, which may greatly enhance the presentation of an algorithm and the underlying data structures. Therefore, AAPE has a potential for promoting the use of computer assisted learning and teaching on data structures and algorithms.

INTRODUCTION

To learn a computer algorithm presented in the text form is often difficult as the reader has to try to *execute* the algorithm mentally. To trace mentally or to understand a complicated algorithm written a text format can be a challenging task to many people. From our experience in teaching algorithms and data structures in a computer science department, we realize that many students experience difficulty in understanding algorithms, especially the recursive ones. We planned to use computer software to assist students in learning various algorithms encountered in the course. Since writing algorithm animation programs from scratch is labour intensive and not cost-effective, we decided to develop reusable tools for this purpose. With the advent of the programming tools, it is believed that program development time can be much reduced. Moreover, the applications programmer need not know about the technical details for programming graphics and animation.

Computer-assisted instruction (CAI) is evolving as an alternative to conventional means of instruction. Algorithm animation programs can be considered as a kind of CAI programs. One of the powerful techniques being used by software developers for CAI is *animation* [Lee, 90]. The term *animation* referenced in this paper actually means *visualization* and *animation*. It is believed that animation is a particularly good means for presenting the execution of an algorithm. Like many CAI programs, the effectiveness of an algorithm animation program depends very much on how well the concept is presented and how much user-interaction is allowed.

The AAPE we have implemented supports the development of animation programs on algorithms involving mainly the data structures: arrays, linked lists, binary trees, and graphs. Further, the software fosters the development of programs which allow much user-interaction, and support the discovery mode of learning.

At the moment, the tools are used mainly for constructing animation programs on topics related to data structures. However, they may also be used to program algorithms involved in other computer science courses such as *operating systems*. To make the software applicable to other problem domains, it is necessary to add more primitives and to make existing ones, if necessary, more general.

Our work on algorithm animation focuses mainly on computer science education. Programs developed through AAPE can be used to support computer assisted learning and computer assisted teaching on the domain of data structures and algorithms. However, as Brown and Sedgewick (1984) pointed out, research in algorithm animation has other applications: 1) the design and analysis of algorithms; 2) advanced debugging and system programming.

DESIGN CONSIDERATIONS

The effectiveness of the programming tools depends on whether they can be used to produce cost-effective animation programs. It implies that AAPE should suit the needs of the programmers and the CAI programs it generates should satisfy the requirements of the student users. Before designing AAPE, we first formulated the following requirements of the algorithm animation programs for CAI applications:

- *Allowing user control.* This is important as different users like to study a topic at their own pace. In addition, the programs should allow the users to control the study sequence of a given number of topics.

- *Allowing much user interaction.* The users should be allowed to supply different input data for doing the animation. In this way, the users can visualize how an algorithm would process individualized data.

- *Making use of audial technique.* One of the most important reason concerning why computer games can excite so many people is that they make good use of audial-visual technique. Thus, the programmer should be allowed to specify a characteristic sound effect or a music to accompany any animation operation.

- *Allowing the user to read the algorithm while doing the animation.* By reading the algorithm, the user may know the correspondence between the textual part of an algorithm and the animation. In fact, the text form of the algorithm and the animating graphics serve to complement each together in presenting an algorithm to the user.

Concerning an applications programmer, AAPE should be equipped with the following features:

- Not requiring the programmer to know how to program graphics and animation. In general, programming graphics and animation is relatively technical and time-consuming. Moreover, not many programmers are keen on this kind of programming.

- Providing a user-interface editing function. In general, programming the user-interface of any interactive system is time-consuming. With the provision of a user-interface editing facility, the programmer can define and modify, without doing any programming, a user-interface for his/her program.

On the basis of the above design considerations, we have designed and implemented AAPE on the IBM PC/AT.

SYSTEM STRUCTURE

AAPE comprises the following components:
1) Screen Editing Subsystem;
2) Interface Unit;
3) Primary Unit;
4) Binary Tree Unit;
5) Linked Lcist Unit;
6) Array Unit;
7) Graph Unit;
8) Audial Unit;
9) Pascal Programming Environment.

Components 2 through 8 can be considered as library units which may be included in the animation program whenever necessary. These units provide different types of functions. In general, the Interface Unit and the Primary Unit have to be included in almost any application.

Screen Editing Subsystem

The main objective of the Screen Editing Subsystem (SES) is to reduce the overhead on user interface programming. SES allows the programmer to define the screen layout of any window-based application, which includes: the definitions of different windows, a horizontal menu and a pull-down menu for each menu option.

The windows can be used for different purposes: (1) To present an algorithm; (2) To serve as a message box; (3) To present graphical objects during algorithm animation; (4) To be used for user input.

SES also provides an editor for the programmer to enter the text form of an algorithm which is an image of one part of the animation program.

Interface Unit

This unit provides facilities for processing the windows, messages, horizontal menus and pull-down menus defined through the *Screen Editing Subsystem.*

It also provides a set of primitives for highlighting statements displayed in the algorithm window while executing an animation program.

Primary Unit

The Primary Unit provides procedures often called primitves for handling the simple graphical objects: circle, arc, curve, line, arrow, and rectangle; an object in the form of an arrow may be used to label some other objects. In essence, these primitives can be used to perform the functions: 1) creating graphical objects and adding them to the object database; 2) deleting graphical objects; 3) drawing the objects on the screen; 4) animating objects on the screen; 5) updating the objects captured in the object database.

During algorithm animation, objects would be created dynamically. For each object being created, it is assigned automatically a unique index. Through this index, any procedure can retrieve information about the object from the database. Each object defined in the database should have the attributes: *position on the screen, field name(s), color* (for display), etc. Some of these values may have to be updated from time to time.

In addition, this unit should also provide primitives for different types of animation operations: 1) moving an object from one location to another; 2) blinking an object a number of times; 3) changing the background color of an object; 4) changing the thickness of a line (an arc, or a curve) object from one end to another to show the direction of movement.

The programmer can use the primitives exported by this unit to program any simple graphical objects for his/her application. As the structured objects are composed of the simple objects defined in this unit, all other units which manipulate structured objects would make use of the simple object primitives. Therefore, this unit must be available whenever other structured units are used.

Binary Tree Unit

This unit provides primitives primarily for the functions: 1) to allow the user to input interactively a binary tree; 2) to draw a binary tree on a certain window; 3) to clear a binary tree; 4) to delete a binary tree; 5) to add a node as a child of a given node in a binary tree.

Graphically a binary tree is made up of simple objects, some animation operations of a binary tree can be achieved through using those primitives *exported* by the Primary Unit.

Linked List Unit

The Linked List Unit provides primitives for the functions: 1) to allow the user to input interactively a linked list; 2) to create a linked list; 3) to draw a linked list on the screen; 4) to clear a linked list on the screen; 5) to delete a linked list; 6) to insert a node to a linked list.

Graphically a linked list is a structured object consisting of a number of nodes and some arrowed lines served as pointers indicating how the nodes are connected. Each node is represented by a rectangle. Therefore, certain animation operations of a linked list can be performed by some of those primitives exported by the Primary Unit. In addition, the Linked List Unit provides primitives for animating node insertion and node deletion respectively.

Array Unit

An array data structure can be represented graphically as a big rectangle containing a number of array elements each represented by a small rectangle. This unit provides primitives for the functions: 1) to allow the user to input interactively an array; 2) to draw an array on the screen; 3) to clear an array; 4) to delete an array. In addition, it provides primitives to animate moving the content of an array element from one location to another.

Graph Unit

A graph can be either directed or undirected. This unit should export the functions: 1) interactive graph input; 2) graph display; 3) clearing a graph on the screen; 4) delete a graph from the object database. As a graph is composed of a number of simple objects, the animation primitives exported by the Primary Unit can be used to animate a graph.

Audial Unit

This unit provides a *sound* primitive and a simple audial database which captures data for producing various sound effects. The sound primitive can be considered as a sound or a music driver, which would use the data passed to it for producing a sound effect or a music. The object code of the primitive is kept resident in memory. If necessary, through using interrupts the code can be invoked periodically while running other program segements. In this way, various sound effects or musics can be generated during algorithm animation.

Pascal Programming Environment

This component is actually the Turbo Pascal programming environment which allows the programmer to write various application programs that can interface conveniently with the above program units for doing algorithm animation.

IMPLEMENTATION

At this moment, we have implemented programming tools to support algorithm animation on the simple graphical objects: circle, rectangle, line, arc, curve, and arrow. Based on the primitives for creating and manipulating these simple objects, we have implemented another suite of primitives for the structured objects: arrays, linked lists, binary trees, and graphs. The following subsections introduce some of the functional components we have developed.

Screen Editing Subsystem

It is a menu-driven subsystem which enables the programmer to define the screen layout of any algorithm animation program.

It allows the programmer to define a number of windows. To define a window, it needs to specify two pairs of coordinates on the screen, one for the upper left corner position of the window and one for the lower right corner position of the window. A window name can be specified as an option. If necessary, the programmer can also specify a message to be prompted at a certain position of a window, which may be used as a kind of input message box. On the other hand, the user can define a message at a certain window used as a kind of output message box. Upon defining one or more windows, the programmer can browse them. If the layout is not satisfactory, it can be modified interactively.

In addition, SES allows the programmer to define a horizontal menu bar with a number of options. For each option, a pull-down menu can be defined interactively. At any time, the programmer can preview and update the user interface. Thus SES supports an incremental definition of a user-interface. Figure 1 previews a sample horizontal menu and the pull-down menus which can be prepared through SES within a minute.

SES is also equipped with a simple full-screen editor for the programmer to define an algorithm for display at a certain window during algorithm animation. The editor generates a line number to each line of text entered. The line numbers would be used to reference the corresponding statements being processed during algorithm animation.

SES stores the window definitions, menu definitions and the algorithm text in three different files.

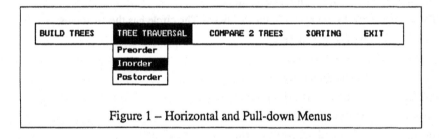

Figure 1 – Horizontal and Pull-down Menus

Interface Unit

This unit provides primitives to load into memory the definitions of the windows, the horizontal and pull-down menus from a file, which are defined and saved through using the SES, and to manipulate the definitions. To facilitate the tracing of the algorithm text, it exports the following primitives:

1) *algload(top, fname)*.

It loads the algorithm from a file specified by *fname* to a list structure pointed to by the algorithm text pointer *top*.

2) *alg(style, size, top, algrec)*.

It displays the algorithm text pointed to by *top* with a specified character *style* and a specified font *size*. Once this primitive is invoked, a record which stores information about the current algorithm window is pushed to the algorithm stack referenced by the pointer *algrec*. The purpose of the algorithm stack is to keep track of the information about different algorithm window positions. The record at the top of the stack contains the position of the current algorithm window.

3) *alghilite(n_1, n_2, algrec, top)*.

It is used to highlight the statements n_1 through n_2 which correspond to the statements currently being executed. If the statements to be highlighted are not shown in the algorithm window, the algorithm text would be scrolled until the statements can be seen.

4) *algclose(algrec)*.

It removes the top record from the stack pointed at by *algrec* and closes the specified algorithm window.

Primary Unit

This unit provides primitives for managing simple graphical objects for algorithm animation. Some of the primitives implemented for creating simple objects are as follows:

1) *addcircle(index, x, y, r, color, shade, label)*.

To create a circle for inclusion in the database. The circle has the attributes:

index: index of the circle;

x, y: coordinates of the circle;

r: radius of the circle;

color: perimeter color of the circle;

shade: color inside the circle;

label: a label in the form of a string inside the circle.

2) *addrec(index, x_1, y_1, x_2, y_2, color, shade, dimen, label$_1$, label$_2$, label$_3$)*.

To create a rectangle object with the attributes:

index: index generated by the machine for the rectangle;

x_1, y_1:   coordinates of the left upper corner of the rectangle;

x_2, y_2:   coordinates of the right lower corner of the rectangle;

color: perimeter color of the rectangle;

shade: color inside the rectangle;

label$_1$,

label$_2$,

label$_3$:   three optional labels inside rectangle.

3) *addline(index, x_1, y_1, x_2, y_2, color, thickness, forward, backward, forlabel, backlabel)*.

To create a line object with the parameters:

index: index generated by the machine for the line object;

x_1, y_1:   coordinates of the first end of the line;

x_2, y_2:	coordinates of the second end of the line;
thickness:	thickness of the line;
forward:	a boolean parameter, if true, there is a forward arrow;
backward:	a boolean parameter, if true, there is a backward arrow;
forlabel:	label adjacent to the forward arrow;
backlabel:	label adjacent to the backward arrow.

Similarly, we have implemented primitives known as *addarc* and *addarrow* for defining the arc and the arrow objects respectively. For the animation of the simple objects, the following are some of the primitives we have implemented:

1) *move(index, xend, yend)*.

It is used to move an object identified by *index* to the position specified by the coordinates *(xend, yend)*. This primitive would move the object in a straight line from its initial position to the specified destination. The movement is normally completed within *n* steps of equal length, each step being delayed by *dt* time units. The step length is predefined. So, the number of steps for completing the movement depends on the distance between the initial position and destination. The time delay for each step is also predefined for different types of machines.

2) *blink(index, n)*.

It is used to cause an object specified by *index* to blink *n* times, each blinking action being delayed by a predefined number of time units.

3) *shading(index, color)*.

It is used to shade an object specified by *index* with a certain *color*.

4) *linethick(index, x_1, y_1)*.

It is used to change the thickness of a line object specified by *index* in a direction starting from the coordinates (x_1, y_1) through a number of line segments, each being of a predefined length and being delayed by a predefined number of time units.

5) *clear(index)*

It is used to clear the graphical display of a given object on the screen.

6) *blinkstring(x, y, str)*.

It makes a given string *str* at position *(x, y)* to blink a number of times each being delayed by a number of time units.

7) *movestring(x_1, y_1, x_2, y_2, str)*.

It moves a string *str* from position (x_1, y_1) to (x_2, y_2) through a number of steps each being delayed by a number of time units.

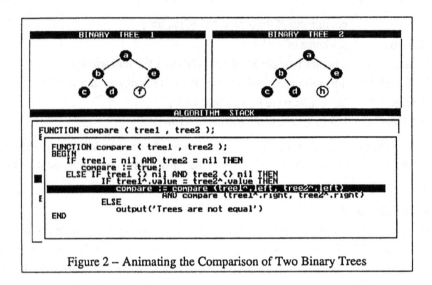

Figure 2 – Animating the Comparison of Two Binary Trees

Structured Object Units

The structured object units include: the binary tree unit, the graph unit, the array unit, and the linked list unit. We have developed primitives for the creation and drawing of these structured objects. Two of the primitives are introduced as follows:

1) *buildtree(root).*

This primitive prompts the user to input a binary tree interactively. It first guides the user to enter data for the root node. Upon defining the root node, the procedure displays it at the current window at a machine-chosen position. Any newly added node becomes the current node. Then, the procedure allows the user to choose, by pressing an appropriate arrow key, to define either the left child node or the right child node. Moreover, the user can move the cursor to the parent node, if any, of the current node by moving the upward arrow key. In this way, the user can define any binary tree. The machine generates a position for each node of the binary tree. The position of each node in a binary tree may be modified from time to time during the interactive input process. If there are too many nodes to fit into a given window, the size of each node would be modified.

2) *buildlist(head, rear).*

This primitive first prompts the user to provide the data: 1) number of fields of each node; 2) maximum field length. Then it prompts the user to define the head node. Subsequently, the primitive allows the user to insert a new node after the current the node by pressing the RETURN key. Any newly defined node is treated as the current node. It also permits the user to make any node on the linked list become the current node by pressing the arrow keys. So this primitive enables the user to define any linked list. Each node is represented by a rectangle whose position being generated by the machine.

As each structured object is made up mostly of simple objects, the animation operations of the structured objects can in general be performed through using the primitives exported by the primary unit. However, the structured object units are also equipped with additional animation primitives.

Figure 2 shows a snapshot of animating the comparison of two binary trees, the operation being based on a single recursive algorithm. The two binary trees can be input by the user during runtime. The number of algorithm windows on the algorithm stack shows the depth of recursion while executing the statement indicated by the light bar. Upon detecting two corresponding nodes of the binary trees to be equal, they are shaded. The user can control the speed of the animation by pressing the SPACE bar. Of course, the diagram cannot show the sound effects and the underlying tree traversal animation.

EVALUATION

AAPE has been used by a batch of 64 computer science majors to develop animation programs on data structures. Such programs can be used to assist students in learning algorithms and data structures. They can also be used by the teacher to supplement his teaching materials on data structures.

The animation programs developed by the students are based on topics related to various algorithms for manipulating the data structures: binary trees, arrays, linked list, and graphs. In general, the animation programs are attractive and considered to be useful for assisting in teaching and learning of data structures and algorithms. Upon implementing the animation programs, the students were asked to give comments on AAPE. In response to a set of questions, their major comments are as follows:

1) With the advent of AAPE, animation program development time can be reduced by 75 percent.

2) The tools are quite versatile as they can be used for programming many of the topics on data structures.

3) The *Screen Editing Subsystem* allows the programmer to define rapidly the user interface which may involve windows, messages, algorithms and menus (horizontal menus and pull-down menus) for an animation program. This facility is very useful as it saves the programmer much time for programming the user-interface.

4) The primitives from the *Interface Unit* permit an easy trace of any algorithm being developed.

5) The primitives exported by the structured object units are very versatile as the programmers need only specify the window for displaying a structured object while defining it. S/he need not concern about the coordinates of the constituent simple objects. Therefore, the primitives are quite easy to use.

6) As the primitives are based on an object-oriented design, the programmer can, in general, access and manipulate any object through its object index. For instance, it is possible to make any object, with index i, blink by issuing the call *blink(i)*.

7) The *buildtree* primitive does not allow the user to label the edge of a binary tree. This is a limitation as some applications may require a binary tree's edges be labeled.

8) The Song Unit is useful as it provides primitives and a library of musics and sound effects, allowing the user to define easily any audial effect for an animation operation.

9) Heap overflow often occurs as the animation programs are run for a long duration. It is suspected that the delete object primitive *delobj* does not properly relinguish the memory of certain deleted objects.

10) If all the bugs are fixed, we would be pleased to use AAPE to develop animation programs for educational use.

11) The documentations for the primitives should be given in greater detail.

The above comments are the major feedbacks to a set of questions posed to our students after they have used AAPE to develop animation programs for a course project.

In addition, some animation programs have been demonstrated to certain faculty staff. They were convinced that such animation programs can be a valuable tool for assisting in teaching and learning the underlying topics.

CONCLUDING REMARKS

AAPE has been designed and implemented for facilitating the development of algorithm animation programs. The software has also been used by a batch of 64 students to develop animation programs on topics related to data structures. These programs make use of some powerful presentation techniques including graphics, animation, audial effects, and algorithm text tracing. Through these techniques, an algorithm can be presented vividly and dynamically. Obviously, such programs have a great potential for assisting in learning or teaching algorithms and data structures. On the other hand, they can also be used by an algorithm designer to observe visually the behaviour of his algorithm. Therefore, AAPE has the potential for promoting algorithm research.

The animation programs developed by our students enable the users supply different input data for processing by an algorithm. In this way, they can explore visually the behaviour of an algorithm. Therefore, the programs support mainly *learning by discovery*, which is a popular mode of learning. The development of an animation program usually takes a long time to complete. However, with the use of AAPE, it has been shown that the programming time can be reduced by more than 75 percent. Thus, AAPE can be considered useful in promoting the use of animation software in the educational arena, particularly in computer science education.

The object-oriented approach in designing the primitives makes the tools easy to use and to maintain. As a result, many of the procedures have the *polymorphism* feature; that is, a primitive can be used for multi purposes. For instance, the *move* primitive can be used to move a line, a circle or any simple object. Thus, the programmer need not remember many names.

Of paramount importance is the provision of the graphical objects creation and display facilities which do not require the programmer to specify the positions of the respective simple objects comprising a structured object. All these positions are generated by the machine, which are relative to a certain graphics window.

As indicated by the feedbacks from our students who have used AAPE, the programming tools are, in general, versatile and easy to use. We would investigate the limitations as mentioned in their comments. If necessary, corrections or improvements would then be made. In addition, we have noticed that the graphs generated by the *buildgraph* primitive is not always satisfactory. At the moment, the user is first prompted to enter the definition of a graph. Then it uses the input data to generate the positions of the graph. The appearance of the resulting graph may look very different from what the user has in mind or drawn on a piece of paper. To remove this limitation, we are trying to develop another graph input procedure to enable user to define the shape of a graph. A mouse input device and a set of icons may be used for this purpose.

REFERENCES

[Lee 90] Lee, M.C. An Abstract Machine Simulator. *Lecture Notes in Computer Science*, *vol 438*, 129-141, Springer-Verlag, 1990.

[Brown & Sedgewick 84] Brown, Marc H. & Sedgewick, Robert. A System for Algorithm Animation. *Computer Graphics*, *18(3)*, 177-186, Association for Computing Machinary, 1984.

ABASE: A Hypermedia-based Tutoring and Authoring System[1]

Jun Li
Computer Science Department
Illinois Institute of Technology
Chicago, IL 60616
321-567-5153

Allen Rovick and Joel Michael
Department of Physiology
Rush Medical College
1750 West Harrison
Chicago, IL 60612
312-942-6426

Abstract

ABASE is a Hypercard-based interactive tutorial program. It is designed to help first year medical students to repair their misconceptions, enrich their knowledge, and integrate what they already know about the major physiological mechanisms involved in acid base regulation. ABASE includes seven problems for the students to solve and four interactive tutorials written as hypercard stacks. It features hypertext, animated summaries, graphical testing routines, and an electronic dictionary. A small scale authoring system -- the ABASE EDITOR is included to provide the instructor with the ability to expand, maintain, and customize ABASE for a particular student group or course.

This paper describes the ABASE program itself, and the authoring system (the ABASE Editor).

[1]This work was supported by the Cognitive Science Program, Office of Naval Research Under Grant No. N00014-89-J-1952, Grant Authority Identification Number NR4422554 to Illinois Institute of Technology, and Grant No. N00014-91-J-1622, Grant Authority Identification Number AA1711319 to Rush Medical College. The content does not reflect the position or policy of the government and no official endorsement should be inferred. Address correspondence concerning this paper to Ms. Jun Li and correspondence concerning the program to Dr. Allen Rovick.

Introduction

ABASE is a Hypercard-based interactive tutorial program [Lij91]. It is designed to help first year medical students to repair their misconceptions, to enrich their knowledge, and to integrate what they already know about the major physiological mechanisms involved in acid base regulation. ABASE includes seven problems for the student to solve and four interactive tutorials organized as hypercard stacks. It features hypertext, animated summaries, graphical testing routines, and an electronic dictionary.

A major feature of ABASE is an Editor that provides the instructor (who may not be a programmer) with the ability to expand, maintain, and customize ABASE for a particular student group or course. This feature is important because it allows instructors to use their own terminology, emphasize different concepts, include their favorite exercises, etc.

ABASE runs on any Macintosh (SE/30 or above). It has two versions. One is for students; the other is for instructors. Users interact with the program by pointing and clicking a mouse or, by typing chemical expressions or text. Pull-down menus are employed in the ABASE Editor designed to be used by the instructor.

ACID/BASE Regulation Problems

ABASE is intended for students who have already studied the function of the components of acid/base regulation to the extent covered in most textbooks of physiology [Ber-Lev88, WES90]. It enables students to evaluate and improve their understanding by providing them with a set of problems to "solve" that involve acid/base disturbances.

Each problem begins with a description of a person who is in some circumstance that causes his/her acid base status to change. Students predict the qualitative effects of this condition on five variables that relate to acid base balance by making entries in a PREDICTION TABLE [Rov-Mic86]. The correctness of these predictions is then checked and errors are identified. An explanation of the mechanisms underlying the correct response is then given for each error or associated group of errors. Each problem ends with two culminating exercises. First, the student is asked to represent the events making up the response to the disturbance on a standard acid base graphical display (a Davenport nomogram [Dav69]). Finally, the program uses the same display to animatedly illustrate the same reactions.

In addition, there are four interactive tutorials. These are question/answer exercises that review the background knowledge that students must have to be able to solve the ABASE problems. Students may do any one or all of the tutorials before they do the problems. And they can, while doing a problem, branch to a relevant tutorial if they want to refresh or improve their understanding of some aspects of acid base regulation before they complete the solution. They may also branch out for a definition of terms. The program flow chart is shown in Figure 1.

The ABASE Program

Because the program needs to provide quick access to related material, play animations, and display graphs, a hypertext (hypermedia) system, hypercard [Goo90], was chosen as the environment for ABASE [Mod89].

The ABASE program consists of Hypercard stacks. These stacks are classified into three categories based on their functions:
- Access Stacks: provide two types of user interface
    Stack "ABASE": access for students
    Stack "AUTHORING": access for teachers
- Resource Stack: contains shared resources
    Stack "ABASE Resource"
- Tutorial Stacks: provide teaching materials
    Stack "Dictionary"

Stack "Problem <name>"

Stack "Lesson <name>"

Each tutorial stack is self-contained in terms of both tutoring material and navigation methods. That is, all information that is necessary for solving a problem or teaching a lesson is stored within that particular stack. There are two ways of traversing a tutorial stack (the student's or the teacher's), each provides a different set of navigation buttons. It is the task of the access stack to set up an appropriate navigation method and provide necessary authoring tools for the teacher.

All tutorial stack names are further tagged with "problem," "lesson" or "dictionary." This is used to inform the Editor for stack "authoring" that this is a stack that it can operate on.

Overview of the Capabilities of the ABASE EDITOR

The Editor provides an interface and the necessary tools for a teacher to modify existing components of ABASE and create new lesson stacks for it.

Upon entering the Editor, the teacher is asked to choose between two options: edit an existing tutorial stack or create new lesson stacks. Then he/she is given an appropriate pull-down menu (see Figure 2, top line). To edit an existing tutorial stack, a file dialogue window is set up listing individual stacks that make up ABASE. Depending on the stack type that the teacher chooses (problem, lesson, dictionary), the corresponding Editing option is added to the pull-down menu and the stack is opened for editing. Table I lists the functions supported by the editor.

When an existing tutorial stack is opened for editing, a backup copy is saved in a file named "Copy of <StackName>" in case the author would like to later discard any modifications that were made or for possible later reference. Also, if changes are discarded, modifications (if any) are saved under a file name "Jou.. <StackName>".

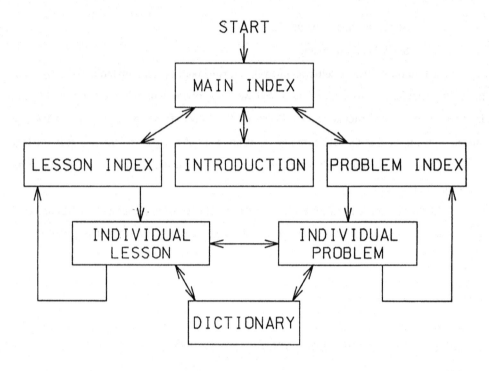

Figure 1. Program Flow Chart

Table I Editor Functions for each Component Type

Component Type	Author can:
Dictionary	1) Modify text (definition) 2) Add/Remove entry
Lesson	1) Modify text 2) Add/Remove question/text segment 3) Create new lesson
Problem	Modify text content

Editing the Dictionary Stack

The Dictionary Stack supports the hypertext functionality of the ABASE program. Every dictionary entry appears as underlined text in the body of the program. A mouse click on an underlined word brings up that item in the dictionary. The Editor supports the following operations:

o Browse:

When the dictionary is opened for authoring, the teacher can freely browse the entries. Definitions can also be edited.

o Add new keyword:

When "Add New Entry" is selected from the "Edit Dictionary" menu, the author is presented with a form (Figure 2) with two fields for entering the keyword and its definition. Clicking on the "ADD WORD" causes the insertion of the new keyword into the dictionary in correct alphabetic order. A click on the "Return" button returns the operation to the dictionary.

o Delete a keyword:

While in the dictionary, the teacher may remove the keyword displayed on the monitor by selecting the option "Delete Current Entry" from the "Edit Dictionary" menu.

Editing the Problem Stacks

The current version of the Editor only supports text editing of the problem stacks. The automation of creation and maintenance of the Prediction Table routines and animated summary routines could be implemented quite easily in the future. However, the possibility of editing the graphic testing routine needs further study to determine if it could be fully automated because it is highly procedure dependent.

Editing the Lesson Stacks

Inside a lesson stack, there are two types of card. One contains pure text and is called a "text card." The other type is a "question card." It contains some text along with a question. ABASE Editor supports the insertion, deletion and update operations on both types of card. The editor also supports four types of questions; they are listed in Table II. For each type of question, an authoring template is created to be used when editing or creating a "question card" (see Figure 3 for an example). When a student uses a lesson stack, ABASE uses a match/explain model. That is, the student's answer(s) to a question is matched to a predefined answer(s) (keyword match/range checking or no match). If there is a match, corresponding explanation text is displayed. By simply filling up (or modifying) a template, a question is created, (or corrected, or customized).

The classification of the questions provides the ability for nonprogrammers to create and customize lesson stacks. But since only limited types of questions are supported, there are restrictions to the ways that the teacher can conduct a tutorial. With the current editor:

o   All questions must take the form specified in one of the four question types.

o   The graphical background is not easily editable.

However, it is not clear that such restrictions would seriously affect the quality of the tutorial program.

Discussion

Tutorial programs can be created using a programming language, an authoring language, or an authoring system [Loc-Car85, Gra85]. *Programming languages* provide the highest degree of flexibility and portability but such systems take a longer time to build because every feature has to be implemented from basic language constructs. Thus, the resulting code is very complex and, consequently, it is hard to maintain and modify.

Authoring languages are code systems uniquely designed for creating instructional programs. The major advantage of an authoring language over a general purpose programming language is that it includes special purpose subroutines necessary to make instructional interactions (such as match, accept, display, etc.). However, they also suffer from serious drawbacks (such as low portability, low execution speed, large disk and memory overhead). On the other hand, *authoring systems* attempt to minimize or eliminate programming by providing a series of menu-driven editors and facilitate instructional design by including instruction templates [Mer87], thereby increasing productivity (reducing development time). Unfortunately, authoring systems suffer from the same problems as authoring languages, in addition to the inherent limitation on instruction design [Mer85].

Even though an authoring system can eliminate the programming work, existing authoring systems are costly to build and are being criticized for lacking "authoring guidance," because most of them include templates for only the most primitive of instructional strategies [Mer85].

Instead of using existing "generic" authoring systems that can be used in different or a very large number of domain(s), we have taken an alternative approach. Using existing technology (Hypercard) we have built a small scale authoring system (the ABASE Editor) within a single and limited domain -- a program that teaches acid/base regulation. This approach makes it possible to tailor the tutorial program to meet specific needs (such as the use of the Prediction Table, hypertext, etc.), and provides enough power to let the system grow and change. The resulting program is expandable and adaptable.

Conclusions and Future Developments

We were able to develop a rather complex tutorial program (ABASE) in a relative short time by using Hypercard. The inclusion of a small scale authoring system increases the program's flexibility and thus improves the quality of ABASE and makes it more acceptable.

Future developments will include the following desirable features.

In the area of Editing the Dictionary:

1) Upon adding a new keyword to the dictionary, it should automatically be underlined in all other stacks.

2) When a keyword is deleted from the dictionary, the underlines should be removed from all tutorial stacks.

In the area of Editing the Problem Stack:

1) The creation and maintenance of the Prediction Table routines and animated summary routines will be automated.

2) The possibility of automating the creation and maintenance of the graphical testing routines will be studied.

In the area of Editing the Lesson Stack:

Addition of more question types.

Table II Question Type Classification

QUESTION TYPE	PURPOSE
FILL	Requires the user to enter (no more than 4) answers; not a multiple choice question.
EQUATION	Requires the user to enter (no more than 4) chemical formulas, the answer(s) is substituted into the equation.
CHOICE	Requires the user to enter one of the choices; the question is a multiple choice one.
RANGE	The question requires a single numeric answer. Explanation text is predefined for answers below/in/above acceptable range.

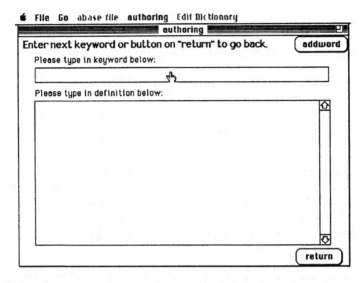

Figure 2. Sample Card Template for Adding New Entry in Dictionary

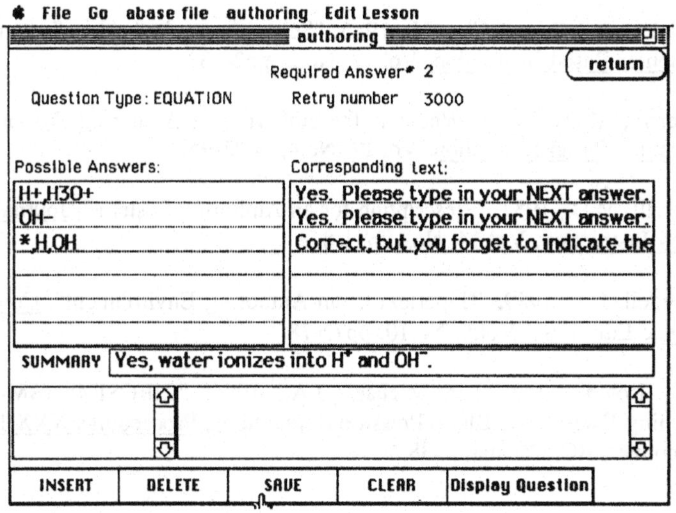

Figure 3. Card Template for Question Modification in Lesson Stack

References

[Bev-Lev88] Berne, R.M., & Levy, M.J., 1988, Physiology, Mosby, St. Louis, 2nd Edition.

[WES90] West, J.B., 1990, Best and Taylor's Physiological Basis of Medical Practice, Williams and Wilkins, Baltimore, 12th Edition, Chapter 32.

[Dav69] Davenport, H.W., 1969, The ABC of Acid-base Chemistry, Chicago, University Chicago Press.

[For-Fre78] Forsythe, A.B. and Freed, J.R., 1978, "Writing Computer-Aided Instruction Lessons: Some Practical Considerations.", Information Technology in Health Science Education, Plenum Press, New York and London, pp523-539.

[Goo90] Goodman, D., 1990, The Complete Hypercard 2.0 Handbook 3rd Edition, Bantam Computer Books, New York, New York.

[Gra85] Graham, S.N., 1985, "Tools for Creating Lessons on a Computer", Computers in Life Science Education, Volume 2, No. 1, pp1-4.

[Lij91] Li, J., 1991, ABASE: A Computer Program that Teaches Acid/Base Regulation, M.S. Thesis, Illinois Institute of Technology, Chicago.

[Loc-Car85] Locatis, C. and Carr, V., 1985, "Selecting an Authoring System", Journal of Computer-Based Instruction, Vol.12, No.2 pp28-33.

[Mer85] Merrill, M.D., 1985, "Where is the authoring in Authoring System?", Journal of Computer-Based Instruction, Vol.12, No.4, pp92-96.

[Mer87] Merrill, M.D., 1987, "Prescription for an Authoring System.", Journal of Computer-Based Instruction, Vol.14, No.1, pp1-8.

[Mod89] Modell, H.I., 1989, "Hypertext as an Authoring Environment", Computers in Life Science Education, Vol.6, No.10, pp73-78.

[Rov-Mic86] Rovick, A.A., and Michael, J.A., 1986, "CIRCSIM: IBM-PC Computer Teaching Exercise on Blood Pressure Regulation", Proceedings XXX IUPS congress, Vancouver, BC, Canada, p138.

A Tool for Developing Intelligent Tutoring Systems

Huang Lianjing

Computer Center, Zhejian Normal University

Jinhua City, Zhejian Province, 321004

P.R. China

Abstract

This paper presents a tool for developing intelligent tutoring systems. The tool which was built upon a combined model of functional and logic programming overcomes some drawbacks of conventional domain-dependent intelligent tutoring systems. We describe some main components of the tool, especially, the student modeler which models student's knowledge both in declarative and procedural aspects. A tutor implemented within the tool is also introduced.

Full version of paper not available in time for printing

Applying computer models of phonological competence to C.A.L.L.

R. LILLY,

Laboratoire de Recherches Phonétiques,

Université de LILLE III, B.P. 149

59650 Villeneuve d'Ascq Cedex

FRANCE

The following paper attempts to show that a computer model of a native speaker's phonological competence, while generating significant improvements to the theory itself provides an adequate framework for intelligent Computer Assisted Language Learning. Allowing automatic error detection, self-adjusting correction and treatment of a large corpus of words, a program incorporating formalized linguistic knowledge does not only offer more simplicity, power and freedom than would more conventional language teaching programs; it also departs radically from a traditionally structuralist approach of C.A.L.L. based on "pattern practice" and conditioning rather than the acquisition of an explicit linguistic knowledge. We will successively discuss two formal rules of English phonology, their computer modelization and their insertion in an experimental teaching program.

1. The phonological framework

1.1 descriptive phonetics

Contrary to some languages with "fixed" stress or accent like Czech which has initial stress [Kuc61], French which has final stress [Del38], or Polish in which words are stressed on the last but one syllable [Jas59], English has a variable accent system. Words can therefore display a variety of stress-patterns, some of which are illustrated hereafter (bold characters represent main stress; the numbers are positioned below the corresponding syllabic peak, 1 representing main stress, 2 secondary stress, 0 absence of stress):

kitchen	revolver	experiment	government
1 0	0 1 0	0 1 0 0	1 0 0
above	ravishing	modulation	phenomenology
0 1	1 0 0	2 0 1 0	0 2 0 1 0 0

In addition, this phenomenon has drastic consequences on the phonology of English, causing numerous vowels transformations (compare for example the pronunciation of the *o* in *melody, melodic* and *melodious*). We can therefore predict a few difficulties for foreign learners, all the more so after reading the following lines by Daniel Jones :

> Generally speaking there are no rules determining which syllable or syllables of polysyllabic English words bear the main stress. The foreign student is obliged to learn the stress of each word individually. He has to learn, for instance, that the main stress is on the first syllable in *photograph*, on the second in *photography*, on the third in *photographic* and on the fourth in *photogravure*. [Jon18:248]

In no way is this an isolated point of view. In *An Introduction to the Pronunciation of English*, another major and detailed work on English phonetics, A.C. Gimson refers only briefly to problems of accent or stress, limiting his approach to a catalogue of possible "word accentual patterns" and carefully avoiding any reference to stress rules. In a 25-line paragraph entitled "Word Accent - Advice to Foreign Learners", he rightly calls attention to the link between stress-patterns and vowel quality, and warns that "the accentual pattern of an extended word form should not necessarily be associated with that of the root upon which it is based" [Gim62:239]. Among thousands of possible illustrations, he interestingly picks out the pair *photograph/photography*, which probably means he had D. Jones's rather discouraging comment in mind. Awareness of a problem may be the beginning of its solution, but remains of little practical help for foreign learners or their teachers.

1.2 a generative approach to phonology

Generative phonology, as defined by Chomsky and Halle [Cho-Hal68], departs radically from such views. Instead of just describing the phonetic (observable) sequences, it considers them as the output of a formal system of transformational rules. In this framework, prior to any rule application, *photograph, photography* and *photographic* share an identical phonological base-form: /fotgræf/. Different endings, however, produce different stress-patterns (102, 0100 and 2010, respectively) which in turn cause originally identical vowels to be processed differently. The phonetic unruliness which perplexed Jones and Gimson is clearly a surface phenomenon. In spite of divergent phonetic forms, related words have a common underlying phonological form and are processed by a set of organized rules. This has far-reaching cognitive consequences. If, contrary to what D. Jones thought, no one is "obliged to learn each word individually", then the internalized grammar of an ideal speaker-hearer, i.e. his phonological "competence", must include (in a still tentative form) phonological representations and transformational rules.

Within this approach, Lilly and Viel have proposed over a hundred ordered rules -and their exceptions- which seem to govern phonological transformations in English [Lil-Vie77]. I have chosen to present here two of the most powerful rules among those. They are responsible for two kinds of phenomena: stress placement and vowel transformations.

1.3 the Stress Rule

It has long been known that English words ending in -ion are stressed on their preceding syllable. Guierre [Gui70] extended this rule to all kinds of suffixes and endings, such as: -eal, -eous, -ia, -ial, -ian, -iar, -iel, -ience, -ient, -io, -iom, -iot, -ious, -ual, -uate, -uel, -uous, etc.. What they have in common is to display two consecutive vowels, the first one being restricted to e, i, or u. The choice of the second vowel is free; any number of consonants, including none, may follow. It is possible to formalize this rule using the now familiar Chomskyan notation:

(i) Stress Rule.

$$V \rightarrow [+ \text{stressed}] \ / \ \underline{\hspace{1cm}} \ C \left\{ \begin{array}{c} i \\ e \\ u \end{array} \right\} V \ (C)$$

This rule reads "*a vowel becomes stressed in the following context: in front of one or more consonants followed by either i, e, or u, followed by any vowel, itself followed by an undefined number of consonants*". It is easy to check that it applies to the following words correctly (stressed vowels are in bold type):

| provincial | election | insomnia | plenteous |
| reaction | mortician | axiom | sumptuous |

1.4 the Tensing Rule

Once stress assignment is completed, another rule applies, which alters the quality of the stressed vowel, through a process called "tensing". Tensing is a general process that turns short (i.e. "lax") vowels into long vowels or diphthongs (i.e. "tense" vowels) under certain contextual conditions. The addition of a "mute e" is one such context:

mat	→	mate
wren	→	serene
sit	→	site
not	→	note
run	→	rune

This same transformation is witnessed each time the Stress Rule applies, provided three conditions are simultaneously met. The rule can be formulated thus:

(ii) Tensing Rule.

$$V \rightarrow [+ \text{ tense}] \; / \; \underline{\hspace{1cm}} \; C^1 \; \begin{Bmatrix} i \\ e \\ u \end{Bmatrix} \; V \; (C)$$

Condition 1: the stressed vowel must be other than i.
Condition 2: there must be only one consonant ("C^1") after the stressed vowel.
Condition 3: the first vowel after C1 cannot be u.

By application of rules (i) and (ii), the following words will show a tense accented vowel. Borrowing from Chomsky and Halle [Cho-Hal68:28] their notational convention for tense vowels (justified because the name of the five vocalic letters A, E, I, O, U is itself "tense"), and using bold type to indicate accent, we obtain the following (correct) result:

nAtion	atrOcious	sEnior	mEdia
rAtio	Union	allUvial	Ocean

On the contrary, the Stress Rule but not the Tensing Rule applies to the following words, because one or more of the three conditions are not fulfilled:

	condition 1	condition 2	condition 3	tensing
trivial	not fulfilled	fulfilled	fulfilled	no
inspection	fulfilled	not fulfilled	fulfilled	no
fluctuate	fulfilled	not fulfilled	not fulfilled	no
dissuade	not fulfilled	not fulfilled	not fulfilled	no

2. The program

2.1 description

An initial version of the program was designed to follow the linguistic formulation precisely without trying to improve on it or add to it. Its aim was to process a word in the same order, indicate whether the rules applied or not and display the result of their application on the screen. For the sake of clarity, the same notational conventions were used:

- lower case standard: neither rule applies   e.g. electric
- lower case bold :   stressed but not tense   e.g. electrician
- upper case bold :   stressed, tense vowel   e.g. comEdian

A very simple program was able to achieve this. The diagram which illustrates its organization (Appendix 1) needs but brief explanations:

2.1.1. The application field of the Stress Rule being wider than that of the Tensing Rule, the transformations are phonologically "ordered" and must be treated accordingly in the program; in that way, only the words which have been successfully stressed by the first rule will be subject to the second.

2.1.2. The term "ending" is usually preferred in the literature to the term "suffix" to define sequences such as *-ion, -ial, -iar, -ual*, etc. because in most cases the root to which they are attached is not an existing word (e.g. *nation, social, familiar, gradual*, etc.). A program, however, which would extract the last three characters of a word - its "ending" - would often fail to find the correct sequence because of further derivations (e.g. *nationally, socially, familiarize, gradually*, etc.). It would also be unnecessarily complicated because not all endings are composed of three characters (consider *-ia, -io, -ious, -eous, -uence* for example) and the program would have to search for two-character sequences, three-character sequences, etc.. The first of these problems can easily be solved by creating a "moveable" window allowing the program to scan the word as a human reader would when looking for the proper sequence. The second can be solved if we notice that the final consonant(s) in the Stress Rule formulation are optional and that final e is erased ("mute") in English: the window only needs to accomodate the two characters of the following sequence:

$$\left\{ \begin{matrix} i \\ e \\ u \end{matrix} \right\} \ V$$

In order to find them in the word *opium*, the window will thus scan "*op*" and "*pi*" before it stops on "*iu*". We will refer to this two-vowel sequence as the Stress Rule Context, since it is this specific environment that causes the Stress Rule to apply.

2.1.3. In order to find the stressed vowel it is now necessary to move a one-character window backwards and check whether its contents are a vowel or a consonant. It should stop on the first vowel it finds.

2.1.4. While looking for the stressed vowel, it is easy to count the number of intermediate consonants. We can also identify the first vowel of the ending and the stressed vowel. We now have the information we need to verify whether the three conditions of the tensing rule are all met: number of consonants < 2; stressed vowel < > i; first vowel of ending < > u.

2.2 testing

Successive versions of the program were tested with a 24000-word corpus [Win72]. Giving a detailed account of the testing procedures and their results is beyond the scope of this study. Not all the problems encountered while testing are of pedagogical interest, and some raise unanswered linguistic questions [Lil91]. Here are, briefly stated, some of the improvements that had to be added to what previously seemed to be a rigorous formulation in a teaching environment.

2.3 English words have to be "read" backwards

It seems natural to follow the normal left to right reading direction when looking for the two-vowel sequence and then only start back in search for the accented vowel. Even though this method is successful with a word like *professionalize*, it fails with a word like *association* where there are two acceptable sequences: the program stops on the first sequence, and incorrectly places primary stress on the second syllable. This suggests that the Stress Rule (like many other rules of English phonology) should work its way backwards from the end of the word.

2.4 initial vocalic sequences

When no vowel precedes the Stress Rule context, the program starts looking for a vowel that does not exist, causing a syntax error. It is doubtful that any student would ever be tempted to place a stress peak on a non-existing syllable. It seems however of pedagogical interest to underline that words exhibiting such sequences in initial-syllable position either contain a digraph (e.g. *field, seal, fruit* ...) or must be treated by a different rule (e.g. *dial, fluent, via* ...).

2.5 rule conflicts

Words such as *anxiety, society, vacuity, oleic, toluic,* while displaying the proper vowel sequence, are not stressed accordingly (compare to *anxious, social, vacuous, oleum, toluene*). The reason for that is the presence of the suffixes *-ety, -ity* and *-ic* which have the general property of placing stress on the preceding syllable. In such a case of conflicting rule application, we must order the rules so that words ending with those suffixes are not subject to the Stress Rule.

2.6 morphological boundaries

Morphological markers can often cause, at least for the program, misleading two-vowel sequences. Words ending in *-y* have a plural in *-ies,* which would cause Stress Rule application if we don't find a way to eliminate them. Many compounds like *whereabouts, whereupon, therein,* etc. entail the same result. Some of these problems have been solved by allowing the program to detect the presence of a prefix or suffix and automatically insert a morpheme boundary (+) between it and the root.

2.7 treatment of exceptions

Because of the rule ordering discussed in **2.1.1**, exceptions to the Stress Rule should be eliminated first. Apart from very few native words (e.g. *television, dandelion, spiritual...*), most "irregular" stress assignments can be accounted for by the origin of the word, whether French (*cavalier, serviette...*), Greek (*museum, panacea...*), Hebrew (*Goliath, Jeremiah...*), or Italian (*Traviatta, virtuoso...*). However, until a satisfactory "foreign word tracer" can be designed to mimic the native speakers' capacity to identify a word's origin, they have to be classified as exceptions. On the other hand, words such as *Italian, onion, precious, special, Spaniard, valiant,* etc., which are stressed on the appropriate syllable but do not exhibit the expected tense vowel, have to be listed as exceptions to the Tensing Rule only.

3. Pedagogical applications

3.1 machines and language teaching

The Language Laboratory and Computer Aided Learning are probably two of the most important teaching tools to have become available to students of languages and their teachers over the past thirty years. In spite of obvious differences - the Language Laboratory allows students to listen to oral stimuli and record their responses while C.A.L.L. has, until recently, been restricted to whatever could be displayed on a computer screen - they often show striking similarities in the way they approach language learning. Most of the work offered to the student is typically based on multiple-choice exercises, structural drills, incomplete sentences to be filled in and (often tedious) repetitive "pattern-practice".

It might well be argued that this type of interaction between student and machine is primarily due to the inherent technological limitations of the media themselves. In the case of C.A.L.L., one would probably add that the programming languages or the authoring systems, whichever are used, are not powerful or elaborate enough. Although there is obviously some truth in that, my contention here is in a more radical way that the pedagogical limitations of the media and the often disappointing quality of commercially available C.A.L.L. software [And-Boy-Rei85] are to be traced back to the theory of language learning to which they historically belong, knowingly or not.

3.2 Applied Structural Linguistics

At one time the dominant theory about language learning, Applied Structural Linguistics is well exemplified by the work of Lado and Fries. Their approach is based on the idea that "to learn a new language one must establish orally the patterns of the language as subconscious habits" [Lad-Fri43:XV]. Those patterns are defined as "the significant framework of the sentence", or the "structural frame" within which new acquisitions will be made by substitution of one or several elements. All the exercises in the above-quoted book propose, like the following, to practice a pattern by "changing some element of that pattern each time" (p. 51, exercise #10):

two months ago	I arrived here two months ago
a year ago	I arrived here a year ago
an hour ago	....
a week ago	....
two days ago	....
five minutes ago	....

Such a learning theory is not only a clear expression of the most mechanical version of structuralism, it is also heavily behaviorist in its philosophy. According to the authors, the linguistic patterns practiced by the student must be "driven intensively into his habit reflexes" and become "subconscious habits".

Approaching language learning as one form of conditioning naturally leads the authors to reject explanations (let alone explicit linguistic formulations) as "talk about language". One of the most often developed themes in their introductions is that "learning a foreign language consists not in learning about the language, but in developing a new set of habits" [Lad-

Fri57:V] or that it is a "mistake to think that understanding the rules of the contruction in a language will result in ability to use the language for communication" [Lad-Fri43:XV].

3.3 using a model of linguistic competence for C.A.L.L.

It is relatively easy to nest a program such as the one described earlier within a larger Computer Assisted Language Learning program, and many versions can be imagined. For example, a word can be submitted and questions can be asked about its phonology. In our program, the student is simply asked to click once on the stressed vowel, or twice on a vowel that is both stressed and tense. The phonological module then processes the word and compares its result with the student's answer. If there is a difference, the student is asked questions corresponding to the error.

3.4 example of student/program interaction
(if student clicks on one item, it switches to boldface)

graduate

- Does the Stress Rule apply to this word ?   **YES**   NO
- Please click on the stressed vowel :   graduate
- Does the Tensing Rule apply to this vowel ?   **YES**   NO
- Click on appropriate tense vowel among the following :   A, E, I, O, U
- Your answer is not totally satisfactory :
  The Stress Rule specifies that "an English vowel is stressed if it is
  followed by i, e, or u, itself followed by any vowel and an
  optional consonant".
  Now identify the first vowel of the Stress Rule Context and click on it :   graduate
- That's correct. This causes the preceding vowel (a) to be stressed.
  It can also cause that vowel to become tense on three conditions,
  which must be fulfilled simultaneously :

  1. The stressed vowel should not be i.
     Is this condition fulfilled ?   **YES**   NO

  2. There should'nt be more than one consonant
     (Two if the second one is a liquid). Is this
     second condition fulfilled?   **YES**   NO

  3. The first vowel of the stress-placing sequence

should not be u. Is the third condition fulfilled ?   YES   NO

- Correct !   Does the Tensing Rule apply then ?   YES   NO

- The word graduate should therefore be represented as : graduate and not grAduate which indicated a tense stressed vowel.

3.5 representation of student and teacher models

In order to achieve a dialogue of this kind, which resembles the one a human teacher might carry out with a student, we clearly have to use the program's analogue of the teacher's explicit phonological knowledge. But a teacher normally adapts his questions to the type of error made by the student. It seems therefore necessary to contruct two models, one corresponding to the "correct" treatment of the word, another corresponding to the student's analysis when it is erroneous. Both models can be viewed as a certain itinerary through a flow chart, each passage through a node of the tree being "recorded" in a variable. With a program incorporating the additions reviewed in **2.3-7**, we could sum up all this information in two matrices. Any discrepancy between the program and student matrices provokes further questions and opens the possibility for the student to correct errors.

test applied to the word "graduate"	program	student	
		try 1	try 2
Is the word an exception to Stress Rule ?.............................	0		
Can -ity, -ety or -ic be found in word ?..............................	0		
Can Stress Rule context be found ?....................................	1		
Position of first vowel of Stress Rule context ?.....................	5		5
Can a vowel be found before a morpheme boundary (+) or a compound boundary (-) are encountered ?.....................	1		
Position of stressed vowel ?..	3	3	
Is the word an exception to the Tensing Rule ?.....................	0		
Condition 1 : Is the stressed vowel < > i ?.........................	1		1
Condition 2 : If there are two intermediate consonants, is the second one r or l and the first one other than r and l ?.........	0		0
Is there only one consonant ?...	1		1
Condition 3 : Is the first vowel of the Stress Rule context = u ?.	1		1
Does Tensing Rule apply ?...	0	1	0
Which tense vowel is it among A, E, I, O, U ?.....................	/	A	/

4. Conclusion

Competence modelling is clearly not the indispensable core of any Computer Assisted Learning program of phonology. Words can be submitted and answers can be checked very easily without it ; but if a more elaborate dialogue between machine and student is called for, then the cost of error analysis and dialogue scripting (even with a small number of words) soon becomes overwhelming, because of the complexity of rule application and student reactions. On the other hand, an explicit model of a native speaker's linguistic competence can apply to an unlimited number of (non-exceptional) words, which in our program can be accessed randomly from a textfile. Because the program not only processes the word, but keeps track of how it reached the result, it can "discuss" the student's answer far beyond a right or wrong judgement and still use simple error analysis and dialogue. The limitations of this linguistically-based approach to C.A.L.L. should not be underestimated and its expandability is a direct function of our present linguistic knowledge. In this respect, electronic teachers and their human counterparts probably have one thing in common : only the unintelligent ones can teach more than they know.

Acknowledgments

I wish to express my gratitude towards Christine Vernet and Jean-Claude Desruque for their help with the technical presentation of this paper and to two anonymous reviewers for helpful suggestions.

References

[And-Boy-Rei85] John R. Anderson, C. Franklin Boyle, Brian J. Reiser. *Intelligent tutoring systems*. Science, 228,1985, pp. 456-462.

[And-Fuc73] Jacques André, Catherine Fuchs. *Ordinateurs, programmation et langues naturelles*. Mame, Paris,1973.

[Bar-Fei81] Avron Barr, Edward A. Feigenbaum. *The Handbook of Artificial Intelligence* (vol. 1). William Kaufman, Los Altos (Ca.),1981.

[Beg-Hog87] Iain M. Begg, Ian Hogg. *Authoring systems for ICAI.* in [Kea87].

[Bra-Ber83] Michael Brady, Robert Berwick (eds.). *Computational Models of Discourse.* M.I.T. Press, Cambridge (Ma.), 1983.

[Cho-Hal68] Noam Chomsky, Morris Halle. *The Sound Pattern of English.* Harper & Row, New York, 1968.

[Del38] Pierre Delattre. *L'accent final en français : accent d'intensité, accent de hauteur, accent de durée.* French Review, 1938, 12, pp. 141-146.

[Gim62] Alfred C. Gimson. *An Introduction to the Pronunciation of English.* Arnold, London, 1962.

[Gui70] Lionel Guierre. *Drills in English Stress-Patterns.* Longman, London, 1970.

[Jas59] Wiktor Jassem. *The Phonology of Polish Stress.* Word, 1959, 15, pp. 252-259.

[Jon18] Daniel Jones. *An Outline of English Phonetics.* Heffer, Cambridge, 1918 (quoted in 9th ed., 1962) .

[Kea87] Greg Kearsley (ed.). *Artificial Intelligence and Instruction.* Addison-Wesley, Reading, Ma., 1987.

[Kuc61] Henry Kucera. *The Phonology of Czech.* Mouton, The Hague, 1961.

[Lad-Fri43] Robert Lado, Charles C. Fries. *English Pattern Practices.* The University of Michigan Press, Ann Arbor, 1943.

[Lad-Fri57] Robert Lado, Charles C. Fries. *English Sentence Patterns.* The University of Michigan Press, Ann Arbor, 1957.

[Lil91] Richard Lilly. *Heuristic value of computer modelling in formal phonology.* Paper presented at the 26th Colloquium of Linguistics, Sept. 1991, Poznan, Poland.

[Lil-Vie77] Richard Lilly, Michel Viel. *La prononciation de l'anglais.* Hachette, Paris, 1977.

[Sle-Bro82] Derek H. Sleeman, John S. Brown. *Intelligent Tutoring systems.* Academic Press, New York, 1982.

[Win72] John Windsor Lewis. *A Concise Pronouncing Dictionary of British and American English.* Oxford University Press, Oxford, 1972.

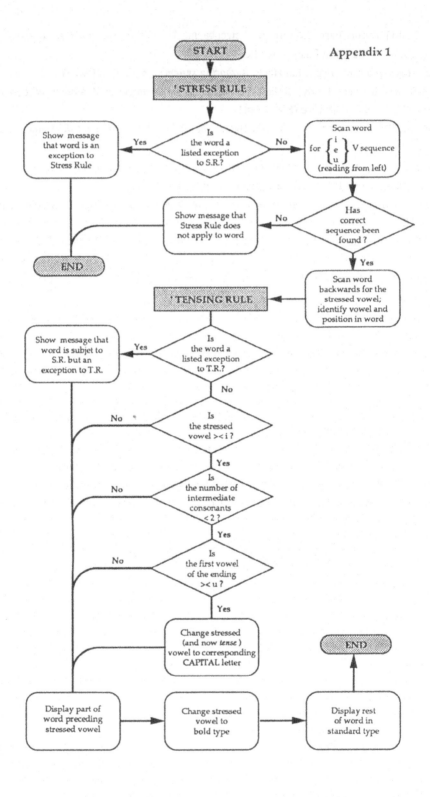

Appendix 1

Vigilance in a Long-Term Cognitive Computing Task:
The Effects of Subject Strategy and Screen Colour on Performance

Lori A. Livingston
Department of Physical Education
Wilfrid Laurier University
Waterloo, Ontario, Canada
N2L 3C5
(519) 884-1970
email: lliving5@wlu.ca

Abstract

The purpose of this study was to determine whether a vigilance decrement would occur in a cognitively-demanding computer task, and whether the strategy employed by the subject and/or the colour complexity of the screen would affect observed performance levels. Adult-aged subjects ($\underline{N}$=60) were randomly assigned to one of three colour conditions (e.g. monochromatic, moderately-coloured, multicoloured) and asked to complete twenty consecutive games of a computerized memory task. Data were gathered by the computer, and subject strategies were determined from the data printouts. Results suggested that subject strategy, but not colour, influenced the overall level of performance and the performance decrement observed over time. Those employing a verbal rehearsal strategy outperformed all other groups by completing the task with the fewest mean errors in the shortest mean time period. Those using a consistent chunking or a variable chunking method were the next best, while those using a combined strategy (chunking and random) or a random technique performed least well. In general, a vigilance decrement was observed.

Introduction

Several attempts have been made to describe vigilance performance in terms of what it is, who it affects, and when, where and why it occurs. Investigators generally agree that the vigilance decrement may be defined as the "within-session deterioration in [performance] efficiency" [Dav-Par82], or, as an overall low or suboptimal level of performance [Cra84], and that humans perform poorly when they must sustain their attention for prolonged periods of time [Par87]. There is markedly less agreement, however, with respect to the time period required, the nature of the task or work environment, and the underlying processes responsible for dictating the ease with which a vigilance decrement can be detected. These differences may be related to the theoretical approach adopted (i.e. basic versus applied) by the investigation in question.

In the 1940s, interest in the study of vigilance was generated in response to a practical problem; that is, the deterioration in performance over time of radar operators in their ability to monitor and detect the movement of enemy vessels. Thereafter, the study of sustained attention underwent what is now a well-documented shift from an applied to a basic research focus. It is only within the last decade that a return to the applied framework has been advocated [Ada87, Wei87] for the advent of computer technology has introduced a real-world vigilance problem into the workplace and the classroom.

Computers demand, by the nature of their technology, that humans perform as passive monitors of information displays. Whether or not a vigilance problem will arise depends on several factors, not the least of which may include the cognitive demands of the task at hand, the organization of the information display, and the conscious deliberate actions of the vigilant actor.

Monitoring tasks have gradually changed in form such that the computer-user is often required to "make judgements of a complex, cognitive nature, rather than of a predominantly perceptual kind" [Cra84]. Communication between the computer and its user begins with the input of visual information. Incoming stimuli and information retrieved from the long-term memory stores are perceived and transformed into a usable form in working memory. From this point onward, information is processed quickly and rapidly, leading to a user response [Wae89]. The information capacity of the working memory is limited, however, to approximately seven items of information [Mil56]. Thus, information displays demanding more resources than what the working memory has to offer may result in a significant form of cognitive stress [Hoc-Gai-Col86].

The visual channel is the primary medium through which computers and humans interact. The grouping of related pieces of information on the basis of colour is often employed in an attempt to reduce cognitive demands on users. In doing so, we exploit the human capacity for perceiving structure and organization [Bae-Bux87]. Furthermore, colour is widely used because it is thought to be motivating and capable of attracting the user's attention [Eng84, Ram-Ram87]. Yet, few secure guidelines exist on the use of colour and many experimental papers are contradictory on its application [Tra-Bow-Set-Pep90].

Clearly, not all possible formats for portraying information lead to similarities in operator effectiveness [Che-Egg-Fle-Sas89] since each individual will bring to the task their own conceptualizations [Nor83] and solution strategies. Task and subject factors interact in determining vigilance performance [Koe-Bri-Hen-Ver89], yet traditional vigilance research has focused to a large extent on only the former.

More recent investigations have pointed to the possible connection between performance and the strategy employed by the vigilant actor. Active, conscious, and directed involvement by a subject while performing the Mackworth Clock Test was demonstrably superior to haphazard or passive involvement [Gia-Qui-Phi-His88]. Others [Koe-Bri-Hen-Ver89] have concluded that the primary discriminating feature between two sets of tasks (i.e. memory, cognitive) was the availability of a phonetic-linguistic code for the cognitive tasks. Thus, there is some suggestion that the amount of effort and the strategy employed may play an important role in determining one's success on a vigilance task. Assessment of such strategies to date, however, have relied on the subjective responses of subjects [Gia-Qui-Phi-His88, Han-War89, Koe-Bri-Zwe-Ver90, Koe-Bri-Hen-Ver89].

The aim of this study was twofold. First, within an applied framework, the investigation sought to determine when and where a vigilance decrement would occur in a cognitively-demanding computer task. Second, two independent variables were of particular interest. The effects of the colour complexity of the screen display and the strategy employed to complete the experimental task were examined.

Methods

The sample consisted of young adult and adult-aged ($\underline{N}$=60) male and female university students and staff. The mean age of the group was 24.3 ($\underline{SD}$=5.4) years. Subjects were prescreened for visual deficits such that those suffering from any form of severe impairment were excluded from the study. Thirty subjects wore corrective lenses while completing the experimental task. Experience in using computers was not a prerequisite for taking part in the study.

An Apple Macintosh II system computer, with a colour monitor, was used to generate the CRT display. The subjects manoeuvred a mouse in order to interact with the computer.

A software package, entitled "Computer Concentration", was designed for the purpose of collecting data for this study. The opening display consisted of a four-by-six matrix of boxes (Figure 1) behind which twelve pairs of objects were individually pictured. The objects were designed so as to semantically differ from each other (e.g. flag, rocket, tree, football, etc.). For each game, the boxes and the objects concealed below them were randomly generated, independent on each other, by the computer.

The software afforded the investigator control over the colour of presentation of the objects and of the covering boxes. The twelve pairs of objects could be presented in a black-and-white or colour format (i.e. three objects each of red, blue, green and yellow). The colour of each individual object remained the same from game to game when the colour option was invoked. The covering boxes in turn would appear either as white boxes with black detail, or as random array of solid colours (i.e. black, red, green, blue, yellow, pink, or cyan). Overall, the software allowed for three differing colour combinations of the covering boxes/objects to be generated. These included: a monochromatic (black-and-white/black-and-white), a moderately-coloured (black-and-white/colour), and a multicoloured (colour/colour) condition.

The game required the subject to select, using the mouse, two boxes at a time in an attempt to match the figures hidden behind them. The object in the first box, once selected, remained uncovered on the display until a second box was selected. when the latter box was opened, both objects would remain on the screen if they did not

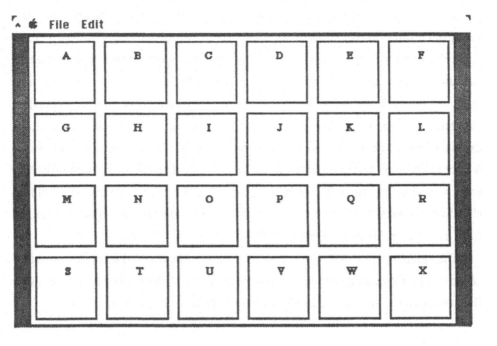

File Edit

A	B	C	D	E	F
G	H	I	J	K	L
M	N	O	P	Q	R
S	T	U	V	W	X

Figure 1. The opening display of "Computer Concentration".

match for a period of 1.2 seconds. After this time, the covering boxes would reappear. However, if a match was completed, the boxes and the objects would disappear leaving blank spaces on the screen. A game was completed when all boxes and objects had disappeared from the screen and the software would automatically generate the next game on the CRT screen.

The subjects were randomly assigned to one of three experimental groups. The design was balanced with an equal number of subjects per group (i.e. n=20). In turn, each group was randomly assigned to one of the three experimental colour conditions.

The experimental task consisted of playing the "Computer Concentration" game twenty times in succession. Subjects were instructed to proceed at their own pace, and to complete each game using as few matching attempts as possible. Upon completion, the subjects were asked to respond to a series of open-ended questions regarding their performance. The questions elicited information pertaining to the strategy used, if any, as well as the approximate time of the onset of fatigue.

Data printouts for each game provided information on the total time on task (i.e.

per game and the overall task), the number of times each object was uncovered, and the specific order in which boxes were selected. Two dependent variables were of particular interest in the analysis. First, the total time required to complete the task was used as an indicator of overall performance efficiency; that is, the more time spent on the task the more inefficient the performance. The second dependent variable, used to assess the performance decrement, was termed the "multiple exposure" error and was defined as any instance in which an object was uncovered four or more times during a single game. The number of multiple exposure errors per game was then determined. From a vigilance perspective, this variable would be classified as a measure of detection latency, or, the number of times that a signal had to be repeated prior to successful detection.

The independent variable of subject strategy was determined from data printouts generated by the testing software. Subjective reports of the strategy employed were then compared to the sequence of moves recorded.

Results

Seventy-seven percent (n = 46) of the subjects reported that the task was fatiguing, but few (n=3) found it difficult. No significant correlations between strategy, colour condition and time on task were found.

Analysis of the objective game data and subjective reports revealed that five different strategies were used to complete the experimental task. These included:

1)   Consistent Chunking (n=22). The pattern of box selections from game to game was consistently the same (e.g. A, B...C, D...E, F) with subjective reports of attempts to memorize the contents of the first four to six boxes. Box selections were always orderly and spatially related.

2)   Variable Chunking (n=10). Boxes were selected in spatially related groups of four to six for memorization, yet the group of boxes selected would vary from game to game (e.g. A, B...C, D...; F, L...R, X; A, F...X, S).

3)   Random Selection (n=6). Boxes tended to be randomly selected from

spatially unrelated locations (e.g. B, K...U, O...R, G...S, A...), and the pattern of box selection displayed no consistency from game to game.

4)   Combined Method (n=11). The subject alternated from a random to a chunking method (consistent or variable) within a game or from game to game.

5)   Verbal Rehearsal (n=11). Subjects used verbal rehearsal to assist them in memorizing object locations. Box selection was either consistently or variably chunked.

Subject reports of strategy used agreed with the objective data in the majority (i.e. 90%) of cases. Six subjects reported using a strategy that was not reflected by the computer-recorded data. In these instances, the computer data was used as the primary evidence of strategy employed.

Statistical Analysis

The time required to complete the experimental task varied from subject to subject, with values ranging from 25.1 to 43.7 minutes. The mean time for the entire sample was 32.2 minutes.

A two-way ANOVA of total time on task revealed a significant difference ($F(4,45)=3.53$, $p<.01$) according to the strategy employed. Effects due to the colour condition experienced and interaction between strategy employed and colour condition were not observed. Those using a verbal association strategy used the least amount of time ($M=29.9$ minutes) to complete the task. The consistent ($M=31.2$ minutes) and the variable ($M=32.2$ minutes) chunkers displayed the next best times, followed closely by those using a combined method ($M=33.4$ minutes). Subjects using the random approach ($M=37.3$ minutes) required the greatest mean time to complete the task. A Tukey HSD test suggested that the mean time observed for the random strategists was significantly different from that of the verbal group and the consistent chunkers.

Multiple exposure errors were tallied and totalled over five blocks of four games each per subject. Mean values were then calculated per block. A two-factor mixed between- and within-subjects repeated-measures ANOVA was used to analyze the data. A between-subjects effect for strategy $(F(4,45)=4.87, p<.002)$ and a within-subjects effect across blocks $(F(4,180)=3.64, p<.007)$ were observed, as was an interaction effect for strategy by block $(F(16,180)=1.78, p<.036)$. The mean number of errors per block of games, calculated according to the strategy implemented, are depicted in Figure 2.

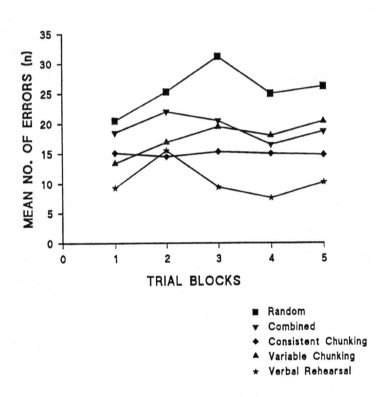

Figure 2. Mean number of multiple exposure errors observed per block of trials according to the strategy employed. An interaction effect was observed.

Post hoc tests revealed that the verbal rehearsal group committed significantly $(p<.01)$ fewer errors than those in both the combined and random groups. The tendency for rapid increases in error followed by rapid declines significantly $(p<.05)$ differentiated the random group from both the consistent chunkers and the verbal rehearsers. Overall, the mean number of errors increased significantly $(p<.05)$ from the time of initiation of the vigil to its end.

Thus, the strategy adopted by the vigilant computer users significantly affected both the mean amount of time spent on task, as well as the mean number of errors observed per block of trials. A significant interaction effect for strategy over time was also observed.

Discussion

The "Computer Concentration" game was modelled after several educational games which are commonly used in the elementary school system for the purpose of developing memory skills in children. Although guidelines are in place as to the maximum duration that students should be allowed to interact with a computer (i.e. approximately 20 minutes per session), vigilance problems were evident for the adult subjects studied herein within one half hour of beginning the task. The number of multiple exposure errors peaked for all groups within either the second or third block (i.e. the fifth to the twelfth games); that is, after the task was approximately twenty to forty percent completed. Regardless of the strategy used, the number of errors which had declined after peaking, once again rose prior to the end of the task. The colour complexity of the display did not appear to significantly affect performance.

Those that utilized a random search and selection strategy displayed a higher mean number of performance errors, and required on the average more time to complete the task than did those who selected more organized approaches to the task. The most efficient overall performance was demonstrated by the group who incorporated a verbal rehearsal strategy. Consistency in performance was best demonstrated by the consistent chunkers who relied on using the same strategy to complete each individual game of the computer task. Four of the five groups observed experienced an increase in mean performance error relatively early in the task, followed by a sharp decline and a second increase as the task neared completion. This decline in error has been likened to a runner catching his or her second wind [Yam85], but as has been demonstrated in other vigilance experiments, the decline is more often than not followed by an increase in mean error performance.

These findings may be surprising to those who have maintained that vigilance does not arise in real-world situations. On the other hand, it may have been that we were just not measuring the appropriate variable. Results such as these emphasize the need to refine old measures [Mil-Tak-Bar-Bro85] while at the same time acquiring new measures that are more closely tied to the structure and processes involved in attention maintenance. The concept of strategy, as studied herein, is just one such potential process which deserves our attention.

The results of this study are in agreement with the findings of others [Gia-Qui-Phi-His88, Koe-Bri-Zwe-Ver90, Koe-Bri-Hen-Ver89] in that the vigilant actors' strategies were associated with detection accuracy. The physical passivity of a computer task must not be generalized to the point of implying cognitive inactivity. Obviously, those subjects capable of increasing the strength of a memory trace via visual input and verbal rehearsal in combination, or the capacity of the working memory store via "chunking" strategies, were able to positively affect their own performances. Yet, unlike previously completed works, this study was able to combine subjective, anecdotal information with objective data in confirming the strategy utilized.

Strategy is a subject-controlled rather than an experimenter controlled variable. This study has incorporated a method of objective measurement in an attempt to better understand one of several cognitive processes involved in human-computer interaction. The extent to which these results may be generalized to other tasks is questionable. However, they do address the need to look beyond the mechanics of interaction and to explore the nature of underlying processes. In studying any form of human cognition, we have to address both the internal (or not so readily observable) and the external (readily observable) behaviours in connection with the task at hand. Traditional vigilance research methodologies (i.e. basic approach) may no longer be adequate to deal with the cognitive nature of today's microcomputer tasks.

References

[Ada87] J.A. Adams. *Criticisms of Vigilance Research: A Discussion*. Human Factors. 1987, Vol. 29, pp. 737-740.

[Bae-Bux87] R.M. Baecker, W.A.S. Buxton. *Readings in Human-Computer Interaction: A Multidisciplinary Approach*. Morgan Kaufmann Publishers, 1987.

[Che-Egg-Fle-Sas89] R.A. Chechile, R.G. Eggleston, R.N. Fleischman, A.M. Sasseville. *Modelling the Cognitive Content of Displays*. Human Factors. 1989, Vol. 31, pp. 31-43.

[Cra84] A. Craig. *Human Engineering: The Control of Vigilance*. In J.S. Warm (Ed.) *Sustained Attention in Human Performance*. John Wiley & Sons, 1984.

[Dav-Par82] D.R. Davies, R. Parasuraman. *The Psychology of Vigilance*. Academic Press, 1982.

[Eng84] E. England. *Colour and Layout Considerations in CAI Materials*. Computers and Education. 1984, Vol. 8, pp. 317-321.

[Gia-Qui-Phi-His88] L.M. Giambra, R.E. Quilter, P.B. Phillips, B.S. Hiscock. *Performance on a Sustained Attention Task as a Function of Strategy: A Cross-Sectional Investigation Using the Mackworth Clock Test*. 1988, Bulletin of the Psychonomic Society. Vol. 26, pp. 333-335.

[Han-War89] P.A. Hancock, J.S. Warm. *A Dynamic Model of Stress and Sustained Attention*. Human Factors. 1989, Vol. 31, pp. 519-537.

[Hoc-Gai-Col86] G.R.J. Hockey, A.W.K. Gaillard, M.G.H. Coles. *Energetics and Human Information Processing*. Martinus Nijhoff, 1986.

[Koe-Bri-Zwe-Ver90] H.S. Koelega, J.-A. Brinkman, B. Zwep, M.N. Verbaten. *Dynamic vs Static Stimuli and Their Effect on Visual Vigilance Performance*. Perceptual and Motor Skills. 1990, Vol. 70, pp. 823-831.

[Koe-Bri-Hen-Ver89] H.S. Koelega, J.-A. Brinkman, L. Hendriks, M.N. Verbaten. *Processing Demands, Effort and Individual Differences in Four Different Vigilance Tasks*. Human Factors. 1989, Vol. 31, pp. 45-62.

[Mil56] G. Miller. *The Magical Number Seven, Plus or Minus Two: Some Limits on Our Capacity for Processing Information*. Psychological Review, 1956, Vol. 63, pp. 81-97.

[Mil-Tak-Bar-Bro85]   J.C. Miller, N.Y. Takamoto, G.M. Bartel, M.D. Brown. *Psychophysiological Correlates of Long-Term Attention to Complex Tasks.* Behavior Research Methods, Instruments & Computers. 1985, Vol. 17, pp. 186-190.

[Nor83] D. Norman. *Some Observations on Mental Models.* In R. Gartner, L. Stevens (Eds.). *Mental Models.* Laurence Erlbaum Associates, 1983.

[Par87] R. Parasuraman. *Human-Computer Monitoring.* Human Factors. 1987, Vol. 29, pp. 695-706.

[Ram-Ram87]   G.K. Rambally, R.S. Rambally. *Human Factors in CAI Design.* Computers and Education. 1987, Vol. 11, pp. 149-153.

[Tra-Bow-Set-Pep90]   D.S. Travis, S. Bowles, J. Seton, R. Peppe. *Reading From Colour Displays: A Psychophysical Model.* Human Factors. 1990, Vol. 32, pp. 147-156.

[Wae89] Y. Waern. *Cognitive Aspects of Computer Supported Tasks.* John Wiley & Sons, 1989.

[Wei87] E. Weiner. *Application of Vigilance Research: Rare, Medium or Well Done?* Human Factors. 1987, Vol. 29, pp. 725-736.

[Yam85] S. Yamamoto. *A Study of VDU Operators' Information Processing Based on Saccadic Eye Movement and Response Time.* Ergonomics. 1985, Vol. 28, pp. 855-867.

Mastering the Machine:
A Comparison of the Mouse and Touch Screen for Children's Use of Computers

Chengdong Lu

Computer Science Department, U-155

The University of Connecticut

Storrs, CT 06269, USA

Telephone: (203) 785-7135

Fax: (203) 785-5572

E-mail: clu@venus.ycc.yale.edu

Douglas Frye

Department of Psychology

New York University

6 Washington Place, Room 306

New York, NY 10003, USA

Telephone: (212) 998-7871

Fax: (212) 995-4018

E-mail: frye@xp.psych.nyu.edu

ABSTRACT

Young children present special problems for the design of instructional computer interfaces. Because they lack the relevant language skills, the keyboard is not an effective input device for preschoolers. If young children cannot operate the computer, then even the best educational software will be unable to make them learn from it. We tested whether the mouse or touch screen provided an effective input device for preschoolers. The children were given four tasks, three of which involved selecting objects on the screen and one that required moving displayed objects. The touch screen showed clear advantages over the mouse on all four tasks. Both devices produced characteristic errors. The children tended to land on the touch screen with more than one finger. They often rotated the mouse while moving it, and had particular difficulty coordinating clicking and dragging. The results argue that the touch screen is the input device of choice for children's early computer use.

1. INTRODUCTION

A primary consideration in the use of computers with children, especially for educational purposes, is whether children are actually able to master the machine. Young children may have difficulty learning from software if they first must learn how to operate the computer. Recent research [Fry-Sol87] has shown that the keyboard can present a very difficult interface for preschoolers. In a first step to improve that interface, the present experiment tested whether the mouse or touch screen, known as indirect pointing device and direct pointing device[Shn87] respectively, might be a more effective input device for young children.

The mouse is now a fairly common auxiliary input device for personal computers. Folklore has it that even two- and three-year olds can make proficient use of the mouse as their main means of interacting with the computer. Although touch screens are currently less widespread, they are a well-established technology [Pic86]. Touch screens would seem to have some advantages compared to the mouse in that there is a direct overlap of the touch screen space and the display screen; in contrast, the mouse requires the child to map from a space on the desk to the space on the screen. Comparisons of the mouse and touch screen with adults has found touch screens are easier for novices to use, but tend to generate more errors and fatigue [Kar-McD-And84].

We compared the mouse and touch screen for preschool children. The children carried out the same four tasks with both devices. The tasks were selected to represent two basic types of operations common to these two interfaces. One operation was merely to select an object or objects on the screen. The other was to select an object or objects, move them to a specified place on the screen and release them. With a graphical or menu interface, these two operations can be made to be sufficient to perform all of the tasks necessary to control the computer.

The two types of operations can be broken down into subcomponents. Selecting an object requires positioning and confirmation. Moving an object adds the subcomponents of dragging and releasing. The two interfaces implemented these subcomponents differently. With the mouse, positioning is done by moving the mouse until the cursor is over the object. Confirmation is accomplished by clicking the mouse button so that the object is highlighted.

Dragging of a selected object is done by moving the mouse with the button held down. Releasing the button releases the object. For the touch screen, positioning and confirmation require touching or landing-on [Pot-Wel-Shn88] the object on the screen so that it becomes highlighted. Dragging and releasing can be done by selecting an object and then sliding one's finger across the screen. Lifting up the finger releases the object.

The four tasks in the experiment were formulated as very simple counting tasks because counting is an activity that preschool children are well practiced at and enjoy [Fry-Bra-Low-Mar-Nic90]. The mouse and touch screen interfaces were presented on two common microcomputers.

2. METHOD

2.1 Subjects

Twelve preschoolers aged 4 to 6 year from a local nursery school participated in the experiment. All were volunteers. All had the consent of their parents.

2.2 Design

Each subject had one session with the mouse and one with the touch screen. The sessions were on different days. Order of the sessions was counterbalanced over the group. A typical session lasted approximately 20 minutes. At the end of the the second session, each child was given a post-experiment questionnaire that asked in part which computer he or she liked better and which one was harder or easier to operate. All of the sessions were videotaped. All of the child's interactions with the computer were automatically recorded in a report file that could be printed out later.

2.3 Equipment

The session with the mouse was carried out on a Macintosh SE computer. The session with the touch screen used an IBM-AT equipped with a commercially available glass capacitive MicroTouch touch screen. The children operated the computers while sitting at two small tables. The mouse could be moved on a mouse pad placed on the top of the table, while the touch screen was mounted on a vertical screen. Both are within easy reach of the child. The programs run on the Macintosh and IBM were written in Allegro Coral Common Lisp and IBM C, respectively. To equate for the difference in screen size (9 inches diagonally for the Macintosh and 13 inches for the IBM), the size of the objects used in the tasks were scaled to each screen so that the proportions were identical. Data from pilot testing with adults was used to add timing loops to the Macintosh programs such that moving the cursor across the smaller Macintosh screen took the same amount of time as moving one's finger across the IBM screen.

2.4 Procedure

There were four tasks in the experiment: Left-Right Counting, Scattered Counting, Corner Counting and Stacking. The tasks were always done in that order. The first three tasks tested selecting an object i.e., positioning and confirmation. The fourth task required that objects be moved so it added the subcomponents of dragging and releasing. In all of the tasks, the objects were white squares displayed on a black screen. Each of the tasks consisted of three trials. In the first trial of each task, the experiment demonstrated what the subject was supposed to do. The two trials that followed were experimental trials. The computer's report file that was automatically created for each subject showed whether the subject selected the right object, selected a blank space (miss) or selected another object (wrong object). The main measure in the experiment was the seek time from one selection to the next.

Left-Right Counting. In the Left-Right Counting task, the initial display was a row of ten white squares with the most left square highlighted. If the subject touched that square, it returned to white, had the number '1' printed on it, and then the second most left square (the one next to the first) was highlighted and so on. At the end of the trial, the whole row of squares was labeled from left to right with numbers '1' to '10'.

    Scattered Counting. Scattered Counting was exactly the same as Left-Right counting except that the ten white squares were randomly scattered all over the screen. The squares were sequentially highlighted in a "random" order. All of the subjects saw the same three orders for the three trials. At the end of each trial, like the Left-Right counting, all of the squares were white and labelled with a number.

    Corner Counting. The objects in the corner counting task behaved the same way as in the first two tasks. Now, however, there were only four objects, one in each corner of the screen. The two experimental trials in this task were each composed of three screens that tested different movements across the display. The three screens are shown in Figure 1. The sequence of highlighting used caused the subject to select objects in each of the following seek directions: up, down, left, right, diagonal up-right, diagonal down-right, diagonal up-left, diagonal down-left. The Corner Counting task was designed to test the subjects' ability to select objects moving in these different directions because there is considerable research showing that young children have trouble processing and producing oblique lines [Ess-80][Fry-Cla-Watt-Watk86].

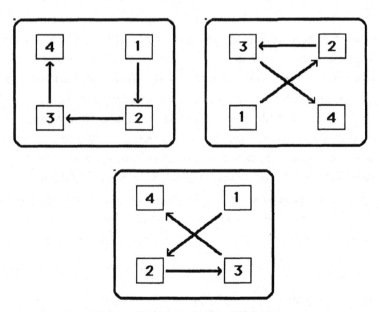

Figure 1. Corner Counting Pattern

Stacking. The Stacking task required the child to move objects. The initial stacking display showed five white square objects, numbered from one to five, arranged on the screen in an invisible cross ('+') pattern. The object numbered '1' was at the center point, the four others at ends of the cross. None of the objects was highlighted. The child had to move the objects to the center according to their numerical order. Movement of the objects on the screen was not constrained in any way. If child moved all of the objects to the center, they formed a stack and the next screen was presented. The two trials in this task were both composed of two screens of stacking, one were the objects were arranged in a '+' and one in an 'x'. These arrangements allowed the same comparison among different line orientations (down, left, up, right, up/right, down/right, up/left, down/left) as was done in the corner counting.

3. RESULTS

Overall. The main measure in the experiment was the time it took the children to carry out the various tasks with the two different input devices. The time results were analyzed in a 2 (Input Device) x 2 (Trial) x 4 (Task) repeated measures analysis of variance. Each of the main effects was highly significant (F's = 87.8, 16.6 and 11.5, respectively, p's < .001)[1]. The findings are shown in Figure 2. The main effects reveal that the children required less time to carry operations on the touch screen as compared to the mouse. In fact, they were three times quicker overall on each move with the touch screen. There was an improvement over trials for both devices. The significant task effect showed a difference among the tasks in difficulty. Post hoc Bonferroni t-tests (p < .05)[2] demonstrated that the moves in stacking took more time than in the other three tasks which did not differ from each other. There was one significant interaction (F (3, 88) = 5.5, p < .002) of trial and task. Analysis of simple main effects showed that the greater time stacking required, compared to the other tasks, was present on the first trial of the four tasks, but not on the second.

---

[1] Analysis of variances indicates that the difference between two input devices, between two trials and among four tasks are proven statistically significant at the probability of greater than 99.9%.

[2] These t-tests have more conservative probabilities to guard against finding chance differences when comparing multiple pairs of means.

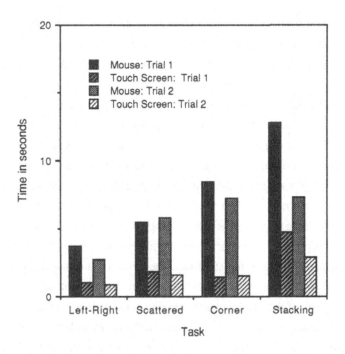

Figure 2. Average seek time for the mouse and touch screen on the four tasks in the two trials.

The children's errors in the experiment were analyzed in a similar 2 x 2 x 4 analysis of variance. Since in this experiment we were interested in the children's ability to use the two interface devices, not how well they could count, errors were defined as the occasions when the children missed an object they were trying to select, rather than when they selected the wrong object. The overall analysis only showed a main effect for task (F (3, 88) = 8.56, p < .001, M 's = 1.75, 2.69, 3.48, 39.12 for left-right counting, scattered counting, corner counting, and stacking, respectively). Post hoc Bonferroni t-tests (p 's < .001) confirmed that the children made more errors on stacking than in any of the other three tasks.

Individual Tasks. The individual tasks in the experiment fairly closely mirrored the overall results. In each of the four tasks, the touch screen required significantly less time than did the mouse. There were significant improvements in times across trials for the left-right counting and stacking but not for scattered or corner counting. It is not surprising that the children did not improve on scattered counting since the arrangement of the objects changed unpredictably across trials. The corner counting may have also been sufficiently complicated such that the children did not detect the pattern in the movements in the first trial.

In the two tasks that might have shown line orientation effects, i.e. corner counting and stacking, only stacking showed a significant line effect (F (3, 184) = 2.8, p < .05, M 's = 8.06, 4.85, 7.99, 6.6 for horizontal, vertical, diagonal left and diagonal right lines). Post hoc Bonferroni t-tests established that the horizontal movements were faster than the vertical and diagonal left. The line orientation effect did not interact with the type of input device.

Qualitative Description of the Errors. Observation of the children and of the videotapes revealed that many of the children were making the same errors with the two input devices. The most common problem the children had moving the mouse was that they would rotate the top of the mouse in the direction they were moving it. Seven of the twelve children showed this problem. Of course, this mistake had the effect of making the cursor move towards the top of the screen instead of to the left or right as the child desired. The children also experience some difficulty in using the mouse to click and drag objects in stacking. The majority of the children had to employ both hands on this task--one to move the mouse and one to hold down the button. Many of the errors with the mouse in stacking were due to the difficulty of coordinating the operation of the button with the movement. Often the children would hold down the button before they had moved the cursor on top of the object and then did not understand why they could not make the object move.

There were relatively few errors with the touch screen on the first three tasks. One drawback that three of the children discovered was that if they placed more than one finger at a time on the touch screen then the landing point was interpreted by the screen as being in between the two touch points. The touch screen also produced errors during stacking. Here the most common problem was that the children did not seem to be able to move their fingers across the screen at a constant speed so that they became disconcerted when the object that was behind their finger would suddenly catch up. Usually in this circumstance they would break contact with the screen and thus have to select and drag the object anew.

Questionnaire Results. Of the twelve children, six liked the mouse better, five preferred the touch screen and one said she like both. Ten of the twelve children thought that the mouse was harder to use than the touch screen.

4. Discussion

The results of the experiment indicate that although the preschool children were capable of using both the mouse and the touch screen, the touch screen provided definite advantages. The children at the beginning were nearly three times faster selecting and moving objects on the touch screen as compared to the mouse. There were no quantitative differences in errors between the two as measured by the times the children missed while trying to touch or click on an object. The children were equally divided as to which they preferred. Almost all of the children thought the mouse was more difficult to operate.

It is conceivable that the touch screen produced better results because the scaling done to compensate for the different screen sizes in the experiment was biased in some way. To evaluate this possibility, we tested an additional 15 5-year-olds. The new study employed a Macintosh II equipped with a MicroTouch touch screen. Because the touch screen on the Macintosh acts as an alternative to the mouse but does not replace it, it was possible to compare the two input devices using the same monitor, computer, and program. All of the children completed two trials of the Left-Right and Scatter Counting tasks for each input device. Since these tasks showed the smallest differences between devices in the first experiment, they were a strong test of the original comparison. The results showed that the touch screen again gave a clear time advantage $(F (1, 56) = 7.82, p < .01, M$'s $= 2.8, 3.5$ for the touch screen versus the mouse) ruling out a screen size explanation of the previous results.

In the original experiment, the task difference findings confirmed that moving objects in the stacking task was more difficult than just selecting them as was necessary in the left-right, scattered and corner counting tasks. Moving objects took much more time and the children made many more errors doing it. These results are in line with the analysis that selecting an object just requires positioning and confirmation whereas moving the object adds the subcomponents of coordinated dragging and releasing. We had anticipated on the basis of the previous literature [1] that when the child was required to select and/or move an object over a diagonal path they might have more difficulty than when they had to move across the screen horizontally or vertically. The only line orientation effect we found was that the children seemed to have the least difficulty with horizontals when they had to move objects in the stacking task.

Because the time differences with the input devices occurred in all four tasks, it would seem that the touch screen's advantage held for positioning and confirmation as was required for the object selection tasks as well as for dragging and releasing that were needed for the object movement task. The most important aspect of the touch screen for the children may be that its space is united with the space on the display screen. As such, the children could select an object merely by pointing to it. They could move the object just by passing their finger along the desired path on the screen. Releasing was done through the simple motion of lifting the finger off the screen.

The mouse, in contrast, required the child to map from a space on the desk to the space on the screen. Even though the children seemed to be able to do this mapping, it allowed the opportunity for more problems to occur. So, for example, when the children went to position the cursor, they may have mapped correctly from the cursor to the screen, but because many of them turned the top of the mouse in the direction they were moving it, they had difficulty putting the cursor on top of the object. The problems were even more apparent in moving objects in the stacking task. Here most of the children had to use both hands on the mouse--one to move it and one to hold down the button--to accomplish the dragging and release of the object. Not surprising, they had particular difficulty coordinating the button click and the movement. A characteristic error was to hold down the button before they had actually selected the object.

The children showed a practice effect over the two short trials in the experiment. It may be that with sufficient experience they would become as proficient with the mouse as they were with the touch screen. However, our results indicate that initially it may be much easier for children to start out using software that can be operated with the touch screen instead of the mouse. The touch screen would be likely to put educational software at the disposal of more children earlier as well as making the hurdles of their first experience with the machine easier to overcome. Of course, economics aside, the best solution would be for computers to have both input devices so that the user, even if he or she were five-years old, would be able to move between the two.

5. REFERENCES

[Ess-80] Essock, E. (1980).*The oblique effect of stimulus identification considered with respect to two classes of oblique effects*. Perception, 9, 37-46.

[Fry-Bra-Low-Mar-Nic89] Frye, D., Braisby, N., Lowe, J., Maroudas, C., and Niocholls, J. (1989). *Young Children's Understanding of Counting and Cardinality*. Child Development, 60, 1158-1171.

[Fry-Cla-Watt-Watk86] Frye, D., Clark, A., Watt, D. and Watkins, C. (1986) *Children's Construction Horizontals, Verticals, and Diagonals: An Operational Explanation of the "Oblique Effect"*. Developmental Psychology 22:213-217.

[Fry-Sol87] Frye, D. and Soloway, E. (1987). *Interface design: A neglected issue in educational software*. In proceedings of CHI+GI 1987 (Toronto, April 5-9). ACM, New York, 93-97.

[Kar-McD-And84] Karat, J., McDonald, J. and Anderson, M. (1984). *A comparison of selection techniques: Touchpanel, mouse and keyboard*. IBM Technical Report TR-51.0166, Austin, Texas.

[Pic86] Pickering, J. (1986). *Touch-sensitive screens: The technologies and their application*. International Journal of Man-Machine Studies, 25, 249-269.

[Pot-Wel-Shn88] Potter, R., Weldon, L. and Shneiderman, B. (1988). *Improving the accuracy of touch screens: An experimental evaluation of three strategies*. In Proceedings of CHI'88 (Washington, D.C., May 15-19). ACM, New York, 27-32.

[Shn87] Shneiderman, B. (1987) *Designing the User Interface: Strategies for Effective Human-Computer Interaction*. Addison-Wesley Publishing Company.

An authoring system for ITS which is based on a generic level of tutoring strategies

Pierre Marcenac

University of La Réunion, IREMIA

Faculté des Sciences, BP N°5

97490 Sainte-Clotilde

La Réunion

Tel : (262) 28-24-14

Fax : (262) 29-00-90

e-mail : marcenac@helios.iremia.fr

Abstract

This paper presents the results of a research which took place at the University of Nice-Sophia Antipolis during the last four years and is now continued at the University of La Reunion. It particularly describes the architecture of an authoring system, EDDI, which aims at providing a basis for the development of Intelligent Tutoring Systems (ITS). The system is not general to any domain to teach, but is more adapted to domains in which knowledge is structured and domains which require a well-known expertise, such as diagnosis.

The architecture of EDDI is object-oriented and is based on the description of a generic level which contains the tutoring strategies. The domain to teach is represented by a set of objects and relationships which form a semantic network.

The originality of the approach is to describe the generic level by looking at the structure of the objects and relationships of the domain to teach which are inspected during the tutoring session rather than the domain itself. For that, the tutoring strategies are classified according to three fundamental categories (strategies for guiding a session, decision strategies and application strategies). The whole architecture is described, a sample example of a tutoring session and some details about the implementation of EDDI are also presented.

Introduction

Today, it is more and more necessary for professionals to have systems which are able to transfer their expertise to different types of learner.

Intelligent Tutoring Systems (ITS) provide a way to train people and help them to become more productive, because they can adapt teaching to the different learners at any stage of the process.

Three distinct components are now well-known in such systems: a knowledge base which describes the domain to teach, a learner model which describes the learner's level and a tutor module which contains the way to transfer the expertise to the learner.

There are some existing tools to create such systems and actual solutions are:

- To create a system "custom-made", which involves a hard work from the system author. Indeed, the author must possess competence in computer science, pedagogy and, of course, expertise.

- To use an expert system, which has a recognized expertise, and to add a learner model and tutoring strategies in order to create an ITS. The aim of authoring systems is to provide a way to help people to build ITS, by defining both general learner model, tutoring strategies and expertise. Our work is integrated in this philosophy, but we suppose that the domain to teach exists in the system and is yet described by an expert.

Bite-Sized Tutor [BoCS 86] is an example of such systems. But, in this system, the generated ITS are organized around padagogical objectives rather than functional components such as the learner model. The domain to teach is separated in "bites", which cover these pedagogical objectives. Conceptual relationships between the different pedagogical objectives are also defined.

So, the tutoring strategies are not directly dependent of the domain to teach, but indirectly through pedagogical objectives.

The definition of a basis for the development of tutoring systems, which have to accomodate their behaviour to different learners, poses the problem of the separation between the domain to teach and the tutoring strategies.

The domain to teach, in our model, is represented with the help of a knowledge representation model, the model DEMO [Heri 86], which describes a set of objects and relationships types, coming from semantic networks, such as aggregation or generalization relationships. A set of inference strategies is also defined to complete the definition of this generic level. Each domain to teach is defined according to this model by an expert before the use of EDDI, i.e. upon the different structures of knowledge defined in the generic level. This leads us to connect the different tutoring strategies to this model, instead of connecting them directly to the expertise. So the generic level both defines the way to build expertises and the way to teach them. This allows us to consider the generic level as an abstraction level with regards to the expertise. We are now going to give more details about this generic level.

1. The shell of EDDI: a generic level

In our approach, we have just seen that all components of ITS are described in a generic level, as independent as possible of the domain to teach. The components which are described in this level represent a learner model and the different tutoring strategies.

1.1. The learner model

A learner model allows ITS to adjust their teaching to the learner, by working with the information the system can get on him and specially about his level on the domain to teach.
A study of J. Self [Self 87] shows that a learner model can be used to correct the learner, to choose the next step and to evaluate the learner. But, if this model is too complex, the system will not be able to exploit it [Self 88].

In our model, we choose to represent the conceptual level of the learner (what he knows), and a trace of the last sessions to be able to correct and evaluate the learner.
It is difficult to develop the conceptual level of a learner for any purpose, and existing models are different according to the problem they tried to solve.
However, even if the reasoning of the learner must follow the expert, we choose to represent the conceptual level by using an "Overlays" technique [CaGo 77]. This technique allows to represent the conceptual level of the learner as a subset of the domain to teach.
So, in our generic level, a learner model is described as a subset of the domain to teach. Then, in each ITS created, the conceptual levels of the different learners will be analysed by tutoring strategies and recognized as subsets of the domain to teach.

1. 2. The tutoring strategies

The major component of the system is a tutor module which is represented by a set of tutoring strategies. In our approach, we decompose these strategies in three categories according to the different functions an ITS has to perform during a tutoring session.

- The first function of a tutor module is to coordinate the whole session between the ITS and the learner. It must first generate a problem for the learner, and then control the interaction between the system and the learner.
To generate a problem to the learner, it is necessary to build a hierarchy of pedagogical objectives, which allows to decompose the domain to teach in different levels of difficulty. This hierarchy is not independent of the expertise and is given by the expert at the same time of the expertise itself.

Then the tutor has to control the interaction between the ITS and the learner and particularly has:

- to know if the learner is right or wrong,
- if he is wrong, to discover the cause of his mistake,
- to correct the learner by executing an intervention which seems to be the best,
- to let him continue or stop him if the problem is solved.

These functions are managed in EDDI by a set of strategies which represents what we call a tutoring session monitor. These strategies are executed in a cycle until the problem has been finished to solve by the learner. The management of the trace of the session is then performed.
The principal objective of the research is to look at the separation of tutoring strategies and the expertise. From a computer science point of view, this separation can be obtain with the help of object oriented approach and subsequent modularity. So EDDI does not take into account different learning theories, and the monitor is quite sample, stopping the learner if his investigations are not good. However, resulting ITS are not too rigid, because of the way the system correct him.
The second point (to discover the cause of the mistake) and the third point (to correct the learner by executing the "best" intervention) form the second and third categories of tutoring strategies and are discussed now.

- To decide which type of tutoring intervention would be applied in order to correct the learner if he is wrong, it is necessary to discover the cause of his mistake. These strategies dealing with the cognitive diagnosis and determining "what to do" are called in our system the "decision strategies", because they really have to decide the intervention to provide and are representative of the performance of the whole system.

An important and original part of this work is to look at strategies which may be connected with the different structures of the knowledge representation model, in order to provide general strategies for several domains. With this point of view, we can note that the decision strategies depend of:

- The object of the domain which is currently inspected by the system when the learner's mistake appears. More particularly, they depend of the structure of the current object environment. Indeed, the study of the different objects and relationships types around the current object allows to know what inference has to be performed to progress towards the solution.
For instance, a structure may indicate that there is something important to deduce at this time, or there is an efficient property to get, etc.

- The behaviour of the learner face with the current situation i.e., face to the learner's choice to continue his reasoning. For example, he may ask for some help, wants to explore others objects to get new values, infers a result, etc.

With these two observations, the decision strategies will be able to abort the undergoing process, in order to guide the learner about one of the right direction to look at. But, sometimes this primary intervention may be proved insufficient i.e., where the behaviour of the learner needs an extensive intervention.
This intervention necessary leads the system to analyse the cause of the mistake, and to transfer him the expertise he needs at this moment.
To analyse the cause of the mistake, decision strategies examine the conceptual level of the learner (which is represented by a subset of the domain to teach) in order to determine if the learner really knows data or reasoning strategies which are here involved in the next reasoning step.

Examples of decision strategies :

- During the problem solving, if the learner involves objects which are not connected in any way with the current one in the network, and there is something important to infer at this resolving step on the current object, then the system has to stop him, because the learner does not really know the current object environment. This mistake can be repaired by providing him some help or asking him a question to activate his memory.

The help that the system can provide comes directly from the study of the different relationships and objects types which are around the current object. For instance, in a medical domain, the system can say "the diagnosis is composed of a clinic observation and a test A and ...".

This information is obtained because the system looks at the current object (the "diagnosis" in this example) and realizes that the current object is surrounded with some aggregation relationships.

When a such relationship is present, the system can provide the message " ... is composed of ...", following the semantics of the relationship. This message is provided by application strategies which will be developed in the next paragraph.

- If the learner involves an object which is connected with the current one, but there is something important to infer at this step, two cases can be considered:

   - If this object is marked in the "overlays" model, which represents the learner conceptual level, then the learner knows that fact, so he would be able to deduce something here.
   In this case, it is judicious to ask the learner about what is to infer at this time, before going to the next step and let him continue. Indeed, if the learner forgets this step in his reasoning, some new facts or new values, which could help him to continue in the right way, will be missing.
   If the learner cannot answer this question, he does not know what is to infer, and the system has to give him some help about it. In this case, the mistake is an indication of a bad reasoning capability.

   - If the object is not marked in the "overlays" model, then the learner does not know what is to infer, and the system has to provide help to the learner. In this case, his mistake will also be considered by the system as a bad reasoning capability.

So, discovering the cause of the learner's mistake is done by looking at the learner model, and particularly at his conceptual level. The system makes then hypotheses about the nature of the mistake as follows:

- Bad control of data: this type of mistake involves bad processes or bad infered facts from the learner. The system detects them by looking at objects which are in the "overlays" model.

- Bad reasoning: this case does not generate, at the other side, any bad facts. The system may detect them by looking at relationships which are in the "overlays" model and by looking at the different relationships which are around the current object. That was the case in the previous example.

Indeed, we have seen earlier that the different objects and relationships which are "around" an object could provide information about what can be done next, in term of reasoning, by looking at the environment of the current object.

The intervention can be done by executing an application strategy. Such strategies are detailed now.

- Application strategies allow to realize the tutoring intervention which has been decided by decision strategies.

This kind of strategies correspond to "How to realize" the intervention according to the type of the mistake.

Like previously, the interest is to look at the interaction between these strategies and the structure of knowledge to be transferred, in order to provide generic tutoring interventions, which are based on the way that the domain to teach have been modeled rather than the domain itself.

With that aim, we can associate each structure in the generic level (objects types, relationships types and sample combinations of them) with different messages, for instance one message for the help to provide and one message for the question to ask to the learner.

The basis structures of the generic level are therefore enriched by semantics and determine an abstraction level with regards to the domain to teach.

Examples of application strategies:

- Strategies which provide some help to the learner:

  - If the environment of the current object X contains relationships such as aggregation ones, then provide to the learner: "X is composed of ...".
  - If the environment of the current object X contains relationships such as generalization ones, then provide to the learner: "X is (or may be) ...".

- If the environment of the current object contains a relationship such as a deduction, then provide to the learner the semantic of this deduction, and verify if he is now able to infer the right result.

- Strategies which provide a question to the learner:

   - If the environment of the current object X contains relationships such as aggregation ones, then ask the learner: "What are the components of X ?"

   - If the environment of the current object X contains relationships such as generalization ones, then ask the learner: "Can you give me the category of X ?".

   - If the environment of the current object contains a relationship such as a deduction, then ask the learner : "What can you deduce at this time ?"

However, an understandable constraint of an ITS is that the domain may have some influence on tutoring interventions and it is sometimes difficult to separate the domain and the way to teach it. So, in our system, some strategies may be directly connected with objects themselves in the domain to teach and could be seen as exceptions of the previous ones. This can be done in the architecture of the system by overloading.

Summary

The capabilities of the system to provide tutoring interventions in order to correct the learner are based on a better understanding of how knowledge is shaped and, of course, on knowledge the system has about the learner (the "overlays model" in the learner model, which is built successively during the different sessions).

Decision strategies are in charge of the choice of the intervention to provide to the learner and must analyse both the learner comportment and the structure of objects which are inspected. The great difficulty is here to discover the cause of the learner's mistake in order to choose the "best" tutoring intervention.

At the other side, application strategies are in charge of the realization of the intervention itself.

The interest of a separation in these two categories of strategies is the modularity of the object environment, allowing the user with the definition of new tutoring strategies (either decision or application strategies).

The strong point of these tutoring strategies is that most of them could be used again for an other expertise, because they depend of the way the exepertise is built. The poor point is the interaction degree between the learner and the system which constitue the actual limitation of EDDI.

2. Architecture of the system EDDI

The learner model and the tutoring strategies are included in a system and integrated in an architecture which describes three levels of representation. The first level describes the generic level and its different components. The second level describes the domain to teach and the different conceptual levels of learners. The third level describes the inference and the tutoring bases of facts.

The figure 1 below illustrates this architecture:

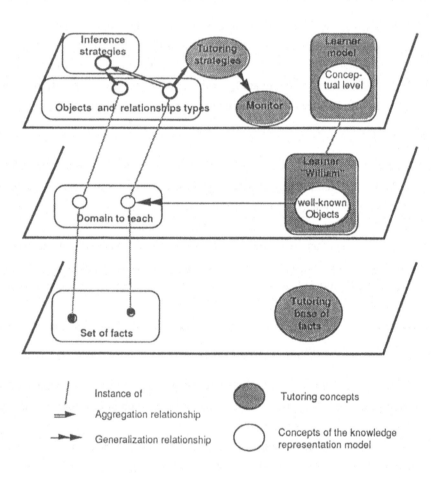

Figure 1: Architecture of the system

The first level describes:

- Generic concepts of the knowledge representation model DEMO i.e., the set of objects and relationships types and sample combinations of them. Some of these structures come from semantic networks, as aggregation and generalization relationships types [Heri 86]. Some inference strategies, which are based on these structures are also described. A more completed description of the inference engine can be found in [CoHe 89].

- The set of tutoring strategies, which represents the decision and application strategies and which are connected to the differents items of the knowledge structure.
- The generic model of the learner, including the description of the conceptual level, which can be seen as the set of objects and relationships well-known by the learner.

This level is independent of the teaching domain and allows the system with using the set of tutoring strategies for different expertises. A more complete description of the architecture of this generic level can be found in [Marc 90].

The second level describes the expertise and the different learners.
The expertise is obtained by application of the upper level to the teaching domain. The expertise is represented by a network of objects and relationships. All objects and relationships in this network are connected with the structures of the generic level by an instancation link. So, all objects of the domain to teach dispose of all tutoring strategies that could be applied on them during the session.

For instance, the representation of "a diagnosis is composed of a clinic observation" is realized by two objects ("diagnosis" and "clinic observation") which are connected by an aggregation relationship. These two objects and the relationship are connected by instanciation with the structures defined in the generic level i.e., an object type (the type "Concept") and a relationship type (the type "Aggregation").

The different learners are created by making a copy of the learner model which has been described in the generic level. For each learner, the conceptual level is represented by the different objects and relationships which are well-known by the learner. This is realized by connecting the objects and relationships of the domain to teach with the object "Well-known Object" by a generalization link. Then, during the tutoring session with the learner "William", the system can know if the current object is controlled by William by following this link.

The third level describes the base of facts of the problem, which is managed by inference strategies, and a tutoring base of facts. The tutoring base of facts is keeping trace of all tutoring interventions which have been applied on the learner and all objects of the domain which have been teached to him.

With this tutoring base of facts, the system can update, after the end of the session, the learner model by adding generalization links between the object "Well-known Object" of the learner "William" and the new objects of the domain that have been learned.

In the system, this update is more complicated, because the system also manages the different tutoring interventions which have been performed on the learner. This allows the system to avoid repetitions in the future and to manage the "best" intervention for learning all different objects of the domain.

3. Some elements of the implementation

The different ideas we have described above have been implemented with a prototype in the object oriented language Loops [BoSt 83]. The different knowledge structures of the generic level are represented in Loops by different classes.

These classes get one or more associated classes describing the different tutoring strategies which could be applied if necessary. The monitor is represented with the help of four classes describing its cycle: control of the inference engine, interpretation of the learner intervention, decision and application strategies.

The different objects and relationships of the domain to teach are specialized from classes describing the knowledge structure.

During the session, if an application strategy is necessary, it is executed by sending a message to the current object of the domain. This one inherits of the right strategy which is connected with the knowledge structure.

A medical expertise, the pulmonary tuberculosis, has been chosen to create an ITS and validate the approach. A sample example of how does the system work is given now.

4. Example of a tutoring session with an ITS created with EDDI

Description of how the system works:

-1- The learner begins a new tutoring session. This is done into the system by sending a message to the monitor.

-2- The first strategy of the monitor is then executed. This one generates a problem which is adapted to the learner by choising an object in the expertise.

-3- Inference strategies of the engine are then executed, allowing the system with knowing the current object environment.

-4- The learner progresses in the problem solving by telling the system the next objects to consider.

-5- The monitor has now to control the learner's progress. It must:

    5-a- consult the structure of the current object,

    5-b- execute tutoring strategies which allow to find the right tutoring intervention by looking at the learner's level (decision strategies),

    5-c- execute tutoring strategies which realize the intervention (application strategies),

    5-d- In this case, store this intervention in the tutoring base of facts.

-6- Strategies of the monitor are then executed again until the entire problem has been solved.

-7- At the end of the session, the management of the learner model is done by looking at the tutoring base of facts.

5. Conclusions

The system we have presented shows how tutoring strategies, which are essentially based on the knowledge structure, can offer an abstraction level towards the expertise and how an object- oriented approach helps in maintaining and evolving it.

However, the system is not complete at the moment and is limited by:

- The possibility of the problem generation: actually, the system is taking into account the learners objectives to generate problems, but is not yet able to manage the best problems.

- The global tutoring strategy: the strategies of the actual monitor are based on an approach where the learner has to follow the strategies of the inference engine and represent a straight tutor.

A practical experience with students will be necessary to measure what could be really learn with the system and its dialogues. Others expertises are now in study with the system to show how useful could be the approach.

References

[Bela 91] : F. BELAID, "Un système explicateur basé sur des formes de connaissances dans une approche objet", thèse, University of Nice-Sophia Antipolis, September 1991.

[BoSt 83] : D. G. BOBROW, M. STEFIK, "The LOOPS manual", Xerox corporation, December 1983.

[CaGo 77] : B. CARR, I. GOLDSTEIN, "Overlays, a theory of modelling for CAI", AI memo 406, MIT 1977.

[CoHe 89] : R. COURDIER, D. HERIN-AIME, "Object-based knowledge and reasoning designed for diagnostics", proceedings of AIPAC'89, Advanced Information Processing in Automatic Control, Nancy, France, Vol 1, 217-221, july 1989.

[Heri 86] : D. HERIN-AIME, "DEMSI", Thèse, University of Nice, september 1986.

[LaYa 87] : R. W. LAWLER, M. YAZDANI, "Artificial Intelligence and Education", vol 1, "Learning environments and tutoring systems", 1987.

[Marc 90] : P. MARCENAC, "EDDI : Contributions aux Environnements de Développement de DIdacticiels", thèse, University of Nice, december 1990.

[NiVi 88] : J. F. NICAUD, M. VIVET, "Les tuteurs intelligents : réalisations et tendances de recherche", TSI, vol 7, (1), 21-45, january 1988.

[Self 87] : J. SELF, "Student models : what use are they ?", proceedings of the IFIP TC3, FRASCATI, Italy, Ercoli & Lewis eds, 73-86, may 1987.

THE USES OF MULTIPLE STUDENT INPUTS IN MODELING AND LESSON PLANNING IN CAI AND ICAI PROGRAMS

Joel Michael, Allen Rovick

Department of Physiology, Rush Medical College

Chicago, Illinois 60612

tel. (312) 942-6426

e-mail: michael@rushvm.bitnet

Martha Evens, Leemseop Shim, Chong Woo

Computer Science Department,Illinois Institute of Technology

Chicago, Illinois 60616

Nahkoon Kim

Dong Duck Women's University

Seoul, Korea

ABSTRACT

Responding appropriately to student errors requires some model of the student with which to determine the most likely cause of the errors. In a conventional CAI program the model is implicit and is represented by the hard-coded relationship between errors and corrective feedback. In an intelligent tutoring system (ICAI program) student modeling can be done dynamically as student responses are generated. In both cases, multiple inputs about causally related variables obtained prior to any tutoring provides a rich source of information about the cognitive state of the student. As a result it is possible to produce a more robust student model and to generate a more effective sequence of lessons to repair the student's misconceptions. Examples of such an approach used in the implementation of both a CAI and a ICAI program are presented.

1. INTRODUCTION

In a tutorial interaction, whether conducted by a human teacher or a machine tutor, each student response elicits some response from the tutor. The particular response selected by the tutor will depend, of course, on whether the student's response was right or wrong. In responding to wrong answers, a tutor is faced with the task of determining, as specifically as possible, the reason for the wrong answer. Student errors may be due to factors as trivial as slips of the tongue or finger [Sup88], may arise from missing or incorrect information in the student's knowledge base, or can be as complex as incorrect ("buggy") problem solving procedures [Bur82]. Ideally, all attempts to remediate a student's wrong answer ought to address the specific cause of the error.

Diagnosing the source of student errors, the building of a student model, is a complex task that requires knowledge of the domain being taught, expertise in teaching in the domain, and information about the student's prior experiences and likely level of domain knowledge. This task is a difficult one for human tutors and still more difficult for machine tutors.

The literature on computers in education [Wen87; Yaz88] suggests a sharp difference between conventional CAI (computer-assisted instruction) programs and ICAI (intelligent computer-assisted instruction) programs. CAI programs carry out no dynamic student modeling, and can only implicitly represent the expert knowledge of a teacher. On the other hand, ICAI programs (intelligent tutoring systems or ITS's) have the potential to build a dynamic model of the *particular* student being tutored from the student's responses [Van88].

We will describe an approach to obtaining multiple student inputs *before beginning tutoring* that provides particularly rich information about the students' cognitive state, and can thus more readily provide information with which to build student models or determine the pattern of response selection. Examples of the use of this approach in implementing both a CAI program and an ITS in the same domain will be discussed.

2.   PREDICTING SYSTEM RESPONSES

We (JM and AR) have spent 15 years developing CAI programs in the areas of cardiovascular [Rov-Mic86], respiratory [Rov-Mic91] and acid/base regulation [LRM92]. These domains are systems having multiple, causally related components arranged in complex pathways that include negative feedback. The behavior of such systems is difficult for students to understand even when they have an understanding of the component phenomena or relationships that are involved. It should be noted that negative feedback systems are not confined to physiology; they are found in other biological domains, in social systems, and in human artifacts.

An understanding of such systems requires that the student have the requisite declarative knowledge about the relationships between individual components, and have the ability to predict the responses of the system to any perturbation.   The basis for understanding such systems is thus the construction of a qualitative, causal mental model of the system [see Gen-Ste83] and the development of an algorithm, a procedure, for correctly "running" it.

Parameter	DR	RR	SS
Cardiac Contractility	0	0	
Right Atrial Pressure	–	+	
Stroke Volume	+	–	
Heart Rate	0	+	
Cardiac Output	–	+	
Total Peripheral Resistance	–	0	
Mean Arterial Pressure	–	+	

Figure 1: The Prediction Table

Although our attempts at using computers to assist our students in achieving such understanding began with the use of a quantitative simulation, MacMan [DGS73], it soon became obvious that it was the ability of students to make *qualitative predictions* about the change (increase/decrease) in system parameters that was important. This led us to the development of what we call the Prediction Table (Figure 1).

The Prediction Table is a user interface with which to collect student responses requiring a minimum of keystrokes (CIRCSIM) or the mouse (CIRCSIM-TUTOR), a device to assist students to structure their thinking about the organization of the system, as well as a tool that enables us to infer a great deal about the students' cognitive state from the pattern of prediction errors that is present.

3. THE CIRCSIM AND CIRCSIM-TUTOR DOMAIN

CIRCSIM [Rov-Mic86], a conventional CAI program and CIRCSIM-TUTOR [SEMR91; WEMR91], an ITS, both assist students in mastering the behavior of the baroreceptor reflex, the part of the cardiovascular system that is responsible for maintaining a more or less constant blood pressure. (These programs are not intended to be used for initial learning about this system; they are to be used only after the student has attended lecture and done the assigned reading.) This is a complex system, made up of a large number of functional components arranged in a complex pattern, and with the overall configuration of a negative feedback system. Figure 2 is a partial representation of the system (it does not include all of the features of the system to be mastered by the student) that we call the concept map; seven of the parameters found in the concept map represent the core features of the system and these parameters are included in the Prediction Table (Figure 1).

Several features of this system need to be pointed out. The number of parameters included in the model is large. Several parameters have multiple determinants (RAP, SV, CO, MAP) and the assignment of priorities to these multiple inputs requires a deep understanding of the system behavior. Two parameters, RAP and CO, interact with each other according to two different relationships (RAP directly determines CO via SV, but at the same time, CO inversely determines RAP). Finally, the structure of this system is that of a negative feedback system such that any change in MAP, the regulated variable, leads to opposing changes in a set of reflexly controlled parameters (HR, CC and TPR) that restores MAP towards its normal value. The complexity of this system results in at least some of the parameters behaving in ways that most students initially find counter-intuitive.

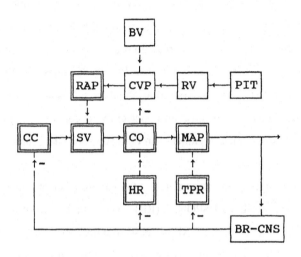

Figure 2: Concept Map of Domain (core features of system in heavy boxes; the negative signs indicate an inverse relationship)

4. THE IMPLICIT STUDENT MODEL IN CIRCSIM

In CIRCSIM the student is asked to predict the qualitative changes that will occur to the seven CV parameters as a result of one of seven different perturbations. The response of the system occurs in three different phases and the student must make predictions about each of them. The immediate response of the system to the perturbation is called the DIRECT RESPONSE (DR) and it always results in a change in MAP. This change then gives rise to a REFLEX RESPONSE (RR) that is organized to restore MAP to its normal level. Eventually, a new STEADY STATE (SS) is achieved which is the "sum" of the DR and RR responses.

It is possible to check the student's predictions one at a time and to respond in some meaningful fashion to each of the 21 possible errors. However, to do so would be to miss the important point about this system; parameters do not change their value independently of one another, and it is the relationships between parameters that we particularly want students to learn. For example, reference to the concept map (Figure 2) shows that the value of CO is determined by SV and HR (CO = SV x HR), a relationship that must always be true. If a student predicts (see Figure 1, DR column) that SV will increase and that HR will not change (whether or not these two predictions are correct) but then predicts that CO will decrease (again, it does not matter whether the prediction is correct), this pattern of predictions reveals a serious misunderstanding about the *relationship*. To respond to an error in CO in isolation would be to miss an opportunity to correct a major source of student misunderstanding (an identical argument can be made about the relationship MAP = CO x TPR).

Another example of the importance of the pattern of errors made by the student can be seen during the REFLEX RESPONSE (RR). The organization of the system is such that any change in MAP (as a DIRECT RESPONSE to a perturbation) will cause HR, CC, and TPR to change in the opposite direction in RR. An error in predicting one of these three parameters suggests a misunderstanding about the particular parameter and its determinant or its role in the reflex. On the other hand, an error in two or three of these parameters (Figure 1, RR column) suggests a misunderstanding about the organization and/or response of the reflex itself.

An analysis of common student errors in predicting the responses of the system led us to create a set of error patterns (present in the *multiple* responses available before tutoring) which, when present, trigger the appearance of text intended to remediate the assumed source of the particular error. This set of error patterns constitutes a kind of implicit, generic student model since it says that certain errors are *most likely to be the result of certain misconceptions or misunderstandings ("bugs")*. And it is this student model that allows us to select a response to present to the student that is most likely to remediate the problem that exists.

5. DYNAMIC STUDENT MODELING AND LESSON PLANNING IN CIRCSIM-TUTOR

5.1 Dynamic Student Modeling

The student modeling unit of CIRCSIM-TUTOR consists of a rule-based modeler and two different kinds of student models: an overlay model and a bug library [SEMR91]. This makes CIRCSIM-TUTOR quite different from both Guidon, which utilizes only an overlay student model, and Debuggy, which models the student only with a list of "buggy" procedures [see Wen87].

5.1.1 The Overlay Model

The overlay model consists of frames representing every parameter and every causal relationship in the concept map; entries in frame slots then show gaps in factual knowledge such as the determinants of causal relationships, the actual determinant (when more than one is present), relationships, values, equations, etc. The student's response is recorded as "c" (correct) or "w" (wrong) in each slot, along with the procedure number, and the response stage (DR/RR/SS). This information will be used by the instructional planner to make decisions based on whether the student knows or does not know about a particular item of knowledge.

5.1.2 The Bug Library

The bug library consists of frames representing each of the bugs we have collected (from experience tutoring students using CIRCSIM, a paper-and-pencil experiment, and from tutoring sessions conducted by JM and AR). The presence of a bug is detected by a particular pattern of prediction errors (see the examples in Section 4).

5.2 Dynamic Instructional Planning

The instructional planner is the central component of the tutor. It is responsible for generating instructional goals, deciding how to teach the selected goals, monitoring and criticizing the student's responses, and determining what to do next at each point during a tutoring session [MEB88]. The instructional planner of CIRCSIM-TUTOR consists of two parts: a lesson planner and a discourse planner. The lesson planner is responsible for generating global lesson plans which are then carried out by the discourse planner. By combining the capabilities of the lesson and discourse planner the system can provide globally coherent and adaptive instruction to the student [WEMR91].

5.2.1 Goal Generation

The generation of tutoring goals is guided by a set of explicit domain-dependent heuristics designed by our domain experts (JM and AR) that ensure that the most serious "bug" is identified and tutored first. Consider the case where the student modeler has determined from an analysis of the RR predictions that the student does not understand the organization of the reflex and also is confused about the causal relationship between RAP and SV and the relationship between SV and CO. The lesson planner retrieves the information from the student model (both "bug" library and the overlay model), applies the goal generation rules, and generates the lesson goals dynamically. The result is a set of lesson goals in the goal stack (Figure 3).

5.2.2 Plan Generation

The lesson planner picks the first goal on the goal stack and expands it into a set of subgoals (i.e., topics) by applying two sets of rules, one for selecting tutorial strategies for achieving goals and the other for selecting pedagogic tactics to execute these strategies. For instance, if the goal is "teach the causal relationship between the two parameters," then the fired strategy rule is "tutor the prerequisites," with the pedagogic tactical rule "ask about: determinants, actual determinant, relationships, and correct value" firing next. The result is the hierarchical plan shown in Figure 4.

Order	Lesson Goals
1.	NEURAL-CONTROL (TPR)
2.	CAUSAL-RELATION (RAP,SV)
3.	CAUSAL-RELATION (SV,CO)

Figure 3: Generated Lesson Goals in the Goal Stack

The subgoals generated at the tactical level are kept in a subgoal stack which is used by the discourse planner to pick the next topic. The tutoring goals remain in force until they are dynamically changed by the planner (because of changes in the student model). This process provides globally coherent, consistent tutoring.

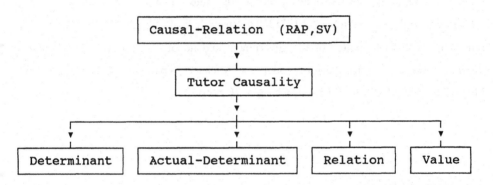

Figure 4: Generated Plan for "Causal-Relation (RAP,SV)"

6.   DISCUSSION AND CONCLUSIONS

CIRCSIM is a conventional CAI program that is nevertheless quite effective at repairing student misconceptions [Mic-Rov91]. We believe that much of its power derives from its ability to detect quite complex "bugs" through.the analysis of multiple inputs in the Prediction Table. Furthermore, the significance of the "bugs" for which it looks has been validated by extensive experience by expert tutors in this domain. Thus, the implicit student model in CIRCSIM, and the lessons that are taught based on the model, both contribute to the effectiveness of this program.

We have implemented an ITS, CIRCSIM-TUTOR, that utilizes the same source of information about the student's cognitive state, the Prediction Table, and a similar "bug" library. This should result in a student modeler that can provide a lesson planner with the information required to most effectively deal with individual students and their particular cognitive problems.

Student modeling remains one of the most difficult problems for developers of intelligent tutoring systems. We believe that the use of multiple simultaneous inputs and the assembly of a "bug" library from the experience of expert human tutors represents an important step in developing this instructional technology.

Acknowledgements: This work was supported by the Cognitive Science Program, Office of Naval Research under Grant N00014-89-J-1952, Grant Authority Identification Number NR4422554 to the Illinois Institute of Technology and Grant N00014-91-J-1622, Grant Authority Identification Number AA1711319 to Rush Medical College. The content does not reflect the position or policy of the government and no official endorsement should be inferred. Address all correspondence to Dr. Joel Michael, Department of Physiology, Rush Medical College, 1750 W. Harrison, Chicago, IL 60612.

7.   REFERENCES

[Bre-Jon88]Barbara Brecht, Marlene Jones. *Student models: the genetic graph approach.* International Journal of Man-Machine Studies. 1988, Vol. 28, pp. 483-504.

[Bur82]Richard R. Burton. *Diagnosing bugs in a simple procedural skill.* In Derek. H. Sleeman, John. S. Brown, (Eds.), *Intelligent Tutoring Systems.* Academic Press, 1982, pp. 157-183.

[DGS73]C. John Dickinson, C. H. Goldsmith, D. L. Sackett. *Macman: a digital computer model for teaching some basic principles of hemodynamics.* Journal of Clinical Computing. 1973. Vol. 2, pp. 42-50.

[Gen-Ste83]Dedre Gentner, Albert L. Stevens (Eds.). *Mental Models.* Lawrence Erlbaum Associates, 1983.

451

[KEMR89]Nakhoon Kim, Martha Evens, Joel A. Michael, Allen A. Rovick. *CIRCSIM-TUTOR: An intelligent tutoring system for circulatory physiology*. In Hans Maurer (Ed), *Computer Assisted Learning (Proceedings of the International Conference on Computer-Assisted Learning*. Springer-Verlag, 1989, pp. 254-266.

[LRM92]Jun Li, Allen A. Rovick, Joel A. Michael. *ABASE: A hypermedia-based tutoring and authoring system*. Paper accepted for presentation at the 4th ICCAL Conference, 1992.

[MEB88]Stuart A. Macmillan, D. Emme, M. Berkowitz. *Instructional planner*. In Joseph Psotka, L. D. Massey, S. A. Mutter (Eds.). *Intelligent Tutoring Systems: Lessons Learned*. Lawrence Erlbaum Associates Inc, 1988, pp. 229-256.

[Mic-Rov86]Joel A. Michael, Allen A. Rovick. *The uses of CBE in teaching the functions of complex systems*. Proceedings of the 27th International Association for the Development of Computer-based Instructional Systems Meeting, New Orleans, LA, 1986, pp. 43-48.

[Mic-Rov91]Joel A. Michael, Allen A. Rovick. *Does use of a CBE program assist students to learn?* Federation of American Societies for Experimental Biology Annual Meeting, Atlanta, GA, 1991, p. A1115.

[Rov-Mic86]Allen A. Rovick, Joel A. Michael. *CIRCSIM: An IBM PC computer teaching exercise on blood pressure regulation*. XXX International Union of Physiological Sciences Congress, Vancouver, Canada, 1986, p. 318.

[Rov-Mic91]Allen A. Rovick, Joel A. Michael. *GASP-PC: A computer teaching program on the chemical control of breathing*. Federation of American Societies for Experimental Biology Annual Meeting, Atlanta, GA, 1991, p. 474.

[SEMR91]Leemseop Shim, Martha Evens, Joel A. Michael, Allen A. Rovick. *Effective cognitive modeling in an intelligent tutoring system for cardiovascular physiology*. Proceedings of the 4th Annual IEEE Symposium on Computer-Based Medical Systems, Baltimore, MD, 1991, pp. 338-345.

[Sup88]Patrick Suppes. *The future of intelligent tutoring systems: problems and potentials*. Presented at ITS-88, Montreal, Canada, 1988.

[Van88]Kurt VanLehn. *Student modeling*. In Martha C. Polson, J. Jeffrey Richardson (Eds). *Foundations of Intelligent Tutoring Systems*. Lawrence Erlbaum Associates Publishers, 1988, pp. 55-78.

[Wen87]Etienne Wenger. *Artificial Intelligence and Tutoring Systems*. Morgan Kaufmann Publishers, Inc., 1987.

[WEMR91]Chong W. Woo, Martha Evens, Joel Michael, Allen Rovick. *Dynamic instructional planning for an intelligent physiology tutoring system*. Proceedings of the 4th Annual IEEE Symposium on Computer-Based Medical Systems, Baltimore, MD, 1991, pp. 226-233.

[Yaz87]Masoud Yazdani. *Intelligent tutoring systems: an overview*. In Robert W. Lawler, Masoud Yazdani (Eds.). *Artificial Intelligence and Education, Vol.1*. Ablex Publishing, 1987, pp. 183-201.

Project NESTOR: New Approaches to Cooperative Multimedia Authoring / Learning

Max Mühlhäuser[1], Joachim Schaper[2]

[1]: Universität Kaiserslautern, FB Informatik, AG Telematik
Erwin-Schroedinger-Str., W-6750 Kaiserslautern, Germany
Phone [+49] (631) 205-2992, Fax ...-2640, email: max@informatik.uni-kl.de
[2]: Digital Equipment GmbH CEC Karlsruhe
Vincenz-Prießnitz-Str. 1, W-7500 Karlsruhe, Germany
Phone [+49] (721) 6902-18, email: schaper@kampus.enet.dec.com

Abstract: The paper reports about Nestor, a prototype of an integrated authoring / learning environment built on locally and remotely distributed multimedia workstations. The four main parts of Nestor are: an object-oriented kernel and hypermedia base system, distributed multimedia support, distributed cooperation support, and generic customizable authoring / learning support. The motivation, background, and organization of project Nestor are described as well as the overall architecture and the four main parts are described. At present, major parts of the Nestor prototype are functional, selected tools and features have led to either software products or public domain software; missing parts are expected in '92. Full integration of all parts, 'serious' courseware development, and evaluation and use are approached in parallel, partly in cooperation with external partners.
Keywords: Computer Aided Instruction, Instructional Design, Authoring / Learning Environment, Object-Orientation, Hypertext / Hypermedia, Navigation, Multimedia, Computer-Supported Cooperative Work (CSCW).

1 MOTIVATION

1.1 Advances In CAI, Instructional Design, and Computing

Considerable efforts are being made to facilitate education and training with computers. Computer aided instruction (CAI)[1] has evolved from inflexible and imperative instructional software to much more adaptive courseware, AI was introduced with intelligent tutoring systems [SEL88, MAL88], and hypermedia is proposed as an approach for structuring the content domain and for modeling the conceptual domain [JON89, JOM90].

Courseware production (courseware engineering) has received increasing attention in the science of Instructional Design (ID) [REI87, WER86]: serious courseware production should follow a detailed and well-described *authoring process* (courseware lifecycle).

---

[1] CAI is used as the embracing term for computer *aided / based instruction / learning / education / training*

In parallel, the underlying technology has advanced a lot: powerful workstations with high-resolution graphics and window-based dialog systems were introduced. Fast local *and* wide-area networks, soon operating in speeds up to 'Gigabits per second', render co-operative work (group authoring / learning) and interactive distance learning feasible. The advent of multimedia workstations (with audio, video and imagery) further promotes co-operative and distance learning and enhances the instructional potential of computers.

1.2 Open Issues In CAI

Despite all these advances, many issues of ID and CAI are unresolved:

- 'Integrated authoring / learning environments' have only recently gained large interest [RBJ88, BNG90, IAL90, HAG92]; much of the above mentioned authoring process is still carried out using paper and pencil or in the authors head, and if more than the implementation phased is 'computerized', then non-integrated tools are used, working on incompatible data.
- Until now, production of 'good' CAI material required a domain expert (experienced in the contents and concepts to be taught), an ID expert (experienced in the authoring process and in ID knowledge such as teaching strategies, courseware structuring / presentation rules, learner models, etc.), a computing expert, media experts for the media used, and a networking / groupware expert if distance learning or group author-ing / learning were to be supported. Usually, the term 'computer aided' means, in a given domain, that programming-level issues are hidden from the user and that expert knowledge (concepts, models, etc.) is 'computerized' in a flexible and reusable way; CAI is still far away from that stage.

Accordingly, it is the goal of project NESTOR to

- enable the creation and delivery of a fully functional authoring / learning environment for the future needs of various educational institutions,
- 'computerize' the ID domain, with an emphasis on cooperative work and multimedia,
- facilitate the use of modern computing and networking technology, thereby protecting investments in courseware development from changes in the underlying technology.

1.3 Project Members And Organization

Nestor is a joint project of German Universities on one side and the Digital Equipment CEC research center in Karlsruhe on the other. The universities include Kaiserslautern, Karlsruhe, and Freiburg. At present, the active Nestor team comprises some ten research-ers and fifty students.

Nestor does not intend to build each and every component of a fully functional environ-ment in productizable quality. Rather, it is based on a common 'architecture' from which

important areas of research or advanced development were identified and investigated. These major areas of research make up four different 'workpackages':
1. Object-Oriented kernel / Hypermedia base system
2. Multimedia support
3. Cooperation support
4. Authoring / learning support.

Orthogonal to the workpackages, Nestor distinguishes two different 'tracks':
- In the *research track*, fields of research were and are investigated following the usual approach (state of the art analysis, modeling, concept and prototype development).
- In the *AD track*, the focus is on robust and easy-to-productize results, in line with standard technology. The areas investigated are smaller; results expected faster.

Obviously, the University partners put a stronger focus on the research track, whereas the Digital Equipment CEC emphasized the AD track (with substantial overlaps).

1.4 Status

In the AD track, Nestor has delivered a large number of software services and tools, some of which were either put into the public domain or turned into products. In the research track, virtually all the conceptual achievements in each of the workpackages were turned into functional prototypes (all built using the programming language Smalltalk-80 [GOR83]). These prototypes, together with services and tools from the AD track, are currently integrated into a Nestor environment prototype for use by selected application sites. In the course of the year 1992, several stages of this integration work will be reached and serious course development will take place. In the meantime, both the research and the AD track will be continued in some selected areas.

2 SYSTEM OVERVIEW

2.1 Basic Design Decisions

Nestor deliberately invested a lot of time and effort into the requirements analysis and early design phases, trying to match the conflicting goals 'use of state-of-the-art technology' (such as multimedia, groupwork, object-orientation, and hypermedia), 'protection in investment' (e.g., through independence from underlying hardware and operating systems), and 'computerization of ID knowledge'.

We can only cite some of the most relevant observations and decisions here which were made during this phase:
- The large number of tasks to be carried out in the authoring process (we identified over forty!) does not justify an equal number of tools in a computer-supported author-

ing environment; rather, generic tools have to be identified which can be customized to do several tasks;

- Object-oriented technology is the most essential part of the Nestor 'software philosophy'; it is considered the only feasible approach to guarantee both extensibility and integration to a satisfying degree (cf. 3.1);
- Apart from object-orientation, the use of hyperstructures (hypertext / hypermedia approaches) is the second most important common philosophy (cf. 3.1);
- The area of hypertext / hypermedia requires more thorough investigation and the development of fundamental formal concepts, as a key to reusable machine-readable descriptions of ID knowledge (cf. 3.4);
- Both the areas of multimedia and of cooperation are dominated by isolated tools and by specialized example applications. Few generic concepts are available, little development comfort is provided, especially if one considers domain experts with little computing / programming knowledge as the 'developers'. Substantial efforts are necessary in both fields to provide generic system support on one hand and user-friendly development support on the other hand (cf. 3.2, 3.3).

2.2 Macro Architecture

From the requirements as outlined above, Nestor developed a shell-structured architecture which allows different levels of functionality to be represented ('general', like collaboration, 'low-level support', like database services, 'high level entities', like authoring process descriptions), so that the architecture can serve as a reference model for an implementation. The building blocks of the architecture are in line with PETE, [DEL91] which is the reference architecture for DELTA an initiative of the european community on learning and technologies. A major issue in the Nestor architecture was the reflection of object-oriented design, used as a common design principle throughout.

Fig. 1 shows the architecture at a macro level which will be explained 'inside out'. The *NICE object kernel* provides basic object-oriented functionality for the other shells. For the first Nestor prototype, NICE is derived from the Smalltalk-80 language.

The next level keeps a set of *kernel extensions*, comparable to modules that can be plugged into the 'NICE object kernel' like extension boards into the backplane of a computer. Each of these 'kernel extension' modules supplies functionality which is orthogonal to all others. Example modules are for example hypermedia support, task support or versioning. Every object in outlying shells of the system can use such functionality. System extensions can be made by plugging new modules into the kernel.

The next shell is split into two parts. The *lower* part, called *system services*, provides access to or implements basic services like databases or network services; the object-oriented encapsulation approach is used to hide the complexity of such services from the user, offering easy-to-use service objects. Support is given for integrating or accessing future services as extensions to the current system. The *upper* part, *'generic tools'*, contains a set of tools through which the author or learner interacts with the environment.

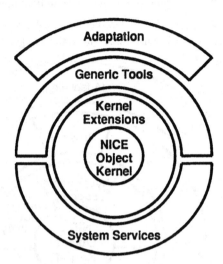

Fig. 1: Nestor architecture, macro level

2.3 Nestor Publications

Much has been published about Nestor, such as results of our very intensive analysis and design phase (e.g., [MÜH90a], [MÜH90b]), details of the research carried out in the individual workpackages (cf. [DÜL91], [BHL91], [RÜD91], [MÜH91], to cite one for each workpackage), comprehensive technical reports and more. In contrast, this paper should be thought of as a brief review of the concrete integrated Nestor environment which is finally on the way. It is considered a valuable reference for individuals who are interested in integrated authoring / learning environments, a field of greatly increasing importance.

3 WORKPACKAGES

3.1 Object-Oriented (O-O) Kernel and Hypermedia Base System

The NICE object kernel provides a 'virtual machine' interface to the 'kernel extensions' in the shell surrounding it. It serves the following four objectives:

1. create a technology independent layer which keeps the residual parts of Nestor (functions, tools and tasks) portable.

2. provide an interpretable runtime environment, so that incremental changes to the system do not require rebuilding the whole system; in addition, an interpreted system

may serve both as a course interpreter, which can load parts of a course incrementally and as (an interpreted) course language, suitable for course distribution, testing etc.

3. serve as the 'central record' for all user interactions with the base system. This is important for both user modeling purposes and configuration management (versioning).

4. allow for the smooth integration of new features (e.g., new tools, new base system functionality, new tasks which 'customize' the system in general).

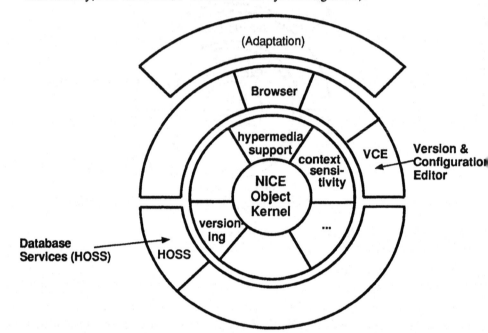

Fig. 2: Nestor modules related to object kernel and hypermedia base syste

A lot of attention has been paid to the use of 'hyperstructures' (Hypertext / Hypermedia systems) recently, as a way of managing information in general, and courseware in particular [SMW88, JOM90]. Hyperstructures allows modeling of the 'units of information' which make up the course material (as 'hyperstructure nodes') *together* with the manifold relations between them (as 'links'), *plus* - of equal importance - relations to and among 'didactic aspects' of this material. As an example one might regard an author writing the learning objectives, connecting them to the corresponding 'semantic networks', determining the significance for instructional strategies, etc. The term hypermedia denotes the combination of 'hyperstructure' information management with support for multimedia information [MUL90]. As such, hypermedia is of central interest in Nestor, and the first and most important kernel extension is the one for 'hypermedia support'.

A particular advantage lies in the Nestor dual o-o / hypermedia approach [DÜL91] which allows a node or link to represent either static information *or* executable code.

The human interface aspect of Nestor o-o / hypermedia workpackage is threefold: 1) a specific human interface exists for every node or link (which is provided as a media-specific editor if the node/link is a known media type, or as an object-class specific human interface), 2) multimedia layouts are generated using a synchronization/layout tool from the multimedia workpackage, and 3) a graphical interface for coping with the overall 'hyperstructure' is provided. This interface is provided as a particular mode of the generic tool 'structure editor'; it allows users to 'browse' through hyperstructure networks and to trigger the individual node/link human interfaces.

The o-o/hypermedia system services consists of an object server called 'HOSS' which provides client/server based storage and retrieval for every object in the system (compare with [SMZ87]); HOSS provides flexible and extensible transaction strategies, ranging from traditional approaches (i.e., strict atomicity and consistency etc.) to very liberal strategies.

Versioning is a kernel extension valuable for both system services (e.g., for implementing backtracking in transactions) and generic tools (e.g., for provision of versions of courses, hypermedia networks, etc.).

The *context sensitivity* kernel extension is a means for complementing the standard encapsulation mechanism for objects which causes identical behavior of objects, independent from the context of usage. In sophisticated courseware authoring or delivery, it is often desirable to have objects behave differently according to the 'environment' context (workstation capabilities etc.), purpose of usage, user's background knowledge, etc.

Object-Orientation has so far proven to be a very adequate base technology for Nestor, providing, e.g., the modularity required in a multi-party multi-year project. Major drawbacks, like lacking support for information modeling, versioning and context sensitivity, have been compensated by the kernel extensions.

The first version of the Nice o-o/hypermedia workpackage excluded versioning and context sensitivity. It has long been prototyped and handed over to all Nestor groups as a basis for their development. Versioning and context sensitivity were investigated in parallel to the general use of the residual workpackage.

Due to the orthogonal concept of the kernel extension shell, generic tools and system services can be built on an arbitrary selection of kernel services.

3.2 Multimedia Support

The multimedia support comprises three classes of generic tools and two system services:

1. The *layout editor* provides support for designing and enforcing the layout of different individual (input or output) media objects (nodes). It helps to organize the screen real estate, i.e. the spatial layout of so-called presentation units (units of information to be taught) and interaction units (control buttons, question forms, etc.).

2. *Score editor:* in such a 'unit', not only the spatial (display) layout has to be organized properly, but also the *timing* of the discrete and continuous media combined; for such synchronization purposes, Nestor offers a 'score editor'. In contrast to e.g., Quick-time™, Nestor offers support for distributed media and enhanced support for 'virtual timelines' which are more flexible than 'hard' real timelines, e.g., when the unpredictable timing of user interactions is to be considered. Harmonization with upcoming international standards such as HyTime are being considered

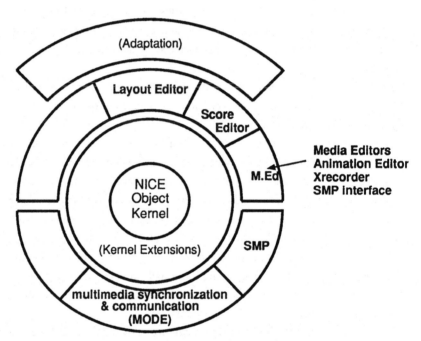

Fig. 3: Nestor modules related to multimedia support

3. *Media editors* feature support for the generation (capturing), modification, and presentation of the media types used: compound document (multifont text, graphics, and embedded 'foreign' media), image, audio, video, animation, and X-Windows I/O. Except for the last three, Nestor imports (provides interfaces to) commercially available tools. For video editing, Nestor provides an interface to SMP (see below). A tool called *Xrecorder* allows recording of display output and user input from/to X-Windows applications, saving them as a special media type 'Xclip' for later playback (again with Xrecorder). An *animation editor* implements rudimentary support for computer based animations. Media editors are developed in the 'AD track'.

4. *SMP (software motion picture);* the video editor just mentioned, allows for display of

video frames on a regular workstation, without the need for dedicated video peripherals. This is due to the system service support given by 'SMP'. SMP supports video capturing, digitalization, compression, storage and transmission via regular devices (i.e., standard hard disks and computer networks), and decompression and dithering/display using standard (gray-scale or color) workstation monitors. For capturing from an analog video source (camcorder, video recorder, laser disk), the author's workstation of course needs to be equipped with special hardware (video framegrabber), but no particular support is needed on the learner side (quality and real-time behaviour are, in fact, a matter of the workstation hardware capabilities, in particular the processor). SMP has largely influenced the *DECmedia* set of products.

5. *MODE (multimedia communication / synchronization* [BHL91], compare with [HSA89]): achieves, network transparency in a distributed workstation environment. In the case of multimedia objects, this means that a user can refer to an arbitrary set of multimedia objects from any workstation in the network, and request operations to be performed on them, without the need to care about the network topology and load, or the current locations of the objects, or special hardware (e.g. for compression/decompression), or the 'target' workstation for i/o (if interactive operations such as 'display' are to be performed). The MODE service developed as part of the research track provides such support. A first prototype was internally released.

3.3 Cooperation Support

As a sophisticated authoring process may involve teams of authors, support for cooperative work is required. In addition, a learner's motivation and acquired skills may be considerably augmented if a course is prepared and executed as a group learning activity, which is best supported by computer means. Finally, even the best courses can not fully replace the interaction of learners and domain experts (called 'tutors' in Nestor), an activity which requires technical support especially in 'distance-learning' scenarios.

In summary, cooperation support is a rather central requirement for advanced authoring / learning environments. Therefore, the ability to develop course-*specific* group learning and tutoring support requires that cooperation support not be 'hardcoded' into dedicated tools. Instead, this functionality has to be made available in the the form of customizable 'building blocks' to the authors so that they can flexibly create the kind of cooperation support they foresee for a course under development. Cooperation support in Nestor provides such generic, reusable 'building blocks' in form of a *kernel extension called 'collaboration'* (see fig. 4).

Specific tools help the author to use the 'collaboration' building blocks to construct the specific cooperative interactions and rules intended. In addition, Nestor system programmers can use these building blocks in order to provide cooperative authoring support (planned in the future as part of 'adaptation', see below). All collaboration tools are integrated into the *'GroupIT'* generic toolset. GroupIT and the collaboration kernel extension are developed in the research track of Nestor ([RÜD91, compare with [KRK88]).

Cooperation support in window-based workstations requires additional system service support which allows to share already exisiting software modules (tools, courseware) among a set of learner workstations. Such support is provided as part of an X-Windows extension package *'shX'* (sharing facility for X-Windows), a major activity within the AD track. shX is complemented with a customization and human interface tool *'shX helper'* which provides several cooperation strategies. At present, two simple such strategies are implemented, a *'polite'* strategy where a user may request control over the application, to be confirmed by the user who owns control (all users see the output of the application, but only one at a time owns control over it), and an *'anarchy mode'* where every user may input to the application at any time.

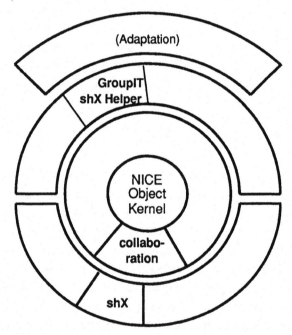

Fig. 4: Nestor modules related to cooperation support

3.4 Authoring / Learning Support

Although the whole Nestor architecture was developed in accordance with authoring/learning related requirements, the shells described above are obviously general enough to be suitable for any other target. Only the outermost shell 'customizes' and 'complements' the architecture for the very specific requirements of authoring/learning. *Customization* means, to a large extent, to provide additions and parameter sets to the generic tools. E.g., the generic tool 'structure editor' can be used, in different customizations, for gathering the learning objectives, for recording a storyboard in preparation of a video shootage, for creating the hyperstructure which represents the contents (domain knowledge) of a course, etc. In order to customize a specific tool, we use:

1. tool-specific customization languages, if available (for highly customizable tools, such as the structure editor mentioned above)
2. specific window / menu layouts, created by use of the generic 'layout editor' tool,
3. templates with pre-defined entries, and
4. computer-assistance for using the tool in the given context (customization).

Complementing, here, relates to four kinds of *processes* or *models*:

1. authoring processes (as introduced in the former sections),
2. instructional strategies (processes which drive the execution of courseware according to instructional design theory, see below),
3. learner models (for acquisition and representation of knowledge about the learners, such as preferences, background and actual knowledge, misconceptions, etc.)
4. instructional transactions, i.e. generic atomic 'building blocks' for courseware (inter)actions, such as 'procedure simulation', 'multiple choice question', etc.

The two general mechanisms used within Nestor for creating processes and models are called *IDObjects* and *PreScripts* ([MÜH91, compare with [ZEL89, STF90]).

IDObjects denote the contents of a Nestor-wide object library, built using the NICE o-o/ hypermedia base system (cf. 3.1). It consists of passive objects, which represent, e.g. the 'instructional transactions' just mentioned or simple learner models ('stereotypes'). It also includes active objects which support, e.g., the first authoring process implemented (a derivate of the authoring process used within courseware development groups of Digital Equipment). IDobjects are developed as part of the 'AD track' of Nestor.

PreScripts are an approach for formal modeling of hyperstructures and navigation. Navigation is the term commonly used for the activity of a user (here: learner) who 'wanders' through a hyperstructure, displaying/executing the nodes s/he is navigating through, and making 'navigation decisions' about the next link. In sophisticated hypermedia-based authoring/learning environments, the navigation support (support for navigation decisions, or even fully system-controlled navigation) implements the above mentioned 'instructional strategies'.

In PreScripts, 'families' of hyperstructures are formally defined with a graph-grammar based approach (cf. [NAG89]), using an easy-to-use graphical interface. As such, PreScripts represent the construction rules for, 'hyperstructures adequate for tutorials', or 'hyperstructures adequate for game-based courses', etc. Along with the construction rules for a family of hyperstructures, the generic navigation rules are stored in the same way-which make up a specific instructional strategy. For example a specific 'tutorial' strategy, a specific 'game-based course' strategy etc. A state-transition based approach is used to describe these navigation rules. In order to build a specific course, an author has to 'instanciate' the construction rules of a family and build a specific hyperstructure of that family (whose nodes and links, by the way, can refer to existing ones). Doing this task, the author 'inherits' the navigation rules from the PreScripts, i.e. he does not need to care about deep ID knowledge and instructional strategies. The two major gains of this approach are as follows:

1. Since instructional strategies are 'programmed' for a whole family of hyperstructures, they become highly reusable
2. The formal models can be used to 'syntax-direct' a graphical editor, so that the author is computer-supported in entering the domain knowledge in a consistent way.

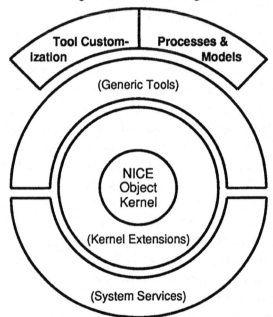

Fig. 5: Nestor modules dedicated to authoring /learning support

4 SUMMARY

A brief overview was presented about Nestor, an approach to a cooperative multimedia authoring / learning environment. As an ongoing multi-party project, Nestor continues to add and enhance components according to the coarse architecture. Major parts of the Nestor prototype are functional. Selected tools and features have led to software products or public domain software. Integration and add-ons are expected in '92. Serious courseware development and evaluation will be approached along with external partners.

5 REFERENCES

[BHL91]   Blakowski, G., Hübel, J., Langrehr, U.: *Tools for Specifying and Executing Synchronized Multimedia Presentations*. Proc. 2nd Intl. Workshop Network &OS Support for Digital Audio and Video, Heidelberg, Germany, Nov. 1991.

[BNG90]   Bessagnet, M.N., Nodenot, T., Gouarderes, G., & Rigal, J.J. (1990). *A New Approach: Courseware Engineering*. in: [WCC90], pp. 871 - 877.

[DEL92]   Commision of the european communities, *DELTA - Exploratory Action - Final Technical Report*, Ref: DE2205 May, 1991

[DÜL91]   Dürr, M., Lang, S.: *Hypertext & Object-Orientation: The Dual Approach*. Proc. BTW'91, Kaiserslautern, 3/1991, 258-270, Springer IFB 270.

[GOR83]   Goldberg, A., & Robson, D. (1983). *Smalltalk 80 - The Language and Its Implementation*. Addison Wesley, Reading, MA etc.

[HAG92]   El Hani, O., Gouarderes, G.: *Standardized Architecture for Integrated Open Courseware*. Proc. ICCAL'92 (this volume), New York: Springer 1992.

[HSA89]   Hodges, M.E., Sasnett, R.M., & Ackerman, M.S. (1989). *A Construction Set for Multimedia Applications*. IEEE Software, January 1989, pp. 37 - 43.

[IAL90]   Ibrahim, B., et al.: *Courseware CAD*. in: [WCC90] pp. 383 - 390.

[JOM90]   Jonassen, D.H., Mandl, H.: *Designing Hypermedia for Learning*. ASI Series, F-67, Berlin: Springer 1990

[JON89]   Jonassen, D.H. *Designing Hypertext for Learning*. in: Scanlan, M., D'Shea, T.: New Directions in Educational Technology, New York: Springer 1989

[KRK88]   Kraemer, K., King, J.: *Computer-Based Systems for Cooperative Work and Group Decision Making*. ACM Comp. Survey 20 (1988), 115-146

[MAL88]   Mandl, H., Lesgold, A.: *Learning Issues for Intelligent Tutoring Systems*. New York: Springer 1988

[MÜH90a] Mühlhäuser, M. *Hyperinformation in Instructional Tool Environments*. Norrie, D., Six, H.: Compuer Assisted Learning. Berlin: Springer 1990, pp. 245 - 264

[MÜH90b] Mühlhäuser, M.: *Issues of Integrated Authoring/Learning Environments*. [WCC90], pp. 419-424

[MÜH91]   Mühlhäuser, M.: *Hypermedia & Navigation as a Basis for Authoring/Learning Environments*. Jl. Educational Multimedia & Hypermedia, 1 (1991), pp. 51-64

[MUL90]   *Multimedia Communications*. Comp.Comm (Special Issue) 13 (1990).

[NAG89]   Nagl, M.: *Graph-Theoretic Concepts in Computer Science, LNCS 411*, Berlin: Springer 1989.

[RBJ88]   Russell, D., Burton, R.R., Jordan, D.S., et al.: *Creating Instruction with IDE: Tools for Instructional Designers*. Xerox PARC, Report No. P88-00076, 1988

[REI87]   Reigeluth, C.M.: *Instructional Theories in Action*. Hillsdale, NJ: Lawrence Erlbaum Ass., 1987

[RÜD91]   Rüdebusch, T.: *Supporting Interactions within Distributed Teams*, Gorling, K., Sattler, C.: Intl. Workshop on CSCW, IFIP COST14, Berlin 1991, pp. 17-33

[SEL88]   Self, J.: *Artificial Intelligence and Human Learning -- Intelligent Computer-Aided Instruction*. London: Chapman and Hall Ltd., 1988

[SMW88]   Smith, J.B., Weiss, S.F.: *Hypertext*. CACM 31 (1988), pp. 816 - 819

[SMZ87]   Smith, K., Zdonik, S.: *Intermedia: A Case Study of the Differences Between Relational and O-O DBS*. ACM SIGPLAN Notices 22 (1987), 452-465.

[STF90]   Stotts, P.D., Furuta, R.: *Hierarchy, Composition, Scripting Languages, And Translators for Structured Hypertext*. in: Streitz, N., et al.: Hypertext: Concepts, Systems & Applications, Cambridge: Univ. Press, pp. 180-193, 1990

[WCC90]   Proc. IFIP Fifth World Conference on Computers in Education, WCCE/90, Sydney, Australia, July 9-13, 1990,

[WER86]   Wedman, F.J., & Ragan, J.T. *Instructional design for developing computer-based learning materials*. AEDS Journal, V.19 (2-3), 1986, pp. 124-136.

[ZEL89]   Zellweger, P.T. *Scripted Documents: A Hypermedia Path Mechanism*. Proc. ACM Hypertext '89 Conf., Pittsburgh, PA, Nov. 1989, pp. 1 - 14.

Design and Implementation of Courseware for Teaching Programming Languages

T. Müldner, R. Blondon

Jodrey School of Computer Science

Acadia University

Wolfville, Nova Scotia, Canada B0P 1X0

(902) 542-2201 Ext. 331

email: solid@aucs.acadiau.ca

Abstract

The first part of this paper describes requirements of courseware for teaching a computer programming language. Besides typical requirements for a CBT material such as interactivity and availability of hypertext facilities, additional needs must be satisfied. For example, courseware in question must be able to interact with tools such as compilers and specialized editors. The second part of our paper deals with the implementation issues of a hypothetical courseware on an IBM PC compatible machine. We examine the feasibility of using existing authoring systems and then describe the implementation of the core program using Asymetrix ToolBook and of the other components using the development tools for the Microsoft Windows 3.0 programming environment. We show that the selected environment can be used to create a powerful learning system which provides a variety of hypertext facilities such as user modifiable links, margin notes, and highlighting. In addition, this system includes a specialized programming editor and a database of examples that are essential for learning a programming language.

1 Introduction

The concept of hypertext has been introduced many years ago [Bus45] but its popularity has grown tremendously during the last few years. At the same time, Computer Based Teaching (CBT) has gained widespread recognition. The interest seems to have been generated by industry and business enterprises. For many years, banks and insurance companies have been using CBT materials to train employees to use new equipment, procedures, forms, etc.

(that's why CBT sometimes stands for "Computer Based Training").

In the past, CBT presentations were based on the "book metaphor", that is they were showing one page (screen) at a time. Lack of interaction with the user and the fact that reading the text from the screen is much slower than from the printed page resulted in a rather limited success of this technology. Lately however, this technology has changed dramatically. More and more CBT materials are becoming highly interactive. Many are also taking advantage of non-standard input/output in a form of multimedia (such as voice I/O, still and live images, etc.). Even more importantly, CBT and hypertext technologies have merged, giving the user the power of well recognized hypertext features such as non-linear, associative organizations and dynamic modifications of selected parts of the material (such as a user-modifiable index).

There are many interesting CBT materials (courseware) which have been developed for teaching university level courses, particularly science courses. Surprisingly, when compared to the amount of courseware developed for courses such as chemistry, physics, and mathematics, there has been very little developed for learning computer science [Mak87]. In this paper, we deal with the problem of designing and implementing courseware to teach computer programming, for example programming in Pascal. Our requirements for such courseware are not trivial. First of all, we wish to provide most of the facilities of hypertext, including links, global margin notes, bookmarks, highlighted text, table of contents, and the index. We demand that all these facilities can be modified by the user, in particular the user could create new links between two parts of the courseware[1]. As for specific needs of our courseware related to its intended role of teaching a programming language, the most basic requirement is to provide the learner with the ability to edit and compile programs without exiting courseware. For this sake, our courseware has to be able to interact with the editor and the compiler. In addition, our approach is example-based (see [Nea89]), that is courseware is to be integrated with the repository of examples. This idea comes from the analysis of a learning process, during which students use examples to understand new concepts. Examples are particularly useful for programmers who have a limited knowledge of a programming language because the example can be used to recall the syntax or semantics of the language. Also, programmers often modify existing code to suit their needs. Thus, a modifiable repository, which is easy to query, would be an enormous help. To support queries, examples may have semantic annotations (see [Nea89]). The above requirements are not typical CBT requirements and we discuss them in Section 2.

We have reviewed several existing authoring systems (programming systems

---

[1]This feature is seldom available in commercial hypertext systems.

specifically designed for creating courseware). While looking for the authoring system that can satisfy our requirements, we have limited our consideration to IBM PC compatible machines. We have found no "ideal" authoring system which would allow us to create the required learning environment. We have chosen the ToolBook authoring system, produced by Asymetrix [Too], because it allows easy interfacing with programming tools that can be developed to run under Miscrosoft Windows 3.0 [Win], and because it allows all requirements described in Section 2 to be satisfied relatively easily. Specifically, ToolBook can be used to develop a driver program, which implements the core of courseware. The remaining components (the editor, the repository of examples, and the compiler) are Windows 3.0 applications which communicate with the driver program through Dynamic Data Exchange (DDE). We present our findings in Section 3 and discuss implementation issues in Section 4. In Section 5 we summarize our experience with the existing authoring systems. In this paper, we assume that the reader is familiar with the basic concepts of hypertext (see [Tom91]).

2 Courseware for Teaching Programming Languages

We claim that courseware for teaching a programming language has to have special features in addition to those available in interactive hyper-documents. Our approach is based on our own experience with the process of learning programming languages and on a series of papers by Neal, see [Nea89]. Below, we describe two sets of requirements which we have developed. The first set includes requirements of an "electronic book" (hyper-document) and is based on our observations of a behaviour of the learner using a classical book. Specifically, learners take advantage of built-in facilities, such as the table of contents, index, and references (both forward and backward). They extend these facilities by making margin notes, "global" notes (on separate sheets of papers attached to the book), inserting bookmarks, and highlighting selected sections.

We wish to provide all of these navigational tools in our courseware with the provision that they can be modified by the learner (this provision does not exist in most hypertext systems). For example, the learner should be able to add new entries to the existing index, create or remove highlighting [Ber86]. References throughout the text are implemented in hyper-documents by links. We use two kinds of links. The first kind of a link connects a selected area of the screen (such as a word or an icon) with a pop-up window. This window is opened when the link is activated (for example by clicking the mouse button on the source of the link). In this paper, we call such a link a *local* link because its destination window appears on the same screen as the source. Local links help to avoid cluttering the screen with an excessive amount of information. Only basic information is shown and the learner can get more information by activating the links. A particular application of local links is to produce help windows (for example, a window containing information about icons). Destination windows may be of different kinds — pop-up windows which disappear when the learner releases the mouse button, sticky windows which stay on the screen until the next time the learner clicks the mouse button, or more permanent windows which have to be explicitly closed (for example, by clicking a special "close" icon within the window). For the second kind of a link, called a *global* link, the destination window appears on a different screen than the source. This type of link may be used when text contains a reference to text in a different section of the material. We require that both kinds of links are available both for the author and the learner. Besides the requirements described above, there are other requirements to help alleviate the well known problems of hypertext, namely cognitive overload and a disorientation in hyperspace (see [Tom91]). To deal with these problems, we require that the controls used to navigate through the courseware be organized as pull-down menus and mouse activated icons. Following the IBM standard, menus usually appear at the top of the screen and icons at the bottom. Since it is easier to access icons than to select items from pull-down menus, the controls that are used most often are invoked by icons, and those that are used less often are invoked by menu items. For example, the control to modify the background color of the screen would be implemented as an item in a pull-down menu while the control to access the index would be implemented as an icon.

The author of courseware should be able to create various visual cues, such as icons, "sliders" (for indicating progress throughout the courseware), etc. Various fonts, foreground colors, and background colors should also be used.[2]

Below we list all facilities which must be available to the author or learner when creating or using courseware:

Requirements 2.1

The following facilities should be available to the author and the learner:
- margin and global notes
- local and global links
- highlighting
- index

---

[2] Note that in this paper we do not discuss other useful features available in most authoring systems for example graphics, animation, answer analysis, etc.

- table of contents
- foreground and background colors[3]
- pull-down menus and icons (author only)
- fonts and formats of the text (author only).
- easy translations into other languages, for example French[4] (author only).

Now, we describe specific requirements related to our goal—creation of courseware for teaching a programming language. As we mentioned before, our approach is example-based. As soon as the user learns a new concept, she or he can experiment with the related example. For this sake, our courseware has to include several components. First of all, an editor should be available for editing source code. This editor should probably be a specialized programming editor with features such as folding functions into their headers (such as in the occam environment). The compiler should be fully integrated with the editor, so that the learner can easily compile the code (for example, by clicking the icon in the editor's window). For programming languages that support separate compilation, even more sophisticated facilities should be available to allow for easy creation of projects consisting of several source files (compare the make facility [Ker84]). The repository of examples would be useful only if the learner can easily locate the required example and then use them in the programming editor. The first issue we have to deal with is that of querying—the learners can find the existing examples if they know what they are looking for. In [Nea89] it has been suggested to add semantic annotations to the programming examples, for instance the annotation "string concatenation". It seems to be appropriate to impose a structure on the set of examples, rather than having a single flat universe. For example, there may be two classes of annotations—a name for the class of examples, such as string, and name of a specific operation within this class, such as concatenate. Indeed, this classification is used in a theory of abstract data types or classes in object-oriented programming (see [Str86]). To facilitate querying, we require that the repository includes a browser which provides a hierarchical view of the existing examples (the idea of a browser is borrowed from the Smalltalk environment [LaL90]). The second issue related to the design of the repository is its interface with the editor. One possibility would be to show the example, and then allow the user to copy it to the editor. We have decided that a better solution would be to

---

[3] Changing colours by the learner is a part of user customization. This customization includes other parts of the user interface such as menus and icons.

[4] The so-called internationalization of courseware can be greatly simplified by constructs built into authoring systems, such as aliases available in ToolBook V1.5.

integrate the editing environment and the repository. This means that once a programming example is located, it is shown in the editor's window. Thus, there may be several editor windows opened at once, and the learner can move from one window to another (for example by moving the mouse pointer). Below, we summarize our requirements related to teaching a programming language:

Requirements 2.2

The following facilities should be available to the learner:
- multi-window editing environment with specialized functions such as folding and (possibly separate) compilation
- repository of examples. Examples can be located using the browser and placed in the editing window. The repository can be modified by the learner by removing existing examples and adding new examples (supplied with proper semantic annotations).

This completes our presentation of requirements for courseware for teaching a programming language. To implement courseware, one can use any programming language, such as C [Ker78] or C++ [Str86], or use a specialized software, called an authoring system. Once we have designed our courseware, we have started looking for an authoring system which would be powerful enough for our purposes. It turned out that this was not an easy task.

3 Authoring Systems

Lack of space prevents us from providing a complete discussion of various authoring systems. Here, we briefly describe why most authoring systems did not suit our needs. The first problem we have encountered was a lack (or limited power) of hypertext facilities. But the real stumbling block was the feasibility of the implementation of Requirement 2.2. Although some authoring systems provide built-in programming languages, these languages are not powerful enough to write specialized tools such as editors. It became clear that we had a choice of either giving up authoring systems and implementing everything in a standard language such as C or C++, or implementing the teaching core of courseware, here called the driver, in an authoring system and interfacing it with other components (such as the editor). The former alternative has been rejected because using the authoring system saves a lot of time and programming effort when implementing frame-based presentations, text, formats, graphics, etc. We have decided to try to interface the existing tools with the driver (for example to request the editor to read a new file and merge it with the file currently being edited). From the beginning of our project, we have decided to consider only authoring systems running on IBM PC compatible machines with 386/486 CPUs, and focused our attention on two authoring systems running under Microsoft Windows 3.0 because most Windows applications can communicate through Dynamic Data Exchange (DDE)[5]. The two systems were IconAuthor [Ico] and Asymetrix ToolBook. We have selected ToolBook for further investigations because (unlike IconAuthor) it comes with its own, object-based programming language (OpenScript) which was powerful enough to implement Requirements 2.1. This choice turned out to be correct, although we could not use the existing tools (for example we could not find editors running as Windows applications). Thus, we have decided to implement our own tools, such as an integrated editor and repository of examples, in Borland C++ [BC++], as Windows applications. This solution would allow us to establish the required communication protocols between the driver and our tools. The next section describes the implementation of Requirements 2.1 using ToolBook.

4 ToolBook Implementation

In this section we provide a brief description of implementation of Requirements 2.1 in ToolBook version 1.5. This authoring system comes with a number of built-in functions, such as creation of pull-down menus, and its own object-based programming language called OpenScript. It is the power and flexibility of this language, combined with enhancements introduced in version 1.5 that allow us to implement the required hypertext facilities.

The ToolBook documentation describes OpenScript as an object-oriented programming language. When building a *book* (ToolBook applications are referred to as books) you normally begin by placing objects (rectangles, text fields, push-buttons, etc.) on the screen. Each of these objects have certain built-in properties which describe the object (eg. an object's "position" property describes that object's screen position). The user can add other properties to each object. These objects may also contain *scripts* which in turn contain *handlers* which are made up of OpenScript statements. These handlers allow objects to respond to *messages*. There are many different kinds of messages, each of which are generated by specific events. As an example, a 'buttonDown' message is generated whenever the left mouse button is pressed down. This message will be sent to the object

---

[5] It should be noted that links described in Section 2 are sometimes called cold links, while links used to transfer data are called warm links (see [Tom91]). Thus, DDE channel can be considered to be warm links.

under the mouse cursor (referred to as the *target*). If the target object contains a 'buttonDown' handler, the handler will be executed, otherwise the message will be sent to the next highest object in the ToolBook object hierarchy (e.g. if a push-button is the target for a message but it doesn't have a handler for the message, the message will be sent to the page, or if the page doesn't have a handler for the message, the message will be sent to the book, and so on). Handlers may send other messages (either built-in or user-defined) to other objects (or to their own object) via the "send" command. They may also use the "forward" command to send the message that they where invoked by to the next highest object in the ToolBook object hierarchy. Messages may carry parameters.

One of the first things that we looked for when selecting an authoring system was its ability to allow the creation of moveable, resizeable windows. ToolBook made this quite easy. Although ToolBook version 1.5 includes a dialog box utility and a Dynamic Link Library (DLL) which allows Windows-style dialog boxes to be easily built and integrated into ToolBook applications, dialog boxes are not resizeable and cannot carry out complex operations. We decided to make our own "windows" by building them out of ToolBook objects. Although these "windows" were not standard Windows-style windows, they served their purpose. The objects which made up the windows were given scripts so that they could send and respond to messages and to manipulate properties of themselves or of other objects. This allowed them to easily interact with other objects, both in the window and in the rest of the book. These objects were *grouped* to make them easier to work with as a whole (e.g. changing the position of the group would move all of the objects together). To simulate the opening and closing of windows, we made the objects either visible or invisible by changing the "visible" property of their group. Many of these windows that we built had to be able to appear on many different pages. To accomplish this, the objects were put in the *background* (in ToolBook, pages can share a common background) and their "drawDirect" properties were set to true. This allowed them to be visible over foreground and other background objects which had their "drawDirect" properties set to false.

Margin and global notes were displayed and edited in windows. By the way of the design of windows as described above, only one window was needed to display all of the notes. Each page had a hidden text field which contained the text of that page's margin notes. There also was a unique page in the book (the first page) which had a hidden field which contained the text of the global notes. These hidden fields contained properties which held the size and position of the window while the window was closed. When the window was opened (shown) the handler which opened it set the size, position, and contents of the window according to the text and properties of the hidden field. When the window was closed (hidden), the handler closing it changed the text and properties of the hidden field to reflect the updated size, position, and contents of the window.

Local links were implemented much like margin notes—only one window was used and a hidden field contained the text and size and position of the window. However, there could be many links and hidden fields to a page. To create a link, its source had to be defined first. This involved selecting text. We had to write our own text selection handlers in order to keep track of what text was selected and to prevent the learner from modifying the selected text. If we had used ToolBook's built-in facilities for selecting text it would have left the text open to modification by the learner and it would have been too easy to loose track of what text was selected. After the source text of the link was established the "create link" mechanism was invoked. It asked whether the link should be local or global. If a global link was desired the learner would be asked which page was the destination of the link. If a local link was desired, a window (like a margin note window) would open to allow the leaner to edit text. Each page had a user-defined property organized as a list which allowed the book to keep track of the sources, destinations, and types of links on that page. When the reader was finished creating a link a line was drawn under the source text. It would seem natural that we would have used the "hotword" object of ToolBook to implement links, but we chose not to. When ToolBook shows where a hotword is it puts a box around it. This box does not indicate whether the hotword opens a window or goes to another page. We decided to draw colored lines under the source text of the links (to indicate their types) and to manage the links ourselves. Different types of links can have different colors of the underlining lines, e.g. forward references use a red color and background references use a green color. After a link was set up it could then be invoked by clicking it. There is also a mechanism to allow the learner to remove links by clicking them.

To prepare text for highlighting, text was selected in the same fashion as selecting the source for a link. To highlight the text, transparent rectangles were created and put over top of the selected text. A user-defined property of the page was used to keep track of the highlighting rectangles. The learner could remove highlighting by clicking on the highlighting rectangles after invoking a "remove highlight" mechanism.

To determine the positions and dimensions of the underlines (for links) and highlighting rectangles, we wrote handlers and functions which utilized the ToolBook function "textFromPoint()" and performed multiple binary searches on the pixels within the selected text's field. Given the fact that OpenScript is not very fast, this operation was quite slow. Our method of underlining and highlighting has, at present, one limitation—text which may be underlined or highlighted is not allowed to move (it may not be in a scrollable field for example). This was done because we have found no simple way to determine how much the underlines and highlighting rectangles should be moved when the text moves. We could remove this particular limitation if we introduced another limitation—that text fields in which links may be created and highlighting may be performed contain only one type and size of font and the font is mono-spaced.

The index and the table of contents windows required a fair amount of message passing between the objects which made up the windows. The index allowed the learner to find, add, and delete references and to add and delete page numbers of references. The table of contents was not modifiable but it allowed the learner to "fold" and "unfold" chapters in order to hide or show sections within a chapter. Most, if not all, of the complexity of the index and table of contents windows was in getting the objects to communicate with each other. In order to simplify the design of these windows they could be implemented as separate books. For example, the index could be in a book all of its own and the main book would then be able to run the index book (in another instance of ToolBook) and communicate with it through DDE. When the window is designed this way there is no need to implement your own move and resize mechanisms for the window.

Over 16 million colors are available in ToolBook, although most display devices cannot display this many. In this case Windows will approximate or dither some of the colors. Colors of objects on the foreground or background may be chosen from these colors. Each background has its own background color. In order for different pages sharing the same background to have different background colors, some mechanism has to be implemented which changes the background color of the background as pages are entered. One limitation on text colors is that all text in a single field must be of the same color.

ToolBook allows easy creation of pull-down menus and icons. The "add menu" and "add menuItem" commands of OpenScript allow menus to be added to the main menu bar. The "remove menu" and "remove menuItem" allow you to remove any menu or menu item from the main menu bar. When a menu item is selected, a message (whose name is the label of the menu item selected) is sent to the current page. A handler for that message can then take action. For creating icons, ToolBook allows objects (and groups of objects) to contain handlers which perform actions when the object is clicked.

ToolBook allows text to be in any font which is available to Windows. It also allows four text styles: bold, italic, underline, and strikeout. These fonts and styles can be mixed within the same text field if desired.

Sometimes courseware must be written in several different languages. ToolBook allows books to be written so that they can easily be modified to support different languages. The *alias* feature allows menus to be designed so that when a menu item is selected, the message sent is not the name of the selected menu item but the alias. This way, when menu items are translated into other languages, the names of their corresponding message handlers do not have to be changed. Part of the documentation of ToolBook version 1.5 is a book entitled "ToolBook Ideas" which, among other things, contains hints on how to design books for international use. ToolBook also supports many different date, time, currency, and number formats.

5 Conclusion

As a result of our research, we have formulated the requirements for a highly interactive hyper-document for teaching a programming language. We have designed the implementation using a combination of an authoring system and standard programming languages. The existing authoring systems have claimed to be easy to use for non-experienced programmers and powerful enough to create interactive CBT materials. Our conclusion is that this is not always the case as we had to resort to Borland C++ to implement some auxiliary components. Nevertheless, some of the facilities available in authoring systems, such as the ease of creation of frame-based presentations and answer analysis, are very helpful indeed. Because many authoring systems for IBM PC compatible machines run under MS-DOS, and because MS-DOS was not designed with inter-program communication in mind, there is sometimes a problem of interfacing the main program with other components. The Windows layer solves the problem of communication but the price is that all tools have to be developed as Windows applications which means that most existing tools cannot be used. Our future research goes in three directions. First, we intend to build a new authoring system which provides hooks to interface any specialized tools without having to use DDE. Second, we are considering UNIX implementations. Finally, we are investigating an enhancement of our courseware with multimedia features such as sound and video.

Acknowledgements

This research was partially supported by NSERC General Grant from Acadia University, 1991. The second author was supported by the SEED'91 program.

Bibliography

[BC++] *Borland C++*. Borland International, 1991.

[Ber86] Mark Bernstein. *The Bookmark and the Compass: Orientation Tools for Hypertext*

Users. pp. 34-45, 1986.

[Bus45] V. Bush. *As we may think.* Atlantic Monthly. July 1945, pp. 101-108.

[Ico] *IconAuthor version 3.0.* AimTech Corporation. 77 Northeastern Boulevard, Nashua, New Hampshire 03062, USA.

[Ker78] Brian W. Kernighan and Dennis M. Ritchie. *The C Programming Language.* Prentice-Hall, Inc. 1978.

[Ker84] Brian W. Kernighan and Rob Pike. *The UNIX Programming Environment.* Prentice-Hall, Inc. 1984.

[LaL90] Wilf R. LaLonde and John R. Pugh. *Inside Smalltalk Volume 1.* Prentice-Hall, Inc. 1990.

[Mak87] F. Makedon, H. Maurer and Th. Ottmann. *Presentation type CAI in computer science education at university level.* Journal of Microcomputer Applications 10 (1987), pp. 283-295.

[Nea89] Lisa Rubin Neal. *A System for Example-Based Programming.* CHI'89 Proceedings. May 1989, pp. 63-68.

[Str86] Bjarne Stroustrup. *The C++ Programming Language.* Addison-Wesley Publishing Company. 1986

[Tom91] Ivan Tomek, Saleem Khan, Tomasz Müldner, Mostafa Nassar, George Novak, and Piotr Proszynski. *Hypermedia — Introduction and Survey.* Journal of Microcomputer Applications. 14, 1991, pp. 63-103.

[Too] *ToolBook version 1.5.* Asymetrix Corporation, 110th Ave., N.E. Suite 717. Bellevue, Washington 98004, USA.

[Win] *Microsoft Windows version 3.0.* Microsoft Inc, 1991.

OBJECTOR, Yet Another Authoring System

Tomasz Müldner, Mohamed Elammari
Jodrey School of Computer Science
Acadia University
Wolfville, B0P 1X0 Nova Scotia, Canada
tel. (902) 542-2201 ext. 331
email: solid@aucs.acadiau.ca

Abstract

In this paper we argue that most commercially available authoring systems are not powerful enough for the development of specialized presentations such as courseware for teaching computer science. We briefly review several existing authoring systems and show their weak points. Then, we describe the design and implementation of OBJECTOR, an object-oriented authoring system. OBJECTOR is an authoring system which has all the required features such as a multi-window environment, text and graphics editors, and hypertext facilities modifiable by the learner. In addition, OBJECTOR is an open system which can be easily modified and extended by the author.

Introduction

There is a growing interest in course delivery supported by computers. This interest has been generated by various applications of computers in remote education, for example the use of electronic mail to provide assignments and gather students answers, and the use of computer conferencing systems to provide on-line interaction between students and instructors. But even more interesting and increasingly popular application of computers in supporting course delivery is the use of computers in the classroom and laboratory to present course material and to interact with the student, see [Cha-She89a, Mer85, She-Lar87]. The latter application has become possible only recently with the development of high-speed processors and large internal and external memories. A computer can be interfaced with many devices to produce still images, live videos and sound. A material for the class presentation can be organized through a specialized computer program. This program allows the instructor to show slides, movies, etc., at the required time during the lecture. The presentation can be highly interactive, with the computer asking questions, judging students answers, and so on. There are many universities which created specialized laboratories to produce and offer courses taught with the extensive use of computers. But the interest is not limited to the academic world; many factories, banks, insurance companies and other enterprises are engaged in computer-based learning and teaching.

In this paper, we are concerned with the development of courseware for teaching science, in particular computer science. We have reviewed several commercially available authoring systems for the Macintosh: Authorware, HyperCard, and Course Builder [CB]. We have also reviewed other systems for MSDOS-based computers: Authorware, cT, IconAuthor [IA], Quest [QU], Tencore [TE], and Toolbook [TO] (for other reviews, see [You84, Col89]).

In Section 1, we describe in details the following five authoring systems: Authorware, IconAuthor, Tencore, Toolbook and Quest. We concentrated on these systems because, in our opinion, they are the best systems for the applications to the post-secondary level education. In Section 2, we describe the basic ideas behind the design of OBJECTOR, an object-oriented authoring system, and in Section 3 we show some details of the implementation of OBJECTOR in the C++ programming language.

1 Review of Several Authoring Systems

Practically all authoring systems described in this paper fall into the category of the Branching Programmed Instruction Model [Mer85]. Courseware consists of a number of lessons, each lesson consists of a number of frames. Thus, this model is based on the a concept of the book. A frame corresponds to a page in the book and branching to turning pages. Each frame may contain various objects, such as text fields, graphic fields, hypertext buttons, etc.

Authoring has become popular when the Apple Company started providing a free Hypercard system with each new Macintosh computer. Hypercard has its MS-DOS counterpart, called Toolbook. These two systems are almost identical, and so in this paper we describe only Toolbook.

Most authoring systems are designed for users with little, if any, programming experience and they provide a point-and-click (PAC) interface to select authoring commands. Few systems provide both, a PAC interface and a textual representation of the authoring language, (AL). There are several variations of the latter technique. In some systems, the user first builds a sequence of frames, using a PAC interface. Then the user can use the AL to attach commands to a frame, or a particular object within the single frame. We will call these systems PACL systems. In other authoring systems there are two levels of authoring. At the first level, the author uses the PAC interface to build a prototype of courseware. The authoring commands selected by the author are saved in textual form. After the prototype has been tested and modified, the author may move to the second level to work with the AL. At that level, it is easier to tune up the details of courseware presentation. Here, we call these systems PAC/AL systems. There are two variations of the PAC systems:

- Flow-line PAC systems, with menu of design icons and flow line. The author selects a required icon from the menu and then places it on a flow line. A design icon can be placed anywhere on a flow line, not necessarily at the end of this line. Also, design icons which are already placed on the flow line can be removed, edited and copied. At any time, courseware represented by icons on the flow line can be executed, or stored in a file.

- Flow-control PAC systems, with menu of icons, but without a flow line. Each icon has input ports and output ports. The user places icons on the screen, and then connects output ports of an icon with the input port of another icon, thereby specifying the flow of control from the former icon to the latter.

Some PACL systems provide a small, special-purpose programming language, others additionally provide the interface to programs in a conventional programming language, such as Pascal or C. The latter option is particularly useful if there is a need to pass data between courseware and the program.

1.1 Development of Courseware

PAC systems are particularly attractive for naive users. Two examples of these systems are Authorware and IconAuthor, both systems use a flow-line PAC interface. Variables and single-dimensional arrays are available through a specialized variable editor, but data types are not supported. All mathematical operations are performed using real arithmetics. Basic mathematical functions are available, for example trigonometric functions. Both systems support control structuresæconditional and iterative statements, created by specialized icons. To give the user a tool to structure courseware, both systems provide composite icons, which are similar to procedures in conventional programming languages. They can input values of global variables and then, upon completion, return values. Course Builder is a similar authoring system, with a flow-control PAC interface.

Quest is a PACL system. It comes with the menu-driven editor and Quest Authoring Language, QAL. A QAL program can be stored in a frame and executed when this frame is entered (the program and the frame can share data). A frame may store up to 500 objects (10,000 bytes), thus QAL programs may have at most 800 lines. QAL is a Pascal-like language and it supports variables of type integer, real, character and string. It also supports arrays, user-defined functions and procedures, conditional and iterative statements and special-purpose commands to draw graphic figures, procedures to clear and fill figures, and finally procedures to operate on libraries.

Toolbook is a PAC/AL system. Its authoring language, OpenScript is practically identical to Hypercard's HyperTalk, and it is an object-based programming language, without inheritance. Tencore is also a PAC/AL system. It provides a menu-driven version called Producer. Unfortunately, Producer does not support variables and so it is not possible to develop courseware based on students responses, for example one in which a student would be asked to enter two numbers, then the sum of these numbers, and finally it would verify whether or not the student's answer was correct. The Tencore AL can be used for such applications, but we have found this language to be difficult to use because of its rather poor design. For example, there are several, syntactically different forms of an assignment statement, depending on whether you assign numbers or strings. Incidentally, cT's programming language is practically identical to that of Tencore's.

IconAuthor and Tencore require specialized interpreters, here called drivers to run applications, that is the author cannot create stand alone applications. Courseware developed using Toolbook comes with the source code, but this code can be removed using a specialized Author Resource Kit, ARK, available from Asymetrix.

Authoring systems that do not support a programming language, that is pure PAC systems are not powerful enough to create more advanced applications. Limitations on existing PACL and PAC/AL systems make it very difficult, and sometimes impossible to create courseware for teaching science, in particular computer science. For example, to develop courseware for teaching a programming language one may wish to develop an interface with existing tools, such as an editor or a database. With this interface, courseware could communicate with the tools, by passing and receiving data. Unfortunately, most authoring systems are "closed", that is they do not supportt communication. Windows 3.0-based systems, such as IconAuthor and ToolBook support a Dynamic Data Exchange, DDE communication. Unfortunately, this support is not always sufficient. For example, it may be necessary to develop a Windows-based editor, and the programming languages that come with these authoring systems are too limited for this purpose. Authoring systems should provide "hooks" to attach routines written in other programming languages. In Sections 2 and 3 we support our claim that the provision of hooks for external routines is not the best solution and it is better to have an authoring system written in an object oriented programming language. For this system, the author can use constructs such as inheritance to add any required features and tools. In what follows, we continue the review of most important features of the selected authoring systems.

1.2 Text and Graphics

Tencore supports four font sizes and different formats such as highlights, underscores, italics, boldface, etc. Fixed and variable spacing (but not proportional) are supported. Quest has similar features, and in addition it has a rather unique feature: a *timed* text, i. e. the text is displayed on the screen, one character at a time, as if someone was typing the text. Time intervals between the two successive occurrences may be set by the author. On the negative side, Quest does not support window-based applications, for example scrolling has to be simulated using programming tricks. None of the systems we have reviewed allows the author to create a multi-window editor that could be used by the learner. IconAuthor has a specialized text editor, with most editing functions. Authorware supports a typical, Macintosh-like editing.

Now, we discuss the graphic constructs. None of the systems evaluated in this paper supports three-dimensional graphics, but all of them support color two-dimensional graphics. Most systems provide specialized editors for object-oriented graphics and the author can include bit-mapped graphics into frames. In IconAuthor, bit-mapped graphics can be displayed on the screen clipped or sized. Some systems allow for transformations of graphic objects (translation, rotation, etc.), for example in IconAuthor, the author can flip figures horizontally and vertically, and invert colors. The area to be affected can be specified as a rectangle or a polygon. A selected area can be erased using an eraser. In Toolbook, the author can create many layers, each layer contains a number of objects. Only objects from the current layer can be accessed, but it is possible to switch between layers.

All authoring systems we reviewed support serial animation, but none of them supported parallel animation. In Tencore, to select an area on the screen to be animated, this object has to be enclosed by a frame, that is it cannot be specified as an object, such as a circle. Steps in the animation and the time between the consecutive steps can be specified (both in discrete units). IconAuthor is particularly powerful for the creation of animated graphics. It provides three specialized programs: Graphics Editor, Animation Editor and a graphics utility program, RezSolution. RezSolution can be used to modify bitmap graphic files, by resizing them and changing the graphic image resolution. Specifically, for any graphic object the following properties can be changed: width, height, number of colors, horizontal and vertical resolution, and the zoom that is the percentage by which the object is enlarged or reduced. RezSolution can also be used to capture the screen.

1.3 Software Interfaces

It is often desired to write a "key handler", that is a routine which is activated when the corresponding key is pressed. Tencore allows the author to write key handlers for up to 10 keys, for example in order to execute a specific unit (in particular to execute first, last, next, previous, the same unit). In IconAuthor any iconware (a complete courseware packaged into a single icon) can be assigned as a handler to the left or to the right mouse button, or to any key on the keyboard. If the mouse is used, a rectangular area on the screen can be assigned, and the iconware is invoked only if the mouse pointer is positioned in this area and the required mouse button is clicked.

For many applications, the author may wish to implement some routines in a general-purpose programming language, such as C, and then call these routines from courseware. For example, if an authoring system lacks statistical routines, these can be written in C. If an authoring system can be interfaced with another programming language, this system can be extended by adding programs in this language. IconAuthor supports DDE to exchange data with other Windows 3.0 applications, and the Dynamic Link Libraries, (DLL) to invoke subroutines written in Microsoft C version 6.0, compiled under Microsoft Windows Software Development Kit. Finally, it supports database interface with DBASE III+ and DBASE IV. In Quest, external programs written in Pascal and C programming languages, and QAL can be called, but these programs do not share data with lessons. (Recall that QAL programs that are attached to frames do share data, but these programs are limited in size.)

Clearly, any Macintosh-based authoring system allows to *cut-and-paste* information presented in courseware, to other tools available on the given system (and from these tools). This is also true for systems running under Windows 3.0. For example, in IconAuthor, any graphic file that can be copied to the Microsoft Windows 3.0 clipboard, can be imported. In addition, in most authoring systems the author can import bitwise files, for example in Tencore two external paint files, PC Paintbrush and Dr. Halo can be imported.

1.4 Questioning and Judging

The most important issues related to questioning and judging are the types of questions supported (multiple choice, true or false, fill-in the blanks, numerical), the placement of a response, and a support for the pointing devices, for example in order to ask the learner to move some objects to the required places on the screen. Quest, IconAuthor, Authorware and Tencore support the above four kinds of questions. In Tencore, for questions that involve numbers, the author can provide ranges for correct and wrong answers. In IconAuthor, the learner's answers can be given through keys or the mouse. Timeout can be specified. The feedback given after the user's answer may involve reverse highlighting the selected area, drawing a box around this area, or both. The author can assign points for correct answers and the system will keep track of the total score. In Toolbook, the author has to write the required routines to handle the question analysis.

In many cases, it is desired to use *inexact matches*. For example, Tencore's author can specify words that will be ignored, or synonyms. By default, Tencore ignores punctuation but this can be changed. The following specifications can be toggled: accept misspelled words, provide markups (indications of misspeled characters), accept extra words, require correct order, ignore case (capitalization), start judging when the user reaches the input limit, and set the maximum length of the input.

1.5 Performance Evaluation and Activities Management

Authoring systems should help in managing student records, building a catalog of lessons, enrolling students in the course, and so on. Also, student answers can be stored in variables and processed using custom programs or built-in statistics program libraries. These libraries may also provide a report generation and regression analysis. In Tencore, Quest and ToolBook, a password can be used to protect students from enrolling. A log is automatically generated when the learner traverses courseware. It saves the date and time the lesson was last used, the total time it was used and the total number of sessions, the score, and produces a report with data on who used the lessons and how far the users have progressed in the lessons. The author can restrict students from retaking the completed activity. Similarly, Quest provides a complete Computer Managed Instruction, CMI package to maintain the list of available courses, register students and monitor their progress.

1.6 Hypertext Facilities

Recently, CBT presentations started using hypertext facilities to support non-linear style of learning. These facilities include links between various objects, and other navigational tools: references, index, table of contents, bookmarks, margin and global notes, help windows, and menus (for more complete description, see [Tom91, Mül91]). Few authoring systems support these concepts, see [Kea88]. For example, ToolBook provides *hotwords* which can be activated to move to another part of the presentation. None of the systems we have reviewed supports learner-modifiable hypertext links.

2 Design of OBJECTOR

The design of OBJECTOR was based on the idea that the author should be provided with a powerful and open development environment. Thus, we have assumed that the author is an experienced programmer, who does not have to resort to PAC-like programming systems. OBJECTOR provides the author with the following facilities:

- mutliple windows,
- various fonts and formats,
- modifiable graphic objects,
- textual and PAC question analysis,
- icons, push-buttons, menus, and scrollbars,
- learner-modifiable hypertext facilities.

Since OBJECTOR is designed to be an open system, we have decided to use an object oriented programming language, C++. This kind of a language seems to be ideal for the above requirements (for the discussion of object-oriented programming in C++, see [Stro91]). In particular, the users of OBJECTOR do not have to memorize information about the various windows, icons, etc., because all the information associated with an object will be encapsulated inside that object. Some of the predefined classes could be used for authoring specialized applications. For example, the classes List, Stack, and Tree could be used to develop courseware on the use of Data Structures in Computer Science. Inheritance can be used to develop specialized classes. In addition, an object-oriented implementation is well suited for *event-driven* environments. (For example, the OpenScript programming language used in ToolBook is an object-based language, used to handle various events, such as the key press, or the mouse click.) Using the C++ implementation of OBJECTOR, authors will be able to implement all features discussed above, in particular user-modifiable hypertext facilities, specialized tools interfaced with courseware, etc. We have decided to use a specific implementation of C++, namely Borland C++ [BOR91], because this implementation allows programmers to develop applications running under Windows 3.0--a powerful and increasingly popular multi-window environment based on the MS-DOS operating system. We have decided to use Windows 3.0 because it provides a multitasking environment, with a consistent "look and feel" across applications. Internally, Windows 3.0 is "almost" an object-oriented system, and the C++ interface makes it easy to use.

3 Implementation of OBJECTOR in C++

Lack of space prevents us from providing a complete description, therefore below we present several selected C++ classes developed to implement the OBJECTOR authoring system.

3.1 Text and Graphics

The three basic classes to manage the text and graphics are Window, Text, and Object. The class Window enables the author to create on the screen multiple windows and to switch between them. The author can also change the attributes of windows, such as the size, the location, the title, etc.:

```
class Window {
        void CreateWindow(...);
        void RemoveWindow(...);
        void MoveWindow(...);
        void RemoveWindow(...);
        void Size(...);

        ...
}
```

The class Text can be used to create various font sizes and formats within windows:

```
class Text {
        void Font(...);
        void Write(...);
        void Size(...);
        void SetOption(...);    -- e.g. Bold
}
```

Finally, the objects of a class Object represent various figures:

```
class Object {
        circle(real x, y, r);
        square(real x,y,w);
        ...
}
```

Note that the author can easily modify the existing class, using inheritance, for example to add new figures, or to define color circles.

3.2 Questioning and Judging

There are several predefined OBJECTOR classes to deal with questions and judging. Here, we list a few classes; first the classes designed to provide authors with templates for questions:

```
class MultipleQuestion;
class TrueFalse;
class FillInBlank;
class matching;
class answer {
        string getInput(void);
        string getInput(int charLimit);
        ...
}
```

The class judge provides optional words, a spelling checker, markups, synonyms, and the support for wild cards:

```
class judge {
        boolean match(...);
        ...
}
```

3.3 Performance Evaluation and Activities Management

In order to enroll a student, the instructor will use the object of the class Instructor:

```
class Instructor {
        string name;
```

```
        string passwd;
        void SetUser(...);
        void EvaluateStudent(...)
};
```

The object of class Evaluate would be used in order to obtain information on the progress of an individual student or the entire class:

```
class Evaluate {
        void ShowScore();
        void ShowMarks();
};
```

For the sake of protection in multi-user environments, students must enter a password to verify whether or not they can use the above routines.

3.4 Hypertext Facilities

The basic class designed to support the hypertext facilities defines a *hotword*, i.e. a word which, when activated (for example by clicking it with the mouse) moves the learner to another screen:

```
class hypertext {
        StringLocation;
        NextFrame;
};
```

Buttons are objects of a class button:

```
class PushButtons {
        void CreateButton();
        void RemoveButton();
        void Enable();
        void Disable();
        void MoveButton();
        ...
}
```

The objects of a class MarginNotes represent *margin notes* that can be created by the learner:

```
class MarginNotes {
        stringfilename;
        void CreateNoteIcon();
        ...
```

}

The contents of a note would appear in a separate window, but would be permanently stored in a file. This is necessary because C++ does not support *persistent objects*, that is objects that do not disappear when the program terminates.

4 Conclusion

At the time this paper was written, we have designed most classes needed to develop OBJECTOR, with the exception of the interface with the external devices. We have implemented and tested some classes, in particular the user interface classes. The future work will concentrate on the implementation of all required classes, and the design and implementation of the hardware interface classes. We will also implement in OBJECTOR a sample courseware for teaching programming languages.

Acknowledgements

This work was partially supported by the fund form the Huggins Science Funds, Acadia University, 1991. The authors of this paper would like to express thanks to the following companies for providing evaluation copies of their software:
TeleRobotics International, Inc. (Course Builder Series Version 4.0), AimTech Corporation (IconAuthor version 3.0), Computer Teaching Corporation (Tencore Producer and LAS), Allen Communication (Quest, Version 3.0), Asymetrix Corporation (ToolBook).

References

[BOR91] Borland C++. Borland International, 1991.

[Cha-She89] Ruth W. Chabay, Bruce A. Sherwood. *A Practical Guide for the Creation of Educational Software*. Center for Design of Educational Software, Carnegie Mellon University, Technical Report No. 89-06, April 1989.

[Col 89] Michael A.J. Collins. *The Hidden Costs of Computer Courseware Authoring Tools*. Educational Technology. June 1989. pp. 46-47.

[Haz87] Margret Hazen. *Criteria for Choosing Among Instructional Software Authoring Tools*. Journal of Research on Computing in Education. Winter 1987. pp. 156-164.

[Kea88] Greg Kearlsey. *Authoring Considerations for Hypertext*. Educational Technology. November 1984. pp. 21-23.

[Mer85] M. David Merill. *Where is the Authoring in Authoring Systems?*. Journal of Computer-Based Instruction. Autumn 1985, Vol. 12, No. 4, pp. 90-96.

[Mül91] Tomasz Müldner and Robin Blondon. *Design and Implementation of Courseware for Teaching Programming Languages.* To appear as a technical report. Jodrey School of Computer Science, Acadia University.

[She-Lar87] Bruce A. Sherwood, Jill H. Larkin. *New Tools for Courseware Production.* Center for Design of Educational Software, Carnegie Mellon University, Technical Report No. 87-05, June 1987.

[Stro91]. Bjarne Stroustrup. *The C++ programming language.* Second Edition. Addison-Wesley Publishing Company, 1991.

[You84] Jerry, L. Young. *The Case for Using Authoring Systems to develop Courseware.* Educational Technology. October 1984. pp. 26-28.

[Tom91]. Ivan Tomek, Saleem Khan, Tomasz Müldner, Mostafa Nassar, George Novak and Piotr Proszynski. *Hypermedia-Introduction and Survey.* Journal of Microcomputer Applications, Vol. 14, 1991, pp. 63-103.

Authoring Systems

[CB] *Course Builder Series Version 4.0.* TeleRobotics International, Inc. 7325 Oak Ridge Highway, Suite 104, Knoxville, Tennessee 37921.

[IA] *IconAuthor version 3.0.* AimTech Corporation. 77 Northeastern Boulevard, Nashua, New Hampshire 03062.

[TC] *Tencore Producer and LAS.* Computer Teaching Corporation. 1713 South State Street. Champaign, Illinois, USA 61820.

[TO] *ToolBook Version 1.5.* Asymetrix Corporation, 110th Ave., N.E. Suite 717, Bellevue, Washington 98004, USA.

[QU] *Quest, Version 3.0.* Allen Communication. 5225 Wiley Post Way. Salt Lake City, Utah 84116.

Design and Evaluation of the SUMIT
Intelligent Teaching Assistant for Arithmetic

Roderick I. Nicolson

Department of Psychology

University of Sheffield

Sheffield S10 2TN, England

tel. +44742 768555 ext. 6547

email: R.NICOLSON@UK.AC.SHEFFIELD.PRIMEA

Abstract

The technique for creating diagnostic tutors for arithmetic has been established for over a decade, but progress towards the creation of an educationally viable system has been disappointingly slow. The SUMIT intelligent teaching assistant for arithmetic was designed explicitly to meet the requirements of classroom arithmetic teaching. Unlike earlier arithmetic tutors, SUMIT is intended to function as a teacher's assistant, rather than a surrogate teacher. It is fully interactive and is able to give adaptive help; to diagnose misconceptions; to generate graded sequences of sums; and to summarise or replay whole user sessions for each of the 'four rules of number'. This paper outlines the design philosophy and the system architecture of the SUMIT system, and it reports two evaluation studies of the classroom effectiveness of the system, demonstrating excellent learning via the use of SUMIT, and a further advantage of the availability of the diagnostic help. It is concluded that construction of intelligent teaching assistants may provide cost-effective and valuable educational resources.

Introduction

The BUGGY Intelligent Tutoring System

Traditional Computer Aided Learning (CAL) programs have been criticised on the grounds that they do not *understand* the domain for which they were devised, and so they cannot give the adaptive help expected of a human teacher. This critique proved the stimulus for the creation of Intelligent Tutoring Systems (ITSs) or, the equivalent term, Intelligent CAL, which did understand its domain sufficiently to provide the same adaptive quality of guidance and instruction as a human teacher. It is generally accepted, following Hartley and Sleeman (1973), that an adequate ITS needs (at least) three components - knowledge of the subject to be taught (domain knowledge); knowledge of the user's current understanding (user model); and knowledge of the appropriate teaching strategies for that domain and user state (pedagogic knowledge). Not surprisingly, given the lack of explicit knowledge about how to construct any one of the three components, ITSs are notorious for promising much and achieving little, but nonetheless they remain a major focus of applications of AI to education.

Arguably the most promising and tractable domain within school education for the application of ITS is that of school arithmetic - the 'four rules of number'. Indeed, the most cited work in the area is the seminal article by Brown and Burton (1978) which demonstrated that it is possible to diagnose 'bugs' or 'malrules' in a child's arithmetic knowledge, and that this diagnostic ability could form the basis of an intelligent arithmetic tutor. Rather surprisingly, this work has never been followed up to produce a system useable within a realistic educational context. With the benefit of hindsight, it is possible to adduce some explanations for this.

Problems of the BUGGY diagnostic system

(i) <u>Lack of the appropriate pedagogical knowledge</u>. Brown and Burton acknowledged explicitly that their system was essentially diagnostic rather than remedial - it was better at identifying what was wrong than knowing what to do about it! As Ruthven

(1985) points out, it is hard to integrate into normal teaching practice a system which merely diagnoses 'Bug 6: larger from smaller', and there is a real danger that confusion will result.

(ii) Unmanageable number of bugs. Brown and Burton appeared to delight in the number of possible bugs that could be identified - they claimed 330 bugs for subtraction alone! Consider the teacher's problem in trying to understand what the diagnosed bug meant, never mind remedying it!

(iii) Lack of immediate feedback. It is a commonplace that a major potential strength of CAL material is the ability to give immediate feedback of correct or error responses. By electing to adopt a retrospective analysis of a set of sums in order to identify consistent bug(s) out of their very large pool, Brown and Burton sacrificed their birthright.

(iv) Bug Instability. This is a problem conceded by Brown and Van Lehn in a later paper (1980. Some bugs appear to be unstable, in that they appear, disappear, and transmute over the course of a session. This unfortunate fact forced them to propose an ambitious 'Repair Theory' which was supposed to explain which bugs would transmute and why, taking the theory further but diminishing any practical value.

(v) Medium-dependence. Brown and Burton's corpus of arithmetic sums was provided from a large pencil-and-paper arithmetic study in Nicaragua. There is no guarantee that the bugs identified for that corpus will transfer to other methods of presentation or teaching, in particular, computer-based methods.

(vi) Pragmatic problems. BUGGY was written in InterLISP and worked on a PDP-KL10. It is highly unlikely that it could be ported to a common educational computer such as the British BBC micro.

(vii) Doctrinaire objections. In a rational world one might expect the above problems to act as a spur rather than a damper to further research. Unfortunately, the prevailing CAL philosophy of this decade has been anti-arithmetic, with well-intentioned objections being made that it is at least as valuable to learn alternative skills such as estimation of change. Change estimation is a useful skill, but arithmetic competence - involving knowledge of the principles of arithmetic together with fluency in the arithmetic processes - is the very bedrock of numeracy. Problems in learning arithmetic should stimulate research to solve them, rather than avoidance behaviour.

Requirements for an Intelligent Arithmetic Tutor

This analysis of the shortcomings of the BUGGY program as a practical tutor of arithmetic leads to the question - what would one expect of an arithmetic ITS? I offer the following suggestions - inevitably they form a personal view:

(i) Target Learning Outcome. Children with minimal understanding of the rules of arithmetic should be able to use the program, and to progress through the intermediate stages of learning to a full understanding both of the principles and the procedures of addition, subtraction, multiplication and division.

(ii) User Interface. The mode of operation must be as close as possible to the standard pencil and paper method normally employed in order to maximise transfer and minimise confusion.

(iii) Feedback. Should be immediate, after every response, in order to pinpoint any errors and to avoid the danger of perseveration of bugs.

(iv) Pedagogic expertise. This should include not only knowledge of how to diagnose and remedy bugs, but also the (more important) knowledge of how to do the sum correctly and how to progress from simple to complex sums in a consistent and effective sequence.

(v) Input of arithmetic sums. The IAT must be capable of adaptive generation of sums at the appropriate difficulty level. It should also be possible to load stored sets of sums from disc.

(vi) Results storage. In addition to standard results summaries presented during the session it should be possible to store a complete 'session log' (including latency information as well as all key presses) on disc which could used subseqently by a teacher either for speeded replay, or replay with just the errors, or could be analysed to give a score/bug breakdown.

(vii) Motivation. The program must of course be motivating and fun to use, though this consideration should be subject to the need for pedagogical integrity.

(viii) Pragmatics. It should run on a micro computer in routine school use.

It is interesting to note that few of these requirements have figured prominently in any of the published Intelligent Tutoring Systems!

THE SUMIT INTELLIGENT ARITHMETIC TUTOR

The remainder of this paper outlines a long-term research programme that we have undertaken in order to meet the above requirements, and presents the results of two recent evaluations of its effectiveness. The basic beliefs behind SUMIT were that it should look and feel the same as 'normal' sums while using the computer power to generate and store sums and answers, offering the immediate feedback of CAL plus the diagnostic and remedial ability of an ITS. In other words, the research was aimed at a synthesis of the traditional approach to teaching arithmetic with the ITS approach by producing a 'glass box' domain expert which followed precisely the traditional teaching progression but was able not only to offer correct advice to the user but also to diagnose and remedy the most common bugs. The research followed an 'evolutionary' strategy, where first a non-diagnostic program (SUMS) was developed and tested exhaustively in the school setting. The diagnostic capability was then 'grafted on' following futher research. The SUMS program is adequately documented elsewhere (Nicolson & Nicolson, 1984); Nicolson et al (1985), and is freely available to British schools via the Council for Educational Technology. Consequently a brief history should suffice here, and I shall then concentrate on the final stages in the creation of SUMIT.

History of the SUMS program

The SUMS program was created jointly with my wife, Margaret K Nicolson, an experienced teacher of middle school arithmetic, and the collaboration involved extensive knowledge engineering studies undertaken over a period spanning three years in which:

(i) the traditional methods of teaching arithmetic were examined and a generalised teaching methodology was abstracted, involving the creation of ten 'grades' of difficulty for each operation, together with rules for the generation of sums at each grade;

(ii) this expertise was then modelled in the form of the SUMS program, a generative semi-expert arithmetic tutor which was able to offer online and appropriate advice to the user (eg. *"You are trying to add the tens column, that is: 3 + 5 + 1 carry, so the result is 9"* and so on, but the help was non-diagnostic in that no effort was made to analyse errors.

(iii) the SUMS program was then extensively tested in the school environment, demonstrating in a formal controlled evaluation impressive improvements both in learning efficiency and in the understanding of arithmetic principles (ref 6).

(iv) SUMS was then made available for free publication by the British Council for Technology. Informal enquiries at four regional centres indicate that the program has been welcomed for use over a wide range of abilities, including children with learning difficulties.

Adding 'Intelligence': the enhancement of SUMS to SUMIT

Early studies had shown that errors made using SUMS were qualitatively different from those reported by Brown and Burton, primarily because of the much more directive nature of the SUMS program - it forces the user to perform the necessary operations in the 'correct' order, and refuses to accept incorrect input. Consequently many bugs just cannot happen at all.

(i) Data Collection. In order to identify which bugs were the most common, SUMS was enhanced to present pre-stored pages of sums, and also to record the complete 'session log' on disc for subsequent analysis. This enhanced program was used to gather automatically a corpus of data relating to over 2000 addition and multiplication sums using 64 children from two Sheffield schools. A total of 1545 errors overall were recorded.

(ii) Bug analysis. The data were analysed by hand independently by two experimenters to identify the bugs involved. A total set of 19 bugs was identified for multiplication and 24 bugs for addition (based on a literature review plus analysis of the data). The bugs were then ranked in terms of frequency of occurrence - in fact 4 multiplication bugs and 9 addition bugs had zero occurrence. Bugs with a frequency of greater than 2% are shown in Table 1.

Addition			Multiplication		
Bug No	% errors	Bug	Bug No	% errors	Bug
1A	32.8%	Forgets to add in carry	1M	23.4%	Puts down carry before digit
2A	24.9	Puts down carry before digit	2M	21.5	Forgets to add in carry
3A	13.0	Arithmetic error (eg. 6+2=9)	3M	20.1	Arithmetic error (eg. 6x7=48)
4A	6.1	Misses out one addend	4M	11.7	Unclassified
5A	5.1	Unclassified	5M	5.1	Extra column problem
6A	4.9	Carries at most 1	6M	3.8	Add digits in LH column
7A	3.1	Extra column problem	7M	3.0	0xN = N
8A	2.4	Carries 0	8M	2.8	0xN -> omit column
Total	92.3%			91.4%	

TABLE 1. The most frequent bugs for addition and multiplication

Notice that the percentage of errors classified is better for addition than multiplication (94.9% vs 88.3% respectively) and that for each operation the remaining set of 7 bugs was sufficient to account for over 80% of all errors made (over 90% of classifiable errors).

(iii) <u>Bug diagnostic criterion</u>. For each of the major bugs a diagnostic criterion plus appropriate remedial advice was identified, and this diagnostic capability was built into the program, thus producing the SUMIT (Sums Intelligent Tutor) suite. Interestingly, the enhancement of SUMS to create SUMIT produced a change of less than 1% in the overall program code.

Evaluation of SUMIT

An initial study, reported in Nicolson et al (1985) demonstrated that SUMS was of great effectiveness for helping children to learn all four of the arithmetic operations. Two recent studies will be described, the first summarising an experiment already carried out, and the second an experiment which will be completed by March 1992, but for which only pilot data are presently available.

Use of SUMIT for group vs individual learning

The first study (based on Nicolson and Darling, submitted) followed a similar format to that reported as Case Study 1 above. A whole class was used again, but this time with the SUMIT program. Given the attested effectiveness of SUMS, it was felt unfair to bar a control group from use of SUMIT, and so the study was designed to investigate the relative effectiveness of individual use as opposed to use in groups of three. As usual, a pencil and paper pre-test (on subtraction) was performed and subjects were split into two matched groups. Subjects in one group used SUMIT individually for three 20 minute sessions, whereas those in the other were randomly allocated to subgroups of three, with each child taking turns to do a sum, again for three 20 minute sessions. Following the three sessions (each one week apart) the children were tested on an exactly equivalent post-test. As expected, SUMIT proved highly effective both in increasing the overall score and in decreasing the number of bugs (the main effects of practice were significant at the .0001 and .01 levels respectively). Interestingly, there was no significant interaction between group and practice — that is, both the individuals and the groups benefited equivalently. The individual data for overall score (out of 32) on pre-test and post-test are shown in figure 1 (with the darker columns indicating the post-test). It may be seen that 12 of the 13 individual subjects improved their scores, whereas for the 15 grouped subjects 9 improved, 4 remained the same and 2 deteriorated. Inspection of the group data shows considerable heterogeneity. Groups 3 and 4 show excellent progress all round, groups 2 and 5 show little overall improvement, and group 1 shows modest improvement. We speculated that the reason for the poor performance of groups 2 and 5 was that one subject was noticeably weaker than the others, whereas groups 3 and 4 have a better mix. Analysis of the experimenter's records supported this conjecture, in that groups 3 and 4 had the best social interaction, whereas in groups 2 and 5 the weakest subject was rather ridiculed and ignored. The overall conclusions of the study were that grouping in threes was most beneficial for subjects of similar ability. If subjects differed widely in ability the social dynamics of the group become especially important, with exclusion of the weakest member the main danger. Nonetheless, it was clear that even one hour of work with SUMIT, spread over three weeks led to significant improvements both in overall performance and in rule understanding.

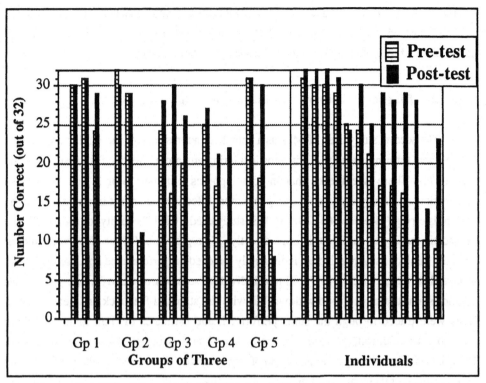

Figure 1. Effectiveness of SUMIT for individuals and groups of three.

The mean and standard deviation data for pre-test and post-test were 20.7 (sd=8.13) and 27.5 (sd=5.04) for the individual group and 21.8 (sd=8.4) and 25.5 (sd=7.19) for the groups of three. These lead to improvements of 0.83 and 0.44 sd units respectively. However, inspection of figure 6 indicates that 9 of the subjects started almost at ceiling, thus artificially limiting the improvement possible. If one limits the analysis to the 17 subjects who initially scored at 75% or less, the pre- and post-test data become 15.5 (sd=5.48) and 25.75 (sd=5.28) for the individuals versus 16.56 (sd=5.64) and 22.78 (sd=8.23) for the groups of three, leading to improvements of 1.87 and 1.10 sd units respectively[1]. Given the very short duration of the study, these are remarkable results, comfortably in excess of the 1

---

[1] it should be noted that the improvement over the period of testing may in part be attributable to generalised practice. However, given the relatively slight improvement (0.28 sd units) of the control group in the longer experiment described in Case Study 1, it seems reasonable to ascribe the bulk of the improvement here to SUMIT.

sd unit of improvement obtained using the LISP tutor and geometry tutor (eg. Anderson et al, 1990), and with the individualised SUMIT tuition approaching the elusive 'two sigma effect' claimed for individualised human tuition by Bloom (1984).

Study 2. Diagnostic help vs non-diagnostic help using SUMIT

The second study uses SUMIT as a vehicle to address one of the fundamental issues in intelligent tutoring, namely, "is diagnostic tutoring any more effective than non-diagnostic tutoring?". There is evidence that in some spheres a human tutor is not able to use information about why a student is erring any more effectively than just information *that* the student is erring (Sleeman et al, 1989). This study used SUMIT's ability to 'switch off' the diagnostic facility to explore this issue directly. Two groups of 9 year old schoolchildren from the same class were selected, individually matched on performance on a pre-test. Both groups then experienced two 30 minute individual sessions of SUMIT, one group with diagnosis and the other group without (but with the standard feedback and help facility). Bugs were traced through the sums performed, and estimates of 'bug longevity' were derived. In addition, performance on a pencil and paper post-test was measured. Comparison of post-test performance and of bug longevity should reveal whether diagnostic help really does help or not, a finding of immense significance for intelligent tutoring systems.

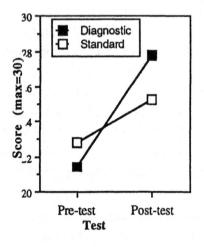 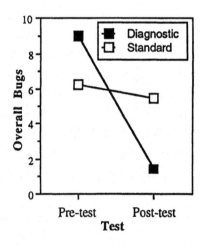

Fig. 2a. Scores for the two groups   Fig. 2b. Bugs for the two groups

The study is reported in detail in Nicolson and Harrop (in preparation). Results for the pre-test and post-test scores are shown in Figure 2a. Several children obtained pre-test scores of 29 or 30, and these were omitted from the analysis of the overall bugs (Fig. 2b). It may be seen that both groups improved as a result of the sessions with SUMIT, and that the diagnostic group improved somewhat more in overall score, and markedly more in terms of the overall bugs. An analysis of variance on the scores indicated a significant main effect of time-of-test [$F(1,20)=10.3$, $p<.01$] but no significant main effect of group, and no significant interaction. An analysis of variance on the bugs data indicated a significant main effect of time-of-test [$F(1,14)=7.0$, $p<.05$], no significant effect of group, but a significant interaction between group and time-of-test [$F(1,14)=4.6$, $p<.05$], indicating that the diagnostic group eliminated their bugs significantly more effectively than the standard group.

We conclude, therefore, that SUMIT with or without diagnostic help is effective in helping children learn the rules of arithmetic, and that the diagnostic help does indeed confer a further advantage in terms of the elimination of bugs.

5. Conclusions

The role of SUMIT is that of intelligent teaching assistant. It was designed as an assistant to a teacher (or parent), providing generative, adaptive support for learning the four rules of number. It frees the teacher from the drudgery of marking, it provides time-saving diagnostic summaries of a child's progress, it allows existing materials to be computerised easily, and it helps any child to learn more effectively. It is explicitly based on existing teaching methodology, and thus fits seamlessly within the classroom. In routine use as an adjunct to normal arithmetic teaching it would probably at worst halve the time necessary for any child to achieve fluency in the four rules of number, thus releasing an hour per week or more for a teacher to address the other, equally important, facets of numeracy. The key to the creation of SUMIT was, in the first place, that the domain is well understood in procedural terms, and, crucially, we had access to a well-developed pedagogical model of how to proceed from the initial state of little knowledge to the desired state of full knowledge.

REFERENCES

Anderson, J. R., Boyle, C. F, Corbett, A.T. and Lewis, M.W. (1990). Cognitive Modeling and Intelligent Tutoring. *Artificial Intelligence,* **42**, 7-49.

Anderson, J. R., Boyle, C. F. and Reiser, B. J. (1985). Intelligent Tutoring Systems. *Science,* **228**, 456-462.

Brown, J. S. and Burton, R. R. (1978). Diagnostic models for procedural bugs in basic mathematical skills. *Cognitive Science,* **2**, 155-192.

Brown, J. S. and VanLehn, K. (1980). Repair Theory: A generative theory of bugs in procedural skills. *Cognitive Science,* **4**, 379-426.

Hartley, J.R. and Sleeman, D.H. (1973). Towards intelligent teaching systems. *Int. J. Man-Machine Studies,* **5**, 215-236.

Nicolson, R. I. (1991). Design and Evaluation of the SUMIT Intelligent Teaching Assistant for Arithmetic. *Interactive Learning Environments,* **1**, 265-287.

Nicolson, R. I. and Nicolson, M. K. (1986). A case study of use of the SUMS program. In M Hope (ed). *Computers and Special Education.* London, Council for Educational Technology.

Nicolson, R. I. and Nicolson, M.K. (1984). *SUMS — interactive middle school arithmetic.* Program suite. London, Council for Educational Technology.

Nicolson, R. I., Bowen, P. and Nicolson, M. K. (1984). Classroom evaluation of the SUMS CAL arithmetic program. *Human Learning,* **3**, 129-136.

Nicolson, R. I. and Darling, E. (*submitted*). Group versus individual instruction using a computer-based arithmetic tutoring program.

Nicolson, R. I. and Harrop, C. (*in preparation*). Diagnosis does help in intelligent tutoring.

Ruthven, K. (1985). The AI dimension? In D J Smith (ed) *IT and education: signposts and* Bloom B.S. (1984). The two sigma effect: the search for methods of group instruction as effective as one-to-one tutoring. *Educational Researcher, 13,* 3-16.

Sleeman, D., Kelly, A.E., Martinak, R., Ward, R.D. & Moore J.L. (1989). Studies of diagnosis and remediation with high school algebra students. *Cognitive Science, 13,* 551-568.

Spelling Remediation for Dyslexic Children using the Selfspell Programs

Roderick I. Nicolson and Angela J. Fawcett
Department of Psychology
University of Sheffield
Sheffield S10 2TN, England
tel. +44742 768555 ext. 6547
email: R.NICOLSON@UK.AC.SHEFFIELD.PRIMEA

Abstract

This paper describes the SelfSpell Hypercard environment for dyslexic children which helps them to learn to spell their problem words. Synthesised speech is used to augment the written text and different levels of help are available at all times. Two versions are available, with one in which the children are encouraged to enter rules to help them remember how to spell each word, and one in which a mastery learning technique is used. Evaluations of the effectiveness of the software indicated substantial improvements with either version in the spelling and motivation of two groups of dyslexic children. The results indicate that, with an appropriate remedial environment, even children with minimal initial spelling ability are able to acquire the spellings of even quite difficult words. The positive results with the mastery-based approach suggest that SelfSpell can help dyslexic children to surmount the barrier of alphabetic coding.

Introduction: Computers and Dyslexia

Developmental dyslexia is characterised by severe problems in reading for children who otherwise appear to be of average or above average intelligence. Interestingly, however, most dyslexic children suffer from even more severe problems in spelling than in reading. Frith (1985) has suggested that dyslexic children have particular problems in mastering the alphabetic stage of reading and spelling, in which the correspondences between letters and their sounds are exploited both for decoding printed words (reading) and for analysing spoken words into their written equivalents (writing). The focus of this paper is an applied one: namely how can we help dyslexic children to spell better? Two studies will be presented, first a demonstration that new technology can be married to good pedagogy to provide a supportive environment (SelfSpell) for adolescent dyslexic children, and second a further investigation of the efficacy of the approach with younger dyslexic children who have made little or no progress with spelling. First it is necessary to provide some background on the technological developments exploited by the SelfSpell program.

The SelfSpell Environment

The early generations of computer hardware had very limited capability for interacting with the user, with the user required to input commands by typing on the keyboard in response to written questions displayed on the computer. Although dedicated programmers made valiant efforts to circumvent these limitations, the fact remained that dyslexic children, with their poor reading and spelling skills, were at a particular disadvantage with such systems. Educational technology has recently taken a major step forward with the introduction of a new generation of affordable but powerful micros such as the Apple Macintosh. In particular, the availability of hypermedia and multimedia environments which allow the smooth integration of text, graphics and synthesised or digitised speech, together with capability for interaction using 'point and click' rather than keyboard text entry, promise a solution to the problems for dyslexic children noted above. The SelfSpell environment represents an initial attempt to use these new developments.

We designed the Selfspell program in an effort to remedy established problems of computer-based presentation for dyslexic children (Thompson, 1985). Our design requirements were that the program should be effective at remedying dyslexic children's most serious difficulties, in particular, spelling problems. Just as important, since motivation contributes crucially to a program's success (eg. Malone, 1981) it should be fun to use! It should give immediate feedback, thus offering no opportunity for persistent errors. It should rely on active learning with the user involved the whole time making active decisions; and it should support a range of forms of learning, including mastery learning. Support available should include synthesised speech to supplement text displays; self-selection of materials using the user's own passages, own spellings and own spelling rules. Furthermore parental support should be encouraged, both for authoring materials and for checking progress.

In order to meet this specification, we developed the program within the Apple HyperCard™ environment, using a 1 Mbyte Macintosh Plus micro. The intention was that the child should be able to use the system unaided much of the time, but with initial support from a parent or teacher. Use of this SelfSpell prototype fell into four distinct phases: first the parent/teacher read an interesting passage slowly to the child, repeating words as necessary, and the child wrote down the words as best he/she could (see figure 1a for a partial transcript). Next the parent/teacher typed the child's version of the passage into the computer, and identified all the 'bugs', making a bug card for each (see Fig. 1b, 1c).

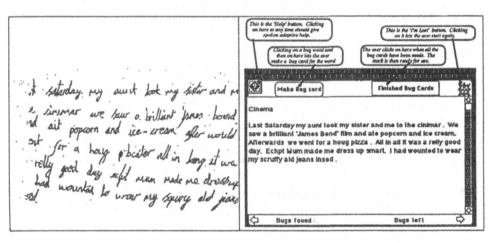

Fig. 1a. A handwritten transcript   **Fig. 1b. Computer version of the transcript**

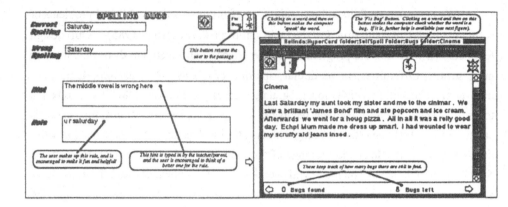

Fig. 1c. Making a Bug Card for 'Satarday'

Fig. 1d. Child's view of the support environment. "Click on a bug"

Next the child went through the passage (helped by the parent/teacher) identifying all the bugs, and for each one thinking up a rule to help them spell it right the next time (in Fig. 1c, the child has typed in the rule 'U R Saturday' to help him remember the 'ur' in the middle).

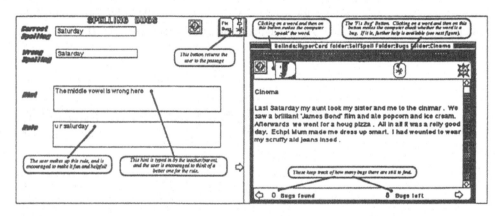

Fig. 1c. Making a Bug Card for 'Satarday'

Fig. 1d. Child's view of the support environment. "Click on a bug"

In the final phase the child went through the passage fixing all the bugs, without human help but with support from the program which could either give a hint, a rule or 'speak' the correct spelling for a bug (see Figures 1d, 1e, 1f - the latter demonstrates the use of scoring to help with motivation). In this version of the program, rule help (eg. U R Saturday in Fig. 1f) was not 'spoken' using synthesised speech, though in subsequent versions spoken help was available if required (via pressing a 'speak' button). All the responses were monitored automatically thus allowing easy record keeping. A novel feature of the program was that all the buttons were programmed to 'say' their name if the user 'hovered' over them with the mouse pointer, and furthermore there was a 'speak' button which used speech synthesis to 'pronounce' any words highlighted.

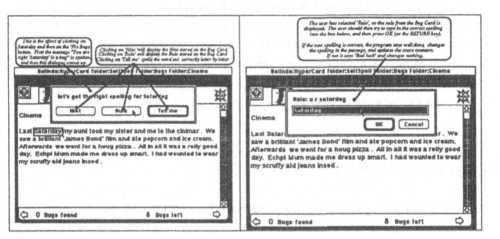

Figure 1e. After selecting Satarday, then clicking on the 'bug' button   **Figure 1f. Going for the rule**

Evaluation Study 1

Informal observations of a few dyslexic children interacting with the program convinced us that it was on the right lines, with the users showing considerable enthusiasm in the use of the program and good improvement in the spellings targetted by it. It was, however, important to undertake a formal evaluation with a good range of dyslexic users, in order to identify whether all the children showed benefits from use of the program, and whether such benefits transferred to the everyday world of pencil and paper work. The study is described in detail in Nicolson, Pickering and Fawcett (1991), and so an overall summary should suffice here.

Participants

The evaluation study was undertaken using a panel of 23 dyslexic children (mean age 13.4). None of them was familiar with use of the Apple Macintosh. An indication of their reading and spelling problems is given in Table 1, which shows their age-normed performance before the study described here. It should be noted that all the children had been diagnosed as dyslexic several years previously (using the standard criterion of an 18 month or more deficit in reading age over chronological age; together with normal or above normal IQ and no primary emotional or neurological problems). By the time of the study several of the children were technically 'remediated' in terms of reading age (ie. their reading age was within 18 months of their chronological age). Nonetheless, even for the 'remediated' children the spelling performance was very poor. The mean reading age was 10.5 years and the mean spelling age was 8.6 years.

Experimental Method

Six interesting passages of about 50 words were constructed, with two passages at 8, 10 and 13 years reading age respectively, using the modified Fogg index (see Lewis and Paine, 1985). For each child the experimenter determined the reading age, and selected the appropriate passage for dictation. The experimenter read the passage aloud with expression, reading a short section at a time, and the child was told to write the words down as carefully as possible, saying them aloud as they wrote them.

Next the child's dictation was typed into Hypercard by the experimenter and bug cards created for each error. Children making less than 8 errors were omitted, and for children making more than 8 errors, their passage was adjusted to have exactly 8 errors. Each child then went through three sessions of the program. Session 1 was used primarily to familiarise the child with the program and to invent rules for each of the bugs. In session 2 the experimenter guided the child through the program, encouraging him/her to identify and fix all the bugs, and in session 3 the child attempted to fix all the bugs with minimal help from the experimenter. Sessions took place one week apart. Parents were often present during the session, but they were not directly involved.

Finally, in order to evaluate the effectiveness of the computer program, the original dictation was repeated one month after session 3. Immediately after completing the passage the child was asked to circle any words that he/she thought were probably spelled wrongly, and, if they thought they could now spell it correctly, to write down the correct spelling. This task was an informal method of checking whether, even if the child could not spell all the words correctly, he/she did at least know which ones were probably wrong. The child's written passage was then scored for errors. A spoken structured interview was conducted for each child and a questionnaire administered to those parents who had been present during the experimental sessions.

Results of the Evaluation

Seven participants made less than 8 errors on the dictation and one was unavailable for further testing and so the following results are based on the remaining 15 children. The mean time spent on sessions 1, 2 and 3 was 65, 24 and 18 minutes respectively, reflecting the initial need to make bug cards, followed by the relatively speedy subseqent completion of the passage. After just three sessions on SelfSpell, the children were able to identify 80% of the bugs; to fix 70% of them immediately and to recall 50% of their rules.

The critical test, however, is dictation performance before and after training. The *overall* dictation errors after training were reduced by about one third (from a mean of 12.0 to 7.5). There was clearly a larger improvement on the 8 bugs targeted for each child, since over two thirds of them were spelled correctly (dictation errors reduced from a mean of 8.0 to 2.6). Indeed, the improvement overall may be attributed entirely to the improved performance on the bugs since the number of errors on untargetted words did not decrease overall. Analysis of the number of errors that the participants circled on their dictations, indicating that they thought they might be wrong, indicated that the participants were aware that their spellings were probably wrong for about half their mis-spellings, but that they were in general not very successful at correcting them.

All 15 children and 8 of their parents completed the questionnaires. Improved motivation and attitude were reported by 75% of the parents, and all the children and parents reported that it was fun to use SelfSpell! Open-ended comments from the comments were uniformly favourable. A selection includes:

She seems to be more aware of spelling mistakes and wants to put them right.
He has a new strategy for remembering correct spellings
He has been checking through his spellings more carefully.
He is more aware of spelling errors and seems to be enjoying reading more.
He seems to have grasped the spelling side and seems to have gained confidence.
N. has had lessons on a one-to-one basis, but has improved more from this method of
   teaching.
Of all the methods that have been used this is the most successful.
The computer talking makes it better and helps them remember what they have written.

Discussion

It seems clear that the Selfspell program was successful in its major objectives. It was fun to do, the participants enjoyed and valued it, as did their parents. It was effective even after one month in improving the spellings of the targetted bugs. In addition, there are also encouraging signs that it aided the children's confidence in that 75% of the parents said they had noticed an improvement in attitude and in confidence.

Study 2. Use of SelfSpell with younger dyslexic children

Study 1 demonstrated clearly that SelfSpell was valuable for adolescent dyslexic children, but it left two questions unresolved; namely whether it would be equally effective for younger dyslexic children whose spelling age was much lower; and whether the use of self-generated rules and a passage-based format were uniquely effective, or whether mastery learning techniques could also prove valuable. This second study investigated both possibilities.

Participants

The participants in this study were seven dyslexic children, aged 10-13 years (mean 11.7) diagnosed as dyslexic between the ages of 7 and 10, on the same exclusionary criteria as the older panel. Their age normed performance in reading and spelling before the study were 8.5 and 6.9 years respectively. Clearly the children in this study had made little or no progress in spelling, with a mean deficit between spelling and chronological age of 4.8 years. Attempts to remediate their spelling performance should therefore provide a stringent test of the efficacy of the spelling program.

Method

In addition to the rule-based approach outlined above a more directive, mastery learning approach is also available under SelfSpell. In this approach a list of words may be typed in (together with their homophone under speech synthesis, and an appropriate context description), and each word is then presented individually from time to time until it has been learned. Immediate feedback is used at all times, and the correct spelling is displayed immediately following any error. The spellings are introduced cumulatively, first with four spellings, then three more when the first four are learned, and so on.

In order to compare the rule-based, undirected approach with the directive mastery learning approach, we decided to test the learning of 20 spellings, with 10 learned using the rule-based approach and a matched set of 10 learned using the mastery approach.

Three training sessions, each of 20 minutes' duration, were run for each set of 10 words for each child. A pencil and paper pre-test on performance was administered by the parents before training began, and an exactly equivalent post-test was administered by the parents one week after the last training session. By contrast with the previous experiment, the spellings were selected by each child's parents as particularly important to him/her, and so the spellings selected were not matched to the spelling age of the child. Consequently, some of the words selected represented a considerable challenge. An example of the spellings made in the second session for one of the participants is given in Figure 3. Farrant was a word of family significance, and the first four words had been mastered in the first session. It may be seen that, in effect, the program requires the user to spell all the words correctly at least three times consecutively, and usually more in that even 'learned' spellings are re-tested from time to time.

CJ Session 2
17/2/91,12:38 pm
Score = 42 out of 53

Word	Spellings on Session 2	Pre-test	Post-test
evidence	evidence,evidence,evidence,evidence	evdans	evidence
farrant	farrant,farrant,farrant,farrant	farant	farrant
orange	orange,orange,orange,orange	oreg	orange
crayon	crayon,crayon,crayon,crayon	craneon	crayon
hospital	hosptil,hosptial,hospital,hopital,hospital,hospital, hospital, hospital,hospital	hosptal	hospital
picture	picher,piture,picture,picture,picture,picture,picture	picher	picture
sense	sense,sence,sense,sense,sense	sencs	sense
reason	resant,reason,reason,reason	resan	reason
kettle	ketal, kettle,kettle,kettle,kettle,kettle	kettal	kettle
perfect	perfcket,perfaket,perfect,perfect,perfect,perfect	pefeckt	perfect

Figure 3. Sample results from Spelling Mastery

Results

The results for each child are given in Table 3. It may be seen that the children scored few marks on the pre-tests, but that both approaches led to excellent learning, as evidenced by the high scores on the post-test. An analysis of variance confirmed that both methods led to highly significant learning, but that when one analyses the proportion of the words that were mis-spelled in the pre-test that were correctly spelled in the post-test, the mastery approach was significantly more effective overall.

Participant	Rule-Based		Mastery	
	Pre	Post	Pre	Post
CJ	1	7	0	10
CE	0	6	0	6
IT	3	7	3	10
MC	0	10	1	10
MS	1	3	5	8
RH	4	6	2	7
TA	1	6	1	9
Mean	1.4	6.4	1.7	8.6

Table 3. Individual results for pre and post tests

As in the previous experiment, an informal questionnaire established that all the children had enjoyed both the Selfspell and Spellmaster program. However, while they found the Selfspell program great fun, 75% preferred the Spellmaster program for the success it engendered. Analysis of the errors on the rule-based words suggested that, although in most cases the children had correctly remembered their rules, for the more complex words the rule alone was insufficient, and they mis-spelled some other portion of the word!

Overall Discussion

It is worthwhile here to consider the theoretical issues underlying the acquisition of spelling in the dyslexic child. Frith (1985) has argued that dyslexic children tend to get locked into the initial, 'logographic' stage for reading, in which performance is based on whole-word recognition, and are unable to make the transition to the phonologically mediated alphabetic stage. This causes severe problems for spelling, which is predominantly a retrieval process and cannot be sustained by the visual route alone. Spelling performance for the younger dyslexics breaks down in the segmentation process, or for the more competent older dyslexics at the stage of phoneme-grapheme translation.

It is therefore particularly encouraging, from both a theoretical and applied perspective, to note that all the children in this study seemed able to use the alphabetic principle when given the appropriate support. Clearly, given sufficient practice and motivation to succeed, even the most intractable spelling problems can be ameliorated to some extent. It appears therefore that the learning processes are largely intact, and that with appropriate support the spelling problem could diminish over time. An interesting parallel can be drawn between these results and those of Bradley (eg. 1988) who demonstrated that early support in phonological processing led to very much better subsequent acquisition of reading. Given early intervention, it seems likely that the initial problems can be substantially alleviated, leading to relatively normal acquisition of spelling skills.

A further issue arises with regard to CAL technology. The dictation system was designed to maximise the child's feeling of 'ownership' over the passages and spellings, ensuring that each child was able to learn truly relevant spellings. A consequence of this design was the need for considerable supportive adult assistance in the initial setting up phase. While this adult support is very desirable, it is also important to have a spelling help facility for children without access to such support, or for teachers who wish to use 'generic' materials suitable for a wide range of users. The success of the mastery learning system offered an opportunity to combine both individual rules and generic spellings, by augmenting the mastery learning of each spelling with a generic rule (available as in the rule-based system) which can easily be modified by the user to one of his/her own choosing. The new system (currently under development) involves a 'resource book' for teachers including a wide range of words to spell, with both pictorial help and spelling hints. A teacher is easily able to add and modify entries in the resource book, and may then rapidly select a set of spellings for any given child. Both pictorial, spoken and rule-based help is then available in addition to the direct algorithm-based learning procedure. We hope that this system will combine the low cost generic potential of the mastery system with the targetted individual 'feel' of the rule-based system.

Conclusion

In conclusion, we have argued that the Apple HyperCard multimedia environment has the potential to provide outstanding support for dyslexic children, using the immediacy and reinforcing effect of computer presentation with digitised or synthesised speech available to avoid reliance on textual presentation. The SelfSpell program proved both fun and effective for all our dyslexic children, including even those with a spelling age of well under 10 years. Both mastery and rule-based techniques proved very effective. We are sure it would prove fun and effective for non-dyslexic children also. We believe that the new developments in educational technology, added to the decreasing cost of such powerful systems, make the development of this type of multimedia environment a practical, affordable and very desirable target for the whole educational system.

REFERENCES

Bradley, L. (1988). Making connections in learning to read and to spell. *Applied Cognitive Psychology*, **2**, 3-18.

Frith, U. (1985). "Beneath the surface of developmental dyslexia". In Patterson K .E., Marshall J. C. and Coltheart M. (eds) *Surface dyslexia* , London Lawrence Erlbaum.

Lewis, R. and Paine, N. (1985). How to Communicate with the Learner. *Open Learning Guide 6.* London, CET.

Malone, T.W. (1981). Towards a theory of intrinsically motivating instruction. *Cognitive Science*, **4**, 333-369.

Nicolson, R.I, Pickering, S. and Fawcett, A.J. (1991). Open Learning for Dyslexic Children using HyperCard™. *Computers and Education*, **16**, 203-209.

Thomson, M.E. (1984). *Developmental Dyslexia: Its nature, assessment and remediation.* London, Edward Arnold.

Using HyperCard to Create
a Flexible Learning Package for Statistics:
Costs, Benefits and Effectiveness

Roderick I. Nicolson & Adrian J. Simpson

Department of Psychology

University of Sheffield

Sheffield S10 2TN, England

tel. +44742 768555 ext. 6547

email: R.NICOLSON@UK.AC.SHEFFIELD.PRIMEA

Abstract

Multimedia programming environments such as HyperCard have the potential to create a new generation of software for flexible learning. This article provides a detailed case study of the development of the HELP-Stats package for learning psychological statistics. HELP-Stats was developed from an existing 10 week laboratory-based statistics course and is intended to provide a complete replication of the desirable aspects of the laboratory classes while adding the immediate feedback, computational support, and adaptive help available in good CAL programs. Controlled evaluations of the effect and affect of the HELP-Stats stacks indicated that even the somewhat inadequate prototypes were more fun and at least as effective as traditional laboratory teaching. Analysis of the costs and benefits suggests that, given careful software engineering, the development costs are comparable with traditional CAL development costs and that the benefits include significant pedagogical and administrative advantages, together with potential resource savings for larger classes or repeated use.

Introduction

Multimedia Teaching: the need for objective evaluation

Hypermedia and multimedia are currently the subject of intense commercial and academic interest. Advocates of multimedia claim that they represent a quantum leap in both ease of use and representational ability, thus providing the potential for a new generation of educational software. Most educational applications of hypermedia have focused on truly innovative projects such as the video/HyperCard Twelfth Night environment (Howard, 1990) developed as part of the Renaissance Project — projects that were made possible only by the advent of hypermedia techniques. There is clearly an important role for such developments, but there is an equally important need to identify the costs and benefits of multimedia enhancements to *routine* teaching methods, so that guidelines for the effective use of the media can be derived. Implicit in this analysis is the need for evaluation of the costs and benefits of such hypermedia teaching enhancements, for it is by this means that estimates of the costs and benefits may be derived. Unfortunately, there has been little or no published research on this issue, and so there are few guidelines validated by objective data.

The HELP-Stats (HyperCard Exercises for Learning Psychological Statistics) project reported here was designed to investigate this issue. In brief, HELP-Stats represents a HyperCard version for an existing 10 week statistics course developed by one of the authors (AJS). Costs and benefits of the HELP-Stats course were derived both from monitoring development time and by means of a formal evaluation in which parallel sessions using HELP-Stats and traditional teaching were undertaken, and users' reactions to the teaching method, together with its effectiveness, were determined.

Applied Statistics: a Rigorous Test for Multimedia Teaching

Statistics learning is traditionally one of the least popular aspects of undergraduate life, seen as a necessary evil rather than an exciting intellectual challenge. Furthermore, statistics teaching is often viewed by University staff as one of the least rewarding lecturing duties (Nicolson, 1991a). The lack of enthusiasm of such staff for their task (and often a lack of expertise also) can lead to highly unsatisfactory educational experiences for all concerned. Statistics learning and teaching is also of necessity a lengthy and effortful process, requiring the mastery of a range of concepts and techniques, most of which are best learned by 'hands on' experience. On the other hand, statistical competence is now acknowledged as a necessity for most disciplines which involve the collection and analysis of data. Almost all psychology departments throughout the country require their students to reach a level of attainment in statistics beyond the merely elementary. Indeed, many other non-mathematical departments do so too, for example departments of biology and geography.

It appears therefore that statistics teaching represents a major challenge for higher and secondary education, being of central importance and yet of little esteem in the eyes of either staff or students. Furthermore, it would seem that statistics teaching might provide an ideal target for development and evaluation of a multimedia teaching package. If the package were effective, it could be widely used as the mainstay of statistics teaching even in the absence of expert statistics teachers. If it proved also to be more fun for the student than the traditional methods, it could have a major effect on their attitude to statistics, thus providing the bedrock for any learning experience.

As with all undergraduate courses in the Sheffield Psychology Department, the statistics course is evaluated each year by the participants, and has had generally satisfactory ratings, within the mid-band of those for other, specialist, courses. However, despite its generally satisfactory nature, the practical work is less than ideal in certain respects because it necessarily relies heavily on support from the class teacher and postgraduate demonstrators. Such support can be inefficient (if the same help has to be given individually to a large number of students) and slow (because the ratio of students to staff is typically high, about 15 to 1). In particular, the high student to staff ratio inevitably leads to delays before many of the students receive feedback on mistakes, with the result that in a long sequence of related calculations errors may accumulate to the detriment of motivation and understanding.

We therefore developed a flexible learning statistics package (using HyperCard) based upon the practical work required in this department, as embodied in the course booklets (a 200 page textbook known as 'the Handbook' and a 'Workbook' comprising 45 pages of exercises). Together, the programs and books form a stand-alone package, but the HELP-Stats system is also capable of being generalised to other statistics courses. As part of the development process, a set of generic tools was devised, to assist in the development itself, and to achieve consistency in the use of the package. Also, students' reactions to the system, and its effect, if any, on their attainment, were assessed as part of the project in a controlled evaluation study.

Pedagogical Issues

The program content was reasonably easily specified, in that it was to be the contents of the existing statistics Workbook, suitably enhanced by hypermedia techniques to allow immediate feedback of error, and so on. However, this begs an important issue encountered in the implementation of teaching by computers, namely the level at which to employ computing facilities. There seem to be two broad schools of thought about how to approach the teaching of applied statistics. One school believes that students cannot grasp the required concepts unless they carry out the detailed calculations themselves. It is claimed that there is no substitute for squaring and summing, for calculating mean squares from sums of squares, and so on. Only with this involvement can the student really appreciate what the statistics imply. An opposing school of thought claims that the drudgery of calculation impedes conceptual understanding and that students get lost in the details. They advocate the use of a computer package (eg Minitab), to which students can offer data and from which they can obtain results. The second school claims that this approach frees the student from drudgery and allows time for exploration and reflection. However, the danger associated with the use of such packages is that they provide answers all too readily, and students can complete assignments without giving any thought to what the package is actually doing computationally, or to the underlying statistical ideas. The process is effectively a bit of magic. One of the objectives of the current project was to attempt to achieve the right balance between the wizardry and the drudgery of these two schools.

A further contentious issue for intelligent tutoring systems and for CAL programs is how directive the program should be. Papert (1980) and his supporters have argued that programs are most effective when seen as a discovery learning environment in which the user can make his or her own decisions, learning from errors, and exploring the space of possibilities. More traditional CAL programs take a more directive line, trying both to pinpoint any errors and to encourage the user to ttake the 'best' route through the learning experience. Our feeling was that the latter approach was more suitable for this application, in that the major perceived drawback of the existing statistics course was the uncertainty as to whether one's calculations were correct, and the frustration involved in finding, three quarters of the way through a tedious calculation, that one's initial step had been incorrect. Consequently, we decided to give immediate feedback following each decision (see Anderson et al, 1990 for a recent discussion of these issues).

Using one of the HELP-Stats stacks

Before considering the results of the evaluation studies, and the stacks and tools created, it is valuable to provide some context by presenting an overview of the program in standard use.

Example of One-factor Analysis of Variance (Week 3)

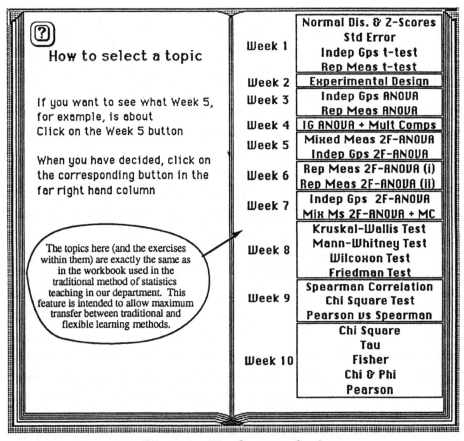

Figure 1. The Contents Card

After an introductory screen, a user interacting with HELP-Stats is presented with the Contents screen (Fig. 1). Clicking on, for example, Week 7 gives a brief overview of the topics available under that heading. In due course the user is expected to select the topic of interest by clicking on the appropriate button. Doing so takes him/her to the relevant stack where a problem is presented. In the present example (Fig. 2), the problem topic is Independent Groups Analysis of Variance in Week 3.

After reading the statement of the problem (which is the same as in the Workbook), the user clicks on the arrow, and is confronted with a template to complete. The template presents the scores to be analysed and requires the computation of certain quantities as a first step towards answering the research question posed in the problem statement. Apart from the calculator, the display is exactly equivalent to that in the workbook. Figure 2 shows the template during the course of solution of the problem. At the stage displayed, two results have been calculated and entered into their fields (see annotations 1 and 2), while a third (annotation 3) is in the course of being dragged to its field. Note that, once the appropriate column of data has been dragged to the column calculator, only two operations are required to obtain $\sum X^2$ — click on data^2, and then on Σ. Examination of the operations required for these computations highlights some of the benefits of the HELP-Stats system.

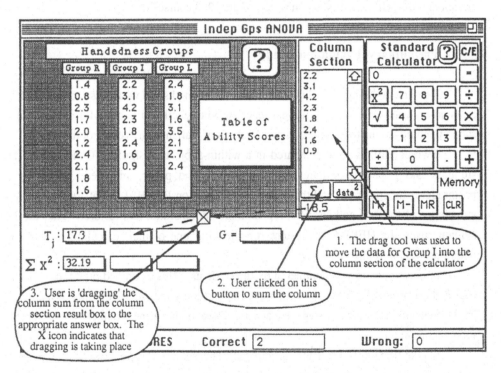

Figure 2. Mid-way through an analysis of variance

In order to complete the problem, the user must then fill in further cards, which support the calculations of F ratios, determining the conclusions, and the graphical display of the data. Space precludes an illustration of the steps involved.

Evaluation Studies

As part of the project, students' reactions to the system, and its effect, if any, on their attainment, were assessed. Students' attitudes to an early version of the HELP-Stats system were initially obtained using two preliminary studies, the first of which is reported below. Subsequently, the main evaluation study examined students performance on, reaction to, and attainment following, the first seven weeks of the 1990 course.

Preliminary Evaluation Study

The first preliminary evaluation study of the strengths and weaknesses of one HELP-Stats stack, compared with traditional teaching via pencil and paper with demonstrator support, employed the topic of one-factor Analysis of Variance, in Week 3 of the course.

Two conditions were compared in a within-subjects design: In Condition A, the students taking part used hand calculators, pen and paper, and were helped by a postgraduate demonstrator and the lecturer; in Condition B, a HELP-Stats program, with knowledge of the data and answers, replaced the demonstrator and lecturer. Thus all the students used the HELP-Stats system for checking one of their calculations, and the traditional system for the other.

A questionnaire was completed by the students. This examined preference for the HELP-Stats program versus the demonstrators, and the good and bad points of using the HELP-Stats program and of using the teachers. These points were obtained as unprompted, spontaneous comments.

On the first day 30 students participated. This session was treated as a pilot run and led to several modifications to the program. On the second day 36 students took part. There were two students to each computer. In answer to the question, "Did you prefer to check your work by using the computer or by asking the teacher?", there was a clear preference for HELP-Stats over the demonstrators. (The alternatives provided were: Computer, No preference, Teacher.) This was true even on the first day, where 57% preferred HELP-Stats and 33% preferred the teacher) although it was beset with teething problems. On the second day the preference for HELP-Stats was overwhelming (72% to 8%).

In their unprompted answers to the question, "What were the good (and bad) points of using the computer?" the students gave the advantages of the HELP-Stats assistance as: immediate checking of intermediate results (42%), speedy feedback (31%), and providing clear organisation of the tasks to be done (24%). On the other hand, disadvantages mentioned were: slow computation (53%), limited feedback (19%), and a danger of discouraging thinking for oneself (13%). These observations resulted in substantial changes being made to certain aspects of the system. In particular, in all subsequent work the data were provided on-screen at the commencement of a problem, and the sequence of operations to be followed was left to the students' discretion. Also, but later on, the 'phrase assembly' method of constructing and checking conclusions was devised.

Students gave the advantages of the teachers as: able to explain why one is wrong, able to answer specific queries, able to judge level of comprehension. The main disadvantage offered was the long wait before the teachers could come to one's aid.

Design of the Main Evaluation Study

The full-scale study was conducted on the first seven weeks of the course, using stacks which taught a number of statistical topics up to two-way analysis of variance (week 7). In this study one group of about 25 students (the HELP-Stats Group) tackled the practicals using the HELP-Stats system for guidance and feedback; a second, independent group of about 35 (the Demonstrator Group) did the practical exercises using hand calculators (or a BASIC program in the case of two-factor ANOVA) and with postgraduate demonstrator help instead of using HELP-Stats.

Results of the Main Evaluation Study

To assess the outcome of the main evaluation study, analyses were conducted on (i) student comments collected from questionnaires distributed during the course, (ii) data on the time taken to complete certain problems, and (iii) performance of the HELP-Stats and Demonstrator groups in the end-of-course pen, paper and calculator 90-minute test in December, and in a similar formal examination which took place in the following June. The comments obtained followed a similar pattern to those reported earlier, with the HELP-Stats group valuing the immediate and informative feedback, but complaining at the slow and tedious operation of the screen calculator. The time data are displayed in Table 1. Note that the HELP-Stats group took significantly longer than the demonstrator group to solve the problems. Of course, this may or may not result in deeper learning and better understanding on the part of the HELP-Stats group. The examination performance data (Table 2) provide evidence that the learning was at least as good for the latter group.

	Demonstrator Group Mean	HELP-Stats Group Mean	F	p
Week 3, No 1	19.57 (23)	29.53 (17)	46.91	.0001
Week 3, No 2	18.78 (23)	35.88 (17)		
Week 5, No 1	38.00 (15)	51.14 (14)	14.81	.0007
Week 5, No 2	27.47 (15)	38.21 (14)		

Table 1. Solution times for problems 1 and 2 in Weeks 3 and 5 of the main evaluation study. (Numbers of observations are given in parentheses.)

Using data from the 90-minute end-of-course test, we examined performance in the Analysis of Variance (ANOVA) questions (since this was the main topic taught by the HELP-Stats system) and also students' total marks. In general, the HELP-Stats group obtained slightly higher scores in the test than did the Demonstrator group, though this difference did not reach statistical significance (see Table 2).

End of Course	Demonstrator Group Mean (N = 34)	HELP-Stats Group Mean (N = 26)	F	p
ANOVA Qs	10.76	12.58	1.74	.19
Total Mark	50.16	53.11	2.04	.16
Examination	Demonstrator Group Mean (N = 36)	HELP-Stats Group Mean (N = 25)	t	p
1-factor Qs	7.44	8.08	0.73	.47
2-factor Qs	18.03	18.16	0.12	.90
Combined Qs	25.47	26.24	0.48	.63
Total Mark	63.30	63.96	0.16	.87

Table 2. Comparative performance on subsequent attainment tests

Six months later, the two groups achieved virtually identical mean scores in the end-of-year exam (see Table 2). Here we examined marks on questions dealing with one-factor ANOVA, two-factor ANOVA, the above marks combined, and also the total marks achieved in the exam. At least the HELP-Stats group, despite teething problems with the system, were not inferior in attainment to the Demonstrator group.

Discussion

Having reviewed the rationale, the content and the evaluation of the research undertaken, it is important to relate the findings back to the issues raised initially, namely the costs and benefits of multimedia educational software, and the implications for developers of such software.

Analysis of Costs and Benefits

We provide separate analyses of the costs and benefits separately for the educational, and the resource perspectives.

(i) Educational Costs and Benefits

The evaluation studies have revealed marked educational advantages. We shall list them for clarity:

> Immediate feedback
> Active Involvement
> Neither 'wizardry' nor 'drudgery'
> More popular than existing teaching method
> At least as effective as existing teaching method
> Compatible with existing teaching methods

The potential educational drawback of any distance learning approach is the lack of access to a human tutor. As is clear from the evaluations, the lack of *need* for access to a human tutor was considered an important advantage of HELP-Stats. It should perhaps be stressed, however, that all students had the benefit of a one hour lecture on the appropriate statistical technique from AJS directly before the practical sessions, and so the approach adopted was flexible learning, involving both human and software presentation, rather than unsupported distance learning. A true distance learning package would probably require redesign of the Handbook material.

Overall, then, in educational terms, the research has been extremely successful, with marked educational benefit, and remarkably little educational cost.

(ii) Resource Costs and Benefits

Clearly a University course is very difficult to cost, depending as it does on issues such as the cost of an academic's time, and the degree of existing material available. It is worth distinguishing two types of costs components: the startup costs (the resources needed to fully prepare a course unit) and the recurrent costs (the resources needed to prepare and re-present the course unit). For each cost it is important to distinguish the overall cost, the cost per student (ie. the overall cost divided by the number of students participating), and the marginal cost per student (ie. the extra cost incurred for each extra student).

(a) *Traditional Method.* For the traditional teaching method we have no data on the original startup costs, in that the course was developed over a period of years. 10 hours per 1 hour lecture is a reasonable guess for a typical startup time for normal lectures (Nicolson, 1991b, §6.1). The startup costs are probably five times this figure for a workbook-based subject such as statistics, in which, in addition to the development of the lectures, the exercises need to be invented, that data calculated and checked, and so on. The recurrent costs are easier to calculate. The system in use was that a group of about 60 students was split into two groups of about 30, and each group undertook the practicals on successive afternoons, with a one hour lecture followed by two hours practical class. The support available during the exercises was the lecturer plus one postgraduate demonstrator. This leads to 3 hours (AJS) plus 2 hours (demonstrator) per afternoon. If we cost a demonstrator at half the lecturer cost per hour (LH), we obtain a total of 4 LH per afternoon, or 8 LH total. Presumably the marginal cost per extra student is the amount of extra demonstrator time required. Since (excluding the lecture) 3 LH units are required for 30 students for the two hours' exercises, the marginal cost per student is 0.10 LH. In fact, in some cases this critically under-represents the cost, in that once the capacity of the laboratory is exceeded, major restructuring is required. This critical number is around 60 for our statistics course, and so further increases might require the spilling over into a third afternoon, at considerable costs in terms of time and timetabling.

(b) *HELP-Stats Method.* The startup costs might include the cost of the necessary computing facilities. The HELP-Stats suite was used satisfactorily with two students per machine, leading to a requirement of 15 machines. Since it runs satisfactorily on a

Macintosh Classic, the total cost would be around $15,000. Of course such a network would be of much wider value in teaching and research, and so we feel that it is not appropriate to include the teaching hardware cost within the overall startup costs. In the present project, the teaching network was already well established.

It is difficult to decide how to estimate the software startup costs. Much of the early work was aimed at designing the necessary tools, such as the drag facility. Now these have been designed, subsequent developments are much faster. However, taking the worst case, the overall programming time, the total time taken was 18 months work, say 70 weeks of 37 hours, for a recent graduate untrained in programming, a total of 2500 hours at approximately demonstrator rate, thus 1250 LH. This resulted in 10 weeks' worth of classes, leading to 125 LH per class, fairly typical of traditional CAL authoring costs (Self, 1985). An extra LH should be added to this total for the lecturer's time in giving the one hour introductory lecture. The marginal cost per extra student appears to be 0, or at least negligible.

An alternative measure of the programming costs is that given by the time taken to create a further laboratory class, once all the necessary tools had been developed. By the end of the project, each week's work was taking exactly one week to prepare (because that was all the time available!), say a total of 40 hours programming, or 20 LH.

Conclusions

The preceding paragraphs provide the background for assessing the achievements of the project. The applied objective of the research presented here was that of constructing a stand-alone flexible learning package for psychological statistics, based on the existing laboratory course. This objective was clearly achieved. The HELP-Stats package was constructed, and it worked, and we are now going over to using it routinely in our undergraduate teaching. The theoretical objectives of the research were to identify whether such a package would be educationally valuable, and whether it would be possible to provide support which concentrated on the important aspects of the statistical computations. The evaluation studies demonstrated that HELP-Stats did satisfy these criteria, being more popular than the traditional approach and at least as effective, with the drag facility and the calculator providing unobtrusive support for routine data manipulation. The wider aim of the research was to assess the feasibility of HyperCard as an environment for constructing viable flexible learning materials. It is clear from our experience that HyperCard has the necessary power to create excellent interactive multimedia learning environments which provide good compatibility with existing teaching techniques but in addition provide significant advantages in terms of immediacy of feedback and flexibility of access. However, despite these advantages, programming in HyperCard is not easy, especially for larger projects, and a thoroughly professional approach to software engineering should be adopted in order to achieve satisfactory results. The costs of HyperCard implementation are roughly comparable with traditional CAL costs. It seems likely that with the continual improvement of multimedia development environments, such facilities will be able to account for a significant proportion of routine teaching requirements. The challenge facing educationalists will be how to design courses in which human teaching and flexible learning provide a constructive synergy rather than coexisting in a wary truce.

References

ANDERSON, J. R., BOYLE, C. F, CORBETT, A.T. AND LEWIS, M.W. (1990). Cognitive Modeling and Intelligent Tutoring. *Artificial Intelligence,* 42, 7-49.

HOWARD, G. (1991). Twelfth Night. Renaissance Project disc UK0304, Coventry Polytechnic.

NICOLSON, R. I. (1991a). Report on the CTI Workshop "Computing and Psychological Statistics: Today and Tomorrow". *CTI Software News,* 3.

NICOLSON, R. I. (1991b). *Guidelines for Effective University Teaching.* Sheffield, University of Sheffield.

PAPERT, S. (1980). *Mindstorms: Children, Computers and Powerful Ideas.* New York; Basic Books.

SELF, J. (1985). *Microcomputers in Education: A critical appraisal of educational software.* Brighton; Harvester Press.

EDUCATIONAL SOFTWARE ENGINEERING : A METHODOLOGY BASED ON COOPERATIVE DEVELOPMENTS

Thierry NODENOT

Laboratoire API, 50 chemin des maraîchers, Université Paul Sabatier,
31062 TOULOUSE, FRANCE
Laboratoire LICIAP, faculté des Sciences, Université de Pau et des Pays de l'Adour,
64000 PAU, FRANCE

Abstract

The development of complex educational software such as learning environments, simulations and intelligent tutoring systems requires a rational approach that looks like those that software engineers call for.

We propose a methodology which allows a real cooperation between the two classes of users concerned about software educational engineering : the pedagogues and the software engineers. This methodology is based on a few straightforward principles such as prototyping, structuring the process of developing software into stages, and the availability of a formal language which allows a communication between the classes of users. It can be used to implement any educational software, from their requirements to their use.

1. INTRODUCTION

Courseware becomes more and more complex and its methods of development follow the same process. In the past, courseware implementation meant little more than designing a few screens and specifying their sequence. Today, such an approach is not suitable for current educational requirements because courseware must not look like drills or tutorials, but like learning environments, complex simulations or intelligent tutoring systems. Their development requires methods which are different from those that software engineers use because these methods are mainly applied by pedagogues with an educational viewpoint, but they are not purely educational because the aim is to develop a software system. *Specific engineering methods for educational software* are required.

Several teams have directed their research towards software educational engineering methodologies. In the United States, we can note the work of [MERRILL-86] for the automated instructional development systems, the work of A. BORK [BORK-84], [BORK-89] which proposes advanced information technology as an aid for courseware development. In Europe, we can quote the work of [SCHOENMAKER-90] which proposes a methodology in which designing an educational system can be done through modelling different aspects of that system at different levels of abstraction, other works which focus on specifying educational software [IBRAHIM-90], or works which give some instructions for the production of a courseware engineering system [CAMCE-90], [BESSAGNET-91].

We noticed the efforts that researchers make to identify and connect the activities proposed to the pedagogues during the development of courseware. But we were surprised that the data processing aspect of such a development was taken into account only at the end of the process, or even ignored. We think that a complex courseware is the result of a narrow cooperation between a team of pedagogues and a team of software engineers : they perform a development which is both educational and data processing oriented.

In this paper, we present a methodology (called MAGE) in which pedagogues and software engineers share out the responsibilities of the development. Such a research comes within the scope of the production of an Integrated Courseware Engineering System or ICES (in French "AGDI") [GOUARDERES-90], [BESSAGNET-90b].

2. THE "MAGE" METHODOLOGY

"MAGE" differs from other educational methodologies :
- it is based, as much as possible, on principles which were put to the fore by software engineering research for the development of business software. The same signs lead to the same cure and problems linked to maintainability, modularity, flexibility, portability and extensibility of courseware should be solved thanks to known software engineering methods which are transposed in an educational context,
- it provides a set of consistent methods which enable the teams of pedagogues and of software engineers to contribute, in turn, to the development of educational software. This requires that the methodology enables both teams to exchange the data of development. To this end, this methodology focuses on the semantics of data which are exchanged by pedagogues and software engineers.

2.1. The principles of the "MAGE" methodology

The functioning of the methodology follows from four principles which are detailed in the next paragraphs. These principles enable us to split the process of development into a sequence of stages, to provide the developers with a model (the "spiral" model) which allows them to achieve the different stages of development, to take into account the particularities of educational software compared to classical applications (three levels of abstraction are required), and to provide the two classes of developers with a formal language that they will use to model the courseware and to exchange their descriptions.

2.1.1.   FIRST PRINCIPLE : A PROCESS SPLIT INTO A SEQUENCE OF STAGES

One of the most important notions we can learn from software engineering is that of separating development decisions. This means that during the development, we limit ourselves to one part of the software at a time. Current research and developments show that five stages are necessary to develop courseware [BESSAGNET-90a], [PENINOU-90], [SCHOENMAKER-90] : the specification, design, implementation, validation and distribution stages. We shall add a stage of maintenance whose purpose is to modify or extend the functionalities of an educational software : it is a repetition of the other stages.

Within the framework of the "MAGE" methodology, both the teams of pedagogues and of software engineers are concerned by these five stages :
- This sequence of stages allows the team of pedagogues to model the educational software from the initial requirements (theme, type of students, educational objectives, ...) to a set of data that can be processed by the program coded by software engineers. Data usually modelled are *educational modules* which divide a CAL session just like chapters and paragraphs split a book ; *learning paths* which define a way between the different concepts that a student must assimilate to satisfy an educational objective ; *instructional transactions* which form the smallest unit of interaction that is still educationally relevant : *graphical and multimedia screens* which are used to interact with students.
- The software engineers use the same sequence of stages to develop a program that can process the previous educational data. The behavior of this program is completely defined by the educational developments of the team of pedagogues.

The two classes of developers achieve, at the same time and in collaboration, the implementation of both the educational data and the program that processes them. This cooperation is directed by the pedagogues who provide, at each stage of the process of development, the educational context in which the software engineers will act.

2.1.2.   SECOND PRINCIPLE : A SPIRAL MODEL OF DEVELOPMENT

Splitting the process of development into stages, as we did in the previous paragraph, is not enough. We must also provide a model which allows the users to achieve and link these different stages : a model for the cycle of development of educational software.

The waterfall life cycle model [BOEHM-76] which is often used to develop educational software is quite limited. Though each stage is matched with a checking phase which allows to ensure that the solution is true to the specifications in entry of the stage, practical use shows that errors which are not detected in the first stages are very hard to dismiss. For the production of an educational software, problems are really complex because two types of mistakes can arise at the same time :

- those of the team of pedagogues when they design the educational objectives, the learning strategies, ...
- those of the team of software engineers when they implement software packages which are supposed to answer the educational aims expressed by the pedagogues.

That's the reason why we have chosen the spiral model [BOEHM-86] to organize the cycle of development of educational software. The main characteristic of this model is the use of prototyping [CHOPPY-88], [VONK-90] to limit the risks of mistakes during the development. Running a prototype enables us, indeed, to understand more easily the behavior of the system, and to promote facilities of communication between the different people who are concerned by the development : the resultant knowledge avoids mistakes during the implementation of the final system.

Applied to educational software development, the spiral model proposes a progression through the same sequence of steps for each level of its elaboration (specification, design, realization, validation, distribution). It is a top-down process in which each cycle begins with the rough identification of requirements, constraints and solutions to implement the different portions of the courseware. The prototyping techniques and tools enable the users to acquire knowledge about the real requirements, and thus, they eliminate most of the sources of risk coming from initial requirements which are incomplete and inconsistent. Then, all depends on the residual risks which are not taken into account by the prototype : whether the developers think that they are important or not, another plan of development will be decided for the next level of prototyping, or for the use of the prototype to choose and implement one solution.

2.1.3. THIRD PRINCIPLE : A MODELLING USING THREE LEVELS OF ABSTRACTION

At each stage of the development, the two classes of users design the educational software by looking at it at different levels of abstraction. An abstraction is a simplified view of a system containing only the details important for a particular purpose. Abstractions are essential for large-scale projects because they must be simplified before they can be understood and synthesized by individual people. For the development of educational software, we shall distinguish three levels of abstraction [GOUARDERES-86],

[SHOENMAKER-90] : *the pedagogic dimension* which is the set of concepts and learning objectives related to the domain in which the educational software will act, *the didactic dimension* which focuses on the different learning strategies that pedagogues foresee to meet the educational objectives (these strategies are more or less learner controlled), *the mediatic dimension* which takes into account the interactions of the student with the educational system during the apprenticeship of the concepts modelled for the domain.

So, the modelling of a courseware defines goals in each of these three dimensions :

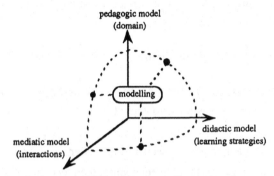

figure 1 : a modelling in a three dimensional space.

We can note that both the pedagogues and the software engineers are concerned by these three dimensions. The concepts and goals that pedagogues put in a prominent position for each dimension of an educational software are part of the program developed by the software engineers : they will be coded as functions, abstract data types, ...

2.1.4. FOURTH PRINCIPLE : A SINGLE LANGUAGE FOR THE WHOLE DEVELOPMENT

During the different stages of development, the two classes of users design descriptions thanks to their particular methods and tools, but the "MAGE" methodology must provide means to store and share these informations between the different methods used in the courseware engineering system. We need a language which supports the integration of both the methods and the classes of users. Our major aim is to provide a language which promotes precise descriptions because this precision is necessary if we want the classes of users to communicate and cooperate but also for the automation of the methodology [McCLURE-89].

The language we have chosen is called "Spec" [BERZINS-90]. Based on the second order logic and abstract data types, it is independent from the type of system which is developed and covers the software life cycle from the specification to the maintenance.

Moreover, its high degree of formalization promotes prototyping, integrity checking of the descriptions, and code generation into high level languages like Ada, C, and Prolog : the "Spec" language is compatible with the spiral model presented in paragraph 2.1.2.

Used in the framework of the "MAGE" methodology, this language allows the sharing of the educational descriptions modelled by each class of users, for each stage of the development (specification, design, ...), and each of the levels of abstraction (pedagogic, didactic and mediatic models) required for a courseware. The study of the language (syntax and semantics) is out of our scope but the different descriptions detailed in paragraph 2.3. show its advanced capabilities.

2.2. Heurism of the "MAGE" methodology

The four principles that we have presented in paragraph 2.1. are combined to build the heurism that the developers will use to apply the "MAGE" methodology :
Begin
    for each stage of the methodology (specification, design, implementation, ...) *loop*
        for each class of users (team of pedagogues, then team of software engineers) *loop*
            for each dimension of the courseware (pedagogic, didactic and mediatic models) *loop*
                - model in the "Spec" language a description matching the aims of the stage and the abilities of the user
                - identify the sources of risk of the description
                While some sources of risk exist *loop*
                    - prototype a solution limiting these risks
                    - modify the description in the "Spec" language to take into account the results of the prototyping process,
                    - identify the remaining sources of risk of the description
                End loop
            End loop
            integrate the descriptions and transmit them to the other class of users
        End loop
        store the description for the next stage
    End loop
End

The use of such a heurism takes more time -initially- to design small and simple applications. However, if one wants to automate the methodology, to change the design for a courseware or to reuse parts of it, one benefits from this approach.

2.3. The practical use of the "MAGE" methodology : an example of development

In this paragraph, we present a concrete example of the use of the "MAGE" methodology. Within the framework of this paper, it is not possible to detail every stage of the development, for each user, and each dimension of the educational software : we shall focus on the pedagogic and didactic models. Our aim is to show that the "Spec" language allows to model educational considerations : we shall detail "Spec" descriptions for the specification stage -because it is the most important in the development process-, then we shall explain how these descriptions are used during the next stages.

2.3.1. INITIAL AIMS FOR AN EDUCATIONAL SOFTWARE

Here is a text which explains the initial requirements for the educational software that a team of pedagogues wants to develop :

"The aim of this educational software is to control that eleven-year-old students know the different properties of *quadrilaterals*. The system must check that the *route* proposed by the student (composed of a sequence of quadrilaterals) respects the given *order*. The orders must be adapted to the abilities of the student, and the goal is to help him *arrange* the different quadrilaterals according to their *geometrical properties* (figure 2)" :

Quadrilaterals

Geometrical properties

figure 2 : an example of route.

2.3.2. THE SPECIFICATION STAGE

FROM THE VIEWPOINT OF PEDAGOGUES

Let us begin by the pedagogic model. The "Spec" description must detail the concepts and the goals which are connected to the domain in which the educational software will be used. From the initial aims, the pedagogues describe the concepts called quadrilateral and geometrical property, the partial ordering operator[1] (to arrange) between the different quadrilaterals : this operator considers the properties of the quadrilaterals to arrange them.

---

[1] The diamond and the rectangle cannot be arranged according to their geometrical properties.

Hence the "Spec" description :

DEFINITION Concepts-and-goals-of-the-pedagogic-model
 	
-- *description of a CAL concept in this courseware : all of them are quadrilaterals*
 	
CONCEPT   cal-concept : type
  WHERE Subtype(cal-concept, quadrilateral)
 	
CONCEPT   quadrilateral : type
 	
-- *description of the geometrical properties of a quadrilateral: has-two-right-angles, has-opposite-sides-equal, and has-4-sides-equal*
 	
CONCEPT   has-two-right-angles(q : quadrilateral) VALUE (b : boolean)
 	
CONCEPT   has-opposite-sides-equal (q : quadrilateral) VALUE (b: boolean)
 	
...
 	
-- *description of the quadrilaterals used in the courseware : ordinary quadrilateral, parallelogram, diamond, rectangle and square*
 	
CONCEPT   ordinary-quadrilateral : type
  WHERE ALL (q : ordinary-quadrilateral ::
       not(has-opposite-sides-equal(q))
       and not(has-two-right-angles(q)))
  Subtype(ordinary-quadrilateral, quadrilateral)
	CONCEPT parallelogram : type
	  WHERE ALL(p : parallelogram ::
	        has-opposite-sides-equal(p))
	  Subtype (parallelogram, quadrilateral)
	
	CONCEPT diamond : type
	  WHERE ALL(d : diamond ::
	        has-4-sides-equal(d))
	  Subtype (diamond, quadrilateral)
	
	...
	
	CONCEPT square : type
	  WHERE Subtype(square, diamond)
	       Subtype(square, rectangle)
	
	-- *description of the goals of the pedagogic model : the operator < means that c2 has all the properties of c1 and others.*
	
	CONCEPT "<" (c1, c2 : cal-concept)
	  VALUE (b : boolean) WHERE b <=>
	            the-properties(c1) < the-
	  properties(c2)
	  goal("<", courseware)
	
	CONCEPT the-properties(c : cal-concept)
	  -- *this concept deals with the geometrical properties of quadrilaterals*
	
	END

The concepts of the didactic model allow the pedagogues to define the different learning strategies that they want the students to use when they learn the quadrilaterals of the pedagogic model. Here, the pedagogues describe the concepts of *route* and of *order*. A refinement of the initial aims (thanks to prototyping) can lead them to classify the orders according to the strategy of arrangement which is proposed to the student. We shall distinguish the *augmentative strategy* in which the student must add geometrical properties to discover new quadrilaterals ant the opposite strategy called a *reductive strategy* :

DEFINITION Concepts-of-the-didactic-model
 	
INHERIT Concepts-and-goals-of-the-pedagogic-model
 	
-- *Description of the concept of route : a route is composed of cal-concepts (quadrilaterals)*
 	
CONCEPT   route : type
  WHERE needed-for(cal-concept, route)
 	
CONCEPT   length(r : route VALUE (n : nat)
 	
-- *Description of the concept of order*
 	
CONCEPT   order : type
 	
CONCEPT   title(o : order)
       VALUE (q : question)
 	
CONCEPT   used-strategy(o : order)
  VALUE (s : strategy)
	CONCEPT is-initial-concept(o : order)
	  VALUE (c : cal-concept)
	
	CONCEPT is-final-concept(o : order)
	  VALUE (c : cal-concept)
	
	-- *Description of the concept of strategy and of its instances*
	
	CONCEPT strategy : type
	  WHERE ALL(s : strategy,
	        SOME(r : route) :: needed-for(r, s))
	  -- *the used strategy can be recognized from the given route*
	
	CONCEPT augmentative : strategy
	
	CONCEPT reductive : strategy
	
	END

Adapting the orders to the routes which are given by a student is a didactic goal that the pedagogues must describe now. Here, they explain what are the criteria that will lead the proposed educational software to choose one order among the others. The "Spec" description tells that "if the route given by the student matches the order, the next order (if there is one) will be more complex. On the other hand, if the route does not match the order, the next order will be simpler. The analysis of a route is achieved through a comparison between the arrangement of the quadrilaterals in the route proposed by the student and the arrangement required by the learning strategy matched to the given order. These orders and their chaining will be described during the educational design.

DEFINITION Didactic-goals
 	
INHERIT concepts-and-goals-of-the-pedagogic-model
 	
INHERIT concepts-of-the-didactic-model
 	
-- *The goal is to know if another order must be proposed to the student, and what order?*
 	
CONCEPT   other-route(r : route, o : order)
    VALUE (b : boolean)
            WHERE   b <=>
    (respect(r, used-strategy(o)) and (SOME(o' : order::
            o' = follows(o)))
    or (not (respect(r, used-strategy(o))) and
    (SOME(o' : order :: o' = precedes(o)))
    goal(other-route, courseware)
 	
CONCEPT   respect(r : route, s : strategy)
    VALUE (b : boolean)
        WHERE ALL(c1, c2 : cal-concept ::
            precedes(c1, c2, r) =>
                precedes(c1, c2, s)
	CONCEPT precedes(c1 c2 : cal-concept, r :
	    route) VALUE (b : boolean)
	    --*true if for the route, c1 appears before c2*
	
	CONCEPT precedes(c1 c2 : cal-concept, s :
	    strategy) VALUE (b: boolean)
	    -- *true if for the strategy s, c1 must appear before c2*
	    WHERE b <=>(s = augmentative and
	            the-properties(c1) <
	                the-properties(c2))
	        or (s = reductive and
	            the-properties(c1) >
	                the-properties(c2))
	
	-- *concepts which are not completely described during this stage but the informations which are given will do the software engineers*
	
	CONCEPT precedes(o : order)
	    VALUE(o' : order)
	
	CONCEPT follows(o : order)
	    VALUE(o' : order)
	
	END

FROM THE VIEWPOINT OF SOFTWARE ENGINEERS

The descriptions of the pedagogues are put at the disposal of the software engineers. The latter interpret them to define the external behavior of the educational system : its functional specification.

From the initial pedagogic goal -the partial ordering operator between quadrilaterals-they deduce the specification of the function "<" which allows to compare the properties of quadrilaterals and the specification of the abstract data type "t-uple" which allows to store these properties. The analysis of the didactic goals allows the software engineers to put to the fore a finite state machine which computes the next order from a given route and its correlated order : thus, the "Spec" description called "Didactic goals" is translated by the software engineers into a machine : it has an internal state which stores the current order proposed to the student and can evolve thanks to transitions of state. Such a description is an important interface between the initial "didactic goals" modelled by the pedagogues, and the piece of code which will implement it. The next "Spec" description shows that the software engineers only "reformulate" the requirements modelled by the pedagogues :

```
MACHINE Didactic-Interface-for-the-Student

INHERIT Concepts-and-goals-of-the-pedagogic-
    model
INHERIT Concepts-of-the-didactic-model
STATE (Current-order : order)
INITIALLY  Current-order = Initial-Order
MESSAGE   analyse  (r : route)
    WHEN     Respect-Order(r, Current-order)
    and
    not(is-the-most-complex(Current-order))
        REPLY     (q : question)
            WHERE q =

            title(follows(Current-order))
            TRANSITION Current-order =
                follows(*Current-order)
WHEN       Respect-Order(r, Current-order)
           and
           is-the-most-complex(Current-order)
           REPLY    Bravo
```

```
WHEN
    not(Respect-Order(r, Current-order)) and
            not (is-the-easiest(Current-order))
        REPLY     (q : question)
            WHERE q=
            title((precedes(Current-order)))
            TRANSITION Current-order =
                follows(*Current-order)
    OTHERWISE REPLY EXCEPTION too-
    difficult-session

CONCEPT   Respect-Order(r : route, o : order)
    VALUE  (b : boolean)
    WHERE b <=>    respect(r, used-strategy(o))

-- the definitions which follow are the same as
    the ones described by the pedagogues

CONCEPT    respect(r : route, s : strategy)
    VALUE  (b : boolean)
    WHERE  ALL(c1, c2 : cal-concept ::
            precedes(c1, c2, r) =>
                precedes(c1, c2, s))

...

END
```

This machine can be used to develop a tutorial or an intelligent tutoring system dedicated to quadrilaterals. It depends on the way the functions "precedes" and "follows" compute the next order proposed to the student :

- if these functions cannot do more than translations in a predefined sequence of orders, then the developers model a tutorial,
- if the choice of the orders is dynamic (depends on the context in which an error occurs, ...), if the system is able to produce orders which are not initially implemented by the pedagogues, then it is probably an intelligent tutoring system.

These choices will be done by the pedagogues during the stage of designing.

2.3.3. THE DESIGN STAGE

FROM THE VIEWPOINT OF PEDAGOGUES

During this stage, the pedagogues are going to describe how the functions "precedes" and "follows" compute the next order that will be proposed to a student. They use the "Spec" language to describe the different classes of orders which are used by the educational software, and the mechanisms allowing their chaining.

This stage has enabled us to put to the fore :
- complex orders (they require that the student combines several geometrical properties), simple orders (they require that the student discovers only one geometrical property), and functions whose aim is to decompose complex orders into simpler ones,
- some mechanisms allowing the automatic generation of orders : when an order defines neither the quadrilateral the student has to discover, nor the geometrical properties he must combine, these mechanisms generate orders that progressively inform the student.

By doing this, we indirectly put to the fore some functions that the software engineers will have to design and implement (the function of decomposition, the function of generation of orders) and data (the initial order, the order which is the objective of the CAL session, the intermediate orders, ...) that the pedagogues will implement during the implementation stage.

FROM THE VIEWPOINT OF SOFTWARE ENGINEERS

Now, the software engineers know all the functions and machines that they have to implement. They must refine and decompose the modules until each one can be coded in the programming language they have chosen : concrete data structures must be matched to the abstract ones (type "t-uple", type "game-of-orders") described during the previous stages, and procedures of access to these concrete data structures must be designed.

2.3.4. THE LAST STAGES OF THE METHODOLOGY

Then, the stage of implementation is quite simple :
- the pedagogues "mediatize" the different quadrilaterals and orders that will be used by the functions "precedes" and "follows",
- the software engineers code their design in the programming language they have chosen (Ada, C, ...).

The validation stage will control the mediatized data -from a pedagogical point of view- and the program which processes them -from a data processing point of view- before the distribution of the educational software to students.

3. THE "MAGE" METHODOLOGY AND THE ICES PROJECT

The methodology is currently implemented with the support of a set of facilities providing an infrastructure for constructing Integrated Project Support Environments :

PCTE (Portable Common Tool Environment) [CAMPBELL-88]. This standardized environment is particularly convenient to define the data repository which will be shared by software engineers and pedagogues. We use HP9000 workstations and the Emeraude product (which is an implementation of the PCTE interfaces) to define the part of the repository which will allow the pedagogues and the software engineers to store "Spec" descriptions. The tools called Lex and Yacc of the Unix environment are used to check the descriptions before they are stored in the repository. We expect that this first stage of our work will be completed by the beginning of 1992. Then, we shall try to solve the problems of mapping the underlying "Spec" descriptions and the different concrete viewpoints that pedagogues will use to model these descriptions in a natural way (cf figure 3). The works of M. RUEHER [RUEHER-87] for the definition of a "multi-shape" model specification suggest a promising solution to this problem.

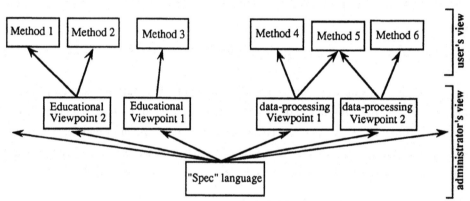

figure 3 : from the methodological level to the user's views.

References

[BERZINS-90] Software engineering with abstractions, V. BERZINS, LUQI, Addison-Wesley publishing company, 1990

[BESSAGNET-90a] A new approach : Courseware Engineering, M.N. BESSAGNET, T. NODENOT, G. GOUARDERES, J.J. RIGAL, Computers in Education, IFIP fifth World Conference on Computers in Education (WCCE'90), juillet 1990

[BESSAGNET-90b], L'AGDI : un environnement de production pour des applications EAO, M.N. BESSAGNET, T. NODENOT, G. GOUARDERES, 3èmes journées internationales du génie logiciel et ses applications, Toulouse, décembre 1990

[BESSAGNET-91], Spécification fonctionnelle d'un atelier de génie didacticiel intégré, M.N. BESSAGNET, Doctorat de l'Université Paul Sabatier, Toulouse, octobre 1991

[BOEHM-76], Software engineering, B.W. BOEHM, IEEE Transactions on computers, vol. C-25, p. 1226-1241, décembre 1976

[BOEHM-86], A spiral model of software development and enhancement, B.W. BOEHM, ACM SIGSOFT Software Engineering Notes, vol. 11, n° 4 p. 14-24, août 1986

[BORK-84], Computers and Information Technology as a Learning Aid, A. BORK, Actes du congrès "Computers and Education : dreams and reality", second Australian computer education conference, Sydney, sept. 1984

[BORK-89], Suggestions for developing Technology based learning material, A. BORK, Interactive learning international, Wiley, janv. 89

[CAMCE-90], The overall Camce Architecture. General requirements and logical architecture of the CAMCE environment, document interne IATIN/CRAI, mars 1990

[CAMPBELL-88], Portable Common Tool Environment, I. CAMPBELL, Computer standards and interfaces, n°8, p. 67-74, North Holland, 1988

[CHOPPY-88], Maquettage et prototypage : panorama des outils et des techniques, C. CHOPPY, revue Génie logiciel & systèmes experts, n°11, mars 1988

[GOUARDERES-86], Présentation et manipulation des connaissances dans le dialogue Homme-Machine en enseignement assisté par ordinateur, G. GOUARDERES, Thèse d'état-Sciences, Université Paul Sabatier, Toulouse, 1986

[GOUARDERES-90], Le projet Atelier de Génie Didacticiel Intégré (AGDI), G. GOUARDERES, T.S.I. - Technique et Science Informatiques, Vol. 9, n°5, octobre 1990

[IBRAHIM-90], Courseware CAD, B. IBRAHIM, A. AUBORD, B. LAUSTSEN, M. TEPPER, Computers in Education, IFIP fifth World Conference on Computers in Education (WCCE'90), juillet 1990

[MERRILL-86], Prescriptions for an authoring system, M.D. MERRILL, Journal of computer-based instruction, vol. 14, n° 1, oct. 1986

[PENINOU-90], Méthodologie de conception, test et réalisation d'un logiciel éducatif dans une approche génie logiciel, A. PENINOU, C. CHOQUET, G. GOUARDERES, Convention GL : actes de la 1ère conférence européenne sur les techniques et les applications du Génie Logiciel, Paris 1990

[RUEHER-87], Un modèle multiforme pour la spécification, M. RUEHER, numéro spécial Bigre+Globule sur les langages de spécification, n°55, juillet 1987

[SCHOENMAKER-90], A Methodology for Educational Software Engineering, J. SCHOENMAKER, E. NIENHUIS, J. SCHOLTEN, J. TITULAER, Computers in Education, IFIP fifth World Conference on Computers in Education (WCCE'90), juillet 1990

[VONK-90], Prototyping : the effective use of CASE Technology, R. VONK, Prentice Hall International Ltd, 66 Wood Lane End, Hemel Hemstead Herdfordshire, 1990

Environmental CAL
for Conversation pattern learning

Ryo Okamoto, Yoneo Yano

Faculty of Engineering Tokushima University

2-1, Minamijyosanjima, Tokushima 770 Japan

tel. [+81] 886 23 2311

e-mail okamoto@n50.is.tokushima-u.ac.jp

Abstract

There are many types of multimedia aids, teaching such things as language conversation and manners required in particular situations. There are few CAL systems which treat such domains. Particularly in companies, the need for this type of CAL systems has been increasing. The characteristics of this domain are such that the typical learning environment which uses the drill and practice method isn't suitable. Therefore we have considered the domain of language activity and described an Intelligent Learning Environment (ILE) which has an indirect instruction mechanism. This environment would aid in the realization of a general and effective CAL system structure, for supporting the learning of language conversation skills. A student would learn the most suitable behavior and utterance for a specific situation through simulation role-playing.

In this paper, we describe some issues in the development of this system: (a) modeling of language activity, (b)structure and (c)instructional procedure in the ILE.

Introduction

There are many CAL systems for language learning at the present time. Particularly in ICAI, many systems have been developed for grammatical study. However, we know that learning about grammar only, is not enough for practical use. When learning foreign languages students do not always have the opportunity to practice, even though practical language skills are needed more and more today. In Japan, it is said that many students have lost their motivation due to a lack of opportunity to practice.

In our research, our purpose is to develop a CAL system that provides practice for beginners. In the development of the system, we focus on these points:

(1) language activities

(2) learning environment

(3) multimedia techniques

Our focus on the process of language activities led us to decide to use simulation, in the form of a role-playing game in our system. We define the script and the plan model for the simulation and describe the domain knowledge in frames.

For our learning environment we have adopted the idea of open-ended learning. In simulations, the student takes part in a story by direct manipulation and interaction. Our system monitors the student's behavior and gives indirect instructions when it is assumed that a student does not understand. We describe this environment for language activities as an ILE.

We adopted multimedia techniques such as sound, graphics and animation to provide motivation for the student to learn.

1. Intelligent Learning Environment

In most instances of ITS research, problem solving learning, utilizing formed and structured knowledge with text, takes a leading part in the type of learning domain. This form of learning is referred to as a well-formed curriculum. On systems applying this method, students are instructed through a measure of drill and practice that uses knowledge transmission with text.

However, in fields which are ill-structured such as language education and solving physics problems which have an extremely complicated structure, it is not sufficient to present students with a text based teaching system for them to be able to understand the subject. Therefore it is desirable that the learning environment makes use of both audio and visual teaching aids.

1.1 Open-ended learning environment

In contrast to systems implementing a well-formed curriculum which are based on the use of drill and practice, systems implementing an open-ended curriculum are based on the trial and error method. Features of domains which are suited to open-ended curriculum are as follows:

· Difficult to present to students with only text based teaching

· Contain knowledge which has an extremely complicated structure

Both environmental CAL and Micro-world are frameworks which are based on the open-ended curriculum. WEST and WUSER are well known environmental CAL systems that adopt game and simulation techniques. The aim of Micro-world [TIM89] proposed by

T.O'shea, is for the student to make acquisition of concepts by experiential learning. In Japan, Ohtuki S. and Takeuchi A. have proposed the Intelligent Education System [OTH87] that provides functions of both Micro-World and ITS.

All the above mentioned open-ended curriculum systems have adopted graphical simulation techniques, and the benefits of this have generally been acknowledged.

1.2 Definition of Intelligent Learning Environment

We considered the features of domains which are suited to an open-ended curriculum, and defined the functions which are required for the open-ended learning environment as follows:

1. Implement the domain using a simulation game including multimedia techniques and direct manipulation.

2. Asses and monitor the student's level of comprehension of the domain, and guide a student by changing the instructional interface appropriately.

3. Ascertain the learning intentions of the student and provide facilities to allow the student to control their own research through the use of Hypertext.

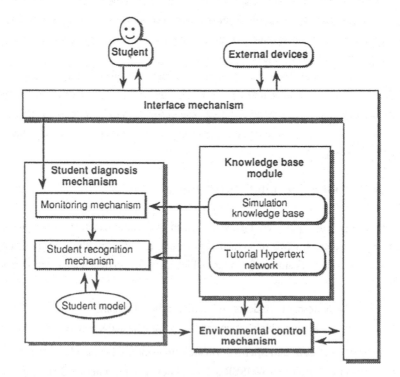

Fig.1 Framework for Intelligent Learning Environment

Fig.1.illustrates the framework necessary for the construction of the learning environment that satisfies all the above functions.

This environment is composed of four mechanisms as follows:

1. Interface mechanism

2. Student diagnosis mechanism

3. Environmental control mechanism

4. Knowledge base module

1. **Interface mechanism** :   This mechanism uses Hypertext to present simulation and initiative research of the domain knowledge to a student. The student controls the progress of the simulation and the process of procuring the domain knowledge by direct manipulation of this interface.

2. **Student diagnosis mechanism** : This mechanism has three sub mechanisms, monitoring, student recognition and student model. The functions of this mechanism are to monitor the students input to the interface mechanism, to refer to the student model to determine the student's level of understanding, and to then utilize this information to update the student model.

3. **Environmental control mechanism** :   This mechanism has two functions, process simulation progress orders and to change the operators. Changing an operator will allow a student to initiate research in a specific area of the domain. These functions are executed by referencing the student model and situation variables, which describe the situation of a simulation, and adopting appropriate instruction strategies.

4. **Knowledge base module** :   There are two knowledge bases, the Simulation Knowledge Base and Tutorial Hypertext, in this module. Both the structure and representations of the Simulation Knowledge Base differ, depending on the domain. The student is guided by the adoption of the instruction strategy, and Tutorial Hypertext must hide the links used to guide the student.

2. Considerations for language activity

We have attempted to apply our ILE to the domain of English conversation learning for students who are not native speakers of English. It has generally been acknowledged that learning foreign conversation requires learning by experiment. Multimedia techniques, particularly sounds, are indispensable to implement this.

We have implemented a prototype English conversation pattern learning system for Japanese students. In this chapter we describe the modelling of language activity, the classifications of acceptable phrases and their degree politeness, and the knowledge of aural comprehension, implemented in our prototype system.

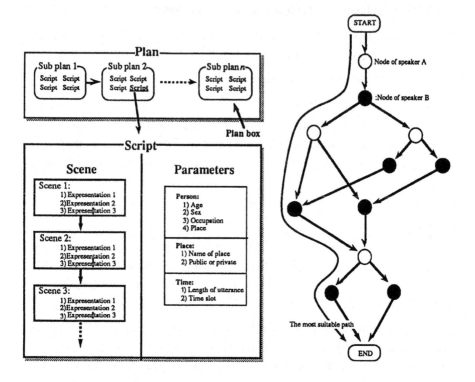

Fig.2 Script and Plan model   Fig.3 Graphic expression of a dialogue

2.1 Simulation model for language activity

The utterance activity is regarded as a time sequence consisting of two segments. First, there is movement to meet the person with whom communications are desired, and this is followed by verbal communications. We defined two aims in the utterance activity according to the segments of the time sequence given above. The aim of movement is to move between different conversation situations, and the aim of verbal communications effectively complete each dialog.

The language activity can be defined as time-sequence of utterances. We referred to the script model of R.Schank [ROG75, and defined a script and a plan model as illustrated in Fig.2. Both the plan and script models are referred to as purpose oriented models. The plan frame has multiple sub-plans, each of which contain multiple script frames. Progression between sub-plans is achieved by satisfying all of the conversational aims within a sub-plan.

Each script frame has a dialogue graph. Fig.3 illustrates an example of a dialog graph, and shows one possible traversal of the graph. A dialog is represented by a graph structure, which has node frames linked to each other and labeled by the conversation aim, and each node contains multiple verbal expressions.

2.2 Instructional purpose in English conversation learning

We define three areas of knowledge necessary in language learning CAL systems:

1. vocabulary and grammar knowledge
2. pragmatic knowledge
3. phonetics knowledge

We considered acceptable phrases of pragmatic knowledge and liaison, which is one area of phonetics knowledge. This knowledge is structured and utilized to progress through a language activity simulation. It is described as sentences in tutorial Hypertext to facilitate student initiated research in the system.

We classified acceptable phrases into five classes by considering the conversational aim, an idiomatic keyword and an appropriate methodology. This is presented in Table 1, which is used to construct the knowledge bases.

We also define a scale of politeness, which has four levels, according to the aim of communications. This definition makes it possible for the system to diagnose the degree of a student's comprehension in acceptable phrases.

Table 1 Types of respectable phrases

Types of acceptable expression	Communication aim	Keyword	Methology
1. indirect	require question proposal	degree of abstraction	additional ideoms
2. representable and prefatory remarks	oppose opinion		prefatory remarks
3. socalizing		subjective and emotional	
4. emphasis	praise thanks	emphasize	
5. weaken	oppose opinion	weaken	

Errors in liaison tend to be main cause for errors in aural comprehension, except for those errors caused by lack of vocabulary and grammar. Two adjoined words are often pronounced as a single word, and it is difficult for a non-native speaker to tell the difference. We defined four types of expressions which have a liaison.

3. English conversation pattern learning system

We have been developing the prototype of an English conversation learning system for non-native speakers. The aim of the system is to teach the students typical patterns in English conversation. Two educational purposes that we have defined are to use 'correct' English in order to complete the conversation aim, and to utilize acceptable phrases according to flow of a conversation.

We implement the system using HyperCard on the Macintosh. HyperCard, which provides an easy method to create a prototype implementation utilizing multimedia techniques, has a large number of benefits .

We adopted a role-playing game to implement the simulation. This method was adopted, as a system based on the ILE allows a student to interactively control the learning environment. We believe that this is necessary to maintain a student's motivation.

We believe that in a conversation learning system, it is indispensable to use sounds for training aural comprehension, and therefore a system must be equipped for sound replay. We utilize the Macintosh sampling resources to record actual sentences because of the clarity of recording. We therefore developed the technique of choosing expressions from the collection stored in the simulation knowledge base when executing a sub-plan. The system produces the choices suited to the situations and uses them for presentation to a student or for system utterance. By utilizing of this technique, the system can create various stories.

3.2 System configuration

Our HyperCard system is composed of multiple HyperCard stacks, each of which is collection of Cards. Procedures, written in Hypertalk, are described in each objects stack, background, card, button and field. Procedures are started by messages, which can be generated by the user's input using the mouse button or by message passing from other objects. HyperCard's stack structure prevents us from describing the system structure as a combination of functional modules as is the case in a procedural language.

Fig.4 illustrates the stack structure which is modularized according to the differences in the interface cards.

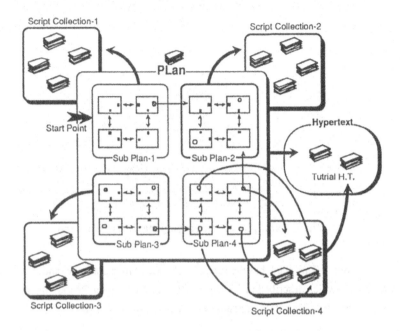

Fig.4   Stack structure of the system

The system is constructed using three kinds of HyperCard stack as follows:

1. Sub-plan stack : This stack contains four interface cards, called moving-space cards, and they are arranged in a 2 x 2 matrix on which a student can move the hero-character freely as in Fig.5. This card illustrates an example of a street containing a number of objects such as people, stores, taxis etc., all of which are button objects.

A student can progress through the simulation by clicking any of these button objects to move the hero-character to them. Menu buttons which have the functions 'require hints', 'save situation', and 'quit learning' are located on the lower part of the card.

The current sub-plan stack is changed when the hero-character has satisfied all of the conversational aims which are contained in that sub-plan stack.
A student can progress through the simulation by clicking any of these button objects to move the hero-character to them. Menu buttons which have the functions 'require hints', 'save situation', and 'quit learning' are located on the lower part of the card.

The current sub-plan stack is changed when the hero-character has satisfied all of the conversational aims which are contained in that sub-plan stack.

Fig.5 Example of moving-space interface card

2. **Script stack** : This stack has the function of simulating a dialogue, and is called by the procedure which described in the object's character-button on the moving-space card of a sub-plan stack. This stack contains two types of card as follows:

1. Dialogue interface card

2. Knowledge base card

The dialogue interface card consists of a graphics window, verbal expression selection button, help button and the set of buttons used to initiate research as in Fig.6.

A student progresses through the dialogue simulation and replays a certain verbal expression's sound resource by choosing a verbal expression from the pull down menu which appears by holding-down the selection button. The items that appear in the pull-down menu are selected by the system from the collection in knowledge base, according to the instruction strategies. The graphics, which assist in describing the situation and in conveying the emotions of the 'dialog companion', are displayed in the graphics window, according to the progress of a dialogue situation. These graphics are stored in the stack as picture resources. The system updates the initiative learning environment of a student by changing the kinds of button, which are contained in the button group to initiate research, according to the updated results of the student's diagnosis.

Fig.6 Dialogue interface card

3. **Knowledge base card** : Verbal expressions are constructed as a dialogue graph, which includes the expressions and attributes of a dialogue. A dialogue graph has multiple nodes which contain a collection of verbal expressions labeled by their communication aim. Each of the nodes and labeled collections have a frame, which is described as a field object in each card. The system searches the fields of these cards and reads in situational verbs for execution of the instruction processes.

Fig.7 Example of initiate search interface field

4. Tutorial Hypertext stack : The aim of this stack is to overcome a situation in which it is impossible for the system to determine the cause of a student's error. Each card of this stack is called by the student's selection from the tutorial interface field. This field has a set of anchor buttons associated with each of the research interface cards of this stack, vocabulary, idiom, liaison and others. These buttons are modified by the environmental control mechanism. For example, the system has judged that a student has the tendency of 'lack of vocabulary', and so the buttons concerned with vocabulary are always located on a card.

4. Realization of Indirect instruction by simulation control

This system controls the progress of the simulation, changing interface card and selection of verbal expressions by indirect instruction. The system has three educational purposes as follows:

1. Progress through Dialogue
2. Communication aim and degree of politeness of acceptable expressions
3. Aural comprehension

Progress through a Dialogue simulation is controlled by the system via indirect instruction. The system refers to a dialogue graph and situational variables which control a simulation situation, and searches for an appropriate 'next node' and 'labeled collection' in accordance with a diagnosis of student's operation.

It is not sufficient for the system to only select an appropriate 'next node', as each 'labeled collection' contains a number of verbal expressions which have a value associated with the degree of politeness as an attribute. Therefore, the system has to carry out a diagnosis so that it can indirectly instruct the student which is the most appropriate 'acceptable expression'.

The system has not only to replay the verbal expression's sound, but must also present what kinds of liaisons are involved in the expression to guide the student to initiate research.

4.1 Simulation control process

The process of indirect instruction has five sub-processes as follows:

1. System utterance process
2. Generate choices process
3. Make operation history process

4. Update student model process

5. Execute instruction strategies process

These sub-process are repeated during a dialogue simulation.

The system refers to the situational variable and a student model and uses inference in this process and there are thirteen situation variables. The student model has five tables, 'History of operations','Understanding levels of communication aim','Understanding levels of politeness', 'Understanding levels of liaison' and 'Tendency of a student'.

4.2 Summary of each sub-processes

1. System utterance process : The system's utterance is chosen by referencing the situation variables. This process carries out two inferences, with respect to the communication aim and the politeness, in the determination of a system's utterance. A sound-resource is replayed and graphics are displayed, which correspond to 'the emotional level' of the situation variable according to the result of the inferences.

2. Choice generating process : The choices are generated for the selection button of verbal expressions. Each node has approximately twenty expressions, and so the system selects a subset of them. The number and level of politeness is established in the situation variables. If the trends in the student's learning process are unclear, the system combines expressions to form a leading question.

3. Operation history making process : After carrying out the two sub-processes mentioned above the system goes into an idle state, waiting for a student's input. A student can select from three operations, 'Choices Button','Help Button' and 'Replay Button' to progress through the simulation. The operation of these buttons is stored as an operation history in the student model. Procedures which are described in these three buttons change according to a situation.

4. Student model update process : This mechanism has two algorithms to calculate values for updating the tables in the student model from a student's progress as follows:

    1. Appropriateness of the communication aim and politeness of the chosen expression for the current situation.

    2. Global information about a students progress.

5. Execute instructional strategies process : The system infers and adopts instruction strategies to rewrite the situation variables. There are four types of instruction strategy, used to establish situation variables as follows:

    1. Priority for communication

2. Priority for politeness

3. Priority for liaison

4. Priority for initiative research

5. Conclusion

In this paper, we have described the development of an application for learning conversation. We defined the ILE to be an open-ended learniing environment. In particular, we described the process of simulation and indirect instruction. We have developed a prototype system for teaching English conversation pattern learning to Japanese beginners. Our next step will be to refine the definition of instruction strategies within the instruction control mechanism. The ILE can be applied to other subjects concerned with language activities, for example, teaching manners required in particular situations.

References

[YAM89] Yamamoto Y, Kashihara A. (1989) Development of KACE, Knowledge Acquisition-type CAI System: Journal of JSCAI Japan 6:12-20 (in Japanese)

[YAM89] Yamamoto Y, Kashihara A. (1989) A Modeling of Knowledge Stability in Open Structured CAI. Trans. IEICE Japan J-72-D-II:9.1459-1471 (in Japanese)

[IKE90] Ikegami I, Yano Y (1990) Development of Knowledge Acquisition Type CAI (KACE II) by Quartet Knowledge Representation. Trans. IEICE Japan D-II vol.173-D-II No.4, 614-625 (in Japanese)

[HAY91] Hayashi T, Yano Y (1991) A Micro World for Kanji Learning. Proc. of 22nd Annual International Conf. International Simulation & Gaming Association (ISAGA'91)

[OTH87] Othuki S, Takeuchi A (1987) A Micro world type CAI and Student model. Computers and education 15-19 (in Japanese)

[ROG75] Roger. C. Shank & Robert. p. Abelson (1975) Scripts, Plans, and knowledge. Proceedings of the 4th IJCAI 151-157

[TIM89] Tim O'Shea (1989) Managements, Martians, and Micro-Words; Learning with and Learning by OOPS. Proceedings of the 4th International Conference on AI and Education, Amsterdam (invited Talk)

Adaptive Navigational Tools for Educational Hypermedia

Brigitte de LA PASSARDIERE

Université Pierre et Marie Curie - PARIS VI

Laboratoire MASI - Equipe SIE, 4, place Jussieu

75252 PARIS cedex 05, France

Tel : 33 1 44 27 53 96, Fax : 33 1 44 27 62 86

e-mail : passardi@masi.ibp.fr

Aude DUFRESNE

Département des Sciences de la Communication

Université de Montréal, Case postale 6128, succ"A"

Montréal, Canada H3C 3J7

Tel : 514 343 73 71, Fax : 514 343 22 98

e-mail : dufresne@iro.umontreal.ca

Abstract

Hypermedia makes it possible to access in a flexible and interactive way large quantities of information. Compared to intelligent tutors, hypermedia learning environments are easier to design. On the other hand, compared to textbooks, they facilitate exploration, simulation and interactive adaptation of the courseware to the user. The flexibility left to the user in hypermedia appears to pose disorientation problems. In this paper we explore how, in the context of education, the interface and especially navigational tools may be used to improve learning. We also present current research on adaptive navigational tools in educational environments: first, the information made accessible should be adapted to the level of the user, eventually unfolding only as he progresses in his learning; second, the interface should reflect the user's progression, using multilevel footprints and advice; finally, the system can offer restructuring facilities to the user for rearranging information as he explores it in order to remember it more easily.

INTRODUCTION

Hypermedia makes it possible to access in a flexible and interactive way, large quantities of information. Compared to intelligent tutors, hypermedia learning environments are easier to design. On the other hand, compared to textbooks, they facilitate exploration, simulation and interactive adaptation of the courseware to the user. The flexibility left to the user in hypermedia appears to pose disorientation problems. While he explores the information network, the user needs to answer questions like : Where am I ? What is important? Where is it ? How do I get there ? [Con87] The research explores how, in the context of education, the interface and especially navigational tools may be used to improve learning.

NAVIGATIONAL TOOLS : A SURVEY[1]

Navigational tools may be defined as all parts of the interface that are designed to help the user choose the relevant information, whether it helps him to discover the scope of information available or to choose a relevant path to get the information he wants [Shn-Kea90]. We will distinguish three kinds of tools : punctual, structural and historical aids. In the context of education, sophisticated navigational tools are important if the aim is to go beyond a mere search for information.

Punctual aids

These aids regroup the very basic and the most classical navigational tools :
- Simple navigational tools inform users of possible connections from the current point. So-called "next", "previous", "first", "last", "home" , etc., are usually displayed on the screen

---

[1] Here is a very brief survey. For more details on this subject see [Nei90, Utt-Yan89].

using their names as in KMS [Aks88] or using icons, as in HyperCard [Goo88] and others systems [Hil86].

- Help buttons are used to improve comprehension of the system. They offer metacommunication information or local contextual help.

- Links point out relationships in the database or the hyperspace. They are usually indicated in bold or italic characters, as icons or as special markers [Utt-Yan89].

Structural aids

These tools give information on the database content and organization. They help the user to orient himself in hyperspace, especially if it is a large and complex one. They are oriented toward the spatial context and help the user to know where he is or how he can reach a given piece of information :

- Overview maps show the database organization at the top or "macroscopic" level. They make links between documents visible by drawing lines between nodes. Such a map is called a *global map* in Intermedia [Mey86, Utt-Yan89] and a *browser* in NoteCard [Hal88]. In fact, they are useful only if the hyperspace is not too large. Otherwise they become difficult to read (small screen size, complex display, etc.).

- Local maps are focused on the current node, i.e. on the user's selected node and show all the documents to which it is linked [Gar86, Gar88, Utt-Yan89].

- Fisheyes can be assimilated to local maps as they are zooming in on the context of the current node. As with a photographic lens, closer objects are bigger and more detailed than further ones [Fur86].

- Filters are used to improve the legibility of maps by reducing the number of links to a display on the screen. For example, in NLS/Augment, it is possible to cut the hierarchy at any level or to control the number of items displayed at each level. It is also possible to write personal filters to select items including a given content/word [Eng-Eng68]. Neptune allows users to generate filtered browsers based on a query [Deli-Sch86].

- <u>Indexes</u> are more hierarchical tools than the previous ones. They give the database a structure. In TextNet, special nodes (called *toc*) are used to organize the text-nodes (called *trunks)* according to the different types of available links [Tri83]. This feature is also present in NoteCards, as it is possible to organize and categorize large collections of notecards through specialized cards called *fixeboxes*. The underlying hierarchy is then displayed by a browser [Hal88]. In GIBIS, the graphical browser is mainly dedicated to a local view of the network, i.e. a zoomed view of the current area of interest with nodes and link in full detail displayed as a hierarchy. The lower right portion of the browser contains a global overview with a rectangular overlay indicating the scope and position of the current local view [Beg88].

Historical aids

These aids are related to the temporal context. They answer the questions as to what has already been seen or what remains to be explored. In educational situations these tools are quite important.

- <u>History trails</u> review the user's activity. They allow him to browse his past activity and support the reopening or the reactivation of documents. In HyperCard, *Recent* offers a way to quickly find a card the user saw recently without forcing him to figure out which stack that card may have been seen in and how to navigate to it [Goo88]. This system maintains a miniature album of the forty-two last cards. In Intermedia, this is achieved by the web view's path, which is a simple linear list of the user's activity [Utt-Yan89]. To give users a more complete temporal context, Intermedia mixes different approaches in the web view which has three major components : a *path*, a *map* and a *scope line*. It also provides three important features : dynamic updating of the user's map, link previewing and shortcuts [Utt-Yan89]. In KMS, the adopted solution for backtracking is rather different. The back command is available as one of the mouse buttons. The user needs only move the cursor to an empty area of the screen, and click the button [Aks88].

- <u>Footprints</u> are system-marks. They are automatically updated when the user passes through a node [Nie90].

- <u>Landmarks</u>, contrary to footprints, are user-marks. These annotations may be added by the user as he progresses, they may serve to highlight important information.

- <u>Progression cues</u> are not very often used in theses systems. They indicate using visual effects what the user has already seen. Progression cues affect an abstraction (map, index or hierarchy) at a level higher than footprints (node).

Two more tools are important in education. The first one concerns context and content <u>identification</u>, the second one <u>tours</u>. Both can be considered as navigational guides, but not all systems have them.

LIMITS OF NAVIGATIONAL TOOLS AND SPECIFIC NEEDS IN EDUCATION

Navigation in education

In the context of education, the concept of navigation may be slightly different from simple information hypertext, since one of the objectives of the system might be to ensure that the user not only sees but also learns a certain amount of relevant information [Jon-Man90]. The interactive potential of hypermedia may be used to include testings, knowledge probing, adapted advices of the system, etc. For efficient communication, the user may be left free to explore according to his preferences and needs but the interface must ensure that information is seen in a relevant order, that no irretrievable errors are encountered and that feedback of the system takes into account the user's level of knowledge.

From this perspective, the tools that help the user to understand the extent of the information and his position in it are very useful, but a form of control might be necessary. For the system to be an efficient didactic agent it must offer more than flexibility. It must also act as a guide, as a testbed and eventually as an evaluator, that might be useful for the student and his teacher, to evaluate and to support the learning process.

Need for some controls of the interaction

If hypermedia systems in education are to be adapted to the user's level of knowledge and if they are to include testing, it is necessary to include some level of control on the part of the system. The control must rest on some knowledge of a model of the task, a model of the tutor and a model of the user's progress. To ensure better learning the user's access to information might be blocked or imposed or he may receive additional advice. The control must be well integrated into the explorative environment so the user is not surprised (for example, if a menu item is added), disoriented or displeased. Control taken by the system may be completely hidden (by help messages being adapted), negotiated with the user (by asking him if he wants more information on something) or made obvious by the interface (items in a menu are made apparent but shown as inaccessible).

Another way to introduce structure in the interaction is to offer navigational tools showing the objectives and suggested path in the curriculum, as well as feedback on the user's progress, so the user himself is encouraged to complete his exploration and learning.

History

For exploration of the user and for the punctual control of the system to be effective, the history of the interaction must be taken into account and eventually made visible to the user through the interface. Information consulted, errors and delays in answering may be considered in the evaluation of the user's competence and in the planning of tutorial interventions. We will show how history trace, may be used, in order to foster a better exploration and learning of the content.

ADAPTIVE ENVIRONMENTS

Adapting the interface's punctual and structural aids to navigation

The expression of the context through structural aids to navigation is the first level of support to navigation. To limit disorientation in the sequential exploration of information in hypermedia, it is important to highlight the context, so the user does not have to remember what he can explore and where he is in the web of information. In education, the expression of the context appears to be especially critical in helping the user structure the information in his mind.

At the card level, titles and graphical cues may be used to indicate the part of the information being explored and also give information on the relative difficulty or position in the hierarchy of information (for example goals vs subgoals, prerequisites for some other information, etc.). At the index level, maps or graphical browser, the same metacommunication is important. It supports the initial orientation of the user and may even suggest a better path of exploration. It serves as an anchor for organizing information in long term memory. It also acts as a checklist and summary to foster remembering through repetition.

Inspired by other learning environments it is important that these pucntual and stuctural aids to navigation evolve as the user gains knowledge, as demonstrated by his exploration and performance in tests. Thus graphical browser could be designed as fisheyes gradually expanding into new areas to be explored. The concept of a genetic organization of information [Gol82] is easily implemented in hypertext and should not cause much disorientation of the user. As in computererized adventure games, it could motivate users to discover new areas to explore as he progresses [Duk74].

Another aspect of the context which the system must take into account is the history of the interaction.

Interface reflecting the historical context

While we studied the learning of procedures on hypertext, it became obvious that if the material to be learned is complex some account has to be made of the user's progress. The system should consider if a page has been seen before or if a mistake in a test has been repeated. We present different ways the system could adapt its feedback and interface to reflect the historical context of the learning process. General features were developed in an environment to support the learning of databases in the Excel spreadsheet called MANUEL EXCEL, where the user is left to explore goals, subgoals and procedures through explanations, examples, exercises and tests [Duf90, Duf91].

The system adapts its feedback and interface to reflect the historical context of the learning process. While previous contextual metacommunication depends only on the organization of the information (task model), the historical context is linked to both the task's model and the user's model. We found that reacting to the historical context was important in an educational environment, because the user does not like learning from a system that does not seem to be learning itself. For example when the system repeats an error message, the user thinks that the system is dumb and even questions the validity of its diagnosis. When he finds himself in a page he has already explored he might resent to be disoriented or think that he has seen everything in that part of the content.

In our experiment, reflecting the historical context to support learning was done in two ways.

First, a user model was used to modify advice and references to information in the knowledge base. A structure for adaptive feedback was designed: for each test and exercise in the system a diagnosis of possible mistakes was made and for each mistake an organized set of didactical interventions could be used. Three kinds of interventions were used : "try again", "give a cue", or "refer to a card". To choose the intervention, the system takes into account the number of local errors in a test as well as the number of trials. The user's model (number of errors and trials) and the general algorithm for selecting interventions are centralized. The task's model is distributed in each card or background, interventions being defined locally as executable lines in a hidden error field and as fields of advice which may be displayed (Figure 1).

```
on <first> <error1> on <first> trial :
        execute <first> instruction> of <first line> of field <error1>
on <second> <error1> on <first> trial :
        execute <first> instruction of <second> line of field <error1>
on <first> <error1> on <second> trial :
        execute <second> instruction of <first> line of field <error1>
.....
on GiveACue <cue1> display field <cue1>
```

Figure 1. Hierarchical structure of advices using distributed fields.

Second, footprints were designed to express the progression in the pages. "Magnifying lens" icons were used to choose subjects. Once chosen they were left highlighted so the user would know what had been done. Experimentation of the system showed two aspects of the footprint to be critical. On the one hand, footprint had to have three states : not seen (white lens) ; partially seen (grey lens) ; and completed (black lens) (Figure 2.). Adding a middle state reduced ambiguity when the user was simply browsing at the beginning of a branch and it also encouraged the user to complete his exploration.

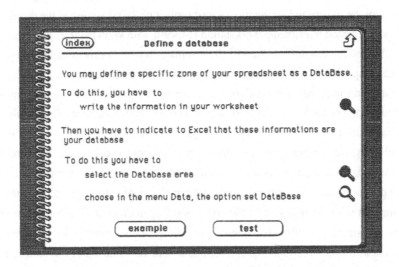

Figure 2. Example of the three step "magnifying lens", serving as
footprints to give historical feedback to the user of his progress.

On the other hand it is important that footprints be edited according to cognitive coherence. This means that when information is being accessed, all paths leading to that information should reflect this. This was made possible by using a dynamic and distributed model. The description of the hierarchy of the task was built at the opening of the stack. This model is being used to help messages from the end of a branch travel upward to all point of access. A consequence of this was that the index reflected the general exploration of the content, thus serving as a summary and as a motivation to complete the exploration.

The tutorial for the Excel spreadsheet was developped without those functionalities and was experimented with 20 university students in Communication. It was then tested with the three-step lens and added feedback with 30 subjects. Following the addition of the various historical feedbacks, statistical analysis of traces of interaction with the system indicates that the exploration of explanations increased significantly (Mean 14,45 vs 19.57 (23 pages), $p <= .01$) [Leb92].

Facilities for the user to restructure the information

Another way to help the user control the complexity of the hyperspace is to let him restructure the information. MULTIWORKS is a large Technology Integration Project supported by the European Community (Esprit project n° 2105) aiming at the development of a low cost integrated multimedia workstation [Mor90] with knowledge engineering facilities for the office of the future [Fog-Sau89]. The application environment includes a set of tools for the development of highly interactive applications. For this environment, a hypermedia based authoring tool called MultiCard was developed, to create and change interactively hypermedia documents containing all simple and combined media available in Multiworks.

Each document is associated to a hypermedia object called a node. Among its characteristics, we can point out that MultiCard does not itself handle the content of the nodes. Instead, by using a protocol, it communicates with different editors that are running separate processes, using a protocol. Each hypermedia node's structure contains the name of the editor that is to be used to edit the corresponding document. The format in which the contents are stored is editor-dependent. Regarding navigational tools, Multicard offers various capabilities for browsing the database. As in some others systems, maps are automatically designed on the screen but can also be reorganized by the user. He can move a node where he wants in the window. All links follow in real time. The user is also allowed at anytime to create new groups. A new group is associated each time to a new window. He can cut and paste as many objects as he wants from one group to another. The screen refreshment is automatic and take into account the last changes. For reasons of complexity and time computing, it has been decided to limit the research of links to levels one and two. This limit makes the design quite fast, even if some information is lost.

In education, we can take advantage of this feature because we can imagine many different types of exercises using it and because the student can organize the database as he wishes and this will improve his memorization.

CONCLUSION

The review of existing tools, as well as our studies in designing interfaces seem to point to a series of recommendations concerning support for navigation in hypermedia environments. Intelligence is the ability to adapt to new situations. It seems that for hypermedia to be adequate as a support for learning, they must offer some flexibility both for the user's restructuring and landmarking and also for the system itself to adjust to the context and user progression.

First, it appears important to ensure that the user completes his consultation of the information. This can be done without constraints to the user simply by offering intelligent footprints expressing the degree of completion. These footprints should follow cognitive more than physical coherence (knowledge as been gained or provided vs. a path has been followed).

Second, since information in hypermedia are highly sequenced, it is important for the system to take this into account and express both the context of the task and the user's historical progression.

Third, if learning is to be more than superficial, and if some problem solving and inference will be demanded of the user, it then becomes important to give him some form of diversified didactic support, by offering advices adpated to his progression.

Finally, it seems important to let the user affect the structure of the information, not only locally using filters but permanently by defining new structures of information. This may help simplify and transform the graphical browser into something more amenable as a summary of and an access to information.

566

REFERENCES

[Aks88] Akscyn R., McCracken D. & Yoder E., *"KMS, a Distributed Hypermedia System for Managing Knowledge in Organizations"*, Communications of ACM, Vol. 31, n° 7, July 1988, pp 820-835

[Beg88] Begeman M. & Conklin J., *"The Right Tool for the Job"*, BYTE, October 1988, pp.255-266

[Con87] Conklin J., *"Hypertext : an Introduction and Survey"*, IEEE Computer, September 1987, pp.17-41

[Deli-Sch86] Delisle N. & Schwartz M., *"Neptune : a Hypertext System for CAD Applications"*, ACM Transactions, 1986

[Duf90] Dufresne A., Jolin N. & Senteni A., *"Hypertext documents for the learning of procedures"*, in Hypertext : state of the art, McAleeese and Green editors, Ablex, 1990.

[Duf91] Dufresne A., *"Ergonomie cognitive, hypermédias et apprentissages"*, Hypermédias et apprentisages conf proc., Paris, Septembre 24-25, 1990

[Duk74] Duke, *"Gaminigs : the future's Language"*, Sage, 1974

[Eng-Eng68] Engelbart D. C. and English W. K., *"A Research Center for Augmenting Humain Intellect"*, AFIPS Conf. Proc., Vol. 33, Part 1, Thompson Books, Wash., 1968

[Fog-Sau89] Forgali G. & Sauter L., *"Multiworks - a MULTImedia Integrated WORKStation"*, in Esprit'89 Conf. Proc., Brussels, Nov 27 - Dec 1, Kluwer Academic Press, 1989, pp.1033-1043

[Fur86] Furnas G., *"Generalized fisheye views"*, in CHI'86 Human Factors in Computing Systems Proc., ACM, Boston, April 13-19, New York, 1986, pp 16-23

[Gar88] Garg P., *"Abstraction Mechanisms in Hypertext"*, Communications of ACM, Vol. 31, n° 7, July 1988, pp.862-870

[Gar86] Garrett N. L., Smith K. E. & Meyrowitz N., *"Intermedia : Issues, Strategies, and Tactics In the Design of a Hypermedia Document System"*, in Computer-Supported Cooperative Work Conf. Proc., MCC Software Technology Program, Austin, Texas, 1986

[Gol82] Goldstein I. P., "The genetic graph : a representation for the evolution of procedural knowledge", in Intelligent Tutoring System, Sleeman and Brown Eds, Academic Press, 1982

[Goo88] Goodman D., *"The Complete HyperCard Handbook, Second Edition"*, Bantam Books, October 1988

[Hal87] Halasz F., Noran T. P. & Trigg T. H., *"Notecards in a Nutshell"*, in Humain Factors in Computing Systems ACM Conf. Proc., Toronto, Canada, April 1987

[Hal88] Halasz F., *"Reflections on NoteCards : Seven Issues for the Next Generation of Hypermedia Systems"*, Communications of ACM, Vol. 31, n° 7, July 1988, pp 836 - 852

[Hil86] Hill B., *"Guide : Hypertext for the Macintosh"*, Owl International Inc., Bellevue, Wash., 1986, pp.25-39

[Jon-Man90] Jonassen D. & Mandl H., *"Designing Hypermedia for Learning"*, Nato, Serie F, Vol. 67

[Leb92] Leblanc, V. (1992). *"Influence de l'organisation graphique et des indices de progression sur la navigation dans un environnement hypertexte"*. Mémoire de maîtrise. Université de Montréal.

[Mey86] Meyrowitz N., *"Intermedia : the Architecture and Construction of an Object Oriented Hypermedia System and Applications Framework"*, OOPSLA'86 Proc., September 1986

[Mor90] Morreto R., *"Multiworks - a MULTImedia Integrated WORKStation"*, in Esprit'90 Conf. Proc., Brussels, Nov 12-15, Kluwer Academic Press, 1990, pp 654-668

[Nei90] Nielsen J., *"The Art of Navigating through Hypertext"*, Communications of ACM, Vol. 33, n° 3, March 1990

[Nor86] Norman D., *"Cognitive Engineering"*, in User Centered System Design : New Prespectives on Human-Computer Interaction, Norman and Draper Eds, Erlbaum, 1986

[Shn-Kea90] Shneiderman B. & Kearsley G., *"HYPERTEXT HANDS-ON : an Introduction to a New Way of Organizing and Accessing Informations"*, Addison-Wesley Publishing Company, 1990

[Tri83] Trigg R. H., *"A Network-based Approach to Text Handling for the On-line Scientific Community"*, PhD Thesis, University of Maryland, 1983

[Utt-Yan89] Utting K. & Yankelovich N., *"Context and Orientation in Hypermedia Networks"*, ACM Transactions on Information Systems, Vol. 7, n° 1, January 1989, pp.58-84

A Tool for Storing and Exploring Ideas

Kudang B. Seminar, Robert N. Robson
Faculty of Computer Science, University of New Brunswick
P.O. BOX 4400, Fredericton, NB E3B 5A3 Canada

Abstract

This paper discusses a tool for organizing and exploring ideas; they may be critiques, comments, opinions, or concepts contributed by different competent people or experts. This tool is very useful in distributed environments, learning and teaching environments, cooperative environments, and multiple expert environments that need to generate, compile, and integrate diverse ideas, and maintain them so that they become collective information available to the public for supervision, consultation, and knowledge acquisition. This tool allows various people living in different places to contribute ideas, explore each other's ideas, and summarize them. The power of the proposed tool lies on its formality (i.e. based on mathematical formulation) and its simplicity. The underlying model for building the tool is the *triangle model* discussed in [SR91a].
Keywords: concept formation, learning environments, symmetric difference, knowledge acquisition, cooperative environments, triangle model.

1 Motivations

Human beings are endowed with different abilities, capacities, and backgrounds, requiring them to learn from one another, consult one another, and to explore each other's ideas. To live in society and interact with others is a natural or inborn characteristic of human beings. The fact that collaborative research is increasing in many disciplines [KGE88, JKTV89] shows the importance of empowering human's will to work together. These natural, observable features are the central motivating points of this paper.

To review topics of high mutual interest, such as to meet goals for verification and validation of on-going development efforts, some programs choose to establish a panel or council of various experts, who typically meet together at times scheduled by the developer. Such a meeting typically starts with participants generating ideas [KGE88, McG90, NDV+91] (e.g., brainstorming). As the resulting ideas, critiques, and suggestions are collected and integrated, dependencies among subareas and dissonant ideas may be discussed and resolved by the group. This will result in many subsequent considerations, such as how to handle the voluminous, diverse ideas that might be forthcoming.

Once adequate ideas have been collected and identified, the experts can be asked to compare and contrast specific entities in order to isolate the salient features of primary ideas or concepts. This technique has been suggested and used in [KGE88, MB89, HPR89, WF90, Sla90, BG91, LF91].

In cooperative learning environments [Tho75, Kag85, AH85, JW86, Sla90], a teacher evaluates the students' understanding by comparing his solution with theirs. Also, a group of students can assist each other by presenting the differences in each other's ideas. The goal is, therefore, to reduce the differences between students' solutions and the correct one (i.e., teacher's solution) [LC89]. We have been applying this difference reduction concept in problem-solving tasks [SR91b]. In learning, a model's knowledge or idea may be augmented by refining, generalizing, or differentiating an existing knowledge component, by adding or substituting a new component, or by integrating several existing components within some larger conceptual work [WF90]. The concept of differences is also utilized in the intelligent tutoring systems for student modeling [Kas89].

Currently, little computer support for ideas recording and exploration is available [NDV⁺91]. Thus, the fact that meetings or learning sessions may end without a clear understanding or record of what was discussed, is left unsolvable. In this paper, we propose a mathematical tool to support comparative (differential) analysis, which further allows the synthesis of new ideas. Differential analysis is very crucial in concept formation (the basic teaching strategy) and data interpretation [JW86]. Differential analysis can also be carried out from the top down. That is, the most general ideas of the discipline are presented first, followed by a gradual increase in detail and specificity. Such a process is called *progressive differentiation* [JW86].

2 The Triangle Model

A thorough discussion of the triangle model appears in [SR91a]. The basic triangle model forms a triangle-shape structure, which is comprised of three nodes, as shown in Figure 1, whose relationships are defined by the following theorem.

Theorem 1 *In the triangle model, each of the three nodes comprising a triangle can be constructed by performing a* **symmetric difference (delta)** *operation on the two other nodes.*

That is, if $A, B,$ and C are the three nodes comprising a triangle, as shown in Figure 1, then the following properties hold:

$$C = A\Delta B \ \leftrightarrow \ A = C\Delta B \ \leftrightarrow \ B = C\Delta A,$$

where Δ denotes the *symmetric difference* operation in set theory [KM76]. Based on set theory, the symmetric difference between two sets A and B is defined as:

Definition 1 $A\Delta B = (A \cap \overline{B}) \cup (\overline{A} \cap B)$

In our model, the nodes depicted as circles are called *version nodes*, whereas the node depicted as a square is called a *delta node*. These distinctive notations are used to aid further discussions. In this paper, each node in the triangle model represents an idea,

Figure 1: The basic structure of the triangle model.

viewed as an object, which is structured as a set of descriptions or attributes. Referring to Figure 1, the nodes A and B represent two ideas, and C represents the symmetric difference (delta) between the two ideas.

Theorem 1 implies that at least two of the tree nodes in the triangle model must be saved in order to preserve all three nodes. Thus, options are available to store the two nodes preferable for a particular policy. For instance, to minimize the space requirement, the two nodes with the smallest size are chosen. Another policy is to select two nodes, one of which contains the most frequently accessed idea (e.g., popular idea), or the most recent idea.

Other important properties of the triangle model are summarized in the following theorems.

Theorem 2 *In the triangle model, applying a union operation ($\cup$) on any pair of nodes always yields the union of two* **version** *nodes.*

Proof :
Referring to Figure 2(a), we can show the following:

1. $A \cup C = A \cup (A \Delta B) = A \cup (A \cap \overline{B}) \cup (\overline{A} \cap B)$
   $= A \cup (\overline{A} \cap B) = (A \cup \overline{A}) \cap (A \cup B) = A \cup B.$
2. $B \cup C = B \cup (A \Delta B) = B \cup (A \cap \overline{B}) \cup (\overline{A} \cap B)$
   $= B \cup (A \cap \overline{B}) = (A \cup B) \cap (B \cup \overline{B}) = A \cup B.$

The union relationship between any two nodes in the basic triangle model is depicted by a dotted line in Figure 2(a).

Theorem 3 *In the triangle model, applying a conjunction operation ($\cap$) on:*

1. *two versions nodes yields the intersection of these two nodes,*

2. *a version node and a delta node, yields the intersection of this version node and the complement of the other version node.*

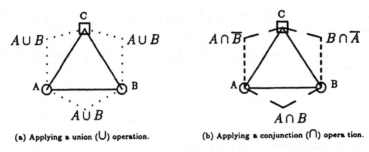

(a) Applying a union (∪) operation. (b) Applying a conjunction (∩) operation.

Figure 2: Properties of union and conjunction operations in the basic triangle model.

Proof :

Referring to Figure 2(b), we can show the following:

- **for case 1**
  It is trivial, $A \cap B$.

- **for case 2**
  - $A \cap C = A \cap ((\overline{A} \cap B) \cup (A \cap \overline{B})) = \emptyset \cup (A \cap \overline{B}) = A \cap \overline{B}$.
  - $B \cap C = B \cap ((\overline{A} \cap B) \cup (A \cap \overline{B})) = (\overline{A} \cap B) \cup \emptyset = \overline{A} \cap B$.

The intersection relationship between any two nodes in the basic triangle model is depicted by a dashed line in Figure 2(b).

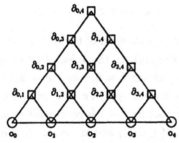

Figure 3: The complete configuration of the triangle model with n = 5.

The triangle model can be extended to capture n ideas as shown in Figure 3. This configuration is defined as a *complete configuration* of the triangle model with $n = 5$ [SR91a], and $\partial_{i,j}$ denoting $O_i \Delta O_j$, where $0 \leq i, j \leq n - 1$.

Definition 2 *A complete configuration is the configuration in which all deltas between every pair of version nodes have been computed.*

A complete configuration is important to allow individuals or groups to review and compare each others' ideas, or to integrate some deltas with respect to one idea into a new idea. Such a configuration is also required when the differences between all pairs of ideas are to be identified quickly for some purpose [SW87, LF91, MH91]. The algorithm for constructing a complete configuration of the triangle model has been discussed in [SR91a].

Theorem 4 *If the delta between A and B is known, and the delta between B and C is known, then the delta between A and C can be computed from the two deltas.*

Proof: $A \Delta C = A \Delta (B \Delta B) \Delta C = (A \Delta B) \Delta (B \Delta C)$.

That is, if $\partial_{A,B} = A \Delta B$ and $\partial_{B,C} = B \Delta C$ then $\partial_{A,C} = \partial_{A,B} \Delta \partial_{B,C}$. Another way of viewing this theorem is that if two triangles have a common node, joining these two triangles on the common node will result in another triangle whose two nodes are the nodes that coincide with the common node. Referring to Figure 3, the triangles $(O_1, \partial_{1,2}, O_2)$ and $(O_2, \partial_{2,4}, O_4)$ can be combined on the common node O_2 to obtain a triangle $(O_1, \partial_{1,4}, O_4)$ whose two nodes O_1 and O_4 coincide with the common node O_2. The operation that performs such a join operation is called the *common join* of two triangles.

The other important properties of the complete configuration are the extensions of the union relationship (Theorems 2) and intersection relationship (Theorem 3). A complete configuration with n version nodes (i.e., O_i's, $\forall i, 0 \leq i \leq n - 1$) has the following properties.

$$O_0 \cup O_1 \cup ... \cup O_{n-1} = O_k \cup \partial_{0,k} \cup \partial_{1,k} \cup ... \cup \partial_{n-1,k}, \tag{1}$$

$$\text{where } 0 \leq k \leq n - 1.$$

Equation 1 can be viewed as an extension of the union relationship by considering all nodes in Figure 3. In this configuration, the union of all version nodes can be obtained from Equation 1 by choosing either $k = 0, k = 1, k = 2, k = 3$, or $k = 4$. Choosing $k = 4$, for example, is equivalent to applying a union operation on all nodes lying in segment $(O_4, \partial_{0,4})$; whereas choosing $k = 2$ is equivalent to applying a union operation on all nodes lying in segment $(\partial_{0,2}, O_2)$ and all nodes lying in segment $(O_2, \partial_{2,4})$.

The equation which can be viewed as an extension of the intersection relationship is captured in the following:

$$O_k \cap \overline{O_0} \cap \overline{O_2} \cap ... \cap \overline{O_{n-1}} = O_k \cap \partial_{0,k} \cap \partial_{1,k} \cap ... \cap \partial_{n-1,k}, \tag{2}$$

$$\text{where } 0 \leq k \leq n - 1, \text{ and } \partial_{k,k} \text{ is excluded.}$$

3   An Illustrative Example

To provide a deeper appreciation of the application of the triangle model, an illustrative example was chosen from a real classroom session at the University of New Brunswick.

Group	Viewpoint	Code	Set Representation
0	- a group of people - share ≥ 1 common characteristic - live in a common geographical area - share ≥ 1 common institution - share ≥ 1 common agency	[a] [b] [c] [d] [e]	$O_0 = \{a, b, c, d, e\}$
1	- a group of people - live in a geographical area - share ≥ 1 common characteristic - interact with each other	[a] [c] [b] [m]	$O_1 = \{a, c, b, m\}$
2	- a group of people - live in a common identifiable area - share ≥ 1 common characteristic - interact with each other	[a] [l] [b] [m]	$O_2 = \{a, l, b, m\}$
3	- a group of people - share ≥ 1 common characteristic - share ≥ 1 common ethnic - share ≥ 1 common function - interact with each other	[a] [b] [n] [f] [m]	$O_3 = \{a, b, n, f, m\}$
4	- a group of people - share ≥ 1 common characteristic - share ≥ 1 common function - share ≥ 1 common environment - share ≥ 1 common religion - share ≥ 1 common culture - share ≥ 1 common interest - share ≥ 1 common life experience - live in a common identifiable area	[a] [b] [f] [g] [h] [i] [j] [k] [l]	$O_4 = \{a, b, f, g, h, i, j, k, l\}$

Table 1: Various definitions of "community", resulting from five groups of students participating in a classroom session.

The goal of the session was to establish the definition and understanding of the concept "*community*". The method was to divide the participating students into five groups, each of which must contribute its own viewpoints. The various concepts contributed by the five groups are tabulated in Table 1. Within the fourth column of the table, each group's viewpoint is denoted as $O_i, 0 \leq i \leq 5 - 1$, in order to be consistent with the notation used in Figure 3.

Referring to Table 1 and Figure 3, the delta between the viewpoints of groups 1 and 2 is designated by $\partial_{1,2} = O_1 \Delta O_2 = \{c, l\}$, which is equivalent to

$$\{live\ in\ a\ common\ geographical\ area,\ live\ in\ a\ common\ identifiable\ area\}.$$

Having isolated these differences, one can further analyze the generality or the specificity of these two points (i.e., c and l). In this case, for instance, c can be viewed as a subset or an instance of l; or l captures the definition of c. This demonstrates how the symmetric difference of two concepts, contributed cooperatively by different groups, can be used to synthesize a more general concept.

The amalgam of the concepts contributed by the five groups is reflected by Theorem 2:

$$O_0 \cup O_1 \cup O_2 \cup O_3 \cup O_4 = \{a, b, c, d, e, f, g, h, i, j, l, k, m, n\}.$$

Whereas the common points shared by all the groups are reflected by Theorem 3:

$$O_0 \cap O_1 \cap O_2 \cap O_3 \cap O_4 = \{a, b\}.$$

4 Comparing One Idea with Others.

It is often the case that an idea (termed as *base*) needs to be compared with other ideas to reveal how this base idea differs from the others. This observation becomes crucial if the *base*, for instance, is a correct or key solution in a group discussion. Using the triangle model such a situation can be depicted in Figure 4(a), where O_4 represents the base. Here, the delta between each $O_i, 0 \leq i \leq 3$, and the base has been computed. By knowing such differences and his own idea, each idea's owner can obtain the base by performing a delta operation on his and the delta between his and the base (based on Theorem 1).

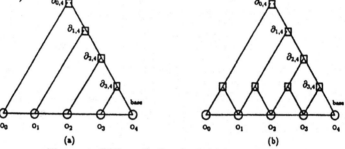

(a) (b)

Figure 4: Differentiating base idea from others.

To illustrate the importance of the triangle model, consider the situation in a learning environment which consists of interconnected terminals controlled by a central computer. Suppose each terminal is assigned to a student and the central computer is assigned to the teacher. Generally, the teacher has prepared the correct solution or idea (i.e., the base) for a particular problem; the teacher expects the students to give their own solutions to the problem by entering the solutions on their own terminals. After all students have entered the solutions, the teacher shows the result of the evaluation to each student by displaying the triangle as shown in Figure 4(a). In this way each student $i, 0 \leq i \leq 3$ can do the following:

- reveal the unmatched points between his and the correct solution (i.e., $\partial_{i,4}$),

- synthesize the correct solution from his and the delta (i.e., $O_4 = O_i \Delta \partial_{i,4}$),

- evaluate the irrelevant points of his solution (i.e., $O_i \cap \overline{O_4} = O_i \cap \partial_{i,4}$, based on Theorem 3),

- evaluate the missing points of his solution (i.e., $\overline{O_i} \cap O_4 = O_4 \cap \partial_{i,4}$, based on Theorem 3),

- compare his solution with each of the other solutions (i.e., by interactively performing the *common join* operation on the base, as shown in Figure 4(b), and further constructing the complete configuration as shown in Figure 3).

On the other hand, the teacher can do the following:

- evaluate each solution of his students (i.e., by viewing all $\partial_{i,4}$'s, $0 \leq i \leq 3$),

- rank the solutions of his students based on the number unmatched points (i.e., the cardinality of each $\partial_{i,4}, 0 \leq i \leq 3$),

- isolate the components which are missing in the solutions of all students (i.e., by finding $O_4 \cap \overline{O_0} \cap \overline{O_1} \cap \overline{O_2} \cap \overline{O_3}$, based on Equation 2.)

In addition to these possibilities, the students and teacher *en masse* can do the following:

- combine all solutions (i.e., $O_0 \cup O_1 \cup ... \cup O_4$),

- find the common points in all solutions (i.e., $O_0 \cap O_1 \cap ... \cap O_4$),

- integrate all solutions given by students so that the differences between each student's solution and the teacher's solution are preserved. This is explored in the next section.

Interestingly, since everyone enters his solution into the computer and lets the computer compute the deltas, students are not afraid of being embarrassed or ridiculed by others, which is an important factor in idea generation [BAC75, OV75, MB89]. This increases the students' motivation to contribute ideas without fear. According to Mc-Graw and Briggs [MB89], confidentiality is a typical problem that must be considered in multiple-expert team. In [NDV+91], confidentiality is attacked by anonymity. In the triangle model, anonymity can be achieved by labeling each node with a secret id known only by the owner.

Another interesting point is that the triangle model can be saved for the purpose of progress monitoring in the subsequent learning sessions. Hence, the teachers and each student are kept cognizant of their progress. As the volume of data increases, the the nodes to be saved must be carefully selected in order to minimize storage requirements. This issue has been discussed in [SR91a].

5 Integrating Object Variants with respect to the Base

When an idea is being reviewed and modified simultaneously by different people, several variants of the idea may result. The problem is how to integrate these variants with respect to the original idea (*base*). That is, how to preserve the changed parts of all variants with respect to the base. In this paper, such an integration is mathematically formulated in the following definition.

Definition 3 *Let X_0 be the base idea, all X_i's, $1 \leq i \leq n$ the variants of X_0, and $M_{X(1;n)}$ the idea obtained from integrating all X_i's with respect to X_0. That is,*

$$M_{X(1;n)} = (X_0 \cap X_1 \cap X_2 \cap ... \cap X_n) \cup (\overline{X_0} \cap (X_1 \cup X_2 \cup ... \cup X_n)).$$

The above definition implies that integration includes all components which do not belong to the base but exist in either one or more variants, plus all components common to the base and all variants. This also implies that if any components of the base are missing from one or more variants, these components are excluded. Suppose, O_0 (in Table 1) is viewed as the base, and $O_i, 1 \leq i \leq 4$ are the variants. Hence, $M_{O(1;4)} = (O_0 \cap O_1 \cap O_2 \cap O_3 \cap O_4) \cup (\overline{O_0} \cap (O_1 \cup O_2 \cup O_3 \cup O_4)) = \{a, b\} \cup \{m, l, n, f, g, h, i, j, k\} = \{a, b, m, l, n, f, g, h, i, j, k\}$. This establishes the definition of "*community*" as the following:

Community is a group of people who share one or more common characteristics, functions, environments, religions, cultures, interests, life experiences, and ethnics; live in a common identifiable area; and interact with each other.

Conceptually, Definition 3 conforms with the one in [HPR89]. However in [HPR89], only two variants can be integrated, whereas our formula allows any numbers of variants to be integrated. Another piece of work [Ber86], treats version integration as extension integration. This requires that the base must be a subset of all variants (i.e., $X_0 \cap X_1 \cap X_2 \cap ... \cap X_n = X_0$). This also implies that deletion of any components of the base is not allowed.

Based on the triangle model, the definition of $M_{X(1;n)}$ can be computed by utilizing all deltas of the variants with respect to the base. This is shown in the following theorem.

Theorem 5 $M_{X(1;n)} = X_0 \Delta(\partial_{X_{0,1}} \cup \partial_{X_{0,2}} \cup ... \cup \partial_{X_{0,n}})$, *where* $\partial_{X_{0,i}} = X_0 \Delta X_i$, $1 \leq i \leq n$.

The proof of the theorem can be found in [KM76]. Combining theorems 1 and 5, we obtain the delta between X and $M_X(1;n)$, denoted as $\partial_{X,M}$ which can be expressed as:

$$\partial_{X,M} = X_0 \Delta M_{X(1;n)} = \partial_{X_{0,1}} \cup \partial_{X_{0,2}} \cup ... \cup \partial_{X_{0,n}}$$

The integration scheme that utilizes Theorem 5 can be graphically depicted in Figure 5.

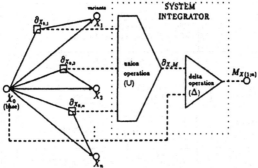

Figure 5: Integrating versions with respect to base.

6 The Invitation Tool

The initiation stage for collaborative work can be categorized into two levels [KGE88]:
the *relationship level* which includes finding partners and sharing background assumptions, and the *task level* which includes generating ideas and planning. Therefore, a
systematic and creative approach to finding new ideas must be found. In this section,
we attempt to support these two levels by designing an invitation tool, as shown in
Figure 6, which is integrated with an electronic mail system.

This enables potentially competent people, living in distant places, to participate in
contributing ideas for a collaborative project or research. Through this tool, interested
people can signal their involvement by acknowledging the invitation and indicating the
appropriate fields of interest or expertise they can contribute. This also allows people to
observe and appreciate each other's personal qualities and professional skills [KGE88,
FGHW88, MB89, Sla90]

This form of invitation can be implemented using templates whose detailed contents
can be filled and modified by both senders and receivers. Information can be stored in
a standard format to facilitate parsing.

The receivers of the invitation can open a window, and are presented with sub-
windows containing subjects of the invitation. All important information such as the
due date, or current command is highlighted. This tool is the first tool to involve
a diverse group of people in the software development process (i.e., equivalent to an
invitation for a conference or workshop). In this way, all interested people are given
an opportunity to contribute their expertise or opinion.

This tool can also be employed to facilitate concept development through learning
centers [Tho75]. In this particular example, the single-object center is the project of
designing a description language for specifying iconic representations of data structures [SR90, RS91]. This approach is effective not only for the purpose of problem-
solving and as an introduction to wide spectrum of language design, but also as a
springboard from which to derive a multitude of concepts about the relationships be-

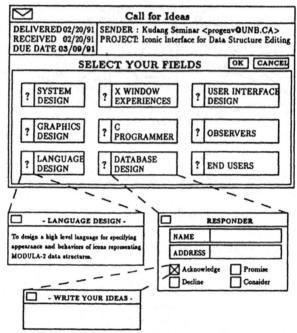

Figure 6: A front end window for calling ideas.

tween various related aspects of a concept [Tho75].

When the reader clicks on an icon containing the ? sign, another sub-window containing the purpose of the corresponding subject is shown. This sub-window may contain other sub-window descendants if necessary. Clicking on the subject itself will cause another window containing an option for reader's involvement. If the reader agrees to become involved in that subject he can click on "acknowledge" and is asked to fill in his name and address. Upon the completion of this query the mail will be automatically sent to the sender whose address is known by the system. The 'X' sign shows the option that a user has chosen. If the option "acknowledge" is selected, a file window is provided for writing ideas or opinions.

It is possible that a reader can be involved in more than one subject. When the sender receives the response, the number of participants in each subject is updated according to the type of involvement (i.e., promise, decline, acknowledge, or consider).

7 Conclusions

A mathematical method for storing and exploring ideas has been described. This paper attempts to relate and translate theories to invention and application in the design of ideas maintenance and exploration which can be useful for enhancing cooperation and education in a large community. The main objective of the tool discussed herein is to provide a general, structural, tool for the exploration of ideas. The basic theorems and definitions underlying the method have been formulated.

Automatic means for contrasting and combining ideas contributed by different people and detecting potential conflicts are urgently required for cooperative work. The triangle model can be utilized to encourage different patterns of thinking, and the development of new ideas [KGE88, JKTV89, McG90, BG91] in an organization which emphasizes idea generation. With this tool, comparing and contrasting techniques can be facilitated in order to isolate the salient features of ideas or concepts. Furthermore, the integration system described herein can be used to produce the combined expertise or ideas from various people.

An attempt is being made to integrate this tool with a hypertext system [Rob92] for supporting cooperative software development projects.

Acknowledgment: The authors wish to thank the anonymous referees whose constructive comments and suggestions contributed to the enhancement of this paper.

References

[AH85] D.M. Adams and M.E. Hamm. *Cooperative Learning - Critical Thinking and Collaboration Accross the Curriculum.* Charles C Thomas Publisher, Springfield, Illinois, USA, 1985.

[BAC75] F.A. Blanchard, L. Adelman, and S.W. Cook. Effect of group success and future upon interpersonal attraction in cooperating interracial groups. *Journal of Personality and Social Psychology*, 31(6):1020–1030, 1975.

[Ber86] V. Berzins. On merging software extensions. *Acta Informatica*, 23:607–619, 1986.

[BG91] S. Bodker and K. Gronbaek. Cooperative prototyping: Users and designers in mutual activity. *International Journal of Man-Machine Studies*, 34(3):453–478, March 1991.

[FGHW88] F. Flores, M. Graves, B. Hartfield, and T. Winograd. Computer systems and the design of organizational interaction. *ACM Transactions on Office Information Systems*, 6(2):153–172, April 1988.

[HPR89] S. Horwitz, J. Prins, and T. Reps. Integrating noninterfering versions of programs. *ACM Transactions on Programming Languages and Systems*, 11(3):345–387, July 1989.

[JKTV89] P.W. Jordan, K.S. Keller, R.W. Tucker, and D. Vogel. Software storming: Combining rapid prototyping and knowledge engineering. *IEEE Computer*, 22(5):39–48, May 1989.

[JW86] B. Joyce and M. Weil. *Models of Teaching.* Prentice-Hall, Inc., Englewood Cliffs, New Jersey 07632, 1986.

[Kag85] S. Kagan. A flexible cooperative learning technique. In R. Slavin et al, editor, *Learning to Cooperate, Cooperating to Learn*, pages 437–460. Plenum Press, New York, NY 10013, 1985.

[Kas89] R. Kass. Student modeling in intelligent tutoring systems - implications for user modeling. In A. Kobsa and W.Wahlster, editors, *User Models in Dialog Systems*, pages 386–410. Springer-Verlag, Berlin, 1989.

[KGE88] R.E. Kraut, J. Galegher, and C. Egido. Relationships and tasks in scientific research collaboration. *Human-Computer Interaction*, 3(1):31–58, 1987-1988.

[KM76] K. Kuratowski and A. Mostowski. *Set Theory: With an Introduction to Descriptive Set Theory*. North-Holland Publishing Company, Amsterdam, 1976.

[LC89] J.F. Lehman and J.G. Carbonell. Learning the user's language: A step towards automated creation of user models. In A. Kobsa and W.Wahlster, editors, *User Models in Dialog Systems*, pages 163–194. Springer-Verlag, Berlin, 1989.

[LF91] J.C. Leite and P.A. Freeman. Requirements validation through viewpoint resolution. *IEEE Transactions on Software Engineering*, 17(12):1253–1269, December 1991.

[MB89] K.L. McGraw and K. Briggs. *Knowledge Acquisition – Principles and Guidelines*. Prentice-Hall, Inc., Englewood Cliffs, New Jersey 07632, 1989.

[McG90]guin90 N. McGuinness. New product idea activities in large technology based firms. *Journal of Product Innovation Management*, 7(3):173–185, September 1990.

[MH91] K. Miriyala and M.T. Harandi. Automatic derivation of formal specification from informal description. *IEEE Transactions on Software Engineering*, 17(10):1126–1142, October 1991.

[NDV+91] J.F. Nunamaker, A.R. Dennis, J.S. Valacich, D.R. Vogel, and J.F. George. Electronic meeting systems to support group work. *Communications of the ACM*, 34(7):40–61, July 1991.

[OV75] M.A. Okun and F.J. Vesta. Cooperation and competition in coacting groups. *Journal of Personality and Social Psychology*, 31(4):615–620, 1975.

[Rob92] R.N. Robson. Using hypertext to locate reusable objects. In *Proc. 25th Hawaii Intl. Conf. Syst. Sciences*, pages 549–557, Kauai, January 7-10 1992. IEEE.

[RS91] R.N. Robson and K.B. Seminar. Visual editing of data structures. In *Proc. Conf. on Software Maintenance*, pages 228–237, Sorrento, Italy, October 15-17 1991. IEEE.

[Sla90] R.S. Slavin. *Cooperative Learning: Theory, Research, and Practice*. Prentice Hall, Inc., USA, 1990.

[SR90] K.B. Seminar and R.N. Robson. An iconic description language: Programming support for data structure visualization. *ACM/SIGCHI Bulletin*, 2(1):70–72, July 1990.

[SR91a] K.B. Seminar and R.N. Robson. A mathematical model for maintaining versions of object data structures. In P. Sadanandan and T.M. Vijayaraman, editors, *Advances in Data Management – Proc. 3rd Intl. Conf. on Management of Data*, pages 127–142. Tata McGraw-Hill Publishing Company Ltd., New Delhi, 1991.

[SR91b] K.B. Seminar and R.N. Robson. Using symmetric difference to aid problem-solving tasks. In *Proc. Annual Computer Science Conf.*, pages 11–21, Halifax, NS, Canada, October 1991. APICS.

[SW87] B. Steinholtz and K. Walden. Automatic identification on software system differences. *IEEE Transactions on Software Engineering*, 13(4):493–497, April 1987.

[Tho75] J.I. Thomas. *Learning Centers*. Holbrook Press, Inc., Boston, USA, 1975.

[WF90] B.Y. White and J.R. Frederiksen. Causal model progression as a foundation for intelligent learning environments. *Artificial Intelligence – An International Journal*, 42(1):99–157, February 1990.

DYNAMIC CAL-COURSEWARE GENERATION WITHIN AN ITS-SHELL ARCHITECTURE

Julita Vassileva
Software Engineering Department
Institute of Mathematics
Bulgarian Academy of Sciences
Academician Bonchev Str. Bl.8
1113 Sofia, Bulgaria

ABSTRACT

This paper presents an attempt to integrate CAL courseware with a domain-independent ITS-shell architecture.

This project follows a recent trend for providing a synthesis of the up to now "rather incompatible fields of authoring systems, intelligent tutoring and hypermedia-based CAL". We see the following advantages of the proposed architecture for "knowledge-based CAL":

1) Dynamic individualized course planning and instruction, which takes into account the student's knowledge and individual characteristics.

2) Ease of updating. The base of teaching materials is separated from the "buffer"-knowledge about how to plan a course. It can be created and updated independently by professionals, that don't need to know about teaching strategies. In the same time teacher-specialists can elaborate the "buffer"-knowledge base. The domain-independent Pedagogical Component allows tuning of the pedagogical strategies. It allows expert-pedagogicians to concentrate on the strategic decisions taken during instruction and the ways the student's individual characteristics can influence them, without knowing anything about the domain.

KEYWORDS: dynamic CAL course generation, ITS-shell, ITS architecture
TOPICS: knowledge-based CAL systems, Intelligent Tutoring Systems

1. INTRODUCTION

The development of individual instructional tools is an example of a multi-dimensional evolution (Wenger, 1987). Some of the most important dimensions are: interaction with the student, individualization of instruction, the palette of presentation methods and pedagogical strategies.

The principal progress of Computer Assisted Learning (CAL) courseware compared to books is in the dimension of interaction. This allows branching of the course of instruction and, therefore, better individualization of instruction. An additional advantage of CAL courseware is the variety of presentation methods, including pictures, videos, sounds, animation, simulations. However, the pedagogical strategies for knowledge communication are either implicitly built-in the course during its design (in traditional CAL courseware) or are absent at all (in microworlds, hyper-systems and other reactive environments).

The advantages of Intelligent CAL systems (ICAL) when compared to CAL software are mainly in the dimensions of interaction and pedagogical strategies. The student is no longer restricted to choosing one of several given answers. The system can analyse any answer and model the student's cognitive state. This allows better individualization, by dynamic generation of instructional material to match the specific student's needs. On the other hand, the explicit representation of pedagogical strategies allows further individualization of instruction with respect to the personal characteristics of the student.

Unfortunately, both inferring the student's cognitive state (student modelling) and defining explicit pedagogical strategies for realistic domains turned out to be extremely difficult. Recently, a wave of skepticism can be noticed among researchers and practitioners about the possibilities of "intelligence" to add much in terms of performance of courseware. However, architectures and ideas from ITS are penetrating the field of traditional CAL (Bierman, 1991).

In our opinion CAL could benefit a lot, if an appropriate architecture is found to create a marriage between traditional CAL presentation methods and interaction and, on the other side, ITS' features of dynamic instructional planning, explicit representation of pedagogical strategies and individual student modelling. The place of this practical "I+CAL" within the evolution of individual instructional tools is shown in table 1.

This paper presents an attempt to integrate CAL courseware with a domain-independent ITS-shell architecture described in detail elsewhere (Vassileva, 1990). This architecture is sketched briefly in section 2. Section 3 describes the structure of the domain knowledge base. The possibilities for dynamic individualized courseware generation, provided by the architecture are discussed in section 4. Section 5 presents a methodology for "plugging in" (already existing) courseware into the architecture (e.g. creating a domain knowledge base) and for tuning the pedagogical strategies of the system.

A system, called TOBIE-CAL is currently being implemented using ready-made base of "screens" from existing CAL-courses.

dimensions indiv. instr. tools	individualization	interaction	presentation methods	pedagogical staratgies
books	weak, e.g.skip chapters	no	text, photos, pictures, exersisses	implicit
CAL	branching	questions, MC-tests	a great variety	implicit or none
ICAL	dynam. generat. of material	student modeling	limited	explicitly represented
practical "I+CAL"				

Table 1.

2. ARCHITECTURE

The architecture of the system is shown in figure 1.

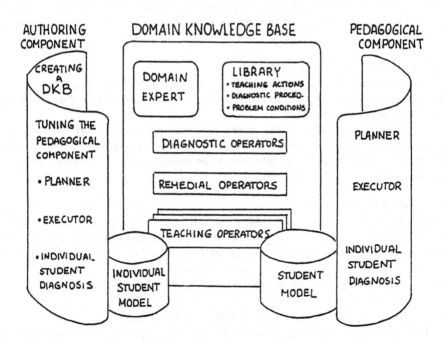

Fig. 1. *The ITS-shell architecture.*

It consists of the following components:

- an invariant Pedagogical Component that plans instruction (dynamically creates a course) and carries out the plan.
- an invariant Individual Student Model, containing three valued parameters: concentration, intellect, motivation and the preferred types of presentation methods.
- a Domain Knowledge Base that can be replaced without changing the rest of the components.
- a Model of the Student's Domain Knowledge which is automatically generated and is the minimum required to allow individualized course generation.
- an Authoring Component for creating/updating the Domain Knowledge Base and for tuning the strategies of the Pedagogical Component for course generation.

The architecture of TOBIE-CAL differs slightly from the general one with respect to the structure of the Domain Knowledge Base.

3. STRUCTURE OF THE DOMAIN KNOWLEDGE BASE

It comprises two parts: a base of teaching materials, roughly corresponding to the "library" in Figure 1, and a "buffer" representation of the domain-specific knowledge. It is needed by the Pedagogical Component to dynamically plan instruction. Thanks to the "buffer" representation, the didactic and domain knowledge become "orthogonal" (Bierman, 1991) and the Domain Knowledge Base can be replaced.

3.1. The base of teaching materials

It contains atoms (text screens, pictures, animations, simulations, procedures that invoke the video-player or tape- recorder) and sub-courses (sequences of atoms to teach a certain element of knowledge).

A special class of atoms (test-atoms) are those intended to test whether or not the student has acquired certain element of knowledge (e.g. MC-test items, questions, problems). The base of teaching materials can be created and updated with conventional authoring tools.

3.2. The "Buffer"

The "Buffer" is needed to represent the structure of the domain knowledge with respect to teaching and to associate it with the corresponding teaching materials in the base. This structure is similar to the associative webs used for knowledge structuring in hypertext systems. However, it is represented in a specific way, oriented towards guided teaching. That's why we shall describe it briefly in the next sections.

3.2.1. The logical structure of knowledge to be taught

The structure of knowledge in any domain can be represented with an AND/OR-graph. The nodes correspond to elements of knowledge, whose possession could be identified by a test-atom. For every node there should be at least one appropriate test-atom in the base of teaching materials.

There are also bug-nodes, corresponding to the common errors that students make when answering the test-atoms and that need a special treatment (when branching is done in traditional CAL courses).

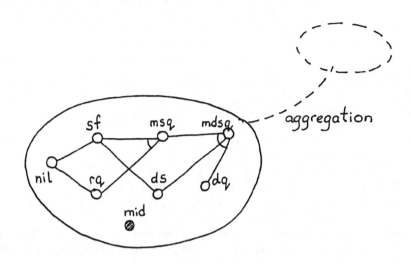

Fig. 2. *Decomposition into partial fractions.*

sf – *denominator decomposable into simple factors;* rq – *recognize non-factorizable denominators;* msq – *denominator containing simple and quadratic factors;* ds – *denominator containing simple factors of higher degree (> 1);* dq – *denominator containing quadratic factors with a higher degree;* mdsq – *denominator containing simple and quadratic factors with higher degrees;* mid – *missing partial fractions with intermediate degrees.*

The not-bug-nodes are linked with respect to precedence in teaching, i.e. the knowledge of a set of nodes can be a prerequisite to learning another node. A course of instruction is associated with one graph and it normally follows these links. We call them "horizontal" links.

The example, shown in figure 2, represents a graph from the experimental implementation of TOBIE-CAL, which teaches the student how to decompose rational functions into sums of partial fractions. Every node represents a certain problem solving skill that should be acquired by the student.

One graph represents a cluster of domain knowledge. Different clusters can be connected with "vertical" links of various types: aggregation, abstraction and analogy (Goldstein, 1982), (Brecht & Jones, 1988), (Greer & McCalla, 1989).

Teaching can temporarily follow the vertical links, when it is appropriate to jump to another cluster of knowledge to use an analogy or define the place of a concept within a more general context.

3.2.2. Representation

The structure of domain knowledge is represented by sets of Teaching Operators (TO). The idea of TOs originates from an early work on instructional planning in intelligent tutoring systems (Peachey & McCalla, 1986). Each set of TOs represents one cluster of knowledge. A TO is similar to a production rule (see table 2) and represents one horizontal link in the graph.

Teaching Operator:

conditions	effects	action		evaluation criteria
		presentation	test	

Table 2.

The condition-nodes should be present in the student model in order to apply a TO (its action is what the student will see). The action has two parts:

• a presentation part - a procedure invoking one atom or a sequence of atoms (sub-course) from the base of teaching materials.

• a testing part - a procedure that invokes a test-atom or a sequence of test-atoms to find out if the student has acquired the knowledge (skill) corresponding to the effect of the TO.

The evaluation criteria contain an indication about the type of the action: animation, text, video etc. or mixed (usually, in case of sub-course) of the TO and the maximum time, allowed for the action.

There are specific TOs, called "remedial operators", whose conditions are bug-nodes. Their effect is to delete the bug-node from the student model and the action is to present appropriate teaching materials to the student.

The vertical links are represented with a special type of TOs, whose action is to invoke another cluster. Information about the type of vertical link is kept in the evaluation criteria of the TO.

The structure of the Domain Knowledge Base is shown in Figure 3. It also demonstrates examples of TOs from the implementation of TOBIE-CAL, whose actions are on two different levels of granularity (atoms and subcourses).

4. COURSE GENERATION AND INSTRUCTION

The Pedagogical Component generates an individual course for the student who has to learn a given element of knowledge (node) within a given cluster, called "a teaching goal".

In doing this it takes into account the student's preliminary knowledge (the student model) and the type of teaching actions he prefers (recorded in the individual student model).

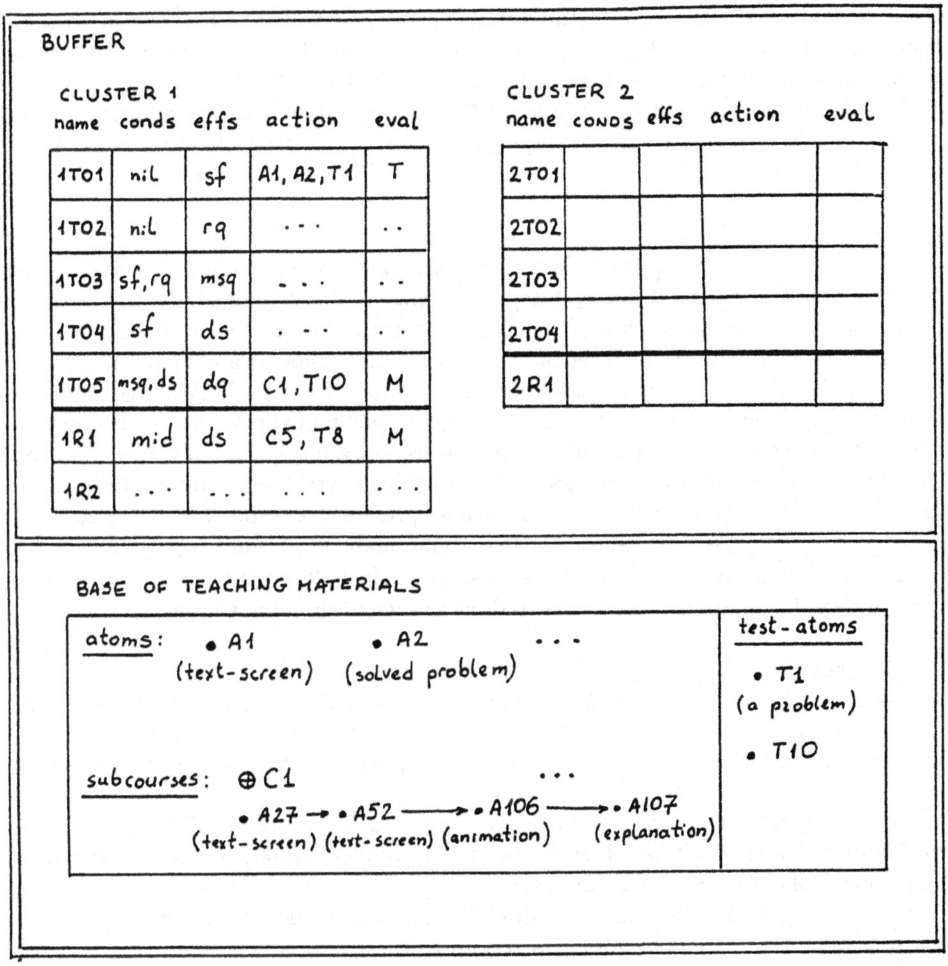

BUFFER

CLUSTER 1

name	conds	effs	action	eval
1TO1	nil	sf	A1, A2, T1	T
1TO2	nil	rq	. . .	. .
1TO3	sf, rq	msq	. . .	. .
1TO4	sf	ds	. . .	. .
1TO5	msq, ds	dq	C1, T10	M
1R1	mid	ds	c5, T8	M
1R2	. . .	. . .	. . .	. . .

CLUSTER 2

name	conds	effs	action	eval
2TO1				
2TO2				
2TO3				
2TO4				
2R1				

BASE OF TEACHING MATERIALS

atoms: • A1 • A2 . . .
(text-screen) (solved problem)

test-atoms

• T1
(a problem)

• T10

subcourses: ⊕ C1 . . .
• A27 → • A52 ──→ • A106 ──→ • A107
(text-screen) (test-screen) (animation) (explanation)

Fig. 3. *The domain knowledge base.*

The course is followed and its plan can be changed dynamically during instruction. The course generation has three phases which are discussed below.

4.1. Initializing the student model (preliminary test)

A preliminary test is generated for the given cluster. Test- atoms are given to the student for every node following the horizontal links. If the student answers correctly to the test- atom, the corresponding node will be added to the student model; in case of anticipated error - the corresponding bug node will be added. The sequence of test-atoms might be not automatically generated, but pre-defined by the author and included in the base as a special TO with no conditions and effects - all nodes in the cluster.

A preliminary test will be given also, if instruction is switched to another cluster (following a vertical link of analogy, specification etc.). A separate student model is created for every "visited" cluster during a dynamic following of a course.

4.2. Course planning

A "plan" is a sequence of TOs which, when applied to the initial state of the student model transforms it into a state, containing the teaching goal. As the TOs are in fact production rules, the task of planning is equivalent to the task of finding a proof of a goal provided with a given set of facts (the student model) and rules (the TOs). There could be several possible paths of nodes leading to the goal. Also, as there are a lot of TOs in the base that have the same conditions and effects, but with different actions, there could be several sequences of TOs for a given sequence of nodes. The one that will become a plan for the course is chosen using several competing criteria: time minimization, best serving the student's learning preferences (type of teaching actions) and requirements, posed by the teacher like: "Skip node X", "Don't use video" etc.

In this way an individualized course planning takes place with respect to the student's different preliminary knowledge and preference of teaching actions.

4.3. Instruction

Instruction consists of executing the actions of the TOs listed in the plan. What the student sees is a sequence of atoms (including test-atoms) that comprise the course. However, this course can change during instruction, because of two types of unexpected events:

1) The student may fail to answer correctly to a test-atom of a TO. In this case the TO's effect-node can't be added to the student model (usually a bug-node is added instead) and plan following can not continue.

2) A TO from the plan makes a call for instruction in another cluster.

In general there are two types of reactions to these events:

• opportunistic, i.e. to serve the needs of the moment. In case 1) an appropriate remedial operator for the bug-node will be executed and the initial plan of the course will be followed. In case 2) the cluster that was called will become the current cluster of instruction. A teaching goal will be assigned, a preliminary test for that cluster will be given to the student (if there is still no student model for that cluster) and a course planning in that cluster will take place. The initial course will not be followed before the teaching goal in the new cluster is accomplished or the time limit for that cluster (determined during course planning) is exhausted.

• plan-based, i.e to reconsider the plan for obtaining the goal. A new plan is always created for obtaining the teaching goal in the following cases:

– if there is no appropriate remedial for the bug-node at hand;

– if there is no bug node that corresponds to the error the student has made (in case 1)

– if time does not allow following of vertical links during instruction (in case 2).

A plan-based or opportunistic reaction is chosen in the other cases by the Pedagogical Component on the basis of information from the individual model of the student. For example, for not-concentrated students it might be better not to switch to different clusters too often, so in case 2) a plan-based reaction will be chosen. The way of choosing an appropriate reaction to a given situation for the particular student is a rather complicated pedagogical problem and we won't try to suggest any solutions here. However, we created a way of defining the type of reaction for a particular type of situation and for all possible combinations of values of the three parameters in the individual student model. The teacher can influence this process by selection of a "character" of the Pedagogical Component (Vassileva, 1992). The "character" influences significantly on the resulting course of instruction.

This is a further step towards the individualization of courseware generation, since the course plan can be changed dynamically. The individual characteristics of the student are taken into account in a way, tuned by the teacher.

5. METHODOLOGY

Users can take three different roles: an author, who creates or replaces the Domain Knowledge Base; a teacher, who tunes the way of courseware generation and instruction according to his own pedagogical style and a student, who faces the result. A special Authoring Component is developed to support the activities of the author and the teacher without the need of programming.

5.1. Creating a domain knowledge base

The task of creating CAL-courseware, is mainly a software engineering one. In our system, as the course is being automatically generated, the task is to represent the knowledge needed for that, so it is a knowledge-engineering task.

The Domain Knowledge Base could be replaced with another one, for a different domain, in two stages:

• Creating/Updating/Using a ready-made Base of Teaching Materials.

The Authoring Component provides means for creating atoms and, in this way, creating and updating the base of teaching materials. It can be coupled with any authoring tool for editing graphics, animation, for including external devices, like video-players and tape-recorders. A ready-made base of atoms can be used or obtained by "slicing" existing CAL-courses.

• Creating the "Buffer" Knowledge Representation.

The following activities can be enumerated:

1) All test-atoms form the base of teaching materials must be analysed and associated to knowledge elements (concepts/skills) that are tested with them. The clusters of domain knowledge containing these knowledge elements (nodes) have to be defined.

2) The pre-requisite links between the nodes within every cluster must be determined and associated with actions (sequences of atoms) of different types. In this way a set of TOs is created.

3) The vertical links between different clusters have to be defined by creating TOs in clusterX that invoke clusterY. The type of the link (generalization/specification, analogy etc.) should be indicated in the evaluation criteria of the TOs.

5.2. Tuning the way of course generation and instruction.

The teacher can influence the way of course planning by assigning the criteria for optimum plan selection and giving weights to them. The way of instruction (e.g. choosing an appropriate reaction to unexpected situations) can be influenced indirectly by means of selection of a "character" of the Pedagogical Component. The teacher interacts with the system via menu-type dialogues.

6. CONCLUSIONS

This project follows a recent trend for providing a synthesis of the up to now "rather incompatible fields of authoring systems, intelligent tutoring and hypermedia-based CAL" (Muehlhauser, 1991). We see the following advantages in it:

1) Dynamic course generation that is individualized, because the student's knowledge and individual characteristics are taken into account.

2) Ease of updating. The base of teaching materials can be created independently by professionals, that don't need to know about teaching strategies. In the same time teacher-specialists can elaborate the base of TOs, the conceptual structure of the domain and the types of links that could be useful for instructional purposes. Expert pedagogicians can concentrate on the strategic decisions and the ways the student's individual characteristics influence them, without knowing anything about the domain.

The advantages of TOBIE-CAL with respect to individualization in comparison with traditional CAL seem obvious. However, the advantages from a software engineering point of view still have to be tested. We hope that the development of a "Buffer"-base of Teaching Operators given a ready-made base of atoms will require less efforts and will be more cost-effective than creating many different courses for the various possible classes of students. However, more experimental evidence is needed which we still don't have.

ACKNOWLEDGEMENT

This work has been partially supported by a contract with the Bulgarian Ministry of Science and Higher Education.

REFERENCES

Bierman D. (1991) To be intelligent or not to be intelligent: is that the question? Proceedings of International Conference on Computer Assisted Learning and Instruction in Science and Engineering, CALISCE'91-Lausanne, pp.25-34.

Brecht B., Jones M. (1988) The Genetic Graph Approach. Int. J. Man- Machine Stud. 28, pp.483-504.

Goldstein I. (1982) The Genetic Graph: A Representation for the Evolution of Procedural Knowledge. In Sleeman D. and Brown J.S. (Eds.): Intelligent Tutoring Systems. Academic Press. pp.51-77.

Greer J., McCalla G. (1989) A Computational Framework for Granularity and its Application to Educational Diagnosis. Proc. ICAI-89, Detroit, pp.477-482.

Muehlhauser M. (1991) Hypermedia Navigation as a Central Concept for Instructional Tool Environments. Proceedings of International Conference on Computer Assisted Learning and Instruction in Science and Engineering, CALISCE'91- Lausanne, pp.177-184.

Peachey D., McCalla G. (1986) Using Planning Techniques in Intelligent Tutoring Systems. Int. J. Man.- Machine Stud. 24, pp.77-98.

Vassileva J. (1990) An Architecture and Methodology for Creating a Domain-Independent, Plan-based Intelligent Tutoring System. Educational and Training Technology International, 27, 4, pp.386-397.

Vassileva J. (1992) Pedagogical Decisions within an ITS-Shell. to appear in Computers & Education.

Wenger E. (1987) Artificial Intelligence and Tutoring Systems. Morgan Kaufmann, Los Altos

CALLGUIDE: using programmable hypertext as a shell for CALL programs

Eve Wilson, Ian Lindley,[1] and Simon Pullen[1]

Computing Laboratory, University of Kent at Canterbury

Canterbury, Kent, CT2 7NF, England

tel. + 44 227 764000 ext. 3628

email: ew@ukc.ac.uk

Abstract

This paper describes a project, Callguide, to investigate the hypertext system Guide as an authoring shell for computer assisted language learning programs. The paper begins by considering the advantages of computers in CALL. It goes on to discuss the interface requirements for a CALL package. The Callguide programs were written, under a hypertext system without audio-visual facilities, to improve the intensive reading skills of advanced students who have A-level or equivalent in English as a Foreign Language and who are additionally motivated by the need to study a technical discipline in the foreign language. Here the discipline is computing, but the techniques would apply equally well to other subjects. The project has largely concentrated on exercises to improve the student's lexical skills and ability to understand, in detail, a technical text. Lexical skills include exercises to recognise antonyms and synonyms, word formation to correspond with part of speech and understanding idiomatic expressions. Discourse skills include maintaining coherence throughout a passage by verb correspondence in tense, mode and aspect, identifying referents of pronouns and relative pronouns, and traditional comprehension exercises including completing Cloze texts and connectivity matrices. A brief user evaluation of the project is followed by a conclusion.

---

[1] Students at the University of Kent at Canterbury, 1988-1991

1 Why CALL?

1.1 The limitations of computers

Many educators still have a largely negative view of the use of computer-based tools to teach subjects other than computer science. Behind programmed learning they see only the theory of conditioning, which results in passive training, not active education. They feel that computers have been introduced not for sound educational reasons but because they produce savings in costs and resources. What intellectual challenge there is belongs to teachers who have to learn how best to exploit the computer in the context of their disciplines. Language teachers feel this particularly acutely: natural language is a complex phenomenon, which has evolved, and continues to evolve, with human beings. The achievements of computer programmers in natural language have fallen far short of those of their colleagues in mathematics and science. Natural language understanding and generation by computer are still largely the subject of laboratory experiment. How can an inanimate machine replace a sensitive and committed human teacher in the essentially interactive process of language acquisition?

1.2 Individual learning

Of course, a computer cannot replace a teacher, and in an ideal world, every pupil would be given material specific to individual needs to be studied with a personal tutor. The traditional classroom can never aspire to this: no group of students is homogeneous. When teaching them collectively, the teacher must compromise, trying to ensure that there is something for everyone, but uncomfortably aware that one or two members are struggling most of the time; one or two are not nearly fully extended, and that the attention of most students wanders from time to time throughout the course of the lessons. It is not a new problem: in the 1960's the traditional language laboratory was developed to allow every student to practise pronunciation skills at the same time. It did not replace the classroom teachers, but allowed them to give a little individual attention to each pupil in turn while the other members of the class were productively occupied. Laboratories with computers instead of tape recorders are an extension of this tradition. They are more flexible than the tape-recorder: in the right environment they can control both audio and visual equipment to give an exciting multimedia environment. Currently, their shortcomings are similar, while not so severe, as those of the simple tape-recorder: spontaneous communications from the student are not yet acceptable. (For a comprehensive history of the development of CALL, see [Cam89] and [Dav82]). However, the computer can enhance lexical and reading skills as the old language laboratory improved pronunciation and fluency in speech. While this may not be the best of all possible worlds, it is an improvement on existing facilities and it is needed. Nuttall reports that moderate readers in their first language can recognise about 50,000 different words while graded readers for students who study English as a foreign language seldom go beyond the 3,500 word level. [Nut82 p 63]. Serious consideration must be given to any system that helps students to embark independently on a reading program to increase vocabulary, improve understanding of grammatical forms and usage, and enhance reading ability and comprehension. Computers can do this, ideally through multimedia systems that can give a student an integrated environment of video, sound and text, but even economical systems restricted to text have their part to play — and sometimes to the student's advantage.

1.3 Feedback

One advantage of a computer over a human being is that users are more likely to seek 'feedback' from a computer than they are from a person. Ashford and Cummings [Ash-Cum83] argue that people fear 'loss of face' in seeking feedback from other people and consequently tend to avoid it, even when the feedback is important to them. Herold et al [Her87] confirm that most people prefer self-generated or task-generated feedback; the computer does not threaten their self-esteem. So users seem to appreciate that the computer is non-threatening, inexhaustible and patient. The major problem is ease of communication. In any CALL system much effort must be made to ensure that this is as easy as possible for the user. Since interaction is mediated by the interface, the first consideration in a CALL project is interface design.

2 Requirements of the user interface

The requirements outlined below owe much to the findings of other workers in the field. It would be invidious not to acknowledge [Rub-Her84], [Whi87], [Rub88], [Shn87] and [Kea88].

2.1 Easy to learn and easy to remember

Foreign language students already have an intellectual discipline that should absorb them entirely. They do not want their concentration on this discipline continually distracted by the demands of an intricate interface.

2.2 Fast Response

Fast response helps to establish user confidence in the system and to maintain concentration on the task in hand. Every action should provoke an immediate observable response; if a delay is expected a message or icon should warn the user. The operating system and window manager should be transparent to them; the CALL program interface as natural and undemanding as possible. Nor do they want to 'waste' even five or ten minutes every session relearning how to use the CALL package; so the interface should be easy to remember.

2.3 Little manual dexterity

Many students do not know how to type. In most countries, keyboarding skills still do not form part of the school curriculum. While teachers might feel it no disservice in to-day's world to encourage students to learn to type, it is hardly fair to require advanced skills incidentally simply because the course is partially dependent on a disparate discipline, on computer-based methods of teaching and training. So might a language learning session degenerate into a keyboard scanning exercise. Learning is likely to be least impeded if the manual skills required are minimal: a pointing device or a touch screen would seem more conducive to a stress-free environment for the student than the traditional keyboard.

2.4 Consistent

The interface must be consistent. The same user action should produce the same effect whatever the task. Inconsistency confuses the user, distracts his attention from the learning process, and reduces his confidence in the program with which he is interacting. Interface inconsistencies often stem from the program designer's desire to tailor performance for every different type of exercise in the CALL package; to vary user dialogue with task so that every program is realised optimally. The resulting system is task-oriented, not user-oriented. It displays the programmers' skills to the bewilderment of the user who sees only one task where the implementor saw many. Good CALL package designers will sometimes forego functional elegance for user consistency.

A second cause of inconsistency can arise where a team of language teachers combine to produce a set of exercises. Often they agree and integrate the language content but do not agree on interface — or agree only in general terms and not detail. A CALL team that wants a coherent package, must appoint an interface manager — and listen to him.

2.5 User control and flexibility

A class for a foreign language may consist of students with widely differing cultural, social, and linguistics backgrounds. This is particularly likely if the students are mature, if they have left their home country to study abroad, if their purposes in learning the language are different. The more advanced the class the more marked the variations will be. For mature students at an advanced level of study in the foreign language, a good CALL package will allow them

a) to select the tasks they do and the tasks they omit

b) to choose the exercises they work through fully and the exercises they complete only partially;

c) to decide how often, and when, they ask for feedback. Boredom dissipates intellectual energy. Advanced students must be free to determine what language skills they need to enhance and to what level and for how long they wish to practise them.

3 Initial parameters of the system

3.1 Design Constraints

The system was designed under two constraints, one voluntary and one involuntary. The involuntary was the absence of audio- or video-equipment, which confined the resulting system to simple hypertext.

The voluntary constraint was to implement no exercise that could not be answered using only a pointing device and completed at least as quickly on the computer as with book and pencil. It was not to be computer-based for the sake of computing but only if the system could offer some improvement over traditional methods.

3.2 The hypertext system

Although only a text handling system was available, the system was powerful: Guide operating under Unix [BEL79] on a workstation. Guide was designed and implemented at the University of Kent at Canterbury by Professor P J Brown [BroPJ86] (A version of Guide for PC's has been implemented by Office Workstations Ltd [OWL88]). Guide possesses several advantages for the CALL undertaking:

i) It is a hypertext system with a variable node size — in contrast with some card-based systems where the amount of text in a node is often limited by the size of the card or window in the hypertext system.

ii) Guide possesses a good variety of the usual pure link buttons associated with hypertext. The more important of these are:

- Definition buttons. which associate a global name or icon with a piece of text and which, when selected, expand in place. The window is reformatted as necessary.

- Usage buttons, which, when selected, take a copy of the text associated with that button name or icon and expand it within the text.

- Glossary buttons, which, when selected, display a copy of the text associated with that button name in a subwindow within the main window.

- Local buttons, which associate a node name with a piece of text relevant only at the point of call. This node name need not be unique.

- Enquiry buttons, which offer the user a choice of links and can be used for implementing menus.

iii) However, in addition to the *link* buttons Guide has *action* buttons, which when selected can initiate Unix shell scripts or other programs: in other words, it is a *programmable hypertext*. This gives it all the power and flexibility of an expert system shell. This facet of Guide was crucial in the implementation of the callguide suite of programs.

3.3 The texts and the exercises

An incongruity of many language learning courses is that the texts around which they are constructed have been artificially contrived to illustrate specific linguistic usages. Their content is frequently irrelevant to the students' interests: most people do not read with the conscious intention of improving language ability. A more natural environment for an advanced student is to structure a foreign language course around another primary interest. This increases student motivation and makes it easier to provide an integrated and coherent sequence of texts. Such courses do exist and two were chosen to furnish the basic texts for this project: Tricia Walker's *Computer Science* in the *English for Academic Purposes Series* [Wal89], and P Charles Brown and Norma D Mallen's *English for Computer Science* [Bro-Mal87].

4 The Callguide Project

The main objective of the project was to design exercises to enhance *intensive reading skills* i.e. *reading for accuracy*; these can be contrasted with *extensive reading skills*, or *reading for fluency* [Bru78]. Leaving aside oral skills, in which, we may assume, a student with A-level English is already proficient, intensive reading requires two main types of skills:

i) lexical skills, and

ii) discourse skills

The exercises were implemented in Guide by Ian Lindley and Simon Pullen as a project in their final year.

4.1 Lexical skills

These are skills that involve recognising words and identifying their meanings.

- *Technical terms*

  A hypertext dictionary was available and the original intention was to link this directly to the texts in the Callguide suite: this would have allowed the student to look up almost every word in the text at the touch of a button. Counsels of those most experienced in language teaching prevailed: students are to be discouraged from too frequent recourse to a dictionary. While the hypertext dictionary is still available on-line the student must request it explicitly and enter the word. For a complete description of the project with the Oxford Advanced Learner's Dictionary [Hor74], see [Wil91]. However, because the text is technical and uses specialist terms that the student cannot be expected to know, technical words and phrases have been automatically linked to a hypertext glossary. The technical terms are shown underlined in the text; when the reader selects a term the main hypertext window splits and the definition of the term appears in the subwindow. See Figure 1, where the term peripheral has been chosen.

- *Synonyms and antonyms*

  Synonym and antonym exercises are useful for testing whether the student really understands how a word can be used. It develops a technique of active reading.

Figure 2 shows a complex synonym — antonym exercise.

In the first three examples, the user decides which word he wants to use by selecting the **synonym** button adjacent to the word. A sentence is displayed. The user points at the word with the same meaning. If the word (or phrase) selected is correct, the sentence is displayed with the synonym in place. If the selection is wrong, the user is given the option to try again. He can at any point opt to look at the right answer by selecting ANSWER.

The next three examples in Figure 2, examples 4-6 on antonyms, work in a similar way.

The remaining exercises in Figure 2, examples 7-9, are examples of using affixes to create antonyms. Here the antonym is not shown in a sentence: the exercise is designed as a multiple choice question. This highlights the limitation of the pointer-only methods. In this exercise, it might have been sounder educational practice not to show the user words that were "wrong" but let him type in the answer without any clues. A similar problem arose in the next exercise where a different solution was adopted.

- *Irregular plurals*

In this exercise, the user is shown words with irregular singular and plural forms — sometimes the word is given in the singular form, sometimes the plural. The user is asked to say which it is, think about the other form, and then simply check to see whether he is right: Figure 3.

- *Idioms*

English idioms and figures of speech are a source of confusion to non-native speakers. Sometimes the reader can guess at the meaning of an idiom because of the context in which it is used, but to learn them all requires an extensive reading course — or a drill exercise of the type shown in figure 4. The user is given a list of idioms. Any one of these may be selected. When a choice has been made, a list of expressions in standard English is displayed and the user can select the expression closest in meaning to the idiom. A user who selects wrongly is given the option of trying again.

- *Word formation*

Many word stems have different forms corresponding with different parts of speech. Often these are shown in an incomplete table, which the student is asked to complete:

educate   *education*   *educable*   *ineducable*

             variation

                         observable

define

In this suite of programs, a set of word forms is displayed together with a set of sentences. The user has to choose the appropriate word for each sentence. There is an option *wrong word*, which allows the users to change their minds and undo a previous selection: figure 5.

4.2 Discourse skills

- Coherence

  A common course of incoherence in the written English of foreign language students is their inability to maintain tense, mode and aspect correspondence among the verbs. This skill can be enhanced using an extension to the technique introduced above. Figure 6 shows a passage to improve a student's understanding of future reference in English. It uses a form of Cloze procedure where gaps are left in the text. A list of words/phrases is displayed; the student may choose one of these to fill each gap. As in the previous exercise, the student may change his mind about a choice he later regrets by reselecting the offending phrase and choosing *wrong word*.

  The same technique may be used to enhance understanding of the use of conjunctions and adverbs to create a well-connected coherent sequence of sentences.

- Pronouns and relative pronouns

  Many foreign language students experience difficulty in assigning the correct referent to a pronoun or relative pronoun. Figure 7 shows an exercise to practise this skill.

- Comprehension

  Ideally one would test the in-depth understanding of a text by encouraging the students to talk about it. Since conversation is not yet part of a hypertext system, other ways had to be found. Efforts were made to introduce as much variety of form as possible into these exercises. Figure 8 shows a straight forward Cloze text, where the student has to choose words or phrases to make sense of the passage with omissions. Figure 9 shows a connectivity matrix, where the student has to mark where a relevant correspondence has been shown between two concepts in the text under consideration. Figure 10 shows simple true/false markers to show whether the adjacent proposition can be inferred from the text.

4.3 Evaluation

Effort was made to obtain user reaction to the package. The earliest, and so far the only, opportunity to do this came at an Open Day at the end of term. Consequently, most of the guinea-pigs were English sixth formers doing Computer Science A-level. An example of the evaluation sheet is shown in Figure 11. Not surprisingly, nobody learned anything about English or Computing. In spite of this, the testers seemed to enjoy using the package and their reaction to other aspects was favourable. A summary of the results of the questions on the numeric scale 1-5 is shown below. There was no agreement about which exercise was most or least enjoyable. the only additional comments that were not positive were about the brevity of the texts.

How easy was the package to use?	4.25
How easy were the menus to use?	4.625
Was the Help facility useful?	3.75
How good was the layout of the texts?	4.25
How useful was the Glossary?	4.25
How varied were the exercises?	3.5
How good were the instructions on how to complete the exercises?	3.75
How good was the layout of the exercises?	4.7

5 Conclusion

The project has proved a worthwhile prototype in using programmable hypertext as an authoring medium for CALL programs. The programs cannot replace interaction with a human teacher; they were solely intended to automate necessary exercises that would otherwise have to be undertaken with paper and pencil. The computer-based system requires little manual dexterity, no keyboarding skills, and is easy to learn and to remember. It has advantages over a paper-based system:

i)   It is fully integrated.

The student can review the text or linguistic explanations at any point while he studies the exercises. Technical terms are instantly available when the text is on display. The student does not have to turn to a different page in the book: he never loses his place.

ii)   It is fast and re-usable.

The exercises can be done as quickly using the mouse as they could with pencil and paper; indeed, unless the student writes in the textbook the computer-based system is quicker. It is also infinitely re-usable: whatever the student has done is obliterated before the exercise is used again. This is not possible with paper-based systems.

iii)   The components are discrete.

In the computer-based system, a single answer can be checked easily; in a paper-based system with back-of-the-book answers it is almost impossible to see only the specific answer needed at that point.

iv)   There is the opportunity to provide personalised monitoring and help systems.

Acknowledgements

I would like to thank Mr. R. C. Saunders for advice on the draft version of this manuscript.

Bibliography

[Ash-Cum83] Ashford, S.J. and Cummings, L.L. "Feedback as an individual resource: personal strategies of creating information" *Organizational Behavior and Human Performance* 32, pp. 370-398, 1983.
[BEL79] Bell Laboratories, *UNIX Time-sharing System: UNIX Programmer's Manual, Seventh Edition, Volume 1*, Murray Hill, N.J., 1979.
[BroCM86] Brown, C.M. *Human Computer Interface Design Guidelines*, Ablex,

Norwood, NJ. 1986.

[Bro-Mul87] Brown, P.C., and Mullen, N.D., *English for Computer Science*, OUP, Oxford, 1987.

[BroPJ86] Brown, P.J., "Interactive Documentation", in *Software Practice and Experience, Vol. 16(3)*, March 1986, pp. 291-299.

[Bru78] Brumfit, C.J., "The Teaching of Advanced Reading Skills in Foreign Languages, with particular reference to English as a foreign language", in Kinsella, V., *Language Teaching and Linguistics Surveys*, CUP, Cambridge, 1978.

[Cam89] Cameron, K., Editor, *Computer Assisted Language Learning: Program Structure and Principles*, Intellect Books, Oxford, 1989.

[Dav82] Davies, G., *Computers, Language and Language Learning*, Centre for Information on Language Teaching and Research, 1982.

[Her87] Herold, D.M., Liden, R.C. and Leatherwood, N.L. "Using multiple attributes to access sources of performance feedback" *Academy of Management Journal* 30, pp. 826-833, 1987.

[Hor74] Hornby, A.S., *Oxford Advanced Learner's Dictionary of Current English*, OUP, Oxford, 1974.

[Kea88] Kearsley, G.P., *Online Help Systems: Design and Implementation*, Ablex Publishing Corporation, Norwood, N.J., 1988.

[Nut83] Nuttall, C., *Teaching Reading Skills in a Foreign Language*, Heinemann Educational Books, London, 1983.

[OWL88] OWL International, *Guide: Hypertext for the PC*, OWL, [Edinburgh], 1988.

[Rub88] Rubin, T. *User Interface Design for Computer Systems*, Ellis Horwood Limited, Chichester, 1988.

[Rub-Her84] Rubinstein, R. and Hersh, H.M. *The Human Factor: designing computer systems for people*, Digital Press Burlington MA, 1984.

[Shn87] Shneiderman, B. *Designing the User Interface*, Addison-Wesley, Reading, Mass, 1987.

[Wal89] Walker, T., *Computer Science*, Cassell, London, 1989.

[Whi87] Whitefield, A. "Models in human-computer interaction: a classification with special reference to their uses in design" *Proceedings of the Second Conference on Human-Computer Interaction* INTERACT87, North-Holland 1987.

[Wil91] Wilson, E., "Using Hypertext as an Interface to the Oxford Advanced Learner's Dictionary" in *Computers and Language 2: Towards 1992*, Sheffield, 1991.

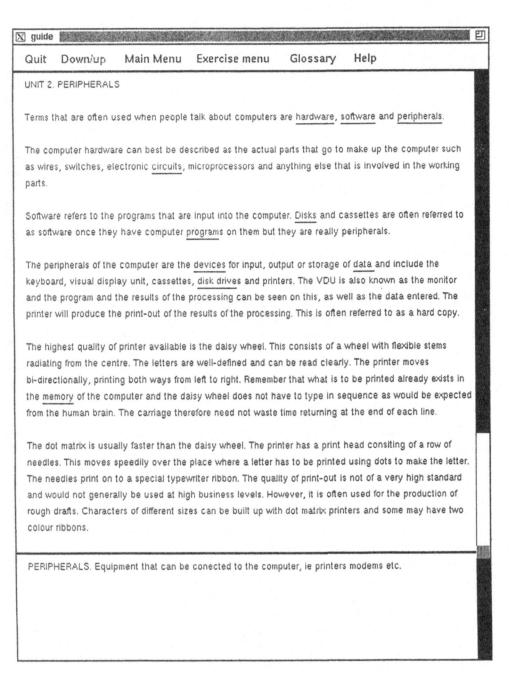

Figure 1: Text with definition of peripherals in glossary subwindow

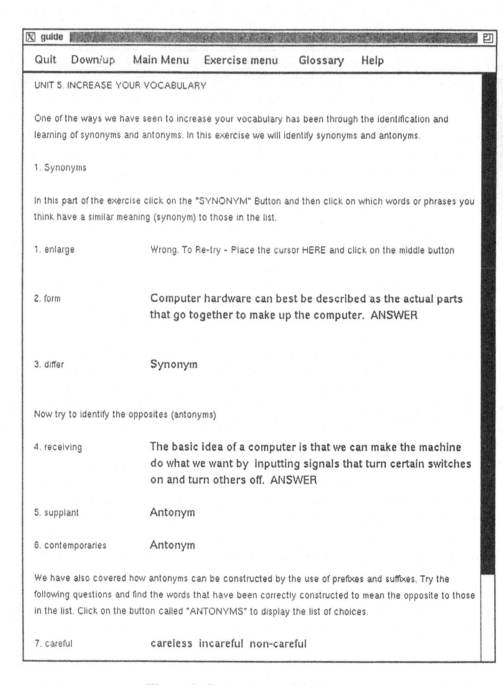

Figure 2: Synonyms and Antonyms

UNIT 4. TEST YOUR GRAMMAR

Everyone is familiar with the letter 'S' to denote the plural in English. There are certain interesting exceptions to the rule, Many of which are scientific or technical terms which have come into English from other languages like Latin and Greek, and which form their plurals in a compleatly different way.
  Below you will find a selection of words. Some are singular, others plural. Make your selection then find out the opposite word.

	Singular	Plural	
matrices	☐	☑	Singular Matrix
syllabus	☑	☐	Plural Syllabi
dice	☒	☐	Singular Die
index	☑	☐	**Opposite**
lens	☐	☐	**Opposite**
aquarium	☐	☐	**Opposite**
radii	☐	☐	**Opposite**
bureau	☐	☐	**Opposite**
axis	☐	☐	**Opposite**
terminus	☐	☐	**Opposite**
formulae	☐	☐	**Opposite**
plateaux	☐	☐	**Opposite**
oasis	☐	☐	**Opposite**

Figure 3: Irregular Plurals

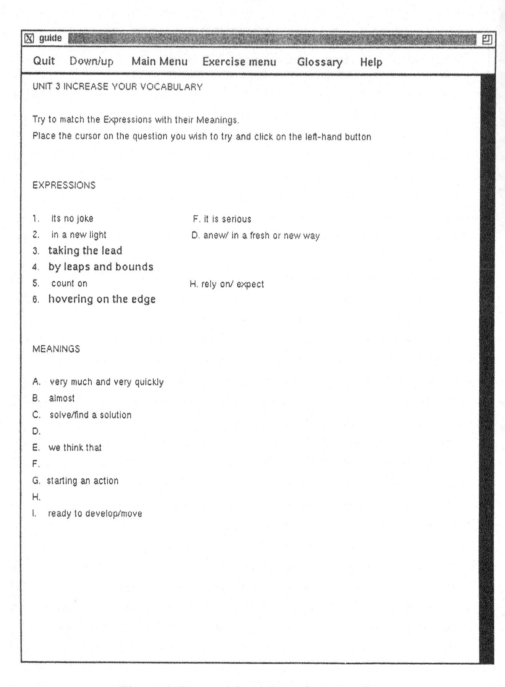

Figure 4: Recognising idiomatic expressions

⊠ guide   ⫽

Quit   Down/up   Main Menu   Exercise menu   Glossary   Help

UNIT 2. TEST YOUR GRAMMAR

If you wish to review the introduction again at any time then click on the words "Review the Introduction".

Review the Introduction

Fill in each blank with the appropriate form of the words.

1. Operations Operate Operator Operational Operationally Operating
    Wrong_Word

    a. A computer can perform mathematical .OPERATIONS   very quickly.
    b. One of the first persons to note that the computer is malfunctioning is the computer
        OPERATOR
    c. The job of a computer operator is to OPERATE   the various machines in a computer
        installation.
    d. The new machines in the computer installation are not yet .OPERATIONAL
    Answers

2. Acceptance Accepts Accepted Acceptable Acceptably Wrong_Word

    a. A computer is a device which ACCEPTS   processes and gives out information.
    b. The students are still waiting for their .... into the Computer Science program.
    c. It is .... to work without a template if the flowcharts are not kept on file.

    Answers

3. Solution Solve Solvable Solver Wrong_Word

    a. It may take a lot of time to find a .... to a complex problem in programming.
    b. A computer can .... a problem faster than any human being.
    c. A computer has often been referred to as a problem ....

    Answers

Figure 5: Variation of word forms with part of speech

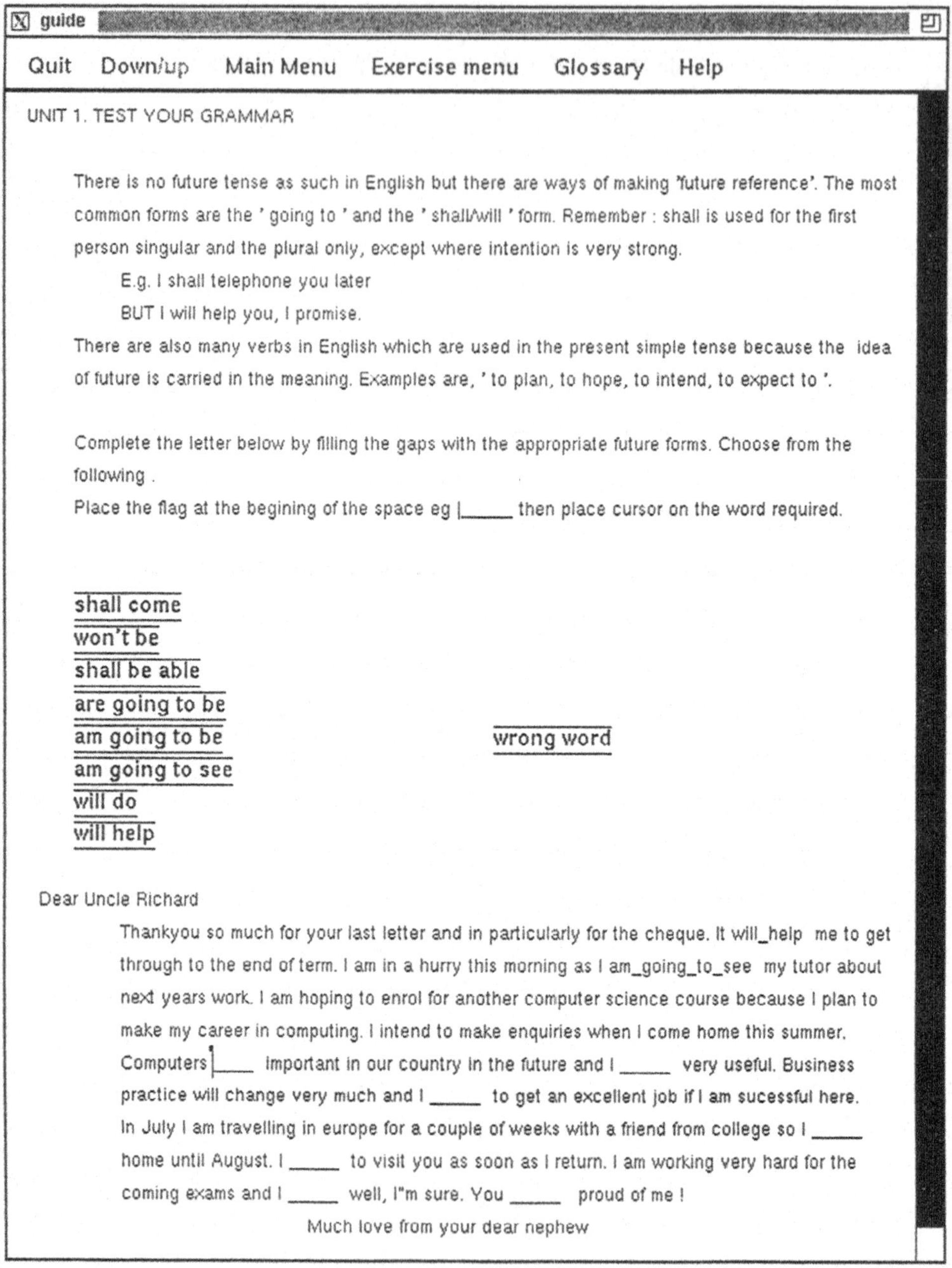

| Quit | Down/up | Main Menu | Exercise menu | Glossary | Help |

UNIT 1. TEST YOUR GRAMMAR

There is no future tense as such in English but there are ways of making 'future reference'. The most common forms are the ' going to ' and the ' shall/will ' form. Remember : shall is used for the first person singular and the plural only, except where intention is very strong.

E.g. I shall telephone you later

BUT I will help you, I promise.

There are also many verbs in English which are used in the present simple tense because the idea of future is carried in the meaning. Examples are, ' to plan, to hope, to intend, to expect to '.

Complete the letter below by filling the gaps with the appropriate future forms. Choose from the following .

Place the flag at the begining of the space eg |_____ then place cursor on the word required.

shall come
won't be
shall be able
are going to be
am going to be   wrong word
am going to see
will do
will help

Dear Uncle Richard

Thankyou so much for your last letter and in particularly for the cheque. It will_help me to get through to the end of term. I am in a hurry this morning as I am_going_to_see my tutor about next years work. I am hoping to enrol for another computer science course because I plan to make my career in computing. I intend to make enquiries when I come home this summer. Computers |_____ important in our country in the future and I _____ very useful. Business practice will change very much and I _____ to get an excellent job if I am sucessful here. In July I am travelling in europe for a couple of weeks with a friend from college so I _____ home until August. I _____ to visit you as soon as I return. I am working very hard for the coming exams and I _____ well, I"m sure. You _____ proud of me !

Much love from your dear nephew

Figure 6: Understanding future reference in English

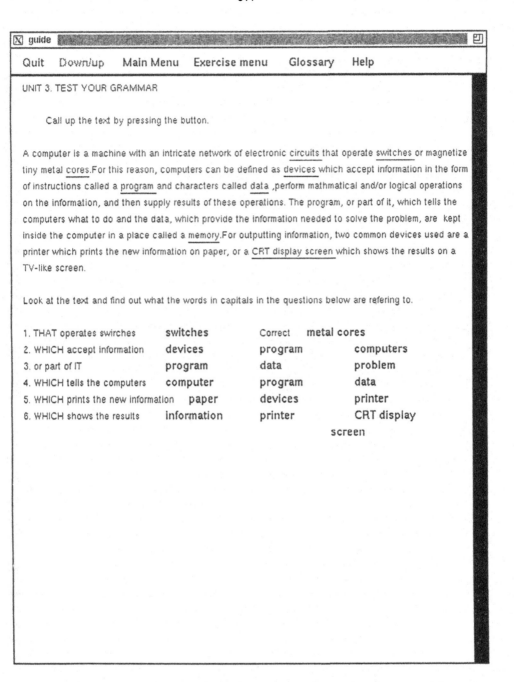

Figure 7: Finding the referent of pronouns and relative pronouns

---

⊠ guide						凹

Quit   Down/up   Main Menu   Exercise menu   Glossary   Help

UNIT 4. COMPREHENSION

Complete the following summary. Words you may need are given below.

1 The aim of a fifth generation computer is to apply reasoning to knowlegde in order to solve highly complex problems.

2 Fifth generation computers comprise a _____ base processor, an _____ mechanism and an _____ user _____ .

3 The processing power of a _____ generation _____ is measured in logical inferences per second.

4 The central _____ of fifth generation computers are _____ knowledge _____ systems.

5 Intelligent _____ interfaces are designed to suit the way of _____ of the _____ rather than that of the _____ .

6 A _____ range of applications is _____ for fifth generation computers, including _____ , intelligent _____ , voice-driven _____ and intelligent _____ guidance system .

intelligent	computer	based	
inference	knowledge	planned	
elements	robots	expert systems	wrong word
thinking	user	interface	
reasoning	complex	word processors	
generation	missile	fifth	

Answers

Figure 8: Cloze procedures to test comprehension

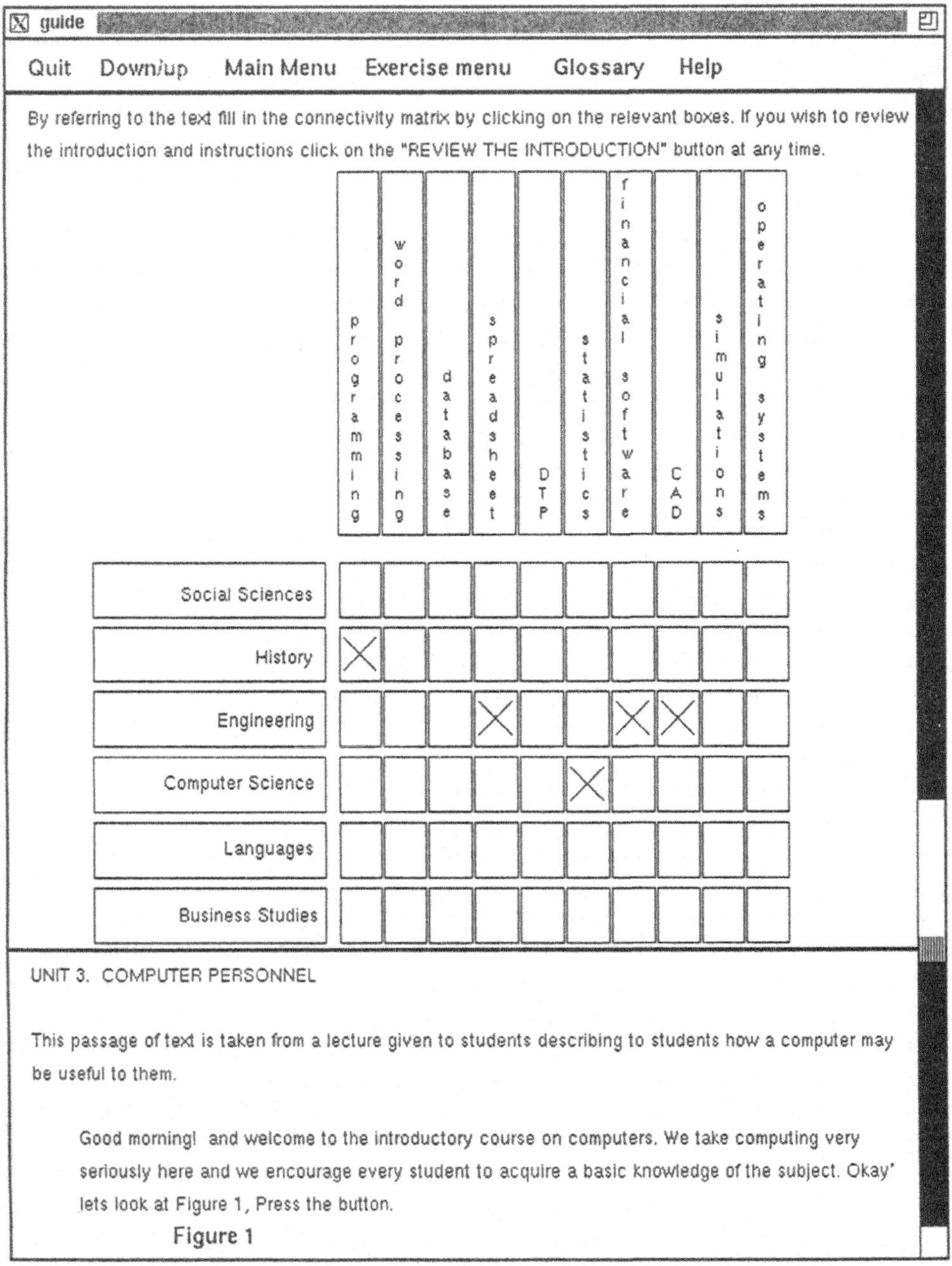

Figure 9: Linking concepts through a connectivity matrix

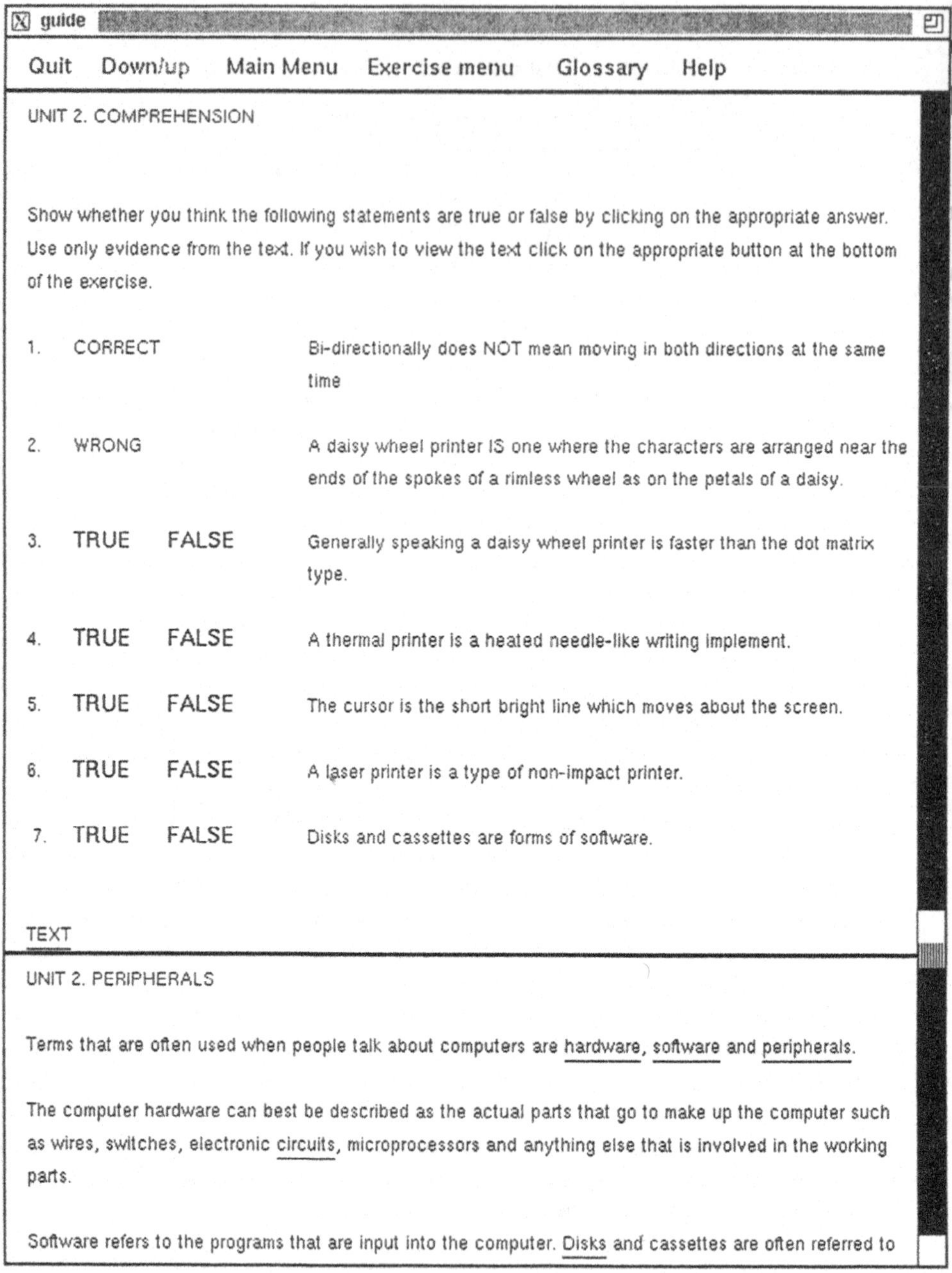

614

☒ guide   回

| Quit | Down/up | Main Menu | Exercise menu | Glossary | Help |

UNIT 2. COMPREHENSION

Show whether you think the following statements are true or false by clicking on the appropriate answer. Use only evidence from the text. If you wish to view the text click on the appropriate button at the bottom of the exercise.

1.   CORRECT   Bi-directionally does NOT mean moving in both directions at the same time

2.   WRONG   A daisy wheel printer IS one where the characters are arranged near the ends of the spokes of a rimless wheel as on the petals of a daisy.

3.   TRUE   FALSE   Generally speaking a daisy wheel printer is faster than the dot matrix type.

4.   TRUE   FALSE   A thermal printer is a heated needle-like writing implement.

5.   TRUE   FALSE   The cursor is the short bright line which moves about the screen.

6.   TRUE   FALSE   A laser printer is a type of non-impact printer.

7.   TRUE   FALSE   Disks and cassettes are forms of software.

TEXT

UNIT 2. PERIPHERALS

Terms that are often used when people talk about computers are hardware, software and peripherals.

The computer hardware can best be described as the actual parts that go to make up the computer such as wires, switches, electronic circuits, microprocessors and anything else that is involved in the working parts.

Software refers to the programs that are input into the computer. Disks and cassettes are often referred to

Figure 10: Inferring the truth of propositions

Evaluation of CALL package.

Please circle your choice of answer.

1 -bad, 2 - poor, 3 - adequate,'4 - good, 5 - excellent

1. Is English your first language?(Y) N

2. If No to Question 1. Did you .find the package valuable for learning English? Y N

4. Did you try all of the exercises? Y(N)

5. Did the package improve your English? Y(N)

6. Did you learn anything about computing?(Y) N

7. How easy was the package to use? 1 2 3(4)5

8. How easy were the menus to use? 1 2 3 4(5)

9. Was the Help facility useful? 1 2(3)4 5

10. How good was the layout of the texts? 1 2 3 4(5)

11. How useful was the Glossary? 1 2(3)4 5

12. How varied were the exercises? 1 2(3)4 5

13. How good were the instructions on how to complete the exercises? 1 2 3 4(5)

14. Which exercise did you enjoy most? e.g. Unit 1. Vocabulary. 2. PERIPHIS INCREASE VOCABULARY

15. Which exercise did you enjoy least? e.g Unit 1. Vocabulary. 2. PERIPHIS. COMPREHENSION

16. How good was the layout of the exercises? 1 2 3 4(5)

Comments: Scrolling the screen is different ~ difficult to gauge. Everything very well explained. Long Instructions are off-putting. Glossary very useful in defining jargon used. No long wait for information or menus to appear. Very good as this is often annoying.

Figure 11: CALL package evaluation questionnaire

Lecture Notes in Computer Science

For information about Vols. 1–529
please contact your bookseller or Springer-Verlag

Vol. 570: R. Berghammer, G. Schmidt (Eds.), Graph-Theoretic Concepts in Computer Science. Proceedings, 1991. VIII, 253 pages. 1992.

Vol. 571: J. Vytopil (Ed.), Formal Techniques in Real-Time and Fault-Tolerant Systems. Proceedings, 1992. IX, 620 pages. 1991.

Vol. 572: K. U. Schulz (Ed.), Word Equations and Related Topics. Proceedings, 1990. VII, 256 pages. 1992.

Vol. 573: G. Cohen, S. N. Litsyn, A. Lobstein, G. Zémor (Eds.), Algebraic Coding. Proceedings, 1991. X, 158 pages. 1992.

Vol. 574: J. P. Banâtre, D. Le Métayer (Eds.), Research Directions in High-Level Parallel Programming Languages. Proceedings, 1991. VIII, 387 pages. 1992.

Vol. 575: K. G. Larsen, A. Skou (Eds.), Computer Aided Verification. Proceedings, 1991. X, 487 pages. 1992.

Vol. 576: J. Feigenbaum (Ed.), Advances in Cryptology - CRYPTO '91. Proceedings. X, 485 pages. 1992.

Vol. 577: A. Finkel, M. Jantzen (Eds.), STACS 92. Proceedings, 1992. XIV, 621 pages. 1992.

Vol. 578: Th. Beth, M. Frisch, G. J. Simmons (Eds.), Public-Key Cryptography: State of the Art and Future Directions. XI, 97 pages. 1992.

Vol. 579: S. Toueg, P. G. Spirakis, L. Kirousis (Eds.), Distributed Algorithms. Proceedings, 1991. X, 319 pages. 1992.

Vol. 580: A. Pirotte, C. Delobel, G. Gottlob (Eds.), Advances in Database Technology - EDBT '92. Proceedings. XII, 551 pages. 1992.

Vol. 581: J.-C. Raoult (Ed.), CAAP '92. Proceedings. VIII, 361 pages. 1992.

Vol. 582: B. Krieg-Brückner (Ed.), ESOP '92. Proceedings. VIII, 491 pages. 1992.

Vol. 583: I. Simon (Ed.), LATIN '92. Proceedings. IX, 545 pages. 1992.

Vol. 584: R. E. Zippel (Ed.), Computer Algebra and Parallelism. Proceedings, 1990. IX, 114 pages. 1992.

Vol. 585: F. Pichler, R. Moreno Díaz (Eds.), Computer Aided System Theory - EUROCAST '91. Proceedings. X, 761 pages. 1992.

Vol. 586: A. Cheese, Parallel Execution of Parlog. IX, 184 pages. 1992.

Vol. 587: R. Dale, E. Hovy, D. Rösner, O. Stock (Eds.), Aspects of Automated Natural Language Generation. Proceedings, 1992. VIII, 311 pages. 1992. (Subseries LNAI).

Vol. 588: G. Sandini (Ed.), Computer Vision - ECCV '92. Proceedings. XV, 909 pages. 1992.

Vol. 589: U. Banerjee, D. Gelernter, A. Nicolau, D. Padua (Eds.), Languages and Compilers for Parallel Computing. Proceedings, 1991. IX, 419 pages. 1992.

Vol. 590: B. Fronhöfer, G. Wrightson (Eds.), Parallelization in Inference Systems. Proceedings, 1990. VIII, 372 pages. 1992. (Subseries LNAI).

Vol. 591: H. P. Zima (Ed.), Parallel Computation. Proceedings, 1991. IX, 451 pages. 1992.

Vol. 592: A. Voronkov (Ed.), Logic Programming. Proceedings, 1991. IX, 514 pages. 1992. (Subseries LNAI).

Vol. 593: P. Loucopoulos (Ed.), Advanced Information Systems Engineering. Proceedings. XI, 650 pages. 1992.

Vol. 594: B. Monien, Th. Ottmann (Eds.), Data Structures and Efficient Algorithms. VIII, 389 pages. 1992.

Vol. 595: M. Levene, The Nested Universal Relation Database Model. X, 177 pages. 1992.

Vol. 596: L.-H. Eriksson, L. Hallnäs, P. Schroeder-Heister (Eds.), Extensions of Logic Programming. Proceedings, 1991. VII, 369 pages. 1992. (Subseries LNAI).

Vol. 597: H. W. Guesgen, J. Hertzberg, A Perspective of Constraint-Based Reasoning. VIII, 123 pages. 1992. (Subseries LNAI).

Vol. 598: S. Brookes, M. Main, A. Melton, M. Mislove, D. Schmidt (Eds.), Mathematical Foundations of Programming Semantics. Proceedings, 1991. VIII, 506 pages. 1992.

Vol. 599: Th. Wetter, K.-D. Althoff, J. Boose, B. R. Gaines, M. Linster, F. Schmalhofer (Eds.), Current Developments in Knowledge Acquisition - EKAW '92. Proceedings. XIII, 444 pages. 1992. (Subseries LNAI).

Vol. 600: J. W. de Bakker, K. Huizing, W. P. de Roever, G. Rozenberg (Eds.), Real-Time: Theory in Practice. Proceedings, 1991. VIII, 723 pages. 1992.

Vol. 601: D. Dolev, Z. Galil, M. Rodeh (Eds.), Theory of Computing and Systems. Proceedings, 1992. VIII, 220 pages. 1992.

Vol. 602: I. Tomek (Ed.), Computer Assisted Learning. Proceedigs, 1992. X, 615 pages. 1992.

Vol. 603: J. van Katwijk (Ed.), Ada: Moving Towards 2000. Proceedings, 1992. VIII, 324 pages. 1992.

Vol. 604: F. Belli, F.-J. Radermacher (Eds.), Industrial and Engineering Applications of Artificial Intelligence and Expert Systems. Proceedings, 1992. XV, 702 pages. 1992. (Subseries LNAI).

Vol. 605: D. Etiemble, J.-C. Syre (Eds.), PARLE '92. Parallel Architectures and Languages Europe. Proceedings, 1992. XVII, 984 pages. 1992.

Vol. 607: D. Kapur (Ed.), Automated Deduction - CADE-11. Proceedings, 1992. XV, 793 pages. 1992. (Subseries LNAI).

Vol. 608: C. Frasson, G. Gauthier, G. I. McCalla (Eds.), Intelligent Tutoring Systems. Proceedings, 1992. XIV, 686 pages. 1992.